ColdFusion MX
Developer's Handbook

ColdFusion® MX
Developer's Handbook™

Raymond Camden
Arman Danesh
Hal Helms
Charles Mohnike
Selene Bainum
Guy Rish
John Colasante
William Baum
Shlomy Gantz
Kenneth N. Fricklas
Matt Liotta
Jen deHaan
Peter deHaan

SYBEX

San Francisco · London

Associate Publisher: Joel Fugazzotto
Acquisitions Editor: Tom Cirtin
Developmental Editor: Carol Henry
Editor: Rebecca Rider
Production Editor: Susan Berge
Technical Editors: Selene Bainum, Raymond Camden, Arman Danesh, Kenneth N. Fricklas, Guy Rish
Graphic Illustrator: Jeff Wilson, Happenstance Type-O-Rama
Electronic Publishing Specialist: Jill Niles
Proofreaders: Amey Garber, Emily Hsuan, Eric Lach, Dave Nash, Laurie O'Connell, Yariv Rabinovitch, Monique van den Berg
Indexer: Nancy Guenther
Cover Design: Caryl Gorska, Gorska Design
Cover Photograph: Akira Kaede, PhotoDisc

Library of Congress Card Number: 2002112934

ISBN: 0-7821-4029-7

Manufactured in the United States of America

10 9 8 7 6 5 4 3 2 1

Acknowledgments

I'd like to begin by thanking my wife. I would not have been able to do this without her support and love. I also want to thank everyone at Sybex, including Tom Cirtin, Carol Henry, and Susan Berge. This book would not have been possible without the amazing effort, patience, and skill of our co-authors. It was wonderful working with them and I hope I get the chance again.

–Raymond Camden

Writing a book of this scope and depth is, undoubtedly, a collaborative effort. I must thank all my co-authors on this project. Their commitment and efforts made this project the success that it has been. I am also grateful to the efforts of the project team at Sybex including Tom Cirtin, Carol Henry, Susan Berge, and the many others who helped in the task of producing this book. Finally, my wife, Tahirih, and son Ethan deserve credit for tolerating the long hours I spent in front of the computer screen.

–Arman Danesh

About the Authors

Raymond Camden is a software engineer for Mindseye, Inc. A longtime ColdFusion user, Raymond is a member of Team Macromedia and a coauthor of *Mastering ColdFusion MX* (Sybex, 2002) and its earlier editions. He also presents at numerous conferences and contributes to online webzines and the *ColdFusion Developer's Journal*. He and Rob Brooks-Bilson created and run the Common Function Library Project (http://www.cflib.org), an open-source repository of ColdFusion UDFs. Ray also formed and helped manage the Hampton Roads ColdFusion User Group (http://www.hrcfug.org).

Arman Danesh serves as the technical manager for The Bahá'í World (http://www.bahai.org), the official website of the Bahá'í International Community, and Bahá'í World News Service (http://www.bahaiworldnews.org), a ColdFusion-driven online news service. Additionally, he is the editorial director for Juxta Publishing Limited (http://www.juxta.com) and manages the ColdFusion-based websites of Landegg International University, a private, international university in Switzerland. He has been working with ColdFusion since 1997 and maintains many other ColdFusion-based websites. Arman has written more than a dozen books, including *Mastering ColdFusion MX* (Sybex, 2002) and its earlier editions, *SAIR Linux & GNU Certified Administrator All-in-One Exam Guide*, *Safe and Secure: Secure Your Home Network and Protect Your Privacy Online*, and *Teach Yourself JavaScript in a Week*. He is pursuing an advanced degree in computer science at Simon Fraser University in Vancouver.

Hal Helms is an internationally known writer, speaker, and trainer on the subject of software development. He is a member of Team Macromedia, serves on the Macromedia Client Advisory Board, and is a monthly columnist for the *ColdFusion Developer's Journal*. Hal has written and contributed to several books, including *Discovering Fusebox 3 with ColdFusion*, *Discovering CFCs: ColdFusion MX Components*, and the *ColdFusion MX Bible*. Hal also publishes the popular free *Occasional Newsletter* available at http://www.halhelms.com. You can reach him at hal.helms@teamallaire.com.

Charles Mohnike has been using ColdFusion to develop commercial websites for more than six years. He operates Zapt Digital Media (http://www.zapt.com), a consulting firm that provides ColdFusion consultation, web application programming, site marketing, and electronic publishing. Among other things, he combines his extensive background in print media and skills in electronic publishing to convert printed documents to digital format and serve them up on the Web. He has written several books on web publishing, including *Sams*

Teach Yourself Macromedia ColdFusion in 21 Days, and has contributed to *Microsoft Bookshelf Internet Directory*, *Wired Digital*, and *Smart TV*.

Selene Bainum has been working with ColdFusion since version 1.5 back in 1996, and with both SQL Server and Oracle for over five years. She has created several dynamic web-based applications for notable clients, including the National Institutes of Health, Citibank, General Electric, and Schlumberger Limited. Selene has spoken at several ColdFusion conferences and seminars across the country, and is a coauthor of *Mastering ColdFusion MX* (Sybex, 2002). She created and maintains WebTricks (http://www.webtricks.com), a well-known tutorial site for ColdFusion, SQL, and JavaScript developers. Since 1998, she has been a member of Team Allaire/Team Macromedia, providing assistance to hundreds of developers on Macromedia's ColdFusion support forums. Selene is also the cofounder and chief software architect of Limited Reality (http://www.limitedreality.com), a software development firm specializing in applications for mobile devices and web platforms.

Guy Rish is a freelance software developer. He holds instructor certificates from Macromedia and Rational Software and has taught in the Multimedia Studies program at San Francisco State University. Most recently, he has been the technical editor or coauthor for various web tools books, including *Mastering ColdFusion MX* (Sybex, 2002), *Dreamweaver MX/Fireworks MX Savvy* (Sybex, 2002), and *Inside Flash MX*. He also writes the article series "Cold Cup O' Joe" in the *ColdFusion Developer's Journal*. Guy has spoken at numerous conferences and user groups (in and out of the U.S.) about the intersection of object-oriented programming and web technologies and practices.

John Colasante is a principal at Solar Productions, Inc., a technology company based in New York City. John has used ColdFusion to build many highly complex and scalable applications for a variety of businesses. On any Sunday you will find him racing. He can be contacted at johnc@solarproductions.com.

William M. Baum is the Chief Technology Officer of GT Alliance, a Macromedia Premier VAR. As one of the youngest licensed NASD brokers in the country, Bill has had an extensive relationship with mission-critical data and systems that he began while working at Shearson American Express (which became Shearson Lehman Brothers). Bill has also been an independent software consultant and has developed management applications for the service industry, in the areas of network engineering, design, and security. In addition, he is proficient in server administration, including load-balancing and clustering technologies, and in database design and administration, including load-balancing and replication, on a variety of platforms. Bill is also an expert in cross-platform connectivity issues, directory services technologies, and application architecture. His comprehensive technical knowledge is currently at work on robust data solutions, many of which involve ColdFusion as the primary client interface.

Shlomy Gantz is founder and president of BlueBrick, Inc., a technology and management-consulting firm based in New York. Before that, he was founder and vice president of technology for CoreActive ACG, a premier Allaire partner. He has over a decade of software development experience and an extensive background in database development and project management. He contributes regularly at technology and management conferences and seminars in the U.S. and Europe. Shlomy has worked with ColdFusion since version 1.5 and is a frequent presenter at ColdFusion conferences and user groups. He is also comanager of the New York ColdFusion User Group. *Mastering ColdFusion 4.5* (Sybex, 2000) benefited from Shlomy's technical editing expertise.

Kenneth N. Fricklas is Chief Technical Officer of Mallfinder Network, a web services company for retail property management companies. Ken, who has been a ColdFusion user since version 1.5 and a Macromedia Trainer, teaches classes on advanced ColdFusion development throughout the U.S. He has presented at Internet World and the Macromedia Developers Conference and serves on the boards of the Boulder Community Network (`http://bcn.boulder.co.us`) and Alt-X Publishing (`http://www.altx.com`). He is also a cofounder of the website Disinformation (`http://www.disinfo.com`). In addition, Ken was a technical editor of Ben Forta's *The ColdFusion 4.0 Web Application Construction Kit*.

Matt Liotta, president and CEO of Montara Software, has been developing applications since he was 12, assisting faculty at Emory University. He built his first web page soon after the release of Mosaic 1.0. Since then he has built a wide variety of ColdFusion-based applications for companies, including Cignify, Consumer Financial Networks, Grizzard Communications, Williams-Sonoma, Inc., and Yipes Communications. He built gMoney's Group Transaction System using an innovative XML messaging architecture similar to the now-popular web services paradigm. At TeamToolz, he designed a highly secure and scalable network architecture to support n-tier distributed applications. He has also implemented a cutting-edge content management system for DevX.

Jen and Peter deHaan have been busy in 2002 writing, contributing to, and editing nine books about Macromedia products for Sybex and other publishers. The deHaans primarily work with ColdFusion, Flash, and ActionScript. Jen mainly uses Flash MX, and is most interested in remoting with ColdFusion, handhelds, and building Flash components. She holds a B.F.A. in art education, as well as honors certification in new media. She will give her first conference presentation in 2003, and you can find her on the web at `http://www.ejepo.com` and `http://www.flash-mx.com`. Peter comes from a computer science background and has been programming for the Web since 1995, focusing on using a mix of client- and server-side technologies to create dynamic and interactive websites. He has used ColdFusion since 1997 to create several e-commerce sites, scheduling systems, web portals, and an inventory system using barcode scanners.

Contents at a Glance

Introduction   *xxvii*

Part I   **Managing Content and Applications**

    Chapter 1:   Designing and Planning a ColdFusion Application   **3**

    Chapter 2:   Troubleshooting and Debugging ColdFusion MX Code   **33**

    Chapter 3:   State Management in a Clustered Environment   **77**

    Chapter 4:   The Fusebox Framework and Development Methodology   **107**

    Chapter 5:   Developing Component-Based Applications   **179**

    Chapter 6:   Creating Search Engines with Verity   **199**

    Chapter 7:   Advanced WDDX   **245**

    Chapter 8:   Application Security Techniques   **285**

    Chapter 9:   Archives and Deployment   **317**

    Chapter 10:   Source Code Management   **333**

Part II   **Advanced Database Integration**

    Chapter 11:   Advanced SQL   **349**

    Chapter 12:   Stored Procedures   **389**

    Chapter 13:   Upsizing Databases to SQL Server   **419**

Part III   **Client-Side Coding**

    Chapter 14:   Using JavaScript and DHTML with ColdFusion   **449**

    Chapter 15:   Working with WAP and WML Clients   **497**

Part IV   **Enhancing Performance**

Chapter 16:   Performance Tuning   **533**

Chapter 17:   Clustering: Load Balancing and Failover   **569**

Chapter 18:   Caching Techniques   **601**

Part V   **Custom Server-Side Coding**

Chapter 19:   Working with Java Objects   **623**

Chapter 20:   Building Java Extensions   **651**

Chapter 21:   Building C++ Extensions   **709**

Chapter 22:   Using cfexecute   **745**

Part VI   **Integrating with External Services**

Chapter 23:   Integrating with Flash MX   **765**

Chapter 24:   Web Services   **837**

Appendices

Appendix A: Configuring ColdFusion for Java   **857**

Appendix B: Understanding UML Class Diagrams   **863**

Appendix C: Using the Code from This Book   **871**

Index   *873*

Contents

Introduction   *xxvii*

Part I   **Managing Content and Applications**   **1**

Chapter 1   **Designing and Planning a ColdFusion Application**   **3**

Gathering Technical Requirements   4
Designing the Application Architecture   6
   Setting Up a Physical Architecture   6
   Designing Databases and Data Models   8
   Creating Tiered Applications   10
   Mapping the Logical Architecture   16
   Identifying Third Party Products   17
Prototyping a Front End   18
Naming Conventions   20
   Naming Variables/Queries/Structures/Arrays   21
   Naming Files/Directories   21
   Naming Database Tables/Columns   22
Comments and Documentation   23
   Using Template Headers   24
   Using a Program Design Language   25
Applying Coding Standards   26
   Cohesion and Coupling   26
   Security Considerations   29
   Using a Methodology   29
   Exception Handling   30
Additional Planning   30
   Project Planning   30
   Backup   31

	Version Control		31
	Integration		31
	In Sum		32
Chapter 2	**Troubleshooting and Debugging ColdFusion MX Code**		**33**
	Interpreting Error Messages		34
		Syntax versus Logic Errors	34
		MX Error Messages	36
	ColdFusion MX Administrator Debug Settings		43
	Debugging in Dreamweaver MX		55
	Implementing Your Own Debugging Template		56
	Tag-Based Debugging		58
		The debug Attribute in cfquery and cfstoredproc	58
		Working with cfsetting showDebugOutput	59
		The cfdump Tag	59
		The cftrace Tag	61
		Logging Errors	64
	Debugging on a Live Server		67
		Using the Error Handlers	67
		Missing Pages	71
		Team Debugging	72
	Some Tips		75
	In Sum		76
Chapter 3	**State Management in a Clustered Environment**		**77**
	State Management with ColdFusion		78
		Managing State over HTTP	78
		CF Variables for State Maintenance	80
	Clustering Fundamentals		83
		Clusters and Sideways Scalability	84
		Clustering Configurations	84
	Guidelines for Clustering in the ColdFusion Environment		85
		Managing CFID/CFTOKEN	85
		Using Session Variables Properly	86
		Inter- and Intra-Session State	87

Setting Up the Cluster Database Walk-Through   89
   Creating the Client Variable Database   89
   Setting the Network Client Connections   90
   Configuring the ODBC Data Source   91
   Configuring the CF Servers to Use the Database   96
   Using the Client Variable Cluster Database   99
Putting Advanced Features to Work   100
In Sum   106

Chapter 4   The Fusebox Framework and Development Methodology   107

A Cautionary Tale   108
Current Software Development Practices   109
   Bad News for Developers   109
   Worse News for the Clients   110
   Of Methodologies and Frameworks   111
What Is Fusebox?   113
   Benefits of Fusebox   113
   Code Reuse with Fusebox   115
A Fusebox Overview   116
   Solving the Complexity Syndrome with Fusebox   117
   The Fusebox Skeleton   121
   Nested Circuits with Fusebox   123
   Defining Circuit Aliases   125
   Exit Fuseactions (XFAs)   126
   Nested Layouts   127
   Query Sims   132
A FLiP Overview   133
   The FLiP Steps   135
   Summing It Up   159
A Sample Fusebox Application   159
In Sum   178

Chapter 5   Developing Component-Based Applications   179

Object-Oriented Concepts within CFML   180
   Instance Construction   180
   Encapsulation   182

Inheritance   183

Polymorphism   187

Applying the Concepts   189

Creating Components   189

An Example of Applying Object-Oriented Design Concepts
to a ColdFusion Application   190

The AddressBook Story   191

Identifying Components   191

Abstracting Component Types   193

The Record Search   194

In Sum   197

Chapter 6   Creating Search Engines with Verity   199

The Basics of Verity   200

Creating Collections   200

Indexing Data   202

Searching an Index   204

The Verity K2 Server   209

Using cfindex and cfcollection   210

Creating Collections with cfcollection   211

Indexing Files with cfindex   211

Indexing and Searching Dynamic Query Results   213

Creating Search Interfaces   219

Presenting Useful Results   219

Paging through Results   229

Helping Users Build Queries   233

Multilingual Indexing and Searching   239

Multiformat Indexing and Searching   240

Automating Indexing   242

Creating an Indexing Template   242

Optimizing Verity   244

In Sum   244

Chapter 7	**Advanced WDDX**	**245**
	Introducing WDDX	246
	The History of WDDX	246
	WDDX Concepts	247
	Exploring the Functionality of WDDX Language Tools	249
	CFML Tools for Working with WDDX	249
	WDDX and CFML Queries	250
	Utilities for Constructing and Displaying Packets	253
	Database Caching with WDDX	254
	The WDDX JavaScript Library	256
	Accessing the Library	256
	Converting CFML into JavaScript	257
	Working with the WddxRecordset Class	260
	Exploring the WddxDeserializer Class	262
	Using the WddxSerializer Class	266
	The WddRecordset Class Revisited	273
	WDDX Syndication	277
	Using WDDX with Moreover.com	278
	Slashdot.org	281
	In Sum	283
Chapter 8	**Application Security Techniques**	**285**
	Before You Begin	286
	Security Basics	286
	Authentication	289
	Authorization	296
	Our Authorization Data Scheme	297
	Roles-Based Security in ColdFusion MX	303
	Building Secure Web Applications	307
	Protecting Input Points	307
	Security through Obscurity	312
	Cross-Site Scripting	312
	In Sum	315

Chapter 9	**Archives and Deployment**	**317**
	Archiving as Part of Deployment	318
	Preparing and Generating an Archive	319
	Defining and Generating an Archive Definition	319
	Creating an Archive Definition	321
	Building an Archive	328
	Deploying an Archive	330
	In Sum	332
Chapter 10	**Source Code Management**	**333**
	What Is Source Code Management?	334
	Locking and Concurrency	335
	Versioning and History	336
	Synchronization	337
	Parallel Projects and Forking	337
	Source Code Management Tools	337
	Using Dreamweaver with RDS	338
	SourceSafe	343
	WebDAV	344
	Other Technologies to Consider	344
	In Sum	346
Part II	**Advanced Database Integration**	**347**
Chapter 11	**Advanced SQL**	**349**
	SQL and Database Basics	350
	Relational Data	350
	The Database Used in This Chapter	351
	Table Manipulation	353
	Create	353
	Alter	355
	Drop	356
	Data Manipulation	356
	Inserting	356
	Updating	360
	Deleting	361

Querying Data	362
select Statements	362
Column and Table Aliases	363
Unique Rows	364
Functions	364
Subqueries	370
Joins	376
Unions	378
Grouping	379
CFSQL	384
Performance Testing	386
Server-Side Debugging	386
GetTickCount	387
In Sum	388

Chapter 12   Stored Procedures   389

Working with Stored Procedures	390
Naming Conventions	390
Creating, Modifying, and Deleting Stored Procedures	391
Parameters	392
Executing Stored Procedures	394
The exec Statement	395
exec Syntax	395
Returning Output Parameters	396
Calling Stored Procedures from ColdFusion	397
Using the cfquery Tag	397
Using the cfstoredproc Tag	398
Using cfstoredproc	400
Input and Output Parameters	400
Multiple Result Sets	402
Advanced Transact-SQL	406
Replacing cfset	406
Replacing cfif	407
Replacing cfloop	409
Replacing cfoutput/cfloop Query	410

	Putting It All Together	412
	In Sum	417
Chapter 13	**Upsizing Databases to SQL Server**	**419**
	What's Upsizing?	420
	Before You Upsize	421
	Do You Need to Upsize?	421
	How Will Users Manage SQL Server Data?	423
	Choosing an Upsizing Method	423
	Using the Access Upsizing Tools	424
	Examining Your Database for Trouble Spots	424
	Running the Upsizing Wizard	429
	Known Problems with the Upsizing Tools	434
	Using SQL Server DTS	434
	Running the DTS Import/Export Wizard	435
	Verifying Your DTS Import	437
	Modifying ColdFusion Applications for Upsized Databases	438
	Modifying SQL Syntax	438
	Working with Identity Columns	440
	Other Differences between Access and SQL Server	443
	In Sum	446
Part III	**Client-Side Coding**	**447**
Chapter 14	**Using JavaScript and DHTML with ColdFusion**	**449**
	Client versus Server Processing	450
	The Server: ColdFusion	451
	The Client: JavaScript	451
	Introducing the Document Object Model (DOM)	452
	Object References	453
	Object Components	455
	Integrating JavaScript and ColdFusion	457
	ColdFusion to JavaScript	457
	JavaScript to ColdFusion	462
	Validating Form Fields	465
	Server-Side Validation	465

ColdFusion's Server-Side Form Validation		467
Client-Side Validation: JavaScript		469
DHTML		482
Considerations		482
Image Rollovers		485
Exploring Styles		488
Hiding/Showing Elements		492
In Sum		496

Chapter 15	**Working with WAP and WML Clients**	**497**
	What Is WAP/WML?	498
	A Typical WAP/ColdFusion Architecture	500
	WML Browser Emulators for the PC	501
	WML Basics	503
	WML Document Structure	503
	The WML Header	505
	WML Syntax Rules	505
	Card Navigation in WML	506
	Intolerance for Coding Errors	510
	Passing URL Attributes Using &	511
	Accessing Variables in WML Using the $	512
	Using WML from ColdFusion	513
	Setting the Content Type with cfcontent	514
	Determining the Browser Type with cgi.http_accept	515
	Working with WML Forms	516
	Handling ColdFusion Errors in a WAP/WML-Friendly Manner	523
	Architecture for a WML/HTML-Capable Site	525
	Prudent Use of cfabort	529
	In Sum	530

Part IV	**Enhancing Performance**	**531**

Chapter 16	**Performance Tuning**	**533**
	Performance Testing	534
	Load Testing Software	535
	Using the Web Application Stress Tool	536

Performance Metrics: What to Measure 540

ColdFusion MX Performance Counters 543

Monitoring Performance: Tools and Methods 544

System Monitor for Windows (Performance Tool) 544

The CFSTAT Utility 545

ColdFusion Administrator Settings 546

Server Settings 546

Caching 549

Client Variables 551

ColdFusion MX Data Source Settings 553

Tuning the Database 555

Database Design 555

Indexes 556

Common Query Pitfalls 557

Profiling ColdFusion MX Templates 563

Profiling Template Execution 563

Using cftrace and getTickCount to Profile within a Page 563

Tuning the Operating System 565

Windows NT/2000 565

Internet Information Server Configuration 566

Solaris and Linux Systems 567

In Sum 568

Chapter 17   Clustering: Load Balancing and Failover   569

High-Availability Systems 570

Clustering 570

Scalability and Reliability 571

Software Load Balancing 572

DNS 573

Round Robin DNS 573

ClusterCATS 574

Windows Network Load Balancing 576

Other Software Load Balancers 577

Hardware Load Balancing 577

Creating a ClusterCATS Cluster   578
  Cluster Requirements   579
  Planning the Cluster   579
  Configuring DNS and IP Address Settings   581
  Installing ClusterCATS   583
  Configuring ClusterCATS   585
Administering a ClusterCATS Cluster   588
  ClusterCATS Explorer   589
  ClusterCATS Server Administrator   590
Testing a ClusterCATS Cluster   591
  Creating a Test Home Page   591
  Testing Load Balancing   593
  Testing Server Failover   594
Content Deployment and Management   596
  Deployment Strategy   596
  Packaging the Content   597
  Delivering the Content   598
  Synchronizing the Web Servers   598
Database Clustering Considerations   599
  Database Replication   599
In Sum   600

Chapter 18   Caching Techniques   601

Identifying Caching Opportunities   602
  Handling Stale Content   604
Using cfcache   604
  Adding the cfcache Tag   605
  How cfcache Works   607
  Handling Dynamic Pages with cfcache   607
Query Caching   609
  Using Query Caching   611
  Query Caching Options   612
  Expiring Cached Queries   614
Caching in RAM   617
In Sum   619

Part V		**Custom Server-Side Coding**	**621**
	Chapter 19	**Working with Java Objects**	**623**
		Introduction to Java Objects	624
		What You Should Already Know about Java	625
		Terminology	625
		Required Setup Examples in This Chapter	626
		Creating Java Objects in CFML	626
		The Greeting Class	626
		Using the cfobject Tag	627
		Using the createObject Function	628
		Working with Java Objects in CFML	629
		Instantiation	629
		Displaying Method Results	632
		Static Members	632
		Handling Exceptions	633
		Class Caching	634
		Overloading	637
		Datatype Conversion	641
		Nested Objects	648
		In Sum	649
	Chapter 20	**Building Java Extensions**	**651**
		Introducing Java Extensions	652
		Rationale for Using Java CFX Tags	652
		What You Should Already Know about Java	653
		Chapter Setup	654
		Installing Java CFX Tags	655
		Java CFXAPI	658
		The CustomTag Interface	659
		The Request Interface	660
		The Response Interface	660
		The Query Interface	661
		Basic Java CFX	662
		Basic Tag I/O	662

Special CFX Attributes   665
Working with Queries   667
Debugging   673
The DebugRequest Class   674
The DebugResponse Class   674
The DebugQuery Class   675
Simple Debugging   675
Query Debugging   677
Advanced Construction   679
Working with Complex Data: Help from WDDX   679
Serializing CFML Datatypes   680
Serializing Query and ResultSet Objects   690
Extending the CFXAPI   695
The Transubstantiator Interface   696
The ComplexRequest Class   696
The ComplexResponse Class   697
A Complex Look   697
CFML Wrapped CFX Tags   699
A Simple XSLT Tag   700
In Sum   707

Chapter 21   Building C++ Extensions   709

Chapter Setup   710
Choosing a C++ Compiler   710
Chapter Sample Code   711
Installing C++ CFX Tags   711
Introducing the C++ CFXAPI   714
The CCFXRequest Class   715
The CCFXQuery Class   716
The CCFXStringSet Class   716
The CCFXException Class   717
C++ CFX Basics   717
The CFX Tag Wizard   718
Basic CFX Construction   718
Portable CFX Construction   724
Returning Variables   731

Working with Queries   734
    Passing a Query   734
    Reference Altering a Passed Query   736
    Returning a Query   740
    Returning Multiple Queries   743
In Sum   743

Chapter 22   Using cfexecute   745

Why Use cfexecute?   746
    Reasons for Using cfexecute   746
Specifying the Application to Be Run   747
    Passing Multiple Arguments to Commands   750
    Using Timeouts to Avoid Endless Loops   753
    Limitations on Executing Applications   756
Effective Use of Output   757
    Storing Output in a File   757
    Capturing the Output in a Variable   759
cfexecute Security Issues   760
    Risks of cfexecute on a Server with FTP/RDS Access   761
    Limiting the Risks of Using cfexecute   761
In Sum   762

Part VI   Integrating with External Services   763

Chapter 23   Integrating with Flash MX   765

Using Flash MX   766
    Building Applications Using Flash   767
    Putting Flash Documents Online   775
    An Overview of ActionScript   776
Integration Using LoadVars   780
    Flash and the LoadVars Object   780
    Building a Mail Application Using LoadVars   782
Flash Remoting MX   788
    Using Remoting for Communication   788
    Your First Flash Remoting Document   789
    RecordSets and Flash Remoting   801

Using the DataGlue Class 803
Building a Dynamic Image Gallery 805
Working with Server-Side ActionScript 815
Web Services and Flash Remoting MX 820
Determining the Weather Using Flash Remoting and Web Services 821
Calculating Distance with Flash, ColdFusion, and Flash Remoting 826
In Sum 835

Chapter 24   Web Services   837

Web Services Defined 838
WSDL 838
SOAP 839
UDDI 839
Interoperability Stack 839
Consuming Web Services 840
Consuming Web Services Automatically with cfinvoke 840
Consuming Web Services Automatically with createObject( ) 843
Consuming Web Services Manually 843
The Process Flow for Consuming Web Services 845
Consuming Web Services Manually with cfhttp and cfxml 846
Consuming Web Services Manually with Apache Axis 849
Producing Web Services 851
Using CFCs 851
The Process Flow for Producing Web Services 854
In Sum 855

Appendices   857

Appendix A   Configuring ColdFusion for Java   857

JVM Requirements 858
Sun Microsystems 858
IBM 858
HP 858
The Administrator's Java Settings 859
Java Virtual Machine Path 860
Memory Sizes 860

	Class Path	860
	JVM Arguments	861
Appendix B	**Understanding UML Class Diagrams**	**863**
	UML	864
	Elements of a Class Diagram	864
	Classes	864
	Types of Relationships	865
	Packages	868
	Notes	869
Appendix C	**Using the Code from This Book**	**871**
	Index	*873*

Introduction

I still remember the day my mother brought home our first computer. It was an Apple IIe with 64K of RAM and a lovely monochrome monitor. More importantly, it came with a stack of floppy disks—most of which were games to which I became quickly addicted. After having trouble with one game in particular (for those who are old enough to remember, it was Bard's Tale), I decided to cheat. But I was more interested in *how* I could cheat and whether it was even possible, than I was in winning the game. I soon discovered a software program that let me actually edit the hex of my saved game, and so began my introduction to the hexadecimal number system.

Next came my first attempts at programming, using what I think was called Applesoft BASIC. As hard as I tried, I couldn't get even the simplest program to work. And the documentation was no help. But then I accomplished a huge leap forward: I read the documentation again, more slowly. I discovered that I had forgotten to hit the Enter key! I was entering a line of code, and then hitting the spacebar until the cursor wrapped to the next line. It was moments like that—both agonizing and exciting at once—that got me into computer programming so many years ago. A language (both computer and spoken) is more than the sum of its parts, more than just its syntax. There is also a "way" or a style that needs to be applied.

Much later, but when the Web was still young (and though it feels like many years ago, it really isn't), I did all of my web application programming in the wonderful Perl language. At that time, using Perl with the Web was a bit difficult—especially when it was time to wrap the Perl code with site formatting. One day, a project came in that required database access. I knew that Perl could do this, but I had no idea how. On a whim, I downloaded a free trial of ColdFusion 2. What a revelation! It was so easy to use that I had a fully functional site up and running in one week!

ColdFusion landed in a sweet spot: It was both powerful and easy to use. In addition, its tag-based syntax melded nicely with HTML. This last point is crucial, and in a way it is this syntax that formed the basis for both ColdFusion's success and its resulting community of programmers. When the World Wide Web started attracting attention from people outside of the government and academia, it seemed that everyone wanted to learn HTML—from middle-school kids to middle-aged used-bookstore owners. You didn't need training in computer science to learn HTML well enough to create compelling websites, and home pages began to pop up like dandelions. Soon, people with backgrounds in medieval French poetry, ecology, and music pedagogy (and, yes, even computer science) found careers as web programmers for companies that suddenly felt the need for a *web presence*.

When the requirement for web pages—driven by the burgeoning world of e-commerce—grew from presenting static presentations to serving up data on demand, ColdFusion was exactly what HTML programmers needed: a language designed to access databases that worked like extensions of good ol' HTML. It was an easy solution to a difficult problem. (Compare a ColdFusion query to a database query in ASP sometime, and you'll see what I mean.)

Despite its ease of use, ColdFusion—especially after the quantum leap of the new version, ColdFusion MX—is a powerful language that attracts professional programmers who need sophisticated solutions for large-scale enterprises. Here's where this book comes in. It's one thing to learn the fundamentals of ColdFusion, and quite another to take your skills to the next level by using ColdFusion along with other, less-easy-to-learn languages such as XML, Java, and C++. Furthermore, large applications need speed and efficiency, and you get that with performance turning, load balancing, and caching—topics that are only touched upon, if addressed at all, in standard ColdFusion books. Other topics, as well, are crucial for the enterprise application developer: security, troubleshooting, writing complex SQL queries, integrating Flash, and designing applications, to name just a few. All these topics and more are found within these pages.

Not all of this book is for everyone: It wasn't intended to be. But every chapter is packed with technical knowledge that gives you what you need to create serious solutions. You might find that one chapter alone is worth the cost of the book because of the time and frustration you save yourself by reading it. Most readers, however, will use various parts of this book at different times, depending on the constantly changing challenges faced by enterprise programmers. The mission of this book is to take you "outside the box" and provide the extra skills you need to be a successful ColdFusion developer in today's demanding environment.

—Raymond Camden

PART I

Managing Content and Applications

Chapter 1: Designing and Planning a ColdFusion Application

Chapter 2: Troubleshooting and Debugging ColdFusion Code

Chapter 3: State Management in a Clustered Environment

Chapter 4: The Fusebox Framework and Development Methodology

Chapter 5: Developing Component-Based Applications

Chapter 6: Creating Search Engines with Verity

Chapter 7: Advanced WDDX

Chapter 8: Application Security Techniques

Chapter 9: Archives and Deployment

Chapter 10: Source Code Management

CHAPTER 1

Designing and Planning a ColdFusion Application

By Shlomy Gantz

- Gathering technical requirements

- Designing the application architecture

- Prototyping your application front end

- Using naming conventions

- Comments and documentation

- Applying coding standards

- Additional planning

For many developers, planning and designing an application is that elusive phase that comes somewhere before coding and after signing the contract. Some developers perceive such up-front research as too expensive or time-consuming, or they believe that they already understand enough of their customers' needs. As a result, there is never enough time devoted to planning, and there is always pressure to start coding. In fact, planning a ColdFusion application is usually done quickly or even not at all. The flexibility of ColdFusion plays into this lack of planning, and many developers choose to go through an iterative approach in which they design the application as they code. This approach usually leads to an endless cycle of coding and debugging.

How many times have you found yourself at the end of a project saying, "I wish I had designed this application differently; it would have saved me so much time" or "I wish I had more time to plan"? Building an application without plans is like trying to build a house with just a hammer, some nails, and a couple of two-by-fours. It's a sure bet that you will either run out of materials, find out that you can't close the bathroom door because the toilet is in the way, or wind up with a house that looks great for the entire summer only to become an indoor swimming pool by the time winter arrives.

Although learning the syntax of the ColdFusion language is important, almost equal emphasis should be given to understanding how the ColdFusion Server works, applying best-practices, and using common design patterns. Planning becomes increasingly important in ColdFusion MX, the brand new and rebuilt version of the ColdFusion Server. Designing your application with the new concepts introduced in ColdFusion MX will help you deliver more scalable and robust applications.

This chapter shows you ways to design and plan your application in advance, which will help you create manageable applications, reduce complexity, and allow for extensibility and code re-use. Here, you'll find application design concepts and best practices that have helped me develop large ColdFusion applications.

Gathering Technical Requirements

You can never have too many requirements. They range from business requirements and functional requirements to technical requirements. While business and functional requirements are ones with which your client can easily provide you, very few clients will be able to give you clear and concise technical requirements.

For most clients, the technical requirements would be something along the lines of they want their application to have 100 percent uptime, they want it to be an ultra-fast download, and they want it to be extremely secure (you've probably heard *that* before...). Although these statements make sense, they do not represent useful technical requirements. In fact, the most important characteristic of a technical requirement is that its parameters can be measured.

Descriptions such as "ultra-fast downloads" should be translated into "an average download time of 2 seconds per page on a 28.8Kbps connection," and statements such as "We should have a very secure site so that no one can steal our credit card numbers" should be translated into "The site will use 128-bit SSL to ensure security on all transactions." By changing those metrics into measurable technical requirements, you are creating a way in which you can measure the technical success of the project later on.

TIP When you are evaluating the client's technical requirements, it is best to ask very specific questions and also provide the client with a list of options and their estimated cost.

At a minimum, a technical requirement document should contain the following items:

- Performance metrics:
    - Maximum/average response time; for example, "Avg. response time must be under 2000 ms."
    - Max number of concurrent sessions; for example, "Application will support up to 50 concurrent user sessions."
- Client side requirements:
    - Browser support; for example, "Application will support IE4.0+ and Netscape 4.0+ for Mac and Windows."
    - Usage of Flash/ActiveX/Java; for example, "Application will not use ActiveX controls or Java applets."
    - Section 508 compliance (accessibility for people with disabilities); for example, "The application will fully comply with Section 508 standards."
- Hardware constraints; for example, "The application will be tested and deployed for Pentium 4 processor hardware with a minimum of 515MB RAM and 40GB of free disk space."
- Data constraints:
    - Estimated number of records in database; for example, "the application will be developed to support up to 1 million products."
    - Estimated number of retrieved records; for example, "the application will retrieve up to 100 records at a time."
- Integration consideration:
    - Third-party product integration; for example, "The application will integrate with fusetalk forums to provide discussion forum functionality."

- Legacy system/database integration; for example, "The web-based system will integrate in real-time with the company's AS400 ordering system."

- Budgetary constraints; for example, "The web-based system will integrate in real-time with the company's AS400 ordering system."

I have yet to encounter requirements that did not change in the course of the project. Clients will eventually change their minds; and this is not only very common, but it is also unavoidable. Though most changes are usually functional, always check their effect on the technical requirements. If change is required, document it.

Designing the Application Architecture

Web application architecture refers to a set of blueprints and models used to map out the various functional, logical, and physical elements of a web application. Just as creating the blueprint for a new building is part of a successful project for an architect, planning your application architecture is an essential part of any successful software project in which you participate. A blueprint will serve as your guide during the development process, and it will help you to avoid critical mistakes in code and design—mistakes that can cost you a lot of time and money.

Good application architecture encompasses both the physical and logical structures of the application and their interaction, and it provides a clear roadmap of solutions to the problems ahead. Although you can easily write ColdFusion code without an architecture, the benefits of spending the time to specify one pays off in the long run. Building an application without specifying its architecture is like driving without a map, the further away you go, the more chances you have of getting lost. Having the right architecture becomes increasingly important as your application scope grows.

Setting Up a Physical Architecture

One of the first things you should plan when you are building a ColdFusion application is the physical environment on which the application will be developed and deployed as shown in Figure 1.1. This becomes even more critical when you're developing for a clustered environment. A good physical architecture should include the following:

- Hardware configuration and specification

- Network configuration

- Operating system information

- Servers and applications

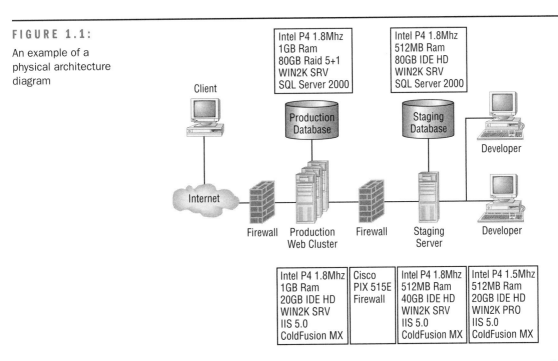

FIGURE 1.1:

An example of a physical architecture diagram

The physical architecture becomes increasingly important when scalability is concerned. In large-scale applications, it makes sense to solve performance issues by adding servers rather than by writing complex code.

The reason for turning to hardware solutions is simple: hardware has a fixed cost while programming is always variable. Estimating development time (especially on optimization projects) is a subject for an entire book, but estimating the cost of hardware is usually a web link or a phone call away. Although adding memory to upgrade the processor will not solve all of your problems, it will involve considerably less effort and time than maintaining highly complex application code does. That comparison alone should make you think of a hardware solution first.

NOTE   Know your environment! Writing code that can easily be deployed across clusters requires you to plan and consider several restrictions that do not exist in a single-server model. Be sure that you are aware of the physical environment on which your ColdFusion MX application will be deployed. And make sure that you understand that environment far enough ahead of time so that you can avoid any significant issues of OS incompatibility, scalability, and database integration.

Designing Databases and Data Models

The following section illustrates the importance of early database planning and choosing the right database and tools for your application. Although this section may refer to specific databases, such as Microsoft SQL Server or Oracle, it applies to all types of databases.

Designing your database prior to development instead of adding fields as you progress will help you find some of the hidden caveats of the data model such as missed data and misinterpretations. In addition, this process will help you identify the main data interactions in your application and gain a general overview without writing one line of code. Designing up front does not mean you cannot add new items later. However, making core architectural decisions ahead of time does allow you to overcome changes in the data model that may arise later on. Such an example is shown below. Suppose your client requests that you build a simple product category tree with only two levels: category and subcategory. He assures you that there will be additional levels to the tree, and that each product can only be in one subcategory. What are your options? Do you

1. Create a Products table with two columns Category and SubCategory—as shown here:

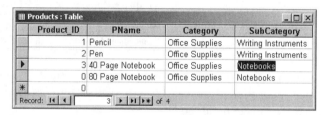

or do you

2. Create a Categories table with three columns—Category_ID, Parent_ID, and Category_ Desc—as shown here:

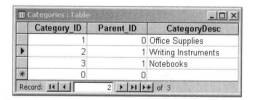

If you chose A, you are right; however, if you chose B, you are also right and probably have some experience working with clients. If there is one thing I've learned in my years of development, it's that clients will always change their minds.

Let me explain this more thoroughly. Option A is simple to implement and answers the client's immediate need. However, if a client requests any change, such as adding another level or a product that can be linked to two categories, you will have to change the database and probably change a lot of code. Even renaming a category would become a hassle, since you would have to rename all the rows with the same category name.

Option B is a bit more complex to understand, but it provides nearly unlimited flexibility and will usually accommodate any parent-child relationship.

Although designing your database in advance is not always possible, always make sure you build the basic data model before you start coding. To do so, you can use tools such as ER/Studio (http://www.embarcadero.com) or even Microsoft Visio. The advantage of using these tools is that they allow you to do *round-trip design*. That means you can reverse engineer an already built database into the tool, automatically producing a diagram based on a previously built database, or you can create a new database from a diagram created in the tool.

TIP   Microsoft SQL Server and Oracle both have their own suite of database design tools. Designing your database in a separate tool allows you to easily generate the same database on different database platforms.

Choosing the right database is equally important, though in some cases the database is actually in a legacy system and cannot be changed. The technical requirements you already gathered and documented will help you in making the right decision.

Although small databases such as Access or mySQL might be sufficient for a small website, most commercial ColdFusion websites use Microsoft SQL Server or Oracle. The differences between these two types of database are in the number of users that can be processed simultaneously, the query execution speed, and number of records the database can reasonably handle. Larger databases have the ability to perform complex operations using triggers, stored procedures, and so on; leveraging those features can increase performance and functionality, but it might reduce the flexibility you have migrating to another platform later on.

To choose the right database, you need to factor in the data model complexity, the amount of data you need to store, and the performance and reliability of the software. Budgetary constraints might also limit you to smaller databases. Make sure you are aware of the constraints of the particular database you choose; this will make it easier to solve performance related issues.

NOTE   See Part II of this book, "Advanced Database Integration," for more information about database techniques.

The Importance of Choosing the Right Database

Making sure that the database interaction is not slowing down your application is one of the first things you should check when you encounter performance related issues.

In one of my consulting engagements, I was brought in to solve some performance issues for a B2B (business-to-business) exchange. Although I was prepared to bring all my code optimization techniques to the table, I quickly discovered that they were using Microsoft Access to store large quantities of data, and they were executing complex queries. Because I knew that a larger database would better handle these queries, I switched them over to SQL Server. This quick and simple migration had a substantial positive impact on performance, and no expensive code changes were needed apart from a few minor queries.

Creating Tiered Applications

Creating separate logical parts, or tiers, in ColdFusion applications has many benefits—from increased scalability to easily manageable code. Tiers can be separated physically on different machines or they can co-exist locally on one machine while maintaining their unique roles.

Although the concept of an *n*-tiered application (multiple tiers in one application) is not unique to ColdFusion, using such an architecture can be extremely beneficial in the long run, especially when you are developing large and complex applications.

Single and 2-Tiered Architectures

The simplest form of a tiered architecture is a single-tiered application; most Windows applications, such as Microsoft Word or Dreamweaver MX, are examples of this type of application. In a single-tiered architecture, all parts of the application are combined in the same physical location.

A more advanced architecture is a 2-tiered application, which is usually based on a simple client-server model. In this architecture, the client makes a service request from another program, and the server fulfills the request.

n-Tiered Architecture

An *n*-tiered application is one that is distributed among three or more separate parts in a distributed network .The simplest form of an *n*-tiered ColdFusion architecture is a 3-tiered architecture (shown in Figure 1.2). A 3-tiered application is organized into three major parts, each of which is distributed to a different place or places in a network. In this model, all tasks and routines are stored in the same ColdFusion template that is requested on the URL. There are no custom tags, CFCs, cfmodules, or cfincludes.

The three common tiers in an *n*-tiered architecture are as follows:

- The Client tier, which is usually the browser
- The Business Logic tier, which is usually a ColdFusion template
- The Data tier, which is usually the database server

FIGURE 1.2:

A diagram of a 3-tiered architecture

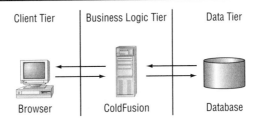

Client Tier   Business Logic Tier   Data Tier

Browser   ColdFusion   Database

Here is the code for a simple 3 tiered architecture:

showMemberList.cfm
```
<cfquery name="qryMemberList" datasource="#request.dsn#">
    select firstname,lastname from members
</cfquery>

<table>

    <tr><td>First Name</td><td>Last Name</td></tr>

    <cfoutput query="qryMemberList">
    <tr><td>#firstName#</td><td>#lastName#</td></tr>
    </cfoutput>

</table>
```

Although a 3-tiered architecture is clearly the simplest way of writing ColdFusion applications and has been the popular model for a long time, new versions of ColdFusion contain features that allow you to build better and more flexible models. Leveraging those new features will allow you to write code that is more scalable, reusable, and simpler to debug.

A more advanced approach is to design 4 or even 5 tiers in your applications, so that they include the following:

- Client tier
- Presentation tier
- Business logic tier
- Data integration tier
- Data tier

Separating the application into additional tiers allows you to scale each tier separately, divide the workload between developers, and have them focus on their unique skill sets (see Figure 1.3). Building 4 and 5 tiered applications allows you to re-use code across the application or even across the enterprise, thus increasing readability and maintainability.

FIGURE 1.3:

A simple 5-tiered architecture

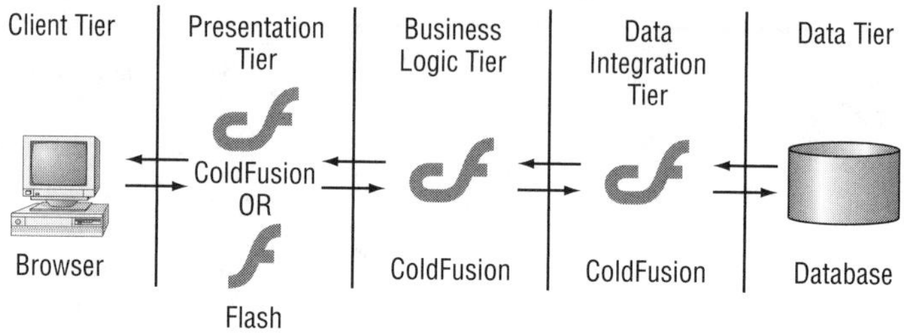

Listings 1.1, 1.2, and 1.3 contain sample code for a simple member listing application. The first template, ShowMemberList.cfm, invokes a component that returns the member recordset from the database. The template then calls two custom tags that apply formatting and simplify presentation. The first tag displays a list of preformatted table headers, the second displays the data.

Listing 1.1   Sample Code for an *n*-Tiered Architecture: Presentation Tier (ShowMemberList.cfm)

```
<!--
   Name:          /c01/ShowMemberList.cfm
   Description:   A template displaying member list from the database
-->

<cfinvoke component="member.cfc" method="getMemberList"
returnVariable="qryMemberList">

<table>
   <cf_UItableHeaders columns="First Name,Last Name">
   <cf_UItableData query="#qryMembers#" columns="#getMembers.columnlist#">
</table>
```

Listing 1.2   Sample Code for an *n*-Tiered Architecture: Data Integration Tier (member.cfc)

```
<!--
   Name:          /c01/member.cfc
   Description:   A cold fusion component retrieving the Member list from the
database
-->
```

```
<cfcomponent>

<cffunction name="getMemberList" access="remote">

    <cfquery name="qryMemberList" datasource="MyDatabase">
        select firstName,lastName
        from Members
    </cfquery>

    <cfreturn qryMemberList>
</cffunction>

</cfcomponent>
```

Listing 1.3   Sample Code for an *n*-Tiered Architecture: Presentation Tier (UITableHeaders.cfm)

```
<!--
   Name:         /c01/UITableHeaders.cfm
   Description:  A custom tag used to display table column headers
-->
<cfparam name="attributes.columns" default="" type="string">

<tr>
    <cfloop list="#attributes.columns#" index="columnIDX">
        <td><cfoutput>#columnIDX#</cfoutput></td>
    </cfloop>
</tr>
```

Although the advantages of writing code this way are not immediately evident, using these techniques allows you to create consistent behaviors in your applications; this consistency becomes increasingly important during the debugging process.

Now that you've seen an example of an *n*-tiered application, take a look at the following, which is an explanation of the common functionality and characteristics of each tier.

Client Tier

The client tier usually consists of a web browser. Making sure you apply the right set of standards (a contradiction in terms) for the right browser is crucial. Internet Explorer, Netscape, and even AOL differ in the way they handle JavaScript, the DOM (Document Object Model), layers, and even HTML tags.

In some cases, the client tier might consist of additional devices such as a cellular phone, handheld, or any other Internet-enabled device. It's common practice among developers working with multiple devices to use one set of modules to retrieve the data and then display client-specific versions of the UI.

Presentation Tier

The presentation tier contains either dynamically generated HTML code or even a Flash application. You can create HTML modules to create common UI (User Interface) elements, and apply display standards across the application. This tier handles all logic related to the way you present data to the user.

Tighter integration of ColdFusion with Flash MX makes it into a popular tool for presentation tiers. When you use Flash, you make it easier for your designers to focus on interaction and design, which allows you, the developer, to focus on the business logic and Data tiers.

NOTE   For more information about Flash MX integration, see Chapter 23 "Integrating with Flash MX."

Business Logic Tier

The business logic tier contains most of the functionality of the application. Most calculations and logical operations will be done in that tier. A set of business rules and processes are created that map out the interaction of users, tiers, or even other systems. These rules vary from e-mail validation schemes to user restrictions and are usually applied through the use of UDFs (User Defined Functions), CFCs (ColdFusion Components), or custom tags. An example of such a rule is validating an e-mail address.

The following listing (Listing 1.4) contains code for a simple e-mail validation UDF. Using a common UDF to perform form validation is a common practice among advanced ColdFusion developers. This ensures that all e-mails will be validated the same way throughout the application, and that changes need only be applied to one template.

Listing 1.4   **Simple E-mail Address Validation Using a UDF (isEmail.cfm)**

```
<!--
    Name:          /c01/isEmail.cfm
    Description:   UDF to validate email address
-->
<cfscript>
/**
 * Tests passed value to see if it is a valid e-mail address (supports subdomain
   nesting and new top-level domains).
 * Update by David Kearns to support '
 * SBrown@xacting.com pointing out regex still wasn't accepting ' correctly.
 *
 * @param str     The string to check. (Required)
 * @return Returns a boolean.
 * @author Jeff Guillaume (jeff@kazoomis.com)
 * @version 2, August 15, 2002
 */
function IsEmail(str) {
        //supports new top level tlds
```

```
if (REFindNoCase("^['_a-z0-9-]+(\.['_a-z0-9-]+)*@[a-z0-9-]+(\.[a-z0-9-
]+)*\.(([a-z]{2,3})|(aero|coop|info|museum|name))$",str)) return TRUE;
   else return FALSE;
}
</cfscript>
```

Most business rules are applied within internal processes that drive the application interaction. These processes may include one or more steps, rules, and process logic associated with those rules. Here's an example of several simple rules for a login process:

- Username must be entered.

- Password must be entered.

- User must exist in the database.

- Password must match the password stored in the database.

The login process may also consist of the following steps, as illustrated in Figure 1.4:

1. Validate required information.

2. Check database for password match.

3. Check database for user.

4. Return message to the user.

FIGURE 1.4:

Login process logical diagram

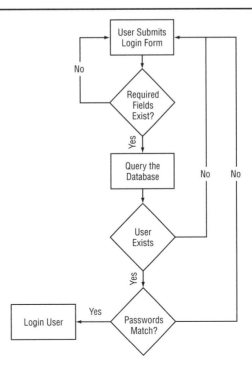

Encapsulating business process logic in CFCs, modules, custom tags, or even EJBs (Enterprise Java Beans) will allow you greater flexibility, extensibility, and reliability. Making sure your business logic is applied consistently throughout your application will also ensure that you will be able to debug or change your application easily.

Data Integration Tier

The data integration tier handles all requests to the data tier. Usually the data tier will consist of a set of `cfquerys` or `cfstoredprocs` stored in a ColdFusion template. In some cases, your data tier might consist of XML documents or files and therefore `cffile` or `cfxml` might be used.

Separating your queries or stored procedures from the presentation or business logic code will enable you or your DBA to optimize the queries in a process parallel to that of your development effort. By using the same template when you are accessing or manipulating the data, you simplify the process of adding or changing database interactions.

How a Simple Query Can Cause Trouble

Several years ago, I was hired to fix a large-scale call accounting application written in Cold-Fusion. To my surprise, many templates had the same `cfquery` at the beginning of the page, with little variations between the templates. The developers simply cut and paste the query every time they created a new template. This habit created what can only be described as maintenance hell. Every time a change was made, it had to be applied to all the templates, which of course created new and unpredictable bugs.

Even if you think you will only be using the query once, consider encapsulating it in a CFC or `cfmodule`. You will often find that doing this will save you many hours of coding and debugging. Building a data integration tier can also save you a lot of time if you later decide to change database vendors.

Data Tier

The data tier usually consists of a database server such as Microsoft SQL Server, Oracle, Access, and so on. If you make sure that the data is stored in a separate tier, you will keep the data independent of your presentation and business logic. The data tier allows other applications to access it, and it allows you to scale and build data clusters as your application needs increase.

Mapping the Logical Architecture

Mapping the business processes and site interactions into logical diagrams will help you simplify complex logical processes and flows. By creating logical diagrams, you can map out potential problems and complexities ahead of time and produce the solution with your client. The benefits become exponentially greater as you face more complex applications and workflows.

In many cases, you do not have to create diagrams for every single function and process. The point at which you stop diagramming and start coding is determined by the complexity of your application. The more complex the backend processes are, the more benefits you will have from mapping them out in advance. I have frequently seen projects go off schedule due to excessive documenting that led to endless discussions. Mapping out simple operations such as add, edit, or delete should only be done if other processes are related.

One of the best tools used to create Logical and Application Flow diagrams is UML (Unified Modeling Language). Creating Activity, Class, Use Case, and Sequence diagrams will provide a clear functional roadmap for your application by visually representing relationships, dependencies and flows. Using UML becomes increasingly beneficial when creating n-tiered architectures, allowing you to map processes and flows among the various tiers.

NOTE   For more information about UML, see Appendix B "Understanding UML Class Diagrams."

NOTE   For a list of UML tools, see `http://www.objectsbydesign.com/tools/umltools_byCompany.html`.

Identifying Third Party Products

One of the biggest improvements in productivity comes from code re-use, but why limit yourself to your own code? There are many ColdFusion developers that are willing to share their code for a minimal fee or no fee at all. These components range from simple form elements to fully functional discussion forums. When you buy a new house, do you build your own refrigerator? Air conditioner? Cabinets? Most of us will use prebuilt appliances and parts in our everyday life. Applying the same logic to application development simply makes sense.

Although your first impulse might be to code everything yourself, using third party products can greatly reduce development time, and most ColdFusion products have an unencrypted version you can customize. ColdFusion MX extensibility is easier than ever. When you are looking for third party solutions, expanding your search beyond ColdFusion to Java and COM objects will increase your chances of finding the right solution.

Some complex applications require custom development and might require features that are not available in commercial third party products. Most third party solutions offer customization services by partners or their own development teams. Consider customizing existing applications rather than building the entire application from scratch.

TIP   The first place to look for third party products is the Macromedia Developer Exchange (`http://devex.macromedia.com/developer/gallery`). You can also find a wealth of information and code on `http://www.cflib.org` and `http://www.cfzone.net`.

Prototyping a Front End

Whether a website is successful or not depends as much on client involvement as it does on the developer's abilities. The biggest obstacle to getting clients involved is that they usually do not understand most of the technical issues involved in building the application. After all, they are not developers and do not have the technical background and experience that you have. Using a prototype can help you get the client involved early on in the development process, thus helping you avoid countless hours of "last minute" changes.

A *prototype* is a fully functional model of the finished application. That is to say it appears to function how it is supposed to, but nothing actually happens on the back end. The prototype demonstrates what the application will do but without requiring any processing resources. Building a prototype is similar to the way architects often build small models to demonstrate the finished building to their clients. Seeing the model or application will help the client understand what the finished product will look like.

When clients are able to see the system, interact with it, and understand what the final result will look like, they will able to provide you with meaningful input that will help you build the right application for them. In fact, many of my clients find it hard to distinguish between the prototype and a live system.

TIP   Dreamweaver MX is one of the most widely used prototyping tools. Using its intuitive WYSIWYG editor, you can easily create and change HTML prototypes.

Changing a prototype is simple, easy, and fast. This process requires basic HTML knowledge and minimal effort when compared to changing a fully coded system. Adding a field is as simple as adding an `<input>` tag to your code. Changing code at the prototype phase has no influence on the final code stability. It will not add any new bugs, and unlike a full blown application change, it will not result in caffeine induced sleepless nights of bug hunting, testing, and frustration.

But the advantages of prototype are not restricted to the client. You will also benefit from building the prototype since you will be able to fully understand the client's vision, hash out any potential issues and interaction complexities in advance, and reduce the risk of last-minute-changes. Developing an application after the prototype is complete allows you to focus on server-side functionality, making it easier to focus on ColdFusion code rather than trying to complete the front end and back end at the same time.

Figure 1.5 shows a prototype page and the corresponding page in the final application. Can you find the difference? (The answer is at the bottom of the diagram.)

A Prototype page and a Final Application page

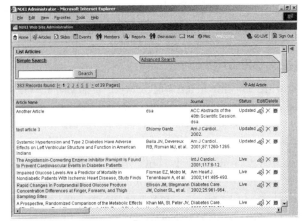

Prototype

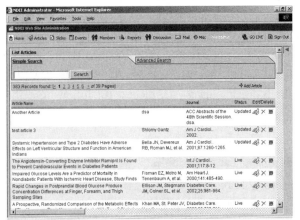

Final Application

Obviously, there is no difference!

WARNING Always develop a 100 percent fully functional prototype. Excluding functionality and creating a partial prototype may create *scope creep* at the beginning of the project. Although this is better than having scope creep after you've started coding, it will still affect the development schedule.

Many times I have had clients go through the prototype only to find out that they needed additional features, or that they needed to change a workflow or process.

TIP   A detailed prototype will save you countless hours of development time. Use it to your advantage and keep the development period as short as possible. That way you shorten the amount of time the client has to come up with those annoying new "little features."

Naming Conventions

When you are working in a team, or even when you are coding alone, make sure you establish clear and defined naming conventions and coding standards. This will allow other programmers to easily understand your code, and it will ensure that even when you look at your application two years from now, you will be able to quickly review and change the code.

A standards document evolves over time and will help new developers understand the way you code, and it will allow you to collaborate more easily. Although the investment in this document is substantial and might be time consuming, the rewards are immediate. By applying common standards, you make another step toward application stability and behavioral consistency.

Some resistance to such standards is natural. Can you honestly say that you have ever seen someone else's code that you thought was as good as your own? Just remember, if you allow team members to contribute to the document; it will become a great learning tool for the junior programmers and an excellent way to elicit knowledge from the more experienced ones.

Standards documents usually include the following items:

- Naming variables/queries/structures/arrays
- Naming files/directories
- Naming application variables
- Naming tables/columns
- Comments and documentation
- Security considerations
- methodology
- Exception handling

NOTE   Sean A. Corfield, Macromedia's director of architecture, has an excellent coding guideline available at `http://www.corfield.org/coldfusion/codingStandards.htm`.

Naming Variables/Queries/Structures/Arrays

A variable name and the variable are essentially the same thing. The "quality" of a variable is largely determined by its name. Consistently choosing the right variable name and applying naming conventions improves predictability and allows team members to understand and integrate your code more easily.

Here is an example of bad variable naming:

```
<cfset x2 = 1>
<cfset theNameOfThePersonInTheDatabase = "John">
<cfset flag = 0>
<cfquery name="AM" datasource="#request.dsn#">
```

And here is an example of good variable naming:

```
<cfset employeeID = 1>
<cfset stFirstName = "John">
<cfset isDelieverd = 0>
<cfquery name="qryAddMember" datasource="#request.dsn#">
```

Good variable names fully describe the entity those variables represent. They are easily readable and their meanings are obvious. Avoid using names with similar spelling or sounds. You should also avoid using names that contain hard-to-read characters such as lowercase "l" and the number 1, or the letter "O" and zero.

TIP Bad variable naming can have a real effect on your application. For example, naming a variable `"form"` in CF5 was allowed, and as a result, some applications have used that name extensively. However, in ColdFusion MX, `"form"` is a reserved name and it will always refer to a structure containing form elements that have been submitted.

Naming Files/Directories

Naming files consistently allows you to easily collaborate with other developers and reduce guesswork about the file's function. The name should represent the function of the file without ambiguity.

Using consistent naming pairs is important. Some of the more common pairs are as follows:

- Add/remove
- Insert/delete
- First/last
- Create/destroy
- Show/hide

Some methodologies, such as Fusebox (see Chapter 4, "The Fusebox Framework and Development Methodology"), specify file-naming conventions and thus allow any developer to easily identify the files and their function in your application. Fusebox uses dsp_*xxxx*.cfm and act_*xxxx*.cfm to better state the template's purpose (display or action).

Organizing files and modules into different directories is also important. Make sure you group templates with similar functions into the same directory, thus allowing easy access to the files you need. In addition, think of what you would rather maintain: one big ColdFusion file or many small templates. The importance of separating logical component into different physical files will be described later on in the "Cohesion and Coupling" section.

Naming Database Tables/Columns

Just as creating a naming standard for variables increases predictability, developing the same standards for tables, columns, and other objects in you database will allow you to develop applications faster and easily identify the needed database elements. The following is a simplified list of the database naming standards that I have applied over the years.

Keep these in mind when you are naming tables:

- Table names should be a clear reflection of the data stored in the table.

- If a table is connecting others in a many-to-many relationship, both "Parent" table names should be used as shown here:

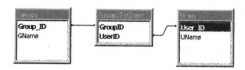

Keep these in mind when you are naming columns:

- The column name should be a clear reflection of the data stored in the table.

- The primary key of a table should contain an indicator, such as the boldfaced letters in these names: **pk**User, User**Code**, User**_ID**.

- The foreign key of a table should contain the same indicator as the primary key it refers to but with a variation. The following examples correspond to the primary key examples given just above: **fk**User, **fk**User**Code**, User**ID** (no underscore).

- Boolean (Yes/No) fields should contain an indicator; for example: Active**_YN**, **is**Active, and so on.

- Fields containing dates or times should contain an indicator; for example Record**Date**, **dt**Record, and so on.

- Never use the special characters ~ , @, #, $, and of course **#**.

- Avoid using spaces. Though some databases allow you to put spaces inside column names, this might cause various problems later on in the application development process while you are trying to output the data in your CF application.

- Do not use reserved words such as system, option, level, and so on.

Comments and Documentation

One of the most frustrating tasks facing a developer is going through someone else's code, either debugging or inheriting a legacy application. This task becomes even more frustrating when the code does not contain any documentation or comments. I frequently find that debugging another developer's code takes a long time because it takes awhile for me to figure out what they were trying to do.

You should apply documentation standards at the beginning of the project. I have often postponed documentation, meaning to do it at the end of the project, only to find out after the project is complete that I never did. You will find, as I have, that good documentation can be a lifesaver, even when you are looking at your own code. This is especially true if you solved a complex problem; make sure to document it on the spot.

First let's look at some examples of bad commenting. The following example is of a simple member list sorting mechanism.

```
getMembers.cfm
<!-- Set a paramenter called sort -->
<cfparam name="sort" default="lastName">
<!-- Query the database -->
<cfquery name="getMembers" datasource="myDatabase">
select firstName, lastName, e-mail from members</cfquery>

<!-- Open an HTML table -->
<table>
    <tr><td><A href="getMembers.cfm?sort=lastName">name</a></td><td><a
href="getMembers.cfm?sort=e-mail">e-mail</a></td>
    </tr>
    <!- loop over the records from the query -->
    <cfoutput query="getMembers">
    <tr><!-- Show the member to the user -->
    <td>#lastName#, #firstName#</td><td>#e-mail#</td>
    </tr></cfoutput>
    <!-- Close the table -->
</table>
(spelling mistakes are intentional)
```

Obviously the comments in this code do not contribute anything to our understanding of the code; indeed, they actually clutter the page with useless information. When comments are made and what the comments are depend on the developer and on the intended audience. The problem gets worse when there is no consistent layout or indentation of code.

Avoid adding comments that simply restate what the code does. For instance, the following command is duplicative and unnecessary:

```
<!-- Loop over records from qryMembers query -->
<cfloop query="qryMembers">
</cfloop>
```

TIP   Making sure that you indent your code can make it more readable. Although HomeSite+ and Studio both have code sweepers that indent your document automatically, it is possible that the code sweeper may encounter problems when it processes code that is not 100 percent valid (missing quotes, missing tags, and so on). Use such features carefully and make sure you have backups.

Do some things in these bad examples look familiar? In these next sections, we'll examine some ways to make sure that your code can be understood by all who read it.

Using Template Headers

One common form of helpful documentation is to begin all code templates with a standard document header describing the purpose of the file, the version, the date it was created, and the date it was updated. Here is an example of such a header:

```
<!--
      Application: www.MyCompany.com
      File:  getMembers.cfm
      Description:   Displays a list of members.
      Author:  Shlomy Gantz (shlomy@sybex.com)
      Date:  4/11/2002
      Revisions:
      09/12/2002 - Added Clickable sorting headers


(c) 2002 Sybex Inc. , This code is owned by Sybex. It may not be copied
in part or in full without the express permission of Sybex Inc.
Sybex reserves all rights to this code.
Contact Sybex at info@sybex.com to discuss any utilization of this code.
-->
```

Documentation can be more than just information for other developers working on the project. In fact, you can use documentation as an opportunity to "show off" by explaining the inner logic of your code and the "beauty" of your solution. And though minimal documentation standards should be enforced, they shouldn't be enforced to the point where the rules are too rigid and are slowing down the development process.

TIP   Set up your default template on HomeSite+ or Studio to include your own template header. This can be done by editing `C:\Program Files\Macromedia\HomeSite+\Wizards\HTML\Default Template.htm`.

Using a Program Design Language

Some coding techniques actually want you to document the code before you start coding. This technique allows you to map out what you are trying to do in plain English using a Program Design Language (PDL). Using a PDL is a simple way of creating minimal documentation before coding. I have often used that technique and found it to be very useful when I have been designing code to handle large and intricate processes. Listing 1.5 is an example of a PDL in action.

Listing 1.5   PDL–Member Listing (getMembers.pdl)

```
<!--
   Name:          /c01/getMember.pdl
   Description:   An initial PDL for member list
-->
Set a default parameter to sort the member list
Get the member list from the database

Display clickable table headers that reload the document with each new sort
Display member list.
```

If you combine the original PDL with the final code, you will get a readable template with meaningful documentation, as is shown in Listing 1.6.

Listing 1.6   The Final Code–Member Listing (getMembers.cfm)

```
<!--
   Name:          /c01/ getMembers.cfm
   Description:   Final member listing template
-->


<!-- Set a default parameter to sort the member list -->
<cfparam name="sort" default="lastName">

<!-- Get the member list from the database -->
<cfquery name="getMembers" datasource="myDatabase">
select firstName, lastName, e-mail
from members
</cfquery>
```

```
<table>
    <!-- Display clickable table headers that resort the list -->
    <tr>
        <td><a href="getMembers.cfm?sort=lastName">name</a></td>
        <td><a href="getMembers.cfm?sort=e-mail">e-mail</a></td>
    </tr>

    <!- Display member list.-->
    <cfoutput query="getMembers">
    <tr>
        <td>#lastName#, #firstName#</td><td>#e-mail#</td>
    </tr>
    </cfoutput>
</table>
```

Using PDL minimizes the effort involved in documenting your code and allows you to simplify complex logical processes by applying a high-level design first. Though it may seem this way sometimes, most of us do not think in code; therefore, laying out the algorithm in plain English is often the first step to solving a complex problem.

> **NOTE**   Some companies and individuals share their standards for the benefit of the developer community. A good example is the Construx coding standard (`http://www.construx.com/cxone/Construction/CxStand_Code.pdf`).

Applying Coding Standards

Have you ever found yourself in a situation in which you have to decide between two different ways to code: one that is generic and flexible but more complex to build, and one that is not as flexible but is easy to build. Regardless of the programming language you use, some concepts and best practices remain the same. Seasoned developers know how to maintain the right balance between flexibility and simplicity in their code.

Coding standards describe the rules and idioms for the construction of ColdFusion code. Using the same construction standard throughout the application will help you more easily identify problems during debugging and testing phases.

Enforcing your coding standards should be done throughout the project by means of a peer review process. Using standards together with peer reviews is also an excellent way to educate junior developers.

Cohesion and Coupling

Cohesion describes the strength of the relationship between the operations in a routine or module. A perfectly cohesive function is round()—it performs only one function that rounds a number. The more functions a routine or module performs, the less cohesive it becomes.

Coupling describes the strength of the relationship between two routines or modules. The more dependent the routine is on other routines, the more tightly coupled it becomes. Writing tightly coupled code reduces flexibility and creates problems when you are changing or optimizing code.

In Listing 1.7, the developer's intention was for the edit link to be restricted to administrators only. I have often seen this type of code in applications that had to be rewritten for lack of flexibility.

Listing 1.7	Tightly Coupled Code Example (GetMembers_Coupled.cfm)

```
<!--
    Name:           /c01/GetMembers_Coupled.cfm
    Description:    An example of tightly coupled code
-->

<cfquery name="getMembers" datasource="myDatabase">
select firstName, lastName, e-mail
from members
</cfquery>

<table>
    <tr>
        <td>name</td><td>e-mail</td><td>edit/delete</td>
    </tr>
    <cfoutput query="getMembers">
    <tr>
<td>#lastName#, #firstName#</td>
<td>#e-mail#</td>
<cfif session.memberName is "administrator">
<td><a href="editMember.cfm?member_id=#member_id#">edit member</a></td>
</cfif>
    </tr>
    </cfoutput>
</table>
```

As you can probably see, the code is not cohesive nor is it loosely coupled, which gives another member permission to edit the user or change the database query, which will involve changing the code, retesting, and redeploying. (The permissions are hard-coded in a `cfif` statement, thus making it hard to change.) Although this might seem like a simple task, if you multiply it by the number of templates in a complete application, you quickly find yourself changing code and chasing bugs for hours on end.

Writing both cohesive and loosely coupled code can greatly reduce the number of bugs, thus making your code easier to maintain and change. By separating the functional parts of the software and decreasing the interdependency of those parts, you break complex operations down to several more manageable elements. You allow those elements to be re-used by other parts of the application and by other programmers, thus avoiding a duplicate effort.

UDFs, CFCs, and custom tags are the tools of choice when you are developing loosely coupled modules.

In the following example, Listing 1.8, both the member list and the user permissions are driven by a CFC that can be re-used throughout the application. Instead of checking for a specific username, the template checks a structure that contains all the user's permissions. Setting such a structure to a session or other type of persistent variable is usually done during the login process.

Listing 1.8   **Loosly Coupled Code (GetMembers_looslyCoupled.cfm)**

```
<!--
    Name:           /c01/GetMembers_looslyCoupled.cfm
    Description:    An example of loosly coupled code
-->


<cfinvoke component="member.cfc" method="getMemberList"
returnVariable="qryMemberList">

<cfinvoke component="authentication.cfc" method="getPermissions"
returnVariable="userPermissions">

<table>
    <tr>
        <td>Name</td><td>e-mail</td><td>edit/delete</td>
    </tr>
    <cfoutput query="getMembers">
    <tr>
<td>#lastName#, #firstName#</td>
<td>#e-mail#</td>
<cfif StructKeyExists(userPermissions, "EditMember")>
<td><a href="editMember.cfm?member_id=#member_id#">edit member</a></td>
</cfif>
    </tr>
    </cfoutput>
</table>
```

You can also apply the concept of loose coupling to the application tiers themselves. By separating your ColdFusion code into user interface and business logic modules, you simplify the development process, create a consistent look and feel, and allow for greater re-use of code.

Security Considerations

You should make sure that security practices are understood and documented before you start coding to ensure that your application will be less vulnerable to hacker attacks. Because new security alerts arise on a daily basis, making sure that your application is protected has become increasingly vital.

Writing secure code becomes even more complex when you are working in a team; but applying standards will help you create a consistently secure application. Just be aware that even one unsecured module is enough to allow a hacker to cause serious damage in your application.

NOTE   See Chapter 8, "Application Security Techniques," for more information about security considerations.

Using a Methodology

The goal of any methodology is to apply a certain level of organization and order to the unstructured and often disorganized world of application development. And although you have already developed your own coding style, you shouldn't disregard these methodologies; some methodologies have many hidden advantages and may prove very useful on many large-scale projects. In addition, using a consistent methodology will make it easier to maintain and extend your application while facilitating collaboration with other developers. Some methodologies will also save you time by solving some of the common issues within their frameworks.

Fusebox

The most widely used ColdFusion methodology is Fusebox, which provides an application framework and has several neat features such as nested presentation layouts and Exit fuseactions. Some developers have extended the original framework with their own modifications, such as creating template execution queues, and have even created a documentation standard using XML (Fusedocs).

Fusebox is very simple to learn and understand and has actually been adapted for PHP, JSP, and even ASP.

NOTE   See Chapter 4 for more information about Fusebox.

cfObjects

Although not as popular as Fusebox, cfObjects allows developers who are familiar with OOP (Object Oriented Programming) models and architecture to apply those to ColdFusion. cfObjects was built to implement inheritance, polymorphism, and encapsulation with CFML.

The framework uses ColdFusion 4.01 features, such as exception handling, collections, and the request scope, to satisfy many of the requirements.

NOTE   For more about cfObjects go to `http://www.cfobjects.com`.

Other Methodologies

Other less known methodologies include BlackBox (`http://www.black-box.org`), Switch_box (`http://www.switch-box.org`), and a less known but very powerful data-driven application framework (`http://www.codebits.com`) by David Medinets.

Exception Handling

ColdFusion provides a full set of error handling tags: `cferror`, `cftry`, `cfcatch`, `cfthrow`, and `cfrethrow`. Applying a consistent error and exception handling methodology will allow your site to present consistent behavior and simplify the debugging process.

There are many ways of handling exceptions both on the client and on the server side. Although client-side validation reduces unnecessary traffic, it creates concerns of browser compatibility. Server-side validation is safer, but it requires additional "trips" to the server and much waiting around on the user's part.

Creating a site-wide exception handler should be a minimum for any ColdFusion application.

Additional Planning

A plan for development implementation is typically created by a project manager, but many ColdFusion developers often join the project manager in this effort. Some additional planning activities not traditionally a part of the developer's scope of responsibilities are discussed in this section.

Project Planning

Although project managers are usually responsible for developing a full project plan, in many cases, a project manager is simply not available. Building a project plan along with resource allocation, schedules, and milestones are essential to the overall project success, however, and developers often absorb this important duty. The plan often includes recommendations for a phased approach in which you implement the total project in logical stages.

NOTE   To learn more about project management, I recommend that you read Steve McConnell's *Rapid Development: Taming Wild Software Schedules* (Microsoft Press, 1996), which is one of the most popular books written on the software development process.

Backup

You set and follow a backup policy only after you have finished and deployed applications, but you should think about backup during development too. Most of us take backup for granted on production sites, but backing up your code on a regular basis during development can be a real lifesaver. Of course it's possible that you'll rarely need the backups you prepare, but Murphy's Law ensures that if you *don't* have them, you'll end up needing them at the worst possible moment.

TIP   HomeSite+ has a user-configurable automatic backup that gives you the option of autosaving files at a certain time interval, and it also lets you recover and restore files that have been backed up.

Version Control

Have you ever fixed a problem in a ColdFusion template only to discover later that you created several new bugs? Do you wish you could somehow go back in time and change the template back to its original state? Version control software allows you to track, retrieve, and manage all versions of your application templates. Many tools available today will easily integrate into your IDE (HomeSite+, ColdFusion Studio), and a simple check-in and check-out feature is now a part of Dreamweaver MX.

NOTE   Using version control is increasingly important when you have several developers working on the same code. However, even when you are working alone, using version control tools can save you time and headaches.

Here are some of the most popular version control tools used by ColdFusion developers:

- Concurrent Versions System (CVS), available from `http://www.cvshome.org/`
- Microsoft's Visual SourceSafe, available from `http://msdn.microsoft.com/ssafe/`
- Starbase StarTeam, available at `http://www.starbase.com/product_starteam/index.cfm`
- MKS Source Integrity, available from `http://www.mks.com/products/sis/`

Integration

Integration points with legacy or third-party systems should be identified in advance. Failing to identify and test integration early on can lead to false assumptions, faulty design, or critical performance penalties.

Consider developing some of the integration modules early, test these integration points with real loads, and make sure they do not break. Integration bottlenecks can scrap entire projects.

Last Minute Integration Failure and Recovery

A company I worked for developed a ColdFusion application that was supposed to be integrated directly with their legacy AS400 system for order processing. The developers managed to connect to the AS400 and assumed that was enough. At the end of the project, they found out that the AS400 was unavailable for several hours each night, which created a vacuum to which orders were sent. The end result was that they had to spend additional time creating a queue that would hold the orders and processes to insure that the orders were not lost.

In Sum

Planning and designing your ColdFusion application is essential in order to create scalable, maintainable, and stable applications. In this chapter, you've learned about issues you should consider before you start coding. We covered subjects such as gathering requirements, designing data models, and creating n-tiered architectures and logical diagrams. We also reviewed prototyping, documentation, and the importance of applying coding standards.

This chapter should serve as a base on which you can build your architectural and planning skills, and it should help you build solid applications in less time and with less effort. In time, these techniques will become second nature and you will be amazed at how you ever built applications without them.

In addition to the technical aspects of planning and design that were covered in this chapter, there are many other nontechnical issues to be planned when you are building a web-based solution. Other parts, such as graphic design and project management, are essential to overall project success and also should be planned to the same extent.

CHAPTER 2

Troubleshooting and Debugging ColdFusion MX Code

By Kenneth N. Fricklas

- Interpreting errors and error messages

- ColdFusion MX and Java

- Visual debugging tools

- The ColdFusion Administrator debugging options

- Debugging in Dreamweaver MX

- Tag-based debugging

- Debugging on a live server

- Team debugging techniques

- Helpful debugging tips

N o matter how much great functionality you've managed to pump into your application masterpiece, your users will view the application as completely unusable as soon as it breaks, no matter what kind of bizarre mistake they've committed to cause the error. We've all seen web-based systems break. We've all gotten 404 errors (missing page), 500 errors (server error) and messages like "An application error has occurred: Please use the Back button." In addition, we've all been annoyed by forms that don't submit properly, pages that break when loading, or links that don't go to the right places.

But errors on your websites are more than just mere annoyances—in fact, they might cause you to lose customers. For instance, consumers may experience true panic when faced with cryptic error messages that appear just after they've enter in their credit card or personal information.

This chapter discusses methods for determining what is happening when something is going wrong with your application. We'll look at the tools ColdFusion MX gives you to help you debug, and we'll examine techniques for debugging in special situations. We'll also cover some tips that will help you avoid bugs and common pitfalls in ColdFusion MX programs.

Interpreting Error Messages

Most errors that you will encounter in ColdFusion MX are called *recoverable errors*, or errors that can be caught and handled programmatically. Following are the official error types in ColdFusion MX.

Type of Error	Description
Program	Code syntax or program logic
Data	User data input errors
System	Database errors, time-outs, out-of-memory errors, file errors, disk errors

In this section, we'll review the indications that ColdFusion MX gives you when each of these types of errors occur.

Syntax versus Logic Errors

It's important to note the difference between syntax and program logic errors. While syntax errors are visible when you load a page, program logic errors are much harder to debug, and frequently it's not obvious that anything is wrong. To give you an example, I recently had an error where options in a `select` control had the wrong values, which caused odd results when I was searching. Though the data was correct, the administrative interface indicated something different than the database. This is an example of a logical error that doesn't have any visual cues other than bad search results.

Here is a simple syntax error:

```
<cfset myName="#Howard">
```

The problem here is that ColdFusion can't parse the single pound sign—in this case it thinks you are beginning the name of a variable—and the parser fails, which causes the kind of syntax error every ColdFusion programmer has seen many times: "Invalid CFML construct found on line *xx*."

Here is an example of HTML code that will cause a program logic error:

```
<b>Choose a recipient:<b><br>
<select name="recipientType">
<option value="M">Female
<option value="F">Male
</select>
```

In this case, the select control passes a value of `"M"` when the user chooses `"Female"`, and a value of `"F"` when the user chooses `"Male"`. The ColdFusion code on the template that processed this form was completely correct, but the values passed to it were backwards from what the user intended. This simple logic error caused invalid results on the form's action page.

Both syntax and logical errors should be caught and corrected during development and alpha/beta testing. The iterative process of correcting mistakes should begin the moment you start typing code. You will find that both syntax and logic errors are more easily caught when you are working with small amounts of code at a time; because of this, Macromedia Training recommends that you implement the "Development Process" when coding. Basically, that's just a fancy way of saying "Type a small amount of code, save it, browse it, and repeat." Coding this way allows you to avoid more complex errors because each smaller bit of code has been verified before it is combined with other bits to form large, complex projects that tend to hide logic errors. Just get into the habit of checking your work as soon as you add something new to a page. Although some errors may slip by, they will hopefully be caught during alpha and beta testing.

Watch Out for Tunnel Vision

An important thing to avoid is *programmer tunnel vision*. Make sure that someone other than you tests your code for logic errors after you write it.

Often programmers are focused so much on fixing the problem immediately at hand that they forget to try paths through code that don't relate to the problem that they are currently fixing. As a result, they frequently break something else in the code. Assuming a small fix won't affect anything else is one of those things that makes intuitive sense, but you just don't do it; it is like pasting blocks of text from copy writers or clients directly into web pages without reading them first. This is how you wind up with great information on your web page like "we expect to tell enjoy summer at this time," which will pass your spell checker just fine.

MX Error Messages

By default, ColdFusion MX displays a good deal of information when an error occurs in your code. Although these MX error messages aren't user friendly, for the most part, they are very developer friendly. As a result, you will not want to display them to end users—especially since they often expose enough information about your application that such a display could be a security risk. (We'll talk later about how to hide these error messages from the user.) However, as a developer, you should get used to seeing them in their full glory.

Default Error Messages

Listing 2.1 has two simple ColdFusion variable assignments and two variable outputs. Note, however, the syntax error—the second variable output is missing a pound sign (#).

NOTE   In several listings in this chapter, line numbers are shown in the code to help provide reference from the debug output.

Listing 2.1   Code with Missing Variable Pound Sign (syntaxError.cfm)

```
01:<!---
02:   Name: /c02/syntaxError.cfm
03:   Description: Simple Syntax Error
04:--->
05:<!DOCTYPE HTML PUBLIC "-//W3C//DTD HTML 4.01
    +Transitional//EN">
06:
07:<html>
08:<head>
09:   <title>Syntax Error</title>
10:</head>
11:
12:<body>
13:
14:<cfset fName="Elvis">
15:<cfset lName="Presley">
16:
17:<font face="Verdana" size="+3" color="#ff0000">
18:<cfoutput>
19:#fName# #lName
20:</cfoutput>
21:</font>
22:
23:</body>
24:</html>
```

Running this code will produce the ColdFusion MX error message in Figure 2.1. This is the output of the default error handler, which is called when an unhandled exception occurs in your code. If ColdFusion MX doesn't know what to do at any point in your code, it stops and dumps this page on the user. In this case, we have a syntax error—ColdFusion MX can't read the code because it can't be parsed correctly.

FIGURE 2.1:

A simple
ColdFusion MX
error message

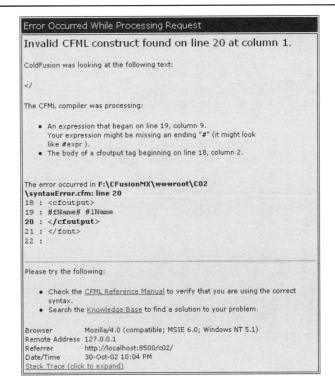

At first glance, the error message seems cryptic. However, as you continue to read it, the problem becomes increasingly clear. The message tells you to look for a missing pound sign and it even tells you on which line you should look (line 20). Then it lists the page name and shows you which line of code it considers to be the problem.

Other error messages are far more descriptive. To see an example, first consider the code in Listing 2.2.

Listing 2.2 **<cftry>/<cfcatch> Nesting Error (nestingError.cfm)**

```
01:<!---
02:   Name: /c02/nestingError.cfm
03:   Description: Badly Constructed TRY/CATCH Block
04:--->
05:<!DOCTYPE HTML PUBLIC "-//W3C//DTD HTML 4.01
   +Transitional//EN">
```

```
06:<html>
07:<head>
08:   <title>Nesting Error</title>
09:</head>
10:
11:<body>
12:
13:<cftry>
14:
15:<cfquery datasource="exampleapps" name="q_Employees">
16:   select firstName, lastName
17:   from tblEmployees_XXXX
18:   order by lastName
19:</cfquery>
20:
21:<cfcatch type="database">
22:   There is a problem with your query.
23:</cfcatch>
24:
25:<font face="Verdana" size="+3" color="#ff0000">
26:Employee List<br>
27:</font>
28:<br>
29:
30:<font face="Verdana">
31:<cfoutput query="q_Employees">
32:#q_Employees.LastName#, #q_Employees.FirstName#<BR>
33:</cfoutput>
34:</font>
35:
36:</cftry>
37:
38:</body>
39:</html>
```

The error message in Figure 2.2 is generated from the code in Listing 2.2. This listing calls the datasource ExampleApps, which is installed by default when you install the example applications in ColdFusion MX. We are running the query inside a <cftry>/<cfcatch> block to catch any problems that develop while the query is being run. However, there's extra code after the cfcatch block, which is illegal syntax.

The nice thing about syntax-related error messages in ColdFusion MX is that they take a stab at telling you where the problem lies. If you set the Enable Robust Exception Handling option in the ColdFusion MX Administrator (discussed in the section "ColdFusion MX Administrator Debug Settings"), you will also see information on the template that ran and an excerpt of the code around which the parser found the error, as seen in Figure 2.3.

FIGURE 2.2:

FIGURE 2.2:

This ColdFusion MX error points out that the tag is not nested correctly and suggests a solution.

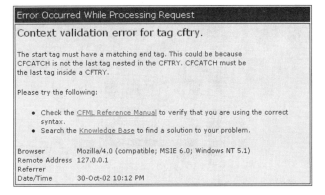

FIGURE 2.3:

ColdFusion MX syntax error, with Enable Robust Exception Handling Information turned on

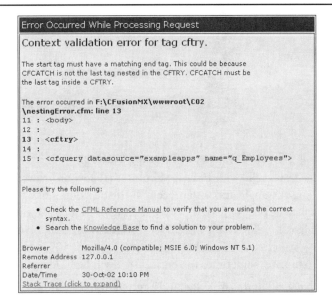

In this figure, you can see that a line number is given and the potentially problematic code is excerpted for you to review. In Dreamweaver MX, the default code view doesn't show the line numbers, but you can turn them on using the View ➢ Code View Options ➢ Line Numbers option, as seen in Figure 2.4.

TIP   To get to a line quickly in your code, use Ctrl+G, which allows you to enter a line number and jump directly to that line of code.

FIGURE 2.4:

Enabling line numbers
in Dreamweaver MX

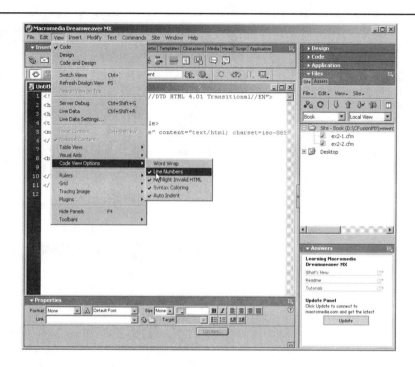

Missing Error Messages in Internet Explorer

Often, especially with Internet Explorer (IE), your browser does not display errors in Cold-Fusion MX applications that occur at the beginning of a template, or ones that result in the template not being parsed. As you'll note in Figure 2.5, one "feature" of IE is that, by default, it hides all useful (to the developer) information about error messages coming from the server. For instance, when ColdFusion returns an error 500, which means an error has occurred in the template, sometimes the entire page will be hidden.

To get rid of this message, in IE, go to Tools ➢ Internet Options ➢ Advanced and turn off the "Show friendly HTTP error messages" option (see Figure 2.6).

You can also avoid this behavior by turning off the "Enable HTTP status codes" option in the ColdFusion Administrator, but this make your pages appear to be successful even when an error does occur. The unfortunate side effect of this is search engines will catalogue your errors, thinking they are normal pages in your application. Try searching for "Application Error" on a search engine sometime, and you'll see what I mean.

FIGURE 2.5:

Internet Explorer error
display

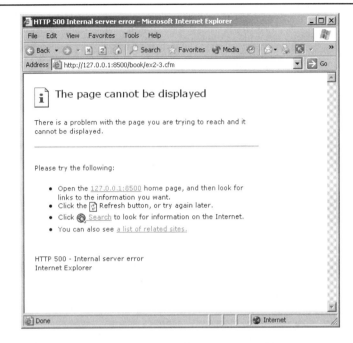

FIGURE 2.6:

Internet Explorer Tools
Dialog

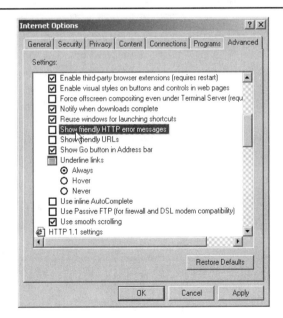

Cryptic Error Messages

An ugly result of the fact that ColdFusion MX is a Java application is that frequently you will receive error messages that look more like Java errors than ColdFusion errors. For example, consider the bad code in Listing 2.3. In this one-line example, we've simply put in a cfinput tag that's not enclosed in a cfform tag. The error you get can be, frankly, scary (see Figure 2.7).

Listing 2.3   **Error That Causes a Java Dump (tagContextError.cfm)**

```
01:<!---
02:   Name: /c02/tagContextError.cfm
03:   Description: Tag Context Error
04:--->
05:<html>
06:<head>
07:<title>Error in content</title>
08:<meta http-equiv="Content-Type" content="text/html;
   +charset=iso-8859-1">
09:</head>
10:<body>
11:<cfinput type="text"   name="bob2">
12:</body>
13:</html>
```

FIGURE 2.7:

Java Context Error

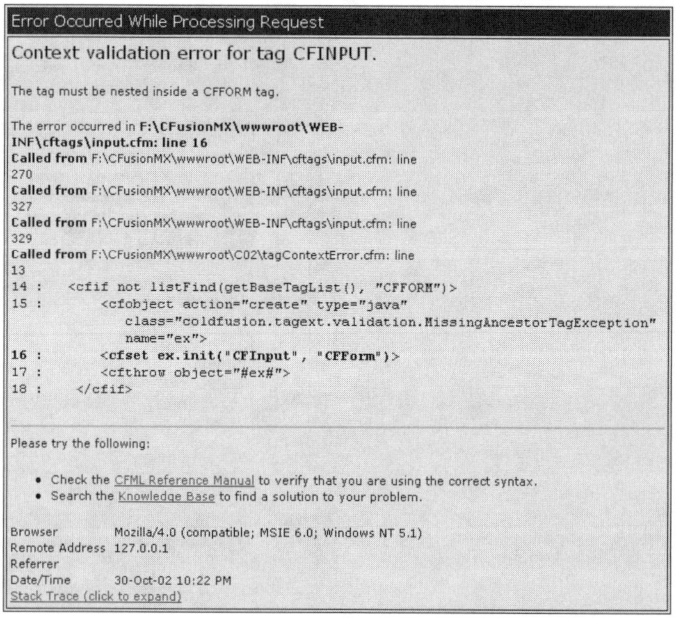

Notice that there is a major difference between this message and what you might have seen in earlier versions of ColdFusion. Because ColdFusion is now built on top of Java (earlier versions were written in C or C++), and because the CFML is now compiled, you may see errors in code that you didn't write! In this case, the code snippet in the error message is an internal error from the `input` tag's own implementation inside ColdFusion MX. The `cfobject` tag in the middle of the listing instantiates and calls a Java object that is an internal part of ColdFusion MX.

Just ignore the odd code that appears in this error; what you care about is right at the top of message. The first two lines tell you all you need to know. The error was in the `cfinput` tag, which should have been inside a `cfform` tag. Down near the bottom of the error output we also see the text

```
Called from C:\CFusionMX\wwwroot\C02\tagContextError.cfm: line 13
```

We can see that the problem was in line 13 of tagContextError.cfm, the file we were editing (we can ignore the rest of the line numbers; they weren't in our file).

Invalid Line Numbers in Error Messages

Line numbers are occasionally off in the debug output. This happens because, as far as ColdFusion is concerned, any text between lines of CFML code isn't worth paying attention to. For this reason, you'll often see an error message that references a line that follows the line in which you're actually interested.

In the debug output shown in Figure 2.7, the compiler claimed line 13 was the problem. When we look at Listing 2.3 we see that line 13 is actually the `</html>` tag, not the line that contained the offending `cfinput` tag (line 11). Since there was no CFML code after line 11, the compiler assumed that all the remaining text was part of that line of code. In fact, adding another line of CFML code after the `cfinput` tag will improve the parser's behavior, causing the parser to return a message that points to the correct line of code. Just remember to look back to the last line of CFML code before the line referenced by the compiler in the error message.

ColdFusion MX Administrator Debug Settings

All the debugging features of ColdFusion MX are controlled by some settings in the ColdFusion MX Administrator (Figure 2.8). In this section, we'll examine these settings and see how we can use them to provide developers with the most useful information available. We'll also see how these settings can help us keep our users from seeing more than they need to when something goes wrong.

FIGURE 2.8:

ColdFusion MX
Administrator Settings

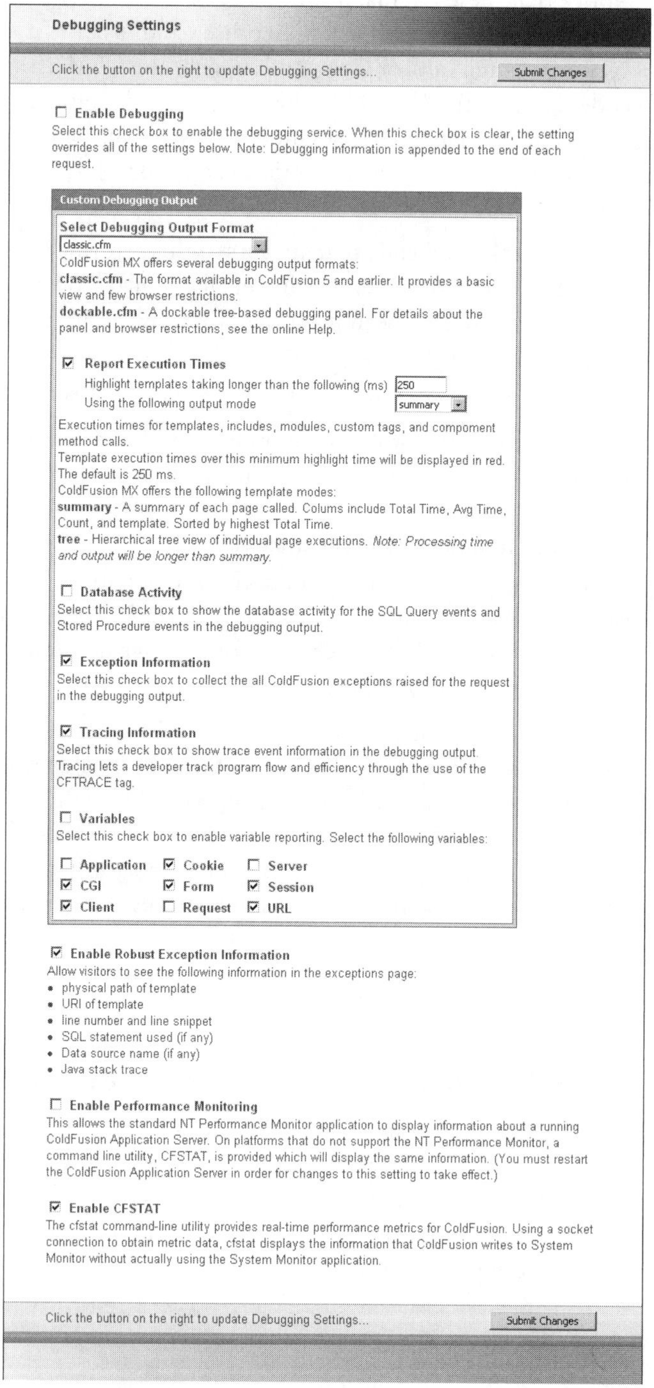

Debugging Settings

Click the button on the right to update Debugging Settings...   [Submit Changes]

☐ **Enable Debugging**
Select this check box to enable the debugging service. When this check box is clear, the setting overrides all of the settings below. Note: Debugging information is appended to the end of each request.

Custom Debugging Output

Select Debugging Output Format
[classic.cfm ▼]
ColdFusion MX offers several debugging output formats:
classic.cfm - The format available in ColdFusion 5 and earlier. It provides a basic view and few browser restrictions.
dockable.cfm - A dockable tree-based debugging panel. For details about the panel and browser restrictions, see the online Help.

☑ **Report Execution Times**
Highlight templates taking longer than the following (ms) [250]
Using the following output mode   [summary ▼]
Execution times for templates, includes, modules, custom tags, and compoment method calls.
Template execution times over this minimum highlight time will be displayed in red. The default is 250 ms.
ColdFusion MX offers the following template modes:
summary - A summary of each page called. Colums include Total Time, Avg Time, Count, and template. Sorted by highest Total Time.
tree - Hierarchical tree view of individual page executions. *Note: Processing time and output will be longer than summary.*

☐ **Database Activity**
Select this check box to show the database activity for the SQL Query events and Stored Procedure events in the debugging output.

☑ **Exception Information**
Select this check box to collect the all ColdFusion exceptions raised for the request in the debugging output.

☑ **Tracing Information**
Select this check box to show trace event information in the debugging output. Tracing lets a developer track program flow and efficiency through the use of the CFTRACE tag.

☐ **Variables**
Select this check box to enable variable reporting. Select the following variables:

☐ Application	☑ Cookie	☐ Server
☑ CGI	☑ Form	☑ Session
☑ Client	☐ Request	☑ URL

☑ **Enable Robust Exception Information**
Allow visitors to see the following information in the exceptions page:
• physical path of template
• URI of template
• line number and line snippet
• SQL statement used (if any)
• Data source name (if any)
• Java stack trace

☐ **Enable Performance Monitoring**
This allows the standard NT Performance Monitor application to display information about a running ColdFusion Application Server. On platforms that do not support the NT Performance Monitor, a command line utility, CFSTAT, is provided which will display the same information. (You must restart the ColdFusion Application Server in order for changes to this setting to take effect.)

☑ **Enable CFSTAT**
The cfstat command-line utility provides real-time performance metrics for ColdFusion. Using a socket connection to obtain metric data, cfstat displays the information that ColdFusion writes to System Monitor without actually using the System Monitor application.

Click the button on the right to update Debugging Settings...   [Submit Changes]

Enable Debugging

The Enable Debugging check box in the ColdFusion Administrator does what you'd expect—it enables and disables the debugging service. When unselected, this setting disables all debug information, including that referenced by the options that follow it. When it's turned on, debugging information will be appended to the end of each page, if available to the user's IP Address (see "Debugging IP Addresses" later in this chapter).

Figure 2.9 is an example of the error shown in Listing 2.1 with debugging turned on.

This is the 'classic' debugging style output, similar to what you've seen in previous versions of ColdFusion. At the bottom of the screen there is now information on how long the page took to run, any exceptions that occurred while the page was running, and environment information about the server and client.

Select Debugging Output Format

ColdFusion MX now offers a new format for viewing debugging output. The new format uses DHTML to render a dockable, tree-based debugging panel in your browser, similar to what you'll see in Dreamweaver MX. After setting the output format to dockable.cfm, you can see your debug information in a floating window (Figure 2.10).

The reason this format is called dockable is that it can be docked using the one of the links at the bottom of the main output window; there are links to Debug This Page and Docked Debug Pane. If you'd prefer a docked frameset style single window setup for your debugging information, click the Docked Debug Pane link and this output will dock to the left of the main window, as seen in Figure 2.11.

There is a small form underneath the Page Overview information at the top of the debug window in the dockable view. This form allows you to enter the name of the next page that you wish to load and debug. Also, if you have multiple browser windows open, clicking Debug This Page at the bottom of any window will make that window's debug information active in the debug window. In this way, you only need to have one debug window at a time open, avoiding confusion.

FIGURE 2.9:

Classic style debug
information

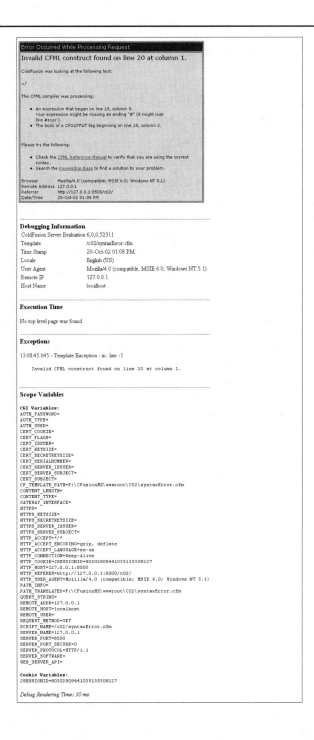

FIGURE 2.10:

Floating debug
information

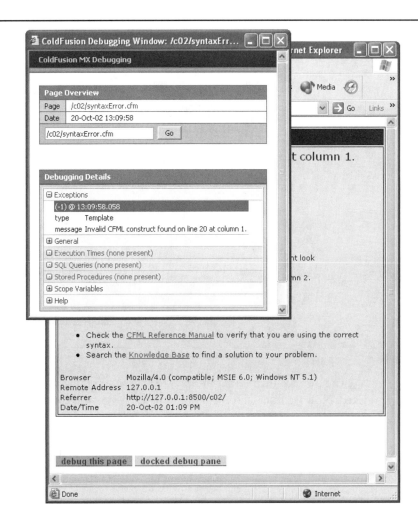

FIGURE 2.11:

Docked debug
information

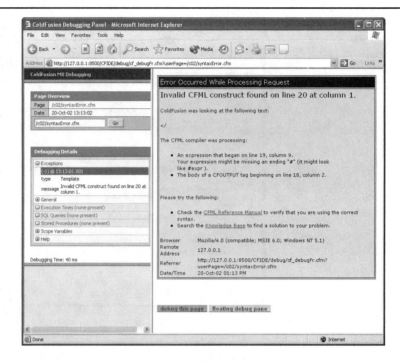

We've now seen three different ways to view your debug information—classic, floating, and docked. Now we'll spend some more time discussing the content of that debug information.

TIP   You can add your own information to the debug output, see the later section "Implementing Your Own Debugging Template."

Report Execution Times

By turning on the Report Execution Times check box in the ColdFusion Administrator, you can get a breakdown of the amount of time it takes to run each template that is called directly or indirectly by the template you are debugging. This includes files that are called via `cfinclude`, `cfmodule`, custom tags, and CFCs. Web services won't be included because they run are in a separate web server request.

You can choose an output mode of Tree or Summary. These actually display the same information, but in slightly different formats. The Tree view shows which files were called by other files, and it displays this graphically; the Summary view displays the information in a simple list. In the Summary view, ColdFusion MX will highlight templates that take a long time to run. (By default, this interval is 250 milliseconds, but you can change this interval to a longer or shorter time as needed.)

Listing 2.4 demonstrates this output.

| Listing 2.4 | Calling a Custom Tag, Include, CFC, and Web Service (mcMain.cfm, mcIncluded.cfm, mcCustomTag.cfm, mcCallCFC.cfm, and myCFC.cfm or myCFCsvc.cfm) |

mcMain.cfm: Master Page

```
<!---
   Name: /c02/mcMain.cfm
   Description: Master page
--->

<cfset myName = "Ken">
<cfoutput>mcMain: Starting.<br></cfoutput>
<cfinclude template="mcIncluded.cfm">
<cfoutput>mcMain: Done.</cfoutput>
```

mcIncluded.cfm: Included Page

```
<!---
   Name: /c02/mcIncluded.cfm
   Description: An included page
--->

<cfoutput>mcIncluded: The time is #now()#.</cfoutput>
<br>
<cf_mcCustomTag>
<cfinclude template="mcCallCFC.cfm">
```

mcCustomTag.cfm: Custom Tag

```
<!---
   Name: /c02/mcCustomTag.cfm
   Description: Trivial custom tag
--->

<Ccfoutput>cf_mcCustomTag: This is a custom tag.<br></cfoutput>
```

mcCallCFC.cfm: Included Page, calls CFCs

```
<!---
   Name: /c02/mcCallCFC.cfm
   Description: An included page that calls a CFC
--->

<cfoutput>mcCallCFC: calling myCFC as CFC.<br></cfoutput>
<cfobject name="mycfc" component="myCFC">
<cfoutput>#myCFC.myFunction("Test Argument")#</cfoutput>
<cfoutput>mcCallCFC: calling myCFC as Service.<br></cfoutput>
<cfinvoke
   method="myFunction" returnVariable="myRet"
   webservice="#CGI.HTTP_HOST#/book/mycfcsvc.cfc?wsdl"
   myArgument="Another Test Argument">
</cfinvoke>
```

```
myCFC.cfm: ColdFusion Component
<!---
   Name: /c02/myCFC.cfm or /c02/myCFCsvc.cfm
   Description: A simple CFC
--->

<cfcomponent>
   <cffunction name="myFunction" access="remote"
       returnType="string">
      <cfargument name="myArgument" type="string"
      required="true">
      <cfset myResult="MyCFCsvc Result =" & arguments.myArgument
      & "<br>">
      <cfreturn myResult>
   </cffunction>
</cfcomponent>
```

The code in Listing 2.4 does this: mcMain, the main program, includes the file mcIncluded
.cfm. That file calls the custom tag mcCustomTag, which includes another file, mcCallCFC (to
make the hierarchy more interesting in the results). Finally, mcCallCFC calls myCFC and
myCFCsvc, both by invoking the CFC as an object and by calling it was a web service (I used
different names to make the output more evident). You can see the result in Figure 2.12.

FIGURE 2.12:

Execution times in
tree format
(floating view)

You can see the order in which the templates were called and how much time was spent in each one. Also note that when myCFC was invoked as a service (myCFCSsvc.cfm) it didn't show up in the output; even though it ran on the same machine as the rest of the code. That is because it wasn't in the *same request to the web server*, so it wasn't part of the debugging session.

Database Activity

Checking the Database Activity check box in the ColdFusion Administrator will cause Cold-Fusion MX to display debugging information about database calls. Figure 2.13 shows information about a query and a stored procedure call.

FIGURE 2.13:

Database activity information (floating view)

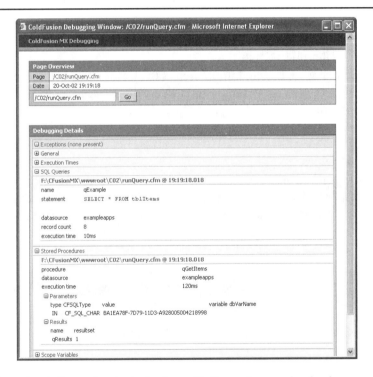

The database debugging information includes lots of information on the database operations, including the name of the query or procedure, how long it took for the query to run, and what the data source name is. Additionally, for queries, it shows the number of records returned (if any) and the actual SQL of the query. For stored procedures, it shows information on all parameters passed to and results returned from the procedures.

TIP   When you are debugging unexpected SQL results, it's a good idea to separate the SQL that's actually running from the code that generates it. The easiest way to do this is to copy the SQL statement from the debug output, stick it in a query on a template, or run it directly from the Dreamweaver MX binding panel, and fix the SQL first. Once you're running the SQL you expect, go back to the code and figure out why it wasn't generated that way.

Exception Information

The Exception Information setting will instruct the debugging service to collect all ColdFusion exceptions raised throughout the life of the request. This is a great improvement over previous ColdFusion versions, which only allowed you to see the one error that was not caught.

Tracing Information

Turning on Tracing Information in the ColdFusion Administrator allows a developer to use the `cftrace` tag. When this is enabled, the debugging service will collect trace events and display them in the debugging output. Trace events let you track variable values and program efficiency. We'll discuss `cftrace` more in the section "Tag-Based Debugging."

Variables

When you enable Variables in the ColdFusion Administrator, you can see the various types of variables that are set after your template runs. This includes `application`, `request`, `cgi`, `server`, `client`, `session`, `cookie`, `url`, and `form` scoped variables. (In ColdFusion 5 you only had access to `form`, `url`, and `cgi` variables.) When all these variable types are enabled, you can see output similar to Figure 2.14.

FIGURE 2.14:

Debugging variable information (classic view)

One of the shortcomings of this feature is that you can't see the details of complex variables. For instance, notice under Server Variables the figure shows OS=Struct (5). The debugging information gives you the name of the variable (OS), and tells you that it's a structure and that the structure contains 5 keys. It doesn't, however, let you see the values of those keys.

If you would like to see the detailed data held within the complex variable, you can use cfdump, discussed in its own section later in this chapter. We'll talk about additional ways to display complex variables for debugging in the later sections on "Implementing Your Own Debugging Template" and "Team Debugging."

Enable Robust Exception Handling

As the Administrator screen indicates, turning on Robust Exception Handling enables you to see lots of information about the environment in which the code is running when an exception occurs. This includes the physical path of the template that is running, the URI of the template (the part of the URL that doesn't include the machine name or the URL parameters), the line number and code snippet that failed, SQL information including the data source of the database that had an error (if any), and a Java stack trace for these types of exceptions.

WARNING   The downside of enabling this feature is that is exposes lots of potentially damaging information to hackers, who can use data source names and disk layout information to their best advantage. I suggest leaving this feature turned off on production servers, but you can enable it on your testing and development machines.

Figure 2.15 shows an example of exceptions displayed in a debug window. Each of these exceptions was caught in a try/catch block, so processing continued normally.

Enable Performance Monitoring and Enable cfstat

These options allow the use of the Windows NT performance monitoring tool and the cfstat command line tool on the server. These tools are discussed in Chapter 16, "Performance Tuning." Both items need to be enabled to use the cfstat utility.

Debugging IP Addresses

When you have Debugging turned on in the Administrator, you can (and should) restrict who can see that output. Debugging information is unsightly to nonprogrammers and can create security issues by exposing potentially damaging information to your site visitors.

The ColdFusion MX Administrator has a second screen that deals with Debugging (seen in Figure 2.16). This feature allows you to restrict debug viewing to specific IP addresses. You must input full IP addresses; no IP masking is allowed. If this setting is left empty, debugging information is available to all browsers on the web server.

FIGURE 2.15:

Exceptions in
Debug view

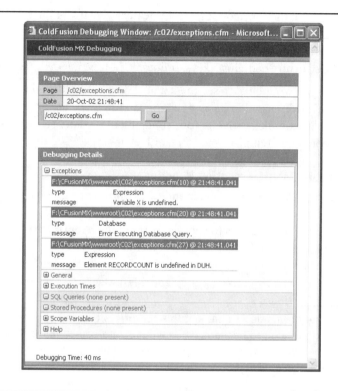

FIGURE 2.16:

Debugging IP Address
screen

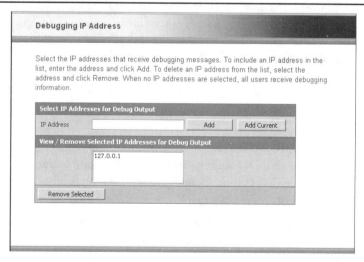

TIP If you have enabled debugging in the ColdFusion MX Administrator, you should also always list at least one IP address in the Debugging IP Address administrator page. If you don't, every person visiting your site will see the debugging information. Adding at least the local-host IP address of 127.0.0.1 is a good idea. If you live behind a firewall and the ColdFusion server is outside of it, you can use the technique discussed in "Debugging on a Live Server."

Debugging in Dreamweaver MX

As noted in the preceding sections, there are three ways of viewing debug output from Cold-Fusion MX code in a web browser: the dockable views and the classic view. If you are using the Dreamweaver MX programming environment, there is another way to view debug output—directly from within Dreamweaver.

Debugging ColdFusion MX in Dreamweaver MX requires that you correctly set up your site's Testing Server definition. Once this is done, click the Server Debug button (the globe with lightning bolt in Figure 2.17) or choose Server Debug from the View menu. This will publish the page to the web server, and display both the results of the page as well as a 'Server Debug' panel in the Results pane.

FIGURE 2.17:

Press the Server Debug button to view debug information in Dreamweaver MX.

Server Debug button

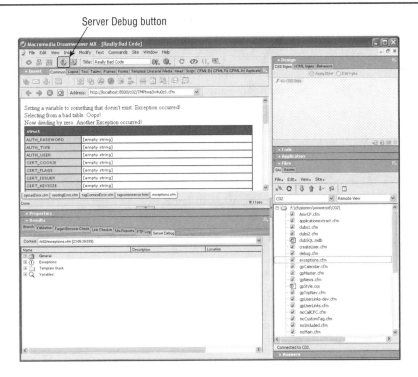

In the Server Debug panel in the Results pane, you can view all the standard debug information as well as any exceptions that occurred when running the page. While viewing this information, you can click the URL of any page that caused an exception, and the page will load into the Code View window.

NOTE   You may have noticed that Dreamweaver MX contains a debugger similar to that of Cold-Fusion Studio 5. It's not for ColdFusion MX, however; it's a JavaScript debugger. You'll find that it is really useful for debugging JavaScript on your pages, by the way.

Implementing Your Own Debugging Template

The files that contain the debug styles exist under *webroot*/WEB-INF/debug . There are three default templates for debugging information. Classic.cfm and dockable.cfm are the templates that are visible in the Administrator. The third, dreamweaver.cfm, contains the template that creates the version of the debugging output used in Dreamweaver MX, and it is hidden from you when you run the ColdFusion MX Administrator. These templates contain the information that is used to display the debug output and trace information collected by ColdFusion MX when running your templates.

Creating your own complete debugging template isn't the easiest of tasks. To do so, you must know ColdFusion MX internals more than they are covered in this book. However, you may find it useful to extend the standard templates by creating your own custom template in the debug directory and by including the other templates as needed. To avoid the complexity of JavaScript, I recommend using the Classic style template for this purpose.

Creating your own template can be extremely useful for displaying data that is defined in your application, especially the data that provides context for the rest of the application. Examples of information you might want to display are user information, shopping cart contents, and path information about the path the user is taking through the application. Listing 2.5 shows some code that creates a user with a couple of attributes (in real life, this would probably come out of a database) and displays his name.

Listing 2.5   **Creating and Displaying a User (createUser.cfm)**

```
<!---
    Name: /c02/createUser.cfm
    Description: Create user example
--->
<cfset getUser = structNew()>
<cfset getUser.name = "Ken">
```

```
<cfset getUser.hobby = "Improvisational Comedy">
<cfset getUser.employeeID = "123123">
<cfoutput>Hello, #getUser.name#</cfoutput>
```

To create a custom debugging template that displays the user information, we create a template in the webroot/WEB-INF/debug directory, which in this case, we'll call mycustom.cfm, seen in Listing 2.6.

Listing 2.6   A Custom Debugging Template (mycustom.cfm)

```
<!---
    Name: /c02/mycustom.cfm
    Description: Custom debugging template
        This file needs to exist in /web-inf/debug/mycustom.cfm
        under the web server root.
--->
<hr>
<h3>Ken's Custom Debugging Template</h3>
<cfif isDefined("getUser")>
    <cfif isDefined("getUser.name")>
        <cfset useName = getUser.name>
    <cfelse>
        <cfset useName = "undefined">
    </cfif>
    <cfdump label="Current User: #variables.useName#"
        var="#getUser#">
</cfif>
<cfinclude template="classic.cfm">
```

In this template, we first display a horizontal line and title to separate our output from the body of the document. Next we cfdump the user's information, checking to make sure it exists so we won't have a runtime error. Finally, we include the file classic.cfm, which contains the standard debugging output.

The last thing we need to do is set the Debugging Output Format in the ColdFusion MX Administrator to the name of our new template.

The results of our custom debug template can be seen in Figure 2.18.

NOTE   If there is a runtime error in the custom debugging template, the template will stop executing at the error and run the default error handler. Any debug output past that point will not be displayed.

FIGURE 2.18:

Custom debug output
showing user variable

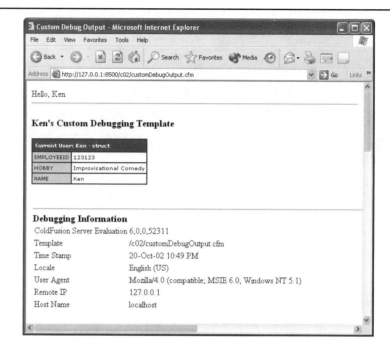

FIGURE 2.18:

Custom debug output
showing user variable

Tag-Based Debugging

Three tags in ColdFusion MX allow you to specify that debugging information should be
shown: cfquery, cfstoredproc, and cfsetting. A function, IsDebugMode(), can be used with
these to allow great control over the display of debug information.

The debug Attribute in cfquery and cfstoredproc

In the following code, we query the exampleApps data source. We've added the debug attribute
to the cfquery tag, as shown.

```
<cfquery datasource="exampleApps" name="q_Employees" debug>
    select firstName, lastName
    from tblEmployees
    order by lastName
</cfquery>
```

Adding the debug attribute results in exactly the same information being displayed as if you
had the Database Activity Debug option set. In this way, you can leave Database Activity
unchecked, and only see query information in your output for the queries in which you are
currently interested.

The `cfstoredproc` tag similarly includes a `debug` attribute that will show information for stored procedures.

Working with cfsetting showDebugOutput

An additional tag, `cfsetting`, is also available to help you optionally turn on debug output via the `showDebugOutput` attribute. Using this tag, you can turn debugging output on and off for a particular page. Note that debugging via `showDebugOutput` will only work if you have Enable Debugging checked in the ColdFusion Administrator. We'll see a cool way to use this in the "Debugging on a Live Server" section.

isDebugMode() Function

The ColdFusion MX function `isDebugMode()` returns true if debugging information can be detected on the current page. This requires that

- Debugging is enabled in the ColdFusion MX Administrator and the current IP address is allowed to see debug output, or

- `cfsetting` has `showDebugOutput` set to yes.

The `isDebugMode()` function allows a clear syntax for allowing the same users who can see general debug information to see your custom debug information. By wrapping debug code in this tag, you can display custom information or log trace information easily. An example of this is presented in the sidebar "`isDebugMode` and `cfdump`."

The cfdump Tag

As mentioned earlier in this chapter, the `cfdump` tag can be used to display detailed information about your complex variables, such as queries, arrays, and structures.

`cfdump` has syntax as follows:

```
<cfdump var = "#variable#" expand = "Yes or No" label = "text">
```

The variable must be contained in quotes, so `cfdump` receives the contents, rather than the name, of the variable.

`cfdump` will display any ColdFusion variable type object, including any system defined structures such as `form`, `cgi`, or `server`. It displayes the data hierarchically. The data is also color coded. In ColdFusion 5, `cfdump` could display simple variables, structures, arrays, queries, and WDDX objects. In ColdFusion MX, it has been extended to handle UDFs, XML data, CFCs and even Java objects.

The `expand` attribute tells `cfdump` whether to expand the information fully when displayed; if left to the default, it will show up initially with all its complex variables' subelement information hidden. You may want to set this to `no` if you are dumping large or deeply nested objects.

Finally, the `label` attribute lets you give the information a title in your output. Since you're passing the contents of the variable to the tag, it can't tell what the variable's name was in your code, so generally you will pass the variable name and perhaps some context information. This is especially useful when you need to dump a variable several times during the execution of a template to see how it changes; you can use the label to indicate where in the code, or on what iteration of a loop, the dump took place.

Earlier, we saw that in the debugging output, the server variables showed up as just a reference to the structure and how many elements it has in it (see Figure 2.14). In order to see the actual contents of these variables, we can add the following statement to our code:

```
<cfdump var="#server#" label="Server">
```

By default, the contents are fully expanded. Clicking the name of any variable, or one of the two structures (`os` and `coldfusion`) will condense that part of the screen and hide the content. In Figure 2.19, the supportedLocales variable has been hidden, and thus its name is displayed in italics.

FIGURE 2.19:

cfdump of server variables

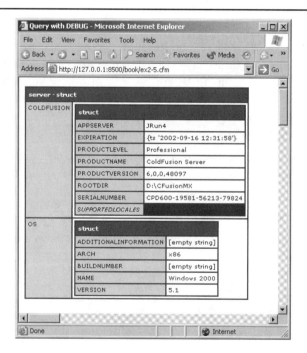

isDebugMode and cfdump

In the following code, the `isDebugMode()` function is used around the `cfdump` tag.

```
<cfif isDebugMode()>
    <cfdump var="#server#">
</cfif>
```

If debugging is turned on in the Administrator, then the `cfdump` tag's results will appear in the page. If debugging is turned off, then the `cfdump` results will not be displayed.

In the past, you could not go live with the `cfdump` tag in your application code. The tag would have either had to be deleted or commented out. Now, using the `isDebugMode()` function, you can leave the `cfdump` tag in place and it will only show for those people who are able to see debugging information.

The cftrace Tag

In ColdFusion 5, we had a server-side debugger that allowed us to set breakpoints, view values at runtime, and see what was happening as the code ran. As ColdFusion MX runs on top of Java, this type of integrated debugging is now unavailable. In order to provide a useful debugging environment and allow simple tracking of the progress of your page, ColdFusion MX introduces the `cftrace` tag.

The syntax of the `cftrace` tag is as follows:

```
<cftrace
    abort = "Yes or No"
    category = "string"
    inline = "Yes or No"
    text = "string"
    type = "format"
    var = "variable_name"
</cftrace>
```

The attributes of the `cftrace` tag work as shown in Table 2.1.

TABLE 2.1: cftrace Syntax

Attribute	Default Value	Description
abort	no	If set to yes, the code will stop running after the `cftrace` statement.
Category	None	User-defined string for grouping trace information.

Continued on next page

TABLE 2.1 CONTINUED: cftrace Syntax

Attribute	Default Value	Description
inline	no	If set, shows the traces in the output code as they occur. Normally, set to the default value of **no**, which displays the trace information at the bottom of the page in the classic or dockable view pane. cftrace will flush all output up to this point before displaying the cftrace information. Complex variable values are only displayed when inline is set to true.
text	None	The text that will be logged.
type	information	Can be information, warning, error, or fatal. Displays an appropriate icon next to the cftrace output.
var	None	The name of a simple or complex variable to display in the trace (similar to cfdump). Complex variables will only display their contents with inline set to yes.

Let's look at a simple example of a form. We want to store an e-mail address in our database if it isn't already there so that we can spam it later (nah, that never happens...). This code can be seen in Listing 2.7 and the output can be seen in Figure 2.20.

Listing 2.7   Simple cftrace Demo—Form Received (showCFTrace.cfm)

```
<!---
    Name: /C02/showCFTrace.cfm
    Description: Display cftrace information
--->

<cfparam name="Form.email" default="demodata@macromedia.com">
<cftrace category="Listing 2.7" inline="yes" text="Value of
    Form.email" var="form.email">
<!--- check to see if the e-mail is in the database --->
<cfquery name="qChkEmail" datasource="exampleApps">
    select EmployeeID from tblEmployees
        where  Email = '#form.email#'
</cfquery>
<cftrace category="Listing 2.7" inline="yes" text="Number of
    matches" var="qChkEmail.recordCount">
<cfif qChkEmail.recordCount eq 0>
    <cftrace category="Listing 2.7" inline="yes" text="New e-mail address">
    <cfquery datasource="exampleApps">
        insert into tblEmployees (email) values ('#trim(form.email)#')
    </cfquery>
<cfelse>
    <cftrace category="Listing 2.7" inline="yes" text="Existing e-mail address">
</cfif>
Thank you for your interest.
<cftrace category="General Information" inline="yes" var="variables">
```

FIGURE 2.20:

cftrace output

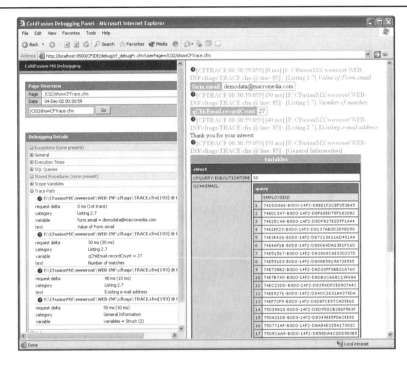

Here, because we've got inline set on for the lines that let us know whether the address existed, we see the trace in the output window telling us that the e-mail did exist already in the database. Under that, we can dump out all our variables by dumping the variable named variables—the struct that contains all our local variables. (Be careful doing this since, as you'll note from the large query that appears in the output, this may be a *lot* of data.) We dump the variables struct inline also, since the contents of complex data types don't appear in the custom debug data.

Looking in the docked debug information pane, we can see detailed information under Trace Path for each of the other traces that we set.

In addition to any text and variables that we output, the cftrace tag adds some other extremely useful information—namely the elapsed time since the last cftrace, and the application name, if one has been set by a cfapplication tag. The template information is very helpful, especially when you are tracing inside a loop, and the elapsed time is excellent for helping us pinpoint where our application is spending its time (we'll come back to this in Chapter 16).

NOTE   At this printing, the cftrace tag in the current version of ColdFusion MX shows the line number within the cftrace tag, rather than the line and template name where the trace was called. This feature should be fixed in a future version.

Although not used in the code listing, an abort="yes" attribute can also be added to the cftrace tag. When used, this attribute will force ColdFusion MX to stop processing any code after the cftrace tag has been run.

> **NOTE**   The Tracing Information setting in the ColdFusion MX Administrator must be checked to enable tracing information in the custom debug output. Even if it's not on, you will still see information from cftrace with the inline attribute set to yes, at the point where it appears in your code. With Enable Debugging off, or if you use the cfsetting show-DebugOutput="No", neither type of information will appear.

cftrace is an excellent tool for helping programmers locate logic errors. Since logic errors often don't produce a visible error message, but rather, just give you the wrong results, cftrace can help you locate the exact location where the problem first occurs.

Logging Errors

The first place to look when you are trying to find out what's going on with your applications is in the log files. Table 2.2 contains a list of ColdFusion MX log files. As you can see, every type of error that happens to your application, from database to mail connectivity, is logged somewhere. In addition, every cftrace call that you use will create a log entry that you can read and refer to later.

TABLE 2.2: Log Files Generated by ColdFusion

Log Filename	Information Recorded
rds.log	Errors occurring in the ColdFusion Remote Development Services (RDS). This service provides remote HTTP-based access to files and databases.
application.log	Every ColdFusion MX error reported to a user. Application page errors, including ColdFusion syntax, ODBC, and SQL errors are written to the log file.
flash.log	Errors from the Flash gateway.
exceptions.log	The stack traces of exceptions that occur in the ColdFusion server.
server.log	Errors that occurred in the communication between ColdFusion MX and your web server.
Customtag.log	Errors generated in custom tag processing.
car.log	Errors associated with Site Archive and Restore Operations.
mail.log	Errors generated by an SMTP mail server.
cftrace.log	All trace information.

The following is the output in cftrace.log from the example in Listing 2.7:

```
"Severity","ThreadID","Date","Time","Application","Message"
"Information","web-22","09/19/02","00:58:50",,"D:\CFusionMX\logs\cftrace.log
    initialized"
```

```
"Information","web-22","09/19/02","00:58:50",,"[190 ms (1st trace)]
    [D:\CFusionMX\wwwroot\web-inf\cftags\trace.cfm @ line: 85] - [Listing 2.7]
    [form.email = demodata@macromedia.com] Value of Form.email "
"Information","web-22","09/19/02","00:58:51",,"[1132 ms (942)]
    [D:\CFusionMX\wwwroot\ web-inf \cftags\trace.cfm @ line: 85] - [Listing 2.7]
[qChkEmail.RecordCount = 27] Number of matches "
"Information","web-22","09/19/02","00:58:51",,"[1132 ms (0)]
    [D:\CFusionMX\wwwroot\ web-inf \cftags\trace.cfm @ line: 85] - [Listing 2.7]
    Existing email address "
"Information","web-22","09/19/02","00:58:51",,"[1142 ms (10)]
    [D:\CFusionMX\wwwroot\ web-inf \cftags\trace.cfm @ line: 85] -
    [General Information] [variables = Struct (2)]   "
```

The cflog Tag

As we've seen, most error types are logged to standard log files, but frequently you may wish to log additional information to keep track of application specific conditions that occur. cflog is a tag that allows you to do exactly that. The syntax is as follows:

```
<cflog
    text = "text"
    log = "log type"
    file = "filename"
    type = "message type"
    application = "application name yes or no">
```

cflog will allow you to log whatever information you want into a specified log file. The file attribute allows you to specify a filename for the log file, such as a custom error log for your application. If you don't use the file attribute, the log attribute can be set to application or scheduler, which will allow you to write to the appropriate standard log file.

The type attribute is the same as that for cftrace; it can be information, warning, error, or fatal information. The log analyzer tool uses this attribute when filtering the logs.

Finally, if the application attribute is yes (the default), the application name from cfapplication, if any, will be logged also.

Using the CFML Code Analyzer

One cool tool that comes with ColdFusion MX is the CFML Code Analyzer. This tool is primarily provided to help you find out what potentially dangerous code you have in a legacy ColdFusion application so that you can check it before you upgrade to MX. Since it reads your code and warns you about any potential problems, it verifies that your code is syntactically correct without you having to actually run the code.

Continued on next page

The CFML Code Analyzer is an option in the ColdFusion MX Administrator. You can run it on an individual file or on an entire directory. Running the tool on a file returns output similar to the following:

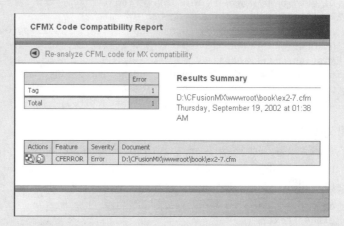

Clicking on the error gives the following output:

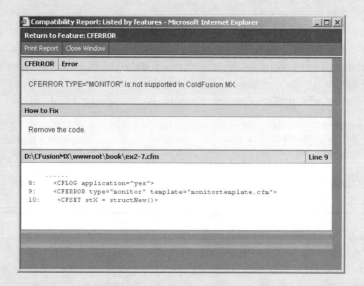

Here you can see there is a problem with a line of code that uses the `monitor` exception type for `cferror`, which is no longer supported in ColdFusion MX.

Debugging on a Live Server

Just because an application has gone live doesn't mean that you will never have to debug it again. First of all, unexpected problems may (and will!) crop up on the production box, or the application may prove to have problems that increase over time and as the site usage increases. The fact that there is really no way to completely control all the environmental factors around your application means that errors probably will turn up on your live server, and they may not even be reproducible on your testing or development server.

You can use both the site-wide error handler and the missing template handler to help you debug your applications and to help your application recover from errors in ways that will be logical to the users who unwittingly manage to break your code.

Using the Error Handlers

You can specify a site-wide error handler and a missing template handler in the ColdFusion Administrator (as shown in Figure 2.21), and its always wise to do so. By creatively anticipating the ways in which a user might arrive at these pages, we can make them intelligently handle many situations that the application as a whole couldn't anticipate.

FIGURE 2.21:

Handler settings in the ColdFusion MX Administrator

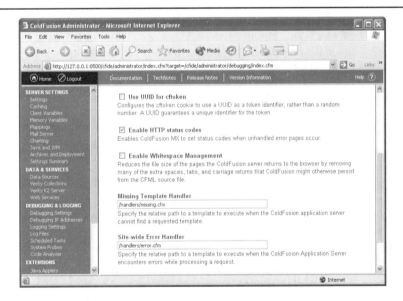

NOTE   Note that the paths to the Site-wide Error Handler and the Missing Template Handler are now relative to your web root and not absolute paths as in previous ColdFusion versions.

The Site-wide Error Handler specified in the ColdFusion Administrator handles errors not explicitly captured by your code. Once your application is on a live server, you have "real" users seeing your code, and they aren't likely to give you a call and let you know what is going on. You may monitor your logs, but in a typical developer situation, you won't do it often or thoroughly enough to really stay on top of intermittent errors. For this reason, I suggest you send yourself an e-mail (I use a special mailbox monitored by several developers) that includes all the information you need to know about your error. We'll see this code below.

At the same time, you can redirect your user to a page that is more useful, or alternatively, you can give them a standard message letting them know that an error has occurred. Either way, they will be less panicked than if they see your error statements. Of course, if you are in the code trying to reproduce the error, you'd probably just as soon see the error on screen instead of waiting for mail to arrive, and then having to delete it.

In addition, it is generally a good idea to have some output tags that will only appear when you are in debugging mode and never be seen by your users. As discussed above, we don't really want to use `cftrace` for this because it will log everything and grow the log files unnecessarily.

I have found that the best way to handle all these issues is by creating a special URL parameter that, when set, forces the application into debug mode using `cfsetting showDebugOutput=` `"yes"`. Let's look at some code, which you can put in your `Application.cfm` file (or your `FuseBox` root application—see Chapter 4), that will let you set up a debugging variable (in the example, `request.debugMode`) for your staff. Testing for this variable and then conditionally using `cftrace` and HTML comments in them gives us lots of options for visible and source-code-only display of debug output.

Listing 2.8 is code for `Application.cfm`, a typical page that uses the debug setting to output some debug data, and finally the default error handler page.

Listing 2.8   **Modal Error Handler (extracts from Application.cfm, dsp_Demo.cfm, error.cfm)**

```
<!---
    Name: /C02/Application.cfm, dsp_Demo.cfm, error.cfm
    Description: Modal error handler
--->

Application.cfm (extract)
<!--- check to make sure that the user is authenticated, and OK
    to debug. If it is, set a request variable indicating that the current user
    is debugging.

    DebugMode can be 0, indicating that it's off, "Trace", indicating
    that the debugger wants to trace, or anything else, indicating that we
    want to show debug output but not trace.
--->
```

```
<cfif getAuthUser() neq "">
   <cfif isUserInRole("Debug")>
   <!--- they are authenticated as being a debugger, check to see
      if they want to --->
      <Ccflock scope="session" timeout="2">
         <!--- if they haven't set it as a url paramenter,
         check the session. We keep the debug going for the
         entire session for convenience, and so you can follow
         links and submit forms --->
         <cfif not isDefined("url.debugMode")>
            <cfif isDefined("session.debugMode")>
               <cfset request.debugMode = session.debugMode>
            </cfif>
         <cfelse>
            <!--- they did define it on the URL, so that
               overrides the session. We now set it in the session
               for the next page load. --->
            <cfset session.debugMode = url.debugMode>
            <cfset request.debugMode = url.debugMode>
         </cfif>
      </cflock>
   </cfif>
<cfelse>
   <cfif isDefined("url.debugMode")>
      <!--- make them log in if you don't do it elsewhere --->
   </cfif>
</cfif>
<!--- set debugMode as a request variable so that we can use it
   everywhere --->
<cfparam name="request.debugMode" default="0">
<cfif request.debugMode neq "0">
   <!--- finally, turn on debug output if we are in debug mode
         --->
   <cfsetting showDebugOutput="yes">
</cfif>
```

dsp_Demo.cfm (sample code)
```
<cfif request.debugMode neq "0">
   <cfoutput><!-- Entering dsp_demo.cfm --></cfoutput>
   <cfif request.debugMode eq "Trace">
      <cftrace category="myError" var="form" inline="yes"
                              text="Form Variables Received">
   </cfif>
</cfif>
```

error.cfm (default error handler template)
```
<!--- if they are a debugger, dump out the error info and abort.
   --->
<cfif request.debugMode neq "0">
   <cfoutput>
   <html><body>
    <h3>Error Occurred While Processing Request</h3><p>
```

```
    <h4>Error Diagnostic Information</h4>
    <p>Template: #Error.Template#</p>
    <p>#Error.Diagnostics#</p>
    <p>Date/Time: #Error.DateTime#</p>
    #TimeFormat(now())#<br>
    Browser: #Error.Browser#<br>
    Remote Address: #Error.RemoteAddress#<br>
    Referrer: #Error.HTTPReferer#<br>
    QueryString: #Error.QueryString#<p>
    form:<br><cfdump var="#form#">
    url:<br><cfdump var="#url#">
    cgi:<br><cfdump var="#cgi#">
    error:<br><cfdump var="#error#">
    </body></html>
    <cfabort>
    </cfoutput>
</cfif>
<!--- not a debugger, show standard error message and send an e-mail with
    lots of environment info --->
Sorry, an error ocurred.  Please press the back button and try again.
<cfmail to="errors@mycompany.com" from="errormessage@#cgi.server_name#"
    subject="Error Encountered - #cgi.server_name#" type="html">
<html>

<body bgcolor="White" text="Black" leftMargin=0 topMargin=0>
<div align="left">

<table border><tr><td>
<b>Site: #cgi.server_name#</b><br>
<br>
URL: http://#cgi.server_name##cgi.script_name#
<br>
Template: #error.template#<br>
<br>
#error.diagnostics#<br><br>
<p>Date/Time: #error.dateTime# #timeFormat(now())#<br>
Browser: #error.browser#<br>
Remote Address: #error.remoteAddress#<br>
Referer: #error.httpReferer#<br>
<cfif isDefined("cgi.http_referer") and
    (cgi.http_referer neq "")>
    (cgi): #cgi.http_referer#
</cfif>
queryString: #listChangeDelims("#error.queryString#", "<br>", ";")#<br>
<cfif len("cgi.http_cookie")>
http_cookie: #cgi.http_cookie#<p>
</cfif>

</td></tr></table><p><hr>
</body></html>
</cfmail>
</cfif>
```

We'll see another way to extend this for teams under "Team Debugging," later in this chapter.

Missing Pages

The Missing Template Handler is always a handy tool to use to ensure that users are always properly greeted when the page they requested does not exist. However, this becomes a problem when a server runs more than one website since there can only be one Missing Template Handler setting per server.

Because I always like each of my domains to have their own Missing Template Handler, I make use of the CGI variable http_host and the cflocation tag to redirect the user to a domain-specific message from the server Missing Template Handler. This technique may also be used in the code in your Site-Wide Error Handler to create a site-specific default error message for each site on a server.

Listing 2.9 shows the code I place in my server's Missing Template Handler when my server is hosting more than one domain.

Listing 2.9   Missing Template Handler with Redirect (error404.cfm)

```
<!---
   Name: /C02/error404.cfm
   Description: Missing Template Handler With Redirect
--->
<!--- first make sure we didn't get here, from here --->
<cfif isDefined("url.lostURL")>
   <h1>Error 404</h1>
   You have arrived at a page that is no longer here.
<cfelse>
   <!--- Locate them to the default page, passing the lostURL
     parameter so that we know if we got here from this same page.
   --->
   <cflocation url="#cgi.http_host#/error404.cfm?lostURL=1">
</cfif>
```

This code simply sends the user to a page called error404.cfm on whatever server they started out on. If there isn't one specific to the host name, it'll come back to this default template (its missing, too). We keep it from looping by adding the lostURL URL parameter to the cflocation URL; if it exists, we know the host didn't have its own error404.cfm page and display a default message.

TIP   Occasionally, you may want to handle a missing template or an unhandled error without returning an error to the user; for example, you were able to make your page do something logical after all. If you want to change the default 404 or 500 return code to a response of "OK" use the cfheader tag as follows: <cfheader statusCode="200" statusText="OK">. This will prevent the user from seeing an error message that may no longer be applicable.

Team Debugging

Programming in teams has its own set of challenges. One issue you'll run into frequently in the latest applications is that a page is often rendered with a control table around the other elements. This means that different developers may be responsible for developing code that handles the individual elements around the page. Take the page in Figure 2.22 as an example.

FIGURE 2.22:

Sample intranet page

This page is broken into four sections; a header that shows the date and contains the date and a navigation bar, a personalized links section, a news area on the left with the sports scores, and a calendar. In a typical development shop, a separate programmer or team would be assigned to create each of those sections. They are then combined into a single table at display time.

In my shop, this typically would be prototyped as an HTML page. Someone then comes up with the breakdown as far as code is concerned, and the code is divided into stubs, which would typically be a table cell in the master document, and each cell would be self contained within a table for display.

It's generally important when you are developing an application like this that you be able to develop your area of the page in context—that is, seeing how it relates to all the other screen areas. The problem is finding a way to allow each user to work in his area of the code without syntax errors and the like breaking the code so that everybody else is disturbed while trying to develop theirs.

The simplest solution to this problem that I've found is to simply include a statement in each area of the page that will include the development code only for the developer working on that area and just include stubs for the rest. As stable cut points occur, the stub is replaced with the stable code, and the development code continues to progress.

This code for the application shown in Figure 2.22 looks like Listing 2.10.

Listing 2.10   **Intranet Master Page (gpMaster.cfm)**

```
<!---
   Name: /C02/gpMaster.cfm
   Description: Intranet Master Page
--->
<link href="ex2-10.css" rel="stylesheet" type="text/css">
</head>
<body>
<table width="400" border="1">
  <tr>
    <td colSpan="2">
    <!--- here comes the nav bar --->
    <cfinclude template="ex2-10topnav.cfm">
    </td>
  </tr>
  <tr>
    <td colSpan="2">
      <!--- here comes the user custom piece --->
      <cfinclude template="ex2-10userlinks.cfm">
    </td>
  </tr>
  <tr>
    <td width="150">
      <!--- table for press information --->
      <cfinclude template="ex2-10news.cfm">
    </td>
    <td width="250">
      <!--- calendar --->
      <cfinclude template="ex2-10calendar.cfm">
    </td>
  </tr>
</table>
</body>
</html>
```

The initial versions of these included files are literally a cut-and-paste from the original HTML prototype. It has just been split into these files.

Next, these files get edited to include either a prototype (if the user is anyone other than the developer) or the development version of the page (if the user is the developer). This looks like Listing 2.11.

Listing 2.11   **Intranet Sub Page: User Links Area (extracts from gpUserLinks.cfm, gpUserLinks-dev.cfm)**

```
<!---
   Name: /C02/gpUserLinks.cfm, gpUserLinks-dev.cfm
```

```
    Description: Prototype file and sample development code file extract.
--->
```

gpUserLinks.cfm Prototype file (HTML only)
```
<!--- only allow Bill to run the live version of this file --->
<cfif (getAuthUser() eq "Bill")>
    <cfinclude template="ex2-7userlinks-dev.cfm">
    <!--- skip the rest of this file --->
    <cfexit>
</cfif>
<!--- prototype follows --->
<table width="400">
    <tr>
        <td colSpan="2"><div align="center"><strong>Welcome To The Friendly
            Web Page, Sample Employee!</strong></div></td>
    </tr>
    <tr>
        <td><a href="department.cfm?deptid=25117" class="pressSubhead">Department
            25117 News</a></td>
        <td><a href="hr.cfm?userID=1" class="pressSubhead">See your benefit
            Information</a></td>
    </tr>
</table>
```

gpUserLinks-dev.cfm Code File
```
<table width="400">
    <tr>
        <td colSpan="2"><div align="center"><strong>Welcome To The Friendly
            Web Page, <cfoutput>#getAuthUser()#</cfoutput></strong></div></td>
    </tr>
.... and so on
```

When the code goes live, all you need to do is replace the file after the first four lines with the code from the development version. This also give you a great way to allow user edits in live code without worrying that every syntax error is going to cause a problem. You simply develop in the –dev version of the file and re-enable the developer.

Note that at my company we've actually taken this a step further. Rather than authenticate to an individual user, in the application.cfm, we check for a URL variable named debugFile. If the URL variable is set and the user is authenticated, we add the name of the file they wish to debug to a structure, stDebugFiles. The check at the top of the included file becomes

```
<cfif isDefined("stDebugFiles") and
    structKeyExists(stDebugFiles, getFileFromPath(cgi.script_name))>
```

This allows any developer to specify any number of files to be debugged in this session at runtime.

Some Tips

Here are some general tips that can help you avoid many common pitfalls when you are developing ColdFusion MX applications:

- If you find that the ColdFusion Server is hanging and you suspect a particular block of code (or call to a `cfx` tag, COM object, or other third party component), you can put a `cftrace` tag before and after the suspect code to log entry and exit.

- Because search engines tend to scramble URLs and take paths through your code that a user who comes into your site through the front page will never hit, it is worth it to check the `cgi.http_referer` value to see if it came from a search engine (for example, Google). If it did, you should output some logical information to a user who hits the invalid URL as a result of an odd or outdated search engine link.

- Similarly, if search engine bots are hitting your pages in unexpected ways, have your error handler check the `cgi.http_user_agent` for the names of common bots (such as GoogleBot). When a search engine hits a page wrong, it a good idea to display a front page or site map page so that the engine will continue through your site in a logical way.

- Be careful with `cflog` and `cftrace`. Using these too much can make your log files increase in size very quickly.

- When you are upgrading from ColdFusion 5 to ColdFusion MX, don't count on structs to automatically alphabetize their elements when you create them. This assumption is a frequent source of errors. In ColdFusion MX, structure elements keep the same order in which you create them.

- Consistently comment code changes. I'd estimate that half of all errors would be avoided if developers did this. If you're not using a source code control tool, or for that matter, even if you are, *always* document changes to your code both at the top of the source code and at the line of code that is changed. Now that ColdFusion is compiled, you have no excuse not to!

- Make sure you use the new `var` attribute of `cfset` when you're defining variables inside a function to avoid overwriting other local variables. These are often the hardest bugs to find in a large application.

- If you have an especially complex code structure for your application, it is frequently helpful to create a URL parameter that, when set, causes your code to include HTML comments at entry and exit from all templates. Then, if you set the URL parameter and read the source HTML, you will know what templates are outputting every line of text. At the top and bottom of each template, use a line similar to the following:

```
<cfif isDefined("url.showTemplate")>
    <cfoutput><!-- Entering dsp_Admin.cfm --></cfoutput>
</cfif>
```

In Sum

ColdFusion MX has continued to improve upon the debugging and troubleshooting tools of the ColdFusion language. In spite of the fact that the ColdFusion 5 debugger is no longer available, it's easier than ever to track down and debug your code through use of the `cftrace` tag, debugging log files, and other features of ColdFusion MX.

We've learned how to interpret the error messages you see, how to use debugging tags and the debug option on database tags, and how to use the log files. In addition, we've covered many tips and techniques for debugging your application. With these tools under your belt, the path to a problem-free application should be a straight one.

CHAPTER 3

State Management in a Clustered Environment

By John Colasante

- State management fundamentals

- Clustering fundamentals

- ColdFusion MX and clustering

- Tips and advanced features

Eventually you're going to want to run your ColdFusion application on more than one server. The main reasons for doing this is to enable a higher level of redundancy and greater load capacity than a single server can provide. *Redundancy* is the ability of the whole system to survive the loss of a component, and *load capacity* refers to the system's ability to give great performance even when many users are making requests at the same time. In this chapter, we'll explore the application requirements for running an application in a cluster of ColdFusion servers.

NOTE   Clustering is a term that has many meanings in the industry. It is most commonly used to describe Microsoft Cluster Server (MSCS). MSCS is a specialized application environment in which two servers cooperate to enable server IP failover in case one of the cluster partners malfunctions. ColdFusion does not take advantage of MSCS, however, and is thus not considered to be a "cluster aware" application. Here, clustering means using several ColdFusion Application Servers to run a single application.

In this chapter, we'll begin by examining some elements of state management and how it relates to ColdFusion. Then we'll look into how to build applications that can run on multiple ColdFusion servers in a cluster. By the end of the chapter, you'll be able to build all of your applications with the principals outlined here to enable them to scale to a ColdFusion cluster with a minimum of additional work required.

State Management with ColdFusion

This section introduces the concept of state management over HTTP and the need for special techniques to maintain application state across requests. ColdFusion MX enables the use of specialized variables to make state management an easy and automatic task for the advanced programmer.

Managing State over HTTP

You have heard over and over that HTTP is a stateless protocol. What exactly does this mean? In the traditional client/server application, there is a database like Oracle or Sybase that holds the user's data and the stored procedures that implement business logic at the database level. Then, there's the application tier, which is the user-run application on the desktop. Common platforms used to build the application tier include Visual Basic and PowerBuilder. The developer decides what logic goes in the application tier and what stays on the server.

In this traditional approach, there is always a connection between the client and the server, and state is maintained between the desktop application and the database at all times. For example, there is a connection string and a login, and then all data passing between the client and server is tracked by the database. This allows the developer to take advantage of special cursors and data structures on the server that are persistent between requests.

The advantages of this traditional approach are that server-side objects are persistent on the server and the application server is usually designed to make this persistence more or less seamless to the programmer. As a result, things like logins are easy to implement, and the data transport is handled automatically.

The disadvantage of the traditional client server model is that the built-in persistence comes at a price of memory and resource usage on the server. Each client might consume a small amount of memory, but for large applications these increments add up quickly. Clustering is usually not supported by common database systems, but it can be added at extra expense and complexity. And these systems are often proprietary, making migrations extremely difficult from one platform to another.

Scalability and Statement Management

We often hear the term *scalability* when referring to server applications. Traditionally scalability referred to a system's ability to handle more load by adding a resource such as additional processors. An example would be adding an additional CPU to a Sun Solaris server to increase the load capacity of an installed Oracle database running on that server. Today it's not uncommon for server computers to be running four or eight CPUs. This type of scalability is called *scaling up*.

In another type of scalability, more servers are introduced to handle the load of an application. This is *scaling sideways,* and it's what we are going to be referring to in this chapter. When we add more ColdFusion servers, we are scaling sideways in an effort to handle more load. This type of scalability is very common in web application deployment and is often called a *web cluster* or *web farm*. Clustered CF servers typically form a topology where several of them serve up identical content from a single database server that connects to each server in the cluster.

This commonly implemented approach does lead to special challenges of state management, however. The built-in state management techniques (session and client variables) were first introduced into CF to work on only one server. Later, the CF server was extended to allow for some new ways to deal with state management in a clustered environment.

In this chapter, we seek to understand a little more about session and client variables and how they can be used in an environment of clustered CF servers. With this awareness of the mechanics of CF's state management capabilities, you will be able to adapt these functions to work in any environment, and even build your own systems from scratch.

In web-based applications, there is usually no constant connection between the browser and the application server. In this case each request from a client browser can be considered a new request. At first this might seem like a grave problem, but there are advantages to this approach.

Because there is no inherent persistence of server objects, there is a very high level of scalability built into this approach. In the case of the typical web-based application, there can be hundreds or thousands of users simultaneously browsing the application, but they may be spending a lot of idle time reading the content. During this idle there is no overhead to the application server. Instant scalability! Further, the data transport is simple and standardized in the form of text-based HTML.

The disadvantage of the web-based approach is that usually the state management must be implemented by the programmer in whole or in part. A crafty programmer will make this an advantage by leveraging techniques that can make the system more powerful and responsive.

CF Variables for State Maintenance

ColdFusion provides several variables for maintaining state between requests. They're called session variables and client variables, and you may have already used them in a single server application. Let's examine the important differences between these two very different variables and see where each can be used to maximum effectiveness in a clustered environment.

Session Variables   These special memory structures are specific to a server and cannot be shared among servers. They are stored in the server's RAM. They take the form of a CF structure, so they can contain complex structures.

Client Variables   These are more flexible but can only consist of simple datatypes like character strings, numbers, and dates. Client variables can be stored in three different ways: as cookies, in the server registry, and in a database. For a cluster approach, the cookies and the database both work well. We shall see this in the sample application examined in the last section of this chapter.

Storing CF State Variables

State variables are most easily maintained on a single server. In fact, without a cluster, CF has all of the right functionality built in to allow you to maintain state in your application from page to page with almost no special programming. It provides a seamless environment for the programmer to create powerful web applications with full blown state management built in; this is one of the important original design goals of the CF server.

Once we move to a multiserver clustered environment, however, we encounter special problems of state variable storage. CF has very different ways of storing session and client variables.

Session Variables

Session variables are stored in the server's RAM. These variables cannot be transferred from one server to another within a cluster. A session variable on a specific server in the cluster is related to the user's session by virtue of the session keys, which are the CFID and CFTOKEN values. CFID and CFTOKEN are special variables that are internally maintained by the CF server. They are available in both the client scope and the session scope. A session key is bound to a browser instance.

In order to use session variables in a cluster, you must configure some front-end device or software that will force a client (a browser) to hit the same server over and over in the context of a single session. That is, when clients visit the cluster, they can land on any server initially, but subsequent requests must go to the same server. If a session is defined in CF to be 20 minutes, then you must make sure that all requests within 20 minutes are sent to the same server in the cluster. The drawback to this approach is obvious. If the server you've been sent to is busy, there is no mechanism for you to move to another server. Usually the session storage is fixed to one server and unless you build special code to transfer it to another server, you are stuck on one single server in the cluster.

The idea of directing a client to the same server in a cluster is also called *session-aware load balancing* and many devices and software can do this. You should not give up on session variables just because of this limitation. Session variables are very powerful.

Client Variables
Client variables are stored in one of three places, but only two are relevant to clusters. The default location is the system's registry, and this location is not suitable for use with a cluster. The system registry is not transferable from one server to another within a cluster. If you intend to use client variables, you must choose another approach. Even if you aren't trying to implement a cluster, you should think beyond the registry for client variable storage. It's OK for small applications, but even large single-server apps can quickly fill the registry and bog down the server and eventually crash it altogether.

The two acceptable storage methods for client variables are as cookies in the user's browser, or in a database. The cookies approach is cluster friendly because nothing is stored on the server, so you need not be concerned with sharing the server-side variables amongst the cluster's servers. With this approach, you do not need any session aware load balancing; you can use plain old round robin DNS (RRDNS). This setup means that each time a request comes into your cluster, the DNS server resolves the IP to the next server in the cluster, vastly reducing the chance of the same client hitting the same server twice in a row. But there is no worry, because the actual values are stored within the cookies themselves. The data is in the browser.

The limitations of the cookies approach are many. First, you may not want your users seeing the data you are storing. By holding the data in client-side cookies, you make it possible for users to snoop their own cookies files and see the exact values. Furthermore, those files could be wiped-out and then the whole effectiveness of the client variable is deleted entirely. Of course using ordinary registry-based client variables does allow the user to delete the CF session tokens (CFID and CFTOKEN), thus orphaning the server-side session, but this is unlikely since the user will not have a clear idea of what values are stored on the server.

The final and best approach for storing client variables is the most cluster aware of all. It utilizes a back-end SQL database capable of high transactional loads to store the client variables. The main reason for the inclusion of this feature is to enable client variables to span more than one server. In the later section "Setting Up the Cluster Database Walk-Through" we'll see how this works

Comparing Storage Methods

Table 3.1 compares the points of the techniques for client variable storage.

TABLE 3.1: Client Variable Storage Methods

Type	Advantages	Disadvantages
Registry	Default option, no configuration necessary	Does not work in a cluster. Hogs the system registry.
Database	Works in cluster	Reliance on external database
Cookies	Works in cluster	Less secure

Allocating CFID and CFTOKEN in a Cluster

As we have discussed already the session keys CFID and CFTOKEN are extremely important, especially when they are installing CF in a clustered environment. Let's take a look at how these variables are generated.

We already know that the CF server generates the session tokens in response to a client that makes a request on a page under session or client control. The session keys are necessary to associate the browser instance with the session on the server or server cluster.

> **TIP**   CFID and CFTOKEN are also referred to collectively as URLTOKEN. As a convenience, CF has a built-in variable session.URLTOKEN, which is equivalent to writing #session .CFID#&#session.CFTOKEN#. You may use them interchangeably.

In the case when you are only using session variables with and no client management, the session variables are unique on each server in a cluster. The CF servers do not share tokens; each server generates the tokens in the following manner:

- CFID is generated as a monotonically increasing number (by one) for each new session to be managed by the specific CF server. There is a registry key called

  HKEY_LOCAL_MACHINE\SOFTWARE\Allaire\ColdFusion\CurrentVersion\Clients\LastID which holds the last CFID that the server gave out. You may find that these keys are out of synch on the multiple servers in the cluster because each server hands out keys from its own cache, independent of the other servers in the cluster. The only time this is not true is when you enable client management and you use a database as the client variable storage location. In this case, the client variable keys are allocated from the central database making it impossible to mix up the CFIDs among servers.

- CFTOKEN is allocated as a random long integer, in the range from 0 to 2147483647.

The combination of CFID and CFTOKEN is sufficiently difficult to guess to make the use of CF sessions reasonably secure. If more security is desired, this setting in the registry

    HKEY_LOCAL_MACHINE\Software\Allaire\ColdFusion\CurrentVersion\Clients\UuidToken

can be set to a value "1." This makes the CF server change its method of generating the CFTOKEN from a simple random integer to a unique global key. The method is especially suited to clusters because the token generated by the server is guaranteed to be unique, which makes it impossible to have duplicate keys in the database. This is achieved via the use of a GUID, or global unique ID algorithm. In ColdFusion MX this setting can be made via the administration interface in lieu of the registry.

Because each server maintains its own LastID, clearly a client session that lives on one server will never by synchronized on another server unless a central database is used to store the tokens. In this case, instead of being generated from its own LastID key in the server's registry, the CFID is generated by adding one to the last value generated from the client's database. The concept is analogous to a database primary key that has been defined as autoNumber (in Access), or Identity (in SQL Server) These types of keys automatically increment by some seed value (in this case, 1) to guarantee that the key shall be unique. When CF creates the client variable database, it does not allocate the autoNumber or Identity property to the columns that hold the CFID. Rather, the CF server increments the keys monotonically on its own.

The structure of the client variable database is simple. There are two tables, CDATA and CGLOBAL. The CDATA table is the critical table in the process because it actually holds the client variable data. The CGLOBAL table holds auxiliary parameters that may not be important to you.

Clustering Fundamentals

Sharing session variables over a cluster of more than one ColdFusion server requires special understanding of how these variables work and their limitations. With a solid grasp of these concepts, the programmer can develop highly scalable applications that can make use of ColdFusion's advanced state management capabilities.

Clusters and Sideways Scalability

Clusters enable your application to handle more load and users. There is a practical limit to the number of simultaneous users that a single server can handle. What exactly do we mean by simultaneous users? Since the HTTP transaction is stateless, a single user does not maintain a constant connection to the database, as we have discussed. So *simultaneous* takes on a new meaning.

Actually, the idea of simultaneous users in a web application is abstract. If you were to analyze the usage pattern of a typical user of your web application, you might see something like this:

1. Hit main page, read contents for 10 seconds.

2. Go to login page; pause there for 5 seconds while entering login information.

3. Visit first page with about a 20-second interval between page views.

4. Log out or just close browser.

So you can see that in a 5-minute session we really only have 10 to 20 page views. If we define a session as a period during which the gap between page views is never longer than some arbitrary timeout (20 minutes is typical), then the spread of hits is relatively sparse. So a single server might be able to handle up to 500 to 600 of these typical users, where a traditional client/server database might handle only 100 effectively. Of course if your usage scenario is different (for example, business users running complex reports), then you may only be able to handle 50 to 100 users per server.

As a first benchmark, try to do some testing to determine the CF server's load based on CPU utilization and keep it below 50 percent sustained. Then build your cluster with the number of servers that will be able to handle your sustained load profile with a safety factor of 3. So if you think a single server can handle 800 users and you anticipate having 2,000 users connected simultaneously, you'll want to start your cluster with about 9 servers on the front end.

Clustering Configurations

Clustering is an important strategy for giving your applications a higher level of reliability and improved load capacity. A single server represents a single point of failure, and this is not an acceptable risk for many applications today. There are various configurations to consider when implementing CF clusters, and there are trade-offs for each configuration.

Using multiple web/CF servers is one of the most traditional architectures for web application farms. Multiple servers, each with identical configurations of a web server and CF server, are placed behind a TCP load balancing hardware device. The type of load balancing device is not of particular importance, but it must support a concept of *"sticky sessions,"* also called persistent sessions or *client affinity*. An even more sophisticated form of client affinity uses the SSL token in the browser header to coordinate the client's transactions with a single server in the cluster. The load balancing device works by recognizing the client and diverting the request to the same server in the cluster within the session.

There are many load balancing devices in use today. It's not possible to explore every one in this chapter, but Table 3.2 takes a look at a few approaches and compares the features of each.

TABLE 3.2: Comparison of Load Balancing Hardware Devices

Device Name	Type	Supports Sticky Sessions?	Supports SSL Affinity?	Notes
Microsoft Windows NT/ 2000 Load Balancing Server (WLBS)	software	No	No	Built into Windows 2000 Advanced Server. Easy setup and administration.
ClusterCATS	software	Yes	No	Built into CF MX. Moderately easy setup.
F5 BigIP	hardware	Yes	Yes	Robust, scalable hardware device. Lots of features; scriptable for highly customized load balancing scenarios.
Cisco LocalDirector	hardware	Yes	Yes	Another popular hardware load balancing device with features for direct integration with CF MX.

Guidelines for Clustering in the ColdFusion Environment

When used properly, CF's built-in state management variables provide all the tools you need to create powerful and reliable web applications. When using these variables in a cluster, there are some guidelines to follow.

Managing CFID/CFTOKEN

The CFID and CFTOKEN are generated by CF and passed to the client in the following fashion:

1. The client browser calls up the CF server's site, for example http://www.mysite.com.
2. The browser sends its cookie payload to the CF server. This always occurs on every HTTP transaction, whether or not the CF server is active. This is a feature of the HTTP cookie spec; the cookies are passed on every round trip.

3. The CF server parses the cookies passed to it in order to determine whether this is a new client or one that has previously visited. The determination is made by examining the CFID and CFTOKEN session keys. If the CFID and CFTOKEN are passed, the client may have visited this server before.

When we discuss a "client," we are talking about an individual instance of a browser. This distinction is important for a number of reasons. If multiple instances of the same browser type (say Microsoft Internet Explorer) are opened by double-clicking the same desktop computer, each instance will share the same set of cookies. For this reason, it is often difficult or impossible for a CF application to distinguish sessions originating from the same computer. If you want to simulate multiple clients from the same computer desktop, you must use two separate browser types, perhaps one instance each of Internet Explorer and of Netscape.

NOTE   The significance of the session key, CFID/CFTOKEN, cannot be underestimated. It is the sole link between the client browser and the application on the server.

If the session tokens are found, then the server must determine what types of session management are enabled in the specific application. Following are two examples of cfapplication tags. These tags are usually placed in a template that gets called once at the top of every request in the application. Possible locations are in the Application.cfm file for non-Fusebox applications, and the app_locals.cfm in the case of a Fusebox application.

```
<cfapplication name="myCFApp"    sessionManagement="yes"
setClientCookies="yes">
```

```
<cfapplication name="myCFApp"    clientManagement="yes"
setClientCookies="yes">
```

In the first example, the cfapplication tag indicates that session management is enabled for the application. The second example indicates client management only. In past versions of CF (before 4.x), when you set clientManagement="yes", the CF server automatically set session management as well, so it was not possible to have one without the other. Since the release of version 4.x, you have been allowed to set them independently. This makes better use of CF server resources by conserving elements that are not required—a welcome change in the interest of more robust performance.

Using Session Variables Properly

Session variables are very powerful and can lend great functionality to your CF application. Because they cannot be shared across servers, however, it is essential that you use a load balancing or clustering technique that supports sticky sessions, or client affinity. Once you have decided to use session variables, you should observe some best practices to ensure that your application is robust, efficient, and fast.

Using Locks

Session variables are also called *shared scope variables* because it is possible for multiple clients to be simultaneously reading from and writing to them. The possibility of this simultaneous access means the CF server can be corrupted and cause an error, or the data value stored in the variable can be corrupted. To avoid this problem, you must lock the session variables with the `cflock` tag. ColdFusion MX has addressed these locking issues, so these locking rules only apply to versions of ColdFusion prior to MX.

`cflock` forces the CF server to single-thread the access to the critical section of code that is delimited by the `cflock` tags, thus restricting the simultaneous reading and writing to memory.

Simplifying the Structure

It's also important to avoid using many session variables and instead encapsulate your session variables into a nested session-instance variable. For example, instead of this:

```
<cfset session.username="joe">
<cfset session.loggedIn="yes">
<cfset session.color="red">
```

try this:

```
<cfset session.user=structNew()>
<cfset session.user.username="joe">
<cfset session.user.loggedIn="yes">
<cfset session.user.color="red">
```

If you create this convenient instance structure, it will be easier to manage your data later. You can copy this instance structure and even transform it into XML format using the WDDX functions without having to worry about anything other than the top level structure, in this case `session.user`. If you didn't use a data structure like this, then packaging the structure would be more complex because you'd have to serialize each variable separately instead of as one combined structure. Get into the habit of creating instance variables like this.

For example, let's say you wanted to wipe out the entire structure associated with the user later, but you still want to preserve the `session.sessionID` that is the session handle. Instead of writing this:

```
<cfset dummy=structClear(session)>
```

you would write

```
<cfset dummy=structClear(session.user)>
```

Inter- and Intra-Session State

Inter-session state refers to client state management that occurs within a session. *Intra-session state* refers to client state management that occurs between sessions. The session is defined as dictated by the `cfapplication` tag. On all servers in the cluster, you must make sure that the session is defined to the same value. This rule applies whether you are using sticky sessions or not.

Taking Advantage of the Session Structure

Session variables are very powerful because they take advantage of the CF datatype called a structure. This makes it possible to hold complex nested datatypes within a session, making the session variable much stronger than the client variable. Client variables can only contain simple datatypes like strings, numbers, and dates. Whether they are stored in the Registry (the default) a database, or in cookies, client variables can only be simple data values. You cannot store complex data structures—only numbers, strings, and dates. Thus, client variables are quite limited. An example of the type of structure you might want to store in a session is a shopping cart, which might be an array of structures. Client variables cannot hold these complex datatypes unless you encode the structure into a WDDX string and then store that string into the client variable.

Cluster Variables and Inter-Session State

Cluster variables are good for storing information that is used between sessions; this type of state management is also referred to as intra-session state. Think of cluster variables as "personalization features."

Cluster variables are typically recalled from the client variable when the user revisits the site, like when you return to a site the next day to check on an order. When the user hits the site or logs in, CFID and CFTOKEN are used transparently to read the client variables from the client variable database storage, and these values are then recalled into a session instance or used directly. The reason to copy the `client` scope into the `session` scope is to make the access quicker during the course of the session. When the user leaves the site or logs out, the updated values can be written back into the client store by assigning the client variables values from the session variables. Using client variables in this manner fits in well with the idea that client variables should be used "write once, read many."

Client variables that belong in the category of cluster variable include the following:

- User preferences that will be recalled upon a revisit to the site

- Past selections that the customer made on previous visits

- Order status that the user might want to view upon returning to the site

---

NOTE   When you use client variables in a cluster with CF MX, you must enable domain cookies. This is set in the `cfapplication` tag, using the parameter `setDomainCookies="yes"`. This setting sends the CFID and CFTOKEN to the browser with domain scope. In other words, the cookie is set with a scope like `.mydomain.com` instead of `www1.mydomain.com`. If you do not enable domain cookies, when the browser is redirected to another host in the cluster, it will lose the session because it cannot read the cookie. This setting only applies when you are not using session affinity.

Setting Up the Cluster Database Walk-Through

In this section, we'll walk through all the steps you need to follow to create the client variable database on a remote SQL Server:

1. Create the client variable database.

2. Set the network connections.

3. Configure the ODBC data source.

4. Configure the CF servers to use the client variable cluster database.

This configuration works well for any number of front-end CF servers; you can even start with one and add more later.

> **WARNING** Although it's possible to use the same server for both the front-end CF server and the client variable database, this approach is not recommended. The client variable database should be set up on a dedicated SQL server to ensure good performance. The client variable tables can be hit with lots of transactions in a short time on a busy application.

It is essential to use a proper SQL database server such as MS SQL Server, Oracle, or Sybase to hold the client variable data, and not a desktop database like MS Access. Access is fine for single server applications, but it cannot handle the multiuser cluster approach, where each server in the cluster is a highly transactional user.

In these examples, we'll be working with MS SQL 7 on a MS Windows 2000 server to hold the client variable database. You can use other types of SQL databases as long as they support ODBC connection to CF MX. In some cases, you may have to tweak the tables after the database is created, and we'll explore that at the end of this section, in "Using the Client Variable Cluster Database."

Creating the Client Variable Database

The first step is to create the database to hold the client variables. Figure 3.1 illustrates the Microsoft SQL Enterprise Manager opened to create a new database, called it CF_Clients.

SQL 7 and later versions can create a small initial database and configure it to grow as needed. This is a good feature to take advantage of if you are not sure how rapidly the client variable database is going to grow. The amount of storage used by the client database will depend on the number of client variables and the size of the actual values. Because client variables can only be simple values such as strings, numbers, and dates, it should be quite easy to estimate the storage amount needed.

FIGURE 3.1:

Creating the client
variable database on
MS SQL Server

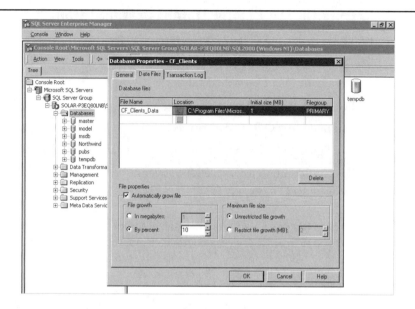

Setting the Network Client Connections

Once the database is created on a CF server, you must establish the communication among
the CF servers and the new database. In this example, we are demonstrating with ColdFusion
for Windows running on a Windows 2000 server.

Connectivity between each server in the cluster and the remote client database server will
vary depending on your platform and network topology, but in most cases, it will be TCP/IP.
It is often necessary to configure the client network protocol to use TCP/IP, ensuring that the
cluster servers can reach the database regardless of reliance on Windows networking components being installed (such as named pipes). For this to work, you must install the network
client part of the SQL server component installation onto each of the CF servers in the cluster.

In Figure 3.2, we see the Client Network Utility as it would appear on any of the CF servers
participating in the cluster. This utility is accessed from the Microsoft SQL Server program
group. It is not necessary to install the entire SQL Server program onto each CF server in
the cluster; you only need to install the client utilities, which are a subset of the entire server
installation located on the SQL Server distribution media. Here in Figure 3.2 we have selected
TCP/IP networking to enable universal connections to the back-end database.

In order to add a new alias to the database server, each CF server will need an alias entered
into the Network Client Utility. We have chosen the name CFCLUSTERDB as shown in
Figure 3.3. The alias name of the database server need not match the actual name of the server

or its domain name. The server name and port are entered in the Computer Name and Port Number fields of the dialog box. The default TCP port for SQL Server is 1433. You can enter either the database server's DNS name or the IP address in the server alias text box.

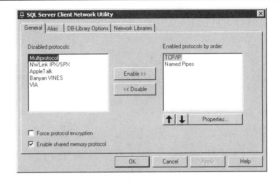

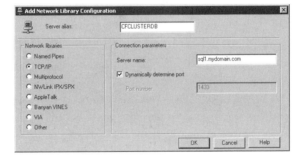

Configuring the ODBC Data Source

Once the alias setup is completed, you can add and configure the ODBC data source. Each of the CF servers in the cluster should use the same data source name for the cluster database to facilitate code sharing among the servers. The Data Sources (ODBC) control panel applet will be used to initially configure the data source; then later, the data source will be associated with the client backing store on each cluster server. The procedure described in this configuration section must be repeated identically on each CF server. The first step is to locate and open the ODBC control panel applet, shown in Figure 3.4. When you select the applet, you will see a list of all the existing ODBC data sources that have already been configured. We are interested in those configured under the System DSN tab (shown in Figure 3.5), since these data sources are not dependant upon user authentication. Each CF server will be connecting to the remote cluster database using the authentication rights of the CF server's domain or user account, but the authentication may be overridden in the data source setup.

Open the ODBC control panel applet under Administrative Tools.

Select from the list of system data sources.

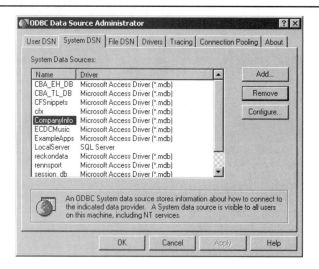

Click Add to configure a new data source. Next you will select the ODBC driver type of the cluster database, as shown in Figure 3.6. In this case, you'll choose SQL Server.

TIP We recommend that you upgrade your system to the latest and greatest Microsoft Data Access Components (MDAC), available at http://www.microsoft.com/data/. Using the latest data access components will ensure the best and most reliable performance from your system.

FIGURE 3.6:

Select the driver.

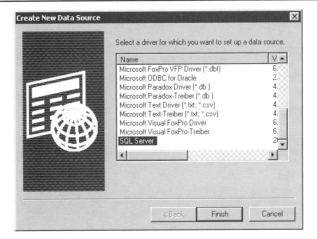

The next few steps cover the creation of the actual data source. In Figure 3.7, we have filled in the name of the data source on each server, in this case ClientStore. (Remember that you'll want to choose an appropriate name that is relevant to what is provided by the data source.) In this figure, note that the name of the SQL Server is the alias that we configured earlier in the Network Client Utility. If you are using named pipes to connect, you can just enter the Net-BIOS name of the SQL server. It is recommended that you configure and use TCP/IP instead of NetBIOS within the SQL Server Client Utility to enable more universal connectivity.

FIGURE 3.7:

Fill in the data source properties.

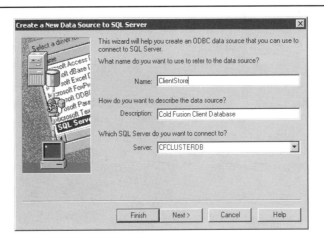

Figure 3.8 shows the authentication options for the data source. These selections are dependent on how you installed the SQL Server and what authentication options you have enabled. If you have allowed Integrated authentication, then you may be able to pass the CF server's authentication credentials over without entering a password. More commonly, you will have

enabled mixed-mode authentication, and you will need to enter the database login ID and password here.

NOTE   Do not be tempted to use the database system administrator account sa when you create datasources. This is a security risk. Instead, create separate user accounts for each application. You should grant each of these accounts the dbo alias in order to give that user full access to the cluster database.

FIGURE 3.8:

ODBC Authentication properties

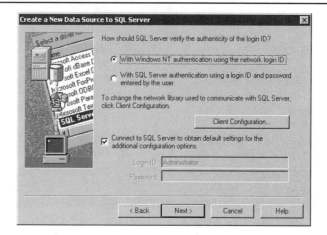

The next step, shown in Figure 3.9, shows the selection of the database once the connection has been established on the database server. The drop-down list at the top will show all currently available databases; select the one you created earlier in this process. This is equivalent to selecting a default database for this connection.

FIGURE 3.9:

Point the cluster ODBC data source to the remote database.

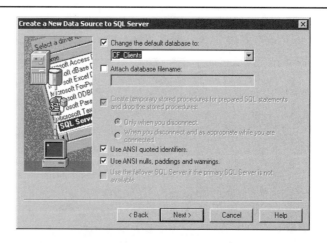

Next up is Figure 3.10, which shows where you select the language and regional settings for the data source. Unless you have a specific reason to change any of these settings, it's best to leave them at their defaults. ColdFusion does not require any changes here.

FIGURE 3.10:

Selecting default language and regional settings

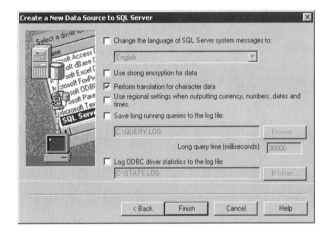

The next step shows the results of the test and verification of the connection (Figure 3.11). If the test succeeded, you are ready to configure the ColdFusion server.

FIGURE 3.11:

Test and verify the connection.

Configuring the CF Servers to Use the Database

Now we are going to configure the CF servers to utilize the client variable repository on the database. The following configuration steps must be performed on each server in the cluster, except for the step where you actually create the database tables (because they only need to be created the first time). If the data source you are using to store the client variables uses a bundled JDBC driver, ColdFusion can automatically create the necessary tables. If your data source uses the ODBC Socket or a third-party JDBC driver, you must manually create the necessary CDATA and CGLOBAL database tables.

If you must create the tables on your own, here is the code to do it (from the Cold Fusion MX documentation).

```
<!---- Create the Client variable storage tables in a datasource.
This example applies to Microsoft Access databases --->

<cfquery name="data1" datasource="#DSN#">
CREATE TABLE CDATA
(
    cfid char(20),
    app char(64),
    data memo
)
</cfquery>

<cfquery name="data2" datasource="#DSN#">
  CREATE UNIQUE INDEX id1
  ON CDATA (cfid,app)
</cfquery>

<cfquery name="global1" datasource="#DSN#">
CREATE TABLE CGLOBAL
(
    cfid char(20),
    data memo,
  lvisit date
)
</cfquery>

<cfquery name="global2" datasource="#DSN#">
  CREATE INDEX id2
  ON CGLOBAL (cfid)
</cfquery>

<cfquery name="global2" datasource="#DSN#">
```

```
CREATE INDEX id3
  ON CGLOBAL (lvisit)
</cfquery>
```

Assuming the tables have been created, go to the CFIDE administration page, available on each server at `http://yourservername/cfide/administrator/index.cfm`.

Once you are in the ColdFusion Administrator, select the link for Datasources in the left panel. You will see a list of the currently configured data sources for the server. This list will include the data source you previously configured within Windows 2000 (ClientStore). Select this data source, click the link, and you will enter the editing page for the data source (Figure 3.12). Here you will check the settings and verify the parameters of the datasource.

FIGURE 3.12:

Verifying the ODBC data source for the cluster database

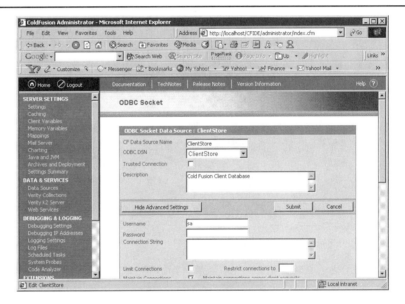

Now it's time to actually select the client storage location. In the left panel, select the link for Client Variables under Server Settings, and you will see all the possible locations for client variable storage. Of course, the default is Registry, but you will also see Cookies here. Because we are going to be using a database, select the ODBC data source that we created earlier to enable it for client variable storage (see Figure 3.13).

Click the Add button to bring up the window shown in Figure 3.14. Here you will most likely accept the defaults. Click Submit Changes. Finally, once the datasource is added as a candidate for client variable storage, you will select its name from the radio button selections and click Apply. Now ColdFusion will use this datasource as the client variable storage location. Repeat this process for each server in the cluster.

FIGURE 3.13:

Select the client
variable storage.

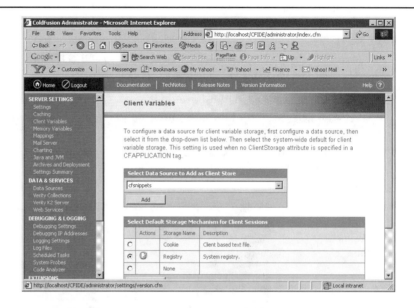

FIGURE 3.14:

Create the client
variable database
tables.

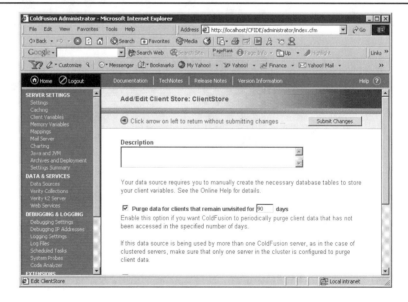

Using the Client Variable Cluster Database

Once you've completed the steps described in the preceding sections, you are ready to begin using the new client variable storage. You will use it just as you would use client variables in the Registry, except now the actual values are stored in the database tables CDATA and CGLOBALS.

The structures of these databases are shown in Figures 3.15 and 3.16. The CFID and CFTOKEN values are stored the CFID field in the form CFID:CFTOKEN, with both values concatenated in the same database field. All of the actual client variable values are concatenated into the DATA field.

Because the data is concatenated into one field, this is a highly denormalized data schema and is not optimized for highly transactional traffic. As a result, you should strive to write into the client variable as seldom as possible. If you do lots of updates to client variables in your application, you may experience database problems such as deadlocks.

FIGURE 3.15:

The structure of the CDATA table

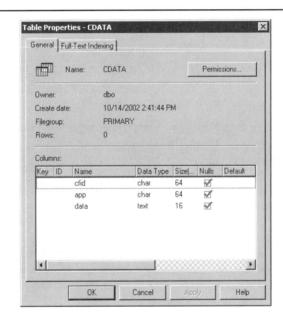

The structure of the
CGLOBAL table

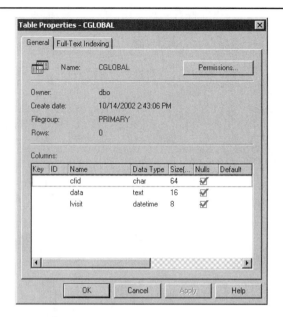

Precautions for Using Client Variables

As we have pointed out, there are a few pitfalls when using client variables. Although the
process is seamless to the user, using only client variables limits overall flexibility somewhat.

Client variables can only store simple values like strings, numbers, and dates. Thus, if you
want to store more complex data, you are required to use a database to store the values. If
you use the more powerful session variables, however, you could create a session variable
using a nested array of structures to represent a shopping cart. But if you are limited to only
client variables, you must make a database table to achieve the same functionality. This can
greatly increase the number of transactions in the database, in turn causing performance
degradation with your application.

Before you commit to a client-variable-only approach, make sure you consider the types of
data and the type of processing you intend to handle. Then make the choice for your cluster
that most efficiently deals with the environment.

Putting Advanced Features to Work

In this section, we'll explore an experimental technique for storing complex datatypes in
the database that can be useful in a cluster scenario. With this approach, there is no specific

reliance on any of the normal CF built-in variables. In fact, you do not need a `cfapplication` tag, since you do not have to set the CF session tokens `CFID` and `CFTOKEN`. We use one anyway in this example to specify that no client cookies are to be set.

NOTE The code presented here is intended as a framework, and for simplicity, we have not attempted to utilize `cflocks` around access to the database tables that read and write the user coded sessions. We have left out this step for illustration purposes and so that we could provide you with alternatives for clustering complex variables. If you intend to implement such an idea, it would be wise to modify the framework to fit your exact application.

Our example begins with the `Application.cfm` file (Listing 3.1). In this file, which is called for every request within the application directory, we are checking to see if the homebrew session ID (SID) is being passed to the template. If it is not, we use CF's function `createUUID` to make a new, globally unique session key. In this application, it is essential that we pass this SID through every link and form action to maintain the session state. If we drop the SID, we will orphan the session in the database.

The database in this example is simple and its structure is shown in Figure 3.17. The SID column holds the session key, and it's represented as a text column. Here's an example of the UUID created by the `createUUID` function:

```
B569FE79-6936-42A3-88A104999868627D
```

You must ensure that the column can hold a text string of at least this length.

FIGURE 3.17:

The structure of the session table

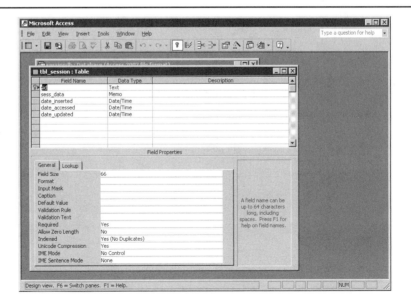

Once the SID is created, a new row in the session database is inserted. The SID is the primary key (PK) and an empty WDDX structure is used as the data payload that goes into the sess_data column. The other columns in the database relate to the creation time and update time of the record. This information can be used to purge older session data from the database and also to keep track of current sessions. For instance, you might track sessions whose hits take place with a timeout no greater than 20 minutes.

Listing 3.1   Example code (Application.cfm)

```
<!---
    Name:          /c03/Application.cfm
    Description:    This file is called for each request, initializing the session
    and populating the database with a new session key if one did not exist.
--->

<cfapplication name="my_sessions" setClientCookies="no">
<cfset sessdsn="session_db">
<cfif not isDefined("url.sid")>
<!--- This user does not have a session SID, so make one for him --->
<cfset sid=createUUID()>
<cfset timeNow=createODBCDateTime(now())>
<cfset emptyStruct=structNew()>
<cfwddx action="cfml2wddx" input="#emptyStruct#" output="wddx_struct">
<cfquery name="PutSID" datasource="#sessdsn#" dbtype="ODBC">
insert into tbl_session (sid,sess_data,date_inserted,date_accessed,date_updated)
    values ('#variables.sid#', '#wddx_struct#', #timeNow#, #timeNow#, #timeNow#)
</cfquery>
<cfelse>
<cfset variables.sid=url.sid>
</cfif>
```

The first template of the sample application is main.cfm (Listing 3.2). Here, we simply output the SID and also set up the call to the next template, another.cfm. Notice the SID is passed in the URL as url.sid.

Listing 3.2   Example code (Main.cfm)

```
<!---
    Name:          /c03/Main.cfm
    Description:    This codeblock is a sample display page to demonstrate the SID
    and how it maintains the user session between requests.
--->

<html>
<head>
<title>Main Page of application</title>
</head>
```

```
<body>
This is the main app page--the menu so to speak.
<br>
<cfoutput>Your sid is: #variables.sid#</cfoutput><br>
Go to another page: <a
href="another.cfm?sid=<cfoutput>#variables.sid#</cfoutput>">Another page.</a>
<cfinclude template="footer.cfm">
</body>
</html>
```

In the template another.cfm (Listing 3.3), we are asking for input from a drop-down list; the user is asked to select a color. This is the first scalar variable that we'll serialize into the database. We use the form in this template to demonstrate the use of a form action that carries the SID.

Listing 3.3   **Example code (Another.cfm)**

```
<!---
    Name:           /c03/Another.cfm
    Description:    This is the second sample page that dumps the wddx packet to
    the browser to prove the session has been deserialized correctly and has kept
    the user data packet intact.
--->
<html>
<head>
<title>Another</title>
</head>
<body>
This is the other page.<br>
Your sid is <cfoutput>#variables.sid#</cfoutput><br>
On this page you are asked to make a choice of which will be saved as a
session.<br>
<form action="form_handler.cfm?sid=<cfoutput>#sid#</cfoutput>" method="post">
<select name="var1">
<option value="Red">Red</option>
<option value="Blue">Blue</option>
<option value="Green">Green</option>
</select>
<input type="Submit" value="Save!">
</form>
<cfinclude template="footer.cfm">
</body>
</html>
```

The form_handler.cfm template (Listing 3.4) introduces the custom tag mysession.cfm (Listing 3.5). There are two "methods" to this tag: one is get and one is set. Setting a variable will serialize it using the CF_wddx function and insert or update the database row corresponding to the session SID. Any type of variable can be serialized in this fashion. Getting a variable does the reverse; it deserializes the variable and places it conveniently into a CF local variable for the calling template to access.

Listing 3.4   **Example code (form_handler.cfm)**

```
<!---
  Name:           /c03/form_handler.cfm
  Description:    This snippet shows the calls to the CF custom tag 'mysession'
  which serializes the session back into the database using the 'set' action.
--->
<html>
<head>
  <title>Saved</title>
</head>
<body>
Your session information <cfoutput>#form.var1#</cfoutput>
<!--- Now write into the database --->
<cfquery name="getPeople" datasource="#sessdsn#" dbtype="ODBC">
select * from people
</cfquery>
<cf_mysession sid="#sid#" action="set" varName="color" varVal="#form.var1#"
datasource="#sessdsn#">
<cf_mysession sid="#sid#" action="set" varName="peopleQuery"
varval="#getPeople#" datasource="#sessdsn#">
This page has also set a session query variable.<br>
<cfoutput>Go <a href="seequery.cfm?sid=#sid#">here</a> to see the display of
it.</cfoutput>
<cfinclude template="footer.cfm">
</body>
</html>
```

Listing 3.5   **Example code (mysession.cfm)**

```
<!---
  Name:           /c03/mysession.cfm
  Description:    This custom tag has two 'methods'. Get is used to retrieve the
  session data from the database and 'set' is used to store it. There is no
  limitation to the type of data that can be stores because structures are
  used. Also, wddx is used to serialized the complex datatypes into strings
  that can be stored in the database memo field.
--->
<cfswitch expression="#attributes.action#">
<cfcase value="get">
  <cfquery name="getSession" datasource="#attributes.datasource#"
  dbtype="ODBC">
  select sess_data from tbl_session where sid='#attributes.sid#'
  </cfquery>
```

```
   <cfwddx action="wddx2cfml" input="#getSession.sess_data#"
   output="sessionStruct">
   <cfset "caller.#attributes.localVar#" = sessionStruct[attributes.varName]>
</cfcase>
<cfcase value="set">
   <cfquery name="getSession" datasource="#attributes.datasource#"
   dbtype="ODBC">
   select sess_data from tbl_session where sid='#attributes.sid#'
   </cfquery>
   <cfwddx action="wddx2cfml" input="#getSession.sess_data#"
   output="localStruct">
   <cfif not structKeyExists(localStruct,"#attributes.varName#")>
      <cfset
      structInsert(localStruct,"#attributes.varName#","#attributes.varVal#")>
   <cfelse>
      <cfset
      structUpdate(localStruct,"#attributes.varName#","#attributes.varVal#")>
   </cfif>
   <cfwddx action="cfml2wddx" input="#localStruct#" output="wddx_struct">
   <cfquery name="putSession" datasource="#attributes.datasource#"
   dbtype="ODBC">
   update tbl_session set sess_data='#wddx_struct#' where sid='#attributes.sid#'
   </cfquery>
</cfcase>
</cfswitch>
```

Finally, the `seequery.cfm` template (Listing 3.6) takes the values that were called out of the database using the `mysession.cfm` custom tag and displays them on the page using the CF custom tag `cf_dump.cfm`. `cf_dump` is available in the CF Developer's Exchange and provides a method for displaying arbitrary datatypes into HTML format.

Listing 3.6   **Example code (seequery.cfm)**

```
<!---
   Name:          /c03/seequery.cfm
   Description:   This code makes use of the 'get' method of the 'mysession'
   custom tag.
--->
<html>
<head>
   <title>See results</title>
</head>
<body>
<cf_mysession sid="#sid#" action="get" varName="color" localVar="color"
datasource="#sessdsn#">
<cf_mysession sid="#sid#" action="get" varName="peopleQuery"
localVar="peopleQuery" datasource="#sessdsn#">
 Here is the query from earlier:<br>
<cf_dump v="color">
```

```
<cf_dump v="peopleQuery">
<cfinclude template="footer.cfm">
</body>
</html>
```

The usefulness of this scenario cannot be understated. By providing a framework for storing arbitrary datatypes in a database using a simple mechanism, we have shown that ColdFusion servers in a cluster can indeed overcome the limitations of ordinary client variables. Although ColdFusion provides the tools to achieve state management out of the box using client variables in a database, you can extend this concept to create powerful homebrew state-management environments using simple CF functions.

In Sum

ColdFusion MX has powerful facilities that allow the programmer to create applications that span multiple servers. But it is up to the programmer to understand the intimate details of how ColdFusion's special variables work in a multiserver environment.

Session variables have scope on a single server. The programmer must ensure that each request to the cluster is directed back to the original server to ensure that state is preserved. Careful use of locks to prevent corruption of the session key is critical in versions of CF prior to MX. Also, use of the built-in "client variable database" is essential to maintaining inter-session state from visit to visit.

Using the techniques introduced in this chapter, you will find that there are virtually no limitations to the size and scalability of your applications. Whether it is just two servers or hundreds, ColdFusion MX will be able to handle the load with ease.

CHAPTER 4

The Fusebox Framework and Development Methodology

By Hal Helms

- Carmen and Bill: a cautionary tale

- The discouraging facts about current software development practices

- The need for methodologies and frameworks

- What Fusebox does for the developer

- Solving complexity

- Key Fusebox elements

- The steps of FLiP

- A sample Fusebox application

In this chapter, you'll learn about the problems of software development for the Web and some of the current attempts to solve these problems. You'll also learn about Fusebox, a framework for developing web applications. Along the way, you'll discover the difference between a framework and a methodology, see the benefits offered by the Fusebox framework, and learn how Fusebox supports code reuse and how it approaches the problem of complexity in software development using a software hub. In addition to all of this, we'll also discuss some powerful features of Fusebox including nested circuits and nested layouts, and we'll talk about how to make Fusebox more flexible with exit action requests (exit fuseactions).

Then we'll look at the Fusebox Lifecycle Process (FLiP), a complementary methodology for approaching web software projects. We'll walk through the 22 steps of a successful FLiP project, and we'll see how FLiP-inspired tools like wireframes and DevNotes can help you determine often-unspoken client requirements. In addition, you'll learn about the dismal failure rate of software projects and how to use prototypes and acceptance tests to reduce this. Finally, you'll read about Fusedocs, an XML-based documentation system that is used with Fusebox, and learn how to ensure success with test harnesses. But first, a story….

A Cautionary Tale

Our story begins with a client and a builder. Let's call the client "Carmen" and the builder "Bill." Carmen wants Bill to create a building—but she's vague on the details. "We're just feeling our way along," Carmen explains. After several meetings, a set of architectural plans is drawn up, and Bill is ready to begin. The foundation is poured. The walls begin to go up. The floors are put down. Then, as the rafters are being put in place, Carmen drops by. "You know what would be nice? If we could make the kitchen larger and maybe make the entryway wider—that would be nice."

"Hmmm…odd that this didn't come up in the requirements meetings," Bill muses, but he understands that things like this sometimes happen. So he lays an additional foundation to support the larger kitchen and revised foyer. Bill's not happy about this—instead of the foundation being a single, integral unit, it's been patched and is far more likely to separate and break under stress, but there's nothing to be done about that.

A week later, Carmen again drops by to check on the progress. "You know what would be nice? If we could make the dining room a lot bigger. This one is just smaller than what we need—yeah, that would be nice." A lot bigger dining room? Another addition to the foundation. More concrete is poured to accommodate the much larger dining room—and again, the strength of the foundation is compromised. Also, the cost of adding to the foundation is higher than Bill originally planned. And now the walls have to be changed, the rafters re-ordered—but still Bill labors on.

When Carmen drives up a week later with some friends, Bill is considerably less happy to see them. "Gee, it's looking good," Carmen tells Bill, "But you know what would be nice? If we could add two bathrooms large enough to accommodate four or five people each. That would be nice." More changes. More cost. Bill's clean, well-thought-out plan has become a hash of additions and penciled-in changes.

Eventually, the building is finished. It's the oddest-looking home the Bill has ever seen. The kitchen can feed 150 people, but where will they sleep? Still, Bill can't worry about that too much. Another job has already fallen behind schedule because of the overruns on this one. Bill just hopes Carmen appreciates what he did for her. It's an odd-looking house to be sure, but Bill complied with what Carmen wanted and the house is finished.

But Carmen *doesn't* appreciate all that extra effort. In fact, she's not too thrilled with Bill at all. Grumbling to herself, Carmen says, "How could it be that my *restaurant* took so long to build and cost so much?"

Current Software Development Practices

Building applications is a risky business. Of late, developers have some discouraging statistics to consider; as for their clients, the facts are even more dismal.

Bad News for Developers

If you're a software developer, the bad news is that studies by the Standish Group and others show failure rates on corporate software projects are as high as 70 percent—an astounding number. As more of the world economy becomes information-based, such numbers are not only embarrassing, but dangerous.

Why do projects fail? Most reasons fall into what developers call *scope creep*—the application grows in size *while* it is being built. In fact, project failure almost never occurs because a technical implementation was too difficult—tools and algorithms abound to solve this sort of problem. What typically sabotages project success is those client-driven midstream changes to the project, like those mentioned in the story about Carmen and Bill.

Clients are almost never aware of the impact such changes have on the system. In addition to the architectural implications of ongoing changes, there is the more subtle effect such changes have on the developers. This effect confirms their fears that *this* project will be like all the others—a monster that has escaped the confines built for it by its creators and now threatens the safety and sanity of the villagers (developers).

It's not that as developers we need help dealing with the frustration of an endless task. The greater problem is that frequent changes indicate that *we don't know what we're building*. Such projects create high stress on all those involved. Faced with no clear plan to follow, developers find themselves trying to anticipate the client's next request. As the statistics show, success in such a venture is rare.

Now consider how such changes will affect the underlying architecture of an application. What may have begun as an efficient architecture gets wrenched out of shape. Change after change to the requirements transmute the original architecture into something awkward, ugly, and fragile. It's bad enough for the people trying to write the application, but we really must pity those who have to maintain the fragile tissue of code that makes the application run.

Worse News for the Clients

Have I convinced you that developers get the short end of the stick? If you put yourself in the client's place, you'll see that things aren't exactly rosy for them, either. Once again, the easiest way to explain this is through a little story.

As the client, you need software to solve a business problem and are counting on the developers to help you. But the developers are uncommunicative—sullen, even. You're asked to provide "requirements documents"—whatever those are—and you have strong suspicions that the developers are mostly concerned with getting you to commit to something even before its ideas have been fully explored.

You'd like to coordinate the rollout of this software with your sales force as well as with marketing, and as a result, you ask the developers, "How long will the rollout take?" Reluctantly and with much prodding, they offer a rough commitment on a deadline—it's a start.

Of course, your boss also wants to know the approximate cost of building this software. When you ask about it, you'd think you just asked the developers if they could spare a kidney! So you have to sort of work out the costs based on the time estimates. The developers "start coding" and you figure you're all on the same page.

Some time goes by. You've attended some meetings and someone gave you a questionnaire to complete, but you really aren't sure what the software will do, exactly. You ask for a progress report—maybe even a peek at the software. Now they look at you as if you've asked them if they could spare a heart.

Then you notice that you've sailed past the initial estimated delivery date. Gathering your courage, you asked, "How far along are we?" Reassured when they tell you that they are 90 percent done, you figure you can wait the few more days until it's done. You'd like to give some input, of course, but it's clear that this won't be appreciated, so you go ahead and take a planned week-long trip. The following Monday you're anxious to see the finished product, but you discover that it's still not done. "How far along are you now?" you ask the developers, and are less than reassured when they tell you 90 percent (again). Your boss isn't happy.

In addition to dealing with your boss, you have to deal with the sales force, which wants to know if the new system will integrate with their ACT files—they've gotta have that. Also, Marketing reminds you that they've already bought advertising space and they expect orders to pick up considerably in 3–5 weeks. They're really excited because they've never before organized such an ambitious advertising campaign—the old system just couldn't handle the increased volume. Now they want to know if they will be able to produce reports by region— that's something they'll really need. In response to these queries, you leave voicemail for the lead developer, reminding him that Marketing needs reports and Sales wants ACT integration. And you're starting to think seriously about your spouse's suggestions about stress reduction.

You manage to put off a planned demo to the partners. Surely by Friday, you pray, the software will be done. But your next stop at the development shop finds them all standing around, drawing pictures on a whiteboard and looking grim.

"So, how are we doing?" you ask.

"We're not doing so well," they tell you, sounding a tad mutinous. "We're trying to figure out how to accommodate all these changes you keep asking for."

"What changes?" you wonder silently. "Say," you offer, "why don't we shift some resources onto this project? The Boss wants to see a demo by Friday." The noise becomes unbearable for a while, and then you're lectured in the strongest terms on the impossibility of this demo. Something about "mythical man-months."

"Well, maybe we can just show what we have so far…" you suggest hopefully. But eventually you realize that all they have so far is a bunch of unfinished code that won't run; in other words, there won't be a demo or anything else on Friday. "Well, about how close are we to being finished?" you ask as gently as you know how. You're not surprised to hear the answer: 90 percent.

Of Methodologies and Frameworks

Much of the reason for the 70 percent failure rate identified by the studies can be traced to the fact that there is no clear process for software development. A great deal of work has been done on new languages and language features, but the study of methodologies has suffered.

NOTE I use the term *methodology* to refer to a planned set of procedures undertaken to produce a desired result. *Framework* refers to a set of code assets that provide services to the developer. We use methodologies and frameworks in order to try to ensure a successful software project—one in which the client gets the software they need.

In the vast majority of cases, the success or failure of a software project is determined before the first line of code is written. With a 70 percent failure rate, the odds are good that you have already been involved in a software project failure. Why did it fail? Probably not because a particular algorithm proved too difficult to implement. Probably not because you were unable to sort a three-dimensional array, execute a particularly difficult SQL statement, or for any other technical reason. In fact, the software may have run just as the developers intended it to—yet it was deemed a failure. What did Shakespeare's Julius Caesar say? "The fault, dear Brutus, is not in our stars, but in ourselves…" Or in this case, perhaps in our methodologies.

Methodologies can be based either on open standards or on a closed or proprietary model. Open-standard methodologies offer several benefits over proprietary approaches.

Coders are given the incentive to become experts in a methodology.   Open-standard methodologies give coders an incentive to become experts in a methodology. Developers know that the time and money they invest in improving their skills in an open methodology will pay off. Even if their current employer doesn't recognize their worth, programmers know that their proven abilities to work within an open standard will attract other offers. Programmers skilled only in proprietary methodology have far less bargaining power.

Development shops find a greater number of available contractors.   Development shops, too, benefit from adopting an open methodology because they find a greater number of available contractors. Shops are more likely to take on more projects when there's no large learning curve to overcome—developers who already know the methodology will be able to step into the project and begin contributing immediately.

Companies can leverage their investment tools.   Open-standard methodologies also let companies leverage their investment in tools. Why invest in one set of tools for one developer using one methodology, when it's unlikely that other developers can also use this tool? With an open standard agreed upon in advance, companies are much more willing to purchase tools. Their investment can be leveraged (and amortized) over many developers (present and future); they need not cater to the personal likes of just one.

Clients can leverage the investment they make in code.   Clients, too, benefit from open standards. The investment they make in code can be leveraged. No one likes "sole source" solutions, and clients are much more likely to invest in coding projects if they have confidence that they can turn to many competent sources.

In short, a public methodology with open standards benefits all involved—developers, development shops, and clients. In the public category, there are several that work with ColdFusion. There is BlackBox (`http://www.black-box.org`), Switch_box (`http://www.switch-box.org`), and cfObjects (`http://www.cfobjects.com`). All three of these are the results of hard work and intelligence on the parts of their creators, and all are worth looking at.

In order to get full utility from a standard however, it must be widely adopted. Without this, a standard is simply an idea. It is the adoption of that idea by people that makes it a standard.

In this regard, one methodology has an enormous advantage over the others: the Fusebox Lifecycle Process (or FLiP) is a specific methodology for creating custom software applications. It's used as a complement to the Fusebox web application architecture.

Fusebox and FLiP advocates number in the tens of thousands, as compared to mere hundreds of BlackBox supporters and the supporters of the other methodologies mentioned here. As a result, there is a vital, active community of Fuseboxers, Fusebox/FLiP training is available, Fusebox publications exist, and the FLiP methodology is international. The remainder of this chapter focuses on the Fusebox/FLiP combination and how it will further your goals for successful software projects.

What Is Fusebox?

Fusebox is a framework for developing software applications that was originally conceived for ColdFusion and has since been expanded to work with Java and PHP. You can learn more online about Fusebox by visiting `http://www.fusebox.org`.

NOTE   Fusebox is the brainchild of many developers including Steve Nelson, Hal Helms, Gabe Roffman, Michael Dinowitz, Robi Sen, and Joshua Cyr.

Computer languages provide the basic components for building an application, but their focus is necessarily on the essentials needed. They don't provide a framework on which to build applications repeatedly. Fusebox is such a framework and it is built on three key principles:

Modularity   Larger applications may be broken into smaller, tightly defined pieces

Severability   Modules are made as independent as possible by eliminating, where possible, fixed references and replacing them with variable references

Clarity   The application programming interface (API) is documented in individual code files through the use of structured comments

Fusebox is widely popular, but popularity alone is no sure guide to success. Although a framework's popularity is very desirable (since this means that more developers skilled in the framework will be available), the framework itself must provide real benefits. Let's take a look at the benefits thousands of developers have discovered in Fusebox, and how they are achieved by the Fusebox principles.

Benefits of Fusebox

As mentioned earlier, a framework must have a good track record in order for it be used frequently. Fusebox has numerous benefits that make it useful to the developer.

One benefit of Fusebox is its ability to build *independent* software modules, which allow individual developers—or separate teams of developers—to work on individual components simultaneously. This type of multitasking is a goal of virtually all frameworks, but few accomplish this task as well as does Fusebox. It means that software can be built faster because the need for serial correlation ("I must wait to do my task until you have finished yours") is greatly reduced.

It turns out that this benefit, also referred to as *severability*, allows both large and small software components to be reused more easily. Apart from the obvious cost benefit of not having to write software more than once, this reusability means that developers can use pretested code, which lowers the risk of failure on a project.

Too often software is designed and built simultaneously, making it all but impossible to build—much less reuse—coherent software modules. Successful software modules are designed with an overall plan in mind. When no such plan exists, software modules become little more than arbitrary code collections and developers cannot reuse them. Fusebox's emphasis on clarity ensures that we know what we're building before we build it.

Another benefit of Fusebox is an integrated documentation/structured comment system known as Fusedoc, a standard I pioneered and which others in the Fusebox community contributed to. Fusedoc comments are written in XML format. A Document Type Definition (DTD) provides structure and allows other software, such as validators and parsers, to work with the Fusedoc.

The Fusedoc tells the coder what the individual file is responsible for, what variables are available at runtime, and what variables the coder is responsible for creating. It forms a sort of "work order" that the programmer works from. In the same way that machinists work on parts without having to know their eventual use, Fusedocs let developers work on code without knowing about the application or even the underlying database. The implications of this are enormous.

Over 25 years ago, Fred Brooks wrote the classic software text, *The Mythical Man-Month: Essays on Software Engineering* (Addison-Wesley, 1975). In this text, Brooks points out that adding people to a project that is late actually increases the amount of time needed to complete the project. The reason? It takes time for those new developers to acquire enough knowledge of the application to contribute. Add in the time for increased communication and coordination to integrate those extra workers, and it's clear that adding more developers only makes a bad situation worse.

Part of the Fusebox framework's planning technique involves separating an application into modules or *circuits*. These modules are then broken into separate code files or *fuses*, and Fusedocs are written for these fuses. An e-commerce site, for example, might have circuits for Login, Products, CompanyInfo, CustomerService, and so on. As you'll see later, circuits can be nested, which allows one large circuit to be split into several smaller, more manageable ones.

At the point of coding, a developer is working on a single fuse. This developer knows what the fuse is responsible for and its input/output parameters but needs little else. Now, if the project begins to run late, additional coders *can* be added without running into the problem Fred Brooks identified. This is possible if we get the code completed by competent developers who don't need to know about the application itself, which means that we can minimize the time needed for the actual writing of code. With Fusebox, that time is typically far less than what any experienced developer would think possible.

Such an abbreviated coding-time requirement radically shifts the equation for software development. Instead of rushing through the requirements, design, and architecture to get to the "real work" of coding, the requirements, design, and architecture *become* the real work. Coding is simply a matter of "scribbling down the details," as Mozart once remarked of the process of writing down the notes already inside his head. The ability to have multiple teams working productively on the same project comes as pure joy to any project manager. It also greatly lessens the stress on the coders, who—freed of the arduous, thankless task of guessing what the client wants—can now concentrate on writing beautiful code.

Fusebox also makes it possible for people with different skills and talents to contribute to the project. A Fusebox project often includes architects, database experts, an art director and graphic artists, interface specialists, HTML/layout specialists, and ColdFusion coders. This arrangement is quite different from other development environments, where the coders must handle all of this by themselves. In addition, Fusebox helps separate an application's logic from its display, and the resulting division of labor allows the project's overall cost, time to completion, and risk of failure to be reduced.

Code Reuse with Fusebox

Reusability is the Holy Grail of programmers. The appeal is obvious—write it once and use it over and over. If only it were so simple in practice. Every framework tries to achieve it, but with only limited success. All that effort, however, has taught us some things about reusability. The most important lesson is that, all other things being equal, it's easier to reuse a little bit of code than a lot.

Consider a code file that does all of the following tasks:

- Queries a database for a list of all users having related information
- Loops over the list checking to see if each user is current in paying their dues
- Sends an e-mail to each user who is late, warning them of the dire consequences of tardiness and suggesting it would *really* be in their best interest to pay
- Sends an e-mail instructing a "customer service representative" to pay a little visit to the tardy payer

Can I reuse this code? Probably not—it does too much and is too complex. The odds are slim that this exact sequence of actions will be needed again. But by breaking the code file into smaller pieces, I have a much better chance of reusing portions of it. For example, the query might be used by several different modules.

Different modules alone don't guarantee reusability, of course. Another impediment to code reuse is application specificity. If I write a user manager circuit—code that handles creating, editing, deleting, and listing users—I will probably need to run some queries that require a data source:

```
<cfquery datasource="UserDB" name="AllUsers">
```

But `"UserDB"` is specific to an application. Rather than hunting down each instance that uses `"UserDB"` (or, scarier, doing a global search and replace), I can create a variable for the data source that is resolved at runtime:

```
<cfquery datasource="#request.DSN#" name="AllUsers">
```

Fusebox carries this further, allowing even page links to be set programmatically, with separate *exit fuseactions* (XFAs) being executed conditionally:

```
<cfif GetUser.recordCount>
    <cflocation url="#self#?fuseaction=#XFA.onSuccess#">
<cfelse>
    <cflocation url="#self#?fuseaction=#XFA.onFailure#">
</cfif>
```

Once an application is built, the real costs begin. Code maintenance normally comprises as much as 80 percent of the total lifecycle cost. Much of this is due to the chronically poor documentation that forces maintenance programmers into detective work. Unless maintenance is planned for, it can quickly spiral into a black hole of costs for a company. More than one company has found itself saddled with obsolete software that is simply too complex and costly to adapt to new circumstances.

Fusedoc, an integral part of Fusebox, is enormously helpful to coders charged with making changes to others' code. Because each code file is well documented, the maintenance task—never a joy—is at least manageable.

A Fusebox Overview

The Fusebox framework is made up of code files that you can download from `http://www.fusebox.org`. The purpose of any framework—including Fusebox—is to provide a base platform that makes writing individual applications easier. Frameworks exist on a different level than the language chosen in which the application will be written. Frameworks are implementations of practices that have evolved over time for dealing with certain recurring problems. The name given to solutions to such problems is *design patterns*. Different design patterns exist to deal with different problems. Fusebox is a design pattern for dealing with the thorniest problem in application development—the problem of *complexity*.

Solving the Complexity Syndrome with Fusebox

Years ago, commercial airplane routing used a *point-to-point* system. If you wanted to go from New York to Los Angeles, for example, you waited until a plane was flying from New York to Los Angeles—from one point (NYC) to another (LA). Point-to-point routing works well when the number of points is small, but as a network grows, it suffers from what we'll call the "complexity syndrome"—one of the major sources of project failure.

Suppose I have a basket with slips of paper containing the names of all the cities, towns, and villages in the world. (It's a big basket.) I draw out three slips and give them to you: Los Angeles, Pine Creek Ridge, Marietta. How many point-to-point routes are there? You might decide to work out the problem on paper, so you abbreviate the locations as LA, PCR, and M. Your scratch paper looks like this:

Simple enough: three points, three routes. Now, let me give you three more slips: Sarasota, London, and Frankfurt. This one takes you a little longer—and it's a lot harder to understand.

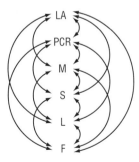

Ready for three more? Add Hong Kong, Sao Paulo, and Perth.

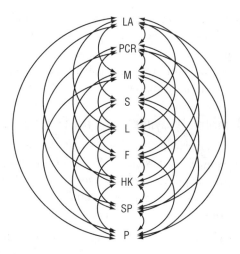

Enter the Hub-and-Spoke System

Gee, I don't mean to be critical, but that's pretty sloppy. It's just about impossible to read, and it took you forever to draw. Plus, I'm pretty sure you missed some routes. I guess it's true what they say: you just can't get good help these days.

So, our problem is one of runaway complexity. With three points, we had three possible routes (or interactions). When we doubled the number of points to 6, we quintupled the number of interactions to 15. When we tripled the number of points to 9, we multiplied the interactions by 12. This is the complexity problem inherent in any system of interaction among individual components.

To solve this particular problem, the airline industry got smart. They went from point-to-point routing to *hub-and-spoke* routing. This makes it so that if you want to travel from Sarasota to Los Angeles on Delta, you'll fly from Sarasota to Atlanta and then from Atlanta to Los Angeles. The hub system reduces the complexity level enormously. Here's the last problem I gave you, recast with a hub-and-spoke solution:

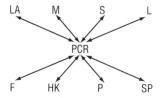

Here, I've taken Pine Creek Ridge and turned it into a hub. The rat's nest from the previous example becomes an orderly, easy-to-maintain system that is simple and clear and allows for expansion without overwhelming the system. (The only cloud on the horizon is that the 358 residents of Pine Creek Ridge are starting to complain about all the noise.)

In software, we have a special name for point-to-point systems: *spaghetti code*. We know it's not a good idea, but what do we replace it with? Fusebox offers a solution: a software hub that relies on multiple, discrete code files to accomplish tasks such as creating a new user or adding an item to a shopping cart. By intention, fuses are simple-minded things—they know virtually nothing of the environment in which they operate. They are nothing but worker bees, carrying out well-defined tasks, oblivious of their neighbors. It follows then that no fuse may call another fuse directly, for how can a fuse call another when it knows nothing of its workmates? For instance, you will never see code like this in a properly constructed Fusebox application:

```
<cflocation url="dsp_ShoppingCart.cfm">
```

Instead, all action requests (fuseactions in Fusebox lingo) are piped to a single hub/circuit. And as a shortcut, the central hub is given the alias, self.

```
<cflocation url="#self#?fuseaction=viewShoppingCart">
```

The hub is implemented as a switch statement. Here is a very small hub that handles the fuseactions newUser, processNewUser, and viewUser. (Some code has been omitted to increase the clarity of the example.)

```
<cfswitch expression="#attributes.fuseaction#">
   <cfcase value="newUser">
      <cfinclude template="dsp_UserForm.cfm">
   </cfcase>
   <cfcase value="processNewUser">
      <cfinclude template="qry_InsertUser.cfm">
      <cfinclude template="act_NewUser.cfm">
   </cfcase>
   <cfcase value="viewUser">
      <cfinclude template="dsp_NewUser.cfm">
   </cfcase>
</cfswitch>
```

Hello Universe

Let's see how circuits, fuses, and fuseactions work together in a real, albeit tiny, application. It's customary to include a "HelloWorld" application when introducing a new technology. Here, I want instead to show you a slightly more complex application—we'll call it "Hello Universe."

To make this application run, you'll need to add Fusebox core files to your application directories and make some changes to those files. Later, I'll explain the files' responsibilities, but for now, you will just download them from http://www.fusebox.org. Before you do so, create a directory under your web root called Universe. Then download the files and place them in this directory. You are now ready to build a Fusebox application.

We begin by asking what sort of behavior the application should have. I want it to display a list of planets in the solar system; each will have a drill-down to another page that welcomes the inhabitants of that particular planet.

Our small application will have only two behaviors (fuseactions): showAllPlanets and welcomeThisPlanet. Next, let's ask, "What does the fuseaction showAllPlanets mean? What will it do?" At this point, we want nothing more than for it to "display a single page that has the planets listed on it." That small, well-defined task is perfect for a single fuse. Since this fuse will only display some information, I'll start the filename with a dsp_ prefix: dsp_AllPlanets.cfm. So we create this code file and place it in the Universe directory:

```
<!--- dsp_AllPlanets.cfm --->
<cfset planets="Mercury,Venus,Earth,Mars,Jupiter,Saturn,Uranus,Neptune,Pluto">
<cfloop list="#planets#" index="aPlanet">
    <cfoutput>
        <a href="#self#?fuseaction=Universe.welcomeThisPlanet&planet="#aPlanet#">
        #aPlanet#
        </a><br>
    </cfoutput>
</cfloop>
```

Notice that whatever planet is chosen by the user will cause a new request to be sent to the file represented by the variable, self. The selection of any planet will cause the same fuse-action value to be sent, as well as a URL variable called planet. The variable, self, points to index.cfm, which needs only to call the software hub downloadable from the Fusebox site.

Open the FBX_Settings.cfm file that you downloaded from the Fusebox site (and which should be in your Universe directory). Place the following code snippet in FBX_Settings.cfm:

```
<cfset self="index.cfm">
```

This should be the only code in FBX_Settings.cfm. Now open the FBX_Circuits.cfm file. The only code in this file should be the following:

```
<cfset Fusebox.circuits.Universe = "Universe">
```

I'll explain what these do later. You'll also need to create an index.cfm file and place it in the Universe directory. The index.cfm file will call the main Fusebox file. If you are running Windows 5.0 or better on a Windows machine, the index.cfm file will need only this code snippet:

```
<cfinclude template="FBX_Fusebox30_CF50.cfm">
```

NOTE   If you're running a different version of the ColdFusion Server, you'll need to use the appropriate FBX_Fusebox30_CFnn.cfm file. You'll learn about this in the following section, "The Fusebox Skeleton."

You're almost ready to run the application. When you do, a bit of magic will occur and the software hub will parse the fuseaction, determining which circuit it belongs to and passing the request portion of the fuseaction (welcomeThisPlanet) to the circuit. The circuit is responsible for determining how to respond to the fuseaction request. It does this by including another part of the Fusebox code, FBX_Switch.cfm (also downloaded from the Fusebox site). For this application, the only code in the switch file is as follows:

```
<cfcase value="#Fusebox.fuseaction#">
   <cfcase value="showAllPlanets">
      <cfinclude template="dsp_AllPlanets.cfm">
   </cfcase>
   <cfcase value="welcomeThisPlanet">
      <cfinclude template="dsp_Hello.cfm">
   </cfcase>
</cfcase>
```

The last bit of code we must write is of this code the dsp_Hello.cfm file, placing it in your Universe folder:

```
<!--- dsp_Hello.cfm --->
<cfoutput>
    Hello, #URL.planet#
</cfoutput>
```

Now that you've got everything set up properly, you can run the application. You start the application by typing this URL into a browser:

```
http://localhost/index.cfm?fuseaction=Universe.showAllPlanets
```

The fuseaction is then parsed, the correct circuit's (in our case, we have only one) FBX_Switch .cfm file is called, and the dsp_AllPlanets.cfm fuse is included. When you click on a link, a new fuseaction request is made—Universe.welcomeThisPlanet. The software hub again does its job and the FBX_Switch.cfm file responds to this new fuseaction and includes the file, dsp_Hello.cfm.

There—that's it—your first working Fusebox application! (If you get stuck with the code, you can download it from http://www.halhelms.com.)

The Fusebox Skeleton

When trying to learn anything, one of the hardest challenges is figuring out the answer to the question, "Where do I start?" Fusebox 3 has a clear answer to this. In any circuit directory, you will have the following files, all of which can be downloaded from http://www.fusebox.org.

FBX_Fusebox30_CFnn.cfm   This file is "frozen"—normally, you would make no changes to it at all. If you decided to go exploring into the depths of Fusebox or needed to make a specific tweak to Fusebox itself, this is where you'd go.

I'm fudging just a little here. In fact, FBX_Fusebox30_CF*nn*.cfm is really only required at the top level. Still, I recommend starting with all these files together in the circuit directory. One advantage of including FB_Fusebox30_CF*nn*.cfm in each directory is that it lets you call the circuits independently for testing purposes. You also need to have an index.cfm file in your home circuit that <cfinclude>s the appropriate FBX_Fusebox30_CF*nn*.cfm file. This ensures that the Fusebox code will run when people type the URL of your site into their browser without specifying the FBX_Fusebox30_CF*nn*.cfm file.

Several Versions of FBX_Fusebox30_CF*nn*.cfm

There are actually several versions of the FBX_Fusebox30_CF*nn*.cfm file corresponding to the different ColdFusion Server versions available:

FBX_Fusebox30_CF40.cfm   Used for the 4.0 or lesser versions of the Windows version of the ColdFusion Server

FBX_Fusebox30_CF45.cfm   Used for the 4.5 version of the Windows version of the Cold-Fusion Server

FBX_Fusebox30_CF45_nix.cfm   Used for the 4.5 version of the Unix or Linux versions of the ColdFusion Server

FBX_Fusebox30_CF50.cfm   Used for the 5.0 and 6.0 versions of the Windows version of the ColdFusion Server

FBX_Fusebox30_CF50_nix.cfm   Used for the 5.0 and 6.0 versions of the Unix and Linux versions of the ColdFusion Server

If you use any version of the FBX_Fusebox30_CF*nn*.cfm file prior to version 5, you will need to include in your home circuit an additional file, SaveContent.cfm, also available from http://www.fusebox.org.

FBX_Settings.cfm   In this file, you place any environment variables that are applicable to an entire circuit. This might include variables such as the operative data source name; the value of self; and variables such as AppRoot, AppImages, and/or AppQueries. Because of the way circuits are nested, children inherit these variables from their parents.

Neither AppRoot, AppImages, nor AppQueries is Fusebox-specific. They just represent my personal (and hopefully obvious) naming scheme.

FBX_Layouts.cfm   This file is responsible for determining which layout file to use. Layouts provide a "skin" for an application. We will discuss these in detail later.

FBX_Switch.cfm   All action in a Fusebox application is sent back to the hub as a fuseaction. FBX_Switch.cfm is a file containing a switch statement that evaluates the expression attributes.fuseaction. This is the file that handles fuseaction requests, delegating and distributing work to various fuses.

FBX_Circuits.cfm   This file, which provides a mapping for resolving nested circuits, must be included only at the top level and in any circuit you wish to call, as in stand-alone fashion.

index.cfm   This may be default.cfm or whatever name your web server uses as its default template. All it does is cfinclude the file FBX_Fusebox30_CFnn.cfm. Alternatively, you can just rename FBX_Fusebox30_CFnn.cfm to your default filename. (See the discussion of FBX_Fusebox30_CFnn.cfm just above.)

Taken together, these files form a Fusebox skeleton that's very useful in getting you started. Creating a new circuit can be as simple as copying the files to a new directory, mapping nested circuits in FBX_Circuits.cfm (if the circuit is to run in "parent mode"), and assigning fuses to fuseactions in FBX_Switch.cfm.

Nested Circuits with Fusebox

Now, I must confess that I hid some issues from you when we examined the "Hello Universe" application by deliberately selecting an application with only one circuit. What happens when you have more than one circuit? How does the Fusebox software hub know where to direct the fuseaction requests?

The answer is different now than it was several months ago. I recommend that you understand both the current iteration of Fusebox (version 3) and the previous one. An application in Fusebox 2 had one home circuit and many subcircuits (Figure 4.1). Although no fuse called another fuse directly, in Fusebox 2, a fuse might well have to call another circuit's hub. For example, if a fuse in Users was called to validate a user login, a Fusebox 2 application could have code resembling this:

```
<cfif MatchUser.recordCount>
    <cflocation url="../store/index.cfm?fuseaction=main">
</cfif>
```

One of the new features introduced in Fusebox 3 is *nested circuits*. Instead of adhering to Fusebox 2's "one home circuit/many child circuits" paradigm, Fusebox 3 allows circuits to exist in a nested directory structure. If we recast the "BooksByHal" application shown in Figure 4.1 into a Fusebox 3 construction, it would look like Figure 4.2.

FIGURE 4.1:

Typical Fusebox 2
directory structure

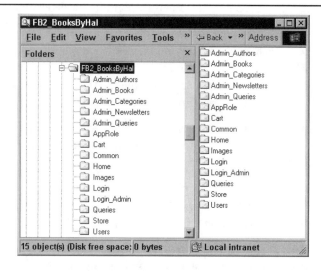

FIGURE 4.2:

The BooksByHal
application's
directories in
Fusebox 3

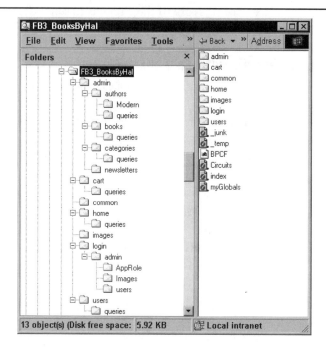

Now, circuits that are logically the children of other circuits are placed directly underneath them. Similarly, variables that are set in the parent circuit are inherited by their children (and grandchildren, and so on). Fusebox 3 was built around the idea of code independence, at both the fuse and the circuit level. This means that someone might take code I wrote to behave as a parent application and use it in another application, where it must function as a child. This new use would require a great deal of flexibility on the part of the circuit code in order to avoid recoding the borrowed circuit—which is something that goes against the spirit of reuse.

In a Fusebox 2 application, any problems involving multiple circuits having the same fuse-actions were resolved by calling the application directly, as you can see here:

```
<cflocation url="//store/index.cfm?fuseaction=main">
```

But with Fusebox 3, a fuse does not know in what context it will be used. The fuse therefore can't know what circuits exist in the application it is part of, or where the appropriate circuit might be located. (If you're wondering, "If the fuse can't know of the existence and location of other circuits, how can it even know of the existence/name of the fuseaction to call?", you've discovered the reason for those XFAs we mentioned earlier. We'll get to those shortly.)

Instead, the fuse calls the home circuit with a fuseaction, and the home circuit must figure out to whom the fuseaction belongs with the following code:

```
<cflocation url="#self#?fuseaction=main">
```

The variable self points to the home circuit, so the action returns to the home circuit with a request of main. But to which circuit does main belong? We could conceivably have a main fuseaction in every circuit.

So we must have a way of specifying the circuit and the fuseaction. And in Fusebox 3 circuits, the fuseaction becomes a compound fuseaction made up of a circuit name and the actual action requested, separated by a dot, as in Admin.main.

Defining Circuit Aliases

We're almost there, but there's still one problem remaining with our solution to complexity. Look at the directory structure for the Fusebox 3 application shown, and you'll see that there is more than one Admin directory. To solve this, Fusebox 3 introduces the idea of *circuit aliases*. Instead of using the actual directory name in a compound fuseaction, a circuit alias is used. If two circuits have the same name, one (or both) can be aliased, and the problem of identical circuit naming is solved.

Fusebox 3's FBX_Circuits.cfm file is a sort of mapping file that resides in the home circuit. Its job is to map circuit aliases with their actual directories. This is implemented as a structure. Each circuit in a Fusebox application must be "registered" by including a mapping for it in FBX_Circuits.cfm. Here is the syntax for an entry in FBX_Circuits.cfm:

```
<cfset FBX.circuit_alias =
"Grandparent_directory_name.Parent_directory_name.Child_directory_name">
```

Now take a look at the `FBX_Circuits.cfm` file for the `FB3_BooksByHal` application:

```
<cfset FBX.circuits.home = "FB3_BooksByHal">
<cfset FBX.circuits.admin = "FB3_BooksByHal.admin">
<cfset FBX.circuits.authors = "FB3_BooksByHal.admin.authors">
<cfset FBX.circuits.books = "FB3_BooksByHal.admin.books">
<cfset FBX.circuits.categories = "FB3_BooksByHal.admin.categories">
<cfset FBX.circuits.newsletters = "FB3_BooksByHal.admin.newsletters">
<cfset FBX.circuits.cart = "FB3_BooksByHal.cart">
<cfset FBX.circuits.main = "FB3_BooksByHal.home">
<cfset FBX.circuits.login = "FB3_BooksByHal.login">
<cfset FBX.circuits.loginAdmin = "FB3_BooksByHal.login.admin">
<cfset FBX.circuits.appRole = "FB3_BooksByHal.login.admin.appRole">
<cfset FBX.circuits.users = "FB3_BooksByHal.users">
```

When a fuse calls a compound fuseaction, it uses the circuit alias name. Some interesting code translates this into the fully qualified fuseaction name. It's as if the circuit, receiving a fuseaction request, says, "You said you wanted `appRole.viewRoles`, but what you really mean is `FB3_BooksByHal.login.admin.appRole.viewRoles`." The request is passed down the directory structure to `appRole`, where the actual fuseaction, `viewRoles`, is processed.

Exit Fuseactions (XFAs)

One issue still needs addressing. We want fuses to be reusable, but no actual reuse can occur if we have fuseactions—even compound fuseactions using circuit aliases—hardcoded into the fuse. To illustrate, let's take a fuse that validates a login. Here's the code with values hardcoded:

```
<cfif MatchUser.recordCount>
    <cflocation url="#self#?fuseaction=Store.main">
<cfelse>
    <cflocation url="#self#?fuseaction=Users.badLogin">
</cfif>
```

But now I want to use it elsewhere. "Elsewhere" might be a completely separate application, but for now let's suppose I want to use it in the same application, in a different context. For example, if a user comes onto my BooksByHal site, I'm hoping they'll decide to log in right away. If they do, I want to take them to my main store page. But some users won't log in right away. I don't want to lose them, so I don't insist on this. However, if they begin checkout, I have to know who they are. For that, I insist that they log in. I don't want a successful login to result in sending the user back to the store's main page, however. In the context of a login occurring from a checkout, I want to send the user back to the checkout.

The Fusebox solution for this is to remove all hardcoded references within fuses themselves, replacing them with variables that bear the value of the appropriate fuseaction. Each fuse defines the conditions under which a fuseaction should be called:

```
<cfif MatchUser.recordCount>
    <cflocation url="#self#?fuseaction=#XFA.success#">
```

```
<cfelse>
    <cflocation url="#self#?fuseaction=#XFA.failure#">
</cfif>
```

Now, the hub's code can set the value of each XFA called for, like this:

```
<cfcase value="validateLogin">
    <cfset XFA.success = "Store.main">
    <cfset XFA.failure = "Users.badLogin">
    <cfinclude template = "/Queries/qry_MatchUser.cfm">
    <cfinclude template = "act_ValidateLogin.cfm">
</cfcase>
<cfcase value="validateLoginFromCheckout">
    <cfset XFA.success = "Checkout.main">
    <cfset XFA.failure = "Users.badLogin">
    <cfinclude template = "/Queries/qry_MatchUser.cfm">
    <cfinclude template = "act_ValidateLogin.cfm">
</cfcase>
```

We've arranged it so that the same fuse, `act_ValidateLogin.cfm`, can be reused in different contexts and in different applications.

Nested Layouts

When circuits are nested, they naturally provide for a mild form of inheritance going "down" the directory tree. Let's say I have an application, one branch of which has a Grandparent circuit containing a Parent circuit that, in turn, contains a Child circuit, which itself is parent to another Grandchild circuit.

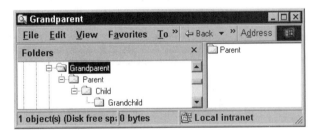

The variables I set in the `FBX_Settings.cfm` file at the `Grandparent` directory will be inherited by all descendant circuits. This inheritance works because `Grandparent`'s `FBX.Settings.cfm` is called first and `Grandchild`'s `FBX.Settings.cfm` is called last. Taking advantage of walking "down" the directory tree, if used judiciously, can mean writing (and maintaining) less code.

Of course (to mangle an old saying), what goes down must come up. So while we walk *down* the directory tree to executing code, we walk *up* the tree to display the results of that code. This precedent lets us use a nested approach to layout, so that the Grandchild's layout is applied first, followed by the Child, Parent, and Grandparent. ColdFusion 5 supports this approach with a new tag set, cfsavecontent, which traps the output within the tags into a variable.

If you execute this code:

```
<cfsavecontent variable="SaveMe">

<form action="#self#?fuseaction=#XFA.submitForm#" method="post">
   Your name: <input type="text" name="fullName"><br>
   Your e-mail: <input type="text" name="e-mail"><br>
   <input type="submit" value=" ok ">
</form>

</cfsavecontent>
```

What you'll see is—nothing. The actual content has been saved as the variable, SaveMe. To see it, I need to dereference the variable SaveMe:

```
<cfoutput>
    #SaveMe#
</cfoutput>
```

Now the content is visible, as shown in Figure 4.3.

FIGURE 4.3:
Outputting the contents of <cfsavecontent>

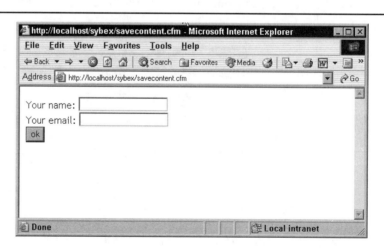

The cfsavecontent tags can be nested, allowing for code like this:

```
<cfoutput>
<cfset self="">
<cfset XFA.submitForm="">
```

```
<cfsavecontent variable="parent">
   <cfsavecontent variable="child">
      <cfsavecontent variable="grandchild">
         <form action="#self#?fuseaction=#XFA.submitForm#" method="post">
            <table
               border="1"
               align="center"
               bgColor="ffffff"
               cellPadding="10">
               <tr>
                  <td>
                     Your name: <input type="text" name="fullName"><br>
                     Your e-mail: <input type="text" name="e-mail"><br>
                     <input type="submit" value=" ok ">
                  </td>
               </tr>
            </table>
         </form>
         <!---end of grandchild--->
      </cfsavecontent>
      <table
         border="1"
         background="stripesHorThin.gif"
         align="center"
         cellPadding="20">
         <tr>
            <td>
               #grandchild#
            </td>
         </tr>
      </table>
      <!---end of child--->
   </cfsavecontent>
   <table
      border="1"
      background="stripesVerThin.gif"
      width="100%"
      cellPadding="30">
      <tr>
         <td>
            #child#
         </td>
      </tr>
   </table>
   <!---end of parent--->
</cfsavecontent>

</cfoutput>
```

When you run *this* code, you'll see…nothing! The content generated by the innermost cfsavecontent tag was hidden in the grandchild variable. Then grandchild was dereferenced within <cfsavecontent variable="child">, and the resulting variable, child, was dereferenced within <cfsavecontent variable="parent">. But nowhere was the parent variable displayed. To fix this, I'll replace the final line of code with two lines:

```
    #parent#
</cfoutput>
```

This produces the output shown in Figure 4.4. I have the grandchild's content, wrapped in the child's layout, in turn wrapped in the parent's layout. Not very elegantly done, I'll admit—but it does hold very exciting possibilities.

FIGURE 4.4:

Outputting an interim step in a nested layout

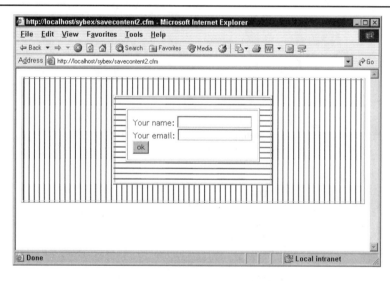

This sort of nesting is built into Fusebox 3. Each circuit can have an FBX_Layouts.cfm file that is used to point to an actual layout file:

```
<cfset FBX.layoutDir = "">
<cfset FBX.layoutFile = "DefaultLayout.cfm">
```

The variable, FBX.layoutDir, is used to point to a specific directory relative to the circuit currently executing. This lets you place you layout files in a separate directory, if desired. If the file set as FBX.layoutFile is in the same directory, FBX.layoutDir would be set to an empty string.

The layout files themselves can provide a "skin" that wraps the content produced by fuses (which are called as a result of executing a fuseaction.)

The presence of FBX_Layouts.cfm is optional. If you don't need or want nesting, you can omit these files from parent directories. However, you will need to have one FBX_Layouts.cfm file somewhere in the circuit tree so that the output saved by the cfsavecontent tag can be displayed finally. Fusebox 3 uses a key named layout in the reserved structure, FBX, as the variable into which cfsavecontent places its contents.

NOTE   This structure is "reserved" only in the sense that Fusebox developers are asked not to use it. There is nothing built into ColdFusion that makes it impossible to overwrite the FBX structure.

If you have no special formatting needs, you can set FBX.layoutfile to DefaultLayout.cfm; that simply displays FBX.layout. The code for DefaultLayout.cfm looks like this:

```
<cfoutput>
    #FBX.layout#
</cfoutput>
```

Because of the order in which the nesting/wrapping is done, variables in children circuits can influence their parent's choice of layouts. This would mean that FBX.layouts.cfm for a parent might have code like this:

```
<cfset FBX.layoutDir="MyLayouts">

<cfif childQuery.recordCount>
    <cfset FBX.layoutFile="SortableTable.cfm">
<cfelse>
    <cfset FBX.layoutFile="DefaultLayout.cfm">
</cfif>
```

What's with Those Attributes?

A curious thing about Fusebox is its use of the attributes scope. Macromedia intended for this scope to be used only by a custom tag when it was referring to variables passed into it. Yet Fusebox uses it quite extensively, even where no custom tag is ostensibly involved. This often strikes people as odd, yet there's an excellent reason for why attributes are used so often in Fusebox code that involves calling the Fusebox application recursively.

From within a fuse fulfilling one fuseaction, I can call the application in midstream, so to speak, and have it execute *another* fuseaction. This isn't done very often, but in certain situations, it proves invaluable.

Continued on next page

> The problem with this technique is that calls to the application as a custom tag will need to pass variables, as in the following:
>
> ```
> <cfmodule template="#Fusebox.rootPath##self#"
>     fuseaction="#XFA.lowInventory#"
>     productID="#lowInventoryItem#"
>     quantity="#quantity#">
> ```
>
> In some situations I would need to refer to these as `attributes.fuseaction`, `attributes.productID`, and so on.
>
> Rather than having conditional code cluttering things up, one of `FB_Fusebox30_CFnn.cfm`'s tasks is to copy all URL and form variables into the `attributes` scope. This lets me always refer to variables passed in either as a form or as a URL variable as one that belongs to the `attributes` scope.

Query Sims

A very useful tool in the Fusebox tool chest is the *query sim* (short for *simulation*). Query sims are record sets that are "built up" from data supplied for the purpose, rather than from the result of a query to a database. In fact, with query sims, neither databases nor ODBC connections are needed. What you *will* need is a custom tag called `QuerySim.cfm`, which is available at `http://www.halhelms.com`. Here's the syntax for using `QuerySim`:

```
<cf_QuerySim>
name_of_query_to_return
comma,delimited,list,of,columns
pipe|delimited|text|matching|columns
pipe|delimited|text|matching|columns
</cf_QuerySim>
```

Here's a query sim being used:

```
<cf_QuerySim>
UsersList
firstName,lastName,address,city,state
Hal|Helms|1960 Stickney Point Rd.|Sarasota|FL
Stan|Cox|null|null|null
</cf_QuerySim>
```

If you use the preceding snippet of code and then send the `UsersList` recordset to Dan Switzer's wonderful `ObjDump.cfm` tag, you'll see that what is returned is, in fact, a true query (Figure 4.5).

```
<cf_ObjDump object="UsersList">
```

Displaying the results
of a query sim

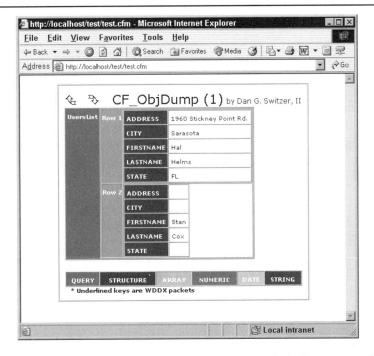

The `null` keyword will return an empty string in the column specified. If you want a blank recordset returned, you would omit the `pipe|delimited|text|matching|columns` altogether.

TIP   Query sims are very useful whenever you need a recordset but you don't have or want to get that information from a database.

A FLiP Overview

FLiP is an acronym for **F**usebox **Li**fecycle **P**rocess. It is a complementary method that provides a series of steps that need to be undertaken to develop any Fusebox application. While Fusebox provides tangible code assets that you can use to build *applications*, FLiP addresses the need to find a reliable method to produce successful *projects* repeatedly.

The FLiP methodology is a complement to the Fusebox framework. FLiP begins with a conclusion—that the extraordinary failure rate of corporate custom software projects is a sign of a deeply flawed approach to building software. What's needed is not another language, or faster compilers, or any more "silver bullets" that promise (and probably fail) to remedy the project's shortcomings. Rather, we need to rethink the entire process, to examine *why* software projects fail. Only then can we build a methodology that supports successful software projects—and that is the only legitimate goal of a software methodology.

Most software projects seem to have adopted Nike's popular advertising slogan: Just do it! The perceived goal is to get coding—and to keep coding until time, energy, and/or money run out. Of course, some requirements gathering is done, and design and architecture play a role, but the emphasis is on coding, as reflected here:

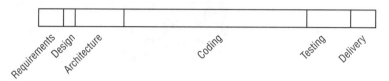

I often remark that, with this approach, we get client feedback at two points in the project—at the beginning of a job, when it's too early to do us much good, and at the end, when it's too late to be of any help. That remarkably high failure rate typically occurs because the delivered software *fails to do what the client needs it to do*.

One approach to the problem is to introduce a formal requirements-gathering method. The most popular of these methods uses the Unified Modeling Language (UML) to abstract client requirements into a dizzying progression of diagrams, each intended to capture the project into a formalized symbology. "If we can get clients to tell us what they need up front," this approach seems to say, "then we can build it." And what approach could be more sensible and levelheaded? Designers trained in the arcane symbology of UML can translate the client's fuzzy concepts into precise, unambiguous documents. (If you're old enough, you may recognize this as the latest version of flowcharting.) As protection against their well-known fickleness, clients are then asked to sign off on these documents.

Unfortunately, many formal approaches fail to account for the fact that *clients* define project success and that those same clients are *not* trained in reading our abstracted language. They look very impressive, these diagrams with their neat boxes and arrows, but they fail in their fundamental task—to communicate with the only arbiters of success, our clients. Though we have done our part in determining what clients want, our logical approach—however appealing its results—still delivers that astonishing 70 percent failure rate. Is it really likely that applying "more of the same" will change that?

"We need to break the development process into bite-sized chunks," say the designers of a new movement taking the development world by storm. Extreme Programming (XP) is the work of Kent Beck and others and has much to commend it. It relies on an intense partnership between developer and client, an iterative approach in which the developer codes a little and deploys a little—and does this over and over again, risking very small failures with each mini-deployment in the hopes of avoiding a major failure at the end. Even so, for most clients, software is something to be used in their business, rather than a process to engage in. XP has some interesting and promising ideas, but it doesn't appear to be a scalable solution to the problem of successfully delivering custom software projects.

FLiP, in contrast, *starts* with the understanding that clients can't tell us what they want *until they see it*. This fact accounts for our failure to get the feedback we need at the beginning of a project, when it's really valuable. Charts and diagrams are a poor excuse for clients actually seeing and touching the product. Prototypes, though, fit the bill very nicely. To a client, the interface to a piece of software *is* the software. Prototypes provide this interface, allowing clients see the software before it's built and letting developers get the feedback they need that's usually obtained only at deployment.

FLiP, then, alters the "Just do it!" approach substantially, placing great emphasis on requirements gathering and design, like this:

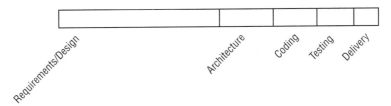

The FLiP Steps

Only after the prototype is completed are we ready to architect the project. To illustrate the FLiP process, we will list the steps in FLiP and then walk through the process of managing a Fusebox project.

1. Meet with the client initially.

2. Create a wireframe.

3. Create a prototype based on the wireframe.

4. Iterate through the prototype using DevNotes.

5. Freeze the prototype.

6. Design acceptance tests.

7. Sign off on the prototype and acceptance tests.

8. Identify exit points.

9. Assign exit fuseactions to the exit points.

10. Identify circuits.

11. Identify fuseactions within each circuit.

12. Identify the fuses needed for each fuseaction.

13. Consolidate fuses where possible.

14. Write Fusedocs.

15. Code fuses.

16. Write test harnesses.

17. Test individual fuses.

18. Integrate fuses into circuits.

19. Test individual circuits.

20. Integrate circuits into the overall application.

21. Test the integrated application.

22. Test for acceptance.

1. Meet with the client initially.

The initial meeting is important in order to size up the prospective client. Just as they must have confidence in me, I must have confidence in them—that they have a clear idea of what they want to accomplish, have a realistic time and money budget, and are committed to the project's success. Throughout the steps presented, the sample project will be to create a website/ application that will be used by a training company to allow students to sign up for classes using the Web.

2. Create a wireframe.

A *wireframe* is a text-only representation of the pages in an application that a user would see. The wireframe has HTML links to other pages so that the client can not only see the pages, but can work through the flow of the application (see Figure 4.6). All graphics are omitted in order to help the client focus on what the application should do. Although a requirements document may be helpful, too often they fail to convey the kind of information needed to ensure a successful application. A wireframe tool that greatly speeds up the page creation process is available at `http://www.bjork.net`.

A rudimentary
wireframe

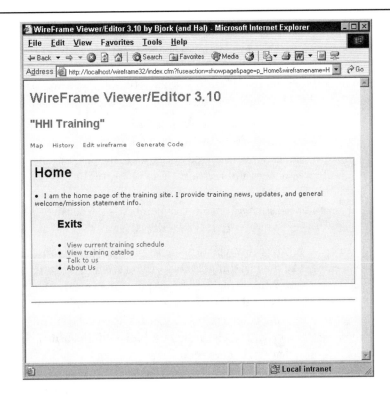

3. Create a prototype based on the wireframe.

Wireframes are wonderful. I liken them to the booster stage of a rocket. Just as booster rockets help a rocket escape the earth's gravity, wireframes help us escape from the weight of our own assumptions about an application. Clients get excited by wireframes; they can actually see their ideas being translated into something concrete. Wireframes are wonderful.

Wireframes are also dangerous. Too often, developers are seduced by the appeal of creating a skeleton, getting client reaction, and jumping straight into architecting/coding an application. In my experience, this is a terrible mistake. Building an application is not only—and maybe not even primarily—a technology exercise, but a political one. For all but the smallest applications, a host of people must have their say. This process, like watching sausage or laws being made, is not something lovely to behold. It's slow, tedious, maddening, frustrating, inefficient—and completely necessary.

The virtue of wireframes is the speed with which you can start to discover customer requirements. But you can only *begin* the discovery process with wireframes. Like the booster rocket separating from the main rocket, the wireframe must fall away once it's done its job, lest it drag us back into the assumptions and ignorance that it helped us escape in the first place. That host of people who must have their say *will* have their say. Your challenge is to make sure this happens before you write the application when their input may be just annoying, rather than after you have invested time and money to code the application, at which point their input can derail the application's deployment entirely. Like it or not, if you are to shepherd a software project to successful deployment, you must accommodate consumer input.

The most successful way of accommodating such input is through the use of a prototype—a sort of full-scale model of the actual application. The prototype can be poked, prodded, and pushed at will. It can be changed once, twice, thrice, be changed back to the original, and then sent off for another set of revisions. The beauty of the prototype is that, to the users, it *is* the application, while in fact, there's nothing to it but HTML and images. That makes changes to the prototype—*necessary* changes, remember—inexpensive. Not free and not pleasant, but relatively cheap. A prototype is a sacrificial lamb.

In order for the prototype to serve its purpose and to protect the project, it must look and feel *exactly* like the real thing. So before you are finished with the prototype, you must have all the content required, and all the graphics and layout. All decisions regarding the application must be answered. If you leave any "wiggle room"—any tiny cracks where the prototype is so close to being complete that it seems silly to delay coding—your client is likely to find that crack and drive a truck through it. Not willfully or maliciously, but because they are clients—and that's what clients do.

NOTE   The wireframe serves as the basis for the prototype, and though there's often correspondence between the two—at least initially—such dialog may not occur at all. A wireframe is typically built by someone not skilled in user interface design, and in the hands of a skilled artisan, the wireframe may undergo substantial changes to make the actual application easier to use and navigate.

Whatever happens at this stage, we can be sure of one thing: the prototype *will* change. I understand and even encourage this because I want to get all the comments and criticisms and concerns out in the open. Everything is in play while the prototype is being worked on. The look and feel can change, functions can be added or dropped—pretty much anything goes. However, while I encourage discussion and change, I continually remind clients that once the prototype is fixed (or "frozen"), the time for change is over. Changes during the prototype phase are cheap; changes after the prototype is frozen are extremely expensive.

Clients sometimes ask me about this: "If it's just a little change, why should it cost so much?" I respond by likening the situation to buying a plane ticket. "If you buy it weeks ahead of time, it doesn't cost much at all. But if you ask for it at the last minute, you'll have to pay a huge premium. Building software works the same way." Silly or not, the analogy mostly works, and as a result, clients try hard to make sure that they have everything fixed before they agree to freeze the prototype.

When is the prototype frozen? Only when both the client's representative and the developer's representative, hopefully a Fusebox architect, agree that the prototype represents exactly what the client wants to see—that all issues and questions regarding the prototype have been resolved. Then the prototype is printed, both the client and developer representatives sign off on it, and architecting the application begins.

FIGURE 4.7:

The finished prototype looks exactly like the finished application

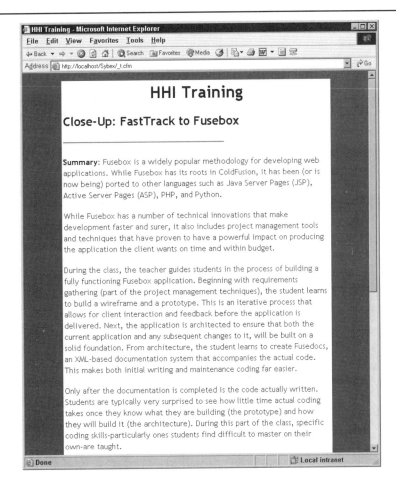

4. Iterate through the prototype using DevNotes.

Prototype evolution is an iterative process. With each agreed to change, the prototype is altered to reflect this request. Since the prototype phase of application development is typically the longest, many changes—e-mail, phone calls, and personal communications among them—are expected. On small projects, this amount of change may be manageable, but on large projects, keeping track of changes can become difficult. Because of this, I created a tool that I dubbed DevNotes that acts as a repository for change requests and all sorts of communication on the project. You can download this from `http://www.grokfusebox.com`.

DevNotes is a small, threaded messaging system, similar in concept (though not in scope) to the message forums used by many companies to provide support and communication within a user community. Users associated with the project (client representatives, developers, and other interested parties) can communicate with each other easily using this system. Ideas, comments, notes, and criticisms can all be expressed with DevNotes, thus reducing the "friction" often associated with keeping track of constant, often rapid, change requests.

FIGURE 4.8:

A prototype with DevNotes

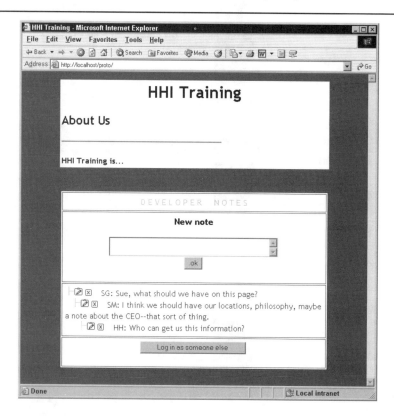

When a note thread is no longer needed—for example, when a request to change the background color has been carried out—the thread can be archived. Later, if someone wants to know how a decision was reached, there is a record.

5. Freeze the prototype.

At the risk of being annoying, let me say again how crucial I consider the prototype to be. If I could only control one aspect of an entire project, I would choose the prototype. If you succeed with the prototype, your chances for overall project success improve; if you fail with the prototype, the odds are overwhelmingly against you.

Make sure you take the prototype very seriously, and don't freeze it prematurely. As the architect, you are responsible not only for making sure that you have the information you need to plan out the application, but you also need to keep the client from making mistakes that will mar the project. I only agree to a prototype freeze when I am sure that the client is aware of any issues, obvious or not, that I thought might have an impact on the project success. We may not be able to keep people from doing dumb things, but we can at least post a sign that warns "Danger: Cliff Ahead."

6. Design acceptance tests.

Although we won't use acceptance tests until the project is completed, it's important to determine by what means we will judge a project's success. Since all issues should have been determined by this point, designing and explaining these tests to your client will greatly help you avoid the common problem of clients changing requirements mid-stream—the dreaded "scope creep." We know we're done with a project when the prototype functions and all acceptance tests complete successfully.

7. Sign off on the prototype and acceptance tests.

Signing off on the prototype and acceptance tests is a ritual I hold to impress on all the importance of the prototype freeze. The sign-off also helps if, later, the client demands to know why a certain functionality wasn't included. I can take out the prototype as evidence that this new item was never identified. That said, no amount of "weasel words" will (or should) protect me if I've done a bad job of guiding the client. If I was an architect designing your house and I failed to ensure that your bedroom had closets in it, I'm sure you wouldn't be appeased by my telling you, "Well, you never said you wanted closets."

8. Identify exit points.

Finally, we're ready to begin architecting the application! The first thing a Fusebox architect does is identify the various exit points on each prototype page. Exit points are ways that a new fuseaction can be triggered. On pages that require user interaction, these points will likely be links or form submissions; on pages processed solely by the system, conditional logic will be employed to decide which of possibly several exit points will be chosen. When identifying a prototype's exit points, I print out each page and circle the exit points. Once this is done, I'm ready to…

9. Assign exit fuseactions to the exit points.

Shortly, I'll explain fuseactions. For now, just think of them as descriptions of what you want the exit point to accomplish. For example, if you click a product to add it to your shopping cart, the exit fuseaction might be `addItemToCart`. If you submit a form that updates your user information, you might choose `updateUserInfo`. The important thing is to make the name of the fuseaction as clear as possible. This is not the time to abbreviate.

10. Identify circuits.

Circuits, as you'll soon see, are just ways to organize fuseactions. Circuits, implemented as directories, help me spot any recurring nouns. For example, say I have the following fuseactions:

```
addItemToCart
removeItemFromCart
displayCart
```

This tells me I probably want to create a separate circuit called `Cart`. We identify circuits to help us keep things straight rather than because the computer needs them. The choice of circuits is more a matter of art and taste than any rigorous selection process.

11. Identify fuseactions within each circuit.

Now, I can take the fuseactions I've identified in the preceding step and fit them into a circuit. (Each fuseaction must have a circuit.) At this stage, I will also identify any fuseactions that are needed by the system but that could not be visually identified.

For example, I may have a prototype page that shows a login form. We can visually identify the Submit button as one exit point for this fuse. Let's say the exit fuseaction is called `validate-Login`. This fuseaction will make use of a query file in order to obtain information on the user whose `userName` and `password` match the ones entered into the login screen. Then, another fuse—let's call it `act_ValidateLogin.cfm`—checks to see if the query returned a user. If a user is found, the login succeeds. If no user is found, the login fails. These two alternatives represent two distinct exit points for the fuse, `act_ValidateLogin.cfm`, a file that has no visual counterpart in the prototype. It is the job of the Fusebox architect to fill in the fuseactions for accomplishing actions that are not represented in the prototype.

There are many different ways of recording the decisions made during this architecture phase. I find a visual outliner to be very helpful. There are several of these "mind-mapping" tools available; I use Visual Mind, which is available at `http://www.visual-mind.com`. Figure 4.9 is a Visual Mind snapshot of my partial outline for the sample project.

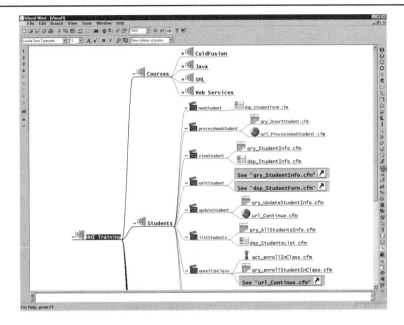

FIGURE 4.9:

Partial visual outline
of Fusebox application
in Visual Mind

12. Identify the fuses needed for each fuseaction.

If fuseactions represent the soul of an application, fuses represent the body. Fuses are the actual parts that perform actions, fulfill intentions and accomplish the goals set forth by the fuseactions. Each fuseaction must have one or more fuses to which control has been delegated. By convention, these fuses have prefixes that provide a clue about what the fuse does.

dsp_   These files primarily handle the display of information to the user. Here is an example of a file that displays a login form to a user:

```
<!--dsp_Login.cfm-->
<form action="#self#?fuseaction=#XFA.submitForm# method="post">
    Your username: <input type="text" name="username"><br>
    Your password: <input type="password" name="password"><br>
    <input type="submit" value=" ok ">
</form>
```

qry_   These files handle database interaction and usually contain a cfquery or cfstored-proc tag. Here is an example of a file that searches a database for a user corresponding to the username and password provided.

```
<!--qry_UserInfo.cfm-->
<cfquery datasource="#request.dsn#" name="UserInfo">
    select
        firstName,
```

```
            lastName,
            userID,
            userGroups
        from
            User
        where
            username = '#attributes.username#'
        and
            password = '#attributes.password#'
</cfquery>
```

act_   These files provide processing without any display aspect. Here is an example of a file that sets a client structure called `CurrentUser` if a user was found, and returns to the Fusebox application with a `success` fuseaction. If no user was found, it returns to the application with a `failure` fuseaction.

```
<!--act_ValidateLogin.cfm-->
<cfif UserInfo.recordCount>
    <cfset str = StructNew()>
    <cfset str.firstName = UserInfo.firstName>
    <cfset str.lastName = UserInfo.lastName>
    <cfset str.userID = UserInfo.userID>
    <cfset str.userGroups = UserInfo.userGroups>

    <cfwddx
        action="cfml2wddx"
        input="#str#"
        output="Client.CurrentUser">

    <cflocation url="#self#?fuseaction=#XFA.onSuccess#" addToken="yes">
<cfelse>
    <cflocation url="#self#?fuseaction=#XFA.onFailure#" addToken="yes">
```

url_   These files are used to handle relocation tasks.

TIP   Some fusecoders do not use url_ files, preferring instead to handle the relocation in the fusebox itself.

Here is an example of a file that returns to the fusebox with different fuseactions depending on a status code that is present to the fuse:

```
<cfif addUser.status EQ "0">
    <cflocation url="#self#?fuseaction=#XFA.successfulAdd#" addToken="yes">
<cfelseif addUser.status EQ "10">
    <cflocation url="#self#?fuseaction=#XFA.attemptedDupe#" addToken="yes">
<cfelse>
    <cflocation url="#self#?fuseaction=#XFA.databaseSNAFU#" addToken="yes">
</cfif>
```

Fuses may be used either individually or in combination. Here is a portion of a fusebox that handles the fuseaction validateLogin:

```
<cfswitch expression="#attributes.fuseaction#">
   . . .
   <cfcase value="validateLogin">
      <cfinclude template="#Approot#/queries/qry_MatchUser.cfm">
      <cfset XFA.onSuccess="Home.welcome">
      <cfset XFA.onFailure="Users.badLogin">
      <cfinclude template="act_ValidateLogin.cfm">
   </cfcase>
   . . .
</cfswitch>
```

13. Consolidate fuses where possible.

Architecting an application in detail provides an opportunity to consolidate fuses. For example, if two query files return very similar information, it may make sense to combine them into one. For instance, with a little foresight, we can use the same file for adding and editing a student in the sample project. This works best when you take the time to fully architect the application before proceeding.

14. Write Fusedocs.

We've all been told *ad nauseum* to comment our code. But what, exactly, should we comment? The advocates of commenting code are often silent on exactly what we should do and why. What Fuseboxers want from code comments is the ability to provide enough information so that a competent programmer, who may know nothing of the application or its underlying database, can write code for the application. This process is sometimes referred to as "programming by contract" because the comments are a sort of "work order" for the coder. The "contract" promises the programmer, "You fulfill this work order and you will be done with the code. You have no responsibility beyond what the document tells you."

Fusedoc is a specification that describes in detail what we're trying to accomplish with comments and how to get it done. With Fusebox 3, Fusedoc goes from a proprietary symbology to the open standard of XML. There is a DTD available at http://www.halhelms.com that provides the formal specification for Fusedoc. We'll take a look at this here.

A Fusedoc is constructed within standard ColdFusion comments. To see what a Fusedoc looks like, take a look at Listing 4.1, which contains a complete Fusedoc for a fuse named act_ValidateLogin.cfm. Following the Fusedoc is the code for this fuse. See what you can gain from looking it over before we examine it in greater detail.

Listing 4.1   **XML Fusedoc for act_ValidateLogin.cfm (act_ValidateLogin.cfm)**

```
<!---
<fusedoc
    version="2.0"
    language="ColdFusion">
    <responsibilities>
        I validate a user login. If MatchUser returns any rows, I create a
        structure with the info returned by the recordset and return to the
        fusebox with XFA.success; else XFA.failure.
    </responsibilities>
    <properties>
        <history
            type="create"
            date="23 Sep 2001"
            e-mail="hal.helms@teamallaire.com"
            role="architect">
    </properties>
    <io>
        <in>
            <string name="self" />
            <string name="XFA.success" />
            <string name="XFA.failure" />
            <recordset name="MatchUser" primaryKeys="userID" />
                <number name="userID" precision="integer" />
                <string name="firstName" />
                <string name="lastName" />
                <number name="userGroups" precision="integer" />
            </recordset>
        </in>
        <out>
            <structure
                name="CurrentUser"
                scope="client"
                format="wddx"
                optional="true"
                onCondition="if MatchUser returns non-empty rows"
                comments="match values in MatchUser to those in the structure.">
                <number name="userID" precision="integer" />
                <string name="firstName" />
                <string name="lastName" />
                <number name="userGroups" precision="integer" />
            </structure>
            <string name="fuseaction" comments="an XFA" />
        </out>
    </io>
</fusedoc>
--->

<cfoutput>
```

```
<cfif MatchUser.recordCount>
   <cfset str = StructNew()>
   <cfset str.userID = MatchUser.userID>
   <cfset str.firstName = MatchUser.firstName>
   <cfset str.lastName = MatchUser.lastName>
   <cfset str.userGroups = MatchUser.userGroups>

   <cfwddx
      action="cfml2wddx"
      input="#str#"
      output="client.CurrentUser">

   <cflocation url="#self#?fuseaction=#XFA.success#" addToken="yes">
<cfelse>
   <cflocation url="#self#?fuseaction=#XFA.failure#" addToken="yes">
</cfif>

</cfoutput>
```

TIP   The first thing you might notice about this fuse is that the Fusedoc is actually *bigger* than the code. Some people might find that odd, but I find that fuses work best (more reusability, easier maintenance, less prone to bugs) when they are small.

The Fusedoc begins with an XML root element called <fusedoc>. The attributes shown are required. Possible subelements are <responsibilities>, <properties>, <io>, and <assertions>. Of these, the only required element is <responsibilities>, but the other elements are also discussed here.

NOTE   The <assertions> element is not currently used. When it's completed and made available, it will provide Fusebox with the ability to check for runtime conditions known as *assertions*.

responsibilities (required)   In responsibilities, the coder describes what the fuse does, in plain language and as clearly as possible. I write my Fusedocs in the first person because it helps me write the responsibilities more clearly and completely. I try to avoid repeating in the responsibilities element anything that will be specified in the io element (coming up).

properties (optional)   The properties section is something of a catch-all. It can contain one or more of three optional elements: history, property, and note. The only restriction is that if you include properties at all, you must include at least one of the optional subelements.

NOTE   A note about the typography used to describe the Fusedoc syntax in this section: The same monospaced font used for code throughout this book is used to describe the element and its attribute names. Square brackets indicate optional attributes. Values for options are in italic. Pipe symbols denote an either/or condition. Default values are in boldface. Elements that allow for a closing tag are shown with that closing tag.

Each element will conform to the following pattern:

```
<element-name
    this="a required attribute"
    [that="an optional attribute"]
    theother="either one value | or another">
```

The subelements of properties are as follows:

```
<history
    type="create | update"
    [date="date in unprescribed format"]
    [author="free text"]
    [role="free text"]
    [e-mail="free text"]>

    I can place any text in here that I wish to.

</history>
<property>
    name="property_name"
    value="free text">
<note
    [author="free text"]
    [date="date in unprescribed format"]>

    I can place any text in here that I wish to.

</note>
```

io (optional)   The io (input/output) section provides concrete information on the variables being passed into and out of the fuse, as well as those persistent variables that the fusecoder needs to be aware of.

TIP   There is no need to include variables that the fusecoder does not need to be concerned with. For example, I typically set a request-scope variable called dsn in my app_locals .cfm file. Unless the fuse deals with queries, though, there's no reason to include this in the Fusedoc.

There are two subelements allowed, one of which must be present if the Fusedoc contains an io section.

```
<in>
</in>
<out>
</out>
```

The in section describes variables that are available to the fuse. The out section describes variables that the fuse is responsible for setting.

Both in and out elements can contain other elements (see Listing 4.2). (Note that the [mask=""] element is reserved for future use.)

Listing 4.2   Syntax for <in>/<out> sub-elements

```
<string
    [name="valid_variable_name"]
    scope="application | attributes | caller | cgi | client | form | formOrURL |
    request | server | session | url | variables"
    [comments="I can type any text here."]
    [mask=""]
    [onCondition="This variable only occurs if certain conditions are true.
    Free text. Example: on XFA.success would indicate that a variable would only
    be set if the XFA.success condition occurred."]
    format="wddx | cfml"
    optional="true | false"
    [default="a value to be used if none is supplied"]
>

<number
    [name="valid_variable_name"]
    scope="application | attributes | caller | cgi | client | form | formOrURL |
    request | server |  session | url | variables"
    [comments="I can type any text here."]
    [precision="decimal | integer"]
    [onCondition="This variable only occurs if certain conditions are true.
    Free text. Example: on XFA.success would indicate that a variable would only
    be set if the XFA.success condition occurred."]
    optional="true | false"
    [default="a value to be used if none is supplied"]
>

<boolean
    [name="valid_variable_name"]
    scope="application | attributes | caller | cgi | client | form | formOrURL |
    request | server | session | url | variables"
    [comments="I can type any text here."]
    [onCondition="This variable only occurs if certain conditions are true.
    Free text. Example: on XFA.success would indicate that a variable would only
```

```
        be set if the XFA.success condition occurred."]
    optional="true | false"
    [default="a value to be used if none is supplied"]
>

<datetime
    [name="valid_variable_name"]
    scope="application | attributes | caller | cgi |client | form | formOrURL |
➡    request | server | session | url | variables"
    mask="a_datetime_mask | m/d/yy"
    [comments="I can type any text here."]
    [onCondition="This variable only occurs if certain conditions are true.
    Free text. Example: on XFA.success would indicate that a variable would only
    be set if the XFA.success condition occurred."]
    optional="true | false"
    [default="a value to be used if none is supplied"]
>

<recordset
    [name="valid_variable_name"]
    scope="application | attributes | caller | cgi | client | form | formOrURL |
➡    request | server | session | url | variables"
    [comments="I can type any text here."]
    [onCondition="This variable only occurs if certain conditions are true.
    Free text. Example: on XFA.success would indicate that a variable would only
    be set if the XFA.success condition occurred."]
    format="wddx | cfml"
    optional="true | false"
>

<array
    [name="valid_variable_name"]
    scope="application | attributes | caller | cgi | client | form | formOrURL |
➡    request | server | session | url | variables"
    [comments="I can type any text here."]
    [onCondition="This variable only occurs if certain conditions are true.
    Free text. Example: on XFA.success would indicate that a variable would only
    be set if the XFA.success condition occurred."]
    format="wddx | cfml"
    optional="true | false"
>

<structure
    [name="valid_variable_name"]
    scope="application | attributes | caller | cgi | client | form | formOrURL |
➡    request | server | session | url | variables"
    [comments="I can type any text here."]
    [onCondition="This variable only occurs if certain conditions are true.
    Free text. Example: on XFA.success would indicate that a variable would only
    be set if the XFA.success condition occurred."]
    format="wddx | cfml"
    optional="true | false"
>
```

```
<list
    [name="valid_variable_name"]
    scope="application | attributes | caller | cgi | client | form | formOrURL |
➡   request | server | session | url | variables"
    delims="one_or_more_single_byte_characters | ,"
    [comments="I can type any text here."]
    [onCondition="This variable only occurs if certain conditions are true.
    Free text. Example: on XFA.success would indicate that a variable would only
    be set if the XFA.success condition occurred."]
    format="wddx | cfml"
    optional="true | false"
    [default="a value to be used if none is supplied"]
>

<file
    path="absolute or relative path as determined by
    the action attribute"
    action="read | write | append  | overwrite | delete | exists | module |
➡   include"
    [comments="I can type any text here."]
    [onCondition="This variable only occurs if certain conditions are true.
    Free text. Example: on XFA.success would indicate that a variable would only
    be set if the XFA.success condition occurred."]
    optional="true | false"
>

<cookie
    [name="cookie_name"]
    [domain="valid_domain"]
    [expires="valid_value"]
    [path="valid_path"]
    [comments="I can type any text here."]
    [onCondition="This variable only occurs if certain conditions are true.
    Free text. Example: on XFA.success would indicate that a variable would only
    be set if the XFA.success condition occurred."]
    optional="true | false"
>
```

Whoo! That may seem like a lot to learn, but you'll find that by referring to the chart in Listing 4.2, you'll master the Fusedoc specs in no time. The tag editors for ColdFusion Studio that are provided at http://www.fusebox.org are particularly helpful when you are trying to learn this information.

TIP   You're very likely to find that writing a Fusedoc for one fuse will spawn a realization that another fuse's Fusedoc is incomplete. This is quite normal—particularly when you are starting out. It may help to use your Visual Mind outline to make notes about <io> variables; they're just notes and so no formal structure is needed. Figure 4.10 is a screenshot from one of mine. Because you have a broad overview of the application using Visual Mind, It's often easier to work out the variables in Visual Mind before writing the Fusedocs.

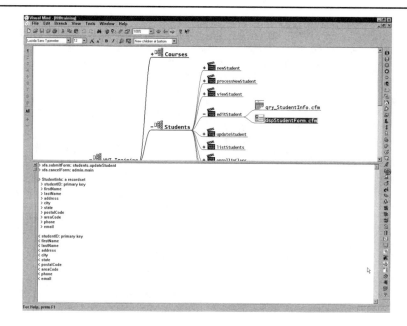

15. Code fuses.

With the Fusedocs for each fuse written, you're ready to write the individual fuses. Programmers are often surprised—and always pleased—to discover that writing code is not frustrating at all, but instead it is rather simple when you know what you're doing.

I said earlier that the goal of a well-constructed Fusedoc was to provide enough information that a competent programmer could write the fuse. Therefore, adding people to a project at this phase is a simple task. Because all the logic and presentation has already been determined, a coder who is unfamiliar with either the application or the underlying database can still write fuses.

TIP   Jeff Peters has written a tool called FuseMinder that reads the output from a visual outliner and produces stubs for code. This can be a real time-saver, giving you a head start on your code development. You can get FuseMinder at http://www.grokfusebox.com.

16. Write test harnesses.

One problem common to development is the discovery of bugs late in the development process—usually at code integration, when the individual files are combined. This is the point at which we're likely to discover a number of problems that reside in the individual fuses. The antidote: create *test harnesses*—small code files responsible for setting up the environment in which individual code files can run and be tested.

For an example, let's go back to our old friend, act_ValidateLogin.cfm and take a quick look at the Fusedoc <io> section:

```
<in>
    <string name="self" />
    <string name="XFA.success" />
    <string name="XFA.failure" />
    <recordset name="MatchUser" primaryKeys="userID" />
        <number name="userID" precision="integer" />
        <string name="firstName" />
        <string name="lastName" />
        <number name="userGroups" precision="integer" />
    </recordset>
</in>
```

Writing a test harness for the fuse is easy in this case; see Listing 4.3.

Listing 4.3   Test Harness for act_ValidateLogin.cfm (tst_act_ValidateLogin.cfm)

```
<!---
    Name:           /co4/tst_act_ValidateLogin.cfm
    Description:    Test harness to ensure that act_ValidateLogin.cfm works
    correctly
--->
<cfset self="Tester.cfm">
<cfset XFA.success="success">
<cfset XFA.failure="failure">
<cfapplication name="test" clientManagement="true">

<!--- test for success --->
<cf_QuerySim>
MatchUser
userID,firstName,lastName,userGroups
100|Hal|Helms|53
</cf_QuerySim>

<!--- test for failure
<cf_QuerySim>
MatchUser
userID,firstName,lastName,userGroups
</cf_QuerySim>
--->

<cfinclude template="act_ValidateLogin.cfm">
```

I save this file as tst_act_ValidateLogin.cfm. As the code reads right now, I can test for success by running the test harness shown in Listing 4.3. I set the variable self to Tester.cfm, a simple file that makes a call to Dan Switzer's custom tag, `Debug.cfm`, available at `http://www.pengoworks.com`. When I run the test harness, `Debug.cfm` produces a new browser window (shown in Figure 4.11) with information I can use to ensure that the fuse is fulfilling the "work order" it received.

FIGURE 4.11:

Running a test
harness using
`Debug.cfm`

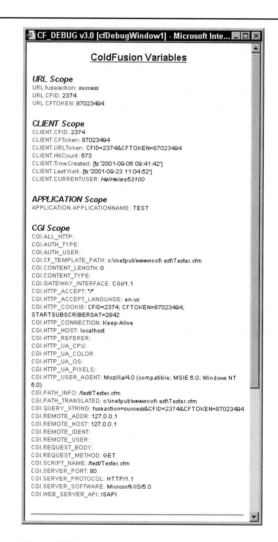

Everything seems to be fine. Now, I'll alter my query sim so that it returns no rows. This time, the code produced shows the fuseaction to be set to the value of `XFA.failure`. When I run the test harness again, I find that it behaves as I intended (Figure 4.12).

FIGURE 4.12:

FIGURE 4.12:

Another test using
a harness

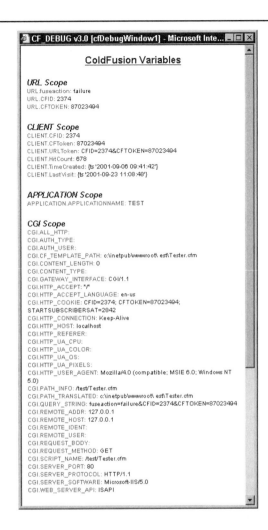

17. Test individual fuses.

When I write fuses, I write the test harnesses along with them. When others write fuses for me, I ask for the harnesses to accompany the fuses. In this way, I can be assured that there are not any gross errors at the unit level.

That said, I also understand that coders aren't testers. The mindset is quite the opposite: Coders are trying to get their programs to *work*, while testers are trying to get those same programs to *break*. This usually means that I get test harnesses that run the code well enough, but without any great stress. For example, here is a test harness for a fuse that adds a product to a shopping cart:

```
<cfset self="Tester.cfm">
<cfset XFA.continue="continue">
<cfset attributes.productID = "3889">
<cfset attributes.productQuantity = "2">
<cfinclude template="act_AddItemToCart.cfm">
```

Running it tells me that the fuse isn't broken—but is it really unit tested? What will happen if productID is not a valid ID? Will the code "degrade gracefully" or will it go down screaming? Or what about the variable productQuantity? What if the user types in "one" instead of "1"? (Stranger things have happened…) What if the user enters "2.3"? Or—here's an interesting question—what happens if the user types in "–3". Do we then owe *them* money?

We can rework our test harness to loop through each of these possibilities to see how the fuse handles it. Here's what the test harness would look like:

```
<cfset quantityList = "one,2.3,-3">

<cfloop list="#quantityList#" index="aValue">
    <cfset attributes.quantity = aValue>
    <cfoutput>
        <b>Evaluation where attributes.quantity = #aValue#</b>
        <br>
    </cfoutput>

    <cftry>
    <cfinclude template="myCFMLpage.cfm">
    <cfcatch>
        <cfoutput>
            #cfcatch.message#
        </cfoutput>
    </cfcatch>

    </cftry>
<hr>
</cfloop>
```

We start by putting all the values we want to try in a list. Then we loop over the list, enclosing our file to be unit tested in <cftry><cfcatch> blocks to trap any errors. Figure 4.13 shows the output we get.

FIGURE 4.13:

Results of a more
robust test harness

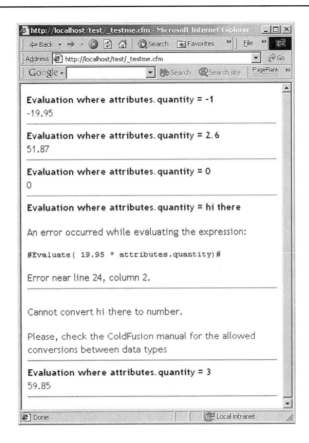

Of course, in a real-world case, you usually wouldn't have only one variable being passed in. In such a case, you could use nested loops to test for every permutation of possibilities:

```
<cfset attributesQuantity = one,2.3,-3">
<cfset attributesMyName = "John,Steve,Nat,Hal">

<cfloop list="#attributesQuantity#" index="aQuantity">
    <cfloop list="#attributes_myName#" index="aMyName">
        <cfset attributes.quantity = aQuantity>
        <cfset attributes.myName = aMyName>
        <cfoutput>
            <b>Results with following parameter values:<br>
            quantity: #aQuantity#<br>
            myName: #aMyName#<br></b>
            <br>
```

```
        <cftry>
        <cfinclude template="myCFMLpage.cfm">

        <cfcatch>
            #cfcatch.message#<br>
        </cfcatch>
        </cftry>
    </cfoutput>
    <hr>
    </cfloop>
</cfloop>
```

NOTE   You may want to check out Jeff Peters's website, http://www.grokfusebox.com. As of this writing, there are rumors that Jeff is working on a tool to automate much of the drudgery of writing test harnesses.

18. Integrate fuses into circuits.

One of the worst things project managers (PM) have to deal with is the last 10 percent of a project. More than one PM has ruefully remarked that "it takes us 6 months to get the first 90 percent done—and another 6 months for the last 10 percent." The problem, of course, is that the project was never actually at 90 percent completion. That 90 percent was a guess, probably at the insistence of management.

To prevent this from occurring, I have a routine of doing daily builds at (hopefully) the same point in the day. I integrate all of the written and tested fuses into their respective circuits and perform a "smoke test," turning on the machine and looking for smoke to come pouring out of the vents.

For fuses that aren't finished yet, I have stub code that says something like, "I'm such-and-so fuse, but I'm not implemented yet." I begin this daily testing very, very early in the development cycle. Initially, of course, I see a lot of almost blank pages declaring their eventual good intentions. But the important thing is that I'm seeing to it that nothing breaks, and with each build I should see a little more functionality implemented. I consider these daily builds to be crucial. Without them, I have no realistic idea of how far along the project has come. An added benefit is that if I'm responsible for others who are helping on the project, I can tell how they're doing, and where to put those extra SecretAgents.com coders to work!

19. Test individual circuits.

Once individual circuits are completed, I begin testing them as a unit. I want to make sure that the individual circuit components work together before I begin integrating circuits. Even at this point, I keep the test harnesses written for the individual fuses. If some issue crops up, I want to be able to isolate the individual fuses and where the trouble lies. Test harnesses are invaluable in this.

20. Integrate circuits into the overall application.

With each circuit tested successfully, a bit more of the overall application picture becomes clear. Just as I do daily builds on the individual components, I want to perform regular integration of circuits. This lets coder, manager, and perhaps even the client judge the progress of the application.

21. Test the integrated application.

After all the circuits have been successfully integrated, I want to test the entire application. I use the acceptance tests designed in step 6, since the client and I have agreed that this is the measure of the application's success. Since the next test coming up is the one that matters the most, I want to know now that the application will do what we promised and what the client expects.

22. Test for acceptance.

Because acceptance tests were designed prior to coding, the chance of misunderstandings between client and developer are greatly reduced. Determination of acceptance tests reflects the understanding that the application is done when the prototype runs. The tests are a formal way of ensuring that this is the case.

Summing It Up

The 22 steps to FLiP make up an ideal project. Obviously, real projects differ—sometimes substantially. For example, if you're working within a corporation, you may not have an introductory meeting (step 1). In addition, you may need to omit some steps and possibly add others that are not shown here.

Although some steps may seem counterintuitive, the steps as described here reflect the experience of many developers and the method they have adopted to produce predictably successful projects.

A Sample Fusebox Application

Hopefully, this chapter has helped you grasp the concepts underlying Fusebox and FLiP. I think you'll agree, though, that there's no substitute for looking at real code to explore the details, so let's write some code. We don't have the space here to develop an entire application, but we'll study a couple of abbreviated circuits to see how things fit together. You can download the entire "Numbers by Vinny" application from `http://www.halhelms.com`. Table 4.1 presents a breakdown of this application.

In my classes on Fusebox, I often have students work on an application for Vinny. Vinny is a "businessman" who runs a "social club" that lets "members" pick numbers and "make contributions." Following are some of the circuits, fuseactions, and fuses from this application so that you can see a Fusebox application (albeit a skeletal one) run.

NOTE Although this application will give you a good sense of how a Fusebox application is put together, there's very little else I can recommend about it! There's no exception checking, no form validation, none of the "stuff that takes time" in programming. There's not a shred of security and even the passwords are stored in their raw state. I'm afraid this is a clear example of "Do As I Say, Not As I Do," and I can only plead for leniency on the grounds of limited space.

TABLE 4.1: Breakdown of the Numbers by Vinny Application

CIRCUIT	FUSEACTION	FUSE(s)
User	new	qry_BlankUserInfo.cfm
		qry_USstates.cfm
		qry_Territories.cfm
		dsp_PlayerForm.cfm
	add	qry_InsertPlayer.cfm
		url_NewPlayer.cfm
Login	login	dsp_Login.cfm
	validateLogin	qry_MatchUser.cfm
		act_ValidateLogin.cfm
	badLogin	dsp_Login.cfm
Player	main	qry_LastWeeksWinningNumber
		qry_LastWeeksPicks
		dsp_PlayerHome.cfm

I'll start by creating the directory structure shown in Figure 4.14.

FIGURE 4.14:

Numbers by Vinny directory structure

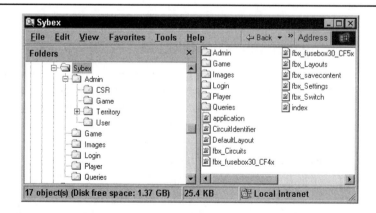

In Sybex\FBX_Settings.cfm (Listing 4.4), I've set a default fuseaction and pointed self at the index.cfm file, as well as doing some other housekeeping chores.

Listing 4.4   Sybex/FBX_Settings.cfm

```
<!---
<fusedoc fuse="FBX_Settings.cfm">
     I set up the environment settings for this circuit. If this settings file
   is being inherited, then you can use cfset to override a value set in a
   parent circuit or cfparam to accept a value set by a parent circuit.
   </responsibilities>
</fusedoc>
--->

<!--- In case no fuseaction was given, I'll set up one to use by default. --->
<cfparam name="attributes.fuseaction" default="login.main">

<!--- useful constants --->
<cfparam name="request.self" default="index.cfm">
<cfparam name="self" default="index.cfm">
<cfapplication name="Sybex" clientManagement="Yes">
```

When I type http://www.localhost/sybex into my browser, the default file, index.cfm, will fire (see Listing 4.5).

Listing 4.5   Sybex/index.cfm

```
<!---
<fusedoc fuse="index.cfm">
     I am not strictly a part of the Fusebox 3.0 specification, but show how a
     default file should deal with Fusebox files.
   </responsibilities>
</fusedoc>
--->

<!--- include the core FuseBox  --->
<cfinclude template="FBX_Fusebox30_CF50.cfm">
```

Within the FBX_Fusebox30_CF50.cfm file, quite a lot of work is being done. One of the actions reads the FBX_Circuits.cfm file, as shown in Listing 4.6.

Listing 4.6   Sybex/FBX_Circuits.cfm

```
<!--FBX_Circuits-->
<!---
<fusedoc fuse="FBX_Circuits.cfm">
     I define the Circuits structure used with Fusebox 3.0
```

```
        </responsibilities>
    </fusedoc>
    --->

    <!--- this file contains all the circuit definitions for the fusebox --->
    <cfset Fusebox.Circuits.home = "Sybex">
    <cfset Fusebox.Circuits.userAdmin = "Sybex/User">
    <cfset Fusebox.Circuits.login = "Sybex/Login">
    <cfset Fusebox.Circuits.player    = "Sybex/Player">
```

Next, the FBX_Fusebox30_CF50.cfm file reads in any existing FBX_Settings.cfm files in the target circuit. Since Login is the target circuit, the only FBX_Settings.cfm file to be read is the one in the Login circuit. In this case, I don't need to set anything specific to the Login circuit, and so I've omitted the settings file from the Login directory. Fusebox 3 is smart enough to understand that FBX_Settings.cfm and FBX_Layouts.cfm files are missing for a reason; no error is thrown.

After trying to include all settings files, the Fusebox file reads the FBX_Layouts.cfm files on the way up the circuit tree. In this case, both Login and Sybex have FBX_Layouts.cfm files. Listing 4.7 shows the one in Login.

Listing 4.7   **Sybex/Login/FBX_Layouts.cfm**

```
<!---
<fusedoc fuse="FBX_Layouts.cfm">
        This file contains all the conditional logic for determining which layout
        file, if any, should be used for this circuit. It should result in the
        setting of the Fusebox public API variables Fusebox.layoutdir and
Fusebox.layoutfile.
    </responsibilities>
    <io>
        <out>
            <string name="Fusebox.layoutDir" optional="false" />
            <string name="Fusebox.layoutFile" optional="false" />
        </out>
    </io>
</fusedoc>
--->

<cfset Fusebox.layoutDir="">
<cfset Fusebox.layoutFile="CircuitIdentifier.cfm">
```

A layout file, CircuitIdentifier.cfm, has been identified as the one to use (see Listing 4.8).

Listing 4.8   **Sybex/Layout/CircuitIdentifier.cfm**

```
<style type="text/css">
table {
    border : thin dashed Silver;
}
</style>

<table cellPadding="10" cellSpacing="10">
    <tr>
        <td>
            <cfoutput>
                <h4>I am the #Fusebox.thisCircuit# circuit</h4><br>
                #Fusebox.layout#
            </cfoutput>

        </td>
    </tr>
</table>
```

The CircuitIdentifier.cfm file uses the variable, Fusebox.thisCircuit, part of the Fusebox 3 API, to identify what circuit it is operating in. I'm outputting this variable so that when we see the generated output, the sources of the various layouts will be clear. Additionally, CircuitIdentifier.cfm outputs Fusebox.layout. Whatever else a layout file does, it must output this variable for display, since Fusebox.layout is the sum total of all preceding fuses and layout files.

Having finished with the Login circuit, Fusebox reads the FBX_layouts.cfm file from the home directory, Sybex (see Listing 4.9). It's identical to the one I used for Login.

Listing 4.9   **Sybex/FBX_Layouts.cfm**

```
<!---
<fusedoc fuse="FBX_Layouts.cfm">

        This file contains all the conditional logic for determing which layout
file
(if any) should be used for this circuit. It should result in the setting of
the Fusebox public API variables, Fusebox.layoutDir, and Fusebox.layoutFile.

    </responsibilities>
    <io>
        <out>
            <string name="Fusebox.layoutDir" optional="false" />
```

```
                <string name="Fusebox.layoutFile" optional="false" />
          </out>
      </io>
</fusedoc>
--->

<cfset Fusebox.layoutDir="">
<cfset Fusebox.layoutFile="CircuitIdentifier.cfm">
```

The `Sybex/CircuitIdentifier.cfm` file is also identical to the one in `Login`.

With all `FBX_Settings.cfm` and `FBX_Layouts.cfm` files accounted for, as well as a default fuseaction (`Login.main`), the Fusebox file "reaches" into the `Login` circuit and reads the `FBX_Switch.cfm` file, shown in Listing 4.10.

Listing 4.10   Sybex/Login/FBX_Switch.cfm

```
<!---
<fusedoc fuse="FBX_Switch.cfm" version="2.0">
      I am the cfswitch statement that handles the fuseaction, delegating work
      to various fuses.
      </responsibilities>
      <io>
          <out>
              <string name="Fusebox.fuseaction" />
              <string name="Fusebox.circuit" />
          </out>
      </io>
</fusedoc>
--->
<cfswitch expression = "#Fusebox.fuseaction#">

    <cfcase value="main,login">
        <cfset displayMessage="">
        <cfset XFA.submitForm="Login.validateLogin">
        <cfset XFA.newPlayer="UserAdmin.newUserForm">
        <cfinclude template="dsp_Login.cfm">
    </cfcase>

    <cfcase value="badLogin">
        <cfset displayMessage="Sorry, but we couldn't
validate you. Try again?">
        <cfset XFA.submitForm="Login.validateLogin">
        <cfinclude template="dsp_Login.cfm">
    </cfcase>

    <cfcase value="validateLogin">
        <cfset XFA.failure="Login.badLogin">
        <cfset XFA.success="Player.main">
```

```
      <cfinclude template="qry_MatchUser.cfm">
      <cfinclude template="act_ValidateLogin.cfm">
   </cfcase>

   <cfdefaultcase>
      <cfoutput>
         I received a fuseaction called <b><font color="000066">"
         #Fusebox.fuseaction#"</font></b> that circuit <b><font color="000066">"
         #Fusebox.circuit#"</font></b> doesn't have a handler for.
      </cfoutput>
   </cfdefaultcase>

</cfswitch>
```

The dsp_Login.cfm file (Listing 4.11) is the code that actually produces content.

Listing 4.11   **Sybex/Login/dsp_Login.cfm**

```
<!---
<fusedoc fuse="dsp_Login.cfm" version="2.0">
      I give the user a form to log in with.
   </responsibilities>
   <properties>
      <history type="create"
         e-mail="hal.helms@teamallaire.com"/>
   </properties>
   <io>
      <in>
         <string name="self"/>
         <string name="XFA.submitForm" />
         <string name="XFA.newPlayer" />
         <string name="displayMessage" />
      </in>
      <out>
         <string name="fuseaction" scope="formOrURL"/>
         <string name="userName" scope="formOrURL" />
         <string
            name="password"
            scope="formOrURL"
            comments="password-encoded field" />
      </out>
   </io>
</fusedoc>
--->

<cfoutput>

<h2>
Login
</h2>
```

```
<strong>#displayMessage#</strong>
<br />

<form action="#self#?fuseaction=#XFA.submitForm#"
method="post">
<table>
   <tr>
      <td align="right">
         Your username:
      </td>
      <td>
         <input type="Text" name="username">
      </td>
   </tr>
   <tr>
      <td>
         Your password:
      </td>
      <td>
         <input type="Password" name="password">
      </td>
   </tr>
   <tr>
      <td colspan="2" align="center">
         <input type="Submit" value=" ok ">
      </td>
   </tr>
</table>
</form>
<br>
New to our social club? Join
<a href="#self#?fuseaction=#XFA.newPlayer#">here</a>.

</cfoutput>
```

Note the use of XFAs in order to set the action property of the form tag and the link to create a new player.

Now is the moment of truth. I write the URL into the browser and see what happens. Take a look at Figure 4.15. Because I set CircuitIdentifier.cfm as my layout file, I can see each circuit involved in this fuseaction request. Since I'm a new user, I click the Join Here link, which returns me to the fusebox with a fuseaction of UserAdmin.newUserForm. Note that UserAdmin.newUserForm is the value of XFA.newPlayer set in the FBX_Switch.cfm file.

The Fusebox file again runs through its processing directives for a new fuseaction, finally calling User\FBX_Switch.cfm (see Listing 4.12).

FIGURE 4.15:

Executing the default
fuseaction

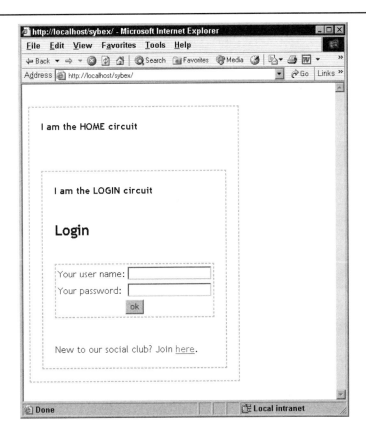

Listing 4.12   Sybex/User/FBX_Switch.cfm

```
<!---
<fusedoc fuse="FBX_Switch.cfm" version="2.0">
    I am the cfswitch statement that handles the
    fuseaction, delegating work to various fuses.
  </responsibilities>
  <io>
    <string name="Fusebox.fuseaction" />
    <string name="Fusebox.circuit" />
  </io>
</fusedoc>
--->
<cfswitch expression = "#Fusebox.fuseaction#">

  <cfcase value="main,newUserForm">
    <cfinclude template="qry_BlankUserInfo.cfm">
    <cfinclude template="qry_USstates.cfm">
```

```
      <cfset XFA.submitForm="UserAdmin.add">
      <cfset XFA.cancelForm="Login.main">
      <cfinclude template="dsp_PlayerForm.cfm">
   </cfcase>

   <cfcase value="add">
      <cfinclude template="qry_InsertPlayer.cfm">
      <cfset XFA.success="Login.validateLogin">
      <cfset XFA.failure="User.duplicateUserFound">
      <cfinclude template="url_AddPlayer.cfm">
   </cfcase>

   <cfdefaultcase>
      <cfoutput>
         I received a fuseaction called <b><font color="000066">
         #Fusebox.fuseaction#"</font></b> that circuit <b><font color="000066">
         #Fusebox.circuit#"</font></b> doesn't have a handler for.
      </cfoutput>
   </cfdefaultcase>

</cfswitch>
```

The code for the fuseaction, newUserForm, is called. The first file included is qry_BlankUser-Info.cfm (see Listing 4.13).

Listing 4.13   **Sybex/User/qry_BlankUserInfo.cfm**

```
<!---
<fusedoc fuse="qry_BlankUserInfo.cfm" version="2.0">
      I return an empty recordset
   </responsibilities>
   <properties>
      <history type="create" e-mail="hal.helms@teamallaire.com"/>
   </properties>
   <io>
      <out>
         <recordset name="MatchUser">
            <number name="userID" precision="integer" />
            <string name="firstName" />
            <string name="lastName"/>
            <string name="address" />
            <string name="city" />
            <string name="state" />
            <string name="zip" />
            <string name="territory" />
            <string name="username" />
            <string name="password" />
         </recordset>
      </out>
```

```
    </io>
  </fusedoc>
--->

<cf_QuerySim>
MatchUser
userID,firstName,lastName,address,city,state,zip,territory,username,password
</cf_QuerySim>
```

This file (qry_BlankUserInfo.cfm) calls a query sim that returns an empty row. I perform this action because I want to use dsp_PlayerForm.cfm (see Listing 4.14) to handle user additions as well as edits. I don't want to use conditional code in the form itself if I can help it (conditional code makes the page longer and messier). Rather than littering the dsp_PlayerForm.cfm with conditional logic, I have designed it to always accept a record set. When I have a new user, I simply pass in a blank recordset. When there is an existing user to edit, I will pass in a recordset containing the user's information.

Next, I call the query, qry_USstates.cfm (not included here due to space limitations). This file calls a query sim to return the names of all the states in America. As you can see, query sims are useful not only as stand-ins while real queries are being written, but in situations where you want to receive a recordset in which the information is fairly static.

Finally, two XFAs are set and, at last, dsp_PlayerForm.cfm is called (see Listing 4.14). The output of this fuseaction is shown in Figure 4.16.

Listing 4.14   **Sybex/User/dsp_PlayerForm.cfm**

```
<!---
<fusedoc fuse="dsp_PlayerForm.cfm" version="2.0">
    I provide a form for editing player information.
  </responsibilities>
  <properties>
    <history type="create" e-mail="hal.helms@teamallaire.com"/>
  </properties>
  <io>
    <in>
      <string name="self" />
      <string name="XFA.submitForm" />
      <string name="XFA.cancelForm" />
      <recordset name="MatchUser">
        <number name="userID" precision="integer" />
        <string name="firstName" />
        <string name="lastName"/>
        <string name="address" />
        <string name="city" />
        <string name="state" />
        <string name="zip" />
```

```
                    <string name="username" />
                    <string name="password" />
                </recordset>
                <recordset name="USStates">
                    <string name="stateName" />
                    <string name="st" />
                </recordset>
            </in>
            <out>
                <string name="fuseaction" scope="formOrURL" />
                <number name="userID" precision="integer" scope="formOrURL" />
                <string name="firstName" scope="formOrURL" />
                <string name="lastName" scope="formOrURL" />
                <string name="address" scope="formOrURL" />
                <string name="city" scope="formOrURL" />
                <string name="state" scope="formOrURL" />
                <string name="zip" scope="formOrURL" />
                <string name="username" scope="formOrURL" />
                <string name="password" scope="formOrURL" />
            </out>
        </io>
    </fusedoc>
--->

<h2>New Player Form</h2>

<cfoutput>

<form action="#self#?fuseaction=#XFA.submitForm#"
method="post">

<input type="Hidden" name="userID"
value="#MatchUser.userID#">
<table border="0" cellPadding="3">
    <tr>
        <td align="right">First name</td>
        <td>
            <input type="Text" name="firstName"
            value="#MatchUser.firstName#">
        </td>
    </tr>
    <tr>
        <td align="right">Last name</td>
        <td>
            <input type="Text" name="lastName"
            value="#MatchUser.lastName#">
        </td>
    </tr>
    <tr>
        <td align="right">Address</td>
        <td>
```

```
          <input type="Text" name="address"
          value="#MatchUser.address#">
      </td>
  </tr>
  <tr>
      <td align="right">City</td>
      <td>
          <input type="Text" name="city"
          value="#MatchUser.city#">
      </td>
  </tr>
  <tr>
      <td align="right">State</td>
      <td>
          <select name="state">
              <cfloop query="USStates">
                  <cfif st is MatchUser.state>
                      <cfset selectState = "selected">
                  <cfelse>
                      <cfset selectState = "">
                  </cfif>
                  <option value="#st#"
                  #selectState#>#stateName#
              </cfloop>
          </select>
      </td>
  </tr>
  <tr>
      <td align="right">Zip code</td>
      <td>
          <input type="Text" name="zip"
          value="#MatchUser.zip#">
      </td>
  </tr>
  <tr>
      <td align="right">Username</td>
      <td>
          <input type="Text" name="username"
          value="#MatchUser.username#">
      </td>
  </tr>
  <tr>
      <td align="right">Password</td>
      <td>
          <input type="password" name="password"
          value="#MatchUser.password#">
      </td>
  </tr>
  <tr>
      <td colspan="2" align="center">
          <input type="Submit" value=" ok ">
```

```
                </td>
            </tr>
        </table>

    </form>

</cfoutput>
```

FIGURE 4.16:

Executing the finished
fuseaction

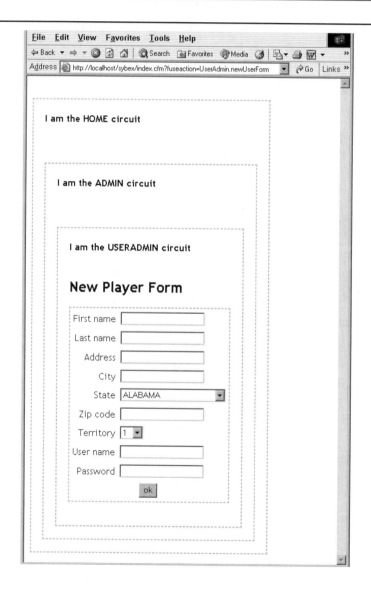

After entering the information for a new user, I click the OK button. Since XFA.submitForm was set to UserAdmin.add, the Fusebox application routes me to the UserAdmin circuit and the FBX_Switch.cfm file. First, the query qry_InsertPlayer.cfm is called. It checks for duplicates and returns statusCode, where 0 means no duplicates were found and 10 means the information submitted already belongs to a user.

I then set XFA.success and XFA.failure (one of which will be called depending on the value of statusCode) and then call url_AddPlayer.cfm (see Listing 4.15).

Listing 4.15   **Sybex/User/url_addPlayer.cfm**

```
<!---
<fusedoc fuse="url_AddPlayer.cfm" version="2.0">
    If statusCode is 0, I return to the fusebox with XFA.success;
    else I return to the fusebox with XFA.failure.
    </responsibilities>
    <properties>
        <history author="Hal Helms" />
    </properties>
    <io>
        <in>
            <number
                name="statusCode"
                precision="integer"
                comments="0 if good; 10 if dupe found" />
            <string name="XFA.success" />
            <string name="XFA.failure" />
        </in>
    </io>
</fusedoc>
--->

<cfif statusCode>
    <cflocation url="#self#?fuseaction=#XFA.failure#" addToken="yes">
<cfelse>
    <cflocation url="#self#?fuseaction=#XFA.success#&username= #attributes.
    username#&password=#attributes.password#" adTtoken="yes">
</cfif>
```

Assuming no duplicates were found, I head off to the home circuit with a fuseaction request of XFA.success, which has been resolved to Login.validateLogin. There, the FBX_Switch .cfm file sets XFAs for success and failure, calls a query file to check for a valid login, and then calls act_ValidateLogin.cfm (see Listing 4.16).

Listing 4.16   **Sybex/Login/act_ValidateLogin.cfm**

```
<!---
<fusedoc fuse="act_ValidateLogin.cfm" version="2.0">
     If MatchUser returns any records, I create
     a structure that mirrors
     the query returned and I call XFA.success; otherwise, I just call
     XFA.failure.
   </responsibilities>
   <properties>
     <history type="create" e-mail="hal.helms@teamallaire.com"/>
   </properties>
   <io>
     <in>
        <string name="self"/>
        <string name="XFA.success" />
        <string name="XFA.failure" />
        <recordset name="MatchUser">
           <number name="userID" precision="integer" />
           <string name="firstName" />
           <string name="lastName" />
           <number name="userGroups"
             precision="integer" />
        </recordset>
     </in>
     <out>
        <structure
           name="CurrentUser"
           scope="client"
           format="wddx"
           optional="true"
           onCondition="on XFA.success">
           <number name="userID" precision="integer" />
           <string name="firstName" />
           <string name="lastName" />
           <number name="userGroups"
             precision="integer" />
        </structure>
        <string name="fuseaction" scope="formOrURL"/>
     </out>
   </io>
</fusedoc>
--->

<cfoutput>

<cfif MatchUser.recordCount>
   <cfset str=StructNew()>
   <cfset str.userID=MatchUser.userID>
   <cfset str.firstName=MatchUser.firstName>
   <cfset str.lastName=MatchUser.lastName>
```

```
        <cfset str.userGroups=MatchUser.userGroups>

        <cfwddx
            action="cfml2wddx"
            input="#str#"
            output="client.CurrentUser">

        <cflocation url="#self#?fuseaction=#XFA.success#" addToken="yes">
    <cfelse>
        <cflocation url="#self#?fuseaction=#XFA.failure#"  addToken="yes">
    </cfif>

    </cfoutput>
```

If a valid user was found, XFA.success (set to Player.main) executes. The Player\FBX_Switch .cfm file finds a fuseaction called main and first calls two queries to retrieve last week's winning number and player's pick. An XFA for makeBet is set, and the file dsp_PlayerHome.cfm is called (see Listing 4.17).

Listing 4.17   Sybex/Player/dsp_PlayerHome.cfm

```
<!---
<fusedoc fuse="dsp_PlayerHome.cfm" version="2.0">
    I greet the user, show them last week's winning number, and let them make
a bet with the default number and amount from any bet made last week.
</responsibilities>
<properties>
    <history type="create" e-mail="hal.helms@teamallaire.com"/>
</properties>
<io>
    <in>
        <string name="self" />
        <string name="XFA.makeBet" />

        <recordset name="LastWeeksWinningNumber">
            <number name="winningNumber" />
        </recordset>

        <recordset name="LastWeeksPick.cfm">
            <number name="numberBet" />
            <number name="amountBet" />
        </recordset>

        <structure
            name="currentUser"
            scope="client"
            format="wddx">
            <number name="userID" precision="integer" />
            <string name="firstName" />
            <string name="lastName" />
```

```
                <number name="userGroups" precision="integer" />
            </structure>
        </in>
        <out>
            <string name="fuseaction" scope="formOrURL" />
            <number name="userID" precision="integer" scope="formorURL" />
            <number name="numberBet" precision="integer" scope="formOrURL" />
            <number name="weekBet" precision="integer" scope="formOrURL" />
            <number name="amountBet" precision="integer" scope="formOrURL" />
        </out>
    </io>
</fusedoc>
--->

<cfoutput>

<cfwddx
    action="WDDX2CFML"
    input="#client.CurrentUser#"
    output="Player">

<h2>Welcome, #Player.firstName#</h2>
<h4>Last week, the lucky winning number was
#LastWeeksWinningNumber.winningNumber#.</h4>

<p>Time to place your bet!</p>
<font size="2">For your convenience, if you
made a bet last week, we've
prefilled your bet form with last week's bet.</font>

<form action="#self#?fuseaction=#XFA.makeBet#" method="post">
    <input type="hidden" name="weekBet" value="#Week( now() )#">
    <input type="hidden" name="userID" value="#Player.userID#">
    <table border="0" cellPadding="3">
        <tr>
            <td align="right">
                Your number
            </td>
            <td>
                <input type="Text" name="numberBet"
                    value="#LastWeeksPick.numberBet#">
            </td>
        </tr>
        <tr>
            <td align="right">
                Your donation
            </td>
            <td>
                <input type="Text" name="amountBet"
                value="#LastWeeksPick.amountBet#">
            </td>
```

```
        </tr>
        <tr>
          <td colspan="2" align="center">
            <input type="Submit" value=" ok ">
          </td>
        </tr>
      </table>
    </form>

  </cfoutput>
```

At the end of this process, we have a user who is registered, logged in, and validated, and can now make "donations" to Vinny's social club, as shown in Figure 4.17. (Remember—you can download the entire working application from `http://www.halhelms.com`.)

FIGURE 4.17:

The player's
main page

In Sum

Fusebox offers developers a well-crafted framework for building web applications. After you determine the circuits, fuseactions, and fuses your application will need, you combine your own application-specific code with the Fusebox core files freely available from `http://www.fusebox.org`. Nested layouts provide a powerful way of separating content from layout.

You can use the Fusebox framework to build anything from simple websites to large, complex applications. Combined with the powerful project management features of FLiP and the free tools available for FLiP, you may find—as thousands of other developers have—that Fusebox provides a great deal of power within an easy-to-learn framework.

CHAPTER 5

Developing Component-Based Applications

By Guy Rish

- Object-oriented concepts within CFML: construction, encapsulation, inheritance, and polymorphism

- Applying object-oriented concepts in your work with CFCs

- An example of applying object-oriented design concepts to a ColdFusion application

One of the most important improvements in ColdFusion MX is ColdFusion Components (CFCs). A CFC is an object-like construct that provides a way to develop reusable components using CFML. Many of the basic tenets of object-oriented software development can be expressed with CFCs; for many ColdFusion developers this opens a whole new field of exploration.

This chapter discusses a number of application-development practices with the intention of helping the novice better apply the new CFC feature. The chapter explores certain CFML language features in some detail, including CFC syntax and tags such as cfcomponent, but it is not meant to be a guide to these features. It is meant to help fine-tune your understanding of CFC concepts and to assist you in discovering ways of applying CFCs to their best advantage.

NOTE   For more extensive coverage of CFCs and tags such as cfcomponent, please refer to Macromedia's own online product documentation or Sybex's *Mastering ColdFusion MX,* by Arman Danesh, et al. (Sybex, 2002).

Object-Oriented Concepts within CFML

A CFC is not a point-for-point class construct to that of other languages. To be sure, it embodies many of the features important to an object-oriented language, such as abstraction and inheritance. On the other hand, CFML can be written without using CFCs, and CFCs are not required to uphold all of the tenets widely held as necessary for object-oriented languages. Thus CFML cannot be considered a pure object-oriented language. This does not, however, prevent you from applying many of the same techniques when you are working with CFCs.

This section of the chapter presents the construction of a few very simple components. These CFCs are deliberately simple to better focus your attention on certain object-oriented characteristics like instance construction, inheritance, overriding, and polymorphism.

Instance Construction

Most object-oriented languages support some mechanism for the initialization of an instance, often called a *constructor*, but CFML does not. There is, however, a workaround that can achieve much the same effect. Any code within the body of the cfcomponent tag that constitutes a component, and that does not belong to a specific function, will be executed when an instance of that component is created by the interpreter. This code can act as the component's constructor.

A simple example of this workaround is shown in Listing 5.1.

Listing 5.1   **Simple Component Construction (person.cfc)**

```
01: <!---
02:     File            /c05/person.cfc
03:     Description      Simple CFC with a constructor.
04: --->
05: <cfcomponent>
06:     <!--- begin "constructor" --->
07:     <cfscript>
08:         constructor();
09:     </cfscript>
10:     <cffunction name="constructor" access="private">
11:         <cfparam name="this.title" default="Citizen">
12:     </cffunction>
13:     <!--- end "constructor" --->
14:
15:     <cffunction name="identify" returnType="string">
16:         <cfset str = "I am a #this.getTitle()#">
17:         <cfreturn str>
18:     </cffunction>
19: </cfcomponent>
```

When the component gets instantiated it immediately executes the `cfscript` block on lines 7–9. This code, which lies between the commented begin and end "constructor" lines, calls the private `constructor` method. This method creates a variable called `title` within the `this` scope. The `title` variable is then properly initialized when there is a call to the `identify` method, as demonstrated in the template in Listing 5.2.

Listing 5.2   **Constructor Demonstration (ConstructorExample1.cfm)**

```
01: <!---
02:     File            /c05/ConstructorExample1.cfm
03:     Description      Demonstrates the instantiation
04:         of a CFC with a constructor-like workaround.
05: --->
06: <html>
07: <head>
08:     <title>Constructor Example 1</title>
09: </head>
10:
11: <body>
12:     <cfscript>
13:         inst = createObject("component",
14:             "handbook.c05.person");
15:         writeOutput(inst.identify());
16:     </cfscript>
17: </body>
18: </html>
```

This example is straightforward enough. An instance of the `person` component is created on lines 13–14, within a `cfscript` block, as the variable `inst`. The string returned from a call to the `identify` method is immediately passed to `writeOutput`. Unfortunately, because component construction is done through an uncontrolled process, it is impossible to create a *parameterized constructor*. A parameterized constructor is a constructor that takes arguments to help determine the way the instance is initialized. Since this kind of functionality does not exist in CFML, additional methods must be created to further initialize internal data, such as loading records from a database. Unfortunately though, the developer must know to invoke these methods as part of the normal usage of the component.

> **WARNING** Notice on lines 13 and 14 of Listing 5.2 that the component is created by specifying the CFC in lowercase. On all non-Windows platforms, ColdFusion MX forces CFCs to be lowercase. This means that it is good development practice to save CFC source files as a lowercase filename as well. In addition, don't use mixed case for names composed of compound words. This will make a component viable on whatever platform it is distributed.

Encapsulation

Encapsulation involves hiding data and other internal mechanisms, and it is one of the pillars of object-oriented development. This act of covering internal variables and allowing them to be accessed only through methods that retrieve (*get* methods) and assign (*set* methods) their values allows an interface for the component to develop. These methods, sometimes called *accessor methods*, become part of a component's interface. You can use these methods to interact with the component data reliably without needing to know how the data is stored or, in some cases, how other values are derived based upon other values passed into the component via accessor methods. As a result of this interaction, you can allow the component to evolve internally without worrying about whether the code that is using the component will break every time you make a subtle change.

An example of the kind of protection encapsulation provides is the hypothetical case of a component that begins by storing a set of strings that becomes a structure, which then eventually evolves into fields within a query. If this data were not hidden behind get and set methods, every time you changed the data storage mechanism, you would need to update all of the templates that were using this component.

> **WARNING** Although it is wise to use accessor methods for interacting with variables, nothing in CFML prevents another developer from circumventing your established interface. Basically, any of the variables that you place in the `this` scope are available through direct access; it is this that makes the act of data hiding more of a conceptual exercise than a reality in CFML.

Listing 5.3 shows an evolution of the person component; it now has two new accessor
methods: getTitle and setTitle.

Listing 5.3   Accessor Methods (person.cfc)

```
01: <!---
02:     File           /c05/person.cfc
03:     Description     Simple CFC with accessor
04:         methods and constructor.
05: --->
06: <cfcomponent>
07:     <!--- begin "constructor" --->
08:     <cfscript>
09:         constructor();
10:     </cfscript>
11:     <cffunction name="constructor" access="private">
12:         <cfparam name="this.title" default="Citizen">
13:     </cffunction>
14:     <!--- end "constructor" --->
15:
16:     <cffunction name="identify" returnType="string">
17:         <cfset str = "I am a #this.getTitle()#">
18:         <cfreturn str>
19:     </cffunction>
20:
21:     <cffunction name="getTitle" returnType="string">
22:         <cfreturn this.title>
23:     </cffunction>
24:
25:     <cffunction name="setTitle">
26:         <cfargument name="newTitle"
27:             type="string" default="Citizen">
28:         <cfset this.title = newTitle>
29:     </cffunction>
30: </cfcomponent>
```

The new methods, getTitle on lines 21–23 and setTitle on lines 25–29, provide a controlled
access point from which you can manipulate the title variable. Another important alteration
occurs inside the identify method on line 17; here the getTitle method is being used to
retrieve the title value instead of accessing the title variable directly. Now even the component
uses its own interface to shield itself from alterations; using the accessor method like this will
likely reduce the number of lines of code that you will need to change at some later date.

Inheritance

Inheritance is one of the core features of component reuse. In fact, it is a natural extension of
the idea of simple reuse. Simple reuse is viable when the component in question can be used

again without its existing functionality being changed. Prior to the formalization of inheritance in programming languages, a component had to be directly altered if the opportunity for reuse did not fit exactly with the component's current functionality. Now, using inheritance, you can create a new component to handle the specific case, and you can amend new functionality to the old without altering the code of the original. The original component is known as the parent or the *superclass*; the new derived component is known as the child or the *subclass*. It can be said that the derived component has subclassed the parent.

Using the subclass to override methods and variables in the this scope is far more useful than adding new methods or altering existing methods in the superclass.

Overriding Methods and Variables

In addition to letting you simply acquire functionality from another component, inheritance allows you to override component methods so that the new subclass you create can use the same method name to create a wholly new method. You would call this new method instead of the method of the same name belonging to the superclass. Externally, the subclass's method would still appear to be exactly like the method it is overriding, with the same access and return type, but its functionality might be decidedly different. This not only applies to methods, but also to the variables in the this scope as well.

The employee component, shown in Listing 5.4, demonstrates overriding a method.

Listing 5.4   **Inherited Component (employee.cfc)**

```
01: <!---
02:     File            /c05/employee.cfc
03:     Description     Simple CFC that inherits
04:            from Person and overrides superclass'
05:            functionality.
06: --->
07: <cfcomponent extends="handbook.c05.person">
08:     <!--- begin "constructor" --->
09:     <cfscript>
10:         constructor();
11:     </cfscript>
12:     <cffunction name="constructor" access="private">
13:         <cfset this.title = "Employee">
14:     </cffunction>
15:     <!--- end "constructor" --->
16:
17:     <cffunction name="identify" returnType="string">
18:         <cfset str =
19:             "Designation is #this.getTitle()#">
20:         <cfreturn str>
21:     </cffunction>
22: </cfcomponent>
```

Line 7 shows the superclass of the component in the `extends` attribute of `cfcomponent`, `person`. Then on line 13, the value of `title` is overridden in the component's faked constructor. Finally, on lines 17–21, the new `identify` method is introduced. Notice that all of the attributes of `cffunction` have the same values at the method definition as they did in `person.cfc` (see Listing 5.3 above), but the actual work done here by `cffunction` is different.

A quick execution of this component, shown in Listing 5.5, displays this new functionality.

Listing 5.5   **Inheritance Demonstration (InheritanceExample1.cfm)**

```
01: <!---
02:     File            /c05/InheritanceExample1.cfm
03:     Description      Instantiating a subclass.
04: --->
05: <html>
06: <head>
07:     <title>Inheritance Example 1</title>
08: </head>
09:
10: <body>
11:     <cfscript>
12:         inst = createObject("component",
13:             "handbook.c05.employee");
14:         writeOutput(inst.identify());
15:     </cfscript>
16: </body>
17: </html>
```

Direct Assignment versus cfparam

Closer examination of the two components `person` (Listing 5.3) and `employee` (Listing 5.4) shows that the override of the `title` variable was done with a direct variable assignment within the components' `constructor` methods. It is important that you understand this because it speaks to the component's lifecycle.

For instance, you could assume that, within the `employee` component, the `title` variable could have defaulted just as easily as it did in `person`. However, because this variable has already been `cfparam`'d into existence by the superclass, `person`, if you try to do so again in the subclass, `employee`, you will not get the desired results.

A new version of the component, `employee2` (Listing 5.6), sets up this condition.

Listing 5.6   **Flawed Employee Component (employee2.cfc)**

```
01: <!---
02:     File            /c05/employee2.cfc
03:     Description      Simple CFC that can be used
```

```
04:            to demonstrate the dangers of using cfparam
05:            to override inherited variables.
06: --->
07: <cfcomponent extends="handbook.c05.person">
08:     <!--- begin "constructor" --->
09:     <cfscript>
10:         constructor();
11:     </cfscript>
12:     <cffunction name="constructor" access="private">
13:         <cfparam name="this.title" default="Employee">
14:     </cffunction>
15:     <!--- end "constructor" --->
16:
17:     <cffunction name="identify" returntype="string">
18:         <cfset str =
19:             "Designation is #this.getTitle()#">
20:         <cfreturn str>
21:     </cffunction>
22: </cfcomponent>
```

Line 13 presents a cfparam of the title variable instead of the direct assignment done with cfset on line 13 of the original employee component, Listing 5.4. Using cfparam like this does not produce the desired effect when executed from the template shown in Listing 5.7.

Listing 5.7   **Demonstrating the Flawed Employee Component (InheritanceExample2.cfm)**

```
01: <!---
02:     File          /c05/InheritanceExample2.cfm
03:     Description    Instantiating a different subclass.
04: --->
05: <html>
06: <head>
07:     <title>Inheritance Example 2</title>
08: </head>
09:
10: <body>
11:     <cfscript>
12:         inst = createObject("component",
13:             "handbook.c05.employee2");
14:         writeOutput(inst.identify());
15:     </cfscript>
16: </body>
17: </html>
```

When this template is run, "Designation is Employee" is displayed quickly in the browser. This may not be what you were expecting if you had the component assigned a value of "Employee" to the title variable. But everything is working as it should, even if it is not what we desired. The variable title does indeed exist already when line 13 in the employee2 component is executed, the variable was `cfparam`'d into existence in the component's super-class, so the call to `cfparam` in `employee2` does nothing; as it should.

Polymorphism

In polymorphism, another major tenet of object-oriented programming, one component outwardly appears like another and can, in some cases, be used just as well as another. Poly-morphism is exhibited by components that all derive from the same superclass somewhere in their line of inheritance. They all, whatever their current form, can also appear as their common superclass.

To exemplify this you need a component that handles other components. Specifically given the example of the component, `greeting`, shown in Listing 5.8 below, designed to handle a person instance through its `greet` method.

Listing 5.8   Polymorphic Friendly Component (greeting.cfc)

```
01: <!---
02:     File            /c05/greeting.cfc
03:     Description      Simple CFC with a method
04:         that uses another CFC instance as an argument.
05: --->
06: <cfcomponent>
07:     <cffunction name="greet" returnType="string">
08:         <cfargument name="who"
09:             type="handbook.c05.person">
10:         <cfset str = "Greetings, #who.getTitle()#">
11:         <cfreturn str>
12:     </cffunction>
13: </cfcomponent>
```

The `greet` method can just as easily accept `employee` component instances as well, because `employee` inherits from `person`. This is successfully demonstrated in the template shown in Listing 5.9.

Listing 5.9   Polymorphic Demonstration (PolymorphExample1.cfm)

```
01: <!---
02:     File            /c05/PolymorphExample1.cfm
03:     Description      Using a superclass as the argument
04:         to a method.
05: --->
06: <html>
07: <head>
08:     <title>Polymorph Example 1</title>
09: </head>
```

```
10:
11: <body>
12:     <cfscript>
13:         greeter = createObject("component",
14:             "handbook.c05.greeting");
15:         who = createObject("component",
16:             "handbook.c05.employee");
17:
18:         writeOutput(greeter.greet(who));
19:     </cfscript>
20: </body>
21: </html>
```

By creating utility components that work with the earliest members of a hierarchy, you can help increase the reusability of the component with later members of the hierarchy. These later descendants can be leveraged within the hypothetical utility component because of their shared lineage.

Now that you understand how polymorphism works you can begin to explore the idea of interface components. Interface components provide a common definition for other components that inherit from them. This allows for other components to treat everything that subclasses the interface component in one common way.

Interface Components

An interface comprises a component's individual API as a whole—all of the methods and all of the public variables. It has already been demonstrated that a component derived of another inherits the interface of the superclass. Some languages, including Java, allow classes to have multiple interfaces without inheritance. Acquiring multiple interfaces is done through special types of classes called interface classes. Interface classes define methods, the method's name, and the arguments, but they do not implement any functionality in these methods. Once these elements are defined, a class can then *implement* these interfaces outside of the regular line of inheritance, which increases opportunities for polymorphic reuse. The implementing class provides the functionality for each of the methods defined in the interface class.

Unfortunately CFCs do not have this kind of capability. But looking at the interface mechanism in other languages might help you design better component hierarchies. For example, if two components have very similar needs, you could standardize and control their interface by having them both subclass from the same component. This other, base component would implement no direct functionality of its own; its only use would be to define the methods, thus establishing a common interface. Each of the subclassing components would have to override these methods in order to implement their own, perhaps diverse, means of manipulating data. The subclasses could, however, be handled identically by other components, because externally, they support the same interfaces.

Interfacing with Components: the MVC Pattern

Sometimes you may wonder whether or not a component should be able to display its own user interface for interacting with its properties and methods. While this may seem like a good idea sometimes, setting a component up this way will quickly prove to be unwieldy as the component becomes larger and/or must address a number of different browsers and devices.

Given a hypothetical collection of components and templates, keeping user interface elements out the component logic is almost always best. In fact, keeping all display logic out of a component but building it such that it provides a rich interface for manipulating its data will make the component more useful to a template that must address multiple display platforms. Components that do this are often called business objects, while the templates that interact with them to create the user interface are called, collectively, the presentation layer. This separation sets the groundwork for the implementation of what is called the Model-View-Controller (MVC) pattern. You don't need advanced knowledge of computer science or years of software development to use this pattern; most web applications implement a portion of this pattern simply by virtue of the rules of the environment.

The MVC pattern identifies three things; the model or component, the view or form page, and the controller or the form action. Although most ColdFusion applications use a form and action to move data in and out of a database, they do not truly implement an MVC pattern. This is because the database does not act like a component does.

Now with the CFC feature of ColdFusion MX, a MVC pattern becomes more fully realized. Now business logic and function can be encapsulated within a component, data can be requested from that component while a form is being created, and when the form posts the action page, the form can interact with the component to pass data into the component. Where the component got that data or what it does it is wholly unimportant to the user interface of the application, the view, and the controller portions of the pattern.

Applying the Concepts

Now that we have reviewed the object-oriented concepts that apply to ColdFusion MX, it is time to learn some ways of applying them. These kinds of discussions can sometimes become very heady when drawn from the more academic crowd, but this will not be the case with this text. Instead, this discussion will be decidedly aimed at practical applications.

Creating Components

Discovering and writing a component are cornerstone tasks of building a component-based system. You begin this discovery process by combing through the requirements documentation.

As you read this documentation you will have to tease apart the details. Some helpful exercises and tips for identifying components from the text are here:

Finding components   If we assume that the project in question has a whole set of business requirements completed, finding components can be rather simple. Merely scanning through the requirements documents will often turn up, usually in the form of the sentences' nouns, the components that need to be created. These components should represent some sort of physical or logical construct, which by definition is what nouns identify.

Identifying methods   Again a grammatical construct will come to our aid when we go to determine the methods that should be created for a given component. Just as a component can be identified from the nouns in the requirements documentation, the methods can be drawn from the actions, or the verbs, associated with those nouns.

Identifying properties   Sometimes a noun is not a component by itself; instead it is an attribute associated with something that is already identified as a component. These cases often occur with component properties, pieces of information belonging to a component. Sometimes it is difficult to determine if these bits of information are wholly subsumed in ownership of a component or if they will eventually become smaller components themselves. This is something that typically evolves over the life of the development cycle. Thus something that started out as a set of strings or a structure within one component might become a whole component in its own right.

Distilling interfaces   Once some of the components, and their methods and properties, of a system have been identified, you can begin to examine what you've identified for commonalities. Larger systems usually mean larger numbers of components, but often many of these objects are similar in nature. Chances are you will be able to see inheritance relationships right away as you look over your list of identified components. This can even lead you to narrowing down reusable interfaces.

Chances are that you will read through the requirements documentation multiple times. You might consider trying to find ways of logically grouping the documentation so that you can focus on specific aspects of the system being described. The denser the documentation, the more passes you will have to make. A separate pass each for finding components, identifying the methods, identifying the properties, and distilling interfaces is not an uncommon approach.

An Example of Applying Object-Oriented Design Concepts to a ColdFusion Application

It is beyond the scope of this book to provide a fully featured example that walks step-by-step through the process of creating business requirements, decomposing it into components, establishing the whole flow of the MVC, and presenting the annotated code listings. Instead, we will skim the surface of these ideas and practices with a story problem: a description of a business need, the creation of some simple components gleaned from the description, the abstraction of those components to create an interface, and finally some templates to provide a search interface.

The example revolves around a project to unify the interface of two corporate address books.

The AddressBook Story

Company X needs to provide a web-based interface that provides unified access to their customer contacts database (the Sales database) and the corporate employee directory (an enterprise-wide LDAP implementation).

The user interface must be browser friendly and require as few plugins and downloadable components as possible so that it will be available to the maximum number of browser types and devices. In addition, users should be able to manipulate the customer and employee data to create new records and to edit and delete existing records. What's more, the user interface should provide a way to handle this data that is as seamless as possible so that the user is unaware of the two different data sources.

Identifying Components

If you reread the preceding description of the AddressBook that you are supposed to create for your client, you can probably pick out the two kinds of entries, customers and employees, easily. These entries seem like two very logical components to construct. However, what you might not be immediately aware of is the opportunity you have to use an interface component.

As you may recall, the point of this AddressBook is to provide your client with a way to manipulate both customers and employees from one interface, despite the fact that the data for these two groups is stored in two different locations. Both the locations have the same kinds of information, but one is stored in the Sales database and the other is in an LDAP server (perhaps Microsoft's Active Directory).

So, first you must identify the common kinds of operations that would be shared by both kinds of records. For simplicity's sake Listing 5.10 defines such an interface.

Listing 5.10   AddressBook Entry Interface (addressbookentry.cfc)

```
01: <!---
02:     File            /c05/addressbookentry.cfc
03:     Description     A CFC that establishes an
04:         interface for the AddressBook application.
05: --->
06: <cfcomponent>
```

```
07:        <!--- begin "constructor" --->
08:        <cfscript>
09:            constructor();
10:        </cfscript>
11:        <cffunction name="constructor">
12:            <cfscript>
13:                this.SEARCH_LASTNAME = 1;
14:                this.SEARCH_CITY = 2;
15:                this.SEARCH_STATE = 3;
16:                this.record = structNew();
17:                this.record.firstName = "";
18:                this.record.lastName = "";
19:                this.record.address1 = "";
20:                this.record.address2 = "";
21:                this.record.city = "";
22:                this.record.state = "";
23:                this.record.zipcode = "";
24:                this.record.phone = "";
25:                this.record.email = "";
26:            </cfscript>
27:        </cffunction>
28:        <!--- end "constructor" --->
29:
30:        <cffunction name="findEntry" returnType="struct">
31:            <cfargument name="searchType"
32:                type="numeric" default="1">
33:            <cfargument name="searchCriteria"
34:                type="string" required="Yes">
35:
36:            <!--- return dummy query --->
37:            <cfreturn this.record>
38:        </cffunction>
39:
40:        <cffunction name="updateEntry">
41:            <cfargument name="key"
42:                type="string" required="yes">
43:            <cfargument name="record"
44:                type="struct" required="yes">
45:        </cffunction>
46:
47:        <cffunction name="addEntry">
48:            <cfargument name="record"
49:                type="struct" required="yes">
50:        </cffunction>
51:
52:        <cffunction name="deleteEntry">
53:            <cfargument name="key"
54:                type="string" required="yes">
55:        </cffunction>
56: </cfcomponent>
```

The addressbookentry interface component defines a structure in the faked constructor (lines 11–27) and defines four methods: findEntry, updateEntry, addEntry, and deleteEntry. You don't actually have to write code for any of these methods within this CFC because these methods are only being used to define an interface. The structure that is defined in constructor will be the format that is returned from the findEntry, and it is this structure that is passed into addEntry and updateEntry.

> **NOTE**   Actually, the statement in the preceding paragraph is a bit misleading. Some additional code was required for the addressbookentry CFC so that it didn't cause the CFML inter- preter to complain. Because the findEntry method returns a query, we had to add a cfreturn to the body of the method and we had to create an empty query object as the value to be returned. This value is unimportant because the addressbookentry compo- nent is not really meant to be instantiated and all of the subclasses will override the findEntry method.

By using the interface established by the addressbookentry component, you can implement the customer and employee components. The actual details of how these components are implemented are unimportant to this example since they will both have the same interface.

Abstracting Component Types

Since there is a common interface for two different records, it makes sense to use a Factory design pattern. Then, based upon the page's request data, either URL parameters or form values, the correct component subclass can be instantiated.

> **NOTE**   A Factory design pattern is a fancy name for a component that knows how to create instances of other components.

recordfactory, shown in Listing 5.11, does this very thing. It implements a single method, create. The create method takes one string argument—the kind of record to create—and returns an addressbookentry instance.

Listing 5.11   AddressBook Record Factory (recordfactory.cfc)

```
01: <!---
02:     File            /c05/recordfactory.cfc
03:     Description     A CFC factory for creating
04:         AddressBookEntry instances.
05: --->
06: <cfcomponent>
07:     <cffunction name="create"
08:         returnType="handbook.c05.addressbookentry">
```

```
09:          <cfargument name="type"
10:              type="string" required="yes">
11:
12:          <cfswitch expression="#lCase(arguments.type)#">
13:              <cfcase value="customer">
14:                  <cfset inst = createObject("component",
15:                      "handbook.c05.customer")>
16:              </cfcase>
17:
18:              <cfcase value="employee">
19:                  <cfset inst = createObject("component",
20:                      "handbook.c05.employee")>
21:              </cfcase>
22:
23:              <cfdefaultcase>
24:                  <cfthrow message="Unknown request!">
25:              </cfdefaultcase>
26:          </cfswitch>
27:          <cfreturn inst>
28:      </cffunction>
29: </cfcomponent>
```

The decision-making process within the `create` method is done via `cfswitch`, which creates either a `customer` or an `employee` instance depending upon the value of the incoming string argument.

The Record Search

You can also construct a simple form search that allows the user to select either Customer or Employee records and the type of search (by last name, city, or state) they want to perform. You can also construct an input field in which the user can enter the string with which to run the search. This is done in the template shown in Listing 5.12.

Listing 5.12   **Search Form**

```
01: <!---
02:     File           /c05/SearchForm.cfm
03:     Description    Find an AddressBook record.
04: --->
05: <html>
06: <head>
07:     <title>Search Form</title>
08: </head>
09:
10: <body>
11: <form name="AddressBookSearchForm" method="post"
12:     action="SearchAction.cfm">
```

```
13:    <table border="0">
14:       <caption>AddressBook Search</caption>
15:       <tr>
16:          <td bgColor="silver">Record Type</td>
17:          <td>
18:             <select name="recordType">
19:                <option value="customer">
20:                Customer
21:                </option>
22:                <option value="employee">
23:                Employee
24:                </option>
25:             </select>
26:          </td>
27:       </tr>
28:       <tr>
29:          <td bgColor="silver">Search Type</td>
30:          <td>
31:             <select name="searchType">
32:                <option value="1">
33:                Last Name
34:                </option>
35:                <option value="2">
36:                City
37:                </option>
38:                <option value="3">
39:                State
40:                </option>
41:             </select>
42:          </td>
43:       </tr>
44:       <tr>
45:          <td bgColor="silver">Search Criteria</td>
46:          <td>
47:             <input type="text" name="criteria">
48:          </td>
49:       </tr>
50:       <tr>
51:          <td align="right" colSpan="2">
52:             <input type="submit" value="Search">
53:          </td>
54:       </tr>
55:    </table>
56: </form>
57: </body>
58: </html>
```

The back end of this form is shown in Listing 5.13.

Listing 5.13   Search Action (SearchAction.cfm)

```
01: <!---
02:     File             /c05/SearchAction.cfm
03:     Description      The action page for the
04:         addressbookentry search.
05: --->
06: <cfscript>
07:     factory = createObject("component",
08:         "handbook.c05.recordfactory");
09:
10:     recordInst = factory.create(form.recordType);
11:
12:     recordData = recordInst.findEntry(form.searchType,
13:         form.criteria);
14: </cfscript>
15:
16: <cfoutput>
17:     <table>
18:         <tr>
19:             <td>First Name</td>
20:             <td>#recordData.firstName#</td>
21:         </tr>
22:         <tr>
23:             <td>Last Name</td>
24:             <td>#recordData.lastName#</td>
25:         </tr>
26:         <tr>
27:             <td>Address</td>
28:             <td>#recordData.address1#</td>
29:         </tr>
30:         <tr>
31:             <td> </td>
32:             <td>#recordData.address2#</td>
33:         </tr>
34:         <tr>
35:             <td>City</td>
36:             <td>#recordData.city#</td>
37:         </tr>
38:         <tr>
39:             <td>State</td>
40:             <td>#recordData.state#</td>
41:         </tr>
42:         <tr>
43:             <td>Zipcode</td>
44:             <td>#recordData.zipcode#</td>
45:         </tr>
46:         <tr>
47:             <td>Phone</td>
48:             <td>#recordData.phone#</td>
```

```
49:            </tr>
50:            <tr>
51:                <td>Email</td>
52:                <td>#recordData.email#</td>
53:            </tr>
54:        </table>
55: </cfoutput>
```

The most important portion of this template exists within the `cfscript` block at the top on lines 6–14. First, a `recordfactory` instance is created on lines 7–8. This instance is then used to create an `addressbookentry` subclass instance on line 10. The `recordfactory` drives its instance creation from the `type` variable passed from the form, the first `select` displayed by `SearchForm.cfm` (Listing 5.12). The `findEntry` method of the `addressbookentry` subclass is then called, passing the two remaining fields (`searchType` and `criteria`) from the form and saving the returned structure to the variable `recordData`.

The remainder of the template (lines 16–55) is the output of the `recordData` structure, formatted in a `table`.

In Sum

The addition of ColdFusion Components to CFML provides a rich feature set that helps you to apply many of the tenets of object-oriented development, such as encapsulation, inheritance, and polymorphism, for the construction of considerably more-sophisticated applications. Of even greater importance is that CFCs provide you with the opportunity to use design patterns, such as MVC and Factory, to increase the stability and flexibility of your ColdFusion MX applications. All of these things will have broad-reaching ramifications for the ColdFusion developer for years to come. More than custom tags and user-defined functions, CFCs will bring a whole new depth of reusability to ColdFusion applications that will far exceed anything to date.

CHAPTER 6

Creating Search Engines with Verity

By Arman Danesh

- Understanding the basics of Verity

- Creating collections and indexing them with `cfcollection` and `cfindex`

- Providing search forms for users

- Indexing and searching multiple languages

- Indexing and searching documents in different formats

- Automatically indexing your collections

- Optimizing your collections

The ColdFusion product line includes the Verity indexing and search engine, which allows you to search the content of your site. With Verity, you can index static documents such as HTML files, Microsoft Word documents, Adobe Acrobat files, and text files, as well as search the contents of database tables using its full-text search abilities.

This chapter reviews the basics of creating collections and indexing data and then searching those indexes; it then goes on to discuss the more general issues of what constitutes a useful, and usable, search engine interface environment for users of your website. These subjects include the following:

- Presenting results in a useful and meaningful way

- Presenting results one page at a time

- Providing query-building assistance

- Indicating file types with icons

In addition, this chapter discusses advanced topics such as automatic, scheduled indexing of content, indexing multilingual content, and optimizing Verity.

The Basics of Verity

Verity is a third-party full text search engine that Macromedia licenses for inclusion in Cold-Fusion Professional and Enterprise servers. Macromedia has integrated Verity into the ColdFusion environment so that you can manage it and index content from the ColdFusion Administrator or using special ColdFusion tags provided for these purposes.

The basic process of using Verity in ColdFusion is as follows:

1. Create a collection   A *collection* is a container for a single set of information that you want indexed and searched. You can have more than one collection and can search them independently. Collections can be created with the `cfcollection` tag or through the Cold-Fusion Administrator.

2. Index data   In each collection, you specify one or more documents or a database query result to be indexed. The index is stored in the collection. Indexing can be done with the `cfindex` tag or using the ColdFusion Administrator.

3. Search the data   Once a set of information has been indexed in a collection, you can search that data in your templates using the `cfsearch` tag.

Creating Collections

The collection is the basis for building searchable content in ColdFusion using Verity. A collection can be used to index a set of documents, such as web pages, Word documents, or text files, or it can be used to index data returned by ColdFusion queries, such as those retrieved from a database table.

You can create multiple collections for your needs, such as creating subject-specific indexes by indexing different subdirectories in different collections, indexing different file formats in different collections, or indexing different database queries in their own collections.

The ColdFusion Administrator allows you to create a collection using the Verity Collections page of the ColdFusion Administrator, which is illustrated in Figure 6.1. Using this page you can create collections in two ways:

By creating a new collection   You should use this if you are using the version of Verity included in ColdFusion. We will assume this is the case throughout this chapter.

By mapping to an existing collection   If you have an existing Verity server, mapping makes its collections accessible from within ColdFusion. These collections are known as external collections.

FIGURE 6.1:

The Verity Collections page of the ColdFusion Administrator

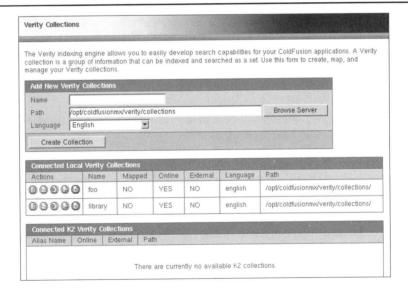

NOTE   In ColdFusion MX, you don't need to manually map external collections. ColdFusion automatically detects and maps these collections.

The steps for creating the collection are straightforward. First, specify a name, path, and language for the collection. The name is used later in your ColdFusion templates to actually search the indexes contained in the collection. The path is the path that Verity can use to store the indexes for the collection; typically it is `C:\cfusionmx\verity\collections\` if you installed ColdFusion in the default location (`C:\cfusionmx\`). The language you specify is the language that will be used when indexing data in a collection, and it is important to choose the language you plan to index, since this will determine how the indexing engine interprets word roots and other lexical structures in the text being indexed.

Having specified the name, path, and language of your collection, click the Create Collection button. The ColdFusion Administrator will create the collection and add it to the list of Connected Local Verity Collections in the bottom part of the Verity Collections page.

There are a few important points to note about your collections. First a collection can only have one language. There is no provision for multilingual collections.

In addition, you do not need to specify a different path for each collection. Verity will create a subdirectory in the location you specify for the collection. For this reason, it is possible, and easiest, to specify the same location for all your collections. Then, if ColdFusion is installed in the default location, the collection `foo` would actually be stored in the directory `C:\cfusionmx\verity\collections\foo\`, the collection `foo2` would actually be stored in the directory `C:\cfusionmx\verity\collections\foo2\`, and so on.

Indexing Data

Once a collection is created, you need to index data in the collection. You can create two types of indexes:

Indexes of static files on disk   This can be done with the ColdFusion Administrator and is discussed in this section.

Indexes of dynamic query results   This must be done with the `cfindex` tag and is discussed later in the section "Using `cfindex` and `cfcollection`."

Indexing static files is a straightforward operation:

1. Identify the index from the Connected Local Verity Collections section in the bottom part of the Verity Collections page.

2. Click the Index icon to the left of the collection name. The ColdFusion Administrator will open the Index Verity Collections page similar to the one illustrated in Figure 6.2.

3. Provide the following information in the indexing form: The file extensions of files you want to index, the path of the directory to index, an indication of whether you want to recursively index subdirectories under the selected index, and a URL for the directory you are planning to index.

4. Click the Submit button. Verity will index the specified files and store them in the collection.

FIGURE 6.2:

Indexing a Verity
collection

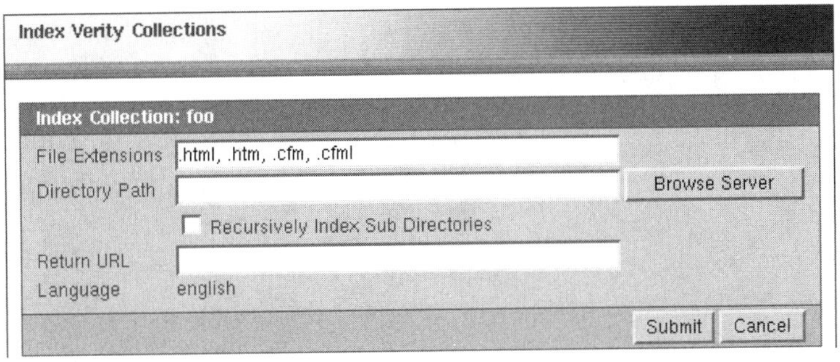

Index Verity Collections

Index Collection: foo

File Extensions	.html, .htm, .cfm, .cfml
Directory Path	[_____] Browse Server
	☐ Recursively Index Sub Directories
Return URL	[_____]
Language	english

Submit | Cancel

Several important points are worth noting regarding the fields in the indexing form.

First of all, Verity can index numerous file formats. You should enter only the extensions of the file types you want to index, separating the extensions by commas. Keep in mind that some formats have multiple possible extensions (such as `.htm` and `.html` for HTML files), and you should enter all that could possibly appear in the directories you are indexing. Among the file formats supported by Verity are the following:

Adobe Acrobat/PDF	Applix Words	CorelDraw
Corel QuattroPro	Encapsulated PostScript	FrameMaker Maker Interchange Format
HTML Files	JPEG	Lotus 1-2-3
Lotus Ami Pro	Lotus Freelance	Lotus Word Pro
Microsoft Excel	Microsoft PowerPoint	Microsoft Rich Text Format
Microsoft Sound/WAV	Microsoft Windows Bitmap	Microsoft Word
MPEG 1	MPEG 2	Portable Network Graphics
QuickTime	Text Files	TIFF (Tagged Image File Format)
WordPerfect		

In addition, all files in the specified directory that match the file extensions you indicate will be indexed. If you select the Recursively Index Sub Directories check box, then all files and all directories below the specified directory that also match the extensions will also be indexed.

The Return URL field indicates which URL, if any, can be used to access the directory being indexed so that Verity can return URLs for files in the search results. For instance, if you are indexing the directory `C:\myfiles` and this directory is accessed through the URL `http://some.host/somefiles/` on your web server, then you would provide this as the Return URL value. Then, if a search returned the file `C:\myfiles\somedir\afile.html` as a result, the URL `http://some.host/somefiles/somedir/afile.html` would returned as the URL for that file.

Finally, you can override the language you chose for the collection at the time of indexing by specifying an alternative language in the Language drop-down list. In ColdFusion MX, the following languages can be indexed:

Arabic	Chinese (Simplified)	Chinese (Traditional)
Czech	Danish	Dutch
English	Finnish	French
German	Greek	Hebrew
Hungarian	Italian	Japanese
Korean	Norwegian	Norwegian (Bokmal)
Norwegian (Nynorsk)	Polish	Portuguese
Russian	Spanish	Swedish
Turkish		

Other Uses of the Connected Verity Collections List

In addition to indexing a collection from the Connected Verity Collections List, you can perform the following functions using the relevant icons that appear next to each collection in the list:

- Repair a corrupted collection

- Optimize a collection; this is discussed later in the section "Optimizing Verity"

- Purge (delete) all index data from a collection returning it to the same state it was in at the time it was created

- Delete a collection and all the index data it contains

Searching an Index

Once an index has been created, it can be searched from your templates using the `cfsearch` tag. Using this tag, you can search both indexes of documents and indexes of dynamic query results. The latter is discussed in the section "Indexing and Searching Dynamic Query Results" later in this chapter.

The `cfsearch` tag takes six possible attributes as outlined in Table 6.1.

NOTE   You can search multiple collections in a single search but only if they are of the same type. You cannot mix regular Verity collections and K2 collections in the same search.

TABLE 6.1: Attributes of the cfsearch Tag

Attribute	Required or Optional	Description
name	Required	Specifies the name of the search query for later reference to the results.
collection	Required	Specifies the name of the collection to be searched. A comma-separated list of collections allows a single search against multiple collections.
type	Required	Specifies the type of search query being specified in the criteria attribute. Possible values are simple and explicit and are discussed later in the section "The Verity Query Syntax."
criteria	Required	Specifies the expression that indicates the data to find in the index.
maxRows	Optional	Specifies the maximum number of results to return from the search results.
startRow	Optional	Specifies the first row of the search results to return.

A search results in a query with the name specified in the name attribute. Each row in the query result has five key columns, as shown in Table 6.2.

TABLE 6.2: Query result columns for Verity searches

Column	Description
URL	The URL of the file
Key	The full path of the file
Title	The title of the file if one was discernable (such as the contents of the <title> ... </title> block in an HTML file)
Score	A score, in the form of a decimal value between 0 and 1 indicating how close a match the result is
Summary	An automatic summary that reflects the best three matching sentences up to a maximum of 500 characters

To illustrate the use of the cfsearch tag, consider the case of a collection called docIndex. The following template searches the collection for the word Hello and displays the results as illustrated in Figure 6.3 with each title as a clickable link to the URL for that document.

Listing 6.1   Displaying Verity Search Results (0601.cfm)

```
<!---
   Name:          /c06/0601.cfm
   Description:    Displaying Verity Search Results
--->
```

```html
<html>
  <head>
    <title>Displaying Verity Search Results</title>
  </head>

  <body>
    <cfsearch
      name="searchResults"
      collection="docIndex"
      type="Simple"
      criteria="Hello">

    <ul>
      <cfoutput query="searchResults">
        <li><a href="#URL#">#Title#</a> (#Score#)</li>
      </cfoutput>
    </ul>
  </body>
</html>
```

FIGURE 6.3:

Searching a collection
and displaying results

The Verity Query Syntax

Verity provides a few basic syntactic forms that allow users to build Boolean queries. Table 6.3 outlines these Boolean operators.

TABLE 6.3: Boolean Operators in Verity Queries

Operator	Example	Alternate Form	Description
and	a and b	None	Results must match both operands to the and operator.
or	a or b	a, b	Results must match either operand to the or operator.
not	not a	None	Results must not match the operand to the not operator.

You can combine multiple operators into large query expressions. However, in doing this, keep in mind that there are orders of precedence that govern the order in which the Boolean operators are evaluated. The orders of precedence state that not is evaluated before and, and then finally or is evaluated. This means that in the expression a or b and c, b and c is evaluated first followed by a or <result of and expression>.

The orders or precedence can be overridden. A subexpression inside parentheses is evaluated prior to the rest of the expression outside the parentheses. Of course, the orders of precedence still apply within the parentheses. As an example of this, in the expression (a or b) and c, a or b is evaluated first followed by <result of or expression> and c.

Using Wildcards

Verity provides support for wildcards in your query expressions. Users can use the following wildcards:

Wildcard	Description
?	Matches any single alphanumeric character
*	Matches zero or more alphanumeric characters
[]	Matches one of the characters contained between the square brackets
{}	Matches all the patterns, separated by commas, contained in the curly brackets
^	When used inside square brackets, indicates that a match should be made for any character not contained in the brackets
-	When used inside square brackets, indicates a range of characters

Most of these special wildcard characters should be familiar to developers who have used Perl's regular expressions.

Simple versus Explicit Queries

Verity supports two types of queries, simple and explicit, that are indicated by the type attributes of the cfsearch tag. These types are as follows.

Simple queries accept wildcard characters, Boolean operators, and alternate forms of Boolean operators. In addition, word stemming is performed so that, for instance, a search for `sea` will find `sea`, but it will also find words derived from `sea` (such as `seas`) but not words that simply start with `sea` without being derived from the word `sea` (such as `season`).

Explicit queries accept wildcard characters and Boolean operators but cannot use the alternate forms of the Boolean operators and do not perform stemming by default. They also support a wide range of additional operators, including the following:

Operators	Description
stem	Performs stemming on the operand
word	Performs a basic word search instead of a complete complex search
thesauras	Includes synonyms of the operand in the search
soundex	Includes words which sound like the operand in the search
typo	Includes words similar to the operand in the search (in other words, it assumes the search term contains a typographical error and should really be a different word)
near	The closer search terms are in a document, the higher the document's relevance score
paragraph	All operands must appear in the same paragraph
sentence	All operands must appear in the same sentence

NOTE A complete list of Verity operators and their syntax and usage can be found in the "Indexing and Searching Data" chapter of the "Developing ColdFusion Applications" section of the ColdFusion documentation.

Verity and cflock

An important point to keep in mind when you are using Verity is that Verity indexes are files, and the operations performed on Verity collections and indexes are file operations. For this reason, it is essential that you use appropriate file locking when using `cfcollection`, `cfindex`, or `cfsearch`. This is done using the `cflock` tag.

When locking your Verity actions, you need to keep the following in mind while crafting your `cflock` tag:

- You should not set your time out values too low as Verity operations can, at times, take several seconds to complete. Otherwise, you may experience frequent timeout errors. The appropriate value will depend on the data you are indexing, the size of your collections, and the speed of your system and its average load.

- You should choose a single lock name to use on all locks from the same collection. One easy approach is to match the name of the lock to the name of the collection.

- You should use readOnly locks for searching and exclusive locks for cfindex and cfcollection.

- You should decide what to do when a timeout occurs. This decision (to throw an exception or continue template processing) really depends on how you code your templates and what will happen if processing continues. You will need to consider this in the context of your application and search template.

A typical cflock tag for Verity searching purposes might, therefore, look like this:

```
<cflock
  timeout="10"
  name="myDocs"
  type="exclusive">
```

The Verity K2 Server

ColdFusion MX includes the Verity K2 Server as well as the standard Verity server. The K2 server offers vastly improved performance over the standard engine and can support larger numbers of simultaneous users and larger indexes. The version included with ColdFusion limits the total number of searchable documents to 125,000 in ColdFusion Professional and 250,000 in the Enterprise version of ColdFusion.

When you first install ColdFusion, the K2 server will not be in use. Configuration of K2 must be done manually before it becomes accessible within ColdFusion. This is done through the k2server.ini file, which can typically be found in c:\cfusionmx\lib\ on Windows systems.

In this file, the value of the vdkHome entry should point to your Verity directory (typically C:\cfusionmx\verity\), and each collection you want to index and search with K2 must be specified in the file. After the collection has been created, you need to add a new section to the k2server.ini file similar to the following:

```
[Coll-4]
collPath=c:\cfusionmx\verity\collections\<collection name>]
collAlias=<K2 Collection Name>
topicSet=
knowledgeBase=
online=2
```

The section name, in this case Coll-4, increments with each new collection added to K2 so that the next collection would be specified with a section named Coll-5. The only crucial entries in each of these sections are the collPath and collAlias entries. The name specified in collAlias is the collection name you will use when you are indexing and searching the collection with cfindex and cfsearch. This name should be different than the collection name you initially used to create the collection. You can continue to use that name to access the collection from within the traditional Verity search engine.

You will also need to manually start the K2 server using this command:

```
c:\cfusionmx\lib\k2server -inifile c:\cfusionmx\lib\k2server.ini.
```

Finally, you need to specify the hostname and port of your K2 server on the Verity K2 Server page of the ColdFusion Administrator. Typically, these values will be localhost and 9901.

Using ColdFusion tags to index data and search it remains the same, so this chapter doesn't specifically address the K2 server. Further discussion of the K2 server can be found in the "Working with Verity Tools" section of the ColdFusion Online Documentation.

Using cfindex and cfcollection

The tasks of creating collections and indexing data do not need to be performed through the ColdFusion Administrator as described earlier. They can be performed programmatically in your templates using the cfcollection and cfindex tags. Most importantly, using the cfindex tag allows you to index the results of dynamic queries, such as those performed against a database. The importance of this should not be overlooked.

When you consider a typical relational database, you can perform searches of the database using SQL. When you perform matches against text fields, you have some limited wildcard capabilities when you use the like keyword in your queries. However, these queries have limited capabilities, are inefficient, and do not provide information about relevance in the results. These differences make Verity a compelling tool for performing searches on query results that are text heavy.

For instance, with Verity searches, a wide range of wildcards are available. As a result, users can easily specify precise binary searches and can search on word stems easily in numerous languages. These features are discussed in the section "The Verity Query Syntax."

One could easily envision several applications of this query indexing and searching integration with the Verity engine, including these:

- Easy searching of text fields in a database

- Indexing and searching of user inboxes using the cfpop tag

- Indexing and searching of remote websites using the cfhttp tag

Creating Collections with cfcollection

The cfcollection tag provides functionality similar to that found on the Verity Collections page. With it, you can create, repair, optimize, delete, and map collections. The tag takes four attributes as outlined in Table 6.4.

TABLE 6.4: Attributes of the cfcollection Tag

Attribute	Required or Optional	Description
action	Required	Specifies an action to perform. Possible values are create, repair, optimize, delete, and map.
collection	Required	Specifies the name of the collection to be created or managed.
path	Required when action is create	Specifies the path where a collection should store its files. This is the same as the path you specify when you are creating a collection through the ColdFusion Administrator.
language	Optional	Specifies the language to use when indexing content in the collection. By default this is English.

In order to create a collection, you will use this tag like so:

```
<cfcollection
  action="create"
  collection="docindex"
  path="c:\cfusionmx\verity\collections\"
  LANGUAGE="English">
```

This tag will create a collection called docindex.

Indexing Files with cfindex

As with the ColdFusion Administrator, once a collection is created it can be indexed. The cfindex tag provides the same basic indexing ability for indexing files that was found in the ColdFusion Administrator but offers more flexibility. In particular, you can manipulate existing indexes in several ways in which the ColdFusion Administrator only allows the complete re-indexing of a collection. With the cfindex tag, you can perform the following tasks:

Task	Action Performed
Update	Updates the index and adds a new key if specified
Delete	Removes index data for a specific file or directory from the index
Purge	Removes all index data from a collection
Refresh	Removes all index data from a collection and then performs new indexing

The `cfindex` tag takes the attributes outlined in Table 6.5.

TABLE 6.5: Attributes of the cfindex Tag

Attribute	Required or Optional	Description
`action`	Required	Specifies the action to perform. Possible values are `update`, `delete`, `purge`, and `refresh`.
`collection`	Required	Specifies the name of the collection to be created or managed.
`type`	Optional	Specifies the type of data being indexed. Possible values are `file` for indexing files, `path` for indexing an entire directory based on specific file extensions, and `custom` for indexing dynamic query results.
`title`	Required when type is `custom`	Specifies either a name for the collection, or, when indexing dynamic query data, the name of the column containing the data to use as a title for each result.
`key`	Optional	Specifies the unique identifier for each item being indexed. When `type` is `file`, this is automatically the filename; when the `type` is `path`, this is automatically the file path and name; and when `type` is `custom`, you can specify the name of the table column containing this unique identifier.
`body`	Optional	When `type` is `custom`, specifies one or more column names, separated by commas, containing data to be indexed. Ignored when `type` is `file` or `path`.
`urlPath`	Optional	Specifies the URL pointing to the directory being indexed when `type` is `file` or `path`.
`extensions`	Optional	Specifies a comma-separated list of file extensions used when `type` is `path` to determine which files to index.
`query`	Optional	Specifies the name of a query to index when `type` is `custom`.
`recurse`	Optional	Indicates if directories below the directory specified in `key` should be indexed as well when `type` is `path`. Possible values are `yes` and `no`.
`external`	Optional	Indicates if the collection was created with native Verity indexing tools outside of ColdFusion (when using a full copy of Verity as opposed to the integrated copy of Verity included with ColdFusion).
`language`	Optional	Specifies the language to use when indexing content in the collection. By default this is English.

Typically, when indexing directories of files on the ColdFusion server, you will use the attributes `collection`, `action`, `type`, `key`, `extensions`, `recurse`, and `urlPath`. For instance, the following tag will index all Microsoft Word documents and WordPerfect documents in the directory c:\mydocs\, which is associated with the URL `http://some.host/mydocs/`, and then it will store the index in the collection `docindex`:

```
<cfindex
  collection="docindex"
  action="refresh"
```

```
type="path"
key="c:\mydocs\"
urlPath="http://some.host/mydocs/"
extensions=".doc, .wpd"
recurse="yes">
```

Later, if you wanted to add the directory c:\otherdocs\ to the index, you could update the collection with this:

```
<cfindex
  collection="docindex"
  action="update"
  type="path"
  key="c:\otherdocs\"
  urlPath="http://some.host/otherdocs/"
  extensions=".doc, .wpd"
  recurse="yes">
```

Indexing and Searching Dynamic Query Results

Handling the indexing and searching of query results with Verity through ColdFusion is slightly different than with the previous examples of indexing files. These differences manifest themselves in several ways:

- You must use cfindex to index the content; you cannot use the ColdFusion Administrator.
- The use of the cfindex attributes differs.
- The content of the columns of the search results differs.

In this section, you will first learn to index dynamic query results and then you will move on to learn about searching those indexes and presenting basic search results.

Indexing Dynamic Query Results

The critical fields of the cfindex tag to use when indexing query results are collection, action, type, body, key, title, and query.

Consider the following definitions of a set of columns for a table named Books in a data source named MyDB:

Columns	Description
ID	Unique ID number for each record
Title	Title of the book
Notes	Description of the book
Country	Country of publication
Value	Price for the record
ISBN	ISBN for the book

When indexing the table, the following is the case: ID is the unique key for each record and Title is the title for each record. Accordingly, to index the contents of the Title, Notes, and Country columns in a collection that already exists called mybooks, you would need to use the following:

```
<cfquery name="bookList" datasource="MyDB">
    select * from Books
</cfquery>

<cfindex
  collection="mybooks"
  action="refresh"
  type="custom"
  query="bookList"
  body="Title,Notes,Country"
  key="ID"
  title="Title">
```

By contrast, consider a different type of query result: a user's inbox on a POP3 mail server. With the cfpop tag, you can do several things:

- Obtain a list of message headers from a POP3 account.
- Obtain the entire content of a single message in a POP3 account.
- Obtain the entire content of all messages in a POP3 account.

The latter is done using the action="getAll" attribute of the cfpop tag. For the POP3 account user1 with password pass1 on the mail host mail.some.domain, the following tag retrieves the content of all messages and places it in the query result named mail:

```
<cfpop
  server="mail.some.domain"
  username="user1"
  password="pass1"
  name="mail"
  action="getAll">
```

This produces a query result with the following columns:

Column	Description
Date	The date of the message as a date object
From	The from line of the message
MessageNumber	The number of the message in the inbox
ReplyTo	The reply to line of the message
Subject	The subject line of the message
CC	The cc line of the message

Column	Description
To	The to line of the message
Header	The complete mail header
Body	The text of the message

Given this, you could index the content of the subject and body fields using the message number as the unique identifier into a collection called `mymail` with the following tag:

```
<cfindex
  collection="mymail"
  action="refresh"
  type="custom"
  query="mail"
  body="subject,body"
  key="messageNumber"
  title="subject">
```

Searching Dynamic Query Results

Having created an index of dynamic query results, searching them is similar to searching an index of files with `cfsearch`. However, the meaning and use of the resulting columns in the search results differs. When results are returned from `cfsearch`, the various columns mean the following:

Column	Description
URL	Ignored for indexes of dynamic query results
Key	The value of the column used to identify each row in the query results that were indexed
Title	The value of the column containing the title for each row in the query results that were indexed
Score	A score, as a decimal value between 0 and 1 indicating how close a match the result is
Summary	An automatic summary that reflects the best three matching sentences up to a maximum of 500 characters

For instance, consider the `mymail` collection used earlier. You can search this index for the word "today" and display a list of matches as follows:

Listing 6.2   Searching and Displaying Dynamic Query Results

```
<!---
  Name:          /c06/0602.cfm
  Description:   Searching and Displaying Dynamic Query Results
```

```
--->
<html>
    <head>
        <title>Searching and Displaying Dynamic Query Results</title>
    </head>

    <body>
        <cflock
          timeout="10"
          name="mymail"
          type="readOnly">
            <cfsearch
            name="searchResults"
            collection="mymail"
            type="simple"
            criteria="today">
        </cflock>

    <ul>
        <cfoutput query="searchResults">
            <li>#Title# (#Score#)</li>
        </cfoutput>
    </ul>
    </body>
</html>
```

Listing 6.2 produces results like those in Figure 6.4.

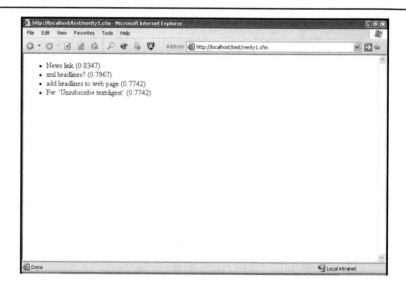

Of course, these results have limited usefulness. In particular, they provide no way to read the message and they do not reflect who sent the message or when. They simply provide the subject line of the message and a score.

We can alter the template to display the basic header information from the message as follows:

Listing 6.3   **Displaying Message Headers in Search Results (0603.cfm)**

```
<!---
    Name:          /c06/0603.cfm
    Description:   Displaying Message Headers in Search Results
--->

<html>
    <head>
        <title>Displaying Message Headers in Search Results</title>
    </head>

    <body>
        <cflock
          timeout="10"
          name="mymail"
          type="readOnly">
            <cfsearch
              name="searchResults"
              collection="mymail"
              type="imple"
              criteria="today">
        </cflock>

        <ul>
            <cfoutput query="searchResults">
                <cfpop
                  server="mail.some.domain"
                  username="user1"
                  password="pass1"
                  name="message"
                  messageNumber="#Key#"
                  action="getAll">
                <li>From: #message.From#<br>
                    Date: #message.Date#<br>
                    Subject: #Title#<br>
                    Score: #Score#<br><br>
                </li>
            </cfoutput>
        </ul>
    </body>
</html>
```

Listing 6.3 generates results like those in Figure 6.5.

FIGURE 6.5:

More useful search
results

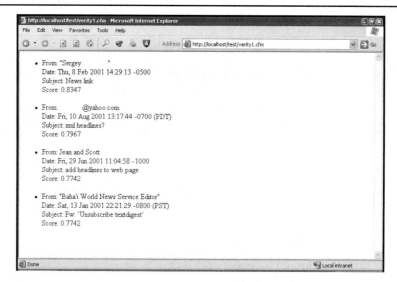

Of course, this still doesn't provide a way to view the actual messages in the results. This requires creating a template for displaying a mail message that receives as input the `messageNumber` in a URL variable. The search template in Listing 6.3 can then use the `Key` column in the search results to create a URL pointing to this new template to display the message. If the template used to display the message is called `viewmessage.cfm` and expects a URL variable called `messageNumber`, then we can change the search template to link to this as follows.

Listing 6.4   Linking to Result Details (0604.cfm)

```
<!---
    Name:          /c06/0604.cfm
    Description:   Linking to Result Details
--->

<html>
    <head>
        <title>Linking to Result Details</title>
    </head>

    <body>
        <cflock
          timeout="10"
          name="mymail"
          type="readOnly">
```

```
        <cfsearch
          name="searchresults"
          collection="mymail"
          type="simple"
          criteria="today">
    </cflock>

    <ul>
        <cfoutput query="searchResults">
          <cfpop
            server="mail.some.domain"
            username="user1"
            password="pass1"
            name="message"
            messageNumber="#Key#"
            action="getAll">
          <li>From: #message.From#<br>
             Date: #Year(message.Date)#-#Month(message.Date)#-
               #Day(message.Date)#<br>
             Subject: <a
               href="viewmessage.cfm?messageNumber=#Key#">#Title#</a><br>
             Score: #Score#<br><br>
          </li>
        </cfoutput>
     </ul>
   </body>
</html>
```

Creating Search Interfaces

So far in this chapter you have reviewed basic uses of the Verity search engine in which a template searches a collection and then simply presents a list of results, possibly with links to the resulting documents. However, there is more to a good search interface than this. There are three main areas you should consider when you are building your search interface:

- Decide exactly what information to present in order to make the search results useful.
- Limit the number of results displayed at any one time and then allow the user to page through the results to avoid a search result display that is overwhelming in its length.
- Consider carefully the way you design your actual search form so that it assists the user to effectively build their queries.

Presenting Useful Results

When you search a collection with the cfsearch tag, the results contain two useful pieces of information. This information can help users decide if any given item in the results is one that they would be interested in investigating further by viewing the document or a related database entry. Specifically, the search results contain the Score and Summary columns.

Many websites have search engines that present the results including a relevance score. For instance, Figure 6.6 illustrates search results on The Baha'i World website (`http://www.bahai.org/`), which includes relevance scores in the search results.

Including relevance scores in search results

What makes these results particularly useful is that they are sorted in decreasing order by the value of the relevance score. This allows users to see those results that Verity thinks are most closely related to the query at the top of the list, then they can scroll through the progressively less relevant documents.

Creating output similar to that found in the Figure 6.6 is simple. As long as a search has been submitted from a form and the form field `Query` contains the search query, then the search processing template would involve code like the following:

Listing 6.5   **Displaying Relevance Scores (0605.cfm)**

```
<!---
    Name:          /c06/0605.cfm
    Description:   Displaying Relevance Scores
--->
<html>
    <head>
        <title>Displaying Relevance Scores</title>
    </head>

    <body>
        <cflock
          timeout="10"
```

```
  name="myDocs"
  type="readOnly">
    <cfsearch
     name="searchResults"
     collection="myDocs"
     type="simple"
     criteria="#Form.Query#">
</cflock>

<cfoutput>Searching for: #Form.Query#</cfoutput>
<hr>
<table border=0 cellPadding=3 cellSpacing=0 width=100%>
    <tr valign=top>
       <td align=left><strong>Title</strong></td>
       <td align=left><strong>Score</strong></td>
    </tr>
    <cfoutput query="searchResults">
       <tr valign=top>
          <td align=left>#Title#</td>
          <td align=left>#Score#</td>
       </tr>
    </cfoutput>
    </table>
  </body>
</html>
```

Listing 6.5 produces results like those in Figure 6.7.

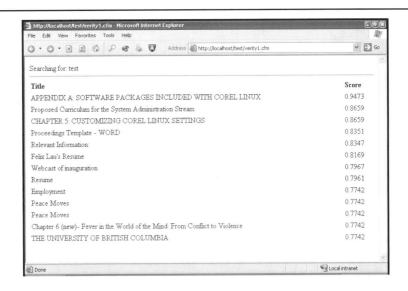

Of course, relevance scores between 0 and 1, such as those produced by Verity, are not as clear as they can be for users. Users will generally find percentage result easier to understand. In this case, you can produce that output by changing the table containing the score so it looks like this:

```
<td align="left">#Int(Score*100)# %</td>
```

This produces results between 0 and 100 and then eliminates any part after the decimal point to produce whole number percentages (see Figure 6.8).

FIGURE 6.8:

Relevance scores as percentages

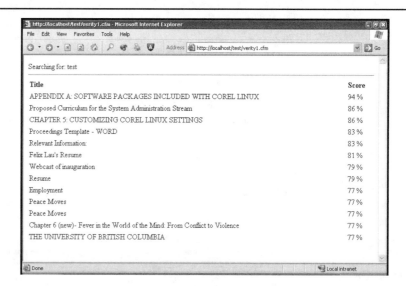

Taking this a step further, there is also the question of how useful the narrow differentiation of percentage scores is. Some sites use iconic representation of relevance on small scales that usually have only five or ten divisions on them. For instance, you can convert the relevance score into one of five iconic representations of relevance; these are illustrated in Table 6.6.

TABLE 6.6:   Illustrating Relevance with Icons

Icon	Score Range	Filename
☐☐☐☐☐	0.8000 to 1.0000	score1.gif
☐☐☐☐	0.6000 to 0.7999	score2.gif
☐☐☐	0.4000 to 0.5999	score3.gif
☐☐	0.2000 to 0.3999	score4.gif
☐	0.0000 to 0.1999	score5.gif

You can convert relevance scores into the appropriate icon filename with the following code in which Score is a column from the search results:

```
<cfset icon = Int(5 * Score) + 1>
<cfset filename = "score#icon#.gif">
```

Therefore, the actual search template could become Listing 6.6, which produces results like those in Figure 6.9.

Listing 6.6   **Displaying Relevance as an Icon (0606.cfm)**

```
<!---
    Name:          /c06/0606.cfm
    Description:   Displaying Relevance as an Icon
--->
<html>
    <head>
        <title>Displaying Relevance as an Icon</title>
    </head>

    <body>
        <cflock
          timeout="10"
          name="myDocs"
          type="readOnly">
            <cfsearch
              name="searchResults"
              collection="myDocs"
              type="simple"
              criteria="#Form.Query#">
        </cflock>

        <cfoutput>Searching for: #Form.query#</cfoutput>
        <hr>
        <table border="0" cellPadding="3" cellSpacing="0" width="100%">
            <tr valign="top">
                <td align="left"><strong>Title</strong></td>
                <td align="left"><strong>Score</strong></td>
            </tr>
            <cfoutput query="searchResults">
                <tr valign="top">
                    <td align="left">#Title#</td>
                    <cfset icon = Int(5 * Score) + 1>
                    <cfset filename = "score#icon#.gif">
                    <td align="left"><img src="#filename#"></td>
                </tr>
            </cfoutput>
        </table>
    </body>
</html>
```

Using icons to illustrate relevance scores

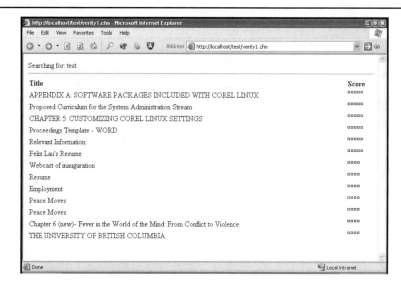

In addition to using scores, you can also use summaries to present useful results. By providing the user with document summaries from Verity's search results, you can help them get a sense of the context and content of each item in the search results before they have to decide whether to proceed with reading a particular document or result item.

The Summary column of the search results contains this information. You can add the summary simply to the previous search template:

Listing 6.7   **Displaying Summaries (0607.cfm)**

```
<!---
    Name:          /c06/0607.cfm
    Description:   Displaying Summaries
--->

<html>
    <head>
        <title>Displaying Summaries</title>
    </head>

    <body>
        <cflock
          timeout="10"
          name="myDocs"
          type="readOnly">
            <cfsearch
              name="searchResults"
              collection="myDocs"
```

```
                type="Simple"
                criteria="#Form.Query#">
        </cflock>

        <cfoutput>Searching for: #Form.Query#</cfoutput>
        <hr>
        <table border="0" cellPadding="3" cellSpacing="0" Width="100%">
            <tr valign="top">
                <td align="left"><strong>Title</strong></td>
                <td align="left"><strong>Score</strong></td>
            </tr>
            <cfoutput query="searchResults">
                <tr valign="top">
                    <td align="left">#Title#<br><font size=1>#Summary#
    ...</Font></td>
                    <cfset icon = Int(5 * Score) + 1>
                    <cfset filename = "score#icon#.gif">
                    <td align="left"><img src="#filename#"></td>
                </tr>
            </cfoutput>
        </table>
    </body>
</html>
```

Listing 6.7 produces results like those in Figure 6.10.

FIGURE 6.10:

Displaying summaries
in search results

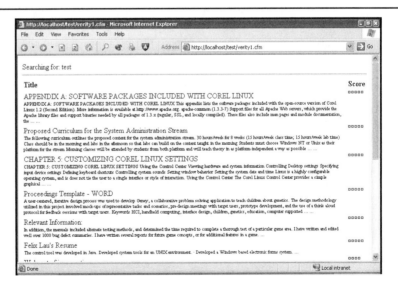

In general, this is useful. However, there are two drawbacks. First, in some document and data sets, the nature of the content will prevent Verity from producing meaningful and useful summaries. These summaries are supposed to consist of the three most relevant sentences from the document or data item; however, there are types of data and documents in which sentences may not be apparent (such as spreadsheet data), and the summaries that result are often hard to read or understand. You should perform a number of test searches against your indexes and see what the summaries look like before using them. The second disadvantage is that by presenting summaries, you are increasing the length of the search results making it harder to quickly scroll through and scan the results list for the appropriate item.

The latter problem can be resolved by providing the user with the option of selectively enabling or disabling summaries. This allows you to let a user decide on the usefulness of the summaries based on their familiarity with the document or data set rather than presume that one approach is better than the other for all users. Allowing the user to enable or disable summaries complicates matters slightly in that we now need a way to pass the summary status into the search template. This can be done through a URL variable called summary, which can have y or n as its values. The cfparam tag can be used to set url.summary to y when the variable is not present so that the search form does not need to indicate the summary status.

After we have set this up, we can add a link at the top of the page so that the user can enable and disable summaries by linking to the same page with a different value for the url.summary variable. However, setting things up this way poses another complication: when users click these links to enable or disable summaries, the actual search query needs to be passed along again to the template so that the search can be re-executed when the template reloads. Initially, the query is passed from a form through a form variable. However, by clicking a link to enable or disable summaries, a user is not submitting a form, so we need another approach. A simple approach is this:

- When users search they submit a query through a form.

- When users click a link to enable or disable summaries, the current query is passed along through a URL variable named query.

- At the top of the template, the following decision is made: If the form.query variable doesn't exist, it is presumed that the query is being passed by URL and the cfparam tag is used to assign the value of url.query to form.query. This allows the actual cfsearch tag to remain unchanged.

The resulting code looks like Listing 6.8 (assuming the name of this template is search.cfm).

Listing 6.8 **Enabling and Disabling Summaries (0608.cfm)**

```
<!---
    Name:           /c06/0608.cfm
    Description:    Enabling and Disabling Summaries
--->
<html>
```

```
<head>
    <title>Enabling and Disabling Summaries</title>
</head>

<body>
    <cfparam name="Form.query" default="#url.query#">
    <cfparam name="url.summary" default="y">

    <cflock
     timeout="10"
     name="myDocs"
     type="readOnly">
        <cfsearch
         name="searcharesults"
         collection="myDocs"
         type="simple"
         criteria="#form.query#">
    </cflock>

    <cfoutput >Searching for: #form.query#</cfoutput>
    <hr>

    <cfif url.summary is "y">
        <a href="search.cfm?query=#form.query#&summary=n">hide summaries</a>
    <cfelse>
        <a href="search.cfm?query=#form.query#&summary=y">show summaries</a>
    </cfif>
    <hr>

    <table border="0" cellPadding="3" cellSpacing="0" width="100%">
        <tr valign="top">
            <td align="left"><strong>Title</strong></td>
            <td align="lef"t"><strong>Score</strong></td>
        </tr>
        <cfoutput query="searchResults">
            <tr valign="top">
                <td align="left">
                    #title#
                    <cfif url.summaryis "y">
                        <br><font size="1">#summary# ...</font>
                    </cfif>
                </td>
                <cfset icon = Int(5 * score) + 1>
                <cfset filename= "score#icon#.gif">
                <td align="left"><img src="#filename#"></td>
            </tr>
        </cfoutput>
    </table>
</body>
</html>
```

The results of Listing 6.8 will look like Figure 6.11 when summaries are enabled and 6.12 when summaries are disabled.

Providing a link to hide summaries

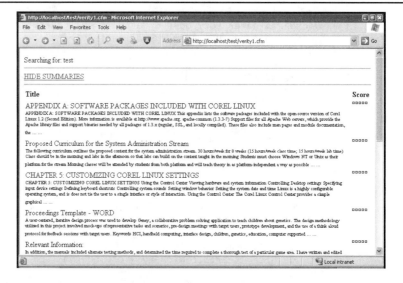

Hidden summaries

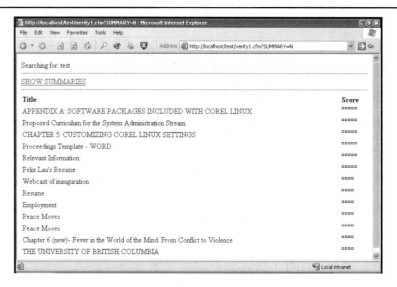

Paging through Results

One of the most useful techniques used by many search engines, from large Internet indexes and catalogues such as Yahoo! and Google to small search systems on personal websites, is to divide search results into multiple pages and then present those pages one page at a time.

For instance, if there are 200 search results, this could be displayed as one, long, 200-item list or as 10 pages, each with 20 items and next and previous page links or buttons. This makes each individual page easier to manage; easier to scan, browse, and scroll; and quicker to load since the size of the page is smaller.

This is achieved with `cfsearch` and Verity by using several features and principles:

- The `maxRows` attribute allows you to limit the number of items returned in your search results. You can use this to specify the number of items to display on each page of your search results.

- The `startRow` attribute allows you to indicate from which row to start returning results. You can use this to specify the first item from the search results to be displayed on any given page.

- It is assumed that indexes are updated infrequently and that if the same query is executed multiple times in a short time span, the exact same set of results is returned. This allows you to perform the same query on each page knowing that the results will be the same as the last time it was performed.

Consider the following simple `cfsearch` tag:

```
<cfsearch
 name="searchResults"
 collection="myMail"
 type="simple"
 criteria="today">
```

If you were splitting the results into pages of 10 items apiece and you wanted to display the third page, the tag would become

```
<cfsearch
 name="searchResults"
 collection="myMail"
 type="simple"
 criteria="today"
 startRow="21"
 maxRows="10">
```

Using this principle we can extend the previous example of searching the index of a POP3 mailbox and displaying the results. Without using paging, the template for performing the search would look like Listing 6.9 assuming that the query was received from a form submission in the `form.query` variable:

Listing 6.9   **Searching a Mail Box (0609.cfm)**

```
<!---
    Name:        /c06/0609.cfm
    Description:  Searching a Mail Box
--->
<html>
    <head>
        <title>Searching a Mail Box</title>
    </head>

    <body>
        <cflock
          timeout="10"
          name="myMail"
          type="readOnly">
            <cfsearch
              name="searchResults"
              collection="myMail"
              type="simple"
              criteria="#form.query#">
        </cflock>

        <ul>
            <cfoutput query="searchResults">
                <cfpop
                  server="mail.some.domain"
                  username="user1"
                  passord="pass1"
                  name="message"
                  messageNumber="#Key#"
                  action="getAll">
                <li>From: #message.From#<br>
                    Date: #Year(message.Date)#-#Month(message.Date)#-
#Day(message.Date)#<gr>
                    Subject: <s
href="viewmessage.cfm?messageNumber=#Key#">#Title#</a><br>
                    Score: #Score#<br><br>
                </li>
            </cfoutput>
        </ul>
    </body">
</html>
```

If we want to provide an interface that pages through the results in batches of 10, we need a way to pass the first item of the current page from template to template. This can be done with the url.startRow variable. When the user submits the form, it is assumed that the starting row should be 1 so that we can use cfparam to set the url.startRow variable to 1.

Using this variable, we can alter our `cfsearch` tag and add links to the next page in the results (when there are more results to display) or to the previous page when the user is not on the first page. The resulting template looks like Listing 6.10.

Listing 6.10   Paging through Search Results

```
<!---
   Name:           /c06/0610.cfm
   Description:    Paging through Search Results
--->
01: <html>
02:     <head>
03:         <title>Paging through Search Results</title>
04:     </head>
05:
06:     <body>
07:         <cfparam name="form.query" default="#url.query#">
08:         <cfparam name="url.startRow" default="1">
09:
10:         <cflock
11:           timeout="10"
12:           name="myMail"
13:           type="readOnly">
14:             <cfsearch
15:               name="searchResults"
16:               collection="myMail"
17:               type="simple"
18:               criteria="#form.query#"
19:               startRow="#url.startRow#"
20:               maxRows="11">
21:         </cflock>
22:
23:         <cfif url.startRow gt 1>
24:             <cfset previous = url.startRow - 10>
23:             <cfoutput>
24:                 <a
href="search.cfm?query=#form.query#&startRow=#previous#">&lt;&lt;previous</a><br
>
25:             </cfoutput>
26:         </cfif>
27:         <cfif searchResults.recordCount gt 10>
28:             <cfset next = url.startRow + 10>
29:             <cfoutput>
30:                 <a href="search.cfm?query=#form.query#&startRow=#next#">next
page&gt;&gt;</a><br>
31:             </cfoutput>
32:         </cfif>
33:
34:         <cfoutput><ol start="#startRow#"></cfoutput>
35:             <cfoutput query="searchResults" maxRows="10">
```

```
36:                    <cfpop
37:                      server="mail.some.domain"
38:                      userName="user1"
39:                      password="pass1"
40:                      name="message"
41:                      MESSAGENUMBER="#KEY#"
42:                      ACTION="GetAll">
43:                      <li>From: #message.From#<br>
44:                         Date: #message.Date#<br>
45:                         Subject: <a
href="viewMessage.cfm?messageNumber=#Key#">#Title#</a><gr>
46:                         Score: #Score#<br><br>
47:                      </li>
48:                 </cfoutput>
49:           </ol>
50:       </body>
51: </html>
```

NOTE   Line numbers have been added to this template for discussion purposes and are not part
of the template code.

There are some important points to note in this listing. First of all, the same technique for
passing along the query in a URL variable as the user pages through the results is employed as
in the earlier example when we discussed hiding and displaying summaries. In this case, we can
see the relevant cfparam tag at line 2 and the query parameters in the URLs on lines 24 and 30.

The cfsearch tag at lines 14–20 may seem strange in that 11 rows are retrieved but only
10 are displayed. This technique allows us to see if there are additional rows beyond the current one being displayed so that we can test to see if the next page link should be displayed
(lines 27–32). This is done by testing searchResults.recordCount to see if it is greater than
10 (in other words, if the search returned 11 rows and we are only displaying 10, then there
must be at least one result on the next page).

In order to test to see if a previous page link should be displayed (as on line 23), we only
need to see if the current url.startRow value is greater than 1. If it is greater than 1, then we
must be on the second page or higher because we increment and decrement the starting row
value in 10s starting at 1 on the first page.

In displaying the next page or previous page links, we calculate the new value for the
startRow URL variable by adding or subtracting 10 from the current url.startRow value.

On line 34, we have changed from an unnumbered list to a numbered list and are using the
startRow variable to ensure that each message in the results is numbered based on its place in
the entire set of search results.

On line 35, `maxRows="10"` has been added to the `cfoutput` loop because we don't want to display all 11 retrieved results but only the first 10.

The end result is pages that look like the one illustrated in Figure 6.13.

FIGURE 6.13:

Paging through search results

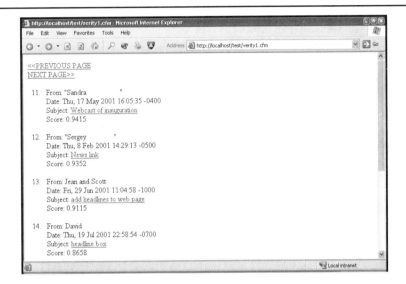

FIGURE 6.13:

Paging through search results

Helping Users Build Queries

Often, sites that have search engines will provide their search form in two tiers: a simple search that appears on all or many pages of the site and contains a single text field for entering a query, plus a button for submitting the search, plus an advanced search page which offers advanced search features and helps and supports users in composing their searches.

Beyond offering simple instructions for building Verity queries based on the Verity query syntax outlined earlier in the section "The Verity Query Syntax," you can help users build Boolean Verity queries.

One approach to this is a form that allows users to specify terms of different types: those that must occur, those from which at least one must occur, and those that should not occur. Using a form with three different fields for these types of terms allows beginning users to build Boolean search queries without using any Boolean search terms such as `and`, `or`, or `not`.

A simple search form of this type can be built using the following HTML code segment:

```
<form method="post" action="search.cfm">
 <table border="0" cellPadding="3" cellSpacing="0">
  <tr valign="top">
   <td align="right">
```

```
              Search terms that must
              be found (separated by commas):
           </td>
           <td align="left">
              <input type="text" size="50" name="and">
           </td>
        </tr>
        <tr valign="top">
           <td align="right">
              Search terms that must
              not be found (separated by commas):
           </td>
           <td align="left">
              <input type="text" size="50" name="not">
           </td>
        </tr>
        <tr valign="top">
           <td align="right">
              Optional search terms, one of which must
              be found (separated by commas):
           </td>
           <td align="left">
              <input type="text" size="50" name="or">
           </td>
        </tr>
        <tr valign="top">
           <td align="right">
               
           </td>
           <td align="left">
              <input type="submit" value="Search">
           </td
        </tr>
     </table>
  </form>
```

This produces a form that looks like the one illustrated in Figure 6.14.

Of course, when this form is submitted to search.cfm, a query will need to be built out of this content. This query should combine all the terms in form.and, form.not, and form.or variables as appropriate, without the items in the Form.not variable; then, and will be used to combine that entire group with a group using or between all the items in form.or. For example, if form.and is "a b c", form.or is "d e f", and form.not is "g h", then the query should be

```
(a and b and c and not g and not h) and (d or e or f)
```

FIGURE 6.14:

An advanced
search form

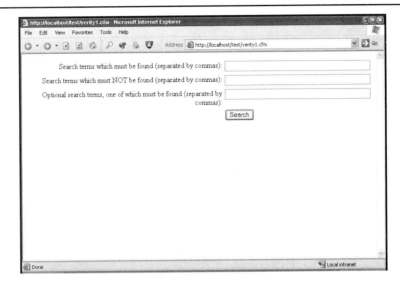

To build this type of query from the three form fields, you can use the fact that ColdFusion can treat strings of text as lists to easily iterate through each form field and extract the individual search terms. For instance, you can extract the terms in the form.and variable and create that section of the query with the following:

```
<cfset query = listGetAt(Form.and,1)>
<cfloop index="Item" from="2" to="#listLen(Form.and)# ">
    <cfset query = query & " and " & listGetAt(Form.and,Item)>
</cfloop>
```

The end result is that the variable query contains the composite query. Similarly, the following code extracts the relevant query in Boolean form from Form.not:

```
<cfset query = query & " not " & listGetAt(Form.not,1)>
<cfloop index="Item" from="2" to="#listLen(Form.not)# ">
    <cfset query = query & " and not " & listGetAt(Form.not,Item)>
</cfloop>
```

To put everything together, the following code segment builds the complete composite query from the three form fields.

```
01: <cfset query="">
02:
03: <cfif listLen(Form.and) gt 1 or listLen (Form.not) gt 1>
04:     <cfset query = "(">
05: </cfif>
06:
07: <cfif listLen(Form.and) gt 1>
```

```
08:    <cfset query = query & listGetAt(Form.and,1)>
09:    <cfloop index="Item" from="2" to="#listLen(Form.and)# ">
10:       <cfset query = query & " and " & listGetAt(Form.and,Item)>
11:    </cfloop>
12:    <cfif listLen(Form.not) gt 1>
13:       <cfset query = query & " and ">
14:    </cfif>
15: </cfif>
16:
17: <cfif listLen(Form.not) gt 1>
18:    <cfset query = query & " not " & listGetAt(Form.not,1)>
19:    <cfloop index="Item" from="2" to="#listLen(Form.not)# ">
20:       <cfset query = query & " and not " & listGetAt(Form.not,Item)>
21:    </cfloop>
22: </cfif>
23:
24: <cfif listLen(Form.and) gt 1 or listLen (Form.not) gt 1>
25:    <cfset query = query & ")">
26:    <cfif listLen(Form.or) gt 1>
27:       <cfset query = query & " and ">
28:    </cfif>
29: </cfif>
30:
31: <cfif listLen(Form.or) gt 1>
32:    <cfset query= query & " (">
33:    <cfset query = query &listGetAt(Form.or,1)>
34:    <cfloop index="Item" from="2" to="#listLen(Form.or)# ">
35:       <cfset query = query & " or " & listGetAt(Form.or,Item)>
36:    </cfloop>
37:    <cfset query = query & ")">
38: </cfif>
```

The logic of this code segment is slightly more complex than simply stitching together the three loops for each of the three form fields. Extra logic is needed to ensure that brackets and Boolean operators are used in the correct locations. Remember that the format of the query is

```
(a and b and not c and not d) and (e or f)
```

This logic works as follows:

Lines 3–5   If there are items in Form.and or Form.not, then the first open bracket is needed. If not, then query only take the form (e OR f) and the first portion of the basic query shown above is left out.

Lines 7–15   If there are items in Form.and, then we need to build the initial Boolean series in the form a and b.

Lines 12–14   If there are items in `Form.and` and also in `Form.not`, then we need an and to join the `a` and `b` list with the `not c` and `not d` list.

Lines 17–22   If there are items in `Form.not`, then we need to build the Boolean series in the form `not c` and `not d`.

Lines 24–29   If there are items in `Form.and` or `Form.not`, then the first close bracket is needed.

Lines 26–28   If there are items in `Form.and` or `Form.not` and `Form.or` has items, then an and is needed to join the first expression in brackets and the second.

Lines 31–38   If there are items in `Form.or`, then we need to build the Boolean series in the form `e or f`.

This code segment can then easily be incorporated into a complete search template such as the one used earlier. Listing 6.11 illustrates the use of icons to represent relevance scores.

Listing 6.11   **A Complete Search Template (0611.cfm)**

```
<!---
    Name:          /c06/0611.cfm
    Description:   A Complete Search template
--->
<html>
    <head>
        <title>A Complete Search Template</title>
    </head>

    <body>

        <cfset query="">

        <cfif listLen(Form.and) gt 1 or listLen (Form.not) gt 1>
            <cfset query = " (">
        </cfif>

        <cfif listLen(Form.and) gt 1>
            <cfset query = query & listGetAt(Form.and,1)>
            <cfloop index="Item" from="2" to="#listLen(Form.and)# ">
                <cfset query = query & " and " & listGetAt(Form.and,Item)>
            </cfloop>
            <cfif listLen(Form.not) gt 1>
                <cfset query = query & " and ">
            </cfif>
        </cfif>

        <cfif listLen(Form.not) gt 1>
            <cfset query = query & " not " & listGetAt(Form.not,1)>
```

```
        <cfloop index="Item" from="2" to="#listLen(Form.not)# ">
            <cfset query = query & " and not " & listGetAt(Form.not,Item)>
        </cfloop>
    </cfif>

    <cfif listLen(Form.and) gt 1 or listLen (Form.not) gt 1>
        <cfset query = query & ")">
        <cfif listLen(Form.or) gt 1>
            <cfset query = query & " and ">
        </cfif>
    </cfif>

    <cfif ListLen(Form.or) gt 1>
        <cfset query = query & " (">
        <cfset query = query & listGetAt(Form.or,1)>
        <CFLOOP INDEX="Item" from="2" to="#listLen(Form.or)# ">
            <cfset query = query & " or " & listGetAt(Form.or,Item)>
        </cfloop>
        <cfset query = query & ")">
    </cfif>

    <cflock
     timeout="10"
     name="myDocs"
     type="readOnly">
        <cfsearch
         name="searchResults"
         collection="myDocs"
         type="simple"
         criteria="#query#">
    </cflock>

    <cfoutput>Searching for: #query#</cfoutput>
    <hr>
    <table border="0" cellPadding="3" cellSpacing="0" width="100%">
        <tr valign="top">
            <td align="left"><strong>Title</strong></td>
            <td align="left"><strong>Score</strong></td>
        </tr>
        <cfoutput query="searchResults">
            <tr valign=top>
                <td align=left>#Title#</td>
                <cfset icon = Int(5 * Score) + 1>
                <cfset filename = "score#icon#.gif">
                <td align="left"><img src="#filename#"></td>
            </tr>
        </cfoutput>
    </table>
</body>
</html>
```

Multilingual Indexing and Searching

At the current time, the version of Verity included with ColdFusion can index and search the following languages:

Arabic	Chinese (Simplified)	Chinese (Traditional)
Czech	Danish	Dutch
English	Finnish	French
German	Greek	Hebrew
Hungarian	Italian	Japanese
Korean	Norwegian	Norwegian (Bokmal)
Norwegian (Nynorsk)	Polish	Portuguese
Russian	Spanish	Swedish
Turkish		

However, any given collection will only use a single language. This provides consistency in how data is indexed and searched within the collection with respect to word roots, grammatical rules, and so on. Accordingly, if you have a multilingual site, you need to give some consideration to a few key issues.

If you have multilingual documents to be indexed, you will need to create a separate collection for each language, and then you will need to index the languages separately into the appropriate collections. In order to do this, you need to give some consideration to how you organize your documents. Because the indexing process identifies documents to be indexed through a directory plus one or more extensions, either the directory or file extension must be used to isolate the documents of a specific language for indexing.

However, it is unlikely that file extensions can be used to distinguish files of different languages. Consider the case of a multilingual website. It is not uncommon to find languages distinguished by replacing a single file, such as `index.html`, with multiple files for each language with names such as `index.en.html`, `index.fr.html`, and so on. However, if you specify `.en.html` as a file extension when indexing files in ColdFusion, no files will be indexed since ColdFusion does not treat an extension with a dot in it as valid. This limitation of Verity prevents extension formats such as `.en.html` and `.fr.html` from being used as the basis for separating files at the time of indexing.

Therefore, the best approach to producing a multilingual website that is easily indexable is to separate the documents for each language into separate directories. This allows you to specify a different directory when indexing each language in order to ensure that only a single language's documents are indexed at one time.

Once this is done, you can create a search form that adds a drop-down list of available languages so that users can select the language to search and you can use this in the search processing template to select the appropriate collection to search.

Multiformat Indexing and Searching

One of the powerful features of the Verity search engine paired with ColdFusion is that it can be used to index so many different popular data formats—from spreadsheets to web pages to word processing documents to Adobe Acrobat files. This means that Verity can be used as a critical component when you are creating an online document repository that includes documents in multiple formats.

You can index multiple document formats in a single indexing operation by specifying multiple document extensions for the various formats at the time of indexing. However, you need to keep in mind that different file formats may produce limited results when searching.

Most notably, Verity will not always be able to identify the title for a document. For instance, in the search results in Figure 6.15, you can see several Microsoft Word documents with no title because Verity could not identify an obvious title in the document. Your search template needs to handle this possibility by checking to see if a title is available and, if not, indicating this to the user as in the following code segment:

```
<table border=0 cellPadding=3 cellSpacing=0 width=100%>
  <tr valign=top>
    <td align=left><strong>Title</strong></td>
    <td align=left><strong>Score</strong></td>
  </tr>
  <cfoutput="searchResults">
    <tr valign=top>
      <td align=left>
        <cfif title is "">
          Title Unknown
        <cfelse>
          #title#
        </cfif>
      </td>
      <cfset icon = Int(5 * score) + 1>
      <cfset filename = "score#icon#.gif">
      <td align=left><img src="#filename#"></td>
    </tr>
  </cfoutput>
</table>
```

FIGURE 6.15:

FIGURE 6.15:

Sometimes Verity cannot determine the title of a document

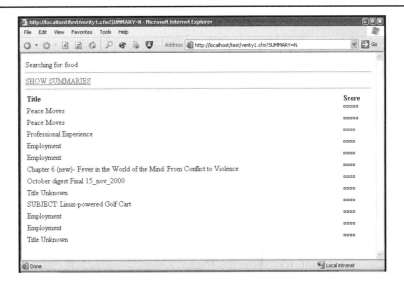

In addition, it is often useful to let users know the type of a file in the search results if you are indexing multiple document types. Search results in ColdFusion don't explicitly indicate the file or mime type for individual search results. Therefore, you will need to use the last three characters of the Key column of the results (which contains the filename) to determine the file type. For instance, if you have indexed just Microsoft Word and Adobe Acrobat files, you could alter the code segment above to indicate the file type as follows:

```
<table border=0 cellPadding=3 cellSpacing=0 width=100%>
   <tr valign=top>
      <td align=left><strong>Title</strong></td>
      <td align=left><strong>Score</strong></td>
   </tr>
   <cfoutput query="searchResults">
      <tr valign=top>
        <td align=left>
           <cfif title is "">
              Title Unknown
           <cfelse>
              #Title#
              <cfif right(Key,3) is "doc">
                 [ Microsoft Word ]
              </cfif>
              <cfif right(Key,3) is "pdf">
                 [ Adobe Acrobat ]
              </cfif>
           </cfif>
```

```
        </td>
        <cfset icon = Int(5 * score) + 1>
        <cfset filename = "score#icon#.gif">
        <td align=left><img src="#filename#"></td>
      </tr>
    </cfoutput>
  </table>
```

The resulting output looks like Figure 16.16 . It would be simple to extend this template to display file type icons instead of a simple text note.

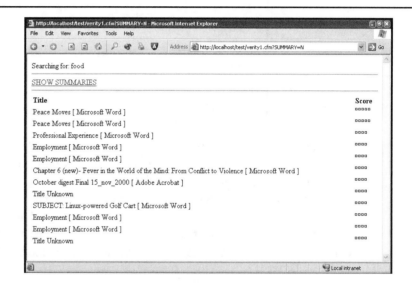

Automating Indexing

If you are using Verity to index and search a data set that changes frequently, you will want to automate the indexing of your data so that you can easily trigger the indexing process or so that you can even schedule the indexing to occur automatically on a regular schedule.

Creating an Indexing Template

An indexing template can be simple: A cfindex tag and some code to tell the user of the template that the indexing is complete. For instance, consider the following cfindex tag:

```
<cfindex
  collection="docIndex"
  action="refresh"
```

```
type="path"
Key="c:\mydocs\"
urlPath="http://some.host/mydocs/"
extensions=".doc, .wpd"
recurse="yes">
```

This could be combined into a simple indexing template, Listing 6.12.

Listing 6.12   An Indexing Template (0612.cfm)

```
<!---
   Name:          /c06/0612.cfm
   Description:   An Indexing Template
--->

<html>
   <head>
      <title>An Indexing Template</title>
   </head>

   <body>

      Indexing c:\mydocs\<br>

      <cflock
       timeout="10"
       name="myDocs"
       type="exclusive">
         <cfindex
          collection="docIndex"
          action="refresh"
          type="path"
          Key="c:\mydocs\"
          urlPath="http://some.host/mydocs/"
          extensions=".doc, .wpd"
          recurse="yes">
      </cflock>

      Done indexing.

   </body>
</html>
```

This template could be invoked by an administrator using a web browser and the appropriate URL, or it could be scheduled to run on a regular basis (such as nightly) using the Scheduled Tasks page of the ColdFusion Administrator.

Optimizing Verity

As you index and update a collection over time, the data stored in the collection's indexes will become inefficient. The optimization function, which can be performed on collections through the ColdFusion Administrator or the `cfcollection` tag, allows for the packing of the data stored in the collections' files into the smallest possible space, thus optimizing the search process. This should be performed as part of routine maintenance and could, for instance, be done after a nightly re-indexing or updating of a collection by including the optimization in the same template that does the re-indexing.

You can optimize a collection with the following tag:

```
<cfcollection
  collection="<collection name>"
  action="Optimize">
```

You can also perform optimization from the Verity Collections page of the ColdFusion Administrator.

In Sum

In this chapter you took your knowledge of the Verity search engine further; you considered not just the mechanics of creating collections, indexing data, and searching, but also more subtle points associated with creating interfaces for search engines, assisting users in building their queries, and handling multiple languages and data formats in our indexes and collections.

CHAPTER 7

Advanced WDDX

By Guy Rish

- Introducing WDDX

- Exploring the Functionality of WDDX Language Tools

- The WDDX JavaScript Library

- WDDX Syndication

This chapter covers a number of topics associated with Web Distributed Data eXchange (WDDX). More specifically, we will concentrate on how WDDX can provide client-side data within the browser in order to create interactive applications. We will explain how this can be done without the need for numerous requests to the web server. As you will see, a number of things are necessary for such an arrangement, and we'll examine each one. In addition, toward the end of the chapter, you'll get to see some examples of WDDX data syndication drawn from existing news-oriented sites on the Internet.

This chapter contains many references to source code, some of which is provided in the chapter and some of which will need to be downloaded from this book's page on the Sybex website (`http://www.sybex.com`). The sheer volume of code associated with this chapter prevents us from including it all in print.

WARNING Although some of the source code that accompanies this chapter will work with any browser, some of the dynamically constructed display elements are written specifically to work with Internet Explorer 5.0 or later.

Introducing WDDX

Web Distributed Data eXchange (WDDX) is an XML vocabulary for exchanging structured data among systems and programming languages.

First, some history.

The History of WDDX

Created by an Allaire team led by Simeon Simeonov in 1999, WDDX was integrated directly into CFML in version 4.0 of the ColdFusion Server. Part of that ColdFusion release was a JavaScript library for working with a subset of WDDX.

Not long after the release of ColdFusion Server version 4, a now defunct website was launched dedicated to distributing and advancing the WDDX technology (`http://www.wddx.org`), and the remainder of the WDDX SDK was introduced along with this website. This SDK provides APIs for Java and Perl, a more complete API for JavaScript, and a COM object for Windows-based languages.

Although this WDDX website provided a central point for distribution, it did not foster the growth of the WDDX community to the degree achieved by Allaire's efforts with other technologies. As a result, there was a spin out of the technology, and a new website was introduced (`http://www.openwddx.org`). This new site, launched in April 2001, offers forums for exchange and enhancement of the WDDX technology, but even these exchanges have had little influence on the enhancement of the WDDX technology. The most important contribution of Open-WDDX.org, beyond this exchange forum, is their download page (http://www.openwddx .org/downloads/), from which you can obtain the latest edition of the WDDX SDK.

Despite the lack of activity demonstrated at the OpenWDDX site, this technology remains widely used. In fact, what is truly remarkable about WDDX is its simplicity and versatility. Even development camps that haven't always been friendly to other Allaire technologies have embraced WDDX. There are now even third-party implementations for other languages, including Macromedia's own ActionScript, as well as those for PHP, Python, Rexx, and even Curl.

In addition to being used with these sometimes disparate languages, many early data syndication efforts, ColdFusion-based or otherwise, used WDDX because of its general-purpose nature. However, over the last couple of years, this usage of WDDX has lessened with the advent of the various XML vocabularies that have been developed to handle specific needs. Although the idea of syndicating content as a generalized data structure has less appeal than specifically crafted XML vocabularies, this does not eliminate the need for such syndication across the board.

WDDX Concepts

There are a few important concepts to understand when working with WDDX: packets, serialization, and deserialization.

Packets

A *WDDX packet* is any string of WDDX tags that is stored in a variable, in a file, or in a database field somewhere. Like any other XML vocabulary, a WDDX packet consists of tags, and these tags enclose textual values. Remember that one of the major purposes for the development of WDDX was to provide data exchange. As a result, rather than implementing innumerable through tags, WDDX identifies nine datatypes: number, string, boolean, datetime, binary, array, struct, recordset, and null. Listing 7.1 shows a WDDX packet that contains many of the legal datatypes that are defined in the WDDX DTD that accompanies the WDDX SDK.

Listing 7.1   A Sample WDDX Packet (sample.wddx)

```
<?xml version='1.0'?>
<!DOCTYPE wddxPacket SYSTEM 'wddx_0100.dtd'>
<wddxPacket version='1.0'>
    <header/>
    <data>
        <struct>
            <var name='aString'>
```

```
                <string>a string</string>
            </var>

            <var name='aNumber'>
                <number>-12.456</number>
            </var>

            <var name='aDateTime'>
                <dateTime>1998-06-12T04:32:12</dateTime>
            </var>

            <var name='aBoolean'>
                <boolean value='true'/>
            </var>

            <var name='anArray'>
                <array length='2'>
                    <number>10</number>
                    <string>second element</string>
                </array>
            </var>
        </struct>
    </data>
```

</wddxPacket>Serialization

The conversion of a specific language's native variable into a piece of WDDX markup for inclusion in a packet is called *serialization*. During the serialization process, the type and value of a variable is converted into a string that is platform and language neutral. Each of the language extensions in the SDK provides a serialization engine.

Deserialization

The conversion of a fragment of a packet into a specific language's native variable is called *deserialization*. During this process, the type and value are determined from the platform and a language-neutral string, and a conversion into implementation-specific content occurs. Each of the language extensions in the SDK provides a deserialization engine.

FIGURE 7.1:

Music database relationship model

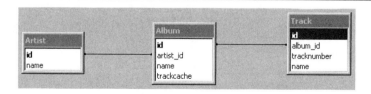

Required Setup for Examples in This Chapter

Much of this chapter focuses on the WDDX libraries that are provided normally as part of the ColdFusion Server. There are, however, specific examples that require the files that are provided only with the complete WDDX SDK. As a result, you must have the SDK installed before you proceed with the examples in this chapter.

Throughout this chapter, we will work with a simple database (shown in Figure 7.1) that keeps track of music CDs. The structure of this database allows the user to track the artist and song tracks associated with a particular album.

To make the examples in this chapter work, you'll need to create a data source called `Music` from within the ColdFusion Administrator. You will need to point this data source at the Microsoft Access database, `MusicLibrary.mdb`. This database can be found with the Chapter 7 code that is available from this book's web page on the Sybex website.

Exploring the Functionality of WDDX Language Tools

A variety of language tools are available for working with WDDX. Some, like ColdFusion's `cfwddx` tag, are already integrated into a language, although most function through APIs provided in the SDK.

After discussing two CFML tools for working with WDDX in more detail, this section will discuss various techniques for using WDDX with CFML query objects. While this is not exclusively the purpose of WDDX, the numerous opportunities available for this kind of handling beg more attention. You will discover that it's not a far reach to cross-apply some of these techniques to other CFML datatypes, such as structures, but one of the largest payoffs will likely come from applying them to query objects.

CFML Tools for Working with WDDX

CFML has two tools for working with WDDX directly: the `cfwddx` tag and the `isWddx` function. The `cfwddx` tag is used for data handling and the `isWddx` function performs sanity checks on strings that might represent WDDX packets.

The cfwddx Tag

The `cfwddx` tag is ColdFusion's only tag for WDDX handling. But this easy-to-use tag provides more than just WDDX interchange with ColdFusion datatypes; it also enables fundamental interoperability with JavaScript.

The cfwddx tag has six configurable parameters, which are listed in Table 7.1.

TABLE 7.1: cfwddx Attributes

Attribute	Description
action	Specifies the type of transformation; actions include cfml2wddx, wddx2cfml, cfml2js, and wddx2js.
input	Specifies the input variable to be transformed.
output	Specifies the variable that will receive the resulting transformation.
topLevelVariable	Specifies the name of the JavaScript WddxRecordset instance to create.
useTimeZoneInfo	Incorporates time zone stamps into the WDDX packet.
validate	Performs integrity checks on the incoming or outgoing WDDX packet.

Four kinds of transformation are possible using the WDDX format of the cfwddx tag:

- The cfml2wddx action converts CFML datatypes into a string of WDDX markup.

- The wddx2cfml action converts WDDX datatypes into a string of CFML datatypes.

- The cfml2js action converts CFML datatypes into text that, when interpreted by the browser, will create the appropriate JavaScript variable and value assignments.

- The wddx2js action converts from a string of WDDX markup into the JavaScript commands needed to create some corresponding variable.

The isWddx Function

The one built-in CFML function that interacts with WDDX packets is isWddx. This function determines whether a packet is well formed, thus indicating whether it can be safely operated on with the cfwddx tag. Here is its syntax:

```
isWddx(packet)
```

The only parameter, *packet*, is a string containing the WDDX packet to be validated. This function returns true or false depending on the well-formedness of the packet.

WDDX and CFML Queries

One common use for WDDX in the ColdFusion environment is for caching database queries. Once a query object has been serialized into a packet, it can be written to a file or written back to the database for later use.

Serializing a query object to a file is a very simple procedure; this is exemplified in Listing 7.2.

Listing 7.2   **Serializing a Query Object (FileExample1.cfm)**

```
01: <!---
02:     Name:        /c07/FileExample1.cfm
03:     Description: Serialize a query to file.
04: --->
05: <cfparam name="fileName"
06:     default="#expandPath("./packet.wddx")#">
07:
08: <cfquery datasource="#request.datasource#"
09:     name="artists">
10:     select * from Artist
11: </cfquery>
12:
13: <cfwddx action="cfml2wddx" input="#artists#"
14:     output="packet">
15:
16: <cffile action="write" file="#fileName#"
17:     output="#packet#" addNewLine="No">
```

This template contains a number of interesting points. The cfparam tag on lines 5 and 6 uses the expandPath function to construct the name of a file in the current directory that will hold the packet generated later. Then lines 8–11 execute a query on the Artist table. The resulting CFML query is then transformed, in lines 13 and 14, into a WDDX packet that is subsequently written to a file (lines 16 and 17).

Once the WDDX serialized query is stored into a file, it can be retrieved on demand. The contents can then be read out and deserialized back into a CFML query. This process is exemplified in Listing 7.3.

Listing 7.3   **Deserializing a WDDX Packet (FileExample2.cfm)**

```
<!---
    Name:        /c07/FileExample2.cfm
    Description: Deserialize a query from a file.
--->
<cfparam name="fileName"
    default="#expandPath("./packet.wddx")#">

<cffile action="read" file="#fileName#"
    variable="packet">

<cfwddx action="wddx2cfml" input="#packet#"
    output="data">

<cfdump var="#data#">
```

Once a serialized file has been written, gaining access to it for later deserialization does not have to be done directly from the filesystem as was demonstrated in Listing 7.3. Files can be drawn from over the network as well. HTTP, FTP, or SMTP connections will all provide the same capability. In addition, the HTTP connection does not require any additional configuration to work if the serialized file is stored in a published directory; this kind of access is exemplified in Listing 7.4.

Listing 7.4   **Retrieving a Packet via an HTTP Connection (HTTPExample1.cfm)**

```
01  <!---
02:     Name:        /c07/HTTPExample.cfm
03:     Description: Deserialize a WDDX packet retrieved
04:         via an HTTP connection
05: --->
06: <cfscript>
07:     function buildHTTPRequest(filename)
08:     {
09:         addressArray =
10:             listToArray(cgi.script_name, "/");
11:         status =
12:             arrayDeleteAt(addressArray,
13:             arrayLen(addressArray));
14:         status = arrayAppend(addressArray,
15:             arguments.filename);
16:         addressList = arrayToList(addressArray);
17:
18:         // concatenation of address
19:         // broken across multiple lines for readability
20:         address = "http://" & cgi.http_host;
21:         address = address & "/";
22:         address = address & listChangeDelims(
23:             addressList, "/");
24:
25:         return address;
26:     }
27: </cfscript>
28:
29: <cfset address = buildHTTPRequest("packet.wddx")>
30:
31: <cfhttp url="#address#" method="GET"
32:     resolveURL="false">
33:
34: <cfwddx action="wddx2cfml"
35:     input="#cfhttp.fileContent#"
36:     output="data">
37:
38: <cfdump var="#data#">
```

Although this template is a bit more involved than the previous two file-based examples, it does essentially the same thing as the `FileExample2.cfm` template shown in Listing 7.2.

Lines 6–27 define a function called `buildHTTPRequest`, which performs some quick work in order to build an address string that picks up a specified file from the same directory as the executing template. The lines after line 27 grab the file via an HTTP connection, transform the recovered WDDX packet into a CFML query object, and dump it for display.

Utilities for Constructing and Displaying Packets

Now that you have a general idea of how to create serialized packets and deserialize them for use, you can be introduced to two utilities that will make some of the work easier for you. PacketBuilder is a simple utility for creating packets from database queries and PacketReader is another simple utility for reading and displaying the contents of serialized files.

Using PacketBuilder

The examples so far in this chapter have been somewhat trivial and have required a certain degree of manual editing. In order to alleviate this manual code-editing part of this process, we need a simple tool that can be used to create WDDX packets for reuse later. PacketBuilder is such a tool and can be summed up as a simple self-posting form, `PacketBuilder.cfm`.

The PacketBuilder form (shown in Figure 7.2) has three edit fields used for input: Packet File, Datasource, and SQL. The Packet File field is the fully qualified local filesystem pathname of the output file to which the query results will be serialized. The Datasource field is the name of the registered ColdFusion data source. The SQL field is the SQL statement to be executed in order to generate the recordset that will be serialized.

FIGURE 7.2:

The Packet
Builder form

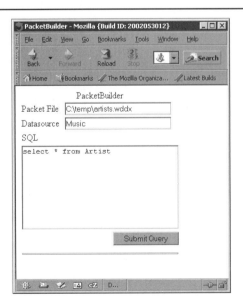

> **WARNING**   PacketBuilder is what is commonly referred to as a "quick and dirty" utility. It should be used carefully, and public access to it from a website should be strictly prohibited. Because it will, without regard to the possible dangers, execute the SQL fed into it, there is a real possibility that the integrity of a database could be damaged.

Working with PacketReader

Just as the PacketBuilder utility answers the need for a simple way to construct packets, the PacketReader utility provides a simple way to display packets. PacketReader is also a template with a self-posting form, `PacketReader.cfm`.

When executed, PacketReader will present the user with a simple form (shown in Figure 7.3). The single field the user must populate is the Filename field, which indicates a file on the local system that will be uploaded to the server for display.

FIGURE 7.3:

The Packet
Reader form

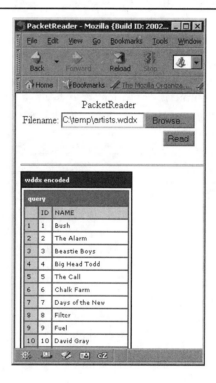

Database Caching with WDDX

There are a variety of ways to perform database caching with WDDX. Stashing serialized query results into a file is one way; another is storing these results directly in the database.

Let's consider database caching for the Music database. As mentioned earlier, there is a relationship that links the Artist table to the Album table and another that links the Album table to the Tracks table. Every time a specific artist's album is looked up, a join occurs between the Artist and Album tables. Then in order for tracks of a specific Album to be retrieved, another join must be made between the Album and Tracks tables. One way to eliminate this second join is by caching the results of join between the Album to Tracks table into the Album table itself. The Album table has a column called trackcache that is meant to hold a packet for that specific purpose.

The caching is initialized through the ColdFusion template TrackCache1.cfm, shown in Listing 7.5. After this cache is established, grabbing all the album tracks for a specific artist's album is a single join instead of two. This approach highlights a number of performance-saving features that could not otherwise be achieved easily or at all. One of the most useful featured used in this example involves caching related rows (in serialized form) within the field of another row, which enables the database to take advantage of specific table storage and indexing methodologies that would not otherwise be available.

Listing 7.5   **Caching Database Records (TrackCache1.cfm)**

```
<!---
    Name:        /c07/TrackCache1.cfm
    Description: Cache all the records from the
        Track table into a special purposed
        field in the Album table to increase
        database perform.
--->
<cfquery name="albums"
    datasource="#request.datasource#">
    select * from Album
</cfquery>

<cfloop query="albums">
    <cfset id = albums.id>

    <cfquery name="tracks"
        datasource="#request.datasource#">
        select
            id, tracknumber, name
        from Track
        where album_id = #id#
    </cfquery>

    <cfwddx action="cfml2wddx" input="#tracks#"
        output="packet">

    <cfquery name="trackcache"
        datasource="#request.datasource#">
```

```
        update Album
        set trackcache = '#packet#'
        where id = #id#
    </cfquery>
</cfloop>
```

The WDDX JavaScript Library

The JavaScript library that comes with ColdFusion Server to be used with WDDX is an abridged version of the one that is provided with the WDDX SDK. That said, this version is all you need to work with the simple WDDX packets that result from most CFML conversions. You should know, however, that although this library can handle almost any CFML datatype, nearly all of its utility is directed at handling applications that need to use data drawn from a database to be used on the client side of a web application. For the packet to be useful on the client side, it must be converted into a technology that can be executed by the browsing client (likely a web browser); this typically means using JavaScript.

The examples in this section demonstrate many of the features of the WDDX JavaScript library. Using the Music database, we'll start looking into the various techniques needed to develop a client/server application that is more robust than the typical kind, one that requires a page request for every minute database interaction.

Accessing the Library

You'll need to do a little setup to make the WDDX JavaScript library work for ColdFusion templates or anything else. First of all, it is important that you make certain that the JavaScript source files are in a published web directory. The typical way to incorporate the library is by using the script tag referencing the source in the head; this is seen in the following snippet:

```
<html>
    <head>
        <title>Snippet</title>
        <script language="JavaScript"
            src="wddx.js"></script>
    </head>
    .
    .
    .
</html>
```

To add flexibility to your ColdFusion templates, place the default WDDX JavaScript library in a directory located within a standard ColdFusion directory mapped off of the web server's root (/ for the base of the published web directories). To do this, replace the `script` line from the preceding snippet with the following:

```
<script language="JavaScript"
    src="/ CFIDE/scripts/wddx.js"></script>
```

WARNING   Notice the capitalization of the directory CFIDE, which is part of the path in the script tag's `src` attribute. On Windows machines case-sensitivity of files and directories is frequently overlooked; this can create problems with templates running on Unix operating system variants where name case is strictly observed.

To work with the advanced portions of WDDX JavaScript library, you must reference additional source files. The source file most specific to this chapter is the deserialization class. This source file is stored in a compressed file, `wddx_software.zip`, in the subdirectory `2__Software_Libraries` found in the WDDX SDK installation. Also contained within this compressed file, `wddx_software.zip`, is a set of directories for each of the languages directly supported—among them is a JavaScript directory. In the JavaScript directory, there are two further subdivisions: `Abridged` and `Original`. The `wddxDes.js` source file from the `Original` subdirectory is the one that you will need for the work in this chapter.

TIP   Because I do most of my JavaScript and WDDX work with ColdFusion, I copy the files `wddxDes.js` and `wddxDesIE.js` into the same directory as the `wddx.js`. For the most part, these files are nearly identical, but there are subtle requirements needed to work with Internet Explorer—hence the separate and suggestively named file, `wddxDesIE.js`.

Converting CFML into JavaScript

Nearly every CFML datatype has some analogous WDDX representation. This is more or less true when you are considering CFML datatypes that have been converted for usage within JavaScript. The WDDX JavaScript library has a number of important classes designed specifically to assist you with handling complex data structures, but not all of the converted CFML datatypes are mapped as well as others.

It will take a little work to investigate how well CFML datatypes will transform into JavaScript datatypes through the use of WDDX conversions. Listing 7.6 shows how this works.

Listing 7.6   **Converting CFML Datatypes to JavaScript DataTypes (DatatypeConversion.cfm)**

```
01: <!---
02:     Name:        /c07/DatatypeConversion.cfm
03:     Description: A demonstration of CFML datatypes
04:         converted into JavaScript datatypes via
05:         WDDX.
```

```
06: --->
07: <cfscript>
08:     // create simple integer
09:     digit = 10;
10:
11:     // create precision number
12:     pi = 3.14;
13:
14:     // create list - multi-line for printing
15:     lst = "Selene Bainum,Raymond Camden,";
16:     lst = lst & "John Colasante,Arman Danesh,";
17:     lst = lst & "Hal Helms,Emily Kim,";
18:     lst = lst & "Guy Rish";
19:
20:     // create array
21:     a = listToArray(lst);
22:     length = arrayLen(a);
23:
24:     // create structure
25:     st = structNew();
26:     // populate structure
27:     st.firstName = listGetAt(a[1], 1, " ");
28:     st.lastName = listGetAt(a[1], 2, " ");
29:
30:     // create query
31:     authors = queryNew("firstName, lastName");
32:     // create array of structures
33:     ast = arrayNew(1);
34:     // populate query and array of structures
35:     for(idx=1; idx lte length; idx=idx+1)
36:     {
37:         tempst = structNew();
38:         tempst.firstName = listGetAt(a[idx], 1, " ");
39:         tempst.lastName = listGetAt(a[idx], 2, " ");
40:         ast[idx] = tempst;
41:
42:         queryAddRow(authors);
43:         querySetCell(authors, "firstName",
44:             tempst.firstName);
45:         querySetCell(authors, "lastName",
46:             tempst.lastName);
47:     }
48: </cfscript>
49:
50: <html>
51: <head>
52:     <title>Datatype Conversions</title>
53:     <script language="JavaScript"
54:         src="/CFIDE/scripts/wddx.js"></script>
55:     <script language="JavaScript">
```

```
56:          <cfwddx action="cfml2js" input="#digit#"
57:              topLevelVariable="digit">
58:          <cfwddx action="cfml2js" input="#pi#"
59:              topLevelVariable="pi">
60:          <cfwddx action="cfml2js" input="#lst#"
61:              topLevelVariable="list">
62:          <cfwddx action="cfml2js" input="#a#"
63:              topLevelVariable="array">
64:          <cfwddx action="cfml2js" input="#st#"
65:              topLevelVariable="struct">
66:          <cfwddx action="cfml2js" input="#ast#"
67:              topLevelVariable="aofs">
68:          <cfwddx action="cfml2js" input="#authors#"
69:              topLevelVariable="authors">
70:      </script>
71: </head>
72:
73: <body>
74: <p>View document source.</p>
75: </body>
76: </html>
```

Though this listing is rather lengthy, there really isn't anything complex about it. The long `cfscript` block running from lines 7–48 sets up a series of seven CFML variables that will be converted to JavaScript content later in the template: a simple integer value, a precision value, a list, an array, a structure, a query object, and an array of structures. Then, within the document head, as previously discussed, the CFML variables are handed off for conversion into JavaScript variables within a `script` block spanning lines 55–70. The display in the browser is of no consequence; the real value comes in viewing the document source to see what became of these converted variables.

The conversion process was not always friendly about preserving the original intent of these variables. In fact, numbers are converted into plain string variables! The conversion of a CFML list is a simple matter, since it is merely converted into a JavaScript string, which makes sense since the underlying CFML datatype for a list is a string. The CFML array correctly became an array. The conversion of the CFML structure, however, provides quite an interesting twist; it becomes a JavaScript object with some public fields. The array of structures does not present anything unexpected when you consider the array and structure conversions, but it is always wise just to check that level of nest complexity. Finally, the query object is transformed into an instance of the special `WddxRecordset` class.

NOTE   cfwddx cannot handle, in any of its various conversion modes, the XML document object datatype that is new to ColdFusion MX.

Working with the WddxRecordset Class

When you use the `cfwddx` tag, you can convert CFML query objects into the initialization strings to create a `WddxRecordset` instance. The `WddxRecordset` class provides a number of public methods; Table 7.2 is a partial list of these.

TABLE 7.2: Some WddxRecordset Methods

Method	Description
addColumn	Adds a column to every row.
addRows	Adds *n* number of rows.
getField	Gets the value of a specific column on a specific row.
getRowCount	Gets the number of rows in the set.
setField	Sets the value of a specific column on a specific row.
wddxSerialize	Serializes the set into a WDDX packet.

A `WddxRecordset` class can have a major impact on the way an application runs from within the browser. When tied to an event on an HTML control, this object can become a powerful tool. It can even allow the display options of a `form` to be adjusted more dynamically.

An example of this kind of dynamic capability can be seen in the excerpts of `LinkedSelect-Example1.cfm`, which are shown in Listing 7.7. Missing from this code are

- The creation of two queries, one against the `Artist` table (called `artists`) and one against the `Album` table (called `albums`)

- The inclusion of some JavaScript files

- The `form` that is the presentation

Listing 7.7   **Dynamic Form Updates Using WddxRecordset (from LinkedSelectExample1.cfm)**

```
01: <!---
02:     Name:        /c07/LinkedSelectExample1.cfm
03:     Description: Using client side cached
04:         recordsets, dynamically update one HTML
05:         select when the other HTML select changes.
06: --->
07: <script language="JavaScript">
08: <cfwddx action="cfml2js" input="#artists#"
09:     topLevelVariable="rsArtists">
10: <cfwddx action="cfml2js" input="#albums#"
11:     topLevelVariable="rsAlbums">
12:
13: function populateAlbum()
```

```
14: {
15:     var loop;
16:     var opt;
17:     var frm = window.document.forms[0];
18:     var artists =
19:         window.document.forms[0].elements['artists'];
20:     var albums =
21:         window.document.forms[0].elements['albums'];
22:
23:     var artist_id =
24:         artists.options[artists.selectedIndex].value;
25:
26:     var recordCount = rsAlbums.getRowCount();
27:
28:     // clear the Album select --
29:     // function from HTMLFormUtil.js
30:     clearSelect(albums);
31:
32:     // top option
33:     opt = new Option;
34:     opt.value = 0;
35:     opt.text = "--- select album ---";
36:     albums.options[albums.options.length] = opt;
37:
38:     if(artist_id != "0")
39:     {
40:         // process through all album records
41:         for(loop = 0; loop < recordCount; loop++)
42:         {
43:             // find related album records
44:             if(rsAlbums.getField(loop, 'artist_id') ==
45:                 artist_id)
46:             {
47:                 opt = new Option;
48:                 opt.value =
49:                     rsAlbums.getField(loop, 'id');
50:                 opt.text =
51:                     rsAlbums.getField(loop, 'name');
52:                 albums.options[albums.options.length] =
53:                     opt;
54:             }
55:         }
56:     }
57: }
58: </script>
```

The elided form contains two select controls, one called Artists that is populated when the template is run with the contents from the query against the Artist table; the other, called Albums, is populated with a single option to act as a placeholder. The onChange event for Artists executes the populateAlbum JavaScript function show in Listing 7.7.

To dynamically update the contents of one `select` based upon the selection from another without a trip to the server, all the data must be shipped to the client side embedded within the page. This can be done by converting the two queries (not shown in this listing), which were created at the beginning of this template, into JavaScript `WddxRecordset` class instances with `cfwddx`. This is done on lines 7–11 in the listing, using the `cfml2js` value for the `action` attribute and specifying an appropriate name for the `topLevelVariable` attribute. When the CFML interpreter processes these two statements, numerous lines of JavaScript code will be created, which can be seen when the page source is viewed from the browser.

You can learn a lot by viewing the page source once the page is rendered in the browser, and you can actually see the JavaScript that is generated by the `cfwddx` transformations.

The `populateAlbum` function, which makes up the majority of the listing (lines 13–57), is fired from the `onChange` event of the `artist select` (part of the `form`, which is not shown) whose job is to update the contents of the `album select`.

Lines 17–21 set up some shorthand work by getting references to HTML objects, such as the `form` and the two `select` controls, that will be manipulated. The selected entry from the `artist select` is retrieved on lines 23 and 24 and is saved to the `artist_id` variable. The value of this selected `option` was populated from the `artist_id` field selected from the `Artist` database table. The record count of the `WddxRecordset` holding the Album records created on lines 8 and 9 is retrieved on line 26. The `album select` is cleared of all entries on line 30 using a function called `clearSelect`, which is kept in an external JavaScript library whose `script` inclusion is elided from the listing. A placeholder entry is created for the `album select` on lines 33–36.

The heart of this function exists on lines 38–56. Here, within this `if`, the records from the `Album` table are matched to the selected entry from the `artist select`. Unfortunately, there is no simple way to query the `WddxRecordset` instance as there is to ask a database for a specific record, so in order to find the albums that belong to a specific artist, you must loop over all of the records and check the `artist_id` variable, whose value was obtained from the `artist select`, against the `artist_id` field in the `rsAlbums` object. When a match is found, a new `option` is programmatically created and added to the `album select`.

Exploring the WddxDeserializer Class

The `WddxDeserializer` class is part of the WDDX JavaScript library that comes with the WDDX SDK; the deserializer resides in its own separate file, `wddxDes.js`. (Internet Explorer users will need to include the `wddxDesIE.js` source.)

As might be expected from its name, the `WddxDeserializer` class takes a packet and transforms it into the appropriate JavaScript object. The performance of this class is more or less acceptable. Indeed, the added flexibility of being able to both serialize and deserialize packets on the client end often means fewer database hits and sometimes even a reduction in page requests.

NOTE   It's a shame that the deserializer is not directly incorporated into the JavaScript library that comes standard with the ColdFusion Server since it's a vital part of doing real client/server work with CFML and JavaScript. The very point and purpose of WDDX is hamstrung in advanced WDDX applications because of this omission.

Just like the other classes in the WDDX JavaScript library, the `WddxDeserializer` class has a small number of methods shown in Table 7.3.

TABLE 7.3: WddxDserializer Methods

Method	Description
deserialize	Converts a packet into the appropriate JavaScript object
deserializeURL	Converts a packet drawn from a URL into a JavaScript object

With our example Music database, each `Album` record's cached track list must be deserialized to be displayed. A simple example of this can be observed in the ColdFusion template, `ShowAlbum.cfm`, shown in Figure 7.4. This screen is not dissimilar to portions of other templates presented in this chapter so far. As with some of these previous examples, Listing 7.8 shows only an excerpt from `ShowAlbum.cfm`.

FIGURE 7.4:

The track list for an album in `ShowAlbum.cfm`

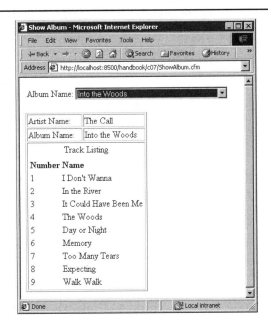

Listing 7.8   **Dynamically Display Album Tracks (from ShowAlbum.cfm)**

```
01: <!---
02:     Name:          /c07/ShowAlbum.cfm
03:     Description: Using client side cached
04:          recordsets, allow for the selection
05:          of an artist and an album from HTML
06:          selects to display the album tracks.
07: --->
08: <script language="JavaScript">
09: function showAlbum()
10: {
11:     var idx;
12:     var length;
13:     var artistIdx;
14:     var artistID;
15:     var albumIdx;
16:     var trackCache;
17:     var tableString = "";
18:     var albumID;
19:
20:     var rsTracks;
21:
22:     var deser = new WddxDeserializer;
23:
24:     var trackSpan =
25:         window.document.all['tracklist'];
26:     var frm = window.document.forms[0];
27:     var albumSelect = frm.elements['albumselect'];
28:
29:     idx = albumSelect.selectedIndex;
30:     albumID = albumSelect.options[idx].value;
31:
32:     if(albumID != "")
33:     {
34:         albumIdx = findIndex(rsAlbums,
35:             "id", albumID);
36:         trackCache = rsAlbums.getField(albumIdx,
37:             "trackcache");
38:         artistID = rsAlbums.getField(albumIdx,
39:             "artist_id");
40:         artistIdx = findIndex(rsArtists,
41:             "id", artistID);
42:
43:         rsTracks = deser.deserialize(trackCache);
44:         length = rsTracks.getRowCount();
45:
46:         tableString += "<table border=\"1\">";
47:         tableString +=
48:             "<tr><td>Artist Name:</td><td>" +
49:             rsArtists.getField(artistIdx, "name") +
```

```
50:                    "</td></tr>";
51:            tableString +=
52:                "<tr><td>Album Name:</td><td>" +
53:                rsAlbums.getField(albumIdx, "name") +
54:                "</td></tr>";
55:            tableString += "<tr><td colSpan=\"2\">";
56:            tableString += "<table>";
57:            tableString +=
58:                "<caption>Track Listing</caption>";
59:            tableString +=
60:                "<tr><th align=\"left\">Number</th>";
61:            tableString +=
62:                "<th align=\"left\">Name</th></tr>";
63:
64:            for(idx = 0; idx < length; idx++)
65:            {
66:                tableString +=
67:                "<tr><td>" +
68:                rsTracks.getField(idx, "tracknumber") +
69:                "</td><td>" +
70:                rsTracks.getField(idx, "name") +
71:                "</td></tr>";
72:            }
73:
74:            tableString += "</table>";
75:            tableString += "</td></tr>";
76:            tableString += "</table>";
77:
78:            trackSpan.innerHTML =
79:                tableString;
80:        }
81: }
82:
83: function findIndex(rs, col, val)
84: {
85:        var idx;
86:        var recordCount;
87:
88:        if(rs.isColumn(col))
89:        {
90:            recordCount = rs.getRowCount();
91:            for(idx = 0; idx < recordCount; idx++)
92:            {
93:                fld = rs.getField(idx, col);
94:                if(fld == val)
95:                {
96:                    return idx;
97:                }
98:            }
99:        }
100:       return -1;
101: }
102: </script>
```

The showAlbum function is triggered off the onChange event of the album select, which is part of the form elided from this listing. In this excerpt, lines 24–27 create variables for shorthand access to parts of the form (and to the form itself) as well as to the span whose contents will be dynamically rewritten to display the album information. The heart of the function is found in lines 32–80 where the specific index from the album select is determined and both artist and track information is gathered and dynamically written to the browser display. This listing is rather lengthy since much of it pertains to the dynamic construction of a table; lines 46–62 begin the table and create the headers, the for loop on lines 64–72 gather the track information from a deserialized packet (discussed later) to build table rows, and finally on lines 74–76 the table is ended.

Additional points of interest within the if statement are the use of the findIndex function and the use of the WddxDeserializer.

A function, findIndex, which is defined on lines 83–101 of Listing 7.8, is used on lines 34 and 40 of the same listing. This function takes a WddxRecordset instance, a field name, and a value to match the field, indicated by the second argument, against. With this information, the function will loop through the WddxRecordset and take the field name specified in the second argument and match it with the value of the third argument. If a match is found, the matched record number is returned; if it isn't found, a –1 is returned.

Specifically, this function is used to locate the record in the rsAlbums that matches the one selected from the form and the rsArtists record that matches the located rsAlbums records artist_id. Once the correct rsAlbums record index is found, it is easy to retrieve the track-cache field using the getField method. This field contains a WDDX packet that needs to be converted, which requires a WddxDeserializer, like the one instantiated on line 22. Once the trackcache packet has been deserialized, on line 43, its contents can be used to dynamically build a table for insertion into the span, which is part of the elided form.

Using the WddxSerializer Class

Although the WddxRecordset class allows for some advanced manipulation of a set of records, once it has gone client-side, there is no way to pass the altered JavaScript object instance back to the server. Fortunately, there is a JavaScript WddxSerializer class to help with this. When passed as an argument to the wddxSerialize method of a WddxRecordset instance, this WddxSerializer instance will enable a WDDX packet to be generated from the data present within the WddxRecordset instance. The resulting packet can then be assigned to a form control, such as a hidden input.

WDDX packets can also be passed as URL arguments. This is unwise and not recommended however, due to restrictions on both the size and the content these packets can contain. The mangling that must take place in order to protect spaces and other nonalphanumeric characters renders the packet useless without additional back-end processing. This back-end processing must also be smart enough to know when not to process, because the contents of a string within a WDDX packet can contain characters that might be purposefully encoded! Worse still, passing binary data can yield unpredictable results.

When working with WddxRecordset instances, there is seldom a need to use WddxSerializer directly. This is because of the tight integration between these two objects. This is not the case, however, when you are dealing with other native JavaScript datatypes. A quick summary of WddxSerializer's methods is available in Table 7.4.

TABLE 7.4: WddxSerializer Methods

Method	Description
serialize	Creates a WDDX packet from the specified object instance or primitive variable
serializeVariable	Serializes a variable
serializeValue	Recursively serializes data
write	Appends the specified data to an existing serialized structure

The point of the WddxSerializer class's existence is to support the creation of the WDDX client side. To better facilitate this, the trackcache needs to be altered to include a field called status_. The point of this field is merely to carry a flag indicating the kind of processing that has been done or needs to be done with an individual record in the trackcache. Listing 7.9 shows the TrackCache2.cfm template; its logic is only marginally different from the TrackCache1 .cfm presented in Listing 7.5.

Listing 7.9   Recaching Database Records to Include Status Information (TrackCache2.cfm)

```
<!---
    Name:        /c07/TrackCache2.cfm
    Description: Cache all the records from the
        Track table into a special purposed
        field in the Album table to increase
        database perform.  Insert an additional
        field into the Track cache for
        later usage in client side editing.
--->
<cfquery name="albums"
    datasource="#request.datasource#">
    select * from Album
</cfquery>
```

```
<cfloop query="albums">
    <cfset id = albums.id>

    <cftry>
        <cfquery name="tracks"
            datasource="#request.datasource#">
            select
                id, album_id, tracknumber, name
            from Track
            where
                album_id = #id#
        </cfquery>

        <cfscript>
            track_recordCount = tracks.recordCount;
            newColumn = arrayNew(1);
            arraySet(newColumn, 1,
                track_recordCount, "R");
            queryAddColumn(tracks, "status_",
                newColumn);
        </cfscript>

        <cfwddx action="cfml2wddx" input="#tracks#"
            output="packet">

        <cfquery name="trackcache"
            datasource="#request.datasource#">
            update Album
            set
                trackcache = '#packet#'
            where id = #id#
        </cfquery>

        <cfcatch type="database">
            <cfoutput>
                There was an error working
                with an Album (id:#id#)
            </cfoutput>
            <cfdump var="#cfcatch#">
            <cfabort>
        </cfcatch>
    </cftry>
</cfloop>
```

Next, we'll look at the WddxSerializer usage through the EditAlbum.cfm template, an excerpt of which is shown in Listing 7.10. This is a little more complicated than might be expected because it is purposefully very similar to ShowAlbum.cfm, discussed previously (see Listing 7.8).

Listing 7.10   **An Interface for Editing an Album's Track Records (EditAlbum.cfm)**

```
01: <!---
02:     Name:        /c07/EditAlbum.cfm
03:     Description: Record editing on the
04:         client side using database records
05:         cached with WDDX.
06: --->
07: <cfif isDefined("form.packet")>
08:     <cfwddx action="wddx2cfml" input="#form.packet#"
09:         output="tracks">
10:
11:     <cfloop query="tracks">
12:         <cfswitch expression="#uCase(tracks.status_)#">
13:             <cfcase value="D">
14:                 <cfquery name="deleteTrack"
15:                     datasource="#request.datasource#">
16:                     delete from Track
17:                     where id = #tracks.id#
18:                 </cfquery>
19:             </cfcase>
20:
21:             <cfcase value="C">
22:                 <cfquery name="createTrack"
23:                     datasource="#request.datasource#">
24:                     insert into Track
25:                         (album_id, tracknumber, name)
26:                     values
27:                         (#tracks.album_id#,
28:                         #tracks.tracknumber#,
29:                         '#tracks.name#')
30:                 </cfquery>
31:             </cfcase>
32:         </cfswitch>
33:     </cfloop>
34:
35:     <cfquery name="albums"
36:         datasource="#request.datasource#">
37:         select * from Album
38:         where id = #tracks.album_id#
39:     </cfquery>
40:
41:     <cfloop query="albums">
42:         <cfset id = albums.id>
43:
44:         <cftry>
45:             <cfquery name="tracks"
46:                 datasource="#request.datasource#">
47:                 select
48:                     id, album_id, tracknumber, name
```

```
49:                    from
50:                        Track
51:                    where
52:                        album_id = #id#
53:                    order by
54:                        tracknumber
55:                </cfquery>
56:
57:                <cfscript>
58:                track_recordCount = tracks.recordCount;
59:                newColumn = arrayNew(1);
60:                arraySet(newColumn, 1,
61:                    track_recordCount, "R");
62:                queryAddColumn(tracks,
63:                    "status_", newColumn);
64:                </cfscript>
65:
66:                <cfwddx action="cfml2wddx" input="#tracks#"
67:                    output="packet">
68:
69:                <cfquery name="trackcache"
70:                    datasource="#request.datasource#">
71:                    update Album
72:                    set trackcache = '#packet#'
73:                    where id = #id#
74:                </cfquery>
75:
76:                <cfcatch type="Database">
77:                    <cfoutput>
78:                        There was an error
79:                        working with an Album (id:#id#)
80:                    </cfoutput>
81:                    <cfdump var="#cfcatch#">
82:                    <cfabort>
83:                </cfcatch>
84:            </cftry>
85:        </cfloop>
86: </cfif>
```

In this listing, the template opens and immediately checks for the posted WDDX packet. If it is present, it is converted into a query (lines 8 and 9) and looped over (lines 11–33). The actions within this loop are determined by the status_ field—the artificial field created within the trackcache by the TrackCache2.cfm presented in Listing 7.9. The records that are flagged to be deleted—indicated by having a status_ value of "D"—are removed from the database (lines 13–19). Records that are flagged to be created—indicated by a status_ value of "C"— are inserted into the database (lines 21–31). The remaining portion of the listing (lines 35–85) rebuilds the trackcache for the album whose tracks were just edited.

Part of the template that was elided from Listing 7.10 is the inclusion of the JavaScript source, `EditAlbum.js`, an excerpt of which is shown in Listing 7.11. All of the client-side logic is contained within this file.

Listing 7.11   **Client-side Logic for Album Editing (from EditAlbum.js)**

```
01: /*
02:     Name:        /c07/EditAlbum.js
03:     Description: A separate JavaScript source to
04:          support the EditAlbum template.
05: */
06: function flagDelete(trackID)
07: {
08:     var record = findIndex(rsTracks, "id", trackID);
09:     if(record != -1)
10:     {
11:         rsTracks.setField(record, "status_", "D");
12:     }
13: }
14:
15: function buildPacket()
16: {
17:     var count;
18:     var frm = window.document.forms[0];
19:     var newName = frm.elements['name'].value;
20:     var newNumber = frm.elements['number'].value;
21:
22:     var serializer = new WddxSerializer;
23:
24:     if(!checkNumber(newNumber))
25:     {
26:         alert('The Track Number must be a number.');
27:         return false;
28:     }
29:
30:     if(newName != "" && newNumber != "")
31:     {
32:         rsTracks.addRows(1);
33:         count = rsTracks.getRowCount();
34:         rsTracks.setField(count, "id", -1);
35:         rsTracks.setField(count, "album_id",
36:             rsTracks.getField(1, "album_id"));
37:         rsTracks.setField(count,
38:             "tracknumber", newNumber);
39:         rsTracks.setField(count, "name", newName);
40:         rsTracks.setField(count, "status_", "C");
41:     }
42:
43:     frm.elements['packet'].value =
```

```
44:          serializer.serialize(rsTracks);
45:
46:     return true;
47: }
```

One of the functions elided from Listing 7.11 is showAlbum. This excluded portion is the same as the showAlbum function of ShowAlbum.cfm (Listing 7.8) except for a couple of slight additions—the form fields. These form fields include check boxes next to each table entry that allow tracks to be flagged for deletion and some text boxes in the last table row that allow a new track to be created. The new functionality of flagging tracks for deletion and submitting new track information is handled with the two functions: flagDelete and buildPacket. You can see the result of these field additions in Figure 7.5.

FIGURE 7.5:

EditAlbum Form

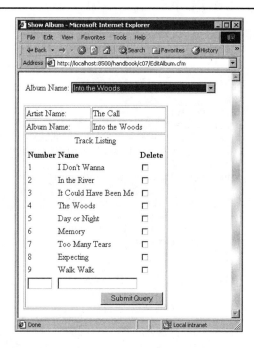

The onClick event for the additional check boxes is linked to the flagDelete function, shown on lines 6–13 of Listing 7.11. This simple function updates the specific Track record in a global WddxRecordset called rsTracks, holding the current and deserialized trackcache and setting its status_ field value to "D".

The buildPacket function (lines 15–47) is the crucial driver of this file. This is how client-side altered content gets back to the server to be updated in the database. Called from the onSubmit event of the form (elided from Listing 7.10), this function uses the WddxSerializer class to convert the global rsTracks into a WDDX packet that can be assigned to a hidden field in the form and posted back to the server. The serializer is created on line 22. The alphanumeric content of the track number field is checked on lines 24–28 to ensure that only numeric content is sent to the database. Lines 30–41 check the text fields that are necessary to create new Track records. If they are in use, a new record is added to rsTrack and populated from the text fields, and the status_ field is set to "C" so that a new record can be created. The entire rsTracks WddxRecordset instance is then serialized and assigned to a hidden form input called packet.

The WddRecordset Class Revisited

One of the extremely powerful features of the WddxRecordset class is its built-in ability to be extended. Using the function registerWddxRecordsetExtension at runtime, it is possible to register new properties and new methods to the WddxRecordset class. This capability exists even in the slimmed-down version of the WDDX JavaScript library that accompanies the ColdFusion Server.

The registerWddxRecordsetExtension function takes two arguments: the label that should be given to the new property or method, and the handle that should be given to the variable or function. It is important to note that added properties will be treated as recordset columns unless their label is prefixed with _private_. To that end, I created a custom WddxRecordset extension to find the index of a record that has a specific value for a specific column: findIndexByColumnValue in the file WddxRecordsetFind.js (Listing 7.12). This is a useful replacement for the findIndex function from the ShowAlbum.cfm (Listing 7.8) template used in the "Exploring the WddxDeserializer Class" section.

Listing 7.12   Custom WddxRecordset Extension (WddxRecordsetFind.js)

```
01: /*
02:    Name:        /c07/WddxRecordsetFind.js
03:    Description: A custom WddxRecordset extension
04:        for doing exact text match lookups of
05:        records.
06: */
07: function wddxRecordset_findIndexByColumnValue(col,
08:     val,
09:     start)
10: {
11:     var idx;
12:     var recordCount;
13:
```

```
14:     if(this.isColumn(col))
15:     {
16:         recordCount = this.getRowCount();
17:         for(idx = start; idx < recordCount; idx++)
18:         {
19:             fld = this.getField(idx, col);
20:             if(fld == val)
21:             {
22:                 return idx;
23:             }
24:         }
25:     }
26:
27:     return -1;
28: }
29:
30: registerWddxRecordsetExtension(
31:     "findIndexByColumnValue",
32:     wddxRecordset_findIndexByColumnValue);
```

Lines 7–28 show a rather simple JavaScript function. This function cannot be called directly because it is designed to be a part of an actual JavaScript class. On lines 14, 16, and 19 it uses the `this` reference indicating an instantiated class. The usage of the JavaScript `this` keyword indicates a reference to the class instance from which the method was invoked, if this function were not incorporated into an instance it would throw a runtime error when the interpreter tried to evaluate `this`.

The function takes three arguments: *col*, the name of the column to match; *val*, the value for which to look; and *start*, the starting index at which to begin the search. The function will return either the index of the exact match, or a –1 if no exact match can be found.

The main driver is in lines 30–32, where the call to `registerWddxRecordsetExtension` is made. Notice that the registration call is not encapsulated in a function. This means that as soon as the source file is included and parsed, the extension will be registered. This extension can be observed in use in Listing 7.13, which is an excerpt of the ColdFusion template `FindAlbum.cfm`.

Listing 7.13   Lookup an Album Record by Name (from FindAlbum.cfm)

```
01: <!---
02:     Name:       /c07/FindAlbum.cfm
03:     Description: Find, in records cached
04:         to the client, through exact text
05:         matches, albums.
06: --->
07: <script language="JavaScript">
```

```
08: function findAlbum()
09: {
10:     var idx;
11:     var length;
12:     var artistIdx;
13:     var artistID;
14:     var albumIdx;
15:     var trackCache;
16:     var tableString = "";
17:     var albumName;
18:     var trackList;
19:
20:     var rsTracks;
21:
22:     var deser = new WddxDeserializer;
23:
24:     var frm = window.document.forms[0];
25:
26:     trackList = window.document.all['tracklist'];
27:     albumName = frm.elements['albumname'].value;
28:
29:     if(albumName != "")
30:     {
31:         albumIdx =
32:             rsAlbums.findIndexByColumnValue("name",
33:                 albumName, 0);
34:         trackCache =
35:             rsAlbums.getField(albumIdx, "trackcache");
36:         artistID =
37:             rsAlbums.getField(albumIdx, "artist_id");
38:         artistIdx =
39:             rsArtists.findIndexByColumnValue("id",
40:                 artistID, 0);
41:
42:         rsTracks = deser.deserialize(trackCache);
43:         length = rsTracks.getRowCount();
44:
45:         tableString += "<table border=\"1\">";
46:         tableString +=
47:             "<tr><td>Artist Name:</td><td>" +
48:             rsArtists.getField(artistIdx, "name") +
49:             "</td></tr>";
50:         tableString += "<tr><td>Album Name:</td><td>" +
51:             rsAlbums.getField(albumIdx, "name") +
52:             "</td></tr>";
53:         tableString += "<tr><td colSpan=\"2\">";
54:         tableString +=
55:             "<table><caption>Track Listing</caption>" +
```

```
56:                    "<tr><th align=\"left\">Number</th>" +
57:                    "<th align=\"left\">Name</th></tr>";
58:
59:            for(idx = 0; idx < length; idx++)
60:            {
61:                tableString += "<tr><td>" +
62:                    rsTracks.getField(idx, "tracknumber") +
63:                    "</td><td>" +
64:                    rsTracks.getField(idx, "name") +
65:                    "</td></tr>";
66:            }
67:
68:            tableString += "</table>";
69:            tableString += "</td></tr>";
70:            tableString += "</table>";
71:
72:            trackList.innerHTML =
73:                tableString;
74:
75:            return false;
76:        }
77: }
78: </script>
```

The FindAlbum.cfm template is not dissimilar to the ShowAlbum.cfm, in Listing 7.8. It has a nearly identical setup of queries and form. The only difference is that instead of selecting an artist and album to be displayed, you need to enter an album name into the text field that will be displayed. When you submit the form, you trigger the call to the JavaScript function findAlbum, shown in Listing 7.13.

Line 27 retrieves the name entered from the text field, and on lines 31–33, that value is used to do a search in the Album recordset. The various pieces of information are obtained, and on lines 45–70, a table is constructed with the Artist name and the Album name. Using the WddxDeserializer discussed earlier, the Album trackcache is then deserialized and displayed within another inner table. In lines 72–73, the string is inserted into a span in the form, similar to what was done in ShowAlbum.cfm (Listing 7.8), and the page displays automatic updates, as illustrated in Figure 7.6.

Naturally, this extension is limited in its uses because performing exact string and numeric matches against content is a less-than-optimal solution. The enterprising developer will take the time to construct a more-powerful extension using JavaScript's built-in regular expression classes.

FIGURE 7.6:

FindAlbum form

WDDX Syndication

WDDX can be a powerful tool for both data and application syndication. Data syndication is the publication of structured data, either though active (push) or passive (pull) methods. Application syndication is a fuzzier term related to the publication of some applications services; in today's terms it can be viewed as a Web Service. Though the topic of syndication is very involved and beyond the scope of this book, we'll look briefly at some resources involved in this subject and some examples of how you can use WDDX for data syndication.

Many news sites provide their headlines and articles in various XML formats, including WDDX. For example, Moreover.com retrieves WDDX news packets, and you'll find custom XML at the geekdom news site Slashdot.org. Since ColdFusion has no built-in support for Slashdot's own Backslash format, you'll need to use XSLT to convert this format into WDDX serialized packets, which will make integration into existing ColdFusion development techniques easier. In addition, though the newer XML capabilities of ColdFusion MX provide excellent opportunities for working with the news packets from Moreover and Slashdot in a variety of ways, for the seemingly simple operation of displaying the headlines and links, the easier CFML query object looping mechanisms will be faster.

Using WDDX with Moreover.com

As mentioned, Moreover.com (http://www.moreover.com) is a popular site that uses the WDDX format for distributing content. Among other formats, this site provides a WDDX news feed for noncommercial use. Not only does Moreover.com support syndication with WDDX, it specifically supports older versions of ColdFusion that had trouble with certain document headers.

Moreover.com supplies WDDX packets with news categories, including links to other WDDX packets that contain headlines and links to news in a specific category.

An example of how you would use the Moreover.com news service is exemplified in Listing 7.14.

Listing 7.14   **The Moreover News Frameset (MoreoverExample.cfm)**

```
<!---
    Name:       /c07/MoreoverExample.cfm
    Description: The frameset for displaying news from
        Moreover.com.
--->
<html>
    <head>
        <title>Moreover News Feed (WDDX)</title>
    </head>

    <frameset border="0" frameBorder="0" rows="100,*">
        <frame name="category"
            src="MoreoverCategories.cfm">
        <frame name="news" src="MoreoverNews.cfm">
    </frameset>
</html>
```

The framed page in Listing 7.14 presents two other templates. The first is Moreover-Categories.cfm (Listing 7.15), which presents an HTML Form select control, populated by the news categories packet drawn from the Moreover.com site.

Listing 7.15   **Moreover News Category Selection (MoreoverCategories.cfm)**

```
<!---
    Name:       /c07/MoreoverCategories.cfm
    Description: Retrieve and build a select
        from the WDDX packet of news categories
        at Moreover.com
--->
<cfhttp
url="http://w.moreover.com/categories/category_list.cf"
```

```
method="get" resolveURL="false">
<cfwddx action="wddx2cfml" input="#cfhttp.fileContent#"
    output="cats">

<html>
<head>
    <title>Moreover News Feed</title>
    <script language="JavaScript">
    function populateNews()
    {
        var frm = window.document.forms[0];
        var category =
            frm.elements['newscategory'];
        var selected = category.selectedIndex;
        var newsURL =
            category.options[selected].value;

        if(newsURL != "0")
        {
            parent.frames['news'].location.href =
                "MoreoverNews.cfm?categoryurl=" +
                newsURL;
        }
    }
    </script>
</head>

<body>
<form action="#null" method="post">
    <select name="newscategory"
        onChange="populateNews();">
        <option value="0">
            --- select category ---
        </option>
        <cfoutput query="cats">
        <option
        value="#urlEncodedFormat(cats.categoryURL)#">
            #cats.category_name#
        </option>
        </cfoutput>
    </select>
</form>
</body>
</html>
```

The first template referred to in the MoreoverExample.cfm (Listing 7.14) is Moreover-Categories.cfm (Listing 7.15); this template retrieves the syndicated news category information from Moreover.com. The retrieved categories are then displayed in a select with a JavaScript function, populateNews, tied to its onChange event. The populateNews function loads the template MoreoverNews.cfm (Listing 7.16) into the second frame passing the selected news category.

Listing 7.16   **Moreover News Headline Display (MoreoverNews.cfm)**

```
<!---
    Name:        MoreoverNews.cfm
    Description: Display all of the headlines from
        a specific Moreover.com news category.
--->
<cfif isDefined("url.categoryurl")>
    <cftry>
        <cfhttp url="#url.categoryurl#"
            method="get" resolveURL="false">
        <cfwddx action="wddx2cfml"
            input="#cfhttp.fileContent#" output="news">
        <cfcatch type="any">
            <cfoutput>#cfcatch.message#</cfoutput>
        </cfcatch>
    </cftry>
</cfif>

<html>
    <head>
        <title>Moreover News Feed</title>
    </head>

    <body>
        <table>
            <tr>
                <th align="left">Headline</th>
                <th align="left">Source</th>
            </tr>
            <cfif isDefined("cfhttp.fileContent")>
                <cfoutput query="news">
                <tr>
                    <td>
                        <a href="#news.url#">
                        #news.headline_text#
                        </a>
                    </td>
                    <td>#news.source#</td>
                </tr>
                </cfoutput>
            </cfif>
        </table>
    </body>
</html>
```

The template MoreoverNews.cfm (Listing 7.16) retrieves the news headlines from Moreover
.com based upon the category passed into the template on the URL. Since Moreover.com
already syndicates in WDDX, it is a small matter to transform the packet into a query object
and display the news headlines in a `table` in the body.

Slashdot.org

One of the great hubs of geekdom news is Slashdot (`http://www.slashdot.org`). A news center primarily for geeks and by geeks, the immense scope of its news topics and popularity
makes it a perfect syndication candidate as well. The sheer volume of traffic at the site, and
the sites to which it links, has even given rise to the term *Slashdot Effect*—or, more simply,
slashdotted. A site is considered slashdotted when, because of an article at Slashdot, the click-
thru traffic to a linked site's web server cannot keep up with the page demand and the server
begins returning errors.

Assisting in the propagation of the Slashdot Effect are the XML syndication files provided
at the site. Using a custom XML vocabulary called Backslash, the news headlines can be syndicated to anyone with a mere HTTP request. To that very devious end, the ColdFusion
template `SlashdotExample1.cfm`, shown in Listing 7.17, demonstrates how to accomplish
this using WDDX.

Listing 7.17   Slashdot Headlines (SlashdotExample1.cfm)

```
01: <!---
02:     Name:       /c07/SlashdotExample1.cfm
03:     Description: Retrieve Slashdot syndicated
04:         headlines and display them.  Using XSLT
05:         to create WDDX packets that can be
06:         converted into CFML datatypes.
07: --->
08: <cfparam name="packetAddress"
09:     default="http://slashdot.org/slashdot.xml">
10: <cfparam name="xslFile"
11:     default="#expandPath("./backslash.wddx.xsl")#">
12:
13: <cftry>
14:     <cfhttp url="#packetAddress#" method="get"
15:         resolveURL="false" throwOnError="yes">
16:
17:     <cffile action="read" file="#xslFile#"
18:         variable="xslFile">
19:
20:     <cfset packet =
21:         xmlTransform(cfhttp.fileContent, xslFile)>
22:
23:     <cfwddx action="wddx2cfml" input="#packet#"
```

```
24:             output="st">
25:
26:     <cfcatch type="any">
27:         <cfoutput>#cfcatch.message#</cfoutput>
28:         <cfabort>
29:     </cfcatch>
30: </cftry>
31:
32: <html>
33:     <head>
34:         <title>Slashdot News</title>
35:     </head>
36:     <body>
37:         <table>
38:             <tr>
39:                 <th align="left">Section</th>
40:                 <th align="left">Headline</th>
41:             </tr>
42:             <cfoutput query="st">
43:                 <tr>
44:                     <td>#st.section#</td>
45:                     <td>
46:                     <a href="#st.url#">#st.title#</a>
47:                     </td>
48:                 </tr>
49:             </cfoutput>
50:         </table>
51:     </body>
52: </html>
```

The first thing this template does is set up some variables for packet retrieval and file handling. Lines 8 and 9 set the address of the Slashdot XML headlines packet, and lines 10 and 11 create the name of the transformation style sheet to convert the headlines packet to WDDX. Then, within a cftry block, lines 13–30, the headlines packet is retrieved and transformed.

The transformation style sheet must be read in, which is also accomplished within a cftry block in lines 17–18. At this point, two transformations take place: Backslash into WDDX and WDDX into a CFML query. The transformation from Slashdot's own format into WDDX is done with the new ColdFusion MX function xmlTransform on lines 20 and 21. Once the content is in a format familiar to the CFML interpreter, it is a small step to transform it into a query, as is shown in lines 23 and 24.

NOTE   There isn't sufficient space here to discuss the contents of the XSLT script used to transform Slashdot's Backslash vocabulary into WDDX. If you wish to learn more about XSLT scripting, you can read the volume of documentation at the World Wide Web Consortium's site (http://www.w3.org/Style/XSL) and in *Mastering XSLT*, by Chuck White (Sybex, 2002).

The remainder of the template shown in Listing 7.17 is straightforward processing that will be familiar to even junior ColdFusion developers. A `table` is created within the body. Within a `cfoutput`, lines 42–49, the query is processed creating a row for each record. Only three fields from the Slashdot packet were used here, but there are several others that are available for various tasks, as described in Table 7.5.

TABLE 7.5: Backslash Fields

Packet Field	Description
Author	Specifies the username of the submitter
Comments	Specifies the number of user comments in response to the posting
Department	Houses a humorous tag line that fictitiously categorizes the posting
Image	Specifies the image file used to visually categorize the posting
Section	Specifies the real category of the article
Time	Specifies when the article was submitted
Title	Specifies the tag of the article
Topic	Specifies a topical categorization value
URL	Specifies the URL link to the Slashdot site for the full body of the article

In Sum

This chapter has covered an assortment of technologies and techniques for using WDDX with ColdFusion applications. The use of WDDX for caching, syndication, and client-side editing of batch records are all complex topics that cannot be adequately addressed by this pedestrian presentation. Nor can we offer the vast amount of performance data and design nuances needed to fully develop these techniques. And we are similarly limited in explaining the many permutations of using WDDX with just ColdFusion. You can, however, launch serious investigations of all these topics from the content presented in this chapter.

CHAPTER 8

Application Security Techniques

By Raymond Camden

- Reviewing security fundamentals for web applications

- What is authentication?

- What is authorization?

- Examining roles-based security in ColdFusion MX

- Building secure web applications

Without a doubt, security is of paramount concern in both the online and the real world today—not only to those of us who build web applications, but also to those who use web applications. An unsecure website is not only dangerous to your business, but it may scare away potential visitors.

In this chapter, we will discuss various methods by which you can add security to a web application. We will begin by covering the basics of security including authentication and authorization. Then we will discuss how to construct safe websites that are protected from malicious attackers and general mischief.

Before You Begin

Before beginning this chapter, you will need to do some setup so that you can run its code.

1. First, if you haven't done so already, you'll need to downloaded the code for this book from the Sybex website and install it to the root folder of your web directory. In this chapter, we will be working with the Chapter 8 folder (c08).

2. The next thing you will need to do is create a data source. To do so, go to the ColdFusion Administrator (which should be found at `http://localhost/cfide/administrator/index.cfm`) and select Data Sources. Name your new data source `cfdev_security` and point it to the Access database named `security.mdb` in the Chapter 8 folder.

NOTE   If your ColdFusion install is running on a different port, be sure to modify the URL above to the point to the correct port. This applies to any URL mentioned in the text below.

Figure 8.1 shows how the data source should be set up.

Security Basics

Security comes down to one basic principle—ensuring that people do only what they are allowed to do. Of course, the devil is in the details. Most web applications need security of some kind or another; for example, consider the following:

• A web-based forum that requires you to log in before posting

• An online bank that requires a login to display the correct account information

• A website that allows users to post comments but requires a special user, known as an editor, to approve the comments before they are published

The design process of any web application should include consideration of security at all times. It's not enough to say that your site will have a certain feature—it is imperative that you also determine who can use the feature and in what way. Let's say your website may contain a static front page, a forums-based application, and a "latest news" page.

In the forums, your visitors can discuss various subjects. You require that visitors register before they can use the forums. This allows you to more accurately trace who is saying what. Later on, we will discuss this aspect of security and refer to it as *authentication*.

The news page displays a list of news articles. These articles are not entered by hand and then uploaded to the server; rather, you use a web-based tool to create, edit, and delete these articles. In this case, no one but you and your business partners are allowed to use this tool. We call this aspect of security *authorization*. Let's take a look at the break down of this setup in Table 8.1.

FIGURE 8.1:

Setting up the data source

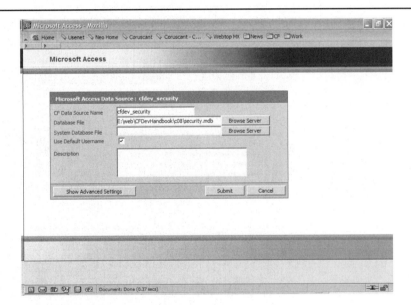

TABLE 8.1: Pages and Security Settings

Page	Task	Security Settings
Home	None.	None. Anyone can view and use this page.
Forums	Users can post messages and interact with other site visitors.	Anyone can use the Forums page, but visitors must register and log in beforehand.
News	Displays the latest news.	None. Anyone can view and use this page.
News Administrator	Allows the user to create, edit, and delete news articles.	Only specific people who have logged in can use this page.

Table 8.1 presents the website in four distinct sections, or *features*. For each feature, we clearly state its purpose and then the particular security settings for that feature.

Let's take a look at a concrete example of this. Imagine a simple content management system. (For more information about content management and web applications, see Chapter 1, "Designing and Planning a ColdFusion Application.") This system consists of a page that displays a list of press releases. The logic behind this page is a simple SQL statement that grabs press releases that have been marked as released. (For now, don't worry about the code. We will discuss that later in the chapter.) Each press release is displayed as just a link and a title.

Open your browser to `http://localhost/CFDevHandbook/c08/index.cfm` and view the sample application (Figure 8.2).

FIGURE 8.2:

Press release list

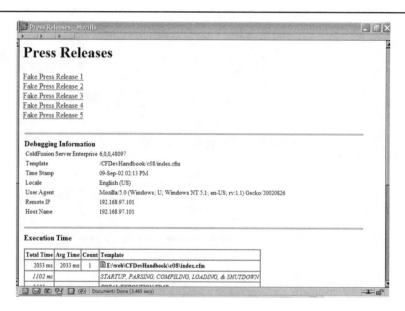

The second page in this sample application contains the actual body of a press release. Each press release in the first page simply links to the second page and passes a URL attribute signifying which press release to load. (Again, we will be discussing this code later in the chapter.) To test this application, simply click any of the links. Figure 8.3 shows one of the press releases.

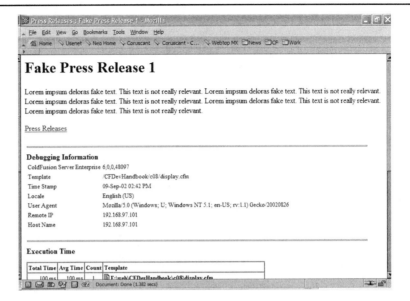

Authentication

At this point, the "public" portion of the site is up and running, but of course we need a means by which we can modify the content of the site. We don't want just anyone doing that, so we need a way to authenticate anyone who's trying to use this administration tool—a way to confirm that a person is who they say they are.

There are multiple ways of doing this. The web server can be set up to require a network login before the user can access a particular folder. You could use various biometrics tools, including fingerprint and retina matching. But the most common way to authenticate a user is the familiar system of requiring a username and password.

The tool to create, edit, and delete press releases can already be found in the code you downloaded from the website, under the CdevHandBook/c08 folder, in a folder named admin. To check out this Press Release Editor (Figure 8.4) tool, open your browser to http://localhost/CFDevHandbook/c08/admin/press_release_editor.cfm. Feel free to modify the existing press releases, or create a few new ones.

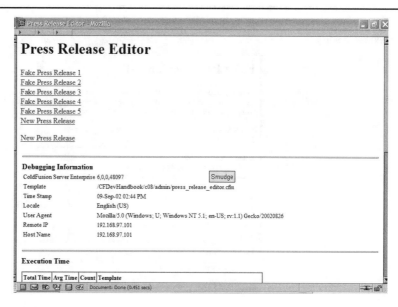

You probably noticed that the Press Release Editor did not ask you to log in. Obviously, this isn't a good thing. Although there's no direct link to this tool from the public website, if someone were to guess the name of the folder (and how hard is it to guess admin?), they would be able to alter the press release database. So the first thing we need to do is protect the admin folder.

ColdFusion will always check for the existence of a file called Application.cfm. If it's not found in the same folder of the template that is being executed, ColdFusion attempts to find it in higher folders. Our goal is to protect the admin folder, so we will begin by adding an Application.cfm file to this folder. Because this file will always be called, we can use it to files within the folder. Listing 8.1 displays the Application.cfm file.

NOTE   If you don't want to type in the code in this listing, simply rename the Application_orig .cfm file that you downloaded from the website. It is already in the admin folder.

Listing 8.1   **Admin Application file (Application.cfm)**

```
<!---
    Name:          /c08/admin/Application.cfm
    Description:    Press Release Editor Security
--->

<cfapplication name="PressReleaseEditor" sessionManagement=true>
```

```
<!--- Handle user logout --->
<cfif isDefined("url.logout")>

    <cflock scope="session" type="exclusive" timeout=3>
        <cfset structDelete(session,"loggedIn")>
    </cflock>

</cfif>

<!--- Process login --->
<cfif isDefined("form.login") and
    isDefined("form.username") and isDefined("form.password")>

    <cfquery name="login" datasource="cfdev_security">
        select
            username
        from
            tblUsers
        where
            username = '#form.username#'
            and
            password = '#form.password#'
    </cfquery>

    <cfif login.recordCount>

        <cflock scope="session" type="exclusive" timeout=3>
            <cfset session.loggedIn = 1>
        </cflock>

    </cfif>

</cfif>

<!--- Is the user logged in? --->
<cflock scope="session" type="readOnly" timout=3>

    <cfif not isDefined("session.loggedIn")>
        <cfinclude template="login.cfm">
        <cfabort>
    </cfif>

</cflock>
```

Arranging for Session Management

The template shown in Listing 8.1 is pretty simple. It begins by defining an application with the cfapplication tag. Session management has been turned on as well. Our security system must keep track of when the user logs in, and session management is the only way to do this over the Web.

Why session management? First, unlike client management, session management will automatically expire. If the user leaves their machine and doesn't return, they will automatically be logged out of the application. By default, sessions will expire after 20 minutes of inactivity. This setting is defined in the ColdFusion Administrator, along with the maximum possible timeout. Since we didn't define the session time out above, users who are authenticated will be logged out if they don't hit the site within 20 minutes.

Logging In and Out

The next portion of the code in Listing 8.1 handles logouts. We will want to provide a way for the user to log out instead of just waiting around for the session to time out. If the URL variable `logout` exists, we remove the `loggedIn` variable from the `session` scope. Where does this `loggedIn` variable come from? This is the variable that will be used to mark someone as being logged in. Therefore the logout action needs to remove this variable so that the "mark" of being logged on is no longer there.

The next block of code will handle login attempts. Here, we check for the existence of three variables: `form.login`, `form.username`, and `form.password`. (Later on you will see these variables set from the login template.) This is a fairly straightforward security check. After we have performed this check, we then pass the form values to the database. If the username and password match, then the query will return one record. That's why we follow the query with a simple check of the query's record count. When the user doesn't provide the correct username and password, the query will have a record count of zero. When the query is successful, the user will have provided a correct username and password. The session variable `loggedIn` is then set to true.

In the next block of code in this listing, you can see where we checked for the `loggedIn` variable. If it didn't exist, a login template would be included and execution would be aborted with the `cfabort` tag.

Why Do We Use cflock Tags?

`cflock` tags are very important when variables that are shared with multiple users are being used, like `application` variables, or when variables are shared with multiple requests, like `session` variables. `cflock` tags help ensure the stability of your ColdFusion application and should *always* be used when accessing (either reading or writing) these variables. For more information, see the online article, "Locking in ColdFusion" at http://www.macromedia .com/v1/handlers/index.cfm?ID=17196&Method=Full.

The good news is that locking is, for the most part, unnecessary in ColdFusion MX. We will continue to use `cflock` throughout the chapter, however, in case you are using an earlier version of ColdFusion.

Let's take a step back and examine the basic flow of the page.

1. When the user requests any file in the admin folder, the first thing that happens is the Application.cfm file executes.

2. We then check to see if the user is in the process of logging out. If so, we remove the session variable that marks the user as being logged in.

3. Next, we check to see whether a user is attempting to log in. If so, we check the database to see if the credentials provided were correct.

4. Lastly, we check to see whether the user has been authenticated. We do this by checking for the session variable. If it doesn't exist, we include a login template and abort.

We've talked about the code aspect of the authentication system, but we haven't discussed the database. In Listing 8.1, we checked a table named tblUsers. If you open this table in Microsoft Access, or connect to the data source with ColdFusion Studio, you'll see that the table only contains two simple columns—username and password—which means the table only contains lists of users and their associated passwords.

Last but not least, let's take a quick look at the login template that Application.cfm includes. Listing 8.2 shows the source of login.cfm.

Listing 8.2   **The log on template (login.cfm)**

```
<!---
    Name:           /c08/admin/login.cfm
    Description:    Login template
--->

<cfoutput>
<form action="#cgi.script_name#" method="post">
</cfoutput>

<h3>Please enter your username and password</h3>

Username <input type="text" name="username"><br>
Password <input type="password" name="password"><br>
<input type="submit" name="login" value="Login">

</form>
```

As you can see, there is nothing much here but a simple form. This is because the authentication logic is actually kept in the Application.cfm file. This template merely handles the display of the login form.

One part that may be of interest is the action attribute of the form tag. Instead of pointing to a specific file, we point to #cgi.script_name#. How does this work? When the user requests a file in the protected directory, it may be the home page, `index.cfm`, or some other page. If the user has been logged out because of inactivity, a nice touch would be to return them to where they were. The variable `cgi.script_name` will contain the name of the file that was requested, not the file currently being run (`login.cfm`). When the user hits the Submit button, they will be sent back to the file they requested. Of course, the `Application.cfm` file will still be called and will still handle security!

To take a look at all these changes, simply go back to your browser and try to view the Press Release Editor again. You should see something like Figure 8.5. This is what we want. Any request for the pages within the folder should force a login.

FIGURE 8.5:

Press Release Editor
with security

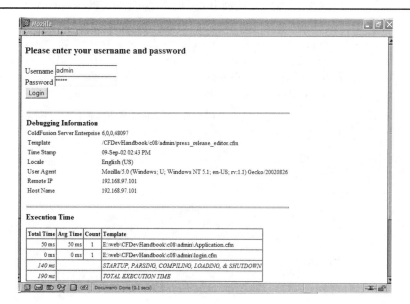

If you want to test the login system, enter **admin** for both the username and the password. These values exist in the database you downloaded from the website. In the real world, however, you would never use a password so simple. (I hope!)

Changing Users and Passwords

If you decide you want to change the password, we have a tool that will handle that. Users and passwords can be considered just like any other piece of content for a website. So since we have a tool to edit press releases, we can edit usernames and passwords in the exact same way.

Because the editor file is a bit large, we will discuss just the important aspects of it. You should take a moment to study the code as a whole before we go into detail on specific parts of it. (You'll find it in the c08/admin/user_editor.cfm file that you downloaded from the Sybex website.) In general, it should look similar to other content management–style applications. Most people have built applications that allow for AED, or Adding, Editing, and Deleting. We get a list of data (in this case, usernames), and we allow users to be added, edited, and deleted.

Let's focus on what makes this template a bit different from the normal content-management-type script. Because usernames should be unique on a system, our user editor should remember the username when editing a user. This way, we can check to see whether the username has been changed, and if so, ensure that it is still unique. The following excerpt shows the simple editor form including the old username:

```
<form action="user_editor.cfm" method="post">
<input type="hidden" name="oldUser" value="#oldUser#">
Username <input type="text" name="username" value="#username#"><br>
Password <input type="text" name="password" value="#password#"><br>
<input type="submit" name="save" value="Save">
<cfif oldUser is not "">
    <input type="submit" name="delete" value="Delete">
</cfif>
</form>
</cfoutput>
```

As you can see, the oldUser value is contained in a hidden form field. There is no need for the administrator to change this value since we are only using it for comparison's sake. If we are editing a new user, the value of oldUser will be blank. You will notice that we do not include a Delete button if this is the case. It doesn't make sense to delete a nonexistent user.

The next important difference we should point out is the use of the cflock tag. The part of the script that handles saving/editing/deleting users is wrapped with this tag:

```
<cflock name="user_editor" type="exclusive" timeout=3>
```

Most people use the scope attribute of cflock, but in our case, we are not locking a shared-memory variable (like the application or session scope). We use the name attribute to create a named lock. The purpose of this lock is to ensure that changes to users are done in a single-threaded fashion. Why? One of the rules of our system is that users must be unique. We can easily write a query to check whether a username already exists. However, if two (or more) people are running the editor at the same time, it's possible that they might both try to save a user with the same username. If this happened, it would then be possible to save both users with the same username. By using cflock, we ensure that this portion of the file can only be run by one particular process. Using our earlier example of the two people trying to use the same username, one person would simply be delayed a few microseconds, and then they would (correctly) get an error message saying that their chosen username already exists.

Finishing Up

The rest of the template really doesn't differ much from the Press Release Editor, so we won't discuss it in detail. However, one thing that was left out of this template is what I call a sanity checker. It is possible to delete all users—but this is not something you would normally want to do. Nevertheless, if the administrator wants to lock up the editing tools, they can. We could also add rules to check for "decent" usernames. For instance, we could add rules to ensure that no spaces exist in the username, or that it begins with a letter, not a number. Again, these mechanisms fall into the category of content management, and the rules employed would change on a case-by-case basis.

Authorization

So far, our security system remains uncomplicated. As long as you have a valid username and password, you can run any of the applications within the `admin` folder. This works fine for many websites, especially those where only a few people are administrating the site. However, consider this scenario:

Your website (the truly exciting listing of press releases) is getting more popular every day. Keeping up with the traffic and requests for new press releases is becoming a more intensive job than what you planned for, and it is seriously eating into your MP3 downloading time. The solution—hire assistants! It is trivial to hire a few grunts...sorry, make that copy writers...create new usernames, and have them toil away creating new content. However, these new assistants may need some guidance. You want them to write those press releases, but before their releases go online, you want to have a chance to approve their content.

And here we arrive at the concept of authorization. Authentication simply ensures that a person is who they say they are. Authorization is what allows us to control what that person can do. In this case, we have two groups (types) of users. The assistants are authorized to create press releases, but they cannot publish these press releases on the website; we will call them Authors. The other group of users are the Editors. These people can approve articles and publish them on the site. They can also do anything the authors can do. Table 8.2 lays out these groups and what they can do.

TABLE 8.2: Groups and Rights

Group	Rights
Authors, Editors	Create and edit press releases.
Editors	Publish, or remove, a press release.
Editors	Delete press releases.
Editors	Add, edit, and/or delete users.

Why do we work with groups? It makes more sense to say what a group can do as opposed to setting up rights for Bob and Mary and Bernice. In terms of writing code, working with groups is just easier than working with individual users. If we designed our code to work around particular usernames, that code would have to be updated every time someone was hired or fired.

Our Authorization Data Scheme

Open up the Access database file and you will notice a table called tblGroups. This table simply lists the groups that exist in our application. As described above, the groups are Authors and Editors.

The other table related to our security system is tblUserGroups. This table simply matches up users and groups. Each row consists of one username and one group. If a person belongs to multiple groups, they will have multiple entries in the table. For our simple system, most people will be in just one group. Since groups will determine what a user can do, we need to grab the groups, if any, to which the user belongs when they log in.

Let's take a look at this new system in the admin_adv folder within the Chapter 8 folder with which we have been working. First we'll examine the enhanced Application.cfm file in Listing 8.3.

Listing 8.3   **Second version of application file (Application.cfm)**

```
<!---
    Name:          /c08/admin_adv/Application.cfm
    Description:    Press Release Editor Security, version 2
--->

<cfapplication name="PressReleaseEditor_Adv" sessionManagement=true>

<!--- Handle user logout --->
<cfif isDefined("url.logout")>

    <cflock scope="session" type="exclusive" timeout=3>
        <cfset structDelete(session,"loggedIn")>
        <cfset structDelete(session,"groups")>
    </cflock>

</cfif>

<!--- Process login --->
<cfif isDefined("form.login") and
    isDefined("form.username") and isDefined("form.password")>

    <cfquery name="login" datasource="cfdev_security">
        select
```

```
                    username
                from
                    tblUsers
                where
                    username = '#form.username#'
                    and
                    password = '#form.password#'
        </cfquery>

        <cfiflogin.recordCount>

            <!--- Grab groups --->
            <cfquery name="getGroups" datasource="cfdev_security">
                select
                    groupName
                from
                    tblUserGroups
                where
                    username = '#form.username#'
            </cfquery>

            <cflock scope="session" type="exclusive" timeout=3>
                <cfset session.loggedIn = 1>
                <cfset session.groups = valueList(getGroups.groupName)>
            </cflock>

        </cfif>

    </cfif>

    <!--- Is the user logged in? --->
    <cflock scope="session" type="readOnly" timeout=3>

        <cfif not isDefined("session.loggedIn")>
            <cfinclude template="login.cfm">
            <cfabort>
        <cfelse>
            <cfset request.sessionGroups = session.groups>
        </cfif>

    </cflock>
```

Let's focus on how this enhanced Application.cfm differs from the original. The cfapplication tag defines the application scope; in this case, we have given it a new name, PressReleaseEditor_Adv, simply to ensure that it doesn't get confused with the original version. The first cfif block handles the logout routine. As before, we remove the session variable loggedIn, which marks the user as being logged in. We also remove the session variable that stores the list of groups to which the user belongs.

The login process has not changed. We still check for the existence and validity of two form variables: username and password. If they are valid, we run a new query that checks the tblUserGroups for any records that match up with the current username and returns a simple query with one column.

```
<!--- Grab groups --->
<cfquery name="getGroups" datasource="cfdev_security">
    select
        groupName
    from
        tblUserGroups
    where
        username = '#form.username#'
</cfquery>
```

We grab this column as a list by using the valueList() function, and we store it in the application scope:

```
<cfset session.groups = valueList(getGroups.groupName)>
```

The rest of the template is the same as the original version except for the login check. As before, we check for the loggedIn variable; however, if the user was logged in, we copy their user groups to a request variable. Since we will be checking the user's groups quite often in the application, and since this variable is stored in a session variable, it is easier to copy it to the request scope so that we don't need to use the cflock tag when we want to check the groups.

So far, so good. Our security system has now been upgraded to check for and store the groups to which the user belongs. Open your browser and connect to the new version of the administrator tool at http://localhost/CFDevHandbook/c08/admin_adv. Log on with the admin username and admin password.

NOTE   If you deleted the admin username when you were playing with the User Editor earlier, switch back to the simpler administrator tool now and re-create the account. For the rest of the examples to work, at least initially, the admin user must exist because it is a member of the Editors group.

We've also added a basic home page for the administrator. Let's take a look at this home page in Listing 8.4.

Listing 8.4   **Administrator home page (index.cfm)**

```
<!---
    Name:           /c08/admin_adv/index.cfm
    Description:    Press Release Editor Home, version 2
--->
```

```
<html>

<head>
    <title>Press Release Administrator</title>
  </head>

<body>

<h1>Press Release Administrator</h1>

<!--- Anyone can run parts of the PR editor --->
<cfif listFindNoCase(request.sessionGroups,"Authors") or
    listFindNoCase(request.sessionGroups,"Editors")>
    <a href="press_release_editor.cfm">Edit Press Releases</a><br>
</cfif>

<!--- Only Editors can edit users --->
<cfif listFindNoCase(request.sessionGroups,"Editors")>
    <a href="user_editor.cfm">Edit Users</a><br>
</cfif>

<a href="index.cfm?logout=1">Logout</a>
```

This page has three links. For each link, we check what groups the user belongs to. Remember that we copied the users' groups to the request scope variable, sessionGroups. This is a list, so the listFindNoCase() function will be used to determine whether the user is in the Authors or Editors group. If so, we display the link. The Edit Users link, however, will only be displayed if the user belongs to the Editors group. Everyone can log out, so the third link will always be displayed.

In order to test the authorization system, we need to create or edit a user and place them in the Authors group only.

The admin_adv folder has a slightly modified version of the user_editor.cfm template that was used in the admin folder.

Let's focus on what has changed in this template from the earlier version. One of the most important changes is the security check:

```
<cfif not listFindNoCase(request.sessionGroups,"Editors")>
    <cflocation url="index.cfm">
</cfif>
```

Recall that we performed a similar check in the index.cfm file before we created the link to this page. Wasn't that good enough? No! Imagine this scenario: A user on your system used to be an Editor, but they made some bad decisions and you demoted them to just being an

Author. But if this user bookmarked the User Edit page, they would still be able to access it despite the link being missing. We will discuss security measures like this in the upcoming section "Building Secure Web Applications."

Now that we've looked at the security check, let's look at another change. The logic that displays all the users has not changed—however, the edit form has. This time we need to grab all the group names when editing a user. This is done by simply querying the `tblGroups` table. We will use this in the edit form as a means of assigning people to groups.

```
<cfquery name="getAllGroups" datasource="cfdev_security">
    select
        groupName
    from
        tblGroups
</cfquery>

<cfset groupList = valueList(getAllGroups.groupName)>
```

The next change is to get the groups the user currently belongs to. This list is set to a local variable, `MyGroups`, that will be blank for a new user.

```
<cfquery name="getMyGroups" datasource="cfdev security">
    select
        groupName
    from
        tblUserGroups
    where
        username = '#url.username#'
</cfquery>

<cfset myGroups = valueList(getMyGroups.groupName)>
```

The next change is in the form itself. After asking for the username and password, we want to display the groups that a user can belong to. We use a `select` tag with the `multiple` attribute to allow us to see and select multiple groups. We loop over all the groups to check to see if the current group is assigned to the user we are editing. The new editor is illustrated in Figure 8.6.

The code that handles saving and deleting users has been updated to handle the presence of groups. The form field that handled the groups was a select box with the `multiple` setting. Because of this, it's possible that no group was selected, and if so, the field won't be passed at all. If the form field exists, it can be one or many groups. If it is multiple groups, they will be in a list, like so: `authors, editors`. We can simply loop over this list and insert a record for each group.

FIGURE 8.6:

The new user editor

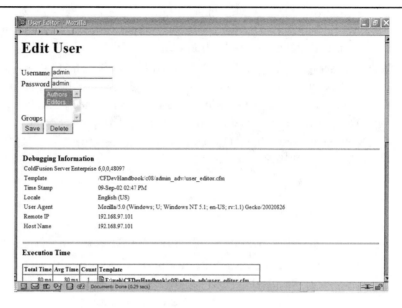

FIGURE 8.6:

The new user editor

For new users, the logic is simple. If form.groups exists (in other words, if *something* was picked), then we insert one record for each group into the tblUserGroups table:

```
<!--- Handle groups --->
<cfif isDefined("form.groups")>
    <cfloop index="group" list="#form.groups#">
        <cfquery name="insGroups"
            datasource="cfdev_security">
            insert into tblUserGroups(username,groupName)
            values('#form.username#','#group#')
        </cfquery>
    </cfloop>
</cfif>
```

Handling existing users is a bit different. For each group that a user is assigned to, one record will exist in the tblUserGroups table. Therefore, re-inserting additional records would corrupt the database table. We could check to see which groups the user used to belong to and delete them if they were not selected again. Then we could add only the groups that are new for the user. The easier solution is to simply delete all records in the table that relate to this user, as shown next. Once we've done that, we can then use the same insertion code we used for new users.

```
<!--- Remove all old groups --->
<cfquery="removeGroups" datasource="cfdev_security">
    delete from
```

```
                        tblUserGroups
                where
                        username = '#form.oldUser#'
        </cfquery>
```

The next change is within the code that handles the deletion of users. The `deleteGroups` query simply cleans up any records associated with the user:

```
<cfquery name="deleteGroups" datasource="cfdev_security">
    delete from tblUserGroups
    where username = '#form.oldUser#'
</cfquery>
```

The user editor was designed only to be used by editors; there, our security check simply ensured that the current user was an editor. The Press Release Editor is a good example of an application that is used by both types of users. Rather than studying the entire template this time, we will focus on the point where groups come into play.

First, the rules we described in the beginning dictate that only editors can publish articles. So in this case, the edit form has the following code block after it asks for the title and body:

```
<cfif listFindNoCase(request.sessionGroups,"Editors")>
    Released <select name="released">
    <option <cfif released>selected</cfif> value=1>yes
    <option <cfif not released>selected</cfif> value=0>no
    </select><br>
<cfelse>
    <input type="hidden" name="released" value=0>
</cfif>
```

We are performing the same, familiar security check. In this case, we want to ensure that the form field for releasing the press release is only displayed for Editors. If the user is not an Editor, the form field is output as a hidden form field instead and is set to false.

If you view the Press Release Editor form for a particular press release, and then you log out and return as a user who is only an Author, you will notice that you no longer have the ability to publish articles.

Roles-Based Security in ColdFusion MX

The security techniques discussed so far are simple—ColdFusion makes it easy to add authentication and authorization to our web applications. With ColdFusion MX, however, we get a new feature called roles-based security. "Roles-based" means the security system revolves around the concept of roles, which for our purposes maps to how we use groups. Basically, a user exists in a role or a set of roles that define what the user does (that is, the user is an author or editor, and so on.)

What we will describe next is a set of tags and functions that make security even easier to work with. For a full discussion of this new feature, see *Mastering ColdFusion MX*, by Arman Danesh et al. (Sybex, 2002).

ColdFusion MX contains the following new security tags and functions:

The cflogin tag   This tag is the key tag for setting up a security system in ColdFusion MX. When placed on a template, the code inside a cflogin tag pair (the cflogin tag must always be used with an end cflogin tag) will *always* be run while the current user isn't logged on. We can use this block of code to force a login form to appear, or to check for a possible login attempt.

The cfloginuser tag   This tag will actually mark a user as being logged in. When this tag is called, you must pass the username, password, and roles for the user. The roles act just like the groups we worked with earlier.

The cflogout tag   This tag does what you might imagine—it logs a user out of the current application.

The isUserInRole() function   This function allows you to test if a user is in a specific role. You can pass multiple roles, but the function will only return true if the user is in all of the roles.

The getAuthUser() function   Returns the name of the current user. If the use hasn't logged in, an empty string is returned.

Now that we've briefly discussed the tags and functions involved, let's talk about how the authentication is persisted. cflogin uses a cookie system. This cookie will last as long as the browser is open or until a specified timeout period has passed. The default timeout is 30 minutes; you can alter it by using the idleTimeout attribute.

Let's take a look at a MX version of the security system we worked with earlier. This application will be stored in the admin_mx folder under c08. Listing 8.5 shows a new Application .cfm file.

Listing 8.5   **MX version of the Application.cfm file (Application.cfm)**

```
<!---
    Name:           /c08/admin_mx/Application.cfm
    Description:     Press Release Editor Security, version 3
--->

<cfapplication name="PressReleaseEditor_MX" sessionManagement=true>

<!--- Handle user logout --->
<cfif isDefined("url.logout")>
```

```
        <cflogout>

</cfif>

<cflogin>

    <!--- Process login --->
    <cfif isDefined("form.login") and
        isDefined("form.username") and isDefined("form.password")>

        <cfquery="login" datasource="cfdev_security">
            select
                username
            from
                tblUsers
            where
                username = '#form.username#'
                and
            password = '#form.password#'
        </cfquery>

        <cfif login.recordCount>

            <!--- Grab groups --->
            <cfquery name="getGroups" datasource="cfdev_security">
                select
                    groupName
                from
                    tblUserGroups
                where
                    username = '#form.username#'
            </cfquery>

            <cfloginuser name="#form.username#"
                    password="#form.password#"
                    roles="#valueList(getGroups.groupName)#">

        </cfif>

    </cfif>

</cflogin>

<!--- Is the user logged in? --->
<cfif getAuthUser() is "">
    <cfinclude template="login.cfm">
    <cfabort>
</cfif>
```

The first change you will notice is the addition of <cflogin> and </cflogin>. As we stated earlier, the code between these tags will always run when the user isn't authenticated. Inside we have the exact same database check; however, this time we use the cfloginuser tag to log the user in. We don't worry about what keys to use in the session scope or anything else like that. We simply run the following line of code:

```
<cfloginuser name="#form.username#"
        password="#form.password#"
        roles="#valueList(getGroups.groupName)#">
```

This MX version is rather clean-cut compared to our earlier code. After the closing cflogin tag, we've added a piece of code that will see if the user has been authenticated, using the getAuthUser() function. If this function returns an empty string, it means the user hasn't been logged in yet. In that case, we force the login form to be included and abort the current process. The only other change is the use of cflogout on top of the script. I think you can see how much easier things are compared to the earlier version (Listings 8.1 and 8.3).

The next piece of our puzzle—authorization—is also much more straightforward in Cold-Fusion MX. We will use only one function, isUserInRole() to describe this process. Listing 8.6 demonstrates how the Press Release Editor home page has been updated to use this new function.

Listing 8.6   **Press Release Editor, MX version (index.cfm)**

```
<!---
    Name:           /c08/admin_mx/index.cfm
    Description:    Press Release Editor Home, version 3
--->

<html>

<head>
    <title>Press Release Administrator</title>
 </head>

<body>

<h1>Press Release Administrator</h1>

<!--- Anyone can run parts of the PR editor --->
<cfif isUserInRole("Authors") or
      isUserInRole("Editors")>
    <a href="press_release_editor.cfm">Edit Press Releases</a><br>
</cfif>

<!--- Only Editors can edit users --->
<cfif isUserInRole("Editors")>
```

```
    <a href="user_editor.cfm">Edit Users</a><br>
</cfif>

<a href="index.cfm?logout=1">logout</a>
```

The only change here is in the check of the user's authorized tasks. We have removed all the checks against request variables to simplify `isUserInRole()` calls. (We also updated the second security checks on both the Press Release Editor and User Editor pages.)

As you can see, security in ColdFusion MX is even simpler to add to an existing web application!

Building Secure Web Applications

In the first portion of this chapter, we explored a custom security system that protected our various administration tools. However, the administration portion of your website isn't the only place where security is needed. There are various things you can do to ensure that every part of your site is as secure as possible.

Protecting Input Points

The Number One security concern for web applications is what I call the *input points*. Input points are simply the variables that are sent back and forth between the web browser and the web server. These include form variables, URL variables, and cookies. The user can manipulate all of these input points. Let's look at a simple example.

In your web browser, return to the public portion of the website at `http://localhost/CFDevHandbook/c08`. (If you deleted all the press releases while playing with the administrator, you'll need to go back there and create some new press releases.) Recall that all we did was grab all the press releases that were published and display them in a simple list. Listing 8.7 shows this simple template.

Listing 8.7   **Press Release Display (index.cfm)**

```
<!---
    Name:           /c08/index.cfm
    Description:    Press Release listing
--->

<cfquery name="getPressReleases" datasource="cfdev_security">
    select
        ID, Title
    from
        tblPressReleases
```

```
        where
              released = 1
</cfquery>

<ntml>

<head>
     <title>Press Releases</title>
</head>

<body>

<h1>Press Releases</h1>

<cfoutput query="getPressReleases">
     <a href="display.cfm?ID=#ID#">#Title#<br>
</cfoutput>

</body>
</html>
```

Notice the query that retrieves the press releases:

```
<cfquery="getPressReleases" datasource="cfdev_security">
     select
           ID, Title
     from
           tblPressReleases
     where
           released = 1
</cfquery>
```

The initial portion of the query is pretty simple—we grab the ID and Title columns from the database. However, notice that the where clause specifies that we should only get press releases that are marked as being released. Let's continue on to the page that displays the press release. Listing 8.8 is the display template.

Listing 8.8   **Display template (display.cfm)**

```
<!---
     Name:          /c08/display.cfm
     Description:   Press Release Display
--->

<cfif not isDefined("url.ID") or not isNumeric(url.ID)>
     <cflocation url="index.cfm">
</cfif>

<cfquery name="getPressRelease" datasource="cfdev_security">
     select
```

```
        Title, Body
    from
        tblPressReleases
    where
        ID = #val(url.ID)#
</cfquery>

<html>

<cfoutput>
<head>
    <title>Press Releases : #getPressRelease.title#</title>
</head>

<body>

<h1>#getPressRelease.title#</h1>

#getPressRelease.body#
</cfoutput>

<p>
<a href="index.cfm">Press Releases</a>

</body>
</html>
```

The script begins by ensuring that the ID value is passed via the query string. This comes from the index file we looked at in Listing 8.7. If the url.ID value does not exist or is not numeric, we push the user back to the index.cfm template. The rest of the template simply grabs the press release and displays it. However, this template has a variety of problems that we haven't prepared for.

Return to your browser and select any of the press releases. Notice the URL in the browser window: http://localhost/CFDevHandbook/c08/display.cfm?ID=5. The URL variable (input point) in this example is ID, and the value is 5. This is what gets passed to the query in our display template. It is a trivial matter for the user to change the 5 to something else, like "0" or "Jacob." If that happens, the browser will automatically push the user back to the press release home page.

But let's consider another example. Change the value to a new number that should not exist in the database, for example, 9999. Wow, an empty page (except for the link back to the home page)! You will see a similar result if you pass the value 0 to the page. So, what happened? Simply put, the query returned had no records because a match wasn't found. True, an error wasn't thrown, but this is certainly not a desirable result.

The fix is easy. If we check the record count returned from the query, we can safely handle this situation. By simply adding this check after the query, we've taken care of the problem:

```
<cfif not getPressRelease.recordCount>
    <cflocation url="index.cfm">
</cfif>
```

Return to the browser and reload, ensuring that the URL still reads ID=9999. This time, the record count check will push you back to the home page.

Ok, so far, so good. The page is getting more bullet proof with every modification. We still have one problem, though. For the next test, we need to return to the Press Release administrator at `http://localhost/CFDevHandbook/c08/admin_adv`. To do so, after logging in, go to the Press Release Editor. Create a new press release and be sure to NOT mark it as released. Take a look at Figure 8.7.

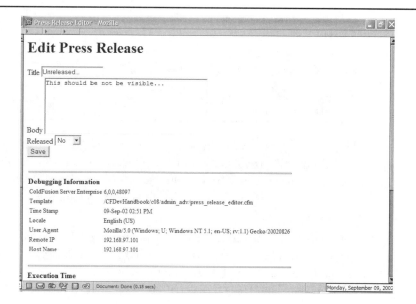

After clicking the Save button, you will be returned to the press release listing. Before the title of each press release is the ID number for that record. Make note of it. As you see in Figure 8.8, the new, unreleased press release is ID number 9. Now return to the public portion of the site, and again select any press release. Change the ID value in the URL to ID 9, and you'll see the press release, supposedly unpublished, show up!

What went wrong? We did have adequate protection on the press release display page. We did restrict the press releases retrieved to only those that were marked as released—but the display page did not honor this. We had covered every other error condition, but this situation could have easily been forgotten. The remedy is to add the same SQL restriction we had on the index page to the display page.

FIGURE 8.8:

The press release we just created has an ID of 9.

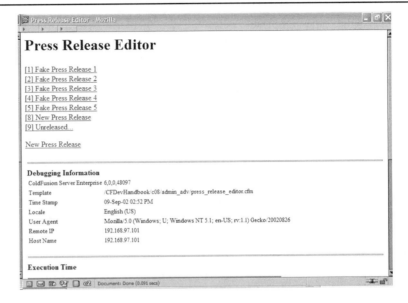

Here is the original query:

```
<cfquery name="getPressRelease" datasource="cfdev_security">
    select
        Title, Body
    from
        tblPressReleases
    where
        ID = #val(url.ID)#
</cfquery>
```

Here is the new query:

```
<cfquery name="getPressRelease" datasource="cfdev_security">
    select
        Title, Body
    from
        tblPressReleases
    where
        ID = #val(url.ID)#
    and
        released = 1
</cfquery>
```

As you can see, the only change is the addition of the `and released = 1` clause. This by itself will force the users away if they attempt to retrieve a press release that has not been released.

This sample illustrates the concept of protecting an application from the manipulation of a URL type input point. Although it's true that URLs are the easiest of the input points to change, it's not that much harder to change form or cookie values. The point is—if the value comes from an outside source, don't trust it!

Security through Obscurity

You've probably heard the phrase "Security through obscurity is *not* security." The idea is that if you hide your security methods instead of building real protection, then you have not really added security to your system. At the same time, security through obscurity can go some of the way toward making life difficult on those who want to cause you harm. It can't be stressed enough that obscuring is not enough by itself. However, anything that slows down the bad guys even a little is worth considering.

Obscurity can mean a few things. Remember our initial folder `admin`? It did require a user to log in, but how many websites use a folder called `admin` to store administration templates? What happens if the authentication system breaks down? If a hacker guesses the folder name, they can access sensitive parts of the website. Therefore, you may want to consider using a different folder name, like `adm` or `control`.

Another place where obscurity can be added is in the URL parameters. In order to display press releases, we used URLs like `display.cfm?id=2` and `display.cfm?id=9`. We could easily take the `ID=N` portion and encrypt it using the ColdFusion `encrypt()` function. This would create a URL something like so:

```
display.cfm?%244%25%5FPT%2A%23R%0A
```

This is a perfectly valid string to pass to the display template, as long as you know how to decrypt it. It looks odd, but the user can still bookmark it just fine. (The encrypt function may return characters that are not URL safe, so be sure to wrap the output with the `urlEncoded-Format()` function.)

As stated, obscurity by itself is not enough, but every step that makes life harder for the bad guys is a good one.

Cross-Site Scripting

Cross-site scripting is just an overblown way of describing a simple problem. Any website that accepts user input—for example, a guest book—can be attacked via that feature. Consider a guest book that simply asks for the guest's name and their comments, like the simple example in the Chapter 8 folder of this book's supporting code. You can view this application by opening a browser and navigating to `http://localhost/CFDevHandbook/c08/guestbook1.cfm`. Figure 8.9 displays the guest book with some sample data in it already.

FIGURE 8.9:

A simple guest book

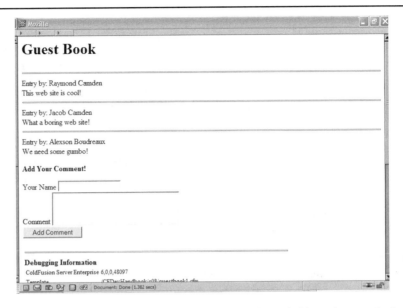

The code isn't that interesting. It basically just takes the two form fields and appends them to a text file. This text file is included in the guest book. However, what if the user enters something unusual for the name, as shown in Figure 8.10.

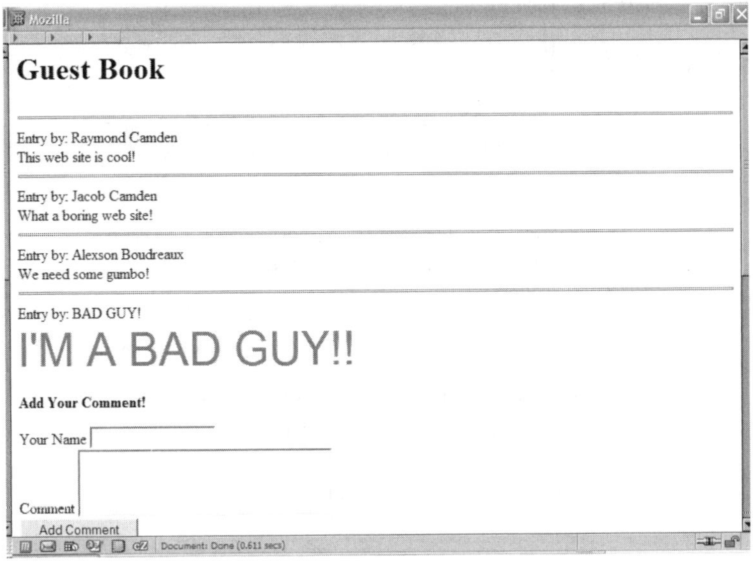

FIGURE 8.10:

A hacked guest book

How did this happen? Instead of entering a simple comment, the user entered this in the text area block:

```
<font face="arial" size="+6" color="red">I'M A BAD GUY!!</font>
    <font face="arial" size="+6" color="red">I'M A BAD GUY!!</font>
```

The user entered not just a comment, but HTML as well. When rendered on the screen, the HTML totally destroys the look and feel of the page. This is, actually, a very minor hack. A worse attack would have used embedded JavaScript that could sniff out cookies set by the original site and send them to another site.

The real issue here is that the code, entered by a stranger, is run as if it were originating from the site. The code is untrusted, but it is coming from a trusted source. Luckily, the fix is quite simple. Here are the lines of code that save the data in guestbook1.cfm:

```
<!--- This will be saved to the text file --->
<cfsavecontent variable="str">
<cfoutput>
<hr>
Entry by: #form.name#<br>
#form.comment#
</cfoutput>
</cfsavecontent>

<cffile action="append" file="#gFile#" output="#trim(str)#">
```

All we do here is create a string—a block of text—that contains the formatted data that is appended to the file. In order to prevent the attack, all we need to do is escape any HTML (JavaScript will be embedded in script tags) using the htmlEditFormat() function. This block of code is from guestbook2.cfm:

```
<!--- This will be saved to the text file --->
<cfsavecontent variable="str">
<cfoutput>
<hr>
Entry by: #htmlEditFormat(form.name)#<br>
#htmlEditFormat(form.comment)#
</cfoutput>
</cfsavecontent>
<cffile action="append" file="#gFile#" output="#trim(str)#">
```

The impact of this change is immediate. Open your browser to http://localhost/ CFDevHandbook/08/guestbook2.cfm. In this case, the hacker's attack was blocked because the HTML was escaped. Figure 8.11 shows how the bad input was changed. (Full listings for both guest books can be found in the c08 folder.)

FIGURE 8.11:

A better guest book

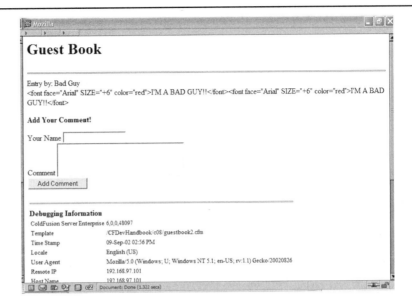

In Sum

This chapter gave a brief overview of what security means to web applications. We covered authentication, which is ensuring that a person is who they say they are; and authorization, the act of restricting what activities groups of people can use. We also covered what steps can be taken to ensure that web applications are not abused by malicious surfers or other nefarious types. The paramount lesson that should be gleaned from this chapter is that security is an all-encompassing concern. Every page in an application will have some relation to your security policy. It is something that should always be on your mind during every phase of development.

CHAPTER 9

Archives and Deployment

By Arman Danesh

- Archiving to achieve efficient application deployment

- Backing up your applications with an archive

- Using your archives

As web applications grow more complex, it is necessary to find ways to easily move them between servers. This process is typically known as *deployment*. A primary goal of efficient deployment includes taking an application from a development or test system and deploying it on a production system without too much headache—*headache* meaning conflicts and incompatibilities between the development and production environments. ColdFusion MX Enterprise Edition provides an archiving and deployment system in the ColdFusion Administrator that makes this a relatively straightforward accomplishment.

A secondary benefit of archiving is that it allows you to back up an application, along with all of its settings, so that it can be restored later in a time of crisis and server recovery.

This chapter runs through the process of creating an archive and then deploying it, typically on another system.

Archiving as Part of Deployment

One of the biggest logistical challenge in the active development of any web application is the migration of an application between systems. You may be moving an application from a development system to a production system or between servers for redundancy or clustering purposes, but, regardless of the reason, the process is often complicated by any number of factors:

- Conflicting directory structures
- Missing or conflicting data sources
- Missing or conflicting directory mappings
- Missing or misplaced custom tags
- Dependencies on components such as Java components

Of course, it is possible to avoid most of these problems by carefully synchronizing environments across systems. You can achieve this by making sure you have matching directory structures and taking care to code in a system independent fashion (such as avoiding absolute path references). Unfortunately, this type of disciplined consistency is not always possible. For instance, a development system might be running Windows while the production server runs Linux or another Unix operating system, or you may not have full control of the environment on one or more of the systems in question.

For this reason, any tools that simplify the process of migrating an application and all its dependencies, such as data sources, directory mappings, custom tags, and Java components, is a valuable resource for web application developers.

ColdFusion MX provides an archiving and deployment facility, managed via the Archives and Deployment page of the ColdFusion Administrator. This feature allows you to bundle an application, its files, and associated resources and configuration information and then easily extract it and deploy it in an organized fashion on another ColdFusion MX system. This capability is useful for migrating applications between ColdFusion MX systems as well as creating application backups so they can easily be restored after disaster recovery.

Preparing and Generating an Archive

ColdFusion provides an easy-to-use Archive Wizard to help simplify the process of building an archive. However, before using the wizard, you should take some important preparation steps. There are some critical pieces of information you need to be aware of to ensure that the application archive you build contains all the necessary components you need to successfully deploy the archive on another system.

In particular, you should know about or assemble the following:

- The Locations of all the critical application directories and files. This includes not just locations where you have stored ColdFusion templates, but also any custom tags, ColdFusion components, HTML files, images, Flash movies, or other files that make up part of your application.
- Server settings that your application relies on. This can include general settings, cache settings, security settings, logging settings, mail settings, and more.
- Directory mappings used by your application.
- Data sources used by your application.
- Verity collections you use in your application.
- Scheduled tasks you have created for your application.
- Registered Java applets used by your application.
- ColdFusion CFX custom tags invoked by your ColdFusion templates.

As a matter of good, structured, application development, you should keep a record of these sorts of resources that each of your applications depend on. If you don't, then before preparing an archive, it is a good idea to review your application and its requirements in these regards so that the archive you build will be complete on the first attempt.

Defining and Generating an Archive Definition

When you have finished preparation and have your resources in place, you'll be ready to start building an archive. The ColdFusion Administrator's Archives and Deployment page is illustrated in Figure 9.1. From this page, you can create new archive definitions, build archives based on these definitions, edit existing archive definitions, and deploy archives to the server.

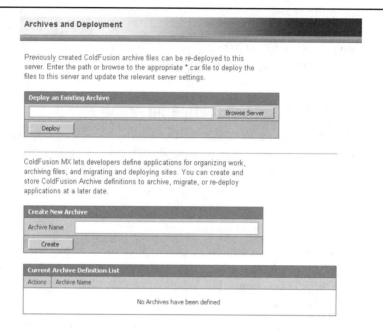

Archives and Deployment

Previously created ColdFusion archive files can be re-deployed to this
server. Enter the path or browse to the appropriate *.car file to deploy the
files to this server and update the relevant server settings.

Deploy an Existing Archive

[Browse Server]

[Deploy]

ColdFusion MX lets developers define applications for organizing work,
archiving files, and migrating and deploying sites. You can create and
store ColdFusion Archive definitions to archive, migrate, or re-deploy
applications at a later date.

Create New Archive

Archive Name

[Create]

Current Archive Definition List

Actions	Archive Name
No Archives have been defined	

This Chapter's Sample Application

In order to illustrate an archiving process for this chapter, you will be walking through archiving and then deploying a hypothetical application. This application meets the following specifications:

- Critical files are stored in `h:\html\com\test\` and `h:\html\apps\test\`, but files in `h:\html\apps\test\temp\` should not be included in the archive since they are temporary and would just add size to the archive without being necessary.

- The application depends on custom tags stored in `h:\html\tags\test\` and that path should be set in the Administrator as a custom tag path.

- The application requires that a mail server be specified in the Administrator.

- The application depends on a single data source named test `testDS`.

- The application depends on a single Verity collection named `testCollection`.

You will be working with this hypothetical application throughout the rest of this chapter.

Creating an Archive Definition

To build an archive, the first step is to create an archive definition. The archive definition specifies all the components of the application that you want included in the archive. Archive definitions are created and edited using the Archive Wizard, which is illustrated in Figure 9.2.

FIGURE 9.2:

The Archive Wizard

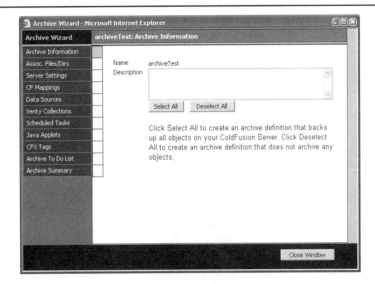

You can access the Archive Wizard in one of two ways:

- When you create a new archive, the ColdFusion Administrator automatically opens the wizard so that you can create an archive definition. To create a new archive, enter an archive name in the Archive Name field in the Create New Archive section of the Archive and Deployment page and click the Create button.

- Click the Edit Archive Definition button (the first button in the Actions column) next to the archive name in the Current Archive Definition List section of the Archive and Deployment page.

In the case of the sample application that you are using in this chapter, you can create a new archive by entering an archive name such as archiveTest in the Archive Name field and clicking the Create button.

The Archive Wizard allows you to work through a series of screens to specify all the information needed for the archive. You select the individual screens from the menu on the left side of the Archive Wizard window. You can work through these pages in any order and skip ones that aren't needed for your application; when you are done, click the Close Window button to close the Archive Wizard.

Creating an Archive Description

The first page of the Archive Wizard is the Archive Information page, which allows you to specify a description for the archive. This description can be used for future reference, serving as a detailed reminder of the contents of the archive. You can enter any text in the Description field. The Archive Information page was illustrated previously in Figure 9.2.

Specifying Files and Directories

The Include/Exclude Associated Files and Directories page (Figure 9.3) is where you specify the files to include in the archive.

FIGURE 9.3:

Selecting files and directories for an archive

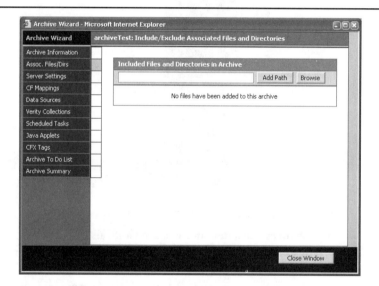

On this page, you can specify a file or directory path and click the Add Path button to add it to the archive. If you select a directory, all files and subdirectories are automatically included in the directory. Once you add a file, this page indicates the files or directories that you have added and it displays a new section called Excluded Files and Directories in Archive. This section allows you to specify subdirectories of included directories that should not be included in the archive.

As an example, consider Figure 9.4. Here you can see that the directories h:\html\com\test\, h:\html\apps\test\, and h:\html\tags\test\ have been added to the archive. However, you don't want to include h:\html\apps\test\temp\. To exclude the directory, enter it in the Excluded Files and Directories in Archive section and click the Add Path button. The Archive Wizard will now display h:\html\apps\test\temp\ in this section as illustrated in Figure 9.5.

FIGURE 9.4:

Included directories
for an archive

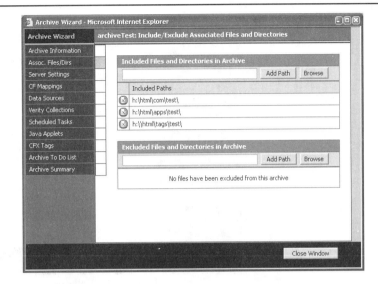

FIGURE 9.5:

Excluding directories
from an archive

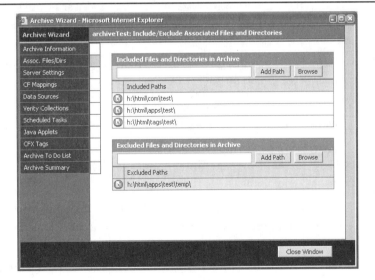

Selecting Server Settings

The Server Settings page allows you to indicate which groups of server settings to include in the archive. This page is illustrated in Figure 9.6.

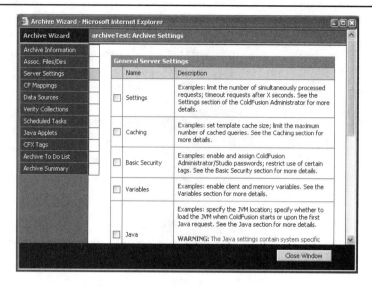

This is the most extensive page of the Archive Wizard because here you can select 10 different groups of settings for inclusion in the archive. The categories you can choose to include are as follows:

Settings   The settings from the Settings page of the ColdFusion Administrator, such as timeout limits and missing template handlers.

Caching   The settings from the Caching page of the ColdFusion Administrator, such as the template cache size and the maximum number of cached queries.

Basic Security   The settings from the Security section of the ColdFusion Administrator. These might include the ColdFusion Administrator password and security settings such as enabled and disabled tags and functions.

Variables   The settings from the Client Variables and Memory Variables pages of the ColdFusion Administrator, such as the location for client variable storage and timeouts for Application and Session variables.

Java   The settings from the Java and JVM page of the ColdFusion Administrator, such as the location of the Java Virtual Machine and the Class Path. Take care in including this information in an archive since it can override system-critical path information that is required for ColdFusion to even start on a system targeted for deployment. For instance, if you include the path to the Java Virtual Machine and this path doesn't match the path on the system where you deploy the archive, then you can render ColdFusion unstartable.

Logging   The settings from the Logging page of the ColdFusion Administrator, such as which pages to log by the time it takes them to complete and the maximum number of log archives.

Mail   The settings from the Mail Server page of the ColdFusion Administrator, such as the mail server and mail logging settings.

Debugging   The settings from the Debugging Settings page of the ColdFusion Administrator, such as which variable scopes to display in the debugging information.

Charting   The settings from the Charting page of the ColdFusion Administrator, such as where to cache charts and how many charts to cache.

Custom Tag Paths   The custom tag path definitions from the Custom Tag Paths page of the ColdFusion Administrator.

In the case of the sample application, you will want to ensure that the Mail settings option is selected as well as the Custom Tag Paths option.

Choosing ColdFusion Mappings

The CF Mappings page of the Archive Wizard, illustrated in Figure 9.7, allows you to specify which mappings to include in your archive. Simply click the check boxes next to the desired mappings to select them for the archive.

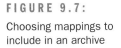

FIGURE 9.7:

Choosing mappings to include in an archive

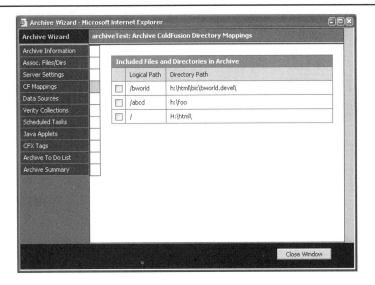

Selecting Data Sources

The Data Sources page of the Archive Wizard is illustrated in Figure 9.8. Here you can click the check boxes next to data sources to include them in the archive. In the case of the sample archive, the testDS data source should be selected as illustrated in Figure 9.8.

FIGURE 9.8:

The Data Sources page of the Archive Wizard

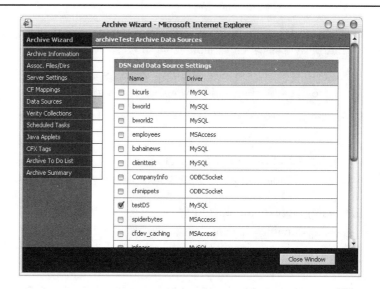

Including Verity Collections

The Verity Collections page of the Archive Wizard allows you to specify Verity collections to include in the archive by clicking the appropriate check boxes as you did with data sources. In the case of the sample application, testCollection should be selected.

Adding Scheduled Tasks

The Scheduled Tasks page of the Archive Wizard is illustrated in Figure 9.9. On this page you can select the individual scheduled tasks that you want to carry into an archive so that they can be scheduled on a target system where the archive is deployed.

Selecting Java Applets and CFX Custom Tags

The Java Applets and CFX Tags pages allow you to choose registered components to include in the archive and register on the target system when the archive is deployed. Selections are made using the appropriate check boxes in a manner similar to the previous screens.

FIGURE 9.9:

Including scheduled
tasks in an archive

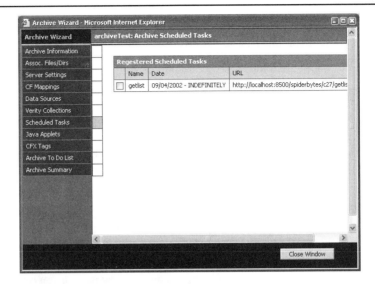

Viewing the Archive Summary

On the Archive Summary page of the Archive Wizard you can view a summary of all the settings you have specified, as illustrated in Figure 9.10.

FIGURE 9.10:

Summarizing an
archive definition

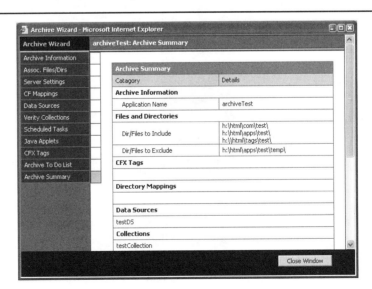

At this point, you can easily return to any page to adjust the settings if the information in this summary doesn't reflect the items you want included in the archive. As you can see in this figure, if you make no selections on a page of the Archive Wizard, that page's section in this summary is left blank.

Building an Archive

Now that you have specified the elements to include in an archive by creating an archive definition, you've made progress, but you aren't finished. In fact, all that you have done is indicate what you want to see included in your archive; you haven't actually created your archive. To do this, you will need to build the archive.

Luckily, this is a simple process. Simply click the Build Archive button (the middle button in Actions column) next to the archive name in the Current Archive Definition List on the Archives and Deployment page of the ColdFusion Administrator. The ColdFusion Administrator will display the Build CAR File Archive window, as illustrated in Figure 9.11.

FIGURE 9.11:

The Build CAR File Archive window

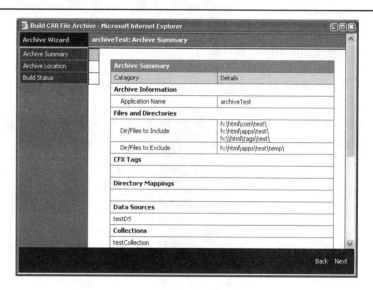

Initially, the Build CAR File Archive window will display the archive summary. Review the settings specified in the summary, and if they are correct, click the Next link in the bottom-right corner of the window. You will be prompted for a location where you want to store the archive file, as illustrated in Figure 9.12.

Enter the complete path and filename of the location where you want to store the archive file. Archive files should have a CAR extension. For instance, you might enter h:\temp\ archiveTest.car as the filename for the archive.

FIGURE 9.12:

Specifying the location
of the archive file

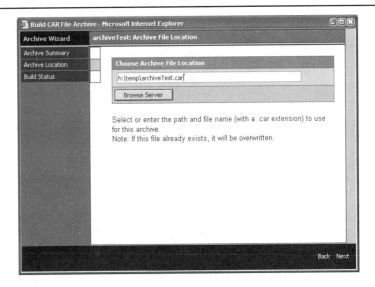

If you specify a filename of an existing archive as the location for an archive you are building, the existing archive will be replaced with the new archive.

NOTE Archives are created on the ColdFusion server. If you access the Administrator from a separate client system, the resulting archive is stored on the server and not on the client. Remember this when specifying the path for storing the archive file.

Once you have entered the location for the archive file, click the Next link. ColdFusion will proceed to build the archive and then it will display a log of the build process, as illustrated in Figure 9.13. The result of the build process should be an archive at the location you specified, as illustrated in Figure 9.14.

Note that the resulting archive file is a binary file that contains all of the data and files you will need to deploy the archive on another system. You can't simply edit or view the archive in a text editor.

TIP Remember that the size of the archive file will be dependent on the number of files, data sources, collections, and other items added to the archive. Potentially, archives can get quite large if the application being archived is large. You should make sure you have sufficient space for the archive in the target location where you are creating the archive file.

FIGURE 9.13:

Logging the build
process

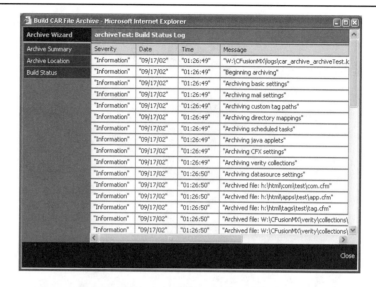

FIGURE 9.14:

An archive file

Deploying an Archive

Once you have created an archive, you can copy the archive file to another ColdFusion MX
server for deployment, or even redeploy it on the same system where it was created. The
process is simple and flexible. The following discussion illustrates deploying the archive from
our sample.

For the purposes of illustration, `archiveTest.car` is stored at `h:\temp\archiveTest.car` on the target server. The directories from the Windows system should end up in the following specified directories:

- `h:\html\com\test\` should become `h:\archiveTest\com\test\`.
- `h:\html\apps\test\` should become `h:\archiveTest\apps\test\`.
- `h:\html\tags\test\` should become `h:\archiveTest\tags\test\`.

To begin deployment, enter the location of the archive (`h:\temp\archiveTest.car`) in the Deploy an Existing Archive field of the Archives and Deployment page of the ColdFusion Administrator and click the Deploy button. The ColdFusion Administrator will display the deployment window as illustrated in Figure 9.15.

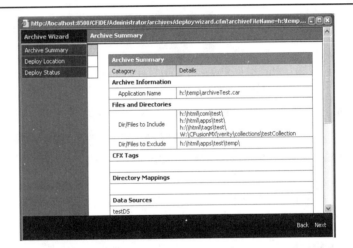

FIGURE 9.15:

The archive summary window

The archive summary window will display a summary of the contents of the archive. Click the Next link in the bottom-right corner to continue with the deployment. ColdFusion will display the Deploy Locations page where you will have the opportunity to adjust the deployment locations of the data from the archive. The items you will be able to adjust here depend on the content you stored in the archive. In the case of the sample application, you can edit the following locations:

- `car.verity.lib` directory, the root ColdFusion MX installation directory
- Each of the paths specified in the bullet list earlier in this section.
- The location for the `testCollection` Verity collection.

Once you have edited the locations, click the Deploy button to deploy the archive. Cold-Fusion will deploy the archive and display a log of the deployment for your reference, as illustrated in Figure 9.16.

Successfully deploying
an archive

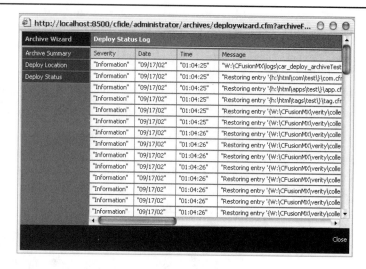

Severity	Date	Time	Message
"Information"	"09/17/02"	"01:04:25"	"W:\CFusionMX\logs\car_deploy_archiveTest
"Information"	"09/17/02"	"01:04:25"	"Restoring entry '{h:\html\com\test\}\com.cfr
"Information"	"09/17/02"	"01:04:25"	"Restoring entry '{h:\html\apps\test\}\app.cf
"Information"	"09/17/02"	"01:04:25"	"Restoring entry '{h:\html\tags\test\}\tag.cfr
"Information"	"09/17/02"	"01:04:25"	"Restoring entry '{W:\CFusionMX\verity\colle
"Information"	"09/17/02"	"01:04:25"	"Restoring entry '{W:\CFusionMX\verity\colle
"Information"	"09/17/02"	"01:04:26"	"Restoring entry '{W:\CFusionMX\verity\colle
"Information"	"09/17/02"	"01:04:26"	"Restoring entry '{W:\CFusionMX\verity\colle
"Information"	"09/17/02"	"01:04:26"	"Restoring entry '{W:\CFusionMX\verity\colle
"Information"	"09/17/02"	"01:04:26"	"Restoring entry '{W:\CFusionMX\verity\colle
"Information"	"09/17/02"	"01:04:26"	"Restoring entry '{W:\CFusionMX\verity\colle
"Information"	"09/17/02"	"01:04:26"	"Restoring entry '{W:\CFusionMX\verity\colle
"Information"	"09/17/02"	"01:04:26"	"Restoring entry '{W:\CFusionMX\verity\colle
"Information"	"09/17/02"	"01:04:26"	"Restoring entry '{W:\CFusionMX\verity\colle

Once you have deployed the archive, you should conduct some basic checks to make sure everything was deployed in the way you intended:

- Check that all your files, including custom tags, are in the right place.
- Make sure that necessary settings were deployed properly.
- Be sure your data sources, mappings, Verity collections, Java applets, and custom tags were correctly registered.
- Test your application.

In Sum

This chapter guided you through an important process in any ColdFusion developer's skill set: being able to archive an application to deploy it on another system.

You learned this skill by becoming familiar with the Archive Wizard. You used this wizard to specify an archive definition and you included a template and a wide range of system settings—including data sources, mappings, and Verity collections—in this definition. With this definition in hand, you built an archive and then learned how to deploy it on a new system while taking into account differences in directory structure and other available resources on the target system.

This archiving and deploying capability of ColdFusion MX is useful for deploying to production systems, mirroring applications across a cluster, and even application backup purposes.

Chapter 10

Source Code Management

By Arman Danesh

- What is source code management?

- Source code management tools

- Manual approaches to source code management

- Building your own source code manager in ColdFusion

As development projects grow more complex, even a single developer can face a source code management dilemma. Developers can lose track of the current versions of files, they can accidentally make changes they don't want to make to a file, or they can even accidentally delete the sole copies of critical source code files.

In the multideveloper context, the problems only compound with problems arising when two developers need to edit the same file, or when they lose track of the history of changes to the source code.

Source code management solutions address these problems. This chapter reviews source code management and the available tools associated with it and discusses how to use some of these in the context of ColdFusion development.

What Is Source Code Management?

Source code management solutions have been widely used in traditional software development environments, both for commercial and open source projects; some large web development firms and projects have similarly used source code management.

At their core, source code management tools are simple in concept: authoritative copies of source code are retained in a central repository. Developers check files out of the repository to edit them and check them back in to release them so that they can be edited by other developers. Additional features may be added in some source code control systems, such as versioning, forking, or other project management features, but at their core, all source code management systems revolve around central code repositories with check-in/check-out capabilities.

Typically, though, most ColdFusion developers are not routinely using source code management tools for the management of their code. Either they are working in individual or small organization contexts where source code management systems are not used, or they are not coming to ColdFusion development from traditional software development backgrounds, and, therefore, they are not familiar with source code management concepts and tools.

However, even an individual developer can benefit from source code management. In particular, it can offer the following benefits to ColdFusion developers:

- Locking and concurrency management
- Versioning and history
- Synchronization
- Parallel projects and forking

NOTE   Forking refers to the notion of splitting source code at some point in its development into two or more parallel projects and working on these development versions separately. In other words, you would move from one track of source code development to two or more parallel and distinct tracks.

Locking and Concurrency

One of the major problems faced in team-based development is how to handle simultaneous editing of the same source code files—this is the concurrency problem. Source code management solutions solve this concurrency dilemma with *file locking*. File locking allows files to be flagged as open and in use when a developer is editing them. There are two main locking strategies that can be used as enforcement mechanisms when another developer attempts to open a locked file: exclusive locks and unreserved locks.

Exclusive Locks

Exclusive locks are occasionally a suitable way to prevent simultaneous editing, and they are fairly simple to implement and manage. When a user has control of a file, no other user can access the file in read-write mode. The file can be viewed or even copied, but it can't be edited or saved by another user until the current lock holder saves the file and releases the lock. This easy solution may seem the ideal protection against concurrent file editing; however, the typical situation is far from this simple.

It's not hard to see that serious contention issues can arise. Consider the following scenario:

1. User A accesses a file for editing and obtains an exclusive lock.

2. User A forgets about the open file or even leaves the office with the file left open and locked.

3. User B is working on a deadline and realizes a critical change needs to be made to the file currently locked by User A.

4. User B cannot open the file because it is held by User A.

5. User B has to wait for User A's return in order to get User A to release the lock so that User B can access the file for editing.

This can become a significant challenge in a large development team where critical work can be damaged or delayed by an exclusive lock being inadvertently retained for long periods of time. It is even possible for a malicious team member to intentionally obtain and retain a lock on a file critical to a rival team member's work just to make it difficult for the rival to complete their work in a timely fashion. This problem becomes even more acute if the development team is distributed. In a colocated development environment, it easier to talk directly to someone that is holding a lock to get the lock released. In a distributed context, however, such as many Internet-based open source development efforts, this type of immediate one-to-one contact can be difficult at best.

For this reason, most high-end, full-featured source code control systems either don't use exclusive locks or offer a choice between exclusive and unreserved locks. Simpler source code control systems may offer exclusive locking capabilities alone.

Unreserved Locks

The solution to exclusive locks' limitations are often referred to as unreserved locks. In the unreserved locking paradigm, more than one user can have a nonexclusive lock on a file. This means more than one user can be editing a file at the same time. Of course, this immediately raises this question: Isn't this the same as having no source code management at all? Enterprise-class source code control systems that use unreserved locks address this by implementing complex, sophisticated algorithms for merging changes and for informing different editors of the same file of changes made by other developers that also have an unreserved lock on the file in question.

These algorithms can track which parts of the file are being changed by different developers and where there is no overlap in the changes; they can then merge all developer's changes into a composite edited file. In addition, when these algorithms determine that it is unsafe to simply merge multiple editors' changes, they can prompt the developers to walk through a manual decision-making process to determine how to merge the changes. As you will see later in the chapter, these techniques are typically used in high-end systems such as SourceSafe (see the upcoming section "SourceSafe") and the Concurrent Versioning System (CVS; see the upcoming section "CVS"). However, these algorithms are complex and not easy to get right. For this reason, they exact a cost either in terms of price or complexity or both.

To bridge the gap between easy-to-implement exclusive locks and complex unreserved locks, some simple systems offer unreserved locks without any file merging capabilities. The best example of this is ColdFusion's own Remote Development Services (RDS) discussed later in this chapter. RDS allows two users to edit a file, but after the first user has a lock, all subsequent users are warned that they are attempting to edit a locked file, at which point they are given the chance of canceling the edit operation. If multiple developers ultimately choose to edit the same file, it is up to the developers to ensure that they don't overwrite each others changes. This is not an effective solution for any large or distributed team because it is easy for problems to occur. However, in a small, colocated development context, this may provide a sufficient middle ground between exclusive locks and unreserved locks with change merging technology.

Versioning and History

Another important feature of many source code management systems is the ability to handle *versioning*. Versioning means that each time a file is opened for editing, the system snapshots a copy of the file before it is edited—the system often will keep an infinite number of such historical snapshots. This allows a development team to backtrack to earlier versions of code in cases where recent changes have actually introduced more problems than they solve.

Also, versioning can generate historical log reports of changes that allow team leaders and administrators to track development processes and cycles that occur in the team. These historical logs can even flag cases in which developers are editing files that they technically shouldn't be editing.

Synchronization

Some source code management solutions provide synchronization features. These features can allow developers to work offline with a local snapshot of a project's code at times when they don't have access to the network or to the source code management server. These features can then help developers synchronize their offline copies of the code with the central repository's copy of the code.

This type of off-line solution typically requires some sophisticated algorithms to determine if it is wise to synchronize a file in either direction. For instance, a user may take a snapshot of a file and proceed to work on it offline. Before they finish working on the file, another developer checks out the same file, edits it, and checks it back in. When the original developer finally goes to synchronize the file, it appears that the offline file should overwrite the version in the repository because its date stamp is newer, but in reality, this would cause the second developer's changes to be overwritten. Because of the need to avoid this conflict, synchronization features are typically tied to systems that offer the sort of change merging technologies described earlier in the discussion of unreserved locking.

Parallel Projects and Forking

High-end systems such as SourceSafe and CVS offer capabilities for project forking and parallel project development. For instance, at some interim point in a project's development, it may be necessary to separate the project into two separate projects that start from the same point in terms of source code but take different paths from that point on.

A source code management system can allow the project to fork so that both teams have the same history and versioning background up to the point that the forking occurs, but from that point on, their changes occur independently and don't affect each other's versions of the project.

Source Code Management Tools

A number of source code management tools exist that can easily be leveraged by ColdFusion developers. In particular, ColdFusion's own Remote Development Services (RDS) provides basic locking capabilities that allow Dreamweaver with ColdFusion to become a basic source code management solution.

Similarly, Dreamweaver can work with Microsoft's SourceSafe source code management system to provide robust source code management capabilities within the ColdFusion environment.

Finally, common source code management platforms, including WebDAV and CVS, can be used to develop ColdFusion applications.

Using Dreamweaver with RDS

ColdFusion Server includes RDS. Often underused, RDS provides an effective mechanism for implementing basic source code control for ColdFusion projects. When you combine Dreamweaver MX with RDS you will be able to perform the following:

- Directly edit files on a ColdFusion Server

- Use unreserved locking to prevent contention problems when multiple developers are working on the same project

- Handle synchronization between offline versions of files and the versions on the Cold-Fusion Server

What is missing in RDS is versioning and facilities to generate historical change logs to track the progress of changes on a file. Still, the basic locking mechanisms of RDS can allow many teams to solve their core problem: how to ensure that two people aren't trying to edit a file at the same time.

Using RDS in Dreamweaver is simple. You just have to configure it when you are defining a site in Dreamweaver. While you are defining a site, you can specify both a local store for files as well as an RDS server and directory, and then Dreamweaver will work with ColdFusion to ensure synchronization and locking.

Configuring RDS

You would use the following steps to configure RDS. These steps assume that you already have a site configured in which you edit local content but that the site is not connected to a remote location through RDS. If you already have RDS configured for your site, you don't need to perform these steps.

1. Edit the site by selecting Site ➢ Edit Sites from the Files panel. Dreamweaver will display the Edit Sites dialog box as illustrated in Figure 10.1.

FIGURE 10.1:

The Edit Sites
dialog box

2. Select the site you want to edit and click the Edit button. Dreamweaver will display the
   Site Definition dialog box for the site you have selected, as illustrated in Figure 10.2. In
   this dialog box, make sure the Advanced Tab is selected and then select Remote Info from
   the Category list on the left and click OK.

FIGURE 10.2:

The Site Definition
dialog box

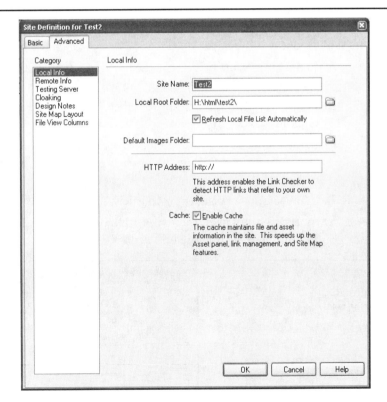

3. In the Remote Info page (Figure 10.3) that results, select RDS from the Access drop-down list and click the Settings button.

FIGURE 10.3:

Editing remote server Information

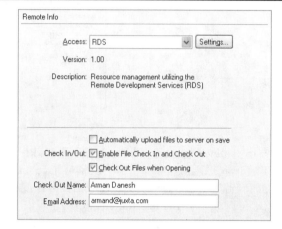

4. Next, Dreamweaver displays the Configure RDS Server dialog box as illustrated in Figure 10.4.

    A. In the Host Name field, enter the hostname or IP address of the ColdFusion server where the production version of the site exists.

    B. In the Port field, enter the port of the ColdFusion server (this is the HTTP port and typically will be 80).

    C. In the Full Host Directory field, enter the directory on the server where the site is stored. This should be the full physical path and not a path relative to the web server root directory.

    D. In the Username field, enter your RDS username.

    E. In the Password field, enter your RDS password and click OK to close the dialog box and return to the Remote Info dialog box.

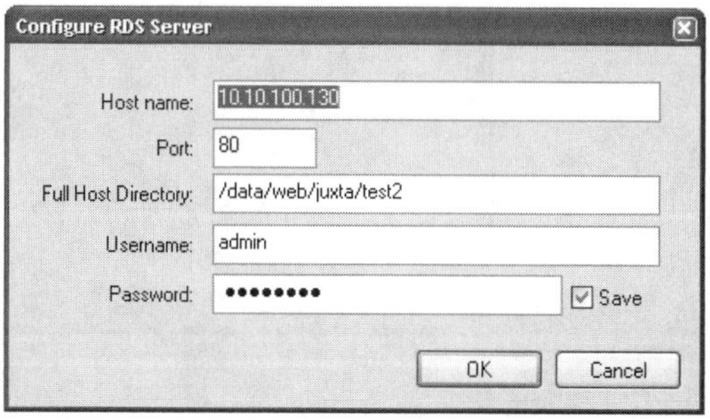

FIGURE 10.4:

The Configure RDS Server dialog box

5. If you are always online and want your changes to be automatically reflected on the server, select the check box "Automatically upload files to server on save" on the Remote Info dialog box.

6. Then click the Enable File Check In and Check Out.

7. Click the Check Out Files when Opening check box.

8. Enter a name and e-mail address to identify yourself to other users when you have the file checked out.

Managing Locks with RDS

Once your site is configured, you will notice some changes when you proceed to work with your site. First, files will appear with a small lock icon next to their names. This indicates that you don't have the file checked out. When you attempt to open the file for editing, Dreamweaver will attempt to check out the file from the RDS server. Once you have successfully checked out the file, the lock will change to a green check mark. If another user has the file checked out, you will see a red check mark in place of the lock.

What happens when you attempt to open a locked file that is checked out by another user depends on how the general preferences of your Dreamweaver installation are configured. Typically, you will be warned of the conflict and offered three options:

- Check out the file anyway.

- View the file (but you will not be able to edit it).

- Cancel the operation.

You need to take care with your choices here. If you choose to override another user's lock, then both you and the other user will be able to edit, save, and check back in the file. This will result in a concurrency problem. Consider the following scenario:

1. User A checks out a file and edits it.

2. User B checks out the same file, is warned about User A's lock, but decides to check out the file anyway and proceeds to edit it.

3. User B saves the file and checks it back in.

4. User A saves the file and checks it back in.

The end result is that User B's changes are lost: User A's version overwrites the version User B saved and checked in.

As you can see, some discipline is required in using RDS as a source code control mechanism because it doesn't enforce locking. It just uses locking to trigger warnings for the user, but the user can still override the locking rendering RDS only effective for remote editing but not for source code control and management.

In order to ensure that you receive these warnings, it is a good idea to make sure Dreamweaver is configured to warn you if you open a file checked out by another user. To do this, select Edit ➤ Preferences, which opens the Preferences dialog box. Select General in the Category list at the left and click OK; Dreamweaver will display the General preferences page as illustrated in Figure 10.5. Make sure that the Warn When Opening Read-Only Files check box in the Document Options section of the page is selected to ensure that Dreamweaver warns you when you open a checked-out file. This will also give you a chance to view the file or cancel the operation instead of actually checking the file out and opening it.

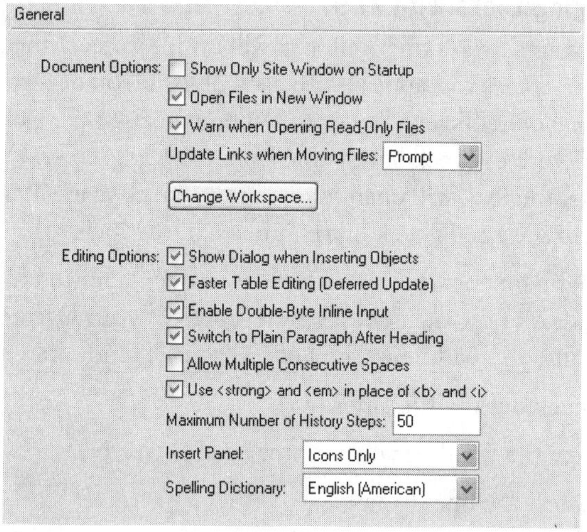

FIGURE 10.5:

Controlling General preferences

```
General

Document Options: [ ] Show Only Site Window on Startup
                  [✓] Open Files in New Window
                  [✓] Warn when Opening Read-Only Files
                  Update Links when Moving Files: [Prompt    ▼]

                  [ Change Workspace... ]

Editing Options: [✓] Show Dialog when Inserting Objects
                 [✓] Faster Table Editing (Deferred Update)
                 [✓] Enable Double-Byte Inline Input
                 [✓] Switch to Plain Paragraph After Heading
                 [ ] Allow Multiple Consecutive Spaces
                 [✓] Use <strong> and <em> in place of <b> and <i>
                 Maximum Number of History Steps: [50    ]
                 Insert Panel:        [Icons Only        ▼]
                 Spelling Dictionary: [English (American) ▼]
```

Dreamweaver also offers several menu options for working with the files and folders in a site that you have associated with an RDS server. When you select one or more files or folders in your site and then open the site menu or when you right click the selected items and view the pop-up menu, Dreamweaver will display five useful options:

Get   This option allows you to download the current version of the file(s) from the RDS server and replace the local copies. This doesn't check the file out.

Check Out   This option lets you check out the file(s) and download the current versions at the same time.

Put   This lets you upload the current local version of the file(s) to the RDS server. This doesn't check the file(s) in.

Check In   This allows you to check in the file(s) and upload them to the server.

Undo Check Out   This cancels the file's checkout status and returns local and remote copies to their original states.

Managing RDS Security

RDS is a quick and useful solution for basic source code management when you are developing ColdFusion applications. However, as with any technology that allows manipulation of content on the server, there are security implications of which you should be aware. Fortunately, ColdFusion provides mechanisms that will allow most administrators to feel comfortable enabling RDS.

Specifically, you can control two levels of RDS security in the ColdFusion Administrator:

Basic Security   In Basic Security, RDS is restricted by a single common password for all users.

Advanced Security   In Advanced Security, you can specify fine-grained access control on a per-file basis so that only the files that you want to make writeable can be overwritten using RDS.

You should consider carefully whether you want to enable RDS, and if you do, you should work carefully with your server administrator to ensure that the security settings are sufficient.

SourceSafe

Visual SourceSafe is Microsoft's enterprise-class commercial source code management solution. If you work in an environment that uses Visual SourceSafe, you can implement Dreamweaver as a client and you can develop against a site managed in SourceSafe in much the same way you can develop against an RDS-based site.

SourceSafe provides numerous high-end features that are critical to teams and can support large development groups. Its capabilities include the following:

- Full versioning support
- Site snapshot capabilities
- Forking development into parallel projects
- Unreserved locking with full reporting of changes across multiple versions so that developers can work on a file and know what other developers have changed
- Full project audit trails
- Full website deployment capabilities that can include link checking and site map generation

To use Visual SourceSafe as a source code control system with Dreamweaver MX, you need to have access to a SourceSafe server as well as the Microsoft Visual SourceSafe client installed on the system running Dreamweaver. As a Microsoft product, SourceSafe is available only for Windows, and this restricts you to working with Windows-based versions of Dreamweaver and with Windows-based source-code control servers.

Configuring Dreamweaver to work with SourceSafe is simple: just choose SourceSafe instead of RDS as the remote data source when you are configuring your site in Dreamweaver and then provide the access information required in the Settings dialog box, such as the database path, the project name, and a username and password.

NOTE   You can learn more about SourceSafe at `http://msdn.microsoft.com/ssafe/`.

WebDAV

WebDAV is an emerging open standard that provides remote editing and management of files on a web server through HTTP. (DAV stands for Distributed Authoring and Versioning.) When WebDAV is fully defined, the WebDAV specification will allow web servers such as Apache and Internet Information Server (IIS) to function as WebDAV servers, and then clients will be able to access files on the server.

WebDAV will provide several capabilities required for robust source code control management including the following:

- Locking with both exclusive and unreserved locks
- XML property tracking to allow data about a file (such as the author) to be tracked
- File system operations such as moving and copying files as well as symbolic linking (similar to shortcuts in Windows)
- Versioning, including full check-in and check-out support and history tracking.
- Parallel development, which can allow parallel development tracks to operate on separate versions of the same project.
- Access control to provide security.

Dreamweaver supports WebDAV for remote site management, and you can work with WebDAV data in much the same way that you work on RDS-based sites. You can select Web-DAV as your access method for a remote site when you configure your site in Dreamweaver.

At the present time, WebDAV is not fully implemented on any platform, but robust Web-DAV implementations are available. WebDAV is commonly used in Apache environments and currently offers locking capabilities, but versioning has yet to be finalized in the standard. You can learn more about WebDAV at `http://www.webdav.org/`.

Other Technologies to Consider

In addition to RDS, SourceSafe, and WebDAV, which are directly supported within Dreamweaver, you can consider turning to other approaches and techniques for source code control for your ColdFusion application development. In the world of team-based software development, a popular source code management platform is CVS, which is an open source software package. Alternately, there are web-based platforms, such as SourceForge, which can give you some of the source code management capabilities you need if you are working on open source software.

CVS

CVS, or the Concurrent Versions System, is a leading source code control platform. An open source project, CVS is widely deployed in Unix and Linux development environments, is used by most open source projects that use source code management, and is used in many commercial, corporate development environments as well. It offers the full range of advanced features found in commercial solutions such as SourceSafe, including unreserved locking with change merging technology, full version histories, offline editing, and synchronization.

Dreamweaver does not provide any integration with CVS, but numerous CVS clients exist for Windows and Unix/Linux systems. Tools exist to publish CVS content to web servers automatically, to integrate with Microsoft Visual Studio, and even to manage Oracle forms through CVS.

CVS offers flexibility but requires a knowledgeable system administrator to install and configure it correctly so that it serves as a useful tool for developers. Typically, ColdFusion development teams will not opt for a CVS-based content management solution unless one of several factors exist:

- They are working in a large development context where CVS is used.

- They are developing and deploying strictly in Unix-based environments.

- They are not using Dreamweaver as their primary development tool but rather use development tools that already integrate CVS support.

- They require advanced features of CVS not offered in RDS or WebDAV or which are too expensive in SourceSafe.

Because of Dreamweaver's close integration with three other source code management possibilities—RDS, SourceSafe, and WebDAV—it makes CVS a hard choice for ColdFusion development unless there are compelling reasons, such as those described above, to adopt an external solution such as CVS.

NOTE   You can learn more about CVS at `http://www.cvshome.org/`.

SourceForge

If you are familiar with the wealth of open source software projects available on the Internet, you have probably encountered some of those projects on SourceForge (`http://sourceforge .net/`). SourceForge is an online community where open source projects can host their work. The platform offers a range of tools to support the development process, including the following:

- Mailing lists and discussion forums for each project
- Bug reporting and tracking tools
- A web-based file release system that helps track download usage for versions of a package
- A variety of systems on which developers can test compile their code
- CVS services for each project including a web-based interface to the CVS repositories

If you are working on an open-source project, it is worth investigating SourceForge. You can gain the benefits of CVS without the complexity of setting up CVS yourself and you can leverage the other useful development tools SourceForge offers.

In Sum

In this chapter, you learned about the techniques and solutions that are available to help individual developers and development teams manage their ColdFusion source code. You learned about the differences between exclusive locks and unreserved locks and the complexity of implementing file merging algorithms to handle unreserved locks.

In practical terms, you learned how Dreamweaver MX makes it easy to leverage ColdFusion's own Remote Development Services for simple source code management or to integrate with SourceSafe or WebDAV for more advanced code management. With RDS you can set up a source code management environment that has unreserved locks without file merging. This means you need to use some human management to prevent concurrency problems but makes Dreamweaver and RDS a good candidate for source code management for small ColdFusion development teams.

Finally, you learned about other available solutions including SourceSafe, CVS, WebDAV, and Web-based solutions such as SourceForge.

PART II

Advanced Database Integration

Chapter 11: Advanced SQL

Chapter 12: Stored Procedures

Chapter 13: Upsizing Databases to SQL Server

Advanced SQL

By Selene Bainum

- SQL and databases basics

- Introducing relational data

- Creating, modifying, and deleting tables

- Inserting, updating, and deleting data

- Retrieving data

- Exploring advanced SQL techniques

- Introducing CFQSL

I f you've built at least one ColdFusion application, chances are good that you've had to connect to a database in order to perform actions such as selecting, inserting, updating, or deleting data. If you've ever used the `cfquery` tag, you've written SQL (Structured Query Language), the de facto language of the relational database world. Even without a lot of SQL experience, you won't find it difficult to retrieve data from a table or to perform other valuable database commands.

ColdFusion makes it very easy to manipulate the data that you pull from a query, but processing data with ColdFusion is not always as efficient as making the database do the work for you. In most cases, the database can perform transactions much more quickly than ColdFusion can. With more complex queries, there are ways to reduce the number of trips that ColdFusion makes to your connected databases.

This chapter explains how to leverage advanced SQL in order to make your ColdFusion applications more efficient. The examples in this chapter are written for Microsoft Access and Microsoft SQL Server. When database-specific code is used here, it will be noted.

SQL and Database Basics

This section sets the guidelines for the SQL code and database studied in this chapter.

SQL is not a case-sensitive language. For instance, the SQL statement

```
SELECT * FROM table_name
```

is the same as

```
select * from table_name
```

In this chapter, database reserved words (`select`, `from`, and so on) will be written in lowercase, as will database functions (`avg`, `count`, `left`, and so on). The names of columns and tables will be in mixed case.

NOTE   Case sensitivity in table and column names as well as in data is handled in various ways by different database packages. Refer to your database documentation for specific information.

A SQL statement is made up of several *clauses*, or statement parts. The SQL:

```
select * from table_name
```

is a `select` statement that contains a `select` clause and a `from` clause. Different types of statements and clauses will be discussed throughout this chapter.

Relational Data

If you are not already familiar with the term *relational data*, you've probably at least heard about *relational databases*. Databases that follow the relational database model are referred to as *relational database management systems (RDBMS)*. Most databases that you'll work with, including Microsoft SQL Server, Oracle, and even Microsoft Access, are relational.

A relational database is a structured collection of two-dimensional tables that are made up of both columns and rows. These tables can have relationships with one another via the table *keys*. There are two types of keys in relational databases: primary and foreign.

Primary key   A *primary key* is a distinct identifier of a table, and therefore its data must be unique for each and every row in the table. A primary key can be either a single column in a table or a combination of columns that form a unique value.

Foreign key   A *foreign key* is a column or group of columns in a table that is present as a primary key in another table. When you add a foreign key to a table, you create a relationship between it and the other table. The table that holds the primary key is often called the *parent table*; the table that holds the foreign key is called a *child table*.

When tables are joined by a relationship, you will need to account for *referential integrity*. Referential integrity ensures that a primary key value cannot be deleted or altered if it is being used as a foreign key in another table. Therefore, if table B has a foreign column of ID that is the primary column of table A, the value of that ID in B must have the same value in the ID column of table A. Most databases check for referential integrity and return an error if an insert, update, or delete statement attempts to violate the integrity.

The Database Used in This Chapter

Throughout this chapter, the code and database examples revolve around a hypothetical application for a video rental system. Figure 11.1 displays the Microsoft SQL Server schema of all the tables associated with this system and their properties.

The video rental system application and its tables are designed to accommodate the following business requirements for the video rental store:

- The store has multiple customers. Customers can be active or inactive.
- The store has multiple movie titles.
- Each movie title can be associated with one movie genre.
- The store can have multiple copies of each movie title. Each copy has its own stock date and cost.
- Each movie copy has a rental status.
- Customers can check out individual movie copies.
- Customers are charged a late fee for movies that are returned late.
- A variety of reports can be created to display desired information. For example, reports can be generated that list all the customers, all of the overdue rentals, the most profitable movies or the most active selections, and so on.

FIGURE 11.1:

The video rental
system database
schema

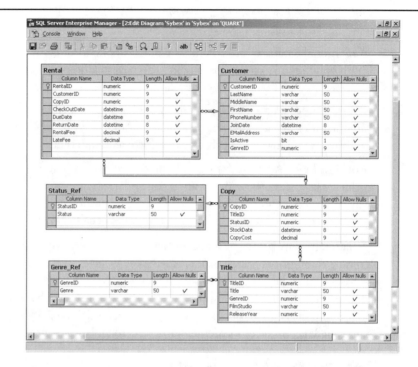

The database used in this chapter has six tables:

Status_Ref   The Status_Ref table is a reference table that holds all the movie status names and IDs. The StatusID column is the primary key of this table. The Status values include available, unavailable, and checked out.

Genre_Ref   The Genre_Ref table is a reference table that holds all of the movie genres and their IDs. The GenreID column is the primary key of this table. The genres include Comedy, Drama, War, Science Fiction, and so on.

Customer   The Customer table holds all the information about the customers, including the date when they joined and whether or not they are *active* (a customer whose account is current and in good standing). The CustomerID column is the primary key of this table.

Title   The Title table holds all the movie titles the video store has in stock. The TitleID column is the primary key of this table. The Title table also has a foreign key on the GenreID column, which creates a relationship between it and the Genre_Ref table. This is a one-to-many relationship because each title can have only one genre, but each genre can be associated with many titles.

Copy   The Copy table holds the data for the distinct copies of all of the titles in the Title table. They CopyID column is the primary key. This table has relationships with both the Title and Status_Ref tables. The Copy table has a foreign key on the TitleID column, which creates a relationship between it and the Title table. Because each copy can be associated with only one title and each title can have multiple copies, there is a one-to-many relationship between these two tables. There is also a one-to-many relationship between the Copy and Status_Ref tables, because the StatusID column is a foreign key in the Copy table. Each copy can have only one status at a time, whereas each status can be associated with many copies.

Rental   The Rental table holds all the current and past rental information and is the core of the application. The RentalID column is the primary key of this table. This table has a one-to-many relationship with both the Customer table on the CustomerID column and with the Copy table on the CopyID column. When a video is checked out, a new record is created in the Rental table with the proper CustomerID and CopyID. The CheckOutDate, DueDate, and RentalFee columns are also populated with the appropriate data. The ReturnDate is left null until the video is returned. If the ReturnDate is later than the DueDate, a LateFee is assessed.

Table Manipulation

In addition to querying and manipulating data with SQL, you can also manipulate your database tables. By using SQL in your cfquery tags, you can create, modify, and delete tables.

NOTE   If you are performing table manipulations in a cfquery and do not expect to return any values, you do not need to use the name attribute of the cfquery tag.

Create

The create table statement allows you to create a table within the data source specified in the cfquery tag. The syntax for the create table statement is as follows:

```
create table table_name (
    column_name data_type[(length)] [null_specifier],
    column_name data_type[(length)] [null_specifier])
```

To specify a primary key on the table, add the constraint clause:

```
create table table_name (
    column_name data_type[(length)] [null_specifier],
    column_name data_type[(length)] [null_specifier],
    constraint key_field primary key (key_field))
```

Give the *null_specifier* a value of null or not null depending on whether the column should accept null values. Primary key fields should always be specified as not null.

Although the syntax of the create table statement does not vary from database to database, the exact datatypes used to create the columns often do vary. For example, the following query will create the Customer table in Microsoft SQL Server:

```
<cfquery datasource="SybexSQL">
create table Customer (
    CustomerID numeric(18, 0) Identity (1, 1) not null,
    FirstName varchar(50) null,
    MiddleName varchar(50) null,
    LastName varchar(50) null,
    PhoneNumber varchar(50) null,
    JoinDate datetime null,
    EMailAddress varchar(50) null,
    IsActive bit null,
    constraint CustomerID primary key (CustomerID))
</cfquery>
```

Next is a Microsoft Access query; note the differences in the datatypes between this query and the preceding SQL Server example:

```
<cfquery datasource="SybexAccess">
create table Customer (
    CustomerID counter,
    FirstName text(50) null,
    MiddleName text(50) null,
    LastName text(50) null,
    PhoneNumber text(50) null,
    JoinDate datetime null,
    EMailAddress text(50) null,
    IsActive yesno null,
    constraint CustomerID primary key (CustomerID))
</cfquery>
```

Check your database documentation for specific datatypes used. Table 11.1 lists some of the Microsoft SQL Server datatypes and their Microsoft Access equivalents.

TABLE 11.1: SQL Server versus Access Field Datatypes

SQL Server Datatype	Access Equivalent
numeric Identity	counter
datetime	datetime
varchar(length)	text(length)
numeric	number
bit	yesno
text	memo

Alter

With the `alter` statement, you can add, alter, and delete columns as well as table constraints. The following query will drop the `FilmStudio` column from the `Title` table:

```
<cfquery datasource="SybexSQL">
alter table Title
    drop column FilmStudio
</cfquery>
```

Conversely, if you wanted to change the datatype of the `FilmStudio` column from alphanumeric to numeric, you would use the `alter column` clause:

```
<cfquery datasource="SybexSQL">
alter table Title
    alter column FilmStudio numeric(18,0) null
</cfquery>
```

The following query adds the `GenreID` column to the `Customer` table so that the user's preferred genre can be stored. Notice that the `column` keyword is not used in the add clause:

```
<cfquery datasource="SybexSQL">
alter table Customer
    add GenreID numeric(18, 0) null
</cfquery>
```

Now that `GenreID` has been added to the `Customer` table, you may want to add referential integrity by making `GenreID` a foreign key and creating a relationship between the `Customer` and `Genre_Ref` tables. You would perform that task by adding a constraint to the `Customer` table. The syntax for adding a constraint is similar to that for adding a column:

```
alter table table_name
    add constraint unique_constraint_name foreign key
        (column_name) references parent_table_name
        (parent_table_column_name)
```

NOTE   The name of the constraint must be unique to the database.

The query used to add the relationship between the `Customer` and `Genre_Ref` table is as follows:

```
<cfquery datasource="SybexSQL">
alter table Customer
    add constraint FK_Customer_Genre_Ref foreign key
        (GenreID) references Genre_Ref (GenreID)
</cfquery>
```

To drop the constraint, use `drop constraint` in the `alter` statement:

```
<cfquery datasource="SybexSQL">
alter table Customer
    drop constraint FK_Customer_Genre_Ref
</cfquery>
```

Drop

The drop statement is very simple:

```
drop table table_name
```

Thus, the following query deletes the `Title` table:

```
<cfquery datasource="SybexSQL">
drop table Title
</cfquery>
```

WARNING   The drop statement permanently deletes both the data and the table definitions without any confirmation prompts. Use it with care.

Data Manipulation

After your database is created and your tables are complete, you'll want to add, edit, and delete data from your tables. These actions are performed by using the `insert`, `update`, and `delete` statements, respectively.

Inserting

To get information into a table, use the `insert` statement. You can only insert data into one table at a time. If you need to insert data into a related table, you must use a separate `insert` statement for each table. The syntax of the `insert` statement is as follows:

```
insert into table_name (textColName, dateColName, numberColName)
values ('textValue', dateValue, numberValue)
```

When inserting data into a table, there is a one-to-one relationship between the columns listed and the values supplied. The order of the values must match the order of the corresponding column names. If you are inserting data for an alphanumeric column, such as for datatypes `varchar` or `text`, you must surround the value with single quotes. Single quotes are not needed (and will cause an error) around numeric values and Open Database Connectivity (ODBC) formatted dates. To format a date, use the ColdFusion `createODBCDate` or `createODBCDateTime` function around the date value.

NOTE   There is no where clause in an `insert` statement because where clauses are used to determine which row(s) are affected by the statement. Since you are inserting a new row into the table, it is impossible to specify existing rows to be affected.

Optional Data

When you are inserting data that isn't required, there is always the chance that you will want to leave a field or value empty. If that is the case, you want to insert `null` into the database as opposed to just an empty value. If you are using Microsoft Access for your database, you must have ColdFusion do the work for you. SQL Server, however, has a function (nullIf) to aid you.

Microsoft Access

The following query will insert a new record into the Customer table. It also will test the optional fields (*form.MiddleName* and *form.EmailAddress*) for value and insert null into the column if they are empty.

```
insert into Customer (FirstName, MiddleName, LastName, PhoneNumber,
    EmailAddress, JoinDate, IsActive)
values ('#form.FirstName#',
    #iIf("#Len(Trim(form.MiddleName))#", de("'#form.MiddleName#'"), de("null"))#,
    '#form.LastName#', '#form.PhoneNumber#',
    <cfif len(trim(form.EmailAddress)) eq 0>
        null<cfelse>'#form.EmailAddress#'</cfif>,
    #createODBCDate(form.JoinDate)#, #form.IsActive#)
```

There are two methods you can use in ColdFusion to return a null value: the iIf function and the cfif tag.

The iIf function evaluates the *condition* and returns the first expression if the condition is true, or the second expression if the condition is false.

```
iIf(condition, string_expression1, string_expression1)
```

The de function delays evaluation of its argument within the iIf and evaluate functions. The following example is from the preceding query. Here, the value of form.MiddleName surrounded by single quotes or the string literal null will be passed to the query depending on the results of the condition.

```
#iIf("#len(trim(form.MiddleName))#", de("'#form.MiddleName#'"), de("null"))#
```

The cfif tag tests whether or not the form field has length and, if it does, it will return the field's value:

```
<cfif Len(Trim(form.EmailAddress)) eq 0>
    null<cfelse>'#form.EmailAddress#'</cfif>
```

Microsoft SQL Server

This next query will perform the same function as the preceding Access query, using the SQL Server function nullIf to enter the correct value for the nonrequired fields.

```
insert into Customer (FirstName, MiddleName, LastName, PhoneNumber,
    EmailAddress, JoinDate, IsActive)
values ('#form.FirstName#', nullIf('#form.MiddleName#',''), '#form.LastName#',
    '#form.PhoneNumber#',
    nullIf('#form.EmailAddress#',''), # createODBCDate(form.JoinDate)#,
    #form.IsActive#)
```

The `nullIf` function tests *expression1* to see if it equals *expression2*. If they match, `null` is returned. Otherwise, *expression1* is returned.

```
nullIf(expression1, expression2)
```

In the preceding query, `nullIf` is used to determine whether or not *form.MiddleName* equals an empty string. If it does, `null` is inserted into the column, otherwise the value of the form field is inserted.

```
nullIf('#form.MiddleName#','')
```

Automatically Generated ID

Most databases have the ability to automatically generate a unique ID for a row when data is inserted into a table. In Microsoft Access, this unique ID is referred to as an `autoNumber`, and in Microsoft SQL Server it's an `Identity`. No matter which database you use, the time will come when you need to know the value of that automatically generated ID immediately after the data is inserted. The next two sections give examples of adding a new row to the `Customer` table with both Microsoft Access and SQL Server.

Microsoft Access

The typical way to get the last inserted ID is to use a `select` query after your `insert` query to retrieve the last value, as shown in the following code. A `cftransaction` tag must wrap all of this to ensure you are getting the correct value. If you are using Microsoft Access, this is the only method you can use.

NOTE The `cftransaction` tag is used to create a single database transaction. If any query within the tag fails, all successful actions preceding it will be rolled back or reversed.

```
<!--- Access Insert Query and ID retrieval --->
<cftransaction>
    <!--- Insert query to create a new row. The ID will automatically be
        created. --->
    <cfquery datasource="SybexAccess">
    insert into Customer (FirstName, MiddleName, LastName, PhoneNumber,
        EmailAddress, JoinDate, IsActive)
    vlaues ('#form.FirstName#',
        #iIf("#len(trim(form.MiddleName))#", de("'#form.MiddleName#'"),
            de("null"))#,
        '#form.LastName#', '#form.PhoneNumber#',
        <cfif len(trim(form.EmailAddress)) eq 0>
            null<CFELSE>'#form.EmailAddress#'</CFIF>,
        #createODBCDate(form.JoinDate)#, #form.IsActive#)
    </cfquery>

    <!--- Select query to retrieve the last ID. --->
    <cfquery datasource="SybexAccess" name="GetID">
```

```
select max(CustomerID) as ThisID
from Customer
</cfquery>

<cfset CustomerID = GetID.ThisID>
</cftransaction>
<cfoutput>#CustomerID#</cfoutput>
```

NOTE   The method shown in this code has to make two trips to the server: one to perform the insert and another to retrieve the ID.

Microsoft SQL Server

With Microsoft SQL Server, you can query the Identity value in the same query as your insert statement, as shown here:

```
<!--- SQL Server Insert Query and ID retrieval --->
<cfquery datasource="SybexSQL" name="InsertCustomer">
set noCount on
insert into Customer (FirstName, MiddleName, LastName, PhoneNumber,
    EmailAddress, JoinDate, IsActive)
values ('#form.FirstName#', nullIf('#form.MiddleName#',''), '#form.LastName#',
    '#form.PhoneNumber#',
    nullIf('#form.EmailAddress#',''), #createODBCDate(form.JoinDate)#,
        #form.IsActive#)
select CustomerID = @@Identity
set noCount off
</cfquery>

<cfset CustomerID = InsertCustomer.CustomerID>
<cfoutput>#CustomerID#</cfoutput>
```

This query introduces two concepts that may be new to you.

set noCount on is used to eliminate the return of the number of rows affected by a query. When several queries are run at the same time, using set noCount on can reduce network traffic because less data is passed between the client and the server. set noCount off is used at the end of the statements to reset the noCount.

After an insert statement, @@Identity contains the value of the last Identity value generated by the statement. In this example, @@Identity contains the value of the CustomerID Identity column in the Customer table. The select statement after the insert statement will store that value in a column called CustomerID, which is the only column and value returned by the cfquery. The CustomerID variable now holds the value of UserID that was created for the inserted data, with only one trip to the database.

NOTE For standard `insert`, `update`, and `delete` queries, you do not need to provide the cfquery tag with the name attribute. However, if you are retrieving the `Identity` column, you'll need to provide a name to recall the value after the `cfquery`.

Updating

The `update` statement is similar to the `insert` statement, in that you can only affect one table at a time and the column names and values must be listed and have a one-to-one relationship. In the `update` statement, however, you must use the = operator to specify the value of each field, and you can add a `where` clause to specify which row(s) will be affected by the update. If you do not use a `where` clause, every row in the table will be updated with the specified values.

```
update table_name
set textColName = 'textValue',
    dateColName = dateValue,
    numberColName = numberValue
where tableIDColumn = tableIDColumnValue
```

You saw the query to insert a row into the `Customer` table in the preceding section. Now look at the following query to update the record by passing in the same information as the `insert` query, only this time the `CustomerID` value is provided so that only the specified record is updated.

```
<cfquery datasource="SybexSQL">
update Customer
set FirstName = '#form.FirstName#',
    MiddleName = nullIf('#form.MiddleName#',''),
    LastName = '#form.LastName#',
    PhoneNumber = '#form.PhoneNumber#',
    EmailAddress = nullIf('#form.EmailAddress#',''),
    JoinDate = #CreateODBCDate(form.JoinDate)#,
    IsActive = #form.IsActive#
where CustomerID = #form.CustomerID#
</cfquery>
```

NOTE The preceding query uses the Microsoft SQL Server `nullIf` function and will not work in Microsoft Access. To perform the same results in Access, replace the `nullIf` function with either the `iIf` ColdFusion function or ColdFusion's `cfif` tag, as detailed in the `insert` example.

NOTE If no rows meet the condition of the `where` clause, no error will occur and no rows will be updated.

Deleting

The query to delete data is much simpler than the queries to insert or update data. You only need to provide the *table_name* and an optional where clause to specify which rows to delete. If you do not provide a where clause, all rows in the table will be deleted. delete uses the following syntax:

```
delete from table_name
where tableIDColumn = tableIDColumnValue
```

The following query will delete the record from the Customer table where the CustomerID equals 59:

```
delete from Customer
where CustomerID = 59
```

This query may not always work, however. The database schema shows that the primary key column CustomerID in the Customer table is a foreign key in the Rental table. If customer number 59 has records in the Rental table, the query will produce the following error:

```
[Macromedia][SQLServer JDBC Driver][SQLServer]DELETE statement
    conflicted with COLUMN REFERENCE constraint
    'FK__Rental__Customer__29572725'. The conflict occurred in database
    'SybexSQL', table 'Rental', column 'CustomerID'
```

You cannot delete a row in a table if the primary key is being referenced in another table and a relationship is defined between those tables. This is to ensure that related data will not be partially deleted. To delete a record from the Customer table, you must first delete data in all related tables. Here's an example:

```
<cftransaction>
    <!--- Delete record from the related table(s) --->
    <cfquery datasource="SybexSQL">
    delete from Rental
    where CustomerID = #form.CustomerID#
    </cfquery>

    <!--- Delete the record itself. --->
    <cfquery datasource="SybexSQL">
    delete from Customer
    where CustomerID = #form.CustomerID#
    </cfquery>
</cftransaction>
```

The preceding code properly deletes all the related data. By using the cftransaction tag, you ensure that none of the data is deleted if an error occurs. If no rows meet the conditions of the where clause in a delete query, no error occurs and no rows of data are deleted.

WARNING   When records are deleted, you get *no* prompt or warning. Records are deleted immediately.

Querying Data

Now that you've seen examples of how to manipulate tables and data, it is time to learn more about the type of query you'll use most often: the `select` statement.

select Statements

In order to retrieve data form a database, you must use the `select` statement. The following clauses can be included in a `select` statement:

- `select`
- `from`
- `where`
- `group by`
- `having`
- `order by`

If used, the `select` clauses must appear in the order just shown. Only the `select` and `from` clauses are required. We'll discuss `group by` and `having` later in this chapter.

The following query will pull all the columns and all the rows from the `Title` table:

```
select *
from Title
```

However, using * in your `select` clause actually slows down the database because it searches for all the possible columns. Even if you want every column returned, it is more efficient to list them individually. Commas must separate column names in the `select` statement:

```
select TitleID, Title, GenreID, FilmStudio, ReleaseYear
from Title
```

If you don't want to return all rows from the table, you can restrict the data retrieved by using a `where` clause as shown here:

```
select TitleID, Title
from Title
where GenreID = 1
```

This query will return just the `TitleID` and `Title` from the `Title` table where the `GenreID` is equal to 1.

You can use multiple conditions in your `where` clause as long as they are separated by either `and` or `or` operators. To clarify the order of processing, it is best to use parentheses as you would if you used multiple conditions in a `cfif` tag. Within queries, parentheses affect what happens in mathematical expressions—they control the order of evaluation. For example:

```
select TitleID, Title
from Title
```

```
where GenreID = 1
    and (TitleID < 12 or Title LIKE 'A%')
```

The % wildcard is used to symbolize any number of characters. So A% means that any values beginning with A will be returned.

The preceding query will again return the `TitleID` and the `Title` columns from the `Title` table. This time, however, the data is even more restricted. A row will be returned only if the `GenreID` is equal to 1 *and* the `TitleID` is less than 12 *or* the `Title` starts with the letter A. By moving the parentheses around, you can greatly change the results of the query.

Finally, the `order` by clause determines how the data will be sorted.

```
select TitleID, Title
from Title
order by Title desc, TitleID
```

Data can be sorted in either ascending (`asc`) or descending (`desc`) order. The default is ascending and it does not require notation. To display data in reverse order, use `desc` after the column name in the `order` by clause. You can reference multiple columns in the `order` by clause including ones that are not in the `select` clause.

Column and Table Aliases

Aliases can be used for columns to provide an alternate name in which the element will be referenced. There are several reasons for giving a column an alias:

- The column name is unsupported by ColdFusion as a variable.

- The name of the column is not descriptive and you want to use a different name.

- You are computing a column based on an aggregate or scalar function (as discussed later in this chapter).

- You are selecting columns from two or more tables with the same column name.

If the name of a column is not formatted so that ColdFusion will support it as a variable name, the column can be referenced by placing it inside of brackets and assigning it an alias. You then refer to the alias after the `cfquery` tag is processed. Use the `as` operator to create a column alias.

Suppose the `Title` table had a column called `Title ID` instead of `TitleID`. The following query would retrieve the data in such a way that it could be output by ColdFusion.

```
<cfquery datasource="SybexSQL" name="GetTitles">
select [Title ID] as TitleID, Title
from Title
</cfquery>
```

```
<cfoutput query="GetTitles">
  #TitleID# - #Title#<BR>
</cfoutput>
```

> **NOTE** ColdFusion variables can contain only letters, numbers, and the underline (_) character. They must begin with a letter.

In addition to column aliases, you can also create aliases for table names. This comes in handy when you are working with more than one table (discussed later in this chapter). It's also helpful if you need to qualify the column names, as follows:

```
select table_name.column_name, table_name.column_name
from table_name
```

Supplying the entire table name before each column can be cumbersome, and you can easily create an alias for your table(s) and use that as the qualifier. To create an alias for a table, place a space after the table name and then the alias. It is not necessary to use the AS operator.

```
select t.TitleID, t.Title
from Title t
```

Unique Rows

In order to pull unique rows from a table, you use the `distinct` keyword. When `distinct` is added to a `select` statement, duplicate rows are discarded. The following query will retrieve all unique last names that are stored in the `Customer` table:

```
select distinct LastName
from Customer
```

If you add additional columns to the `select` statement, the `distinct` keyword will only retrieve unique combinations of the specified columns.

Functions

Like ColdFusion, SQL databases have many functions that can help you format data and perform mathematical operations. There are two types of functions: aggregate and scalar.

Aggregate Functions

Aggregate functions are used to summarize data. For the video store example, you would use aggregate functions to determine the average late fee paid, or the total number of times a particular movie has been rented. The following paragraphs explain the aggregate functions that are associated with most databases.

> **NOTE** You must create an alias for each aggregate function in your `select` clause in order to retrieve the value in ColdFusion after the query.

The avg Function

The avg function can be used to produce an average value from all of the values in a numeric column. It will ignore null values in the specified column and they will not be factored into the resultant value. To determine the average late fee in the Rental table, you would use avg as shown here:

```
<cfquery datasource="SybexSQL" name="GetAverage">
select avg(LateFee) as AverageLateFee
from Rental
</cfquery>

<cfoutput>#GetAverage.AverageLateFee#</cfoutput>
```

The count Function

The number of records in a table can easily be counted by querying all the rows and by using RecordCount:

```
<cfquery datasource="SybexSQL" name="GetCount">
select *
from Title
</cfquery>

<cfoutput>#GetCount.RecordCount#</cfoutput>
```

However, if you only want to know the number of rows in the table and do not need the entire record set, it is much more efficient to determine the number of rows using the count function, passing in * instead of a specific field name:

```
<cfquery datasource="SybextSQL" name="GetCount">
select count(*) as DataCount
from Title
</cfquery>

<cfoutput>#GetCount.DataCount#</cfoutput>
```

Now DataCount represents the number of rows in the Title table.

Keep in mind that you shouldn't use RecordCount when you are trying to return a count of all rows using count. This is because even if no rows are in the table, the RecordCount will always be 1. However, if there are no rows, the value of DataCount will be zero. To get a count of all rows meeting a specific condition, you will need to use a where clause to restrict the data.

You can also use count to determine the number of rows in which a specific column has a value that is not null, as shown here:

```
select count(EMailAddress) AS EMailAddressCount
from Customer
```

The preceding query will return a count of rows in the `Customer` table that do not have null values in the `EMailAddress` column. In order to determine the number of distinct values in a column, use the `distinct` keyword:

```
select count(distinct LastName) as NumLastNamesUsed
from Customer
```

`NumLastNamesUsed` will return the number of distinct `LastName` values in the `Customer` table.

The max Function

The `max` function is used to determine the maximum value of a numeric, date, or character field. When used against a character field, the resultant value will be the one with the highest values based on the ASCII character chart.

Here is an example from our video-rental database:

```
select max(LateFee) as MaximumLateFee
from Rental
```

This query will return the highest late fee paid by a customer for a late movie return.

The min Function

The `min` function is used to determine the minimum value of a numeric, date, or character field. When used against a character field, the resultant value will be that with the lowest values based on the ASCII character chart.

```
select min(LateFee) as MinimumLateFee
from Rental
```

The preceding query will return the lowest late fee a customer paid for a late movie return, excluding null values.

The sum Function

The `sum` function can be used to total the numeric values in the specified column. In order to determine the total late fees paid, use `sum`:

```
<cfquery datasource="SybexSQL" name="GetFees">
select sum(LateFee) as TotalLateFees
from Rental
</cfquery>

<cfoutput>#GetFees.TotalLateFees#</cfoutput>
```

The `TotalLateFees` variable is a total of all the values in the `LateFee` field. If you wanted to determine the total late fee for only a specific set of users, add a `where` clause to the query.

Scalar Functions

Using scalar functions can greatly reduce the amount of ColdFusion code you need to write both in the query and in the output. Scalar functions allow you to format the data at the database level before it is returned to ColdFusion. This can help save processing time.

NOTE For a complete list of ODBC-supported scalar functions and the version of the driver that supports them, visit `http://www.microsoft.com/msdownload/platformsdk/sdkupdate/` to download the MDAC SDK. If you are using native drivers to connect to your database, check your database documentation for the correct functions to use.

One function that SQL and ColdFusion share is the `left` function. It has the same syntax in both environments:

```
left(string, count)
```

The value returned will be the first *count* characters of the *string*, starting from the left. One use of the `left` function is to group data by its first letter, as in the movie title listing in Figure 11.2.

FIGURE 11.2:

Data grouped by first letter

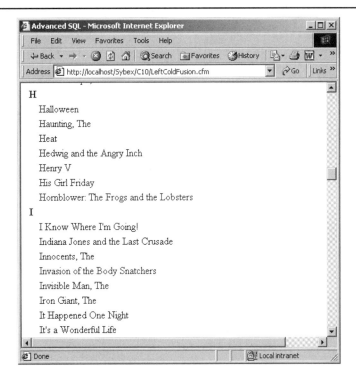

This grouping can be obtained using two different methods. The first method (shown in Listing 11.1) queries all the movie titles from the `Title` table.

Listing 11.1   **Using the ColdFusion left Function (c1101.cfm)**

```
<!---
    Name:          /c11/c1101.cfm
    Description:   Queries all the titles and uses
                   the ColdFusion left function
                   to display the first letter of each.
--->
<!--- Query the titles. --->
<cfquery datasource="SybexSQL" name="GetTitles">
select Title
from Title
order by Title
</cfquery>

<!DOCTYPE HTML PUBLIC "-//W3C//DTD HTML 4.0 Transitional//EN">

<html>
<head>
    <title>c1101.cfm</title>
</head>

<body>

<!--- Initialize the FirstLetter variable. --->
<cfset FirstLetter = "">

<table border="0">
    <!--- Loop through the query results. --->
    <cfoutput query="GetTitles">
        <!--- If the first letter of the title is not
              the same as the FirstLetter variable,
              set the variable and display the letter. --->
        <cfif left(Title,1) is NOT FirstLetter>
            <cfset FirstLetter = Left(Title,1)>
            <tr>
                <td colspan="2"><b>#FirstLetter#</b></td>
            </tr>
        </cfif>
        <tr>
            <td>   </td>
            <td>#Title#</td>
        </tr>
    </cfoutput>
</table>

</body>
</html>
```

In the query output, you must set a placeholder (called *FirstLetter* in this example) that will hold the value of the current first letter of the group being displayed. You use the ColdFusion left function to determine that value. Each time that first letter changes, the grouping heading will be displayed with the titles underneath it.

You can simplify your code by using the SQL left function in your query to retrieve both the Title and a new column called FirstLetter, which contains only the first letter of the title. Listing 11.2 shows this method.

Listing 11.2   Using the left Database Function (c1102.cfm)

```
<!---
    Name:           /c11/c1102.cfm
    Description:    Queries all the titles and uses
                    a database function to return
                    the first letter of each.
--->
<!--- Query the titles and the first letter
    of each. --->
<cfquery datasource="SybexSQL" name="GetTitles">
select Title, Left(Title,1) AS FirstLetter
from Title
order by Title
</cfquery>

<!DOCTYPE HTML PUBLIC "-//W3C//DTD HTML 4.0 Transitional//EN">

<html>
<head>
    <title>c1102.cfm</title>
</head>

<body>

<table border="0">
    <!--- Loop through the query results and use
        the group attribute to display each distinct first letter. --->
    <cfoutput query="GetTitles" group="FirstLetter">
        <tr>
            <td colspan="2"><b>#FirstLetter#</b></td>
        </tr>
        <cfoutput>
            <tr>
                <td>   </td>
                <td>#Title#</td>
            </tr>
        </cfoutput>
    </cfoutput>
</table>

</body>
</html>
```

Because the `FirstLetter` variable is now part of the record set, you can use the `group` attribute of the `cfoutput` tag to display the group heading, and its subsequent titles, by nesting `cfoutput` tags.

Subqueries

A *subquery* is a query that is used within another query. Subqueries can be used in both the `select` and `where` clauses of another query.

select Clauses

A subquery in a `select` clause is often used to retrieve summarized data. For example, you might want to retrieve the results of an aggregate function that references data in columns/rows other than just the ones specified in the `select` statement and its `where` clause.

Figure 11.3 displays each customer, the date they joined, the earliest customer join date, and the difference in days between the two dates.

FIGURE 11.3:

Customer join dates

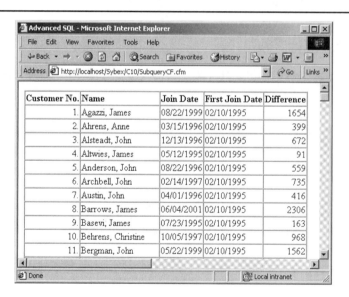

Without a subquery, you would need two `cfquery` tags to get the necessary data. In addition, you would have to use a `cfset` tag for each user to determine the date difference (See Listing 11.3).

Listing 11.3   **Combining Data from Two Queries Using ColdFusion (c1103.cfm)**

```
<!---
   Name:         /c11/c1103.cfm
   Description:  Query the first join date and
```

```
                    query all the customer information to
                    compare the two.
--->
<!--- Get first join date. --->
<cfquery datasource="SybexSQL" name="GetDate">
select min(JoinDate) as FirstDate
from Customer
</cfquery>

<cfset FirstDate = GetDate.FirstDate>

<!--- Query the customers. --->
<cfquery datasource="SybexSQL" name="GetCustomers">
select CustomerID, FirstName, LastName, JoinDate
from Customer
order by CustomerID
</cfquery>

<!DOCTYPE HTML PUBLIC "-//W3C//DTD HTML 4.0 Transitional//EN">

<html>
<head>
   <title>c1103.cfm</title>
</head>

<body>

<table border = "1" cellpadding="1" cellspacing="0">
   <tr>
      <td><b>Customer No.</b></td>
      <td><b>Name</b></td>
      <td><b>Join Date</b></td>
      <td><b>First Join Date</b></td>
      <td><b>Difference</b></td>
      <!--- Loop through the result set and display them. --->
      <cfoutput query="GetCustomers">
        <cfset DateDifference = DateDiff("d", FirstDate, JoinDate)>
        <tr>
           <td align="right">#CustomerID#.</td>
           <td>#LastName#, #FirstName#</td>
           <td>#DateFormat(JoinDate, "mm/dd/yyyy")#</td>
           <td>#DateFormat(FirstDate, "mm/dd/yyyy")#</td>
           <td align="right">#DateDifference#</td>
        </tr>
      </cfoutput>
   </tr>
</table>

</body>
</html>
```

By using a subquery and a scalar function (see Listing 11.4), you can achieve the same results using only one query and omitting the cfset tag.

Listing 11.4   **Combining Data Using a Subquery (c1104.cfm)**

```
<!---
    Name:            /c11/c1104.cfm
    Description:     Query the first join date and the customer
                     data using a subquery to compare the data at once.
--->
<cfquery datasource="SybexSQL" name="GetCustomers">
select CustomerID, FirstName, LastName, JoinDate,
    (select min(JoinDate) as FirstDate from Customer) as FirstDate,
    DateDiff(dd, (select min (JoinDate) from Customer), JoinDate)
        as DateDifference
from Customer
order by CustomerID
</cfquery>

<!DOCTYPE HTML PUBLIC "-//W3C//DTD HTML 4.0 Transitional//EN">

<html>
<head>
    <title>c1104.cfm</title>
</head>

<body>

<table border = "1" cellpadding="1" cellspacing="0">
    <tr>
        <td><b>Customer No.</b></td>
        <td><b>Name</b></td>
        <td><b>Join Date</b></td>
        <td><b>First Join Date</b></td>
        <td><b>Difference</b></td>
        <cfoutput query="GetCustomers">
            <tr>
                <td align="right">#CustomerID#.</td>
                <td>#LastName#, #FirstName#</td>
                <td>#DateFormat(JoinDate, "mm/dd/yyyy")#</td>
                <td>#DateFormat(FirstDate, "mm/dd/yyyy")#</td>
                <td align="right">#DateDifference#</td>
            </tr>
        </cfoutput>
    </tr>
</table>

</body>
</html>
```

where Clause

You can also use subqueries in your where clause as an easier way to determine which rows should be selected, updated, and/or deleted.

As mentioned in the earlier section about deleting, you must often delete related data before you delete the actual record you want to purge. This isn't difficult if you know which record(s) of the parent table you want to delete, but it can be more confusing if those rows are unknown. Let's say you want to delete all the customers that joined before 1996 from the Customer table. You must first determine which CustomerID records can be removed and then delete them from the child tables before you can delete them from the parent table. Without subqueries, you would need to write the code shown in Listing 11.5.

Listing 11.5   **Deleting Data Using a where Clause (c1105.cfm)**

```
<!---
    Name:         /c11/c1105.cfm
    Description:  Delete data using a where clause.
--->
<!--- Set a date. --->
<cfset DeleteDate = CreateDate(1996, 1, 1)>

<cftransaction>

    <!--- Query all the customers who meet the delete requirements. --->
    <cfquery datasource="SybexSQL" name="GetCustIDS">
    select CustomerID
    from Customer
    where JoinDate < #CreateODBCDate(DeleteDate)#
    </cfquery>

    <!--- Create a list with all of the customer IDs returned. --->
    <cfset DeleteList = ValueList(GetCustIDs.CustomerID)>

    <!--- Delete the related data. --->
    <!--- You must use cfif in case no records were returned in
     the GetCustIDs query. --->
    <cfif GetCustIDS.RecordCount NEQ 0>
        <cfquery datasource="SybexSQL">
        delete from Rental
        where CustomerID in (#DeleteList#)
        </cfquery>
    </cfif>

    <!--- Delete the customers. --->
    <cfquery datasource="SybexSQL">
    delete from Customer
    where JoinDate < #CreateODBCDate(DeleteDate)#
    </cfquery>

</cftransaction>
```

The example in Listing 11.5 uses one query to find the `CustomerID` of all the customer records that match the delete criteria. You then store these IDs in the variable `DeleteList`. Since the values after the `in` operator cannot be empty, you must first make sure you have records to delete from the child table by using the `cfif` tag. With all this in place, you can delete the parent record.

in/not in Keywords

By using the subquery in Listing 11.6 with the `in` operator, you can simplify your Cold-Fusion code.

Listing 11.6   **Deleting Data Using a Subquery (c1106.cfm)**

```
<!---
   Name:          /c11/c1106.cfm
   Description:   Delete data using a subquery.
--->
<!--- Set a date. --->
<cfset DeleteDate = CreateDate(1996, 1, 1)>

<cftransaction>

   <!--- Delete the related data by using a subquery to only delete
    records matching the delete requirements. --->
   <cfquery datasource="SybexSQL">
   delete from Rental
   where CustomerID in (
      select CustomerID
      from Customer
      where JoinDate < #CreateODBCDate(DeleteDate)#)
   </cfquery>

   <!--- Delete the customers. --->
   <cfquery datasource="SybexSQL">
   delete from Customer
   where JoinDate < #CreateODBCDate(DeleteDate)#
   </cfquery>

</cftransaction>
```

This example uses a subquery with the `in` operator to determine which child records to delete directly within the `delete` statement. Because the subquery is permitted to return no values, you no longer need to use `cfif` conditional logic. If no records are returned in the subquery, no records will be deleted.

Conversely, to delete all records that were not returned in the subquery, you would use the `not in` operator as opposed to `in`.

NOTE   When you are using a subquery with the `in` operator in a query's where clause, the subquery can return zero, one, or more rows, but only one column can be specified in that subquery's `select` statement.

exists/not exists Keywords

Another subquery option uses the `exists` keyword. In contrast to `in`, which will retrieve zero, one, or more values of a single column, the `exists` keyword will determine whether or not any data was retrieved in the subquery. `exists` will return true if the results are nonempty, and `not exists` will return true if the results are empty.

The query in Listing 11.7 performs the same delete operation as in Listing 11.6, but it uses `exists` instead of `in`.

Listing 11.7   **Deleting Using a Subquery with exists (c1107.cfm)**

```
<!---
   Name:          /c11/c1107.cfm
   Description:    Delete data using a subquery with exists.
--->
<!--- Set a date. --->
<cfset DeleteDate = CreateDate(1996, 1, 1)>

<cftransaction>

   <!--- Delete the related data by using a subquery only to delete
    records matching the delete requirements. --->
   <cfquery datasource="SybexSQL">
   delete form Rental
   where exists (
      select CustomerID
      from Customer
      where JoinDate < #CreateODBCDate(DeleteDate)#
         and Customer.CustomerID = Rental.CustomerID)
   </cfquery>

   <!--- Delete the customers. --->
   <cfquery datasource="SybexSQL">
   delete from Customer
   where JoinDate < #CreateODBCDate(DeleteDate)#
   </cfquery>

</cftransaction>
```

In the first `delete` statement of this example, you are checking to scc if there are any records in the `Customer` table that meet the delete requirements (that the current `CustomerID` also exists in the `Rental` table). In this case, using `exists` is actually more efficient than using in. When you use `in` or `exists` in a query, the subquery is processed for each row within the table specified in your `delete` query. With `in`, every row is returned from the subquery's table each time the subquery is processed; with `exists`, only the rows that are related to the table specified in the `delete` query will be returned, thus creating less network traffic. Typically, the results of `in` and `exists` will be the same.

Joins

Frequently the data you want resides in two or more tables in your database. The two ways to accomplish this retrieval are using joins and unions. Let's look first at joins.

Suppose you want to query all the movie titles in the Action genre, and you know that the `GenreID` for Action is 1. You would use the following query:

```
select TitleID, Title
from Title
where GenreID = 1
```

What if you don't know the `GenreID` of the Action genre, but you just know that the genre was named Action? In that case, you would have to join the two tables. There are two types of joins: inner joins and outer joins.

Inner Joins

Inner joins return only matching rows from two or more tables. They are based on equality. Inner joins are the most common type of joins. Typically, two tables are joined by setting the matching fields in the `where` clause to be equal to each other:

```
select T.TitleID, T.Title, G.Genre
from Title T, Genre_ref G
where T.GenreID = G.GenreID
    and G.Genre = 'Drama'
```

Notice that the tables are assigned aliases and that the column names are qualified with those aliases. If you did not join the two tables together on the `GenreID`, you would retrieve a Cartesian product, which returns all possible combinations of rows.

```
select T.TitleID, T.Title, G.Genre
from Title T, Genre_ref G
where G.Genre = 'Drama'
```

Instead of returning approximately 40 rows, the Cartesian product query will return over 200.

You can also join tables together using `inner join` in the `from` clause. The following query will return the same results as the preceding one:

```
select T.TitleID, T.Title, G.Genre
from Title T inner join Genre_ref G
ON T.GenreID = G.GenreID
where G.Genre = 'Drama'
```

NOTE   The query that uses the `inner join` syntax will return the same results as the one that does not. Deciding on which syntax to use depends on personal preference and/or the database package you are using.

Outer Joins

Since inner joins only return rows that have matching values in each table, you can use an outer join to pull data from two or more tables where it may exist in only one. There are two types of outer joins, left and right.

Left Outer Join

The most common outer join is the left outer join. To create a left outer join, use the `left outer join` operator as opposed to `inner join`. When two tables are joined using a left outer join, all the rows are returned from the first table specified—the left table—and related data in the right table if it exists. If matching data does not exist, null values are returned for the columns selected from the right table.

The following query will return all `CopyID` values from the `CopyTable` and any related `RentalID` values from the `Rental` table if they exist. If there is no correlated data, `null` will be returned for the `RentalID` value:

```
select C.CopyID, R.RentalID
from Copy C left outer join Rental R
on C.CopyID = R.CopyID
order by R.RentalID
```

Right Outer Join

Using the `right outer join` operator produces the opposite results of using the `left outer join`. All values from the right table are returned, as well as matching values from the left table. If there is no matching data, null values will be returned for the columns selected from the left table.

The following query reverses the order in which the tables were listed in the query just discussed for the `left outer join`, but it will produce the same results because it uses the `right outer join` operator:

```
select C.CopyID, R.RentalID
from Rental R right outer join Copy C
on C.CopyID = R.CopyID
order by R.RentalID
```

NOTE   Some database packages use different syntax to process outer joins. Please check your database documentation for the proper syntax.

Unions

Unions are used to merge the results of two or more `select` statements into one result set, by means of the `union` operator placed between each `select` statement. With unions, each `select` statement must select the same number of columns in the same order. Each merged column must contain the same datatype.

By default, the `union` operator normally removes all duplicate rows. In order to return all rows, duplicates included, use `union all`.

Unions are underutilized in ColdFusion development because much of the work that's traditionally done with a `union` can easily—but not necessary more efficiently—be done in ColdFusion code.

This next example queries all the users. Because the `IsActive` field has a value of either 0 or 1, the `cfif` tag is used to nicely format the data returned.

```
<cfquery datasource="SybexSQL" name="GetUsers">
select FirstName, LastName, IsActive
from Customer
order by LastName, FirstName
</cfquery>

<table>
    <cfoutput query="GetUsers">
        <tr>
            <td>#LastName#</td>
            <td>#FirstName#</td>
            <td><cfif IsActive EQ 1>Yes<cfelse>No</cfif></td>
        </tr>
    </cfoutput>
</table>
```

The same effect can be reached with a `union` operator and without using `cfif` logic to format the data.

```
<cfquery datasource="SybexSQL" name="GetUsers">
select FirstName, LastName, IsActive, 'Yes' as ActiveStatus
from Customer
where IsActive = 1
union all
select FirstName, LastName, IsActive, 'No' as ActiveStatus
fromCustomer
where IsActive = 0
order by LastName, FirstName
</cfquery>
```

```
<table>
    <cfoutput query="GetUsers">
        <tr>
            <td>#LastName#</td>
            <td>#FirstName#</td>
            <td>#ActiveStatus#</td>
        </tr>
    </cfoutput>
</table>
```

In this example, the union merges the results of two select statements. The first select statement returns all customers who are active and uses the literal constant 'Yes' as the ActiveStatus column. This column doesn't exist in the table and exists only in the record set. The second select statement returns all customers who are inactive and has a value of 'No' for the ActiveStatus column. ActiveStatus is used to output the nicely formatted status of the user.

Notice that there is only one order by clause for the two select statements. With a union, you can use one order by clause at the end of the query to sort the entire record set as desired.

NOTE   Some database packages require the use of column position numbers rather than column names in the order by clause when a union is used. If this is the case, the order by clause in this section's example would be order by 1. Check your database documentation to determine which method is supported.

Grouping

Because data can be grouped both in the query and in the cfoutput tag, it can be confusing to determine which technique you should use when. Grouping in the query works fine if you want to just display summary results, but if you want to see the details, you should group in the cfoutput tag.

Group in Query

Grouping in a query introduces two new clauses used in the select statement: group by and having. In a group by query, only column names, aggregate functions, and/or constants can be used in the select clause. Every column and constant that is not an aggregate function must be listed in the group by clause. The having clause is used to create conditions based on an aggregate function.

```
select column_name, expression
from table_name
where column_condition
group by column_name
having expression_condition
order by column_name
```

If you wanted to determine how many movies each customer returned late, and the total amount of late fees they paid, you could write a query that uses the group by clause. You can further restrict the results to include only those customers who returned more than one movie late, so the nondelinquent customers will not be included in the list. Listing 11.8 shows an example of this process.

Listing 11.8   **Grouping Data in a Query (c1108.cfm)**

```
<!---
   Name:           /c11/c1108.cfm
   Description:    Group data within a query.
--->
<!--- Query the data, group within the query. --->
<cfquery datasource="SybexSQL" name="GetSummary">
select C.CustomerID, C.FirstName, C.LastName,
  count(R.RentalID) as TotalLate, sum(R.LateFee) as TotalLateFee
from Customer C, Rental R
where C.CustomerID = R.CustomerID
  AND R.LateFee is not null
group by C.CustomerID, C.FirstName, C.LastName
having count(R.RentalID) > 1
order by C.LastName, C.FirstName
</cfquery>

<!DOCTYPE HTML PUBLIC "-//W3C//DTD HTML 4.0 Transitional//EN">

<html>
<head>
   <title>c1108.cfm</title>
</head>

<body>

<table border = "1" cellpadding="1" cellspacing="0">
   <tr>
      <td><b>Customer No.</b></td>
      <td><b>Name</b></td>
      <td><b>No. Late</b></td>
      <td><b>LateFees</b></td>
      <cfoutput query="GetSummary">
         <tr>
            <td align="right">#CustomerID#</td>
            <td>#LastName#, #FirstName#</td>
            <td align="right">#TotalLate#</td>
            <td align="right">#DollarFormat(TotalLateFee)#</td>
         </tr>
      </cfoutput>
   </tr>
</table>

</body>
</html>
```

The select clause retrieves three columns and two aggregate function expressions. Following the group by rules, the three column names are listed in the group by clause. This ensures that the number of RentalID values and the sum of the LateFee column will be combined when the CustomerID, FirstName, and LastName match. This means only one record will be returned for each customer.

The having clause further restricts the query: It only applies to the records where the number of RentalID values that are late for each user is greater than one. You cannot use aggregate functions in the where clause.

Figure 11.4 shows the results of the query in Listing 11.8.

FIGURE 11.4:

Grouped data

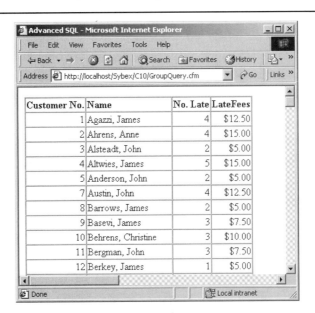

Customer No.	Name	No. Late	LateFees
1	Agazzi, James	4	$12.50
2	Ahrens, Anne	4	$15.00
3	Alsteadt, John	2	$5.00
4	Altwies, James	5	$15.00
5	Anderson, John	2	$5.00
7	Austin, John	4	$12.50
8	Barrows, James	2	$5.00
9	Basevi, James	3	$7.50
10	Behrens, Christine	3	$10.00
11	Bergman, John	3	$7.50
12	Berkey, James	1	$5.00

Group in Output

Grouping in the query will help return summary results, but it is not always the best solution for reports where details are desired. To show details and summaries combined, grouping in the output is a much better choice. For instance, to build a report that would find the details of all movies returned late for each user, including the title, the date it was checked out, the original due date, the date it was actually returned, and the individual late fee, you would select multiple rows for each customer and group them in the output. The code in Listing 11.9 will retrieve the desired information and display both the details and summary results.

Listing 11.9   **Grouping Data in the Output (c1109.cfm)**

```
<!---
    Name:           /c11/c1109.cfm
    Description:    Group data in the output.
--->
<!--- Query the data. --->
<cfquery datasource="SybexSQL" name="GetDetails">
select C.CustomerID, C.FirstName, C.LastName,
  R.CheckOutDate, R.ReturnDate, R.DueDate, R.LateFee, T.Title
from Customer C, Rental R, Copy CC, Title T
where C.CustomerID = R.CustomerID
  and R.LateFee is not null
  and R.CopyID = CC.CopyID
  and CC.TitleID = T.TitleID
  and exists (
      select CustomerID, count(RentalID)
      from Rental
      where CustomerID = C.CustomerID
      group by CustomerID
      having count(RentalID) > 1)
order by C.LastName, C.FirstName
</cfquery>

<!DOCTYPE HTML PUBLIC "-//W3C//DTD HTML 4.0 Transitional//EN">

<html>
<head>
   <title>c1102.cfm</title>
</head>

<body>

<table border = "1" cellpadding="1" cellspacing="0">
   <tr>
      <td><b>Movie Title</b></td>
      <td><b>Checkout Date</b></td>
      <td><b>Due Date</b></td>
      <td><b>Return Date</b></td>
      <td><b>LateFee</b></td>
      <cfoutput query="GetDetails" group="CustomerID">
         <tr>
            <td colspan="5"><b>#CustomerID#. #LastName#, #FirstName#</b></td>
         </tr>
         <!--- Initialize/reset the TotalLateFee counter for each customer
            looped through. --->
         <cfset  TotalLateFee = 0>
         <cfoutput>
            <tr>
               <td>#Title#</td>
               <td>#DateFormat(CheckOutDate, "mm/dd/yyyy")#</td>
               <td>#DateFormat(DueDate, "mm/dd/yyyy")#</td>
               <td>#DateFormat(ReturnDate, "mm/dd/yyyy")#</td>
```

```
          <td align="right">#DollarFormat(LateFee)#</td>
        </tr>
                      <!--- Add the current late fee to the total late
                        fees for the customer. --->
        <cfset TotalLateFee = TotalLateFee + LateFee>
      </cfoutput>
      <tr>
        <td colspan="4"> </td>
        <td align="right"><b>#DollarFormat(TotalLateFee)#</b></td>
      </tr>
    </cfoutput>
  </tr>
</table>

</body>
</html>
```

The query in Listing 11.9 will return all customers who have more than one late movie and the details for each late movie. The subquery is used to determine which customers have more than one movie returned late. If you wanted to return all customers, regardless of the number of late returns, that condition and subquery could be excluded.

By nesting the cfoutput tags, both detail and summary data can be displayed. The outermost cfoutput tag requires the query attribute to specify which query will be used, and it requires the group attribute to specify by which column the data will be grouped/summarized. The innermost cfoutput tag accepts no attributes. If this example used more than two nested cfoutput tags, the other cfoutput tags would require the group attribute and could not use other attributes.

Figure 11.5 displays the customer report with both the details and the summary.

FIGURE 11.5:

Report with details

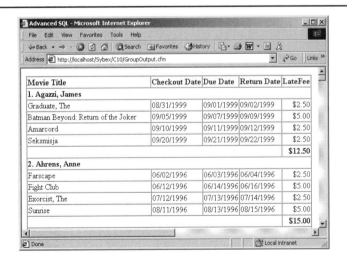

CFSQL

CFSQL—ColdFusion SQL—introduced in ColdFusion 5, allows you to perform a "Query of Queries." CFSQL can be used for many tasks such as reducing or reordering record sets that are results of `cfftp`, `cfhttp`, `cfldap`, `cfpop`, `cfquery`, `cfsearch`, or `cfstoredproc` tags. You can also use CFQSL to perform joins or unions on two or more queries, including queries that are run against different data sources.

In order to query another query, you must use the `dbtype` attribute in the `cfquery` tag and set the value to `query`:

```
<cfquery dbtype="Query" name="GetDisplay">
SQL
</cfquery>
```

The table name used in the SQL code will be the name of the query that you are querying against.

A common task that many developers need to tackle at one point or another is to break up a result set over multiple pages. This is usually done with large listings of search results when the desire is to keep the page loading time to a minimum. The most common way to do this is to output only a certain number of rows in a query's loop or output, and pass the starting row back and forth via next and previous links.

This method won't necessarily produce the desired results, however, if you are using the `group` attribute in `cfoutput`. For example, using the Scalar Functions example from Listing 11.1 to display each letter's grouping, how would you display one letter's records on a page? The letter *A* may have 10 records, while *B* could have 20. There isn't one number you can use to break up the output without inconsistent results, because displaying 15 records per page could display too many records for one letter and not enough for another.

The code in Listing 11.10 demonstrates the use of CFSQL to properly break up grouped output.

Listing 11.10   Using CFSQL (c1110.cfm)

```
<!---
   Name:          /c11/c1110.cfm
   Description:   Using Query of queries to display
                  the correct number of records on each page.
--->
<!--- Query all the titles. --->
<cfquery datasource="SybexSQL" name="GetTitles">
select Title, Left(Title,1) as FirstLetter
from Title
order by Title
</cfquery>
```

```
<!--- Set the default Display to A. --->
<cfparam name="Display" default="A">

<!--- Query only the display items for the full query --->
<cfquery dbtype="Query" name="GetDisplay">
select Title, FirstLetter
from GetTitles
where FirstLetter = '#Display#'
</cfquery>

<!--- Initalize the LinkList variable. --->
<cfset LinkList = "">

<!--- Loop through the numeric values of the letters of the
    alphabet and create a list with a link to each. --->
<cfloop from="65" to="90" index="Index">
    <cfset LinkList = ListAppend(LinkList,
        "<a href='c1110.cfm?Display=#Chr(Index)#'>#Chr(Index)#</A>", "|")>
</cfloop>

<!DOCTYPE HTML PUBLIC "-//W3C//DTD HTML 4.0 Transitional//EN">

<html>
<head>
    <title>c1110.cfm</title>
</head>

<body>

<cfoutput>#LinkList#</cfoutput>

<table border="0">
    <tr>
        <td colspan="2"><b><cfoutput>#Display#</cfoutput></b></td>
    </tr>
    <cfoutput query="GetDisplay">
        <tr>
            <td>   </td>
            <td>#Title#</td>
        </tr>
    </query>
</table>

</body>
</html>
```

In Listing 11.10, the GetTitles query is the same query used in the Scalar Functions example to pull all the titles and the first letter of each title. Because this same query will run each time the page is reloaded and will return the same results, you may want to cache the query or store it as a session variable to reduce processing time. The subsequent cfparam tag sets a default value of A for the *Display* variable. The first time this page loads, it will display the titles that begin with the letter A. The GetDisplay query will retrieve all the records that were returned in GetTitles that begin with the letter that matches the Display variable. Figure 11.6 shows the results.

FIGURE 11.6:

Grouped record set on multiple pages

Performance Testing

Sometimes the decision about whether to have your database or ColdFusion do the processing can be made by comparing the performance of the two. Two techniques for performance testing are *server-side debugging* and the ColdFusion GetTickCount function.

Server-Side Debugging

By turning on server-side debugging in the ColdFusion Administrator, you can view useful information such as the queries that were processed, the number of records each query returned, and how long each query took. You can also see the total processing time for the page.

Experiment with different versions of a query. Compare pages that use more SQL processing versus those that use more ColdFusion processing; what you observe in this comparison will help you determine which method is best for a particular task.

TIP	When using ColdFusion's server-side debugging, it is a good idea to refresh the page several times in a row, discarding the first set of values and calculating the average of the other tries.

Refer to the ColdFusion Administration documentation for instructions on how to turn on server-side debugging and what debugging options are available.

Figure 11.7 shows an example of the values returned with server-side debugging:

FIGURE 11.7:

Server-side debugging

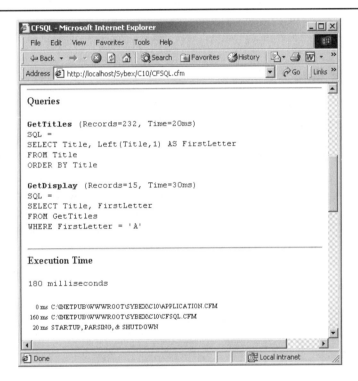

GetTickCount

The GetTickCount function in ColdFusion returns a millisecond counter. By retrieving the tick count both before and after a block of code and subtracting the start count from the end count, you can determine how many milliseconds of processing were required for that block of code. Here's an example:

```
<cfset StartTime = GetTickCount()>
. . .
<cfset EndTime = GetTickCount()>
<cfset TotalTime = EndTime - StartTime>
<cfoutput>#TotalTime#</cfoutput>
```

As in the server-side debugging example, it is a good idea to refresh the page a couple of times and average the values.

For an example, look back to the `select` clause examples in the "Subqueries" section. The first example used two queries and additional ColdFusion code; it took an average of 230 milliseconds to process. The second example, which relied more on the database, took an average of only 170 milliseconds to process.

NOTE   The processing times stated here were generated by a particular system. Performance on your own system may differ.

In Sum

In this chapter you have learned (or reviewed) many SQL and database topics, both basic and advanced. Using the example database in this chapter, you have seen how to manipulate tables, either by creating new ones or by modifying or deleting existing ones. You have also learned how to manipulate data by inserting, updating, or deleting it from database tables.

A critical function for any ColdFusion developer is to know how to select the data you want from a database in such a way that you can usefully output it to the user. This chapter explained complex database concepts such as scalar functions, joining tables, grouping data, and subqueries. You also saw how to query the results of an existing query using CFQSL. Finally, this chapter covered some useful techniques for debugging and optimizing your SQL.

The next chapter will delve more deeply into SQL by demonstrating how to create and utilize stored procedures in order to get the most out of your database.

CHAPTER 12

Stored Procedures

By Selene Bainum

- Introducing stored procedures

- Naming, creating, and modifying stored procedures

- Executing stored procedures

- Working with stored procedures in ColdFusion

- Replacing complex ColdFusion code with stored procedures

Database stored procedures are perhaps one of the most underutilized optimization techniques in the realm of ColdFusion/database programming. Perhaps this is because it takes a bit of time and effort to learn how to put stored procedures to work and quickly develop Cold-Fusion applications that call them. However, the effort you will expend to learn and practice stored procedures is well worth it. As explained in Chapter 11, "Advanced SQL," the database can process transactions much more quickly than can ColdFusion. In many cases, entire blocks of code and several discrete queries can be combined into a single stored procedure. Applications that use stored procedures tend to run more efficiently and are more modular than those that don't.

This chapter attempts to demystify stored procedures for ColdFusion developers. We'll review the basics of creating/calling these procedures and then we'll look at how to replace complex ColdFusion code blocks with a single stored procedure. Though many stored-procedure concepts are similar for different databases, each database technology usually has its own flavor of the SQL language. For example, Microsoft SQL Server uses Transact-SQL and Oracle uses PL-SQL.

The examples in this chapter are written for Microsoft SQL Server 2000. For specific information on other SQL languages, refer to your database's documentation. These examples use the same video rental database that was outlined in Chapter 11. Please refer to that chapter for the database schema and table definitions.

WARNING   Because the SQL in this chapter is written for Microsoft SQL Server 2000, it may not all work with SQL Server 7.

Working with Stored Procedures

In order to create a stored procedure, you must run Transact-SQL statements on your SQL Server database. This can be done in several ways: by using SQL Server tools such as Enterprise Manager or SQL Query Analyzer, by running a query from the Database tab in Cold-Fusion Studio, or by running a query from within a ColdFusion cfquery tag. Using the SQL Server tools is much easier, but all three methods will produce the same results.

This section reviews the basics—naming and creating—of stored procedures.

Naming Conventions

Before you can create a stored procedure, you must choose a name for it. There are certain restrictions on what names you can give to your stored procedure and other database objects:

• Object names must be unique. You cannot create a stored procedure with the same name as an existing table in the same database.

• The first character must be a letter, an underscore (_), or a pound sign (#).

NOTE A stored procedure's name that begins with the # character denotes a temporary stored procedure. Working with temporary stored procedures is outside the scope of this book. Check your database documentation for more information.

- Subsequent characters can be letters, numbers, the "at" sign (@), the dollar sign ($), or the underscore (_).

Stored Procedures versus Standard Queries

Why should you choose to use stored procedures over standard queries? There are several reasons; the following are the most important:

- Stored procedures will process more quickly than the same code passed as a query because the code is already precompiled within the database.

- You can use stored procedures to replace logic that you would normally perform within ColdFusion, such as conditional logic and looping.

- By creating a stored procedure, you are essentially creating the database version of a custom tag that you can call from within any page in your application. If you need to change your business logic, you need only alter your stored procedure; you don't have to change ColdFusion code multiple times throughout the application.

NOTE In this chapter, all stored procedure names will begin with *sp_* to easily distinguish them as stored procedures.

Creating, Modifying, and Deleting Stored Procedures

In Transact-SQL, the syntax for creating stored procedures is very simple. When you first create a stored procedure, you use the `create procedure` statement:

```
create procedure stored_procedure_name as
sql_code
```

For example, to create a stored procedure that simply returns all the users in the `Customer` table, the following SQL code is all you would need:

```
create procedure sp_ReturnCustomers as

select * from Customer
```

The `create procedure` statement will only work as long as you are creating a new stored procedure that does not exist in the database. If you try running the `create` statement again after the procedure has been created, you will receive the following error:

```
There is already an object named 'sp_ReturnCustomers' in the database.
```

In order to modify an existing stored procedure, use the `alter procedure` statement:

```
alter procedure sp_ReturnCustomers as

select * from Customer
```

Other than using `create` rather than `alter`, the syntax is the same for both creating and modifying stored procedures.

To delete a stored procedure, you use the `drop procedure` statement:

```
drop procedure stored_procedure_name
```

The following statement will remove the `sp_ReturnCustomers` stored procedure from the database without warning or prompting you.

```
drop procedure sp_ReturnCustomers
```

Parameters

Stored procedures support two types of parameters: input and output. Input parameters are used to pass values into your stored procedure when it is executed, and output parameters are used to retrieve values.

Like all identifiers, names of parameters have certain restrictions:

- Variables must begin with the @ symbol.

- Creating variables that begin with @@ should be avoided because some Transact-SQL functions begin with @@.

- After the initial character, the remaining characters in the variable name can be letters, numbers, the underscore (_), the "at" sign (@), and the pound sign (#).

NOTE   Parameters that are passed to and from a stored procedure are also considered variables within the stored procedure.

NOTE   Parameters can take the place of constants only. They cannot be used in your SQL code to replace the names of tables, columns, or the names of other database objects.

Input Parameters

One of the more beneficial features of ColdFusion is that it gives you the ability to create dynamic SQL statements by using variables within a query. This functionality is not limited just to ColdFusion; you can also create dynamic SQL within your stored procedures.

For instance, consider the following query:

```
<cfquery datasource="SybexSQL" name="GetInfo">
select FirstName, LastName, EMailAddress
from Customer
where CustomerID = #CustomerID#
</cfquery>
```

This query will run just fine as long as the `CustomerID` variable exists before the query is run. Just as in other programming structures, the variables in stored procedures need to be defined before they are called. In other words, in order to use a variable in a stored procedure, you must first pass it in as a parameter. A good analogy involves a ColdFusion custom tag that does not have access to the variables in the page that called the tag (with the exception of Request variables). As a result, attributes must be passed into the custom tag. In Transact-SQL, such attributes are known as *input parameters*.

Input parameters are values that you pass to your stored procedure. In order for the stored procedure to know what values to expect, you must include all parameters in your `create/alter` statement:

```
create or alter stored_procedure_name
    (@parameter_name datatype [=default] [output],
    @parameter_name datatype [=default] [output]
    ) as
sql_code
```

There are several guidelines for assigning parameters to a stored procedure:

- Use commas to separate the parameter definitions.

- Assign each parameter a datatype. The datatypes used for parameters are the same datatypes used to create/alter database tables.

- Consider assigning the parameter a default value. If you set a default value for a parameter, it need not be assigned a value when the stored procedure is executed. You can only assign a constant value or `null` to a parameter value.

- Follow the parameter declaration with the `output` keyword if the stored procedure is to return the value of that parameter.

- Optionally, use parentheses, like those used in the syntax example just discussed, to help your code's readability.

The following stored procedure will produce the same results as the query that was discussed at the beginning of this section. Here, the `@CustomerID` variable is defined as an input parameter with a datatype of `numeric`. The parameter has not been assigned a default value, so its value is required when the stored procedure is executed.

```
create procedure sp_GetCustomerInfo
    (@CustomerID numeric) as
```

```
select LastName, FirstName
from Customer
where CustomerID = @CustomerID
```

NOTE   An example of an input parameter with a default value assigned is discussed in the upcoming section, "Executing Stored Procedures."

Output Parameters

Often you won't want to return just a single result set from a stored procedure. Instead, you may find that you want to retrieve just one value, or multiple values, and then output it/them. This can be accomplished using output parameters.

In ColdFusion, to return/display the value of a parameter, you simply use the cfoutput tag, as shown here.

```
<cfset ThisCustomerID = 3>
<cfset NextCustomerID = ThisCustomerID + 1>
<cfoutput>#NextCustomerID#</cfoutput>
```

This code creates a value for NextCustomerID that is the value of ThisCustomerID plus 1. The value is then displayed using cfoutput.

The stored procedure to produce the same result is slightly different:

```
create procedure sp_ReturnValue
    (@ThisCustomerID int,
    @NextCustomerID int output) as

set @ThisCustomerID = @ThisCustomerID + 1
set @NextCustomerID = @ThisCustomerID

return @NextCustomerID
```

This procedure, sp_ReturnValue, uses two parameters, as does the preceding Cold-Fusion code. In this code, @ThisCustomerID is defined as a parameter with datatype int. @NextCustomerID is also defined with a datatype of int, but it is followed by the output keyword. Since the stored procedure will return this result, the output keyword must be used.

The value of @NextCustomerID is calculated (the set statement is discussed later in this chapter), and then the return statement returns the value after the stored procedure is processed. Each stored procedure can return multiple values.

Executing Stored Procedures

As mentioned earlier, stored procedures can be called several ways. Executing stored procedures from within ColdFusion will be discussed in the upcoming section, "Calling Stored

Procedures from ColdFusion." This section focuses on executing stored procedures using SQL, such as in SQL Server's Query Analyzer or using the database tab in ColdFusion studio.

The exec Statement

Stored procedures are called, or executed, using an exec statement.

NOTE   The exec keyword is a shortened version of the execute keyword; both work the same.

Before you see an actual stored procedure, you must become familiar with the syntax for the exec statement, which is as follows:

```
exec stored_procedure_name [@parameter_name = ]
    parameter_value [output] [default],
    [@parameter_name = ] parameter_value [output] [default]
```

exec Syntax

This isn't quite as complicated as it looks. The following list explains the rules of this syntax:

- The name of the stored procedure immediately follows the exec keyword.
- Commas must separate the parameters passed into the stored procedure, and these parameters must have been defined when the stored procedure was created.
- The parameters can be passed in as values or as name/value pairs. If a name/value pair is used for one of the parameters, all subsequent parameters must also be name value pairs.
- If name/value pairs are not used, the parameters must be passed into the stored procedure in the exact order in which they were declared when the stored procedure was created. If they aren't, an error will occur.
- If name/value pairs are not used and you wish to use just the default value of a parameter, you must pass the default keyword for that parameter. However, if you are using name/value pairs and you wish to have the procedure use that default value, you do not need to refer to variables that have a default specified by the stored procedure.
- null can be passed as the value for any parameter that can accept null values.
- If the parameter is an output parameter, it must be followed by the output keyword.
- The values of output parameters passed into a stored procedure must be variable names. The variable will hold the value of the returned parameter after the stored procedure is executed.

To see these rules in action, take a look at the following stored procedure. It has three input parameters, one of which has been assigned a default value:

```
create procedure sp_RentalInfo
    (@GenreID numeric,
```

```
    @FromDate datetime = '1-1-1998',
    @ToDate datetime) as

select G.Genre, T.Title, count(R.RentalID) as RentalCount
from Genre_Ref G, Title T, Copy C, Rental R
where G.GenreID = T.GenreID
AND T.TitleID = C.TitleID
AND C.CopyID = R.CopyID
AND G.GenreID = @GenreID
AND R.CheckOutDate between @FromDate AND @ToDate
group by G.Genre, T.Title
```

There are several correct ways to execute this stored procedure. The first method just passes in the values of the input parameters. Because the names are not specified, the values must be passed in the following order: @GenreID, @FromDate, @ToDate:

```
exec sp_RentalInfo 7, '1/1/2001', '11/11/2001'
```

If you wish to use the default value for @FromDate (which returns all records beginning on January 1, 1998), you would use the default keyword:

```
exec sp_RentalInfo 7, default, '11/11/2001'
```

In a third method, these same values can be passed using name/value pairs:

```
exec sp_RentalInfo @GenreID = 7, @FromDate = default,
    @ToDate = '11/11/2001'
```

However, with name/value pairs, you no longer need to use @FromDate if you wish to use the default value. SQL Server will know which values are being passed based on the parameter names and will use default values for missing parameters:

```
exec sp_RentalInfo @ToDate = '11/11/2001', @GenreID = 7
```

By using name/value pairs, you can also change the order in which you pass in the parameters:

```
exec sp_RentalInfo @ToDate = '11/11/2001',
    @GenreID = 7, @FromDate = '1/1/2001'
```

All of the preceding exec statements are perfectly valid for calling the same stored procedure. In order to choose the best method, you will need to look at what data you have to pass and how you want to pass it.

Returning Output Parameters

The statements you need to use to execute a stored procedure that returns output parameters are slightly more complicated. Because you must pass in a variable as the output parameter in your exec statement, that value must first be declared. For instance, in order to execute the `sp_ReturnValue` stored procedure that was described in the earlier section on output parameters; you would first need to run the following code:

```
declare @NextID int
exec sp_ReturnValue 3, @NextID output
```

Here, `@NextID` is passed as the value for `@NextCustomerID`. After the stored procedure is run, the `@NextID` variable will hold the value of the `@NextCustomerID` that was returned from the stored procedure. Notice that the `output` keyword is used after `@NextID` to let the stored procedure know it will be returning a value into that variable.

Calling Stored Procedures from ColdFusion

The preceding section described how to execute stored procedures from within Query Analyzer. But how do you call them from ColdFusion? There are two tags you can use to do this: `cfquery` and `cfstoredproc`.

Using the cfquery Tag

Prior to the introduction of ColdFusion 4.0, using the `cfquery` tag was the only way to call stored procedures from ColdFusion. Though `cfquery` is no longer the preferred method, it is still heavily used. To explain this further, we will refer back to our sample video rental database.

As an example, `sp_GetInfo` will retrieve information about all of the customers in the `Customer` table. This procedure takes no parameters and returns only a single result set.

```
create procedure sp_GetInfo as

select CustomerID, FirstName, LastName, EMailAddress
from Customer
```

To call this stored procedure using the `cfquery` tag, you would only need to use an `exec` statement, like so:

```
<cfquery datasource="SybexSQL" name="GetInfo">
exec sp_GetInfo
</cfquery>
```

In this example, the result set would be stored as a query named `GetInfo`. You could then loop over or output this result set just as you would any other standard query result set.

The following block alters this procedure so that it only retrieves information about a particular customer. In this case, we now have to pass in the `@CustomerID` parameter to the stored procedure:

```
alter procedure sp_GetInfo (@CustomerID numeric) as
```

```
select CustomerID, FirstName, LastName, EMailAddress
from Customer
where CustomerID = @CustomerID
```

To run this stored procedure using cfquery, you would need to supply a value for @CustomerID when the stored procedure is being executed:

```
<cfquery datasource="SybexSQL" name="GetInfo">
exec sp_GetInfo #CustomerID#
</cfquery>
```

It is also possible to use cfquery to execute stored procedures that return output parameters. Refer again to sp_ReturnValue; the following code would retrieve the value of @NextCustomerID as computed in the stored procedure and save it to the ColdFusion variable @NextID:

```
<cfquery datasource="SybexSQL" name="GetValue">
exec sp_ReturnValue 3, NextID output
</cfquery>
<cfoutput>#NextID#</cfoutput>
```

Using the cfstoredproc Tag

Since the arrival of ColdFusion 4.0, using the cfstoredproc tag has become the recommended method for executing stored procedures from ColdFusion. By using the cfstoredproc tag, you can eliminate the complications associated with the exec statement.

Before we get into examples that illustrate the use of the cfstoredproc tag, you need to become familiar with some of its attributes, of which there are many. The most common ones are listed in Table 12.1. For a full listing of the tag's attributes, refer to the ColdFusion documentation.

TABLE 12.1: cfstoredproc Attributes

Attribute	Description
procedure	Required. This is the name of the stored procedure in the database.
datasource	Required. This is the name of the data source used to access the database.
returnCode	Optional; values can be Yes or No (the default is No). If Yes is set as the value, the cfstoredproc.StatusCode variable will be populated with the stored procedure's return code.

In addition to these attributes, you need to be familiar with a couple of variables. After a stored procedure is called with the cfstoredproc tag, there are two variables set by ColdFusion: cfstoredproc.ExecutionTime and cfstoredproc.StatusCode. cfstoredproc.ExecutionTime returns the number of milliseconds it took for the stored procedure to execute. cfstoredproc.StatusCode contains the return code returned by the stored procedure; this value will only exist if the returnCode attribute of the cfstoredproc tag was set to true.

Table 12.2 lists the return codes for SQL Server that could be returned by the cfstoredproc .StatusCode variable.

TABLE 12.2: SQL Server Return Codes

Return Code	Meaning
0	The execution was successful.
1	A required parameter was not specified.
2	An invalid parameter was specified.
3	An error occurred getting a value.
4	Invalid null value found.

NOTE   Check your SQL Server documentation for more information on return codes.

Now that you are more familiar with the details of this tag, let's look at the two tags that can be nested within cfstoredproc: cfprocparam and cfprocresult.

The cfprocparam Tag

If you want to pass parameters into a stored procedure or return them using the cfstoredproc tag, you must nest at least one cfprocparam tag within the cfstoredproc tag. This tag specifies information about the parameter, such as the datatype, name, and value. The attributes if the cfprocparam tag are listed in Table 12.3.

TABLE 12.3: cfprocparam Attributes

Attribute	Description
type	Optional. This indicates whether or not the parameter is in, out or inOut. Default is in.
variable	Required for out and inOut parameters. This is the name of the variable that will hold the returned value.
dbVarName	Required for named notation. This is the name of the parameter as defined in the stored procedure.
value	Required for in and inOut parameters. This is the actual value being passed into the stored procedure.
cfSQLType	Required. This is the datatype that is bound to the parameter. Common datatypes include: CF_SQL_BIT, CF_SQL_CHAR, CF_SQL_DATE, CF_SQL_FLOAT, CF_SQL_INTEGER, CF_SQL_NUMERIC, CF_SQL_VARCHAR.
maxLength	Optional. This is the maximum length of the parameter.
null	Optional. Possible values include Yes or No. If Yes is specified, the value of the parameter is passed in as null and the value attribute is ignored.

Refer to the ColdFusion documentation for a complete list of tag attributes and CFSQL datatypes.

The cfprocresult Tag

The cfprocresult tag takes a result set returned from a stored procedure and assigns it to a ColdFusion result set that you can use in other tags, such as cfoutput and cfloop. If the stored procedure returns multiple result sets, you can specify which result set you wish to access with each cfprocresult tag. With this feature, a single stored procedure can create several ColdFusion result sets.

The cfprocresult tag has only three attributes (see Table 12.4).

TABLE 12.4: cfprocresult Attributes

Attribute	Description
name	Required. This specifies the name in which to store the query result set.
resultSet	Optional. This identifies which result set in the stored procedure is returned. The default is 1.
maxRows	Optional. This specifies the maximum number of rows returned to the result set.

Using cfstoredproc

This section describes how to call stored procedures using the cfstoredproc tag and its attributes, which were described in the preceding section.

Input and Output Parameters

As you learned earlier in the chapter, values can be passed into stored procedures and values can also be returned. Both input and output parameters can be passed to a stored procedure using the cfprocparam tag.

Let us refer yet again to sp_ReturnValue:

```
create procedure sp_ReturnValue
    (@ThisCustomerID int,
    @NextCustomerID int output) as

set @ThisCustomerID = @ThisCustomerID + 1
set @NextCustomerID = @ThisCustomerID

return @NextCustomerID
```

The code in Listing 12.1 can be used to execute this procedure.

Listing 12.1   Using the cfstoredproc Tag (c1201.cfm)

```
<!---
    Name:           /c12/c1201.cfm
    Description:    Use the cfstoredproc tag
                    to execute a stored procedure.
--->
<!--- Execute the procedure. --->
<cfstoredproc
    datasource="SybexSQL"
    procedure="sp_ReturnValue"
    returnCode="Yes">
    <cfprocparam
        dbVarName="@ThisCustomerID"
        value="3"
        cfSQLType="CF_SQL_INTEGER"
        type="In">
    <cfprocparam
        dbVarName="@NextCustomerID"
        variable="NextID"
        cfSQLType="CF_SQL_INTEGER"
        type="Out">
</cfstoredproc>

<!DOCTYPE HTML PUBLIC "-//W3C//DTD HTML 4.01 Transitional//EN">

<html>
<head>
    <title>c1201.cfm</title>
</head>

<body>

<!--- Display the output the variables. --->
<cfoutput>
    The next id is: #NextID#<br>
    The stored procedure took #cfstoredproc.ExecutionTime#
        Milliseconds to execute.<br>
    The return code is: #cfstoredproc.StatusCode#
</cfoutput>

</body>
</html>
```

The cfstoredproc tag tells ColdFusion to go to the SQL Server data source and execute the sp_ReturnValue stored procedure. The first cfprocparam tag passes in a value for @ThisCustomerID. The second tag tells the stored procedure to store the returned value of @Next-CustomerID into the NextID ColdFusion variable. Within the cfoutput tag, the value of NextID is displayed. Because returnCode was set to Yes within the cfstoredproc tag, a value is returned for cfstoredproc.StatusCode. Figure 12.1 shows the results of the code.

FIGURE 12.1:

Displaying results of
the cfstoredproc tag

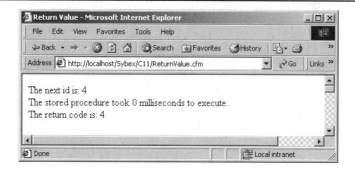

Multiple Result Sets

There may come a time when you want to call a stored procedure that will return more than one result set. For instance, consider the following:

```
create procedure sp_MultipleRecordsets as

select CustomerID, FirstName, LastName
from Customer
order by LastName, FirstName

select TitleID, Title
from Title
order by Title
```

This stored procedure queries all the customers in the Customer table and all the titles in the Title table. This is a simple stored procedure and does not require any input parameters, but it does return more than one result set.

To execute this stored procedure using cfquery and to display the results returned, you would use the following code:

```
<cfquery datasource="SybexSQL" name="GetRecords" maxRows="3">
exec sp_MultipleRecordsets
</cfquery>

<p><b>Records:</b></p>

<table border="1">
   <tr>
      <cfloop list="#GetRecords.ColumnList#" index="Column">
         <td><b><cfoutput>#Column#</cfoutput></b></td>
```

```
            </cfloop>
        </tr>
        <cfoutput query="GetRecords">
            <tr>
                <cfloop list="#GetRecords.ColumnList#" index="Column">
                    <td>#Evaluate(Column & "[" & CurrentRow & "]")#</td>
                </cfloop>
            </tr>
        </cfoutput>
    </table>
```

In this code, the cfquery tag will execute the stored procedure and store the results in the result set named GetRecords. The maxRows attribute will be used to limit the number of records returned. The rest of the code will dynamically loop through the ColumnList of the result set and display column headers as well as the data for each row returned, and this output will be nicely formatted in a table, as shown in Figure 12.2. As you can see in this figure, the only records the query returned were from the first select query in the stored procedure, which is the one that queried the Customers table.

FIGURE 12.2:

Displaying a single result set

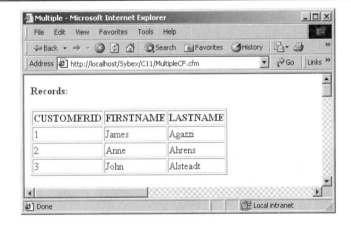

As you learned earlier, the cfstoredproc has a nested tag called cfprocresult that allows you to retrieve multiple result sets from a single stored procedure while assigning each a unique name that ColdFusion will be able to access. Listing 12.2 displays how to return multiple result sets using cfstoredproc and cfprocresult.

Listing 12.2   **Using cfstoredproc to Return Multiple Result Sets (c1202.cfm)**

```
<!---
    Name:          /c12/c1201.cfm
    Description:   Use the cfstoredproc tag
```

```
                     to return multiple results sets from a
                     stored procedure.
        --->

        <!--- Execute the stored procedure. --->
        <!--- Use a cfstoredproc tag for each result
           set returned. --->
        <cfstoredproc
           datasource="SybexSQL"
           procedure="sp_MultipleRecordsets">
           <cfprocresult
              name="Customers"
              resultSet="1"
              maxRows="3">
           <cfprocresult
              name="Titles"
              resultSet="2"
              maxRows="3">
        </cfstoredproc>

        <!DOCTYPE HTML PUBLIC "-//W3C//DTD HTML 4.01 Transitional//EN">

        <html>
        <head>
           <title>c1202.cfm</title>
        </head>

        <body>

        <p><b>Customers:</b></p>

        <!--- Loop through the Customers result set to display
           all the columns and rows returned. --->
        <table border="1">
           <tr>
              <cfloop list="#Customers.ColumnList#" index="Column">
                 <td><b><cfoutput>#Column#</cfoutput></b></td>
              </cfloop>
           </tr>
           <cfoutput query="Customers">
              <tr>
                 <cfloop list="#Customers.ColumnList#" index="Column">
                    <td>#Evaluate(Column & "[" & CurrentRow & "]")#</td>
                 </cfloop>
              </tr>
           </cfoutput>
        </table>

        <p><b>Titles:</b></p>

        <!--- Loop through the Tables result set to display
           all the columns and rows returned. --->
```

```
<table border="1">
   <tr>
      <cfloop list="#Titles.ColumnList#" index="Column">
         <td><b><cfoutput>#Column#</cfoutput></b></td>
      </cfloop>
   </tr>
   <cfoutput query="Titles">
      <tr>
         <cfloop list="#Titles.ColumnList#" index="Column">
            <td>#Evaluate(Column & "[" & CurrentRow & "]")#</td>
         </cfloop>
      </tr>
   </cfoutput>
</table>


</body>
</html>
```

By using cfstoredproc with the cfprocresult tag, you are able to successfully retrieve all of the result sets generated by the stored procedure. The maxRow attribute is used in each cfstoredproc tag to limit the number of records returned in each result set. As with the cfquery example, the results from each result set are dynamically displayed by using the ColumnList attribute of each result set. Figure 12.3 displays the return of the multiple result sets.

FIGURE 12.3:

Multiple result sets from a stored procedure

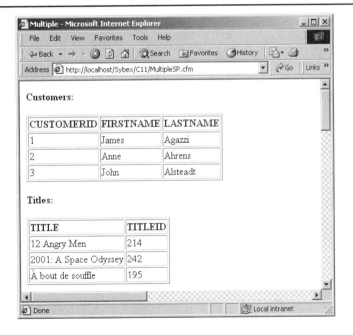

Advanced Transact-SQL

Transact-SQL is integral to Microsoft's SQL Server. All applications that communicate with SQL Server do so with Transact-SQL. Like most programming languages, you can perform many common tasks with Transact-SQL, much as you would in ColdFusion. This section highlights some of the advanced Transact-SQL techniques you can use to write stored procedures.

NOTE   For more detailed information on Transact-SQL, refer to the Transact-SQL Help that is included with Microsoft SQL Server.

Setting variable values, looping over a record set or through some values, and using conditional processing techniques are not unique activities to ColdFusion. These techniques have been around as long as programming languages have existed. It will come as no surprise, then, to find out that you can push processing to your stored procedure in order to save processing time, minimize trips to the database, and ease general wear and tear on your application.

The following sections demonstrate how Transact-SQL and ColdFusion compare to one another, allowing you to write stored procedures that replace logic currently performed by ColdFusion.

Replacing cfset

Variables can be set in Transact-SQL just as they can in ColdFusion using the cfset tag. Before you set a variable, you must first consider the variable name. Like ColdFusion, Transact-SQL has certain restrictions on the names of variables. (See the "Parameters" section earlier in this chapter for more information.)

Unlike Cold Fusion, though, Transact-SQL variables must be declared before they are set. You must both declare the name of the variable and assign it a datatype. These variable datatypes are the same datatypes you use when you are creating or modifying database tables. The syntax to declare variables is as follows:

```
declare @variable_name datatype, @variable_name datatype
```

You can declare several variables in one declare statement as long as they are separated by commas. If you prefer to break up your code for formatting reasons, the declare statement can be divided. For example, the following code is processed by the database exactly the same as the preceding single-line statement:

```
declare
   @variable_name datatype,
   @variable_name datatype
```

Once a variable has been declared, it can be set using the set statement:

```
set @variablename = value
```

The following code will declare a variable called @RentalFee, assign it a data type of float, and set its value:

```
declare @RentalFee float
set @RentalFee = 3.99
```

You can also set a variable to equal the results of an arithmetic expression. Here are the arithmetic operators used by Transact-SQL:

Operator	Meaning
+	Addition
–	Subtraction
*	Multiplication
/	Division
%	Modulo

The following are all valid set statements, assuming the variables specified have all been declared:

```
set @MyVar = @MyVar + 1
set @EvenOdd = @TotalRows % 2
set @TotalCost = @Quantity * @Price
```

It is also possible to set a variable equal to a value retrieved from a query. These statements:

```
declare @CustomerCount
select @CustomerCount = count(*)
from Customer
```

accomplish the same as these:

```
<cfquery datasource="SybexSQL" name="GetCount">
select count(*) AS TotalCount
from Customer
</cfquery>
<cfset CustomerCount = GetCount.TotalCount>
```

Replacing cfif

Conditional logic is certainly not something restricted to ColdFusion programming and the cfif tag. Transact-SQL, like most languages, also makes use of if/else logic. Unlike Cold-Fusion, there is no such thing as else/if—like ColdFusion's cfelseif tag—in Transact-SQL; however, you can easily combine else and if on the same line to obtain the same results.

The syntax for the equivalent of if/else logic in Transact-SQL is as follows:

```
if boolean_expression
    sql_statement | sql_block
```

```
else
    sql_statement | sql_block
```

You can also nest if statements to mimic else/if logic:

```
if boolean_expression
    sql_statement | sql_block
else if boolean_expression
    sql_statement | sql_block
else
    sql_statement | sql_block
```

Within the if statement, *boolean_expression* represents a condition that will be evaluated to either TRUE or FALSE when the statement is run. If a condition is met—it returns TRUE—either a SQL statement or statement block will be processed. A statement is a single Transact-SQL statement.

If you have multiple tasks you want to perform if a condition is met, you must create a block by using the begin keyword before the set of statements and by including the end keyword afterward:

```
begin
    sql_statement
    sql_statement
end
```

The following code determines how many videos a given customer has rented and sets the customer's "level." If the customer has rented 15 or more videos, they will also receive a 15 percent discount on future rentals.

```
declare
    @NumRentals int,
    @Level varchar(25),
    @Discount int

set @Discount = 0

select @NumRentals = count(RentalID)
from Rental
where CustomerID = @CustomerID

if @NumRentals < 5
    set @Level = 'Bronze'
else if @NumRentals >= 5 AND @NumRentals < 15
    set @Level = 'Silver'
else
    begin
        set @Level = 'Gold'
        set @Discount = 15
    end
```

Once our variables are declared (@CustomerID was an input variable passed into the procedure), we query the number of rentals the customer has and save that value into the @NumRentals variable. Conditional logic is then used to determine the customer's discount level and whether or not they should receive a discount.

Notice that the else statement contains the keywords begin and end around its content. This ensures that both the SQL statements it includes will be processed if the condition is met. If begin and end were not used to create a block of code in the else statement, only the setting of the level would be affected by the conditional logic. The setting of the discount would execute for each customer. Thus, regardless of their level, they would receive the discount. As you can see, failing to block your statements can dramatically affect your results.

The Transact-SQL conditional logic could be used to replace the following ColdFusion code:

```
<cfset Discount = 0>
<cfquery datasource="SybexSQL" name="GetRentals">
select count(RentalID) as TotalRentals
from Rental
where CustomerID = #CustomerID#
</cfquery>
<cfset NumRentals = GetRentals.TotalRentals>

<cfif NumRentals LT 5>
    <cfset Level = "Bronze">
<cfelseif NumRentals GTE 5 AND NumRentals LT 15>
    <cfset Level = "Silver">
<cfelse>
    <cfset Level = "Gold">
    <cfset Discount = 15>
</cfif>
```

Replacing cfloop

Unlike the multiple types of loops available with ColdFusion's cfloop tag, in Transact-SQL, looping is performed using the while statement. Like if/else conditional logic, the while statement only affects the first Transact-SQL statement after the while statement, unless begin and end are used to create a block. Like the cfbreak tag, there is a break keyword that can be used to exit the loop. There is also a continue keyword that will cause the loop to restart, ignoring any code that follows the keyword.

The syntax for while is as follows:

```
while boolean_expression
    sql_statement | sql_block
[break]
    sql_statement | sql_block
[continue]
```

The *boolean_expression* condition is the same type of expression you would use in the if statement. As long as the expression evaluates to true, the loop will continue to process.

Replacing cfoutput/cfloop Query

Looping over a query result set is one of the most commonly used functions of ColdFusion using either cfloop or cfquery. Like many other ColdFusion tasks, looping over the result set can also be performed in SQL.

In order for Transact-SQL to be able to access the results of a query, you must declare a cursor to hold the results. This process typically involves the following six steps:

1. Declare a variable for each column that will be returned in the query. Make sure the datatype of the variable is the same (or larger, such as allowing more characters than the field in the database) as the datatype of the column being returned.

2. Use the declare cursor statement to associate a cursor with the select statement. Names of cursors must follow the naming restrictions for identifiers.

3. Open the cursor using the open statement.

4. Use the fetch into statement to save the values of the individual row saved into the declared variables.

5. Loop through the result set using the while statement. Use SQL statements and code blocks to process the values in the row.

6. Close the cursor using the close statement. When you are finished with the cursor and will not need to access it or open in again, purge it using the deallocate statement.

The syntax for looping over a result set of a query is as follows:

```
declare
    @variable1 datatype,
    @variable2 datatype

declare cursor_name cursor for
select_statement

open cursor_name

fetch next from cursor_name into
    @variable1,
    @variable2

while @@fetch_status = 0

    begin
```

```
        sql_statement | sql_block

        fetch next from cursor_name into
            @variable1,
            @variable2

    end

  close cursor_name
  deallocate cursor_name
```

The `fetch next` statement fetches the next row from the cursor and increments the current row to the row returned. By calling `fetch` before the `while` loop, you are retrieving the first row's values for processing. `@@fetch_status` is the status of the last cursor fetch. If the value is 0, the statement was successful. After your SQL statements in the `while` loop are executed but before the block ends, the next row of the cursor is fetched. If the fetch is successful, the loop continues to process. When the loop is in the last row of the cursor, the `fetch next` statement returns a status code of –1, meaning it tried to fetch a record beyond the last row in the result set. At this point the loop will be exited.

If we added a column to the `Copy` table called `EarnedValue`, we could use the following ColdFusion code to set that value equal to the total value of rental fees for each copy in the database.

```
<cfquery datasource="SybexSQL" name="GetCopies">
select CopyID
from Copy
</cfquery>

<cfloop query="GetCopies">
    <cfquery datasource="SybexSQL">
    update Copy
    set EarnedValue =
        (select sum(RentalFee)
        from Rental
        where CopyID = #CopyID#)
    where CopyID = #CopyID#
    </cfquery>
</cfloop>
```

This code loops over the `GetCopies` result set and updates the `Copy` table with the appropriate `EarnedValue` amount. It makes one trip to the database to retrieve all of the copies and then makes a subsequent trip for each record returned.

The following actions can be performed in a single stored procedure:

```
create procedure sp_SetEarnedValue as

declare
    @CopyID int,
    @EarnedValue float

declare c_Copy cursor for
select CopyID
from Copy

open c_Copy

fetch next from c_Copy into
    @CopyID

while @@fetch_status = 0

    begin

    update Copy
    set EarnedValue =
        (select sum(RentalFee)
        from Rental
        where CopyID = @CopyID)
    where CopyID = @CopyID

    fetch next from c_Copy into
        @CopyID

    end

close c_Copy
deallocate c_Copy
```

Putting It All Together

Let's walk through an example of what you've learned here about stored procedures and the individual aspects that make up useful Transact-SQL.

Every so often, the video store likes to update the status of its customers. If customers have not rented a movie within the last year, their status is updated to be inactive. If they have more than one movie that is past due, their status is also set to inactive so they are prevented from renting another movie until their account is reconciled.

The typical way to perform this action in ColdFusion is to query all the active customers and then perform queries for each customer, to determine how many movies they rented in the last year and how many unreturned movies are past due. If the customer meets the requirements for a status change, their record is updated. See Listing 12.3 for the ColdFusion code that could be used to accomplish all of this.

Listing 12.3   Using ColdFusion to Perform Multiple Tasks (c1203.cfm)

```
<!---
   Name:         /c12/c1203.cfm
   Description:  Using ColdFusion to perform multiple tasks.
--->

<!--- Set RowsUpdated to 0 --->
<cfset RowsUpdated = 0>

<cftransaction>

    <!--- Create a cursor to hold the result
       set from a query that retrieves the
       active customers --->
    <cfquery datasource="SybexSQL" name="GetCustomers">
    select CustomerID, JoinDate
    from Customer
    where IsActive = 1
    </cfquery>

    <!--- Loop through the GetCustomers result set --->
    <cfloop query="GetCustomers">

        <!--- Reset the value of the variables --->
        <cfset InLastYear = 0>
        <cfset NumLate = 0>

        <!--- Select the number of movies rented in the last year
           by the customer and store the value in the
           @InLastYear variable --->
        <cfquery datasource="SybexSQL" name="Rentals">
        select count(*) AS InLastYear
        from Rental
        where CustomerID = #CustomerID#
        AND CheckOutDate > DateAdd(yyyy, -1, GetDate())
        </cfquery>

        <cfset InLastYear = Rentals.InLastYear>

        <!--- Select the number of movies the user has late ---> 
        <cfquery datasource="SybexSQL" name="GetLate">
        select count(RentalID) as TotalLate
```

```
      from Rental
      where CustomerID = #CustomerID#
      AND ReturnDate is null
      AND DueDate < getDate()
      </cfquery>

      <cfset NumLate = GetLate.TotalLate>

      <!--- If InLastYear is 0 or NumLate is greater than 1,
         make the user inactive --->
      <cfif InLastYear EQ 0 OR NumLate GT 1>

            <cfquery datasource="SybexSQL">
            update Customer
            set IsActive = 0
            where CustomerID = #CustomerID#
            </cfquery>

            <cfset RowsUpdated = RowsUpdated + 1>

      </cfif>

   </cfloop>

</cftransaction>

<!DOCTYPE HTML PUBLIC "-//W3C//DTD HTML 4.01 Transitional//EN">

<html>
<head>
   <title>c1203.cfm</title>
</head>

<body>

<cfoutput>
   #RowsUpdated# customers made inactive.
</cfoutput>

</body>
</html>
```

Listing 12.3 makes one trip to the database to retrieve all the active users, makes two more trips for each user to determine their rental history, and makes yet another trip if their record needs to be updated. Depending on the number of customers in the database, this page could make several hundred trips to the database.

All of this processing can be put into one stored procedure. Listing 12.4 is the stored procedure that performs the same logic as Listing 12.3.

Listing 12.4   **Using a Stored Procedure to Perform Multiple Tasks (c1204.sql)**

```
/*
   Name:           /c12/c1204.sql
   Description:    Create the sp_UpdateStatus stored procedure
*/

-- Create/alter the procedure
create procedure sp_UpdateStatus (@RowsUpdated int output) as

-- Declare the variables to be used
-- and their datatypes
declare
   @CustomerID numeric,
   @JoinDate datetime,
   @InLastYear numeric,
   @NumLate datetime,
   @IsActive bit

-- Set @RowsUpdated to 0
set @RowsUpdated = 0

-- Create a cursor to hold the result
-- set from a query that retrieves the
-- active customers
declare c_Customer cursor for
select CustomerID, JoinDate
from Customer
where IsActive = 1

-- Open the cursor
open c_Customer

-- Store the values from the first row of the
-- result set into variables
fetch next from c_Customer into
   @CustomerID,
   @JoinDate

-- Loop through the remaining rows in the cursor
while @@fetch_status = 0

  begin

      -- Reset the value of the variables
      set @InLastYear = 0
      set @NumLate = 0

      -- Select the number of movies rented in the last year
      -- by the customer and store the value in the @InLastYear
      -- variable
```

```
select @InLastYear = count(*)
from Rental
where CustomerID = @CustomerID
and CheckOutDate > DateAdd(yyyy, -1, GetDate())

-- Select the number of movies the user has late
select @NumLate = count(RentalID)
from Rental
where CustomerID = @CustomerID
AND ReturnDate is null
AND DueDate < GetDate()

-- If @InLastYear is 0 or @NumLate is greater than 1,
-- make the user inactive
if @InLastYear = 0 OR @NumLate > 1
    begin

        update Customer
        set IsActive = 0
        where CustomerID = @CustomerID

        set @RowsUpdated = @RowsUpdated + 1

    end

    -- Fetch the next record into the variables
    fetch next from c_Customer into
        @CustomerID,
        @JoinDate
end

-- Close and deallocate the cursor
close c_Customer
deallocate c_Customer

return @RowsUpdated
```

The stored procedure *sp_UpdateStatus* performs the exact same processing logic as Listing 12.3, while making only one trip to the database. This procedure can then be called from your ColdFusion page as Listing 12.5 demonstrates.

Listing 12.5   **Calling a Complex Stored Procedure from ColdFusion (c1205.cfm)**

```
<!---
    Name:          /c12/c1205.cfm
    Description:   Calling a complex stored procedure from ColdFusion
--->

<!--- Execute the stored procedure. --->
<cfstoredproc
```

```
        datasource="SybexSQL"
        procedure="sp_UpdateStatus">
        <cfprocparam
            variable="RowsUpdated"
            cfSQLType="CF_SQL_INTEGER"
            type="Out">
</cfstoredproc>


<!DOCTYPE HTML PUBLIC "-//W3C//DTD HTML 4.01 Transitional//EN">

<html>
<head>
    <title>c1205.cfm</title>
</head>

<body>

<!--- Display the results. --->
<cfoutput>
    #RowsUpdated# customers made inactive.
</cfoutput>

</body>
</html>
```

By calling *sp_UpdateStatus* from Listing 12.5, you can perform the same tasks as in Listing 12.3 while making only one trip to the database. Depending on the number of records you are working with, using the stored procedure can take only a fraction of the time as using ColdFusion with basic queries does.

In Sum

In this chapter, you've learned the basics about stored procedures, as well as a taste of some of the more advanced stored procedure and Transact-SQL topics. You've also learned how to utilize tags such as `cfstoredproc`, `cfprocparam`, and `cfprocresult` to efficiently execute stored procedures from ColdFusion.

Many times developers will being a project using only the `cfquery` tag and standard SQL queries, promising to go back and replace their queries and code with stored procedures when they are finished. Unfortunately, that rarely happens.

It is best to inject stored procedures into your application as you are developing so that you can take advantage of them throughout your application. You will also increase performance and efficiency. Optimization of code and processing time is very important to your application. It is often cheaper to write well-formed efficient code than to have to improve the hardware on your server.

CHAPTER 13

Upsizing Databases to SQL Server

By Charles Mohnike

- What is upsizing?

- Before you upsize

- Using the access upsizing tools

- Using SQL Server DTS

- Modifying ColdFusion applications for upsized databases

When you began learning about ColdFusion development, it's likely you pictured a future of, well, writing ColdFusion applications. But by this point, you've realized that writing code represents only a fraction of your work—no doubt, you spend nearly as much time serving as a jack-or-jill-of-all-trades, with tasks including basic systems administration, web server administration, and most frequently, database-related tasks. Most of us didn't come to Cold-Fusion as database or SQL experts, but many have since learned more than we bargained for about the nuances of databases.

Likely, one of the tasks that lands often on your desk is database maintenance—keeping the database running smoothly and at peak efficiency (after all, if the database goes down, it's probable that someone will blame your application). In many cases, this means dealing with an application that has grown in size and traffic since it came to life on your development server so long ago.

Microsoft Access and other file-based database applications make excellent data sources when you're prototyping a site or a site that will host a limited amount of traffic: file-based databases are inexpensive, easy to modify, and they get the job done. But sooner or later you'll encounter a project where Access data sources create a bottleneck and can't take the strain. That's the time to consider *upsizing*.

What's Upsizing?

First, a basic definition: *upsizing* is a term that has come to describe the process of migrating a database from a one user at a time file-based database application to a multiuser, client/server database application.

Upsizing differs from simply *importing* or *exporting* a database from one application to another because the goal of an upsizing operation is to transfer the database's schema and records, and most important, to preserve other elements like datatype specifications, relationships, views, and default values. In contrast, importing or exporting a database usually transfers table structures and data alone, leaving you to manually re-create relationships and other important items in your new database.

Most often, upsizing is used to describe the migration path between Microsoft Access and Microsoft SQL Server. Why? Because Microsoft uniquely offers both single-user and multi-user database applications, making it possible to replicate a database between them and still preserve most characteristics of the original.

NOTE   If you're starting with a non-Microsoft database, you can still use the information in this chapter to upsize to SQL Server. Most OLE DB- or ODBC-compliant databases can be upsized using SQL Server's *Data Transformation Services (DTS)*. DTS gets the job done, but as you'll read in later sections, it doesn't preserve elements like primary key designations, default values, and so on.

This chapter will help you answer these questions:

- Do I really need to upsize?
- What are the primary differences between file-based applications like Access and server-based applications like SQL Server?
- What methods are used for upsizing, and which one is best for my project?
- How can I make sure my upsized database preserves all the attributes of my original?
- What changes do I need to make to my ColdFusion applications once I've upsized?

Before You Upsize

Don't jump immediately into the process of upsizing a database before addressing a few fundamental questions—such as, does it even need to be done? Understanding what will be achieved from the migration is important to really understanding the process. The basic question may have precipitated from a performance problem or security concerns, but blindly assuming the need to upsize may not bring the desired results.

This section addresses the basic questions of whether to upsize.

About the Microsoft Data Engine (MSDE)

If you don't have direct access to a SQL Server database (for example, if you're working in a development environment and plan to migrate your application later), you can still approximate a SQL Server environment on your local machine: Microsoft's Office 2000 and XP, Visio 2000 and 2002, and Access 2000 and 2002 CDs all include a tool called the Microsoft Data Engine (MSDE), which is essentially a scaled-down version of SQL Server 7.0. MSDE doesn't have its own user interface but instead is accessed via the interface in which it's embedded (usually either Access or Visio).

Databases created or upsized into MSDE are directly compatible with SQL Server, making MSDE an excellent tool for identifying potential upsizing problems before you deploy your database to a production server, or as an interim solution until SQL Server is available.

All upsizing issues and methods described in this chapter also apply to MSDE. You'll find the MSDE installer in \sql\install\setup on your Office, Visio, or Access CD.

Do You Need to Upsize?

Before you begin, it's important to consider whether your project really requires upsizing. There are literally thousands of ColdFusion applications throughout the Web that are running just fine on Access data sources. Access database's are well-suited to smaller applications that don't receive lots of traffic or require frequent user input. As mentioned earlier, Access is less expensive than SQL Server and requires virtually no maintenance other than frequent backups.

With that said, let's look at some of the differences between the two applications. Consider each of these items to determine whether your application might benefit from a database upsize.

Security   Access does allow you to secure entire databases and individual tables, but security is handled from within the application. SQL Server integrates with Windows operating system security, giving users just one login to access both their network and their databases. This method simplifies security administration and adds an additional layer of protection since users can't access your databases without first logging onto the server.

Performance   Access was designed for single users or very small workgroups, meaning that it doesn't perform well when multiple users are reading or writing data concurrently. Again, this may not be a problem for low-traffic sites, but it does present a problem on sites that offer many user-input forms or serve lots of traffic. SQL Server processes queries in parallel (using multiple native threads within a single process) and offers much better performance.

Scalability   SQL Server provides support for very large databases, up to one terabyte, which is much larger than the current limit for an Access database (currently 2 gigabytes in Access 2000 and 2002). In addition, many ColdFusion developers who use large Access databases on busy sites have reported problems with file corruption.

Dynamic backups   SQL Server allows you to perform dynamic backups of a database while it's in use, meaning that you don't have to require all users to exit their applications when backups execute. This gives you the ability to have your ColdFusion data sources available 24/7. Access, on the other hand, does not allow file copies while the database is in use.

Recoverability   When your operating system crashes or the power goes out, SQL Server uses an automatic recovery mechanism to restore your database to its last consistent state—without user intervention. Access databases must be restored from previous backups, meaning that data written between the backup and the crash will be lost.

Commit and rollback   Commit and rollback are critical features in enterprise applications because they ensure that no data is written to a database unless all changes within a transaction are successful. SQL Server treats all database changes within a transaction as single unit of work—either an entire transaction is completed, or the entire transaction is rolled back and all changes are undone. Though Access doesn't support this feature natively, ColdFusion does allow you to approximate it with the `cftransaction` tag.

True client/server performance   SQL Server is designed as a true client/server database, meaning that your data resides on a server that may be remotely accessed by many client computers. For ColdFusion developers, this means that your queries, triggers, and stored procedures may be processed by a different physical machine than your ColdFusion templates, usually resulting in better performance for your applications and less wait for your users. By contrast, Access files usually reside on the same machine as your ColdFusion applications and are processed by the same physical server.

How Will Users Manage SQL Server Data?

Another important consideration before upsizing is how your users will access the database. It is likely that you will find that you do most of your reading and writing via ColdFusion output templates and web-based input forms. But if your Access database resides on an intranet, you may have users who are accustomed to working with it directly, via Access forms, reports, and so on. Unless you plan to re-create all of your existing Access forms as web forms or design a custom Visual Basic interface to handle your SQL Server data, you'll have to deal with the problem of SQL Server having no equivalent form or report interface.

The good news is that the upsizing process allows you to automatically create a rudimentary client/server-like application (an Access *project* or .adp file) that can use your original Access forms, reports, macros, and modules to work with data residing on a SQL Server. The bad news is that the resulting application is not truly client/server. Much of the processing is still handled by the Access client, which can slightly impede performance in environments that comprise large datasets or slow client machines.

In most situations, the drawbacks of using Access project files to manage SQL Server data are minor, but it's important to consider them before you make the move. You'll learn more about project files in a later section, "Using the Access Upsizing Tools."

Choosing an Upsizing Method

Access and SQL Server offer two methods for upsizing your databases, each with its own benefits and drawbacks. The method that is best for your project will depend on the complexity of your database, your version of Access (or other database application), and whether or not you want to create an Access client/server project (.adp) file during the upsizing process.

Microsoft Access Upsizing Tools   A set of optional components that come with Access 95 and later. In general, using these tools is the preferred upsizing method because they offer the clearest path to SQL Server, accurately preserving database elements like default field values, primary key designations, data relationships, datatypes, and so on. However, the upsizing tools can be very "stingy" and will require that you carefully inspect your database for trouble spots before you run your upsize process. Using the Access Upsizing Tools requires more preparation and real-time supervision than the second method, using DTS.

Data Transformation Services   Available in SQL Server's Enterprise Manager, DTS is the recommended alternative to the Access Upsizing Tools even though it does not preserve primary key designations, relationships, default values, or queries that may exist in your original Access database. While DTS transfers only the database schema and/or data, it's still preferable to a no-frills file import because it offers additional capabilities (for example, mapping datatypes and creating custom `insert` queries to control where your data goes). Moreover, DTS is the *only* upsizing method available if you're starting with a non-Microsoft database or an Access version older than 95. DTS uses OLE DB or ODBC data sources to transfer the data, making it fairly versatile with non-Microsoft files.

You'll learn more about both methods in the following sections.

Using the Access Upsizing Tools

Before you proceed with this section, you'll need Access 95 or greater, and you'll need to be upsizing to SQL Server 6.5 or later, or MSDE.

NOTE   To use the upsizing tools with SQL Server 6.5, you'll need to have Service Pack 5 for SQL Server installed.

Access Upsizing Tools are your most powerful ally when you are migrating to SQL Server, but if you use them, you will need to think ahead and you will need to manipulate them to get a good clean transfer. In most cases, they're preferable to SQL Server's Data Transformation Services (DTS) because they create the most accurate copy of your database and are able to preserve default values, primary key designations, relationships, and so on. Really, the only time you *wouldn't* want to use the Access Upsizing Tools is if you had tried to use them in the past and had encountered errors that couldn't be fixed using the pointers in this section.

The complete upsizing process will require four steps:

1. Examine your database for potential trouble spots.

2. Run the Upsizing Wizard.

3. Review the report generated by the Wizard.

4. Re-create any objects, default values, and so on that weren't successfully upsized.

Examining Your Database for Trouble Spots

The Access Upsizing Tools can save you lots of time when you are migrating your databases, but they're far from perfect. There are several features in Access that are not supported in SQL Server, and vice versa, so it's important to take a close look at potential trouble spots before you run the Upsizing Wizard.

Start by opening your Access database in design view, as illustrated in Figure 13.1.

FIGURE 13.1:

Examining table
properties in Access's
table design view

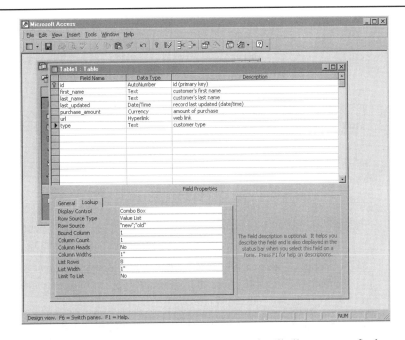

Inspecting the content prior to running the Upsizing Wizard will allow you to find many of the non-compatible points. Reviewing everything from the column naming convention to the validation rules will give you an opportunity to identify some of the things that won't migrate and will have to be recreated manually.

Examining Your Fields and Their Properties

Check your Access tables for nonstandard field names. Access may let you get away with spaces and non-alphanumeric characters, but SQL Server will be pickier. It lets you use non-alpha characters, but it requires that you delimit your identifiers with square brackets ([])—which can be a pain when you're building queries in ColdFusion. Also ensure that your field names don't use SQL reserved words like desc, asc, and, and or. For obvious reasons, these can create problems later.

Open up each of your tables and inspect the settings for your fields' DefaultValue and ValidationRule properties. Access allows you to use Visual Basic (VB) functions for these properties, but SQL Server uses a different language called Transact-SQL (or TSQL). Some of the functions translate just fine, but unsupported functions can cause problems in the upsize. For example, if you've used an Access VB function for DefaultValue that has no corresponding function in TSQL, the Upsizing Wizard will skip the entire table. Table 13.1 lists the Access VB functions that will successfully transfer to SQL Server.

TABLE 13.1: Access VB Functions that Transfer to SQL Server

asc()	cvdate()	minute()	sgn()
ccur()	date()	mod	str()
cdbl()	day()	month()	time()
chr$()	hour()	now()	trim$()
chr()	int()	right$()	trim()
cint()	ltrim$()	right()	ucase$()
clng()	ltrim()	rtrim$()	ucase()
csng()	mid$()	rtrim()	weekday()
cstr()	mid()	second()	year()

If a field's `ValidationRule` is successfully upsized, its `ValidateText` value will be as well. Avoid apostrophes in `ValidationText` properties since they'll be converted to double quotes.

Check the `AllowZeroLength` properties. These properties won't be upsized, so it's a good idea to note the fields that use them so that you can manually create the necessary constraints in your SQL Server database later.

`Indexed` properties will upsize correctly, though the behavior of indices is slightly different in SQL Server. If this property is set to `Yes (Duplicates OK)`, the wizard will create a non-clustered index on SQL Server; if it's set to `Yes (No Duplicates)` a unique, nonclustered index will be created.

> **NOTE**   If your Access database shows `indexed` *and* `required` property values for a field that contains a null value in more than one record, the wizard will migrate only your table's structure and ignore the data within.

Make note of any `Lookup` fields that may be present in your table. In Access, you can use `Lookup` fields to display values selected from a query, a table, or from a predefined text list. Since SQL Server doesn't have `Lookup` functionality, it will simply import the value stored in the field, rather than the corresponding value that may be associated with it.

Examining Your Datatypes

Datatypes present the most common problem area when you are upsizing, so it's important to spend some time understanding how they're mapped from Access to SQL Server. Though ColdFusion largely ignores datatypes, the SQL statements you use in your `cfquery` statements aren't as accommodating. Table 13.2 shows how datatypes get translated.

TABLE 13.2: Corresponding Data Types in Access and SQL Server

Access Datatype	SQL Server Datatype
autonumber or number (long)	int (with the IDENTITYqualifier)
byte	smallint
currency	money
date/time	datetime
hyperlink	ntext (Unicode; hyperlink functionality is dropped)
memo	ntext (Unicode)
number (decimal)	decimal
number (double)	float
number (integer)	smallint
number (long)	int
number (replicationID)	uniqueidentifier
number (single)	real
ole object	image
text	nvarchar (Unicode)
yes/no	bit (0 or 1)

Watch Out for Unicode Fields

Note in Table 13.1 that hyperlink, memo, and text datatypes are converted to datatypes beginning with an *n*. Those are Unicode datatypes, which can cause trouble later if you're running ColdFusion Server for Linux and Solaris. The culprit is the Merant SQL Server driver, which doesn't convert Unicode datatypes (nchar, nvarchar, ntext) correctly. Your queries will return an error like the following:

```
ODBC Error Code = S1000 (General error)
[MERANT][ODBC SQL Server Driver]Unicode conversion failed
```

Unfortunately, until Merant issues a fix for its SQL driver, the only solution is to avoid Unicode datatypes when you are connecting to SQL Server from ColdFusion on Linux or Solaris platforms. To do this, you can manually change *n* datatypes (such as nvarchar and ntext) to varchar after your database has been upsized to SQL Server.

Examining Your Queries

In a normal upsizing, queries that may be present in your Access database are not migrated to SQL Server. However, if you plan to use the Upsizing Wizard's "Create a new Access client/server application" option, the wizard will attempt to migrate any queries it finds.

In general, `select` queries are converted to SQL Server views, while unparameterized action queries (append, delete, make table) are converted to stored procedures. The wizard will ignore these types of queries altogether:

- Union queries
- Crosstab queries
- SQL pass-through queries
- Queries that reference form values
- Queries that perform an action (append, delete, update) that require extra parameters
- Queries that perform an action and include nested queries

The wizard will also ignore some Access query properties because they have no SQL Server equivalents:

Description	Record Locks	Subdatasheet Expanded
Filter	Recordset Type	Subdatasheet Height
Link Child Fields	Run Permissions	Subdatasheet Name
Link Master Fields	Source Connect String	Unique Values
Max Records	Source Database	Unique Records
ODBC Timeout		

Similarly, if your queries contain Visual Basic functions, the wizard will attempt to map the functions to their SQL Server equivalents. If no equivalents exist, the query won't be upsized. Table 13.3. shows the Access functions that can be mapped to SQL Server.

NOTE The Upsizing Wizard only attempts to map your Visual Basic functions if they occur in the `select` portion of your query. If they occur in the `where` clause, the query is ignored.

TABLE 13.3: Access SQL Functions that Can Be Mapped to TSQLFunctions

avg()	count()	lcase()	min()	space$()
ccur()	csng()	left()	minute()	str$()
cdbl()	cstr()	len()	month()	sum()
chr$()	cvdate()	ltrim$()	right$()	ucase$()
chr()	day()	max()	right()	ucase()
cint()	hour()	mid$()	rtrim$()	weekday()
clng()	lcase$()	mid()	second()	year()

Examining Your Security Settings

Because Access and SQL Server use two entirely different systems in which to implement security, none of your database's security settings will be upsized. However, it's important to check your database and table security settings to be sure that you have correct permissions on the objects to be migrated.

Choose Tools ➤ Security ➤ User and Group Permissions (see Figure 13.2) and ensure that all tables to be upsized have at least Read Design permission for the user performing the upsize. If you try to upsize objects without correct permissions, the wizard will silently skip them.

FIGURE 13.2:

Examining security settings in an Access database

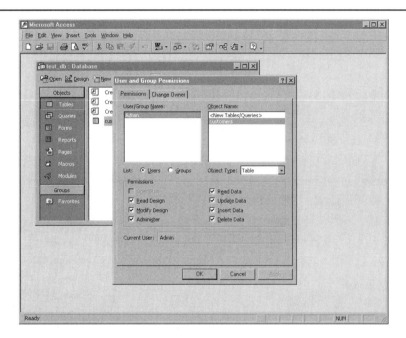

Running The Upsizing Wizard

Once you've identified any potential trouble spots and made the necessary modifications, actually performing the upsize is a fairly straightforward task. Start by choosing Tools ➤ Database Utilities ➤ Upsizing Wizard. If you haven't run the wizard previously, Access will may request its installation CD to install any files need for the Upsizing Tools that it doesn't find present on the system.

NOTE   If you get an "Overflow" error when you run the Upsizing Wizard for the first time, you may need to update your Office installation with a couple of files. This is discussed in the Microsoft Knowledge Base Article Q279454 (available at `http://support.microsoft` `.com/default.aspx?scid=kb;[LN];Q279454`). You'll need Office Update SR-1 and the Access 2000 and SQL Server Readiness Update. Both are available at `http://office` `.microsoft.com/downloads/`.

The wizard's dialog boxes are fairly self-explanatory, so we won't spend a lot of time on them here. The first screen simply asks if you prefer creating a new SQL Server database, or if you'd rather upsize to a database that already exists. The second screen requests the name of a SQL Server on your network, valid login information, and the name of that database you wish to create.

NOTE   When you use the Access Upsizing Tools, your SQL Server must be configured to use the "SQL Server and Windows" authentication method rather than "Windows Only." You'll find this setting by right-clicking the server in SQL Server Enterprise Manager, and then choosing the Security tab.

SQL Server Authentication

SQL Server provides for two different modes of user authentication, SQL Server login and the Windows system login.

SQL Server, like most high-end database servers, provides its own user and group management system independent of external structures. Individual users and groups can be assigned various rights to databases, database content, and even database files devices. These rights almost wholly exist without any influence from external systems. While some users and groups preexist in any stock SQL Server installation, new ones will likely have to be created for the specific application at hand. SQL Server can also authenticate user logins against the operating system's login mechanisms as well. Called the Windows login, instead of matching passwords against the internal catalog of user information, it is matched against the operating system's lower-level system.

If the wizard successfully connects to your SQL Server, you'll see a list of tables in your Access database and be prompted to select those you want to upsize. The resulting dialog box demands a little more attention. It's pictured in Figure 13.3.

FIGURE 13.3:

Choosing Table
Attributes to Upsize

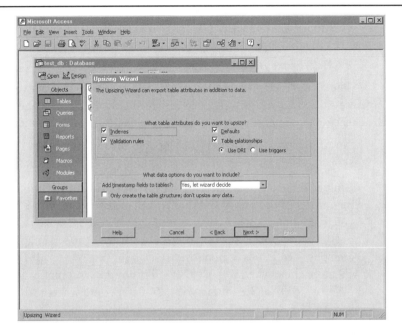

FIGURE 13.3:

Choosing Table
Attributes to Upsize

The check boxes in Figure 13.3 control the following actions:

Upsizing Indexes   When this option is enabled, any Indexes in your Access tables are migrated to SQL Server. If your index name contains any illegal characters, they will be replaced by the underscore (_) character during upsizing.

Upsizing Default Values   When enabled, the Default Values defined for your fields will be migrated.

Upsizing Validation Rules   When this option is enabled, all table, record, and field rules to be upsized as `update` and `insert` triggers.

Upsizing Table Relationships   Relationships can be upsized in one of two ways. Selecting Declarative Referential Integrity (DRI) creates the relationships as your tables are created; this is usually the best choice for most databases. Selecting Triggers will add support for cascading updates and deletes, or for cross-database referential integrity.

Adding Timestamps   It's usually best to allow the wizard to add timestamps as it sees fit. When used, this feature will allow records to be automatically timestamped each time they're updated. This can increase performance with tables that contain large memo fields, floating-point numeric fields, or OLE objects.

Create Table Structure Only   Enabling this feature is useful in testing. The wizard will go through all the motions of an upsize except for moving the actual records in your database. If you're upsizing a large database, this can allow you to quickly check to see if things are working before you wait for the longer import.

The final screen prompts you to choose whether to make any changes to your existing Access database, for example, whether to simply upsize the database or whether to create a client/server application using Access as a front-end tool. Your choices are as follows:

No Application Changes   This upsizes the tables only and doesn't create the client/server application.

Link SQL Server Tables To Existing Application   With this option, your tables are migrated to SQL Server and then linked back to your Access file using ODBC. This allows you to continue to use Access to read and write data, as well as run your existing reports, queries, and forms. Note that this is not a true client/server application. Your Access queries aren't upsized in this option; they remain in your Access file and thus are executed by the client machine when you use them. This option automatically appends _local to your original Access tables so that you don't later confuse them with the migrated SQL Server versions.

SQL Server tables that are linked to an Access front-end via ODBC can't be redesigned. If you think you'll need to modify your table designs, choose the Create a New Access Client/Server Application option.

Create A New Access Client/Server Application   This option creates an entirely new Access project, or .adp file. All tables and queries in your Access database are upsized to SQL Server. All forms, reports, macros, and so on are automatically modified to work with the SQL Server data and are saved in the new project file. The project is linked back to your SQL Server tables using ActiveX Data Objects (ADO) connections.

When you're done, click the Finish button to begins the upsizing process and/or to create of your new Access project file.

The Upsizing Wizard allows you to upsize databases unattended. When it's used with large databases, the longer transfer time may trigger an ODBC Timeout error. To prevent this, increase the QueryTimeout value in the system registry or disable it by setting it to 0. You'll find the registry key at HKEY_LOCAL_MACHINE\Software\Microsoft\Jet\4.0\Engines\ODBC\QueryTimeout.

NOTE   Upsizing very large tables may max out SQL Server's transaction log. In these cases, the table is skipped and an error is generated in the Upsizing Report. While there really is not a product-version independent fix, one way to help avoid this is to clear the log prior to upsizing.

Reviewing the Upsizing Report

If the Wizard encounters errors during the upsizing process, it won't stop to let you know. The wizard is designed to run unattended, so it will instead note any problems and display them in a report when the entire upsizing action is complete. The report contains details on all of the actions that failed, except those that were skipped due to permissions problems (see "Examining Your Security Settings" in the previous section). A sample report is shown in Figure 13.4.

FIGURE 13.4:

The upsizing report lists tables that failed to upsize.

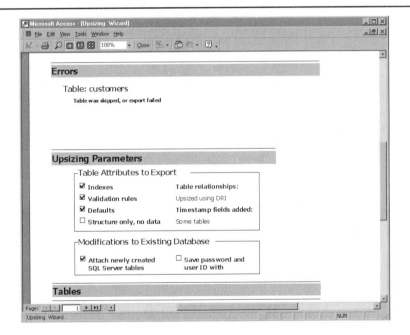

Re-creating Objects that Weren't Upsized

Despite your best efforts and extensive pre-examination of your database, it's not uncommon for some objects to fail the upsize process. Most often these are queries, and they generally fail because they contain functions or properties for which there are no SQL Server equivalents. For excessively complex queries, sometimes the only solution is to rewrite the query as a view or as a stored procedure using TSQL, the syntax used by SQL Server (refer to the list of resources in this chapter's "In Sum" section).

Missing tables are easier to remedy. Table upsizes most often fail due to unsupported functions, so carefully check the field properties of your original table in Access's design view and try to upsize again. Note that you can use the Upsizing Wizard on a single table, so you can keep trying until you identify the problem.

NOTE   If all else fails, you can use DTS, the alternate upsizing method also discussed in this chapter. Since it lacks many features of the wizard, it is less error-prone and will ignore unsupported functions (as well as all default values, relationships, and so on).

Known Problems with the Upsizing Tools

It is beyond the scope of this text to provide a complete list of all of the possible pitfalls and problems that can occur with the Access Upsizing Tools. Summarizing the differences between two different products across five versions collectively (SQL Server 6.*x*, SQL Server 7.*x*, SQL Server 2000, Access 2000, and Access 2002) is more than a little challenging. However, Microsoft's online Knowledge Base provides a number of different articles, from the Access perspective that address some of the more unusual circumstances.

- For Access 2000, visit `http://support.microsoft.com/default.aspx?scid=kb;en-us;` Q325019.

- For Access 2002, visit `http://support.microsoft.com/default.aspx?scid=kb;en-us;` Q328319.

Using SQL Server DTS

The second upsizing method, SQL Server's Data Transformation Services (DTS), doesn't offer the flexibility of the Access Upsizing Tools. In fact, DTS is much closer to a standard file import in the sense that it just re-creates your Access tables, minus "frills" like primary keys and relationships, and it then populates them with your data. But it's still an extremely useful tool in some situations, particularly when the Upsizing Tools fail, or when you need to upsize a non-Microsoft database.

Data Transformation Services *do not*

- Automatically replicate primary keys.

- Replicate validation rules or default values.

- Preserve relationships.

- Upsize any queries from the Access database.

Data Transformation Services *do*

- Create a basic table structure.
- Allow for some manual mapping and/or custom scripting.
- Work significantly faster than the Access Upsizing Tools.
- Allow you to upsize tables that fail with the Access Upsizing Tools.
- Work with any OLE DB or ODBC data source.
- Allow you to reverse the upsizing process and export SQL Server databases as Access files.

Unlike the Access Upsizing Tools, DTS doesn't require you to perform any special preparations before you upsize your Access database. It works through either an OLE DB connection or an ODBC data source, so it's essentially accessing your database the same way ColdFusion does. It uses SQL commands behind the scenes to create replicas of your original Access tables and then transfers the data using Visual Basic functions.

Running the DTS Import/Export Wizard

DTS can be started either from its Start Menu icon, or by logging onto a SQL Server in Enterprise Manager and choosing Tools ➤ Data Transformation Services ➤ Import Data. In either case, the opening dialog box will ask from where you wish to copy data, as shown in Figure 13.5.

FIGURE 13.5:

Choosing a source
to upsize in
SQL Server DTS

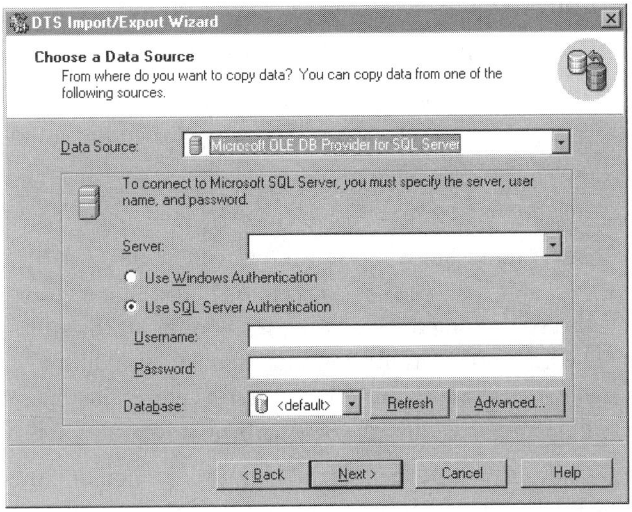

The following steps will walk you through it:

1. Selections in the data source box will vary depending on the OLE DB and ODBC drivers installed on your machine. To import an Access file, choose ODBC. If the Access database is already set up as a data source, you can select it from the list; if not, the wizard will guide you through the standard Windows ODBC setup. If the database requires a login, you'll need to supply the username and password.

2. After you finish filling out the Choose a Data Source step, and click Next, the wizard will prompt you to select a destination source; most likely this will be the SQL Server OLE DB driver. In the boxes that follow, select or type the name of the SQL Server and provide any authentication data it may require. Note that you may use either Windows authentication or SQL Server authentication with DTS. Next, select either an existing database or choose New and supply a database name. The wizard will ask you to define sizes for both the data file and the log file; the default of 2MB is usually sufficient for upsizing the average-sized Access database.

TIP   A good rule of thumb is to triple the size of your Access file to get the data file size; then halve it to get the log file size.

3. After you have selected the appropriate size, press Next and you're given the option to either allow the wizard to automatically upsize your data, or to use your own custom SQL query to handle the transfer. Unless you need specific control over the way your tables are created, it's safe to choose the "Copy" option.

4. Press Next again and you'll see a dialog box like the one in Figure 13.6.

   This screen allows you to select the tables you wish to upsize, either one-by-one or via the Select All button. It also presents one of the most important options available in DTS—the Transform button.

5. Click the button next to one of the table names and you'll see a screen like Figure 13.7.

   The Column Mappings tab allows you to customize the datatype and required status ("Nullable") for each of your table's fields. If you've experienced problems with datatype conversion using the Access Upsizing Tools, this feature alone may make DTS worthwhile. The Edit SQL button allows you to manually edit the SQL command that will create your table. Click the Transformations tab to get similar, manual control over the way your data will be imported into the new table by way of Visual Basic functions.

6. Finally, choose Next and you'll have the option of either running the upsize process immediately or scheduling it for a later time and date.

FIGURE 13.6:

Selecting tables
and transforming
data in DTS

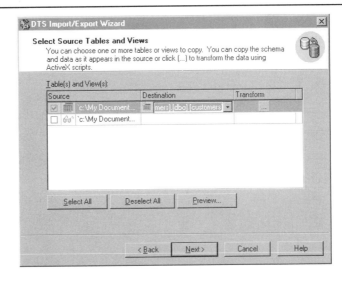

FIGURE 13.7:

Altering column
mappings and SQL
statements in DTS

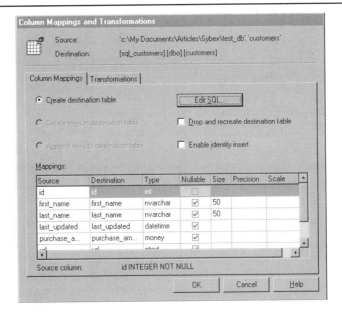

Verifying Your DTS Import

Since DTS uses such a bare-bones approach to upsizing, it's also relatively trouble-free. Only occasionally will you encounter errors, and the majority of those will be mismapped datatypes or the result of an Access Lookup field that didn't translate as expected.

Still, before you begin using your new database in an application, it's important to make sure your data remained intact. Use SQL Server's Query Analyzer or another SQL-compatible tool and run some basic select queries on your new tables. Watch closely for common errors like these:

- Truncated text or memo fields
- Date/time fields stored as text datatypes
- Missing records

You may also need to do some design work on your tables to re-create the following elements:

- Primary key designations
- Default values and constraints
- Relationships
- Indexes

Modifying ColdFusion Applications for Upsized Databases

Once you've successfully converted your database to SQL Server you're almost home. The final step is to alter your existing ColdFusion applications to work with your new database, taking into account the slight differences between Access data sources and SQL Server.

Modifying SQL Syntax

If you're using SQL Server for the first time, one thing you'll immediately notice is that the error messages generated by its ODBC or OLE DB drivers are much more detailed than those displayed by Access. You'll come to appreciate that verbosity as you begin to search your application for SQL statements that use syntax unique to Access and must be changed. Consider this simple query used with an Access data source:

```
<cfquery name="delete_customers" datasource="sampledata">
    delete * from customers where id = #url.id#
</cfquery>
```

Pretty basic stuff—but that query will throw an error when used with SQL Server. You now need a query like the following. Note the missing asterisk after `delete`.

```
<cfquery name="delete_customers" datasource="sampledata">
    delete from customers where id = #url.id#
</cfquery>
```

Table 13.4 displays some common differences between Access SQL statements and their SQL Server counterparts.

TABLE 13.4: Comparing SQL Statements between Access and SQL Server

Access	SQL Server
delete * from table	delete from table
select distinctRow	select distinct
where x like 'foobar'	where x like '%foobar%'

Access and SQL Server also support different SQL functions, as listed in Table 13.5. Note that these apply to SQL functions only—not ColdFusion functions.

TABLE 13.5: Comparing Commonly Used SQL Functions between Access and SQL Server

Access	SQL Server
ucase()	upper()
lcase()	lower()
trim()	rtrim(ltrim())
instr()	charIndex()
now()	getDate()
int(x)	convert(int,x)

You might be tempted to simply convert your SQL functions to ColdFusion functions so that you no longer need to worry about database versions. Don't forget, however, that since you're now working with a true client/server data source you might want to let SQL Server do some of the function work and thus relieve some stress from the machine hosting your ColdFusion templates.

WARNING Using a global search-and-replace across your templates is a great approach for changing Access queries to their SQL Server equivalents. But use extreme caution when working with functions: Globally replacing the SQL function ucase() can also replace part of the ColdFusion function #ucase()#, which is probably not what you want.

Also remember that when your Access yes/no fields were upsized, they were assigned the bit datatype in SQL Server. For example, this query works in Access:

```
<cfquery name="get_new_customers" datasource="sampledata">
   select last_name from customers where new = TRUE
</cfquery>
```

but needs adjustment to the bit datatype (0 or 1) in SQL Server:

```
<cfquery name="get_new_customers" datasource="sampledata">
   select last_name from customers where new = 1
</cfquery>
```

SQL's string concatenation operator will also require some adjustments. The following Access query combines the string `first_name` followed by a space, then `last_name` as the new string `full_name`:

```
<cfquery name="get_customer_name" datasource="sampledata">
   select (first_name & " " & last_name) as full_name
   from customers
</cfquery>
```

SQL Server uses a different concatenation operator, the plus (+) sign and requires single quotes around text strings (in this case a space):

```
<cfquery name="get_customer_name" datasource="sampledata">
   select (first_name + ' ' + last_name) as full_name
   from customers
</cfquery>
```

Working with Identity Columns

When you upsize a database that uses Access's autonumbering feature, in most cases that field is converted to SQL Server's `int` datatype and designated as an *identity* or *ID* field. You can confirm this by viewing your table's properties in SQL Server Enterprise Manager (see Figure 13.8).

FIGURE 13.8:

Examining table properties in SQL Server Enterprise Manager

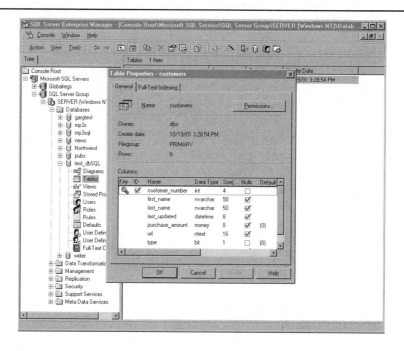

In the figure, note that the field `customer_number` from this upsized database has the ID box checked and is designated as a primary key (as it was in the original Access table). This creates the same behavior as Access's autonumbering feature, meaning that when new records are inserted, `customer_number` doesn't need to be supplied; instead it will be numbered incrementally by SQL Server, and each record has a unique primary key.

But take a look at the same table upsized with DTS. It's shown in Figure 13.9.

FIGURE 13.9:

Examining a table
upsized with DTS

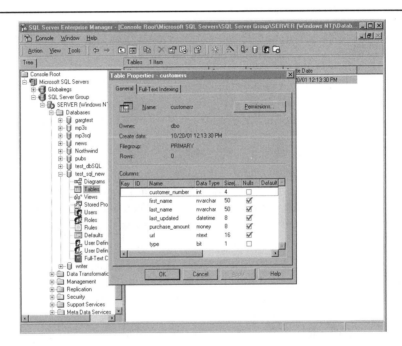

DTS has made the `customer_number` field required (the Nulls box is unchecked) but the field isn't designated as a primary key or as an identity field. Without the `identity` designation, records that are inserted in the future won't automatically receive a sequential `customer_number`; this may create problems if the insert queries in your ColdFusion application assume that it will. Your first thought might be to add the `identity` designation manually, but SQL Server doesn't allow `identity` to be added to existing fields—it can only be added when a field is created.

Creating a New, Sequential Identity Field

It might also occur to you that you could create a new temporary field in the table, say `customer_number_temp`, with a SQL statement like this:

```
alter table customers
    add customer_number_temp int primary key identity not null
```

This assigns the necessary `primary key` and `identity` designations and lets SQL Server automatically assign identity numbers to your records. Then you could drop the existing `customer_number` field,

```
alter table customers
drop column  customer_number
```

and then rename the column using the SQL Server command `sp_rename`:

```
exec sp_rename 'customers.customer_number_temp', 'customer_number', 'column'
```

This gives you a new, autonumbered primary key, but remember that the new identity numbers have been added to your existing records sequentially. This method works fine if `customer_number` isn't used as a foreign key in any other tables in your database. But if your original `customer_number` values were used in relationships, say as a foreign key in another table, this would create a problem because your records would have been renumbered sequentially. For these cases, read on to the workaround described in the next section.

Manually Generating Sequential IDs

When you need to preserve the original Access `autonumbered` values with your existing records, you can use a method that was common to ColdFusion development in the days before SQL Server had an `identity` attribute. You can leave your existing IDs as they are and use Cold-Fusion and/or SQL Server to generate new, sequential IDs for records you may insert in the future.

One of the most common approaches to this method is to create a new table in your database that will do nothing but keep track of the last ID number assigned to your records. This table will contain fields corresponding to the field names for all of your tables that need to have sequential IDs generated. For example, the sample database pictured in Figure 13.9 has just one table, `customers`, so you would use SQL to create a new table called `last_id` containing just one field called `customers`.

```
create table last_id
(customers int not null)
```

You then populate that field with just one number—the value of the last sequential ID that exists in the `customers` table. This SQL snippet assumes that the last existing record in the customers table has the `customer_number` 121:

```
insert into last_id (customers) values (121)
```

Once the `last_id` table is created and populated with its single record, you can use it to generate new sequential IDs in your customers table. Using this method, your application might use a series of queries like these when inserting a new customer record:

```
<cfquery name="get_last_id" datasource="customers_sql">
   select customers from last_id
</cfquery>
```

```
<cfquery name="update_last_id" datasource="customers_sql">
   update last_id
   set customers = #IncrementValue(get_last_id.customers)#
   where customers = #get_last_id#
</cfquery>

<cfquery name="insert_customer" datasource="customers_sql">
   insert into customers
   (customer_number, first_name, last_name)

      values (#IncrementValue(get_last_id.customers)#,
      '#first_name#', '#last_name#')

</cfquery>
```

Note that these queries are purposely left verbose to show the principles at work; depending on the needs of your application, you might instead consolidate them into a custom tag or a SQL stored procedure. The first query fetches the last ID value used in the customers table (as stored in the last_id table), or 121. The second query increments the value in the last_id table to 122, readying it for future operations. The third inserts a sample customer record, using the 122 value as the customer_number. The next time these queries run, they will select the value 122, increment it to 123, and so on.

You may wonder why it's necessary to store the last ID values in a table; why not just select the last ID number from the customers table (rather than a separate last_id table), increment it by one, and then perform the update? The reason is that if there is any lag time between selecting the last ID and inserting the new record, the last ID could be inaccurate. By writing the values to a table, you can ensure that each insertion gets assigned a unique ID value.

Other Differences between Access and SQL Server

Even if a database is seemingly successfully upsized, this does not guarantee that the ColdFusion application will interact with the database as smoothly as before the upsizing. Subtle actions that were left to be handled by the database instead of the application logic itself may manifest themselves in some uncomfortable ways.

While numerous things can be discussed regarding the differences between Access and SQL Server, many of these items will not affect a ColdFusion application directly. Two items that certainly will, though, are the entry of longer text into a shorter field and nullable column values.

Text Truncation

With Access data sources, when you try to insert a text string into a field that has a length shorter than your string, the text is simply truncated and Access doesn't report an error. SQL Server is more particular about the length of strings, and it will show you (or your users) a detailed error when a text string is too long to be inserted. The quickest way to avoid such errors is to use some simple client-side validation and limit your form fields to match the length of your table's text fields.

For example, if a table "messages" contains a subject field defined as the datatype varchar(50), you might use some code like this in its input form:

```
<form action="some_action.cfm" method="post">
   Input Your Text Here:
   <input type="text" name="subject" maxLength="50">
   <input type="submit">
</form>
```

You might instead take advantage of SQL Server's generous error reporting and create a more sophisticated server-side validation method using cftry. This method catches the error on the form's action page rather than the form itself:

```
<cftry>

<cfquery name="insert_message" datasource="messages">
   insert into messages (subject) values ('#form.subject#')
</cfquery>

<cfcatch exception="database">
      <h3>The subject of your message exceeds 50
      characters.  Please use your browser's "back" button
      and supply a message subject of 50 characters or
      less.</h3>

</cfcatch>

</cftry>
```

A third option is to duplicate the original functionality of Access, simply truncating the text to the required length at the time it's inserted:

```
<cfquery name="insert_message" datasource="messages">
   insert into messages (subject) values ('#left(form.subject, 50)#')
</cfquery>
```

Null Values

When you originally created your database in Access, it's possible that you may have relied on its default behavior in the Allow Zero Length property when you created your fields. For example, take a look at the field properties for last_name in Figure 13.10.

By default, Access sets Allow Zero Length to "No" when you create new fields. Your Cold-Fusion application may have been using this feature as a rudimentary form of error-checking, for example, throwing an error when a user tries to submit a form with a blank field. But when you upsize a database using either the Upsizing Tools or DTS, the default behavior is different. Take a look at the SQL Server database properties pictured in Figure 13.11.

FIGURE 13.10:

Access defaults to not allow zero length

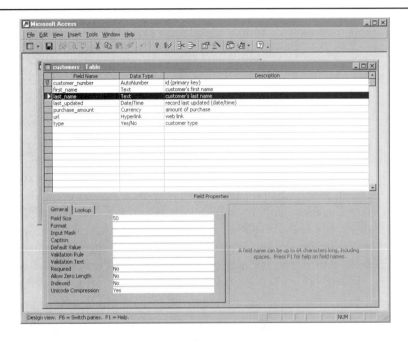

FIGURE 13.11:

SQL defaults to allow null values

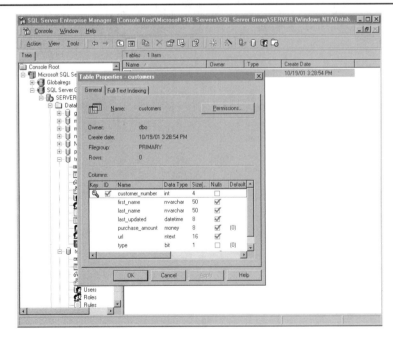

The `last_name` properties shown in that field *will* accept null values, so a ColdFusion application wouldn't thrown an error if a record was inserted without a defined `last_name`.

If this creates a problem in your application, you could redefine the field properties with a SQL `alter table` statement:

```
alter table customers
alter column last_name nvarchar(50) not null
```

In Sum

Upsizing from Microsoft Access to Microsoft SQL Server can make your ColdFusion applications more stable, easier to develop, and ready for any amount of traffic you can send their way. The process can initially seem daunting—after all, no one likes to tamper with a database that's already working—but the payoff is well worth the effort. If you're willing to spend the time up front examining your Access database for trouble spots and choosing an upsizing method that suits your project, you can help ensure a more seamless upgrade to SQL Server, one that will require only minor changes to your existing ColdFusion application.

Here are some additional resources for help with upsizing efforts.

- You'll find the complete documentation for SQL Server 2000 at Microsoft's Books Online Site: `http://www.microsoft.com/sql/techinfo/productdoc/2000/books.asp`.

- Superior Software for Windows (SSW) offers a product called SSW Upsizing PRO that can scan your Access databases for many of the trouble spots detailed in this chapter: `http://www.ssw.com.au/ssw/UpsizingPRO/`.

PART III

Client-Side Coding

Chapter 14: Using JavaScript and DHTML with ColdFusion

Chapter 15: Working with WAP and WML Clients

Using JavaScript and DHTML with ColdFusion

By Selene Bainum

- Discussing client-side versus server-side processing

- Introducing the Document Object Model (DOM)

- Integrating JavaScript and ColdFusion

- Exploring Form Field Validation

- Introducing DHTML

Several years ago, many developers were hesitant to add JavaScript and Dynamic HTML (DHTML) to their web applications out of fear that they would be alienating large audiences whose browsers weren't able to process or view such advanced code. At that time, there was a huge difference between the capabilities of Netscape Communicator and Internet Explorer, and the majority of developers decided to forego the flashy user experience—such as Active X controls, JavaScript and VBScript and extreme graphics—and focus more on the functionality of their programs.

That scenario no longer holds true. Although web developers still need to be concerned with browser compatibility and other issues, nowadays, common elements such as JavaScript form field validation, image rollovers, and cascading style sheets (CSS) are handled similarly by most browsers. Also, other functions, such as hiding and showing elements, can be coded easily to allow for cross-browser compatibility.

This chapter explains how to enhance your web applications using JavaScript and DHTML, and it demonstrates how you can use ColdFusion to make developing such enhancements easier. In addition, we'll introduce the core of JavaScript, the Document Object Model (DOM). We'll also discuss how to integrate customized JavaScript form validation with the `cfform` tag and how to pass JavaScript values to ColdFusion, and then we'll introduce the concepts of DHTML and styles.

NOTE Some of the examples in this chapter involve the video rental database scenario introduced in Chapter 11 "Advanced SQL."

NOTE For complete JavaScript and DHTML references, check out *Mastering JavaScript Premium Edition*, by James Jaworski (Sybex, 2002). You can also find an excellent reference to HTML, JavaScript, and DHTML online at Microsoft's MSDN Library—`http://msdn.microsoft.com/library/`.

Client versus Server Processing

The title of this section suggests that there might be a war between server-side processing and client-side processing. This isn't the case, although the two sides don't always work as closely as we would like. What we're doing here is taking a concise look at the client- and server-related roles played by ColdFusion and JavaScript so that we can understand ways to make them play nicely together.

The Server: ColdFusion

A ColdFusion page is processed when a browser makes a request to a web server. The web server software—IIS, Netscape, Apache, and the like—will recognize that the ColdFusion Application Server must process the requested page. The ColdFusion Application Server software processes the CFML and sends the results back to the web server, which in turn sends the page back to the browser. When the page is finally loaded in the browser, it no longer contains any CFML. The code that is returned is primarily just HTML and JavaScript—and anything else that wasn't processed by ColdFusion.

ColdFusion is completely unaware of and uninterested in the web browser. This is both good and bad. The upside is that because ColdFusion pages are processed on the server, there are few cross-browser capability issues. Compatibility issues can arise with the HTML or JavaScript that is sent back to the browser as standard HTML, but with the exception of cfform objects, the developer controls much of the HTML and/or JavaScript created.

On the downside, ColdFusion doesn't know anything about the properties of the browser. It is unaware of frames and has no access to any JavaScript variables. One of the most common complaints from ColdFusion developers is that ColdFusion lacks a target attribute in the cflocation tag. This means that unless ColdFusion knows that a frame exists, there is no way it can send the user there.

The Client: JavaScript

JavaScript is a language that is processed exclusively by the browser. This can be a problem when you want to make sure the code will be processed properly and consistently for users on different platforms who are using different browser types and versions. Because of the advances in web browsers over the years, many of the functions you want to perform will be processed very similarly on the various browsers.

Because the client browser processes JavaScript, it runs very quickly. This is largely because no trips back to the server or the database to run the code are needed; as all code is loaded into the browser when the page loads. Keep this in mind when you are writing JavaScript. The more JavaScript code you write, the longer the page will take to actually load in the browser. The size of the page isn't just the HTML that is used to display your page, but also all the underlying code such as JavaScript.

Since ColdFusion pages are processed before the JavaScript is returned to the browser, you can "build" your JavaScript using ColdFusion. You can create JavaScript by looping over queries or lists or by using the values of ColdFusion variables, just as you would with HTML. Examples of creating JavaScript with ColdFusion will be presented later in the chapter.

Introducing the Document Object Model (DOM)

The *Document Object Model (DOM)* is a term you have probably already heard, even if you aren't quite sure what it is. The DOM is an application programming interface (API) for documents such as HTML and XML. The DOM defines the structure of the document and the way in which its objects are accessed and manipulated. Objects within the document can include—but are certainly not limited to—frames, tables, forms, and their child objects.

TIP   For complete, up-to-date information on the DOM, visit the World Wide Web Consortium (W3C) at http://www.w3c.org.

Before you can access objects in your document using JavaScript and DHTML, you have to know how to reference them. The easiest way to do this is to gain a basic understanding of the DOM. Since a model is a plan for the organization of objects, it can be represented graphically, in a hierarchical manner. Figure 14.1 shows a portion of the DOM that is supported by most browsers.

FIGURE 14.1:

The DOM

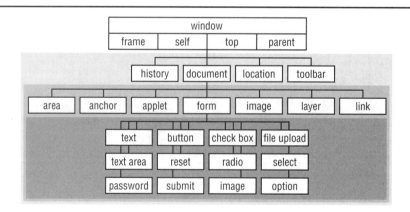

Object models can be applied to subsets of the entire document as well. The following code is a basic HTML table:

```html
<table>
    <tr>
        <td>A</td>
        <td>1</td>
    </tr>
    <tr>
        <td>A</td>
        <td>1</td>
    </tr>
</table>
```

The table represented here can be broken down into objects. The table itself is an object that contains row objects, which contain column objects that contain elements. Figure 14.2 is a graphical representation of these objects.

FIGURE 14.2:

Table object model

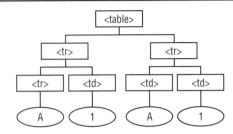

Object References

After a document is loaded into the browser, all of the objects are stored in memory and can be easily accessed and controlled with scripts (usually JavaScript). In order for JavaScript to access these objects, they need to be referenced; the best way to reference objects is by using names.

Each object you want to reference, whether it is a text box, an image, an area, or another item, must be assigned a name. Objects are assigned names using the name attribute of the object's tag. The naming conventions for objects are very similar to the ColdFusion naming conventions:

- Object names cannot contain spaces.
- They may contain only letters, numbers, and the underscore (_) character.
- Objects names must start with a letter.
- When assigned to the name attribute, the name of the object must be inside quotes.

WARNING Unlike ColdFusion variables and object names, object names in JavaScript are case-sensitive. An object named MyObject is different from another object named myobject.

Once you have named your objects, you can reference them using JavaScript's dot-separated syntax, in which the period is used to separate the components of the hierarchy as is shown here:

```
object.object.object
```

When you reference an object, you start at the top of the DOM and work your way down. Most JavaScript references will start with the document object. Keep in mind that the window object is technically the "top" object in the DOM but is usually omitted in most JavaScript references. Since only one document can be contained in a window at any time, the window reference is redundant.

Listing 14.1 creates a basic form.

Listing 14.1   Basic HTML Form (c1401.cfm)

```
<!---
    Name:           /c14/c1401.cfm
    Description:     Create a basic form.
--->
<!DOCTYPE HTML PUBLIC "-//W3C//DTD HTML 4.01 Transitional//EN">

<html>
<head>
    <title>c1401.cfm</title>
</head>

<body>

<form action="ServerSide.cfm" method="post" name="MyForm">
    Username: <input type="text" name="Username"><br>
    Birth Date: <input type="text" name="BirthDate"><br>
    Over 21? <input type="radio" name="Over21" value="Yes">Yes
        <input type="radio" name="Over21" value="No">No
    <input type="submit" name="Submit" value="Submit"
</form>

</body>
</html>
```

Figure 14.3 displays the object model for this form, within the document object. Using the graphical hierarchy of the form, it is quite simple to create the references for the various objects. Simply replace each connecting line with a period. The farther down in the model you travel, the more "dots" you will use. Table 14.1 lists the objects and their references.

FIGURE 14.3:

Form object model

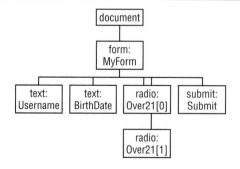

TABLE 14.1: Objects and References

Object	Reference
form: MyForm	document.MyForm
text: Username	document.MyForm.Username
text: BirthDate	document.MyForm.BirthDate
radio: Over21[0]	document.MyForm.Over21[0]
radio: Over21[1]	document.MyForm.Over21[1]
submit: Submit	document.MyForm.Submit

NOTE   Multiple objects that share the same name, such as select-box options, radio buttons and check boxes, are referenced with the object index number in brackets immediately following the object name. Unlike ColdFusion, JavaScript indexes start with 0 and increment up. A check box with three elements will have indexes of 0, 1, and 2.

Object Components

HTML objects are defined by their components. To the browser, every text box is different, even though one might look exactly like another in the browser. The three components used by the browser to define objects are their properties, methods, and event handlers.

Properties

Almost any object can be characterized by its properties. For instance, you can easily describe an automobile as being blue, having two doors, and using an automatic transmission. HTML objects can be described the same way. The form in Listing 14.1 contains a text box named Username. The name of that text box is one of its properties.

Properties are usually defined in name/value pairs, though it is possible for a property to have no value. If we were to represent the above-mentioned car as a tag, for instance, it would look like this:

```
<automobile color="blue" doors="2" transmission="automatic">
```

The automobile is defined by the following properties: color, doors, and transmission.

If we add the value attribute to the Username form field, the object's tag would look like this:

```
<input type="text" name="Username" value="Jdoe">
```

This object now has two properties: name and value. These properties can also be referenced using the dot syntax, as follows:

```
document.MyForm.Username.name
document.MyForm.Username.value
```

These references will point to the name and the value of the object respectively.

NOTE Even if you don't create an attribute for an object, its property can still be referenced. For example, if you omitted the `value` attribute from an `input` object, you could still reference the `value` property. It would just have an empty value.

It is important to note that the references are pointing to and pulling from memory, and not necessarily referring to what is coded in the HTML. When the document is loaded into the browser, `document.MyForm.Username.value` will return `Jdoe`. If the user changes the value of the form field by typing in a value, `document.MyForm.Username.value` will then return the value entered by the user. In other words, properties of objects can be changed by the user as well as by your scripts.

Methods

Although properties describe the characteristics of an object, methods relate what an object can do. A document can write, a form can submit, a text box can have the text within it selected. All of these actions are methods of their objects. Method names are similar to property names except that they are followed by a pair of parentheses.

Some methods need no direction other than to be called. Other methods, however, require instructions in the form of *parameters* or *arguments*. Both these terms mean the same thing and are interchangeable.

To submit the form in Listing 14.1, you would add the `submit()` method to the object's reference, like so:

```
document.MyForm.submit()
```

To select the text in the `Username` text box, you would add the `select()` method to the reference:

```
document.MyForm.Username.select()
```

To write text to a document, you need to provide a little more instruction. The `write()` method takes a string parameter:

```
document.write("Hello World")
```

This statement will write the text "Hello World" to the document.

Each type of object has its own set of methods, some similar to or the same as those used by other objects, and some quite different.

Event Handlers

Events area actions that take place in a document, related to a particular object. Events are usually triggered by the action of the user. An *event handler* is a way of controlling what happens to an object when it accessed by an event. Like object methods, event handlers are denoted by a set of parentheses and are preceded with the word on. The event handler for a document's loading, for example, is onLoad().

Event handlers take an action attribute, which specifies what you want to happen when the event is triggered. A common task on the Web is to have the cursor focus in a particular form field when the page loads. To have the cursor appear in the Username field of our form, we would call its focus() method. This call would be passed in as an attribute to the document body's onLoad() event handler:

```
<body onLoad="document.MyForm.Username.focus()">
```

When the page loads, the body's onLoad() event handler will trigger the focus() method of the Username field, placing the cursor in the field.

NOTE   You'll find a complete listing of Internet Explorer's HTML/DHTML objects and their properties, methods, and events in Microsoft's MDSN Library at http://msdn.microsoft .com/library/default.asp?url=/workshop/author/dhtml/reference/objects.asp. You'll find Netscape's at http://www.mozilla.org/docs/dom/domref/dom_intro.html.

Integrating JavaScript and ColdFusion

Now that you know a little more about JavaScript and how it works, you're better prepared to understand how ColdFusion and JavaScript can—and cannot—communicate with each other.

ColdFusion to JavaScript

As mentioned in the beginning of the chapter, you can build JavaScript using ColdFusion. A good example of how this might work can be seen in the interaction between select boxes, referred to as *related selects*. When two or more select boxes are related, the value of one depends on the value of the other. For instance, in the video rental database, each movie title is assigned to a genre such as Science Fiction, Drama, War, Romance, and so forth. In order to narrow down a list of movie titles by genre, you can create two select boxes, one that lists the genres and the other that lists the titles.

When the page loads, the Genre select box will be populated with all of the genres retrieved from the database and the Title select box will be empty, as demonstrated in Figure 14.4. Once a particular genre is selected, the Title select box is populated with all the titles that belong to that genre. Figure 14.5 displays some of the values that appear in the Title select box after the Drama genre is selected. If another genre were selected, the Title select box would be repopulated with only the titles belonging to the newly selected genre.

FIGURE 14.4:

Related selects

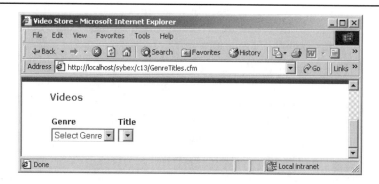

FIGURE 14.4:

Related selects

FIGURE 14.5:

Related selects
displaying values in
a second box

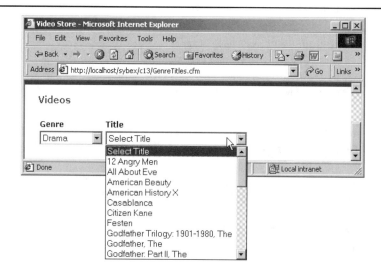

There are several key elements to the related-select process:

- A JavaScript array for each element in the parent select box.
- A parent select box with an onChange() event handler.
- A child select box.
- A JavaScript function that is called by the parent select box's onChange() event handler; this function will populate the child select box.

In the video store application, the database comprises six genres, so the page needs six JavaScript arrays, one that holds the movie titles for each genre. The following code snippet is the JavaScript code used to create the array for the Drama genre (the second element in the Genre select box) and populate it with movie titles:

```
// Create the array
GenreArray2 = new Array();

// Populate the array
GenreArray2[1] = "12 Angry Men";
GenreArray2[2] = "All About Eve";
GenreArray2[3] = "American Beauty";
GenreArray2[4] = "American History X";
GenreArray2[5] = "Casablanca";
GenreArray2[6] = "Citizen Kane";
GenreArray2[7] = "Festen";
GenreArray2[8] = "Godfather Trilogy: 1901-1980, The";
GenreArray2[9] = "Godfather, The";
GenreArray2[10] = "Godfather: Part II, The";
GenreArray2[11] = "Goodfellas";
GenreArray2[12] = "It's a Wonderful Life";
GenreArray2[13] = "L.A. Confidential";
```

You'll notice that this code is awfully repetitive. Because the data we want to display is stored in a database and the JavaScript code created is repeated for each element, it is very easy to generate it using ColdFusion. Listing 14.2 presents the code used to create the related select boxes.

Listing 14.2   Related Select Boxes (c1402.cfm)

```
<!---
    Name:          /c14/c1402.cfm
    Description:   Created select boxes that are related
                   to each other.
--->
<!--- Select the genres and titles codes. --->
<cfquery name="GetGenreTitles" datasource="SybexAccess">
select G.GenreID, G.Genre, T.TitleID, T.Title
from Genre_Ref G, Title T
where G.GenreID = T.GenreID
order by G.Genre, T.Title
</cfquery>

<!DOCTYPE HTML PUBLIC "-//W3C//DTD HTML 4.01 Transitional//EN">

<html>
<head>
    <title>c1402.cfm</title>
```

```
    <script language="JavaScript">
<!--
// For each genre, create an array to hold the titles.
// Each genre array will be identified by an index.
<cfset counter = 0>
<cfoutput query = "GetGenreTitles" group = "Genre">
    <cfset counter = counter + 1>
    // Create the array
    GenreArray#counter# = new Array();
    <cfset i = 0>
    // Populate the array
    <cfoutput>
        <cfset i = i + 1>
        GenreArray#counter#[#i#] = "#Title#";
    </cfoutput>
</cfoutput>

// Function to populate the titles for the genre selected
function populateTitles() {
    // Only process the function if the first item is not selected.
    if (document.VideoForm.GenreID.selectedIndex != 0) {
        // Find the selected index for the genre
        var ThisGenre = document.VideoForm.GenreID.selectedIndex;
        // Set the length of the titles drop-down
        //equal to the length of the genre's array.
        document.VideoForm.Title.length =
            eval("GenreArray" + ThisGenre + ".length");
        // Put 'Select Title' as the first option in the title drop-down
        document.VideoForm.Title[0].value = "";
        document.VideoForm.Title[0].text = "Select Title";
        document.VideoForm.Title[0].selected = true;
        // Loop through the genre's array and populate the title drop-down.
        for (i=1; i<eval("GenreArray" + ThisGenre + ".length"); i++) {
            document.VideoForm.Title[i].value =
                eval("GenreArray" + ThisGenre + "[i]");
            document.VideoForm.Title[i].text =
                eval("GenreArray" + ThisGenre + "[i]");
        }
    }
}
//-->
</script>
</head>

<body>

<h1>Videos</h1>

<form name="VideoForm">
<table border="0">
    <tr>
```

```
            <td><b>Genre</b></td>
            <td><b>Title</b></td>
        </tr>
        <tr>
            <td>
                <select name="GenreID" onChange="populateTitles()">
                <option value="0">Select Genre
                <cfoutput query="GetGenreTitles" group="Genre">
                <option value="#GenreID#">#Genre#
                </cfoutput>
                </select>
            </td>
            <td>
                <select name="Title" size="1">
                </select>
            </td>
        </tr>
    </table>
    </form>

</body>
</html>
```

The first thing this page does is query the video rental database for all the genres and their titles. Using a join, one query will pull all the data needed for the form. The JavaScript immediately following the `script` tag will be run when the page loads, since that code is not included within a function. By looping over the output of the query, you can use ColdFusion to create the JavaScript that is sent back to the browser. By examining the following lines closely, you can follow how the JavaScript is being created.

```
<cfset counter = 0>
<cfoutput query = "GetGenreTitles" group = "Genre">
    <cfset counter = counter + 1>
    // Create the array
    GenreArray#counter# = new array();
    <cfset i = 0>
    // Populate the array
    <cfoutput>
        <cfset i = i + 1>
        GenreArray#counter#[#i#] = "#Title#";
    </cfoutput>
</cfoutput>
```

By using the `group` attribute of the `cfoutput` tag, an array will be created for each genre. Inside the nested `cfoutput` tag, an element will be added to that array for each title associated with that genre. After the script is run, a total of six arrays will have been created, each containing all the associated titles as elements.

By using ColdFusion to create the arrays, you can save yourself a lot of typing and you can ensure that the data will be up-to-date because it is pulled from the database each time the page loads.

The populateTitles() function is called when the value of the GenreID select box is changed. This function first makes sure the currently selected value is not the first option, because it has no associated array. If an actual value is selected in the GenreID select box, then populateTitles() sets the number of elements in the Title select box equal to the number of elements in the selected genre's array. It then loops through the array and sets the options in the Title select box equal to each element in the array. When the value of the GenreID select box is changed, the process will repeat.

JavaScript to ColdFusion

From the example in Listing 14.2, you can see that it is very easy to pass ColdFusion values to JavaScript. By using the same techniques you employ to create HTML, you can also create JavaScript. However, it is not quite so easy to pass information in the other direction, from JavaScript to ColdFusion.

Often, developers wish to trigger ColdFusion processing by a JavaScript event handler; for example, they want a database query to be run if a select box value is changed. The goal of putting a cfquery tag inside a JavaScript function is to run the query when the function is called. However, since the ColdFusion code is processed on the server, the query is run on the server and the JavaScript function will be empty when the page loads. JavaScript cannot trigger ColdFusion code on that page to be processed. However, JavaScript can successfully trigger other events, such as the opening of a new window or the processing of a hidden frame in the window. These actions will allow you to process a ColdFusion page, thus processing ColdFusion code.

When you pass JavaScript variables to a ColdFusion page, you can do so using either hidden form fields or URL variables. In the example of related selects in Listing 14.2, the page only lists the titles for each genre. But what if we want to know how many copies are available for each title when that title is selected? By adding an onChange() event to the Title select box, we can open a new window, to which we can pass a value retrieved using JavaScript:

```
<select name="Title" size="1" onChange="getCopies()">
```

The onChange() event handler will call the getCopies() function.

```
// Function to open a new window to return the number of copies of the title.
function getCopies() {
    var ThisTitleNum = document.VideoForm.Title.selectedIndex;
    var ThisTitle = document.VideoForm.Title[ThisTitleNum].value;
    window.open("c1403.cfm?Title=" + escape(ThisTitle), "CopyWindow",
        "height=150, width=300");
}
```

This function retrieves the name of the selected title and opens a new window that will load c1403.cfm. In order for this page to know what title it should be accessing, the title is passed to the page as a URL variable. The JavaScript escape() method is used to ensure that the value is formatted appropriately for a URL. This method is similar to ColdFusion's urlEncoded-Format function.

Listing 14.3 is the code used in c1403.cfm.

Listing 14.3   Displaying Count of Copies (c1403.cfm)

```
<!---
    Name:          /c14/c1403.cfm
    Description:   Pop-up window to display the number
                   of available copies for each window.
--->
<!--- Query the number of copies for the title. --->
<cfquery name="GetCount" datasource="SybexAccess">
select count(C.CopyID) as CopyCount
from Copy C, Title T
where C.TitleID = T.TitleID
and T.Title = '#URL.Title#'
</cfquery>
<!DOCTYPE HTML PUBLIC "-//W3C//DTD HTML 4.01 Transitional//EN">

<html>
<head>
    <title>c1403.cfm</title>
<script language="JavaScript">
function process() {
    window.close();
}
</script>
</head>

<body>

<center>
<cfoutput>
    <br><br>
    <b>There are #GetCount.CopyCount# copie(s) of #URL.Title#.</b><p>
</cfoutput>
<form>
    <input type="button" value="Close" onClick="process()">
</form>
</center>

</body>
</html>
```

c1403.cfm will query the number of copies available for the title, based on the value passed in the URL. For the title *Goodfellas*, you can see that there are three copies in the store (Figure 14.6). Clicking the Close button will close the window.

FIGURE 14.6:

Number of copies

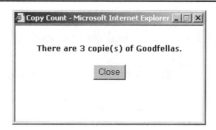

We can take this example a step further and send the number of copies calculated in c1403.cfm back to the originating window. In order to display the number of copies, we'll add another field to the form in Listing 14.2, this time a text box named NumCopies.

```
<input type="text" size="5" name="NumCopies">
```

We then modify c1403.cfm to send the number of copies back to our form.

Instead of having the onClick() event handler of the Close button close the window, it will now call a function called process():

```
<input type="button" value="Close" onClick="process()">
```

The process() function will populate the originating form's NumCopies field and then close the window:

```
<script language="JavaScript">
function process() {
    self.opener.document.VideoForm.NumCopies.value =
        <cfoutput>#GetCount.CopyCount#</cfoutput>;
    window.close();
}
</script>
```

You'll notice that the reference used to access the NumCopies field on the originating form is longer than other references displayed in this chapter. Because the field is not within the current document, the window in which the form field is located must be referenced. Because this window was opened by NumCopies' document, the field can be referenced by adding self .opener. to the beginning of the reference. Once the process() function runs, the NumCopies field in the originating form will contain the number of copies available for the selected title. Figure 14.7 displays the value of the NumCopies field in the form.

FIGURE 14.7:

Number of copies
displayed in the form

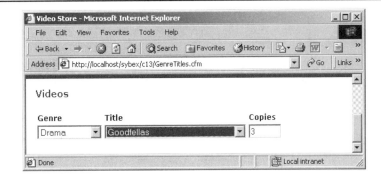

Validating Form Fields

Forms are a major part of almost any dynamic web application. When your application uses forms, however, you need to ensure that the form has been properly completed to avoid errors when the form is processed. You can do this processing on the client using JavaScript or on the server using ColdFusion, but JavaScript validation may be easier for the user. For instance, if the form is not properly filled out, the user will be alerted before the form is processed and the browser will not leave the form, making it much easier to make changes. However, server-side validation is more reliable because it is the only way to ensure that the correct data has been passed. If the user's browser does not support JavaScript or an error occurs, invalid data could be sent to the form's action page. If you use JavaScript validation, it is always preferable to back it up with server-side validation.

Server-Side Validation

To set up server-side validation, you will want to verify that all the required fields are filled in and that any other special validation rules are applied when the form is processed. The code displayed in Listing 14.4 is a very basic form and its server-side validation. To make the handling of errors easier, the form posts to itself. If there are any errors, the form will be refreshed with the error message at the top. The form fields will contain the same values that the user entered. Although this validation isn't as easy for the user as JavaScript validation, it is still a good method to use because the user is returned to the form with the errors displayed and the values they entered still retained in the fields.

Listing 14.4   **Basic Form with Server-Side Validation (c1404.cfm)**

```
<!---
    Name:           /c14/c1404.cfm
    Description:    Displays a basic form and uses server-side
```

```
                        validation to ensure that it was filled out properly.
--->
<!--- Initialize the ErrorMessage variable. --->
<cfset ErrorMessage = "">

<!--- If the form was not submitted, set empty fields  --->
<cfif not IsDefined("form.Submit")>
   <cfset Username = "">
   <cfset BirthDate = "">

<!--- Form was submitted. --->
<cfelse>
   <cfset Username = form.Username>
   <cfset BirthDate = form.BirthDate>

   <!--- Perform validation. --->
   <cfif not len(trim(Username))>
      <cfset ErrorMessage = ErrorMessage &
         "<li>Please enter a username.</li>">
   </cfif>
   <cfif not len(trim(BirthDate)) or not IsDate(BirthDate)>
      <cfset ErrorMessage = ErrorMessage &
         "<li>Please enter a valid birth date.</li>">
   </cfif>

   <!--- If the error message is empty, process and do cflocation. --->
   <cfif not len(trim(ErrorMessage))>

      <!--- Process Form. --->
      <cflocation url="AnotherPage.cfm">

   </cfif>

</cfif>

<!DOCTYPE HTML PUBLIC "-//W3C//DTD HTML 4.01 Transitional//EN">

<html>
<head>
   <title>c1404.cfm</title>
</head>

<body>

<!--- If there is an error message, display it. --->
<cfif len(trim(ErrorMessage))>
   <cfoutput>
      The form contained the following errors:
      <ul>#ErrorMessage#</ul>
   </cfoutput>
</cfif>
```

```
<form action="ServerSide.cfm" method="post">
   <cfoutput>
      Username: <input type="text" name="Username" value="#Username#"><br>
      Birth Date: <input type="text" name="BirthDate" value="#BirthDate#"><br>
   </cfoutput>
   <input type="submit" name="Submit" value="Submit"
</form>

</body>
</html>
```

ColdFusion's Server-Side Form Validation

ColdFusion has had built-in server-side form validation since the beginning. Back in the early days of ColdFusion development (anyone remember version 1.5?), server-side validation was all the rage. We employed hidden form fields, which ColdFusion then used to determine if the form was properly filled in.

A basic form using this method is created in Listing 14.5.

Listing 14.5   **Form Using ColdFusion's Server-Side Validation (c1405.cfm)**

```
<!---
   Name:         /c14/c1405.cfm
   Description:  Creating a form using ColdFusion's
                 server-side validation
--->
<!DOCTYPE HTML PUBLIC "-//W3C//DTD HTML 4.01 Transitional//EN">

<html>
<head>
   <title>c1405.cfm</title>
</head>

<body>

<form action="ServerSideValidate.cfm" method="post">
   <input type="hidden" name="Username_required"
     value="You must enter your username">
   <input type="hidden" name="BirthDate_date"
      value="You must enter a valid date for your birthdate">
   Username: <input type="text" name="Username"><br>
   Birth Date:  <input type="text" name="BirthDate"><br>
   <input type="submit" value="Submit">
</form>

</body>
</html>
```

In order to ensure that the Username is filled in, you create a hidden form field named Username_required. The value is the message that will be displayed for the user if the field is left empty. The _required is a suffix you add to a hidden field name to ensure that the associated field has been filled in by the user. The other suffixes that are used are _integer, _date, _range, _float, _time, and _eurodate. In the form presented in Listing 14.5, the BirthDate field is only validated as a date. To make it required, we would need to create a hidden form field named BirthDate_required. Figure 14.8 shows the results of an incorrectly filled-in form.

FIGURE 14.8:

Results of ColdFusion's server-side validation

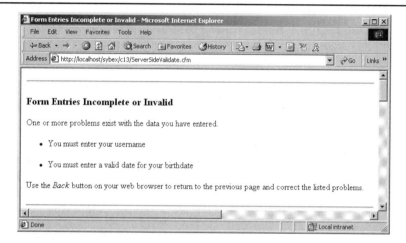

This type of validation isn't used very often, although it is still supported by ColdFusion and is included in the ColdFusion documentation. Even if you don't use ColdFusion's server-side form validation, you still need to know about it and understand how it works. ColdFusion treats all form fields that end with these reserved suffixes as *validation fields*. As such, they are treated differently on the form action page. If you choose to name your form fields using these suffixes—a field called Birth_Date, for instance—you need to be aware of the following rules:

- The form fields ending in validation suffixes are not included in the form.FieldNames variables; instead, a comma-delimited list of all form fields is passed to the action page. (They are, however, still listed in the form scope.)

- Form fields ending in validation suffixes are ignored in the cfinsert and cfupdate tags. Data contained in these fields will not be passed to the database.

- If you use cfparam to set a default value for a form field ending with a validation suffix, the existing value will be overwritten with the value supplied by the cfparam tag, even if the user filled it in on the form.

To make it easier on yourself, try to avoid naming fields using the reserved suffixes. Many developers have spent hours and hours trying to determine why their code isn't working as expected, when the real cause is that one of rules mentioned above has been broken.

Client-Side Validation: JavaScript

In order to save valuable processing time for the user and the server, client-side form field validation using JavaScript is the best way to go. When the user submits the form, JavaScript determines if it is filled in properly. Because the code is already loaded into the browser, this validation occurs immediately. If there is an error on the form, the user is alerted—usually with a JavaScript alert box—and the form is not actually be submitted. If there are no errors, the user probably isn't even aware that the validation took place and the form is submitted as normal.

Figure 14.9 shows the Customer Information form that will be used as the JavaScript validation example. Here, the fields that have labels in bold are required, and the others are not. The JavaScript validation should ensure that the form will not be processed if any of the required fields are left empty. Since the form states that no more than three genres can be selected, an additional validation check will be needed to ensure that this business rule is met.

FIGURE 14.9:

Customer Information form

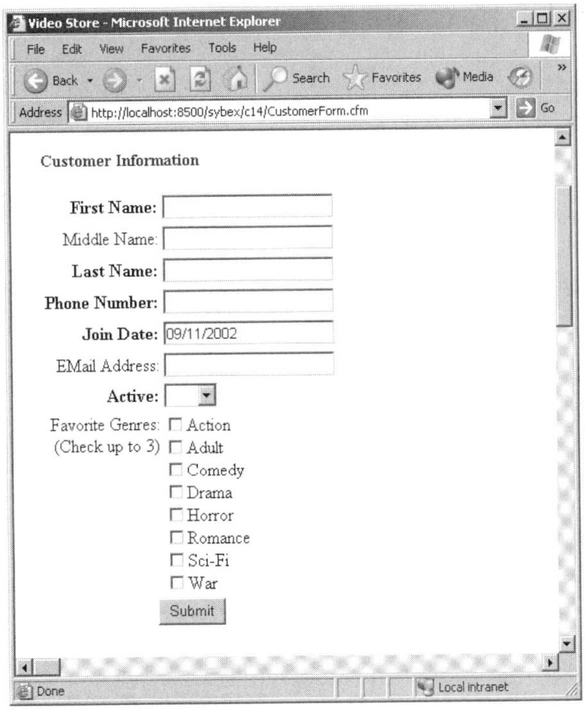

The first step in adding JavaScript processing to a form is to add an onSubmit() event handler to the form tag:

```
<form action = "CustomerForm.cfm" method="post" name="CustomerForm"
    onSubmit="return checkForm()">
```

When the form is submitted, the JavaScript checkForm() function will be run and its result will be returned. If the function returns true, the form will be submitted. If the function returns false, the form will not be submitted and the user will be notified.

Listing 14.6 contains the code used to create the form displayed in Figure 14.9 and the JavaScript used to validate it.

Listing 14.6   Customer Form and JavaScript Validation (c1406.cfm)

```
<!---
    Name:          /c14/c1406.cfm
    Description:   The Customer Information form and the JavaScript
                   code needed to validate it.
--->
<!--- Query all the Genres. --->
<cfquery name="GetGenres" datasource="SybexAccess">
select GenreID, Genre
from Genre_Ref
order by Genre
</cfquery>
<!DOCTYPE HTML PUBLIC "-//W3C//DTD HTML 4.01 Transitional//EN">
<html>
<head>
    <title>c1406.cfm</title>
<script language="JavaScript">
function checkForm() {

    // Check the first name.
    if (!document.CustomerForm.FirstName.value) {
       alert("Please enter a first name.");
       return false;
    }
    // Check the last name.
    if (!document.CustomerForm.LastName.value) {
       alert("Please enter a last name.");
       return false;
    }
    // Check the phone number.
    if (!document.CustomerForm.PhoneNumber.value) {
       alert("Please enter a phone number.");
       return false;
    }
    // Check the join date.
    if (!document.CustomerForm.JoinDate.value) {
```

```
      alert("Please enter a join date.");
      return false;
   }
   // Check isActive.
   if (document.CustomerForm.IsActive.selectedIndex == 0) {
      alert("Please select a status.");
      return false;
   }
   // Check the genres.
   var numChecked = 0;
   for (i=0; i<document.CustomerForm.GenreID.length; i++) {
      if (document.CustomerForm.GenreID[i].checked == true) {
         numChecked++;
      }
   }
   if (numChecked > 3) {
      alert("Please select no more than 3 genres.");
      return false;
   }
   // Return true if everything passed.
   return true;
}
</script>
</head>

<body>

<h1>Customer Information</h1>

<!--- Display the form. --->
<form action = "process_page.cfm" method="post"
   name="CustomerForm" onSubmit="return checkForm()">
  <table border="0">
    <tr>
      <td align="right" class="Required">First Name:</td>
      <td><input type="text" name="FirstName" maxLength="50"></td>
    </tr>
    <tr>
      <td align="right">Middle Name:</td>
      <td><input type="text" name="MiddleName" maxLength="50"></td>
    </tr>
    <tr>
      <td align="right" class="Required">Last Name:</td>
      <td><input type="text" name="LastName" maxLenth="50"></td>
    </tr>
    <tr>
      <td align="right" class="Required">Phone Number:</td>
      <td><input type="text" name="PhoneNumber" maxLenth="50"></td>
    </tr>
    <tr>
      <td align="right" class="Required">Join Date:</td>
```

```
    <td><input type="text" name="JoinDate"
      value="<cfoutput>#DateFormat(now(), "mm/dd/yyyy")#</cfoutput>"
      maxLenth="50"></td>
  </tr>
  <tr>
    <td align="right">EMail Address:</td>
    <td><input type="text" name="EMailAddress" maxLenth="50"></td>
  </tr>
  <tr>
    <td align="right" class="Required">Active:</td>
    <td>
      <select name="IsActive">
        <option value="" selected> 
        <option value="1">Yes
        <option value="0">No
      </select>
    </td>
  </tr>
  <tr>
    <td align="right" valign="top">Favorite Genres:<br>(Check up to 3)</td>
    <td>
      <cfoutput query="GetGenres">
        <input type="check box" name="GenreID"
          value="#GetGenres.GenreID#">#GetGenres.Genre#<br>
      </cfoutput>
    </td>
  </tr>
  <tr>
    <td colspan="2" align="center">
      <input type="submit" name="Submit" value="Submit">
    </td>
  </tr>
</table>

</form>

</body>
</HTML>
```

The JavaScript function in Listing 14.6 uses conditional processing (if-else statements) to determine whether or not each field is properly filled in. The first four conditional statements pertain to the text boxes of FirstName, LastName, PhoneNumber, and JoinDate. The following statement checks to see if the Username field was filled in:

```
if (!document.CustomerForm.FirstName.value)
```

In order to understand what is happening here, let's examine how ColdFusion would perform the same function on the action page once the form is submitted:

```
<cfif not len(trim(form.FirstName))>
```

In ColdFusion, you can determine whether or not a variable has value by wrapping the `len()` and `trim()` functions around it. The `trim()` function will remove all leading and trailing spaces and the `len()` function will return the length of the remaining value. If the value is empty, the `len()` function will return false, otherwise true. By using the `not` keyword, the `cfif` statement will only be met if the form field has no value.

The JavaScript statement works exactly the same way. The conditional statement accesses the value property of the `Username` text box by calling `document.CustomerForm.FirstName`
`.value`. If the form field has no value, `document.CustomerForm.FirstName.value` will return false. Otherwise, it will return its value, which will be translated to true. The bang symbol (!) is the same as using `not` in ColdFusion. If the value of the form field is empty, the condition is met and the code within the conditional statement is processed. If the condition is not met, the user is alerted to their error and false will be returned by the function, thus blocking the submission of the form.

Because the `IsActive` form field is a drop-down select box, its validation is handled differently. When a select object does not have a specified size, the elements are displayed in a drop-down box. By default, the first element is always selected. To ensure that the user actually selects an element, you will want to have the first option contain an empty or blank value. By default, that blank value will be selected. You can then validate that object by determining which option is currently selected, as follows:

```
if (document.CustomerForm.IsActive.selectedIndex == 0) {
    alert("Please select a status.");
    return false;
}
```

As noted earlier in the chapter, JavaScript indexes start with 0; 0 represents the first option in a select object. The `selectedIndex` property of a select object returns the index of the currently selected object. The `if` statement shown here determines whether the `selectedIndex` is 0. If it is, the user has not selected an option and the form submission is halted.

The final test in the script is to ensure that no more than three genres have been checked.

```
// Check the genres.
var numChecked = 0;
for (i=0; i<document.CustomerForm.GenreID.length; i++) {
    if (document.CustomerForm.GenreID[i].checked == true) {
        numChecked++;
    }
}
if (numChecked > 3) {
    alert("Please select no more than 3 genres.");
    return false;
}
```

The first step in the above script is to determine how many genres have been checked. We start out by creating the numSelected variable and assigning it an initial value of 0. By accessing the length property of the GenreID check box group, you can loop through the group. (Because the indexing starts at 0, you want to loop from 0 and end just before the actual length. If there were 8 elements, you would loop from 0 to 7.) For each element, the script accesses the checked property to determine whether or not it has been checked. If so, the numChecked variable is incremented. If after all of the check boxes have been tested, the num-Checked variable is greater than 3, the user is alerted and the form submission is halted.

You may have noticed that a critical validation was missing from the JavaScript code just discussed—the JoinDate form field was tested only to ensure that it was filled in, but not to see if that value actually contained a date. In reality, if there was no server-side validation to test the value on the form's action page, a nasty ODBC error could follow. If you've ever worked with dates in JavaScript, you know that it can be a very painful task. This is because JavaScript lacks many of the elegant date functions we take for granted in ColdFusion. The complexity of that topic is beyond the scope of this chapter. Never fear, however; you can easily ensure the user has entered a valid date by using ColdFusion's cfform tag and its validation scripts.

Integrating Custom JavaScript with cfform

Many ColdFusion developers could not live without cfform, and for a good reason. With cfform, you can include extensive JavaScript validation on your forms without knowing any JavaScript at all. Not only can you verify that text boxes are filled in, you can ensure that the entered value is a date, time, integer, telephone number, social security number, zip code, or other particular value. If the cfform and cfinput tags were used in the validation form in Listing 14.6, the first four validation tests would be able to be eliminated.

If you've used cfform before, however, you know that there are limitations. Basically, cfform cannot ensure that a user has selected a drop-down box value, and it cannot limit the number of check box elements or multi-select elements selected.

NOTE   The cfselect tag does have a required attribute, but it can ensure that an option is selected only if the size is set to at least 2. A drop-down box cannot be automatically validated using cfform.

Because of these limitations, many developers experienced with JavaScript prefer to simply use the form tag and write their own validation scripts. However, this is not only time consuming, it is unnecessary. Customized JavaScript validation functions can be easily called from a form created with the cfform tag.

Consider the following `cfform` tag:

```
<cfform action = "CustomerForm.cfm" method="post" name="CustomerForm">
```

When ColdFusion processes this tag, it sends the HTML form tag back to the browser:

```
<form name="CustomerForm" action="CustomerForm.cfm" method=post
    onSubmit="return _CF_checkCustomerForm(this)">
```

ColdFusion automatically creates the onSubmit() event handler for the form tag and calls the _CF_checkCustomerForm() function that was also generated by ColdFusion. If you view the source of a page created with the cfform tag, you'll see an extensive amount of JavaScript that has also been created.

If you wanted to use cfform to perform some validation, but you also use the checkForm() function to validate the IsActive and GenreID form fields, you would add the onSubmit() event handler to the cfform tag. This was performed on the HTML form tag in Listing 14.6, as shown in these lines:

```
<cfform action = "CustomerForm.cfm" name="CustomerForm"
    onSubmit="return CheckForm()">
```

NOTE   The method attribute is not necessary in cfform because the method will always be set to post.

When this page is returned to the browser, the form tag returned would look like this:

```
<form name="CustomerForm" action="CustomerForm.cfm" method=post
    onSubmit="return _CF_checkCustomerForm(this)">
```

Notice that this is the exact same syntax that was returned using cfform, but it doesn't involve adding the onSubmit() event handler. What happened to that event handler? It is not lost. At the end of the _CF_checkCustomerForm() function that ColdFusion has created, the following line is added:

```
return checkForm()
```

Once all of the cfform validation has been processed and the data has been validated, our checkForm() function will run and validate the remaining fields. Keep in mind that the function will only be processed *after* all the cfform processing has been completed.

By allowing cfform to handle the bulk of the JavaScript validation, the checkForm() function can be reduced to the role shown in Listing 14.7. This shows that by using the validation features provided by cfform, you can greatly reduce the amount of JavaScript code you need to write.

Listing 14.7   **Integrated Custom JavaScript with cfform (1407.cfm)**

```
<!---
    Name:           /c14/c1407.cfm
    Description:    Integrating customized JavaScript with cfform.
--->
<!--- Query all the Genres. --->
<cfquery name="GetGenres" datasource="SybexAccess">
select GenreID, Genre
from Genre_Ref
order by Genre
</cfquery>

<!DOCTYPE HTML PUBLIC "-//W3C//DTD HTML 4.01 Transitional//EN">

<html>
<head>
    <title>c1407.cfm</title>
<script language="JavaScript">
function checkForm() {
    // Check IsActive.
    if (document.CustomerForm.IsActive.selectedIndex == 0) {
        alert("Please select a status.");
        return false;
    }
    // Check the genres.
    var numChecked = 0;
    for (i=0; i<document.CustomerForm.GenreID.length; i++) {
        if (document.CustomerForm.GenreID[i].checked == true) {
            numChecked++;
        }
    }
    if (numChecked > 3) {
        alert("Please select no more than 3 genres.");
        return false;
    }
    // Return true if everything passed.
    return true;
}
</script>
</head>

<body>

<h1>Customer Information</h1>

<!--- Display the form. --->
<cfform action= "process_page.cfm"
    name="CustomerForm" onSubmit="return checkForm()">
    <table border="0">
```

```
<tr>
  <td align="right" class="Required">First Name:</td>
  <td><cfinput type="text" name="FirstName" maxLength="50"
    required="yes" message="Please enter a first name."></td>
</tr>
<tr>
  <td align="right">Middle Name:</td>
  <td><cfinput type="text" name="MiddleName" maxLength="50"></td>
</tr>
<tr>
  <td align="right" class="Required">Last Name:</td>
  <td><cfinput type="text" name="LastName" maxLength="50"
    required="yes" message="Please enter a last name."></td>
</tr>
<tr>
  <td align="right" class="Required">Phone Number:</td>
  <td><cfinput type="text" name="PhoneNumber" maxLength="50"
    required="yes" message="Please enter a phone number."></td>
</tr>
<TR>
  <td align="right" class="Required">Join Date:</td>
  <td><cfinput="text" name="JoinDate"
    value="#DateFormat(Now(), "mm/dd/yyyy")#"
    maxLength="50" validate="date"
    required="yes" message="Please enter a valid join date."></td>
</tr>
<tr>
  <td align="right">E-Mail Address:</td>
  <td><cfinput type="text" name="E-MailAddress" maxLength="50"></td>
</tr>
<tr>
  <td align="right" class="Required">Active:</td>
  <td>
    <select name="IsActive">
      <option value="" selected> 
      <option value="1">Yes
      <option value="0">No
    </select>
  </td>
</tr>
<tr>
  <td align="right" valign="top">Favorite Genres:<br>(Check up to 3)</td>
  <td>
    <cfoutput query="GetGenres">
      <input type="check box" name="GenreID"
        value="#GetGenres.GenreID#">#GetGenres.Genre#<br>
    </cfoutput>
  </td>
</tr>
<tr>
  <td colspan="2" align="center">
```

```
                <input type="submit" name="Submit" value="Submit">
            </td>
        </tr>
    </table>

    </cfform>

    </body>
    </html>
```

Working with Function Libraries

When you create JavaScript validation functions for your forms, you'll be sure to notice one thing: repetition. Over and over again, you will end up creating functions that are exactly the same or only slightly different from functions you've created before. Do yourself a favor: Instead of copying and pasting your functions from one form to another, build a JavaScript library so that you can write your functions once and reuse them as need be.

If you view the source of a page that includes the cfform tag, you'll notice that the function called in the onSubmit() event on the form calls other functions to perform the validation. There is one function to ensure that a text box has value, another to make sure a value is a date, and so on. You can do the same thing. To create your own library, create a page that you can include from any form on your site. When the form loads, your library will be loaded as well. Whenever you determine you need a new validation function, add it to your library and all your forms will have access to it.

In order to be included in a library, functions must be independent of the form and/or field names for which they are being used. You can reference objects dynamically, however, by passing in the name of the form and the name of the field you wish to validate. The following code (taken from Listing 14.6) contains two script tags, one that is written on the page containing the form, and the other from the library being included.

```
<!--- Script written on form page. --->
<script language="JavaScript">
function checkForm() {

    // Check the first name.
    if (!textBoxRequired('CustomerForm', 'FirstName')) {
        alert("Please enter a first name.");
        return false;
    }
    // Return true if everything passed.
    return true;
}
</script>
<!--- Script included from library. --->
```

```
<script language="JavaScript">
// Checks whether a text box is filled in.
function textBoxRequired(FormName, FieldName) {
    var hasValue = eval("document." + FormName + "." + FieldName + ".value");
    return hasValue;
}
</script>
```

For the moment, we are just going to examine validation of the FirstName field on the form. The textBoxRequired() function is one included in the library. It can be used to test whether any text box on any of your forms has value. In order to know which text box it is validating, the function needs to receive two parameters, *FormName* and *FieldName*. The function creates a variable called *hasValue*. The value of the form field is determined dynamically based on the values of the *FormName* and *FieldName* parameters that were passed to the function.

The JavaScript eval() method works much the same way as ColdFusion's evaluate() function. The eval() method will create a string and evaluate the value of that string; in this case, it will return true if the field has length and false if it does not. By returning the value of the hasValue variable, the function returns true if the field was filled in and false if it was not.

In order to call textBoxRequired(), the checkForm() function makes a function call. The following line calls the function and tests its value:

```
if (!textBoxRequired('CustomerForm', 'FirstName'))
```

This code calls the textBoxRequired() function, passing in CustomerForm as the value of the *FormName* parameter and FirstName as the value of the *FieldName* parameter. Because of the bang symbol, the condition is met if the function returns false.

In order to validate multiple fields using the textBoxRequired() function, you would have a separate conditional statement for each field with only the field name and, if desired, a different alert message.

A Sample Library

Listing 14.8 is an example of a JavaScript validation function library.

Listing 14.8   JavaScript Library (c1408.cfm)

```
<!---
    Name:          /c14/c1408.cfm
    Description:   JavaScript library
--->
<script language="JavaScript">

// Function 1
// Checks whether a text box is filled in.
```

```
function textBoxRequired(FormName, FieldName) {
   var hasValue = eval("document." + FormName + "." + FieldName + ".value");
   return hasValue;
}

// Function 2
// Checks whether a drop-down value was selected
// Assumes the first options is blank.
function dropDownRequired(FormName, FieldName) {
   var itemSelected = eval("document." + FormName + "." + FieldName +
      ".selectedIndex");
   if (itemSelected == 0) {
      return false;
   } else {
      return true;
   }
}

// Function 3
// Checks whether the right amount of check boxes were checked in a group
// If FieldMin is not 0, at least one must be checked.
// If FieldMax is 'no', there is no maximum
function checkBoxValidate(FormName, FieldName, FieldMin, FieldMax) {
   var numOptions = eval("document." + FormName + "." + FieldName + ".length");
   var numChecked = 0;
   for (i=0; i<numOptions; i++) {
      if (eval("document." + FormName + "." + FieldName +
         "[" + i + "].checked") == true) {
         numChecked++;
      }
   }
   if (isNaN(FieldMax)) {
      FieldMax = numOptions;
   }
   if (numChecked < FieldMin || numChecked > FieldMax) {
      return false;
   } else {
      return true;
   }
}

// Function 4
// Checks whether the right number of options were selected in a multi-select
// If FieldMin is not 0, at least one must be seleted.
// If FieldMax is 'no', there is no maximum
function multiSelectValidate(FormName, FieldName, FieldMin, FieldMax) {
   var numOptions = eval("document." + FormName + "." + FieldName + ".length");
   var numSelected = 0;
   for (i=0; i<numOptions; i++) {
      if (eval("document." + FormName + "." + FieldName +
         "[" + i + "].selected") == true) {
         numSelected++;
```

```
        }
    }
    if (isNaN(FieldMax)) {
        FieldMax = numOptions;
    }
    if (numSelected < FieldMin || numSelected > FieldMax) {
        return false;
    } else {
        return true;
    }
}

// Function 5
// Checks whether or not a text area was filled in, or is within the
// number of characters. If FieldMin is not 0, there must be a value.
// Set FieldMin to 1 if it is required, but no other minimum length.
// If FieldMax is 'no', there is no maximum.
function textAreaValidate(FormName, FieldName, FieldMin, FieldMax) {
    var fieldLength = eval("document." + FormName + "." +
        FieldName + ".length");
    if (isNaN(FieldMax)) {
        FieldMax = fieldLength;
    }
    if (fieldLength < FieldMin || fieldLength > FieldMax) {
        return false;
    } else {
        return true;
    }
}
</script>
```

This library contains five validation functions. The first one, textBoxRequired(), was explained earlier. The second function, dropDownRequired(), will ensure that an option other than the first one in a drop-down box was selected. The remaining three functions are slightly more complicated but are also much more versatile:

The checkBoxValidate() function   This function is sued to validate a series of check boxes. It takes in two additional parameters, *FieldMin* and *FieldMax*. *FieldMin* will hold the value of the minimum number of boxes that need to be checked; the value will be 0 if the field is optional. *FieldMax* will hold the maximum number of boxes that can be checked. In the case of GenreID on our Customer Information form, that value would be 3. If the value is passed in as no, all of the boxes can be checked if the user so chooses, and as a result, the FieldMax variable is changed to the number of boxes in the check box group. If the number of boxes actually checked does not fall within the desired range, the function will return false.

The multiSelectValiate() function   This function works exactly the same way as the checkBoxValidate() function, except that it validates a select box that has the multiple attribute set.

The `textAreaValidate()` function   This final validation function will validate a text area field. It also takes in the *FieldMin* and *FieldMax* parameters. In addition to testing whether the text area was filled in, it can also check for a minimum or maximum specified length. This function is especially useful if you want to ensure that users don't enter too much data into the text area.

If you are interested in a JavaScript function library but are hesitant to write your own, you'll find a wealth of web resources on this topic. Many sites have libraries you can download and use for free. These sites in themselves are also great examples on which you can base your own code.

NOTE   An excellent JavaScript API that interacts nicely with ColdFusion can be found at PengoWorks.com at `http://www.pengoworks.com/index.cfm?action=qForms`.

DHTML

Dynamic HTML (DHTML) can be a confusing concept in web development. Before the term DHTML became well known, many ColdFusion developers thought that their applications created dynamic HTML. After all, every time a particular ColdFusion page was loaded in a browser, the underlying HTML could be different. There were many variables, ranging from security permissions to user input to search filters, used to determine what code was presented.

This process hardly used Dynamic HTML, however. Even if your application dynamically serves up HTML based on certain variables, the HTML does not change once it is in the browser. The user cannot change the look of the page. Once the page loads, the HTML is static.

With DHTML, the HTML or its presentation can actually change after the page is loaded in the browser. Events, usually trigged by the user, can make objects appear and disappear and cause images and styles to change. By using HTML, JavaScript, and cascading style sheets (CSS), the complexity of user interface design is almost limitless.

Considerations

Before you update all your pages to use the latest and greatest that DHTML has to offer, there are a few considerations to keep in mind.

Browser Compatibility

DHTML relies on the browser to do the work. Since not all browsers are created equally, this can cause some issues for you. Netscape and Internet Explorer each have their own DOM, which means that code that works beautifully in Internet Explorer could bomb out in Netscape and vice versa. Throw AOL's browser and Opera into the mix and you can run into serious incompatibility problems.

Some code, including the JavaScript form field validation discussed in this chapter, is cross-browser compatible and will work in all current browser versions. When you start moving elements around a page, however, things can get a bit hairier. In order to create cross-browser applications, you'll need to provide code that can be processed by both Netscape and Internet Explorer. And after you've created the page, you will need to tell the browser which code to process by determining which browser the user is running.

Browser Test: JavaScript

Since JavaScript interacts with the browser, you can easily test the browser using JavaScript. Listing 14.9 contains an example of a JavaScript browser test.

Listing 14.9   JavaScript Browser Test (c1409.cfm)

```
<!---
    Name:           /c14/c1409.cfm
    Description:    Perform a JavaScript test when the page
                    loads to determine which browser the user is using.
--->
<!DOCTYPE HTML PUBLIC "-//W3C//DTD HTML 4.01 Transitional//EN">

<html>
<head>
    <title>c1409.cfm</title>
<script language = "JavaScript">
<!--

// Test to see if the browser is Netscape or IE
ns = (document.layers)? true:false;
ie = (document.all)? true:false;

// Create pointer variables
function init() {
    if (ns) block = document.blockDiv;
    if (ie) block = blockDiv.style
}

function createDHTML() {

    if (ns) {
        // Netscape JavaScript
    }
    if (ie) {
        // Internet Explorer JavaScript
    }
}
//-->
</script>
</head>
```

```
<body onLoad="init()">

   <!--- code --->

</body>
</html>
```

The init() function, which is called when the document loads, tests whether the browser is Internet Explorer or Netscape. The value of ns will be true if the browser is Netscape and false if it is not. The reverse holds true for the value of ie. Because these variables were declared outside of a function, any JavaScript function on your page will have access to them. The createDHTML() function will only run the code that is appropriate for the browser.

One of the benefits of the JavaScript browser test is that it is quick. However, there are disadvantages as well. If the browser is Internet Explorer, all the JavaScript code required for Netscape is included in the page. If there is a lot of code to test, using the JavaScript test could increase both the size of the page and the amount of time it takes to load into the browser. Also, the user has access to even more of your code by viewing the source.

Browser Test: ColdFusion

By performing the browser test in ColdFusion, you can send the page to the browser with only the necessary code. This will decrease the page loading time. It will also keep the user from seeing all of your code (although, of course, the rest of it would be visible from within another browser).

ColdFusion cannot talk to the browser to find out its identity, but there is another way to determine browser type: using a CGI variable called USER_AGENT that contains the browser information. The following code will output the value of CGI.USER_AGENT:

```
<cfoutput>#cgi.user_agent#</cfoutput>
```

In Internet Explorer 5.5, the code would produce the following results:

```
Mozilla/4.0 (compatible; MSIE 5.5; Windows NT 5.0)
```

Although this is a nice feature, the string returned certainly isn't easy to work with. In order to simplify things, you can use a custom tag called CF_BrowserSimple. This tag takes no parameters and returns two variables, browserName and browserVersion:

```
<CF_BrowserSimple>
<cfoutput>
   Browser: #browserName#<BR>
   Version: #browserVersion#
</cfoutput>
```

This code, when run on Internet Explorer 5.5, will produce the following results. As you can see, the results are much easier to work with and will greatly aid you in returning the correct code to the browser.

```
Browser: MSIE
Version: 5.5
```

NOTE   The CF_BrowserSimple tag, written by Albert Popkov, can be downloaded from Allaire's Developer Exchange at `http://devex.macromedia.com/developer/gallery/`.

When to Use DHTML

It is best to use DHTML when you know your audience. The two most ideal scenarios are when you are dealing with a corporate intranet and you have control over the browsers installed on the employees' computers; or when an application that you are dealing with requires a specific browser. An example of such an application would be online banking provided by a bank. One of the prerequisites for using the application is that the user has the proper browser. Users who want to access the online application will be more than happy to make sure that they have the browser type and version required. On the other hand, if Joe User comes to your site as a casual browser and finds out that he needs to upgrade to view it properly, he'll most likely just leave your site and not come back.

A good way to determine who is visiting your site is to view your web server's logs. If you find out that only five percent of the traffic is using non-DHTML-compliant browsers, this may be enough encouragement for you to forge ahead and alienate that small audience.

When Not to Use DHTML

If your site needs to support a wide range of browsers, DHTML may not be the best choice for you. Many government and other high-security institutions restrict browsers from supporting JavaScript, a key element in DHTML. As a result, pages may not function as expected, severely limiting the user's experience.

Because all of the DHTML code is loaded when the browser loads, page size is another issue. If you know that a large number of your users dial in over a modem, you'll want to keep that in mind when you are creating your pages. Plugging a lot of JavaScript and images into your page can drastically increase the amount of time it takes your page to load.

Image Rollovers

Image rollover is the term used to describe the process of changing the source of an image on an action, usually when a mouse moves over or off of the image in question. This is most often used in site navigation. The images will start out in the Off position. When the mouse is moved over the image, the source will change and another image will appear. When the mouse rolls off the image, the original image will reappear. When a mouse moves over an item, that triggers an `onMouseOver()` event. When the mouse rolls off, it is an `onMouseOut()` event.

Image rollovers are perhaps the most commonly used functions of DHTML. Almost all browsers handle them well using the same code. They have become a very recognized feature of many web sites. To illustrate image rollovers, take a look at the following figures. Figure 14.10 shows what the Video Store navigation looks like when the page loads. In Figure 14.11, you can see how the navigation looks when the mouse is moved over one of the images.

FIGURE 14.10:

Standard page header

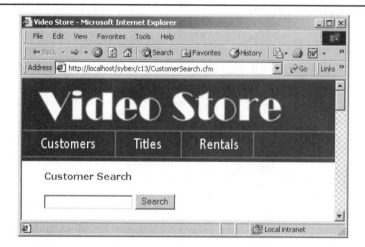

FIGURE 14.11:

Standard page header with an imaged turned on

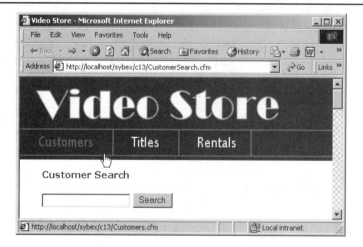

To change the source of your images, you need to display the images in HTML, include the onMouseOver() and onMouseOut() event handlers, and provide the JavaScript to change the source. Here is an example of what this would look like:

```
<script language = "JavaScript">
// function to "Turn on" the image on a mouse over
function showImage(ImageID, ImageName) {
    document["Image" + ImageID].src = "images/" + ImageName;
}
</script>

<table border="0" cellPadding="0" cellSpacing="0">
   <tr>
      <td><a href="Customers.cfm"
         onMouseOver="showImage(1, 'customers_on.gif')"
         onMouseOut="showImage(1, 'customers_off.gif')"><img
         src="images/customers_off.gif" name="Image1"
         border="0"></a></td>
      <td><a href="Titles.cfm"
         onMouseOver="showImage(2, 'titles_on.gif')"
         onMouseOut="showImage(2, 'titles_off.gif')"><img
         src="images/titles_off.gif" name="Image2" border="0"></a></td>
      <td><a href="Rentals.cfm"
         onMouseOver="showImage(3, 'rentals_on.gif')"
         onMouseOut="showImage(3, 'rentals_off.gif')"><img
         src="images/rentals_off.gif" name="Image3"
         border="0"></a></td>
   </tr>
</table>
```

In this example, the images are displayed within a table to help with the placement, each image and link call is in its own table cell, and all the images start out in the Off position. All the Off images end in _off for clarification. Each image also has a name so that JavaScript can change the image source. The onMouseOver() and onMouseOut() events are added to the a tag. The onMouseOver() event calls the showImage() JavaScript function and passes in a value for the *ImageID* and *ImageName* parameters, with the *ImageName* being the name of the On image. The onMouseOut() event calls the same function, but it passes in the Off image.

The JavaScript function showImage() takes the *ImageID* and the *ImageName* parameters. *ImageID* helps tell the function which image to effect, and *ImageName* tells it what image to use as the new source.

The HTML that displays the images and the links can very easily be created using Cold-Fusion. The following code queries the menu items from the database and then creates the table columns using cfoutput:

```
<!--- Query the level 1 items. --->
<cfquery name="GetMenuItems" datasource="SybexAccess">
```

```
select Item, MenuURL, ImageOn, ImageOff
from Menu
where MenuLevel = 1
order byOrderNum
</cfquery>

<table border="0" cellPadding="0" cellSpacing="0">
   <tr>
      <cfoutput query="GetMenuItems">
         <td><a href="#GetMenuItems.MenuURL#"
            onMouseOver="showImage(#GetMenuItems.CurrentRow#,
            '#GetMenuItems.ImageOn#')"
            onMouseOut="showImage(#GetMenuItems.CurrentRow#,
            '#GetMenuItems.ImageOff#')"><img
            src="images/#GetMenuItems.ImageOff#"
            name="Image#GetMenuItems.CurrentRow#"
            border="0"></a></td>
      </cfoutput>
   </tr>
</table>
```

The GetMenuItems query retrieves the level 1 navigation items from the Menu table. Using cfoutput, a table cell is created for each menu item. The GetMenuItems.CurrentRow variable is used to help name the image as the *ImageID* parameter that gets passed to the showImage() function.

Exploring Styles

One of the three main components of DHTML is cascading style sheets. *Cascading style sheets* control the visual presentation of a web page. Style sheets are made up of rules that describe how page elements will be displayed. These rules typically apply to HTML objects, but custom rules can be created as well.

There are two parts to a rule, a selector and a declaration. Consider the following rule:

```
b {
   font weight: bold; color: blue;
}
```

The *selector* specifies to which objects the style will be applied—in this case, the B tag. The *declaration* assigns the style. Style declarations must be within the curly braces and consist of a property and a value. The property and value are separated by a colon and are followed by a semicolon. In the case above, text within the b tag will be bold and blue.

Applying Styles

There are three ways to apply style sheets to an HTML page: by using inline styles, embedded style sheets, or external style sheets.

Inline Styles

Inline styles are added to the HTML tag for each object that will use the style. The `style` attribute of the object is used. For instance, this code will make the text within the b tag bold and blue:

```
<b style="font-weight: bold; color: blue;">Text</b>
```

This method is perhaps the least preferable of the three. One of the most helpful features of a style sheet is that you can use one to control the look of your entire website. In contrast, if you put inline styles in all your HTML objects, you'll have to go through and change them all whenever you want to change the color of your text.

Embedded Style Sheets

A style sheet can be embedded in your document by enclosing the rules within the `style` tag. The `style` tag must be placed within the `head` tag of the document. The following code will embed the styles in your page so that each object that has an associated rule will use the style. In this case, all the text on the page within b tags will be bold and blue.

```
<head>
    <title>Document Title</title>
    <style type="text/css">
        b {
            font-weight: bold; color: blue;
        }
    </style>
</head>
```

The downside of using embedded style sheets is that you must include the code in each document in which you want to implement the styles. Using ColdFusion however, you can simplify this process. You can create a ColdFusion document that contains your `style` tag and the rules within them, and then include that page within the `head` tags of your documents using the `cfinclude` tag. If you are using a standard header throughout your site, you'll only need to include it there.

External Style Sheets

External style sheets are perhaps the most common type of style sheets used on the Web. External style sheets allow you to have all of your styles in one location, without the use of ColdFusion.

The style rules are all placed in a single document with a `.css` extension. To include the styles in a document, add the `link` tag within the document's `head` tags:

```
<head>
    <title>Document Title</title>
    <link rel="stylesheet" href="StyleSheet.css" type="text/css">
</head>
```

Custom Rules

Sometimes you'll want to apply a style to an element that may not be contained within a specific HTML object. Or, you might use the same HTML object on your page several times but want each one to use its own styles. On these occasions, you can create *custom rules*.

Custom rules have a selector that is preceded with a period. To apply that rule, include the class attribute in the HTML object naming the custom rule. Consider this example:

```
.Error {
    color: red;
}

<span class="Error">There has been an error</span>
<b class="Error">There has been an error</b>
```

Here the code contains a custom rule for Error and shows two different examples of applying it. The span tag is used primarily to assign customized style rules to an object, usually text. Because the span tag has no styles of its own, it is an ideal custom style wrapper. In the case of the B tag, adding the class attribute to the tag will apply the Error rule after the B rule has been applied. The end result will be text that is bold and red.

Style Precedence

When an object has several different rules applied to it, the precedence in which the styles are applied can be quite important. Styles cascade down the DOM, and objects that are children of other objects in the hierarchy will inherit their parent's styles unless the child has its own selector. Using the class attribute on an object will override the styles specified by that object's selector. Note, however, that if the object's selector has a declaration for a specific property and the custom rule does not, the style for that property will still show through. That is why the b tag in the example above is bold and red as opposed to just red.

Controlling Styles with ColdFusion

ColdFusion has long been used to create the look and feel of a web application. One of the most basic ways to handle styles is to create variables in the Application.cfm page and utilize them throughout the site. This way you can change colors and fonts in only one place without having to change many lines of code.

```
<!--- Application.cfm --->
<cfset Request.BodyColor = "ffffff">
<cfset Request.FontFace = "Verdana">
<cfset Request.FontSize = "2">

<!--- Page Code. --->
<body bgColor="#<cfoutput>#Request.BodyColor#</cfoutput>">
```

```
<font style="<cfoutput>#Request.FontFace#</cfoutput>"
    size="<cfoutput>#Request.FontSize#</cfoutput>">
    Text
</font>
```

This method can be replaced by having ColdFusion process the style sheets. Normally, this replacement would not be necessary. The very nature of style sheets makes them flexible and easily changed. One reason to have ColdFusion process the style sheets, however, is to allow the styles to change on a user-by-user basis, for example, to create a customized appearance for a particular user who has logged into the site. By creating a form that allows users to select/ enter their style preferences, you can store those values in your database. You can then create session variables to hold those values and insert them into the style sheet.

The following code will query the user's preferences, create session variables to hold the values and insert them into the style sheet:

```
<!--- Application.cfm --->
<cflock scope="Session" type="exclusive" timeout="5">
    <cfparam="Session.Initialized" default="false">
    <cfset Request.SessionInitialized = Session.SessionInitialized>
</cflock>
<cfif not Request.SessionInitialized>
    <!--- Query the styles. --->
    <cfquery name="GetStyles" datasource="#Request.DS#">
    select BackGroundColor, FontSize
    from UserPref
    where UserID = #UserID#
    </cfquery>
    <cflock scope="Session" type="exclusive" timeout="5">
        <cfset Session.BackGroundColor = GetStyles.BackGroundColor>
        <cfset Session.FontSize = GetStyles.FontSize>
        <cfset Session.Initialized = true>
    </cflock>
</cfif>
<cfset Request.SessionBackGroundColor = Session.BackGroundColor>
<cfset Request.SessionFontSize = Session.FontSize>

<!--- ColdFusion pages. --->
<head>
    <title>Document Title</title>
    <cfinclude template="StyleSheet.cfm">
</head>

<!--- StyleSheet.cfm --->
<style type="text/css">
body, p, td, b, i, li, h1, h2, h3, h4, a:link, a:visited: a:hover, a:active {
    font-family: Verdana, Arial, Helvetica, sans-serif;
```

```
      font-size: <cfoutput>#Request.SessionFontSize#</cfoutput>px;
      color: black;
      font-weight: normal;
   }
   body {
      background: <cfoutput>#Request.SessionBackGroundColor#</cfoutput>;
      margin: 0 0 0 0;
   }
   </style>
```

Hiding/Showing Elements

One of the most useful features of DHTML is hiding/showing elements within a document. With the click of a mouse, one element can disappear and another can appear. This is accomplished by changing different styles so that the visibility of particular objects toggles between visible and hidden.

NOTE   The example for this section will be written for use in Internet Explorer. For information on how to write DHTML for Netscape, a good Internet resource is Netscape's DevEdge Online at `http://developer.netscape.com/tech/dynhtml/index.html`.

One application of hiding and showing elements can be to page through the results of a record set. This is typically done using ColdFusion. Each time the page loads, the query is run, returning all results. Using the `startRow` and `maxRow` attributes of the `cfoutput` tag, only the desired number of records are displayed on each page. The user is then presented with links to go back and forth in the record set. Those links would pass the starting row of that page in order for the proper rows to appear. Figure 14.12 displays the titles from the video store with 10 titles displaying per page.

If this technique is used in ColdFusion, the query is usually rerun each time the page is loaded, although the query could be cached to save processing time. Also, each page load requires a trip to the server to process the ColdFusion code. If you use DHTML, you can run the query once and eliminate the need for ColdFusion to process each page.

When the page loads in the browser, a block is created for each "page" of results using the span tag. These blocks are placed on top of each other in the exact same position. The first block is set to be visible and the remaining blocks are hidden. When a particular page number is clicked, that page's block is made visible and all other blocks are hidden. This ensures that only one block is visible at a time. Because the blocks all share the same positioning, the "page-to-page" switching is instantaneous and invisible to the user. Because the page doesn't need to go to the server to process the code, the movement from page to page happens immediately.

FIGURE 14.12:

Displaying partial
record sets

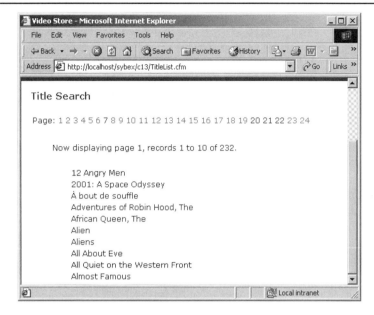

Listing 14.10 displays the code used to hide and show the particular blocks of titles.

Listing 14.10   Displaying Partial Record Sets (c1410.cfm)

```
<!---
    Name:          /c14/c1410.cfm
    Description:   Displaying partial recordsets using DHTML
--->
<!--- Set the defaults for the parameters --->
<cfparam name="startRow" default="1">
<cfparam name="PageNum" default="1">

<!--- Select the titles. --->
<cfquery name="GetTitles" datasource="SybexAccess">
select TitleID, Title
from Title
order by Title
</cfquery>

<!--- Set the number of records to display on each page. --->
<cfset OnEachPage=10>

<!--- Determine how many pages will be displayed. --->
<cfset NumPages=Ceiling(GetTitles.RecordCount / OnEachPage)>
<!DOCTYPE HTML PUBLIC "-//W3C//DTD HTML 4.01 Transitional//EN">
```

```
<html>
<head>
   <title>c1410.cfm</title>
   <style type="text/css">
   .Vis1 {
      visibility: visible;
   }
   .Vis2 {
      visibility: hidden;
   }
   </style>
<script language="JavaScript">
// function to show a page
function showPage(obj) {
   <!--- Loop through the pages to hide the blocks. --->
   <cfloop from="1" to="#NumPages#" index="ThisPage">
      <cfoutput>Page#ThisPage#Div.className="Vis2";</cfoutput>
   </cfloop>
   // Show the block selected
   obj.className="Vis1";
}
</script>
</head>

<body>

<h1>Title Search</h1><p>

<!--- Display the current record count --->
<table border="0">
   <!--- Begin next/previous links. --->
   <!--- The links are just a JavaScript function.  --->
   <!--- The 'ThisPage' variable tells the function --->
   <!--- which block to display. --->
   <tr>
      <td>Page:</td>
      <cfloop from="1" to="#NumPages#" index="ThisPage">
         <cfoutput>
            <cfset PageNumStart=(((ThisPage - 1) * OnEachPage) + 1)>
            <td><a
               href="javascript:ShowPage(Page#ThisPage#Div)">#ThisPage#</a>
               </td>
         </cfoutput>
      </cfloop>
   </tr>
</table><p>
<!--- End next/previous links. --->

<!--- Loop through the number of pages and create a block
   for each 'page'. --->
<cfset startRow=1>
```

```
<cfloop from="1" to="#NumPages#" index="ThisPage">
    <!--- Set the end row of the current block. --->
    <cfset endRow=startRow + onEachPage - 1>
    <cfif endRow gt getTitles.RecordCount>
        <cfset endRow=getTitles.RecordCount>
    </cfif>
    <cfoutput>
        <span id="Page#ThisPage#Div"
            style="position:absolute; left:50px; top:225;"
            class="<cfif ThisPage eq 1>Vis1<cfelse>Vis2</cfif>">
        <!--- Display the current block info. --->
        Now displaying page #ThisPage#, records #StartRow# to
            #EndRow# of #GetTitles.RecordCount#.<p>
    </cfoutput>
    <table border="0">
        <!--- Begin results. --->
        <tr>
            <td valign="top"
                colspan="<cfoutput>#evaluate(NumPages + 2)#</cfoutput>">
                <table border="0">
                    <cfoutput query="getTitles"
                        startRow="#startRow#" maxRows="#onEachPage#">
                    <tr>
                        <td>     </td>
                        <td>#Title#</td>
                    </tr>
                    </cfoutput>
                </table>
            </td>
        </tr>
        <!--- End results. --->
    </table>
    </span>
    <cfset startRow=startRow + onEachPage>
</cfloop>

</body>
</html>
```

Much of the code used in Listing 14.10 is the same as what would be used in ColdFusion to paginate through a result set. In this case, however, each "page" of result sets is created in the document; they are just not all visible.

By looping over the number of pages needed to display the result set, we create a span object for each page. As you can see, the positioning of all of these blocks is the same. Each block is uniquely named based on the page number. Within each block, the startRow and maxRows attributes of the cfoutput tag are used to display the appropriate titles on each page.

Above the page blocks are the numbers of all of the possible pages. These numbers are hyperlinks; clicking the number will make the appropriate page's block appear while it hides all the other blocks. This action is accomplished by calling the showPage() function and passing in the name of the block to make it visible. The showPage() functions sets the class of all of the blocks to Vis2 to hide them. The block passed into the function then has its class changed to Vis1, making it the only block visible.

NOTE   This code and logic can be applied to many other tasks, such as creating multipart form wizards and collapsible menus. The code for such tasks can be complex, but you can get help from many resources on the Web that not only provide extensive JavaScript tutorials, but include the code for free download and use. An excellent one is at http://www.javascript.com. This site offers great tutorials as well as links to many other resource sites.

In Sum

In this chapter, you've learned quite a bit about JavaScript and DHTML and how to integrate them with ColdFusion. Certainly, there is still a lot to learn on the subject, but you should now have a good understanding of how the client and server components interact, and this knowledge should allow you to create rich user interfaces for visitors to your sites while allowing you to employ some of the best features of DHTML and ColdFusion.

CHAPTER 15

Working with WAP and WML Clients

By Arman Danesh

- What is WAP/WML?

- WML browser emulators for the PC

- WML basics

- Using WML from ColdFusion

An emerging trend is the area of wireless-enabled websites and content that can be delivered directly to handheld devices. These devices include mobile phones and personal digital assistants (PDAs) that use existing wide-area digital networks such as the PCS networks that is commonplace in most urban centers. Using a combination of the Wireless Application Protocol (WAP) and the Wireless Markup Language (WML), it is possible to build interactive applications for this wireless space. You can build applications specific to the wireless space or extend your existing HTML applications by adding WML support to them.

The complete dynamic power of ColdFusion can be leveraged in building these applications. This chapter provides a brief introduction to WAP and functions as a short introductory tutorial on the basics of WML. It also addresses some fundamental issues you need to be aware of when you are developing WML applications using the ColdFusion environment.

What Is WAP/WML?

WAP and WML together form a platform for the delivery of interactive web and web-like content for wireless devices. The entire wave of mobile phone providers that offer wireless web services today are using the combination of WAP and WML to make this possible.

WAP is a collection of protocols designed to deliver content to wireless devices just as HTTP delivers web pages to web browsers. WML is used to specify the structure of the content sent to wireless devices just as HTML defines the structure of the web content sent to web browsers.

How do they fit together? WAP is a collection of protocols designed for delivering content for mobile devices. This content is usually represented using WML. WAP is designed to accommodate several unique proprieties of wide area wireless networks, including:

- Limited processing power and memory on handheld devices
- Limited display size on handheld devices
- Limited bandwidth on wide area wireless networks
- Lack of a consistent stable connection on wide are wireless networks
- Limited data input modalities on handheld devices
- Diverse types of wireless networks
- Diverse operating systems in mobile devices

WAP has become the default standard protocol suite for these purposes, and the vast majority of hardware manufacturers and service providers have committed to WAP for their wireless web offerings. WAP ensures that devices from most hardware vendors will work with the services offered by any service or content provider in the wireless web space.

WML, on the other hand, is a simple XML-based markup language that is similar to HTML but is focused on producing documents optimized for the microbrowsers found in small hand-held devices on wireless networks. WML is optimized for producing documents that can be parsed and rendered in a small memory footprint on these small displays and using minimal bandwidth.

A typical page created in WML and rendered on a WML browser is illustrated in Figure 15.1.

FIGURE 15.1:

A WML document

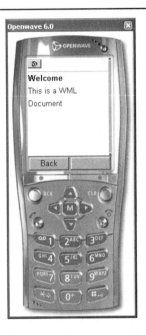

Now take a look at Figure 15.2, which illustrates the relationship between WAP/WML, HTTP, and web servers. Architecturally, it is not possible to directly deliver content from today's web servers to handheld devices. Not only are most web application servers incapable of delivering WML content, they also cannot speak WAP directly on wireless networks. Instead, content is sent through gateway devices that are responsible for bridging requests and responses between the WAP and HTTP networks and, in some cases, translating HTML to WML—although many web servers will directly generate WML to be sent via the gateway to the client device. (WAP gateways are discussed in a later section.)

FIGURE 15.2:

The relationship
between wireless
devices, gateways,
and web servers

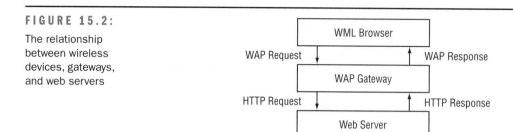

A Typical WAP/ColdFusion Architecture

For the real-world deployment of WAP/WML applications using ColdFusion, you will need an architecture that is slightly more complex than the generic WAP architecture just described (see Figure 15.3 for a typical example). This is because the ColdFusion environment must be considered. The major components of this architecture are WAP gateways, WML browsers, HTTP servers, and application servers.

FIGURE 15.3:

A typical ColdFusion-
based WAP
architecture

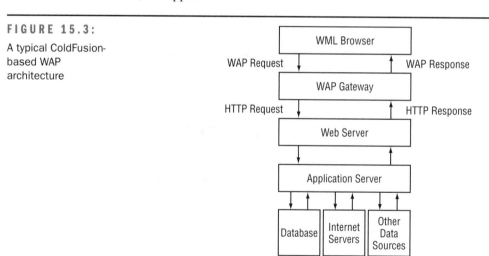

WAP Gateways

WAP gateways play the role of converting requests from WAP to another protocol such as HTTP. Because HTTP is not optimized for mobile devices or wireless networks, it is necessary to use another protocol (WAP) to translate between the two. When a client browser makes a request for a URL, it is sent to a WAP gateway provided by the user's wireless service provider. The gateway converts it into an HTTP request and sends it to the appropriate web server.

When the requested item is returned by HTTP, the item is re-encoded into a WAP transaction and is sent back to the client browser. This separation of WAP and HTTP through the gateway allows you to build WAP/WML-enabled applications using the same platforms you use to build your HTTP/HTML applications—without adding any special support to those servers. The WAP gateways are typically deployed by wireless service providers for their clients.

WML Browsers

These are typically embedded in hardware on the handheld devices. There are numerous WML browsers on the market today that are licensed and used by various hardware makers, and they all support the basic WML standard. Typically, you can develop WML applications and test them using WML browser emulators (discussed in a later section) without having to employ actual handheld devices for early testing. During the final stages of testing you'll want to test performance and functionality through an actual WAP gateway.

HTTP Servers

Your actual WML documents will be served by your standard HTTP server just as HTML documents are. For static WML documents, this will mean creating the appropriate MIME type entries in the server's configurations so that WML documents are associated with the `text/vnd.wap.wml` MIME type. We'll take a closer look at the MIME type in the later section on the WML header.

Aside from ensuring that WML documents have the right MIME type, an HTTP server can serve WML documents as easily as it can HTML documents.

Application Servers

The application server, in this case ColdFusion, can be used to build WML or HTML documents and can access the same array of dynamic external data sources for both. Just as CFML (ColdFusion Markup Language) and HTML co-exist in templates destined for HTML browsers, WML and CFML can co-exist in templates destined for WML browsers.

WML Browser Emulators for the PC

In order to develop WML applications without access to a WML gateway and the mobile hardware that supports WML and WAP, you can test your WML applications using WAP/WML browsers. Following are two such browsers you can try:

- Klondike WAP Browser for Windows at `http://www.apachesoftware.com`
- WinWap at `http://www.winwap.org`

These Windows-based browsers are nice tools because they look and feel like a basic web browser. For instance, take a look at the Klondike WAP Browser for Windows, which is illustrated in Figure 15.4. However, this similarity to web browsers also detracts from their value as development testing tools. To really see what your application will look like on typical mobile devices such as mobile phones, you need an emulator.

FIGURE 15.4:

The Klondike WAP
Browser for Windows

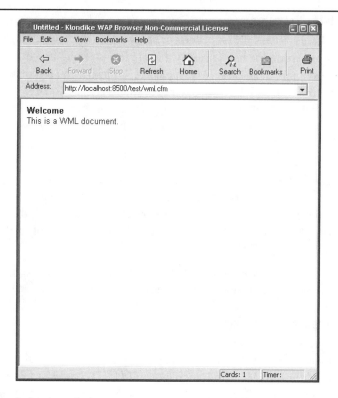

Emulators emulate the behavior of a browser on a specific hardware platform so that you can test your applications against the most common handheld devices on the market. Some emulators require that you also run a WAP server or gateway for access to your WML files; others allow you to browse local files or directly access HTTP servers. There are three principal emulators available today:

Ericsson's WapIDE SDK Browser at `http://www.ericsson.com/developerszone`

Nokia's Mobile Internet Toolkit at `http://www.forum.nokia.com`

OpenWave's SDK at `http://www.openwave.com`

In this chapter, all screen examples use the OpenWave Simulator because it can directly communicate with an HTTP server without the use of an intervening WAP gateway. This allows you to directly test your ColdFusion-based WML applications in the same way that you currently use a web browser to test your ColdFusion-based web applications.

WML Basics

A complete tutorial for WML is beyond the scope of this chapter. Instead, we will provide enough knowledge of WML so that you can generate a WML applications using ColdFusion.

If you want a complete introduction to WML, consider *Getting Started with WAP and WML*, by Huw Evans and Paul Ashworth (Sybex, 2001) or *WAP Development with WML and WMLScript* by Ben Forta, et al., from Sams.

WML provides for text presentation, image delivery, user interaction, and navigation. Now we will take a brief look at the structure of WML documents, the basic syntax of WML tags, and some key WML tags.

WML Document Structure

WML applications are built out of cards collected into decks, where a single WML file is a deck of one or more cards. Navigation occurs between cards. This bundling of multiple cards into a single deck in a file is akin to bundling multiple HTML pages into a single file instead of storing them in separate files. This makes sense in WML because the screen limitations of handheld devices will mean that each card is inherently smaller than the average HTML page. In addition, you will want to minimize traffic between the handheld device and server because of the slow, unstable nature of the wireless networks typically used by handheld devices.

Decks are sent as a single packet (although there is a maximum size to the deck). No matter how many cards are in the deck or how large the deck is within its limits, this single packet takes the same time to transmit. Therefore, loading a deck with the most cards and data possible utilizes the limited bandwidth of wireless networks to its best possible advantage.

A prototypical example of deck utilization is the generation of search results. In HTML this would typically be two-tiered, with a list of results being generated and sent to the user. The user then clicks links to view the details of a result, which are then retrieved from the server.

Consider an example dialog where a user views two items from the results list:

1. The server sends the results list to the browser.

2. The user clicks one result, which generates a request to the server and a response returning to the browser.

3. The user returns to the results list (which is likely cached).

4. The user clicks a second result, which generates a request to the server and a response returning the browser.

The end result is three transactions between the browser and server at a minimum.

In the deck-and-card model of WML, the search results list and the details of each result could each be a card in a single deck sent as a single file to the browser. Then, the user could navigate the search results list and the details of each result without any more transactions with the server.

The basic structure of a WML document looks like the following:

```
<wml>
    <card>
        <p>
            text of the card
        </p>
    </card>
</wml>
```

Note the following important characteristics of the basic document:

- Every WML document starts with an opening <wml> tag and ends with the closing </wml> tag.

- Every WML document contains at least one card, and each card is demarked by the opening <card> and closing </card> tags.

- Text must be enclosed in <p> and </p> tags. You cannot have text hanging alone as many developers do in HTML. The browser will not assume that the tag is a paragraph and will generate an error.

Taking this simple WML document a step further, a deck of multiple cards simply means you have more than one card block in the document:

```
<wml>
    <card id="cardA">
        <p>
            text of the card A
        </p>
    </card>

    <card id="cardB">
        <p>
            text of card B
        </p>
    </card>
```

```
<card id="cardC">
   <p>
      text of card C
   </p>
</card>
</wml>
```

Notice the use of the id parameter of the card tag to distinguish the cards. These identifiers can be used to address a particular card in a URL or link uniquely. If the URL of a card were myserver/mydoc.wml then the second card would be addressed as myserver/mydoc.wml#cardB.

The WML Header

In addition to the basic document structure just described, each WML document must have a header identifying the XML version and WML document definition being used. The header looks like this:

```
<?xml version="1.0" encoding="iso-8859-1"?>
<!DOCTYPE wml PUBLIC "-//WAPFORUM//DTD WML 1.3//EN"
"http://www.wapforum.org/DTD/wml13.dtd" >
```

In this chapter, this header will be omitted from the individual code listings presented. Keep in mind, though, that each WML deck file must start with this header.

WML Syntax Rules

Although WML looks a lot like HTML, WML browsers are not tolerant of inconsistent or loose coding practices. You need to adhere strictly to coding standards in building your WML documents; otherwise, WML browsers will have trouble and generate errors.

Following are some important basic syntax rules:

- When assigning values to tag parameters, you cannot have space around the equal sign. Thus <card id="cardA"> is valid, but <card id = "cardA"> is not.

- Each parameter in a tag must be separated from the preceding parameter and the next parameter by one or more spaces. You cannot have two parameters flush with each other as in "id="cardA"title="This is Card A".

- Take care when nesting tags. Sometimes, HTML browsers will be tolerant of code blocks such as some text. WML browsers, however, do not allow this type of mismatched opening and closing tags in nested code.

- Tags are case sensitive. It is especially important that the case of opening and closing tags match (`<p>`*some text*`</P>` is not legal). As a matter of code coding style, stick to lower case tags.

- Values of tag parameters must be enclosed in quotes. HTML browsers are tolerant of omitted quotes in some cases, but WML browsers do not tolerate this in any case. In other words, you cannot use `<card id=cardA>` instead of `<card id="cardA">`.

Perhaps the most important syntax requirement is that all tags must have closing tags. That means this code is valid:

```
<p>
    some text
</p>
```

but this is not:

```
<p>some text
```

Of course, this raises a question: What happens with tags that are typically not thought of as having closing counterparts? One tag that appears in both HTML and WML is the `br` tag for a line break. In WML, you must close this tag even though no text appears between the opening and closing tags:

```
<p>
    some text
    <br></br>
    more text
</p>
```

There is a short form available for use when you don't have any text between the opening and closing tags: Simply include a forward slash at the end of the opening tag, as done in the following:

```
<p>
    some text
    <br />
    more text
</p>
```

NOTE   If you know XML, the `<br />` tag will be familiar to you. WML is an XML-based language and, like all XML, this is the way you close a tag that stands alone.

Card Navigation in WML

Navigation in WML is similar to navigation in HTML. The most basic form of navigation involves the use of URLs. For instance, you can navigate to the URL `http://www.juxta.com/`, in which case the WAP gateway will be instructed to retrieve whatever document is at the specified URL, using HTTP.

You can also use URLs to access new documents or individual cards within the current or other documents. To specify a specific card in a WML document, designate a URL such as `http://myserver/mydoc.wml#mycard` where `mycard` is the identifier of the desired card.

To create links for navigation purposes, you have two mechanisms:

- The HTML-style a tag
- The anchor tag block

Linking with the a Tag

You can use the a tag for linking just as you would in HTML. You can link to an external document or to another card within the current WML deck. Here are your choices:

- To link to an external document, use the document's URL.
- To link to a specific card in an external document, include the card in the URL after the # symbol.
- To link to a specific card in the current document, use a tag of the form `<a href="#cardname">`.

Let's consider a simple example: you have a deck with three cards. The first card contains a menu of the other two cards as shown in Listing 15.1.

Listing 15.1   A Deck with Three Cards (1501.wml)

```
<!---
    Name:          /c15/1501.wml
    Description:   A deck with three cards
--->
<wml>
    <card id="menu">
        <p>
            <b>Main Menu</b>
            <br />
            <a href="#cardA">Card A</a>
            <br />
            <a href="#cardB">Card B</a>
        </p>
    </card>

    <card id="cardA">
        <p>
            This is Card A
        </p>
    </card>

    <card id="cardB">
        <p>
            This is Card B
```

```
          </p>
        </card>
      </wml>
```

The end result is a menu similar to that on the left in Figure 15.5, which can link to the other two cards (Card B is illustrated on the right in Figure 15.5).

FIGURE 15.5:

Linking to another card in the current deck

Linking with the anchor Tag

The anchor tag allows you to indicate the text that will appear as a link without providing a mechanism to directly indicate the target URL of the link. In its basic form, the anchor tag looks like this:

```
<anchor>
    link text
</anchor>
```

However, this doesn't tell the browser where to go when the link is selected by the user. You provide this information by placing one of several possible tags within the anchor block. The tag we are interested in is the go tag, which is used to specify a URL for the link:

```
<anchor>
    link text
    <go href="url" />
</anchor>
```

You may be wondering, "Why should I use <anchor> instead of <a>?" With the anchor tag, you are not actually specifying a simple URL link as you are with the a tag; instead, you are specifying a task. In the preceding example, the go tag is the task; but there are other tasks, including the following:

<prev />   Returns to the previous document in the history list when the link is selected

<refresh />   Refreshes the current document

Linking with Access Keys

With both the a and anchor methods of linking, you can specify a keypad key which can be used to activate the link. The keypad keys you can specify are the 10 keys on the numeric keypad plus the # and * keys. You do this with the accessKey parameter for both tags.

In the earlier example with three cards, where the first is a simple menu of links to the other two cards, you could add access keys to the menu as shown in Listing 15.2.

Listing 15.2   A Deck with Three Cards and Access Keys (1502.wml)

```
<!---
    Name:          /c15/1502.wml
    Description:   Using access keys
--->
<wml>
    <card id="menu">
        <p>
            <b>Main Menu</b>
            <br />
            <a href="#cardA" accessKey="1">Card A</a>
            <br />
            <a href="#cardB" accessKey="2">Card B</a>
        </p>
    </card>

    <card id="cardA">
        <p>
            This is Card A
        </p>
    </card>

    <card id="cardB">
        <p>
            This is Card B
        </p>
    </card>
</wml>
```

Not all browsers will display the relevant numeric shortcut for the user, so it is probably a good idea to add your own numeric shortcut indicators, as shown in Listing 15.3. The results look like Figure 15.6.

Listing 15.3   **Displaying Numeric Key Shortcut Indicators (1503.wml)**

```
<!---
    Name:          /c15/1503.wml
    Description:    Using Numeric Key Shortcuts
--->
<wml>
    <card id="menu">
        <p>
            <b>Main Menu</b>
            <br />
            <a href="#cardA" accessKey="1">Card A [Press 1]</a>
            <br />
            <a href="#cardB" accessKey="2">Card B [Press 2]</a>
        </p>
    </card>

    <card id="cardA">
        <p>
            This is Card A
        </p>
    </card>

    <card id="cardB">
        <p>
            This is Card B
        </p>
    </card>
</wml>
```

Intolerance for Coding Errors

Remember one very important point when developing WML applications: WML browsers are extremely intolerant of errors in your code. There are several reasons for this, but the most significant are listed here:

Strict code standards   By adhering to strict code standards, browsers ensure compatibility with the code they will encounter—even if the developer tested it on another device or browser emulator.

Small memory footprints   Because of the small memory footprint and processing limitations of handheld devices, WML browsers cannot be designed to handle numerous exception cases as is done with most HTML browsers. Instead, the approach taken is just to throw an error when code doesn't match the WML standard exactly.

For these reasons, you need to be extremely careful to make sure that your code is error free. In HTML, you often can assume the browser applies lax code parsing so that you can get away with loose coding techniques. You can't do this with WML. With WML you need to be disciplined and write clean code.

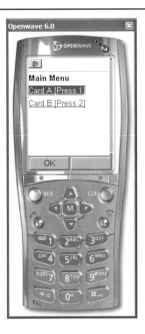

FIGURE 15.6:

Specifying access keys for links

Passing URL Attributes Using &

Like HTML URLs, WML URLs can pass variables at the end of the URL, using the following form

```
http://some.server/somedoc.wml?var1=value1&var2=value2&...
```

However, an anomaly in some WML browsers may cause them to create errors when they render pages with this type of WML. The error is caused at the ampersand in the query string at the end of the URL. In the case of the OpenWave emulator, the error appears as illustrated in Figure 15.7.

Ampersands in URLs
can cause rendering
errors in some
browsers.

This can be resolved by coding such URLs using & rather than simply an ampersand,
like this:

```
http://some.server/somedoc.wml?var1=value1&amp;var2=value2&amp;...
```

This causes the browser to render an ampersand as part of the URL. The desired URL is
made accessible without generating any rendering errors when the page is displayed.

Accessing Variables in WML Using the $

WML allows you to create and reference variables in your cards and decks. A variable is global
to a deck and can be accessed anywhere in the deck. You use the setvar tag to create a variable.
The following tag

```
<setvar name="myvar" value="Foo">
```

creates a variable named myvar and assigns the value Foo to it. The actual value of the myvar
variable can then be accessed with $(myvar) as shown in Listing 15.4.

Listing 15.4   **Creating and Using Variables (1504.wml)**

```
<!---
    Name:          /c15/1504.wml
    Description:    Using Variables in WML
--->
```

```
<wml>
   <card id="setvalue">
      <setvar name="myvar" value="Foo">
      <p>
         The myvar variable has been set.
         <br />
         <a href="#showvalue">See the variable</A>
      </p>
   </card>

   <card id="showvalue">
      <p>
         The value of myvar is: $(myvar).
      </p>
   </card>
</wml>
```

Variables can also be used to access the values entered in WML forms, as outlined later in the section "Working with WML Forms."

Using WML from ColdFusion

Now that you have a broad sense of WML and the way WML documents are built, we will consider some basic issues related to building WML documents using ColdFusion.

Just as you build HTML content for web browsers with ColdFusion, there is nothing to prevent you from building WML content for WAP-enabled devices. Just like HTML content, this WML content can ultimately be generated based on database queries, POP3 mailboxes, and any other dynamic content normally used within your ColdFusion applications.

The only difference is that you would build WML code with your ColdFusion template instead of HTML code. For instance, consider the simple ColdFusion template in Listing 15.5.

Listing 15.5   **Generating Dynamic WML with ColdFusion (1505.cfm)**

```
<!---
   Name:         /c15/1505.cfm
   Description:  Generating Dynamic WML
--->
<cfcontent type="text/vnd.wap.wml">
<wml>
   <card>
      <p>
         <cfoutput>
            Today is #Year(Now())#-#Month(Now())#-#Day(Now())#
         </cfoutput>
      </p>
   </card>
</wml>
```

This template generates a dynamic WML document with the current date that would ultimately look like the one in Figure 15.8.

The process of working with WML from ColdFusion does have some unique aspects of which you need to be aware. These are addressed in this section.

Setting the Content Type with cfcontent

In the ColdFusion-based WML document above (Listing 15.5), notice the first line:

```
<cfcontent type="text/vnd.wap.wml">
```

This tag is used to set the MIME type of the outgoing document generated by WML. By default, the ColdFusion document goes out with a MIME type that the browser will treat as HTML. But the WML browser needs the appropriate WML MIME type, which is text/vnd.wap.wml.

This means that the complete header, which needs to appear in every WML document generated by ColdFusion, should look like the following:

```
<cfcontent type="text/vnd.wap.wml">
<?xml version="1.0" encoding="iso-8859-1"?>
<!DOCTYPE wml PUBLIC "-//WAPFORUM//DTD WML 1.3//EN"
"http://www.wapforum.org/DTD/wml13.dtd" >
```

Determining the Browser Type with cgi.http_accept

As you build applications in ColdFusion, it may be useful to determine whether the browser is a WML browser or simply a standard web browser. Specifically, you'll want to do this when you are using ColdFusion to build a single application that delivers content to both HTML and WML browsers. In this case, you will want to determine what type of browser is requesting a document so that you can send the correct version. Sending an HTML document to a WML browser will generate errors; and if you sent a WML document to an HTML browser, the browser would just ignore most of the tags.

The simple approach is to check to see if the browser is a WML browser, and if it isn't, assume that it is an HTML browser. This can be done with the cgi.http_accept variable that is generated with each query from the browser client. The variable indicates the type of content it accepts by indicating the MIME types. So, if a browser indicates vnd.wap.wml in the cgi.http_accept variable of a request, we can assume that the browser is a WML browser.

The test for this is fairly simple:

```
<cfif cgi.http_accept contains "vnd.wap.wml">
    take action for a WML browser
<cfelse>
    take action for an HTML browser
</cfif>
```

Shortcomings of cgi.http_accept

The cgi.http_accept approach to determining whether a browser is an HTML browser or a WML browser has limitations. Up until this time, the technique has been widely used because it is effective. However, it has remained effective only while no browsers supported *both* WML and HTML. Such browsers are emerging today, which means that cgi.http_accept will indicate both MIME types.

Consider the case of the Opera browser, which now supports WML and HTML. Of course, because Opera is a full-scale HTML browser, you wouldn't want to send it a WML document when an HTML one is available. However, our earlier code segment that tested for a WML browser will do exactly this. Similarly, if a mobile device browser supports basic HTML for when WML documents are unavailable, you wouldn't want to send an HTML document when a WML is available, since WML documents are optimized for the wireless handheld environment.

To get an absolutely accurate sense of what kind of browser is requesting a document, you could use cgi.user_agent—but then you need to maintain a list of all possible browsers, their user agent signature, and the particular document type you want to send to each browser. This will be cumbersome and hard to maintain as new browsers and browser versions are released. For this reason, most applications still use cgi.http_accept to decide if WML should be sent to the browser, or if HTML is more appropriate.

Working with WML Forms

So far, all the WML documents we have seen are static and involve no significant interactivity with users. Just as in the HTML world, real interactivity with users begins when you start to leverage forms. Forms allow users to send data of their choosing to your applications, and the application must be ready to process it and send some data back in response. WML provides a forms mechanism, as well, which you can use in conjunction with ColdFusion to develop interaction in your WML applications.

A simple WML form involves one or more text fields entered by the user and then submitted to the server. To build this type of form, you need two items: the text fields, and the code that handles the form submission. In WML, form elements such as text fields appear in the normal p tag blocks. There are no specialized form blocks.

So, the WML document in Listing 15.6 produces a form with two text fields (one for a person's name and another for a phone number).

Listing 15.6   **A WML Form with Multiple Text Fields (1506.cfm)**

```
<!---
    Name:          /c15/1506.cfm
    Description:   Multiple text fields in forms
--->
<wml>
    <card>
        <p>
            Enter Your Name:
            <input name="username" type="text" />
            Enter Your Phone Number:
            <input name="phone" type="phonenum"/>
        </p>
    </card>
</wml>
```

NOTE   The type attribute of the input tag requires some explanation. Depending on the input method available on the device used to access the WML form, the type attribute helps indicate what type of data will be entered in the field. On a phone, this helps distinguish whether the number keys should cycle through letters or just display numbers. Possible values of type are text, phonenum, or password.

Listing 15.6 actually produces a two-step dialog with the user in which they are first prompted for their name and then for their phone number. On some devices, a simple form is displayed for the user to fill in, as shown in Figure 15.9.

FIGURE 15.9:

A simple form

Once the user completes the entry of data, the form is submitted. Our example so far, however, does not have an indication of where or how to submit the form. This is achieved by adding a do block to the card. You have two choices here: Move on to another card in the same deck when the form is submitted by the user, or send the form input to another WML file altogether.

Let's start with the single deck. For instance, if we wanted to simply display the data entered by the user, we could create a second card for display purposes and use the do block to redirect the user there. This is shown in Listing 15.7.

Listing 15.7   Using do (1507.cfm)

```
<!---
    Name:          /c15/1507.cfm
    Description:   Using the <do> tag
--->
<wml>
    <card id="getData">
        <do type="accept" label="GO">
            <go href="#showData" />
        </do>
        <p>
            Enter Your Name:
            <input name="username" type="text" />
            Enter Your Phone Number:
```

```
            <input name="phone" type="phonenum" />
        </p>
    </card>

    <card id="showData">
        <p>
            Hi $(username), your phone number is $(phone).
        </p>
    </card>
</wml>
```

This deck is simple to understand. First, the `getData` card is displayed and the user enters the appropriate data. When they are done, they select the GO link as illustrated on the left in Figure 15.10. When they select the GO link, the user is redirected to the `showData` card. The `showdata` card uses WML variables to display the contents of the two form fields in its text, as illustrated on the right in Figure 15.10.

FIGURE 15.10:
A GO link is on the left; on the right, data is displayed from a form field.

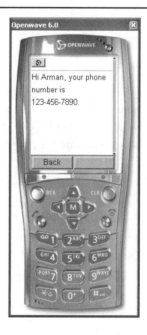

This technique can be taken a step further. When you simply redirect to another card, you can do only a limited amount of serious processing of user input data. However, by submitting the form data to another WML document, you can process the data on the server. If the WML document accepting the form submission is actually a ColdFusion template, you can process the submission and generate a dynamic response to the user.

To submit to a document, our form template becomes something similar to Listing 15.8.

Listing 15.8   Submitting to Another Document (1508.cfm)

```
<!---
    Name:            /c15/1508.cfm
    Description:     Submitting to another document
--->
<wml>
    <card id="getdata">
        <do type="accept" label="GO">
            <go href="http://some.server/processform.cfm" method="post">
                <postfield name="username" value="$(username)" />
                <postfield name="phone" value="$(phone)" />
            </go>
        </do>
        <p>
            Enter Your Name:
            <input name="username" type="text" />
            Enter Your Phone Number:
            <input name="phone" type="phoneNum" />
        </p>
    </card>
</wml>
```

We have made the following changes in Listing 15.8:

- The showdata card has been removed.

- The go tag has been altered to submit the data to processform.cfm, by means of a POST request instead of the default GET request that is normally done with the go tag.

- Two postfield tags have been added to the go block, which assign a value to a name for submission by the POST method. Notice that the postfield tags are the actual fields being submitted. The input fields are not; instead, their values are assigned to the postfield fields using WML variable references of the form $(username).

The result is that these form fields become accessible in our processform.cfm template, just as they would be if they had been submitted from an HTML form as Form.username and Form.phone. For instance, in Listing 15.9, the form would determine a user's city and display that based on the area code of the phone number (for three main Canadian cities). The result is that ColdFusion processes the form input and outputs the user's city and area code based on that input as illustrated in Figure 15.11.

Listing 15.9   Processing Form Input and Displaying the Results (1509.cfm)

```
<!---
    Name:            /c15/1509.cfm
    Description:     Processing form input with ColdFusion
--->
```

```
<wml>
  <card>
    <p>
      <cfoutput>
        <cfset city="Toronto">
        <cfif left(Form.phone,3) is not "416">
          <cfset city="nowhere">
        </cfif>
        <cfif left(Form.phone,3) is "604">
          <cfset city="Vancouver">
        </cfif>
        <cfif left(Form.phone,3) is "514">
          <cfset city="Montreal">
        </cfif>
        Hello, #form.username# from #city#.
        Your area code is #left(Form.phone,3)#.
      </cfoutput>
    </p>
  </card>
</wml>
```

FIGURE 15.11:

Processing form input with ColdFusion

You can use form input from WML in the same way you would from an HTML form, as the basis for

- inserting data into or querying a database
- dynamically building a new form for the user
- dynamic actions such as generating e-mails

Using Selection Lists

Just like their HTML counterparts, WML forms can include selection lists. These use `select` and `option` in a manner that should be familiar to HTML developers. For instance, Listing 15.10 presents a simple selection list to the user and then displays the chosen item when the user finishes. The result is a selection list like the one in Figure 15.12 on the first card.

Listing 15.10   **Selection Lists in WML (1510.cfm)**

```
<!---
    Name:           /c15/1510.cfm
    Description:    Using WML Selection Lists
--->
<wml>
    <card id="getData">
        <do type="accept" label="GO">
            <go href="#showData" />
        </do>
        <p>
            Select Your Area Code:
            <select name="phone">
                <option value="Vancouver">604</option>
                <option value="Toronto">416</option>
                <option value="Montreal">514</option>
            </select>
        </p>
    </card>

    <card id="showData">[showData]
        <p>
            You have selected the $(phone) area code.
        </p>
    </card>
</wml>
```

These selection lists can also allow for multiple selections with the `multiple="true"` parameter, as shown in Listing 15.11.

FIGURE 15.12:

Presenting a
selection list

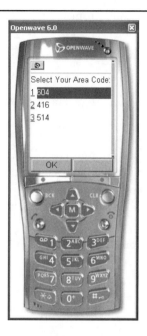

Listing 15.11   Multiple Selections in a Selection List (1511.cfm)

```
<!---
   Name:          /c15/1511.cfm
   Description:   Allowing multiple selections in WML
--->
<wml>
   <card id="getData">
      <do type="accept" label="GO">
         <go href="processform.cfm">
            <postfield name="phone" value="$(phone)">
         </go>
      </do>
      <p>
         Select Your Area Code:
         <select name="phone" multiple="true">
            <option value="Vancouver">604</option>
            <option value="Toronto">416</option>
            <option value="Montreal">514</option>
         </select>
      </p>
   </card>
</wml>
```

In this case, it is important to realize that the list of selections is returned as a semicolon-separated list rather than a comma-separated list as it is by the HTML selection list. This raises the need to account for the semicolon in your form processing code:

- If you plan to treat the value of the form field as a list, you will need to specify the semicolon as a delimiter in your loops or list-related functions.

- If you plan to use the list in an SQL query of the form SELECT ... WHERE ... IN, then you need to first convert the semicolons to commas in the results, as shown here:

```
<cfset newPhoneList = listChangeDelims(form.phone,",",";")>
```

Then you could use newPhoneList in your SQL query.

NOTE   Remember, as well, that if the values in the list received from a selection list in a form are text values, and you want to use them in an SQL query, you need to wrap single quotation marks around each element in the list. You can use listQualify to do this: <cfset newPhoneList = listQualify(newPhoneList,"'",",","ALL")>.

Handling ColdFusion Errors in a WAP/WML-Friendly Manner

When building WML with ColdFusion, take care to handle all ColdFusion errors gracefully. The code generated by ColdFusion for display in the browser is HTML code that is not accepted by WML browsers and will generated browser errors. For instance, here is the daunting typical source code of a ColdFusion error message:

```
</TD></TD></TD></TH></TH></TH></TR></TR></TR></TABLE></TABLE>
</TABLE></A></ABBREV></ACRONYM></ADDRESS></APPLET></AU></B>
</BANNER></BIG></BLINK></BLOCKQUOTE></BQ></CAPTION></CENTER>
</CITE></CODE></COMMENT></DEL></DFN></DIR></DIV></DL></EM></FIG>
</FN></FONT></FORM></FRAME></FRAMESET></H1></H2></H3></H4></H5>
</H6></HEAD></I></INS></KBD></LISTING></MAP></MARQUEE></MENU>
</MULTICOL></NOBR></NOFRAMES></NOSCRIPT></NOTE></OL></P></PARAM>
</PERSON></PLAINTEXT></PRE></Q></S></SAMP></SCRIPT></SELECT>
</SMALL></STRIKE></STRONG></SUB></SUP></TABLE></TD></TEXTAREA>
</TH></TITLE></TR></TT></U></UL></VAR></WBR></XMP><HTML><HEAD>
<TITLE>Error Occurred While Processing Request</TITLE>
</HEAD><BODY><HR><H3>Error Occurred While Processing
Request</H3><P> <TABLE BORDER><TR><TD><H4>Error Diagnostic
Information</H4><P>Just in time compilation error<P> An unknown
attribute '<b>kdjjflkd</b>' has been encountered at document
position (6:12) to (6:19) while processing tag CFINCLUDE. This
tag can only take the following attributes:
<ul><li>TEMPLATE</ul><p>The last successfully parsed CFML
```

```
construct was a CFINCLUDE tag occupying document position (6:1)
to (6:10).<p>The specific sequence of files included or
processed is:<code><br><strong>h:\html\test\wml1.cfm
     </strong></code><P><P>Date/Time:
10/01/01 02:07:16<BR>Browser: Mozilla/4.0 (compatible; MSIE
6.0b; Windows NT 5.1)<BR>Remote Address:
127.0.0.1<P></TD></TR></TABLE><P><HR>
</BODY></HTML>
```

Obviously, you need to take special care to trap and handle ColdFusion errors in your WML templates to avoid sending these error messages to the browser. You can do this with the cferror tag, with which you can display some or all the information available about the error to the user. Or you can mail the error to your system administrator. Alternately, you can use the site-wide error handler configured through the ColdFusion Administrator. This error handler is the catch-all for errors not otherwise explicitly handled by cferror or cfthrow.

To illustrate error handling simply, consider the case of using the cferror tag with type= "Request". This will handle all major errors in your template and allow you to create a special error template that has no ColdFusion code in it. The cferror tag must appear in each template and indicates the type of error to handle in a special way, along with a custom ColdFusion template that should be invoked instead of allowing ColdFusion to simply display the error when it occurs. Accordingly, the cferror tag is usually placed in an Application.cfm file to ensure it is part of every ColdFusion document in your application.

The cferror tag would look like the following, specifying the relative URL to your own error-handling template:

```
<cferror type="Request" template="/errortemplate.cfm">
```

Then, the actual error handling template could look like the following, and the result would be a screen like the one Figure 15.13, when a ColdFusion error occurs in your application.

```
<wml>
    <card>
        <p>
            An error has occurred.
            Contact <cfoutput>a@b.c</cfoutput>
        </p>
    </card>
</wml>
```

FIGURE 15.13:

Handling ColdFusion
errors gracefully

Architecture for a WML/HTML-Capable Site

Typically, you will be generating both WML and HTML from your application in order to provide access to the widest possible audience. Although in some cases you may be using ColdFusion to produce WML-only applications, traditional practice is to extend existing HTML applications by adding WML support to them.

You have already seen how you can use the cgi.http_accept variable to distinguish between WML and HTML browsers. The question remains, what is the best way to architect your site to use this information effectively? There are three main approaches you can consider, as described in the following sections: all-in-one templates, shared directories, and separate directories.

All-in-One Templates

The notion of all-in-one templates is that a single template produces both your HTML and WML code. The advantage is that the same URL applies to all browsers and all users—in theory any user should receive the correct form of a document. For instance, the following is a simple all-in-one template:

```
<cfif cgi.http_accept contains "vnd.wap.wml">
```

```
<cfcontent type="text/vnd.wap.wml">
<?xml version="1.0" encoding="iso-8859-1"?>
<!DOCTYPE wml PUBLIC "-//WAPFORUM//DTD WML 1.3//EN"
"http://www.wapforum.org/DTD/wml13.dtd" >
<wml>
   <card>
      <p>
         Hello World
      </p>
   </card>
</wml>

<cfelse>

<html>
   <body>
      <p>
         Hello World
      </p>
   </body>
</html>

</cfif>
```

The all-in-one template has several limiting disadvantages. In particular, you cannot set up WML-specific error-handling mechanisms because any error-handling mechanism you create will also be sent to the HTML browser. Similarly, if you make mistakes in your templates, HTML code could unintentionally be sent to a WML browser.

Another issue is template editing. When both the HTML and WML code are in a single template, that template can grow quite large and become hard to read and edit.

Shared Directories

Another approach to the site architecture is to have multiple versions of a document in a directory. For instance, suppose you have a URL for an HTML application that is `http://my.server/mydir/index.cfm`. You can switch to the following model:

- `index.cfm`, which is a template to detect the browser type
- `index_wml.cfm`, which is a template for WML browsers
- `index_html.cfm`, which is a template for HTML browsers

Therefore, in our example in the "All-in-One Templates" section, `index_wml.cfm` would be as follows:

```
<cfcontent type="text/vnd.wap.wml">
<?xml version="1.0" encoding="iso-8859-1"?>
```

```
<!DOCTYPE wml PUBLIC "-//WAPFORUM//DTD WML 1.3//EN"
"http://www.wapforum.org/DTD/wml13.dtd" >
<wml>
    <card>
        <p>
            Hello World
        </p>
    </card>
</wml>
```

And, similarly, `index_html.cfm` would be

```
<html>
    <body>
        <p>
            Hello World
        </p>
    </body>
</html>
```

Then, you need to consider how to build `index.cfm`. You have two choices. The first is to redirect the user to the appropriate template with `cflocation`:

```
<cfif cgi.http_accept contains "vnd.wap.wml">
    <cflocation url="index_wml.cfm">
<cfelse>
    <cflocation url="index_html.cfm">
</cfif>
```

This has the advantage of allowing the two templates to contain different error handler `cferror` tags so that you can generate WML-specific and HTML-specific error-handling mechanisms. However, handling form submissions can be difficult, and it would be necessary to build code to re-encode all form variables into URL variables and pass those in the `cflocation` URLs. This can become cumbersome or difficult depending on the complexity of the form data.

Your second alternative for building `index.cfm` is to include the appropriate templates with `cfinclude`:

```
<cfif cgi.http_accept contains "vnd.wap.wml">
    <cfinclude template="index_wml.cfm">
<cfelse>
    <cfinclude template="index_html.cfm">
</cfif>
```

The problem with this method is that it is essentially identical to the all-in-one template approach discussed earlier, where only a single error-handling mechanism is provided for.

In both of these `index.cfm` procedures, code management is made easier because there are separate files for your WML and HTML versions of a page. You don't have to contend with a single large page with both versions of the document.

Separate Directories

A third approach is to create separate directories for your WML and HTML templates. Therefore, the URL `http://my.server/wml/` might be the root of the WML version of your application, and `http://my.server/html/` might be the root of the HTML version of your application. Thus, the WML document `http://my.server/wml/mydocs/index.cfm` corresponds to the WML document `http://my.server/html/mydocs/index.cfm`.

The initial document logic works like this:

1. When a user requests `http://my.server/`, a default `index.cfm` file checks for the browser type and redirects the user to the appropriate directory for their browser:

    ```
    <cfif cgi.http_accept contains "vnd.wap.wml">
        <cflocation url="wml/index.cfm">
    <cfelse>
        <cflocation url="html/index.cfm">
    </cfif>
    ```

2. Once a user is navigating within a directory tree, it is assumed that they are using the same browser and can continue that navigation.

This approach to WML/HTML site architecture has several advantages:

-   The WML and HTML versions of your application are kept distinct and separate. You can drop in a completely new version of one without affecting the other.

-   Each version of the application can use its own error-handling mechanism.

-   Each version of the application can use its own browser-specific `Application.cfm` file. This allows you to place your WML-specific `cfcontent` tag and XML header in the `Application.cfm` file and have it apply to all your WML code.

One issue does need to be addressed, however. What if, for example, a user is browsing the application with a web browser and records a URL from that version of the site and later tries to open it on their WML phone? Then the user will be receiving the HTML version of the site on the WML browser, which violates the intended purpose of this application separation.

You can handle this problem by performing a small check in the `Application.cfm` files for the WML and HTML versions of your application. In the HTML version of your application, you might include the following code in the `Application.cfm` file:

```
<cfif cgi.http_accept contains "vnd.wap.wml">
    <cfset goodUrl = replace(cg.script_name,"/html/","/wml/","one")>
```

```
        <cflocation url="#goodUrl#">
    </cfif>
```

This code segment takes the relative URL of the current template; replaces the /html/ path with /wml/, which creates a URL for the corresponding WML document; and then redirects the user's browser to that location.

A similar check can be used in your WML Application.cfm file:

```
<cfif cgi.http_accept does not contain "vnd.wap.wml">
    <cfset goodUrl = replace(cgi.script_name,"/wml/","/html/","ONE")>")>
    <cflocation url="#goodUrl#">
</cfif>
```

NOTE The emergence of XML and the XSLT transformation model now allows a new approach to the problem of generating different output for HTML and WML browsers: build your documents in XML and then create two different XSLT style sheets that respectively transform the XML to WML or HTML as appropriate. If you are interested in adopting this approach, consider reviewing the coverage of ColdFusion's XML-handling capabilities in *Mastering ColdFusion MX*, by Arman Danesh et al. (Sybex, 2002).

Prudent Use of cfabort

If your ColdFusion logic uses cfabort to terminate processing at a specific point in a template for certain cases, you need to take extra care when doing this in a WML template. It is essential that you properly close all tags in your WML documents.

So, if you are testing a form field as follows in HTML, you can usually get away with the resulting unclosed tags:

```
<html>
    <body>
        <cfif Form.Phone is "">
            <p>Please provide a phone number</p>
            <cfabort>
        </cfif>
        Form processing code
    </body>
</html>
```

But if you use this same logic in WML, you'll end up with this:

```
<wml>
    <card>
        <cfif Form.Phone is "">
            <p>Please provide a phone number</p>
            <cfabort>
        </cfif>
```

```
        Form processing code
    </card>
</wml>
```

This means that the closing `</card>` and `</wml>` tags will not be included in the data sent to the browser if the `cfabort` tag is executed. Therefore, you must include redundant closing tags as needed before a `cfabort` tag, as shown here:

```
<wml>
    <card>
        <cfif Form.Phone is "">
            <p>Please provide a phone number</p>
            </card></wml>
            <cfabort>
        </cfif>
        Form processing code
    </card>
</wml>
```

Dreamweaver MX Support for WML

We can't end this chapter before mentioning support for WML coding in Dreamweaver MX. Dreamweaver supports your WML development as follows:

- Drop-down tag completion assistance for WML tags, like that provided for HTML and CFML tags

- A WML tags category, and subcategories in the tag chooser, for a quick way to find the right WML tag

This makes DreamWeaver MX an ideal development environment for both your HTML-based ColdFusion applications and your WML-based ColdFusion applications.

In Sum

This chapter functions as a brief tutorial on the basics of WML application development for WAP-enabled devices. Though short on in-depth study of development in WML, the chapter informs you about the issues and techniques involved in building WML applications in Cold-Fusion, and it discusses how to integrate those, if needed, with your existing HTML applications. With this foundation, together with the aid of a detailed guide to the WML language, you should be able to develop WML applications for the wireless web market.

Part IV

Enhancing Performance

Chapter 16: Performance Tuning

Chapter 17: Clustering: Load Balancing and Failover

Chapter 18: Caching Techniques

CHAPTER 16

Performance Tuning

By William Baum and Kenneth N. Fricklas

- Performance testing

- Monitoring Performance: tools and methods

- ColdFusion Administrator settings

- Tuning the database

- ColdFusion MX template profiling

- Tuning the OS

hroughout most of this book, we've been primarily concerned with ColdFusion programming. In this chapter, we'll be departing from that pattern and turning to some other factors that affect your application's overall performance and help you get the most out of your application and your server. Improved application performance is a function of many interactions between an application, server, network, and operating system—the challenge is to determine which of these elements is causing problems, so we can deal with them. We'll cover ways to measure performance, to isolate which components are causing specific problems, and of dealing with those performance problems.

Here in Chapter 16 we'll look at ways to improve the overall speed and efficiency of your application and your server. This chapter explains important topics necessary to accomplish the following steps of the performance tuning process:

1. Monitor

2. Test

3. Measure

4. Document

5. Adjust

6. Repeat

We'll begin by discussing tools that measure exactly how our application is performing so that we can tell where it needs tuning. Next, we'll discuss which tools we can use to figure out which system resources are causing the problems we've encountered. We'll also learn how the ColdFusion MX Administrator settings affect the systems performance and how to tune them for our individual application. Finally, we'll look at how each part of our environment—the database, the code, and the operating system—affects our application, and what to do to improve performance by modifying each. When we're done we'll know how to tell if something is wrong, how to figure out what's causing the problem, and how to start correcting the issues to make our program run at its best.

Performance Testing

The only way to truly establish the performance capabilities of your application and its hardware and software configuration is to test it under load. The best way to do this is with one of any number of load testing software packages. This section presents some tools you can use to test performance, and it looks at the metrics those tools measure and how they affect your application's performance. It also looks at the performance counters provided by ColdFusion MX.

The Testing Environment

Although it is possible to develop a ColdFusion application with a single computer, it's not really feasible to do performance tuning without a testing environment that approximates the production environment as closely as possible. At a minimum, you should use a separate computer for the client and the server.

Bear in mind that an essential element of a development environment is some sort of source control or change management system. There are lots of solutions available that range from very simple, and either freeware or very inexpensive, to very sophisticated and quite expensive. As your development skills increase, so will the complexity of your projects, and you will get to a point at which some sort of revision control system is essential. As many developers have found, it's much better to have such a system in place before you need it than after it's too late. See Chapter 10, "Source Code Management," for more information.

Load Testing Software

Load testing is an industry unto itself, and the many products that are available vary greatly in capability, features, ease of use, and cost—especially cost. Products range from being free to costing millions of dollars, depending on the product and the number of virtual simultaneous users you need to simulate.

All load testing software uses the same basic philosophy: simulate a web browser by sending requests to the server, collect performance and error statistics, and then present a report of the results (frequently with graphs, breakdowns by function, and so on). Most packages can employ a client-server architecture in which you can create a cluster of client machines that are controlled by a central console. This allows a web server or a cluster of web servers to be subjected to a much greater load than could be accomplished with a single machine performing all of the requests.

Some of the more popular load testing tools include the following:

- Microsoft's free Web Application Stress Tool (WAST), available from `http://webtool
.rte.microsoft.com/`.

- Microsoft's Application Center Test (the supported version of WAST that is part of Visual Studio .NET), available from `http://msdn.microsoft.com/vstudio/techinfo/articles/
developerproductivity/apptesting.asp`.

- Astra LoadTest and LoadRunner from Mercury Interactive, available from `http://
www-heva.mercuryinteractive.com/products/testing/`.

- SilkPerformer from Segue Software, available from `http://www.segue.com/html/
s_solutions/s_performer/s_performer.htm`.

- The e-TEST suite from Empirix (formerly RSW Software), available from `http://www.empirix.com/`.

- WebLOAD from RadView Software, Inc., available from `http://www.radview.com/products/WebLOAD.asp`.

- OpenSTA, HTTP/S Load, available from `http://www.opensta.org/`. This is a free, open source load test tool that is part of the Open System Testing Architecture.

Using the Web Application Stress Tool

A good tool for your first foray into load testing is Microsoft's Web Application Stress Tool (WAST), shown in Figure 16.1. It's easy to use, readily available from Microsoft, and it's free. This simple stress tool is extremely useful. It is quite flexible in the methods it employs to assist you in creating a script for testing. With it, you can manually enter all the URLs, record a session with your browser, read in unique entries from a web log file, or simply pick files from a directory tree. WAST also allows you to monitor cookies for multiple simulated users, as well as to request delays and host header information.

NOTE   If you want to play with WAST on your local machine, you can't use 127.0.0.1 as your local address; use 'localhost' instead when you are recording.

FIGURE 16.1:
Microsoft's WAST startup screen

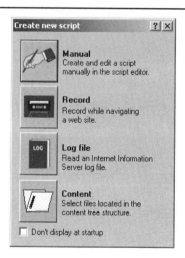

To get a better idea of how to use this tool, let's review an example that I set up to test the performance of the Tack2 Store sample application that is provided with ColdFusion. In this example, I chose to use the Record method, which tracks movement though the application as it runs. As I stepped through the application with the web browser, the tool recorded all of the requests to the server (as shown in Figure 16.2). Notice that WAST has recorded all of the requests that were sent from the browser to the server, including all images and URL parameters. After these requests were recorded, I created page groups by entering names into the group field. This allows us to view the various performances of the application's parts by grouped function. As you can see in the Group column, I created groups for the checkout and search parts of the application.

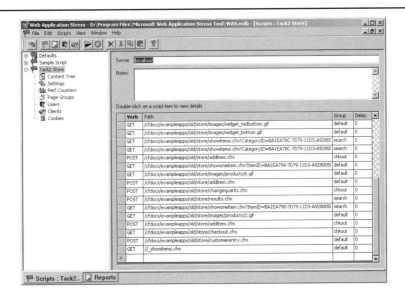

Simulating multiple sessions in an application is straightforward if your application tracks sessions with cookies. If your application uses URL parameters as session identifiers, and you want to measure multiple simultaneous ColdFusion sessions, you would have to actually record multiple sessions in order to send the different URL tokens. WAST shows its ASP heritage here, meaning it deals much better with cookies as session identifiers.

The recorded script shown in Figure 16.2 is simply a linear list. If you run the test as is, it will repeatedly step through the requests in order and collect statistics, and all pages will receive the same number of hits. If you would like to modify the script, you can create page groups such as the "checkout" and "search" groups seen in Figure 16.2, which will allow you to distribute the requests between the page groups, simulating pages that are more popular than others. You create the page groups from the primary script page by simply filling in the Group field. Once you've entered the groups, you can set the percentage of hits each group will receive, as seen in Figure 16.3.

FIGURE 16.3:

Setting percentage
of hits for the
page groups

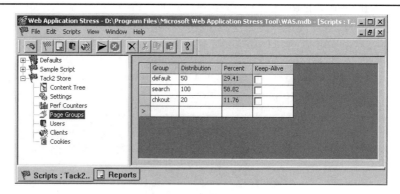

In addition to the default statistics, WAST can collect performance data from any of the
Microsoft Windows performance counters on the client or server machines. Listing 16.1
shows you a partial look at the reports for this test.

NOTE   You'll need to turn on Enable Performance Monitoring in the Debugging Settings of the
ColdFusion Administrator in order to collect this data.

Listing 16.1   **Partial Listing of Web Application Stress Results for the Tack2 Sample Application**

```
Overview
========================================================================
Report name:              1/28/2003 11:53:51 PM
Run on:                   1/28/2003 11:53:51 PM
Run length:               00:01:01

Web Application Stress Tool Version:1.1.293.1

Number of test clients:   1

Number of hits:           7103
Requests per Second:      118.22

Socket Statistics
------------------------------------------------------------------------
Socket Connects:          7139
Total Bytes Sent (in KB): 3507.39
Bytes Sent Rate (in KB/s): 58.38
Total Bytes Recv (in KB): 22813.31
Bytes Recv Rate (in KB/s): 379.70

Socket Errors
------------------------------------------------------------------------
Connect:                  0
```

```
Send:                          11
Recv:                          0
Timeouts:                      0

Page Summary
Page                           Hits    TTFB Avg  TTLB Avg  Auth
================================================================
GET //_showitems.cfm           223     148.97    158.59    No
GET /cfdocs/exampleapps/old/st 240     118.75    140.21    No
GET /cfdocs/exampleapps/old/st 239     180.19    199.79    No
GET /cfdocs/exampleapps/old/st 238     178.72    178.82    No
GET /cfdocs/exampleapps/old/st 237     196.86    196.95    No
GET /cfdocs/exampleapps/old/st 236     202.84    202.94    No
GET /cfdocs/exampleapps/old/st 235     168.59    192.76    No
GET /cfdocs/exampleapps/old/st 235     191.27    191.37    No
GET /cfdocs/exampleapps/old/st 235     184.70    184.76    No
GET /cfdocs/exampleapps/old/st 233     180.39    182.61    No
GET /cfdocs/exampleapps/old/st 232     212.88    212.91    No
GET /cfdocs/exampleapps/old/st 231     218.71    218.80    No
POST /cfdocs/exampleapps/old/s 223     141.49    177.04    No
POST /cfdocs/exampleapps/old/s 223     152.89    172.13    No
...
```

In this example, the test ran for one minute, and the application sustained 7103 hits, or just over 118 per second with 11 errors, probably an acceptable rate. We could extrapolate and assume that the application could sustain over 10 million hits per day, but we would be wrong. Although we have put a load on the server and it has executed a great number of requests, we have not simulated real world application performance. What we have simulated is 5 copies of the same ColdFusion session in 5 different browser windows on the same machine connected to the web server via a 100MB connection, not to mention the miraculous user capable of filling out forms and clicking links 40 times a second. In other words, what we have simulated is possible only in the simulation.

You can use the detailed listing of time spent per template as a starting point to figure out which templates are taking an inordinately long time to run. Then you can profile those templates (see "Profiling ColdFusion MX Templates" later in the chapter) to improve slow running code.

There are many settings available in WAST that will help you make the simulation more realistic, but you will never simulate a population of users with complete accuracy. Only trial and error can tell you which settings are most important for your particular application.

TIP   Though load testing is invaluable (some would say essential), it can yield misleading results if there are any errors in your testing methodology. However, if there are portions of your application that are limiting its performance, load testing should make this immediately apparent to you.

Performance Metrics: What to Measure

Before you can do anything to improve the performance of your application, you have to be able to measure it. Otherwise it will be very difficult to determine the effect that any configuration changes you make have on performance.

Performance is affected by each of the resources an application consumes within its operating environment, including CPU, memory, network, and disk. This section discusses the key factors you can use to monitor and measure the consumption of these resources.

CPU Utilization

A high CPU utilization on the web server or database computer indicates that the server is nearing its performance limits. In your performance testing, this will be a key factor that you will need to determine how much load to throw at the server. Although a high CPU utilization is expected when the server is under a heavy load, if it appears under other circumstances, it is indicative of a serious problem with your application or server.

On web servers, you should expect CPU utilization to increase with load, although this relationship is usually not exactly linear. CPU utilization of 10 percent at a given load does not mean that the application will sustain 10 times that load. The only way to determine the maximum load for an application platform is to increase the load until performance suffers to an unacceptable level, and this can occur either before or after the CPU reaches 100 percent utilization.

On database servers, inordinate CPU utilization might mean that you have at least one poorly tuned database. See "Tuning the Database" later in this chapter for more information.

Keep in mind that on Windows machines, virtual memory and disk operations appear as idle time, and therefore they won't bring up the measured CPU utilization. As a result, memory and database issues (discussed in later sections) can bring your performance down to unacceptable levels without ever affecting the CPU.

NOTE   You should also monitor CPU utilization on the testing client machine(s). If the testing client machine(s) exhibits overly high CPU utilization, you might have to streamline your testing procedures or spread the testing among additional client machines to get meaningful results.

Memory Allocation

High memory allocation is relative to a number of factors and can vary greatly from application to application. On a web server, memory usage is influenced by a great number of things, including a number of ColdFusion Administrator settings (details in "ColdFusion Administrator Settings" later in the chapter).

In general, memory should not rise with load in a linear fashion; instead, it should rise to a level that remains fairly stable as load increases. (This is because your application is running a limited, constant maximum number of threads. More queued requests don't increase the amount of stuff that's actually running.) Several load-related factors, however, will increase the amount of memory the server needs to allocate. For web servers, if you have client and/or session tracking enabled, the ColdFusion Server process will allocate additional memory for each new client or session that it detects. This can be a huge problem if you have any errors with client or session integrity. For instance, if you are tracking your sessions with URL tokens and you fail to pass a URL token anywhere in your application, you just created a new session on the server. Pay particular attention to this with load testing tools because an error in the testing script can falsely indicate a memory allocation problem in your server. It's quite possible to think you have a memory leak when you actually have an excessive number of sessions or clients created.

The most important thing to watch when analyzing the effect of memory on your application's performance is virtual memory paging. If your application is using too much virtual memory, it becomes disk-bound, and that disk is far slower than internal memory. On your application servers, be very careful with the number and size of session variables, cached queries, and so on, because these can grow significantly as the number of sessions and queries escalates. On the database servers, high memory utilization usually indicates a poorly tuned database or poorly written SQL queries in your application. This will be especially noticeable with very large or complex databases.

NOTE Remember that memory is cheap. Don't eliminate caching to lower memory usage unless your machine simply can't support more RAM. It's generally much cheaper to add RAM than to redevelop code.

Network Traffic

You will want to measure the network traffic—inbound, outbound, and total—for all network adapters in all servers.

Inbound traffic to the web server is generally insignificant when compared to the outbound traffic, which is our primary focus when monitoring. On the web and database servers, the outbound network traffic should rise in a direct linear relationship to the load on the server. Therefore, you would expect to get a proportionate number of bytes out for every additional request to the server. As the output per input lowers, you should expect to see an increase in failed or timed-out requests. This is either an indication of a problem, or merely that the server is performing at capacity.

Watching the traffic between the web server and the database server under varying loads can be quite helpful in spotting or diagnosing database problems as well.

NOTE   One point of network architecture to consider here—it's a really good idea to have multiple network adapters in your web servers so that you can isolate the network traffic between the web server and the database server(s) from the Internet and general LAN traffic. This ensures that the connection between the web server and the database server is as fast and clean as possible, and that HTTP traffic between the web server and clients does not interfere with database queries, and visa versa.

Disk Activity

For web servers, disk performance does not usually cause a bottleneck unless your application uses an extremely large number of ColdFusion templates, image files, and so on, or does substantial file-based I/O.

NOTE   If your application server delivers a great deal of image files, consider moving the images to a dedicated server. This will avoid some competition for memory, disk, and CPU cycles between the web server process and the ColdFusion server process, and it can yield a significant performance improvement. Also, a caching hard-drive controller on that image server can make an enormous improvement in performance.

Other than delivering files, unusually high disk activity is generally indicative of a problem, usually a memory or operating system configuration problem. All modern operating systems (basically anything that can run ColdFusion) are very efficient in their use of hard drives, and they allocate enough memory for disk caches so that most files are only physically read from the disk once, and are thereafter supplied from the disk cache. A web server, even under heavy load, shouldn't be thrashing its disks.

Disk activity can be, but isn't necessarily, more of a performance factor for database servers than web servers. If the database is well designed and well tuned and the database server has ample memory installed, it is quite possible for the majority of database operations to be served from the memory or disk cache. Of course, when the database is very large and complex, a certain amount of disk activity can't be avoided.

Excessive disk activity or poor disk performance can sometimes be difficult to measure. Among the best methods for determining whether this might be a problem for your application is to simply watch the disk lights under load. If any are glowing fairly solidly for significant periods of time, further investigation is warranted. If you press a key on the keyboard, and the hard drive flashes for 30 seconds before you see a response on the screen, you can be pretty sure it's a virtual memory issue. It is important that your servers spend their time servicing requests, not swapping their memory to and from the disk.

ColdFusion MX Performance Counters

ColdFusion MX provides a group of performance counters that provide an excellent source of information about what is going on within your application under load. Most of these counters will only produce meaningful results when the load on the server is within the server's performance limits. If the server is being subjected to a load beyond what it can handle, as can occur during load testing, that fact will become apparent from these results, but the numbers themselves won't be terribly useful. The order of importance of these factors will vary from application to application, reflecting the fact that applications stress the server in different ways and have different limiting factors.

ColdFusion's performance counters can be monitored via the Performance/System Monitor tool in Windows, and via the CFSTAT utility on other platforms. We'll discuss the tools in the next section, but first let's examine what benchmarks they measure.

Number of running requests   The number of ColdFusion requests actually being processed by the server. Requests that are waiting for external responses from databases or cfhttp requests are also included in this count. If your application uses a number of external connections, you will probably want to increase the number of simultaneous connections allowed in the ColdFusion Administrator. Otherwise, your server could spend most of its time waiting for other servers.

Number of queued requests   The number of ColdFusion requests not running at the moment because they are in line waiting for other requests to finish. This number should remain quite low except for periods of high activity—*load spikes*. Pay close attention to the number of queued requests along with the average queue time (discussed momentarily). When requests are received faster than the server can process them, they are lined up in the queue. If the queue grows too much, they may even be lost. For further information, please see the upcoming section, "ColdFusion Administrator Settings."

Number of timed out requests   In a perfect world, everything is working properly, and requests never time out. In the real world, however, requests do time out, and they usually time out because an external connection fails. This can be anything from a remote database connection to a failed cfhttp request, or even a bad DNS server connection.

Average request time   The average amount of time, in milliseconds, that the ColdFusion server spent processing each request. This is the total time spent running the request, including the queue time and the database transaction time.

Average queue time   The average amount of time, in milliseconds, that all queued requests spent in the input queue.

Average database time   The amount of time it took ColdFusion MX to complete an individual database operation. For most ColdFusion applications, this number will be representative of the primary limiting factor. Poor ColdFusion performance is almost always caused by bad database performance or virtual memory overload. Please see the section "Tuning the Database."

Database hits per second   The average number of database operations performed per second. This is the best measure of overall database work being performed by the server.

Page hits per second   The number of web pages, per second, that the server is currently processing. Note that this includes CFC calls because they generate a separate call to a page on the server.

Bytes incoming per second/Bytes outgoing per second   The average number of bytes being transferred between the ColdFusion MX Server and the web server. These will generally equate to the total size of requests received, and the total size of ColdFusion output to the web server service, respectively. This measurement is quite different from that of the total network traffic because it only includes actual ColdFusion input and output. These figures do not include images and other requests served directly by the web server service.

Monitoring Performance: Tools and Methods

There are several ways to monitor the performance of your server(s), both for load testing your application prior to deployment, and for monitoring the health and performance of your production systems on an ongoing basis. Among the factors to consider when you are choosing the tools and methods for monitoring your server are the timeliness and clarity of the information presented, and the impact of the monitoring on the server.

In this section, we discuss System Monitor for Windows and the CFSTAT utility, the stand-alone ColdFusion Statistics tools. If you are running ColdFusion MX on a J2EE platform, it is also possible to monitor the performance of ColdFusion by tracking the underlying Java runtime with tools specific to that Java platform or SNMP.

System Monitor for Windows (Performance Tool)

System Monitor in Windows 2000/.NET (known as Performance Monitor in earlier versions) allows you to view real-time performance data from any number of performance counters in graphical, report, or histogram form. This tool is available only on Windows platforms.

You can save off data from System Monitor for comparisons across various load levels. In fact, you may find it useful to compare System Monitor information to server log files in order to determine which templates cause heavy load, though this is a labor intensive process.

TIP Try to avoid running the Windows System Monitor on the web server and viewing the resulting graphical display from a remote machine using a tool like pcAnywhere. System Monitor itself, as well as remote control tools such as pcAnywhere, can cause a significant load on your server. System Monitor can be made significantly less intrusive by running it on a remote machine and allowing it to collect the performance statistics from the web server remotely. This is usually practicable only if the System Monitor client machine has a local area connection to the web server machine. Firewall and latency issues frequently eliminate this as a viable method for monitoring web servers from across the Internet.

The CFSTAT Utility

A frequently overlooked, but very useful method for looking at ColdFusion performance statistics is the CFSTAT utility. Available on all versions of ColdFusion, CFSTAT for ColdFusion MX is located by default in the C:\CFUSIONMX\bin directory on Windows platforms, and in /opt/coldfusionmx/bin on Unix flavored servers.

To use CFSTAT, you must have access to a command line on the server, either locally, or by telnet or rlogin. CFSTAT will check statistics once, or you can set a repeat interval by specifying a number of seconds as an argument, for example **cfstat 5** will check the statistics every five seconds. You can enter **cfstat -h** for more options.

Listing 16.2 shows you the results of running the CFSTAT utility on a moderately loaded web server, while checking statistics every second.

Listing 16.2   **Output of CFSTAT on a Lightly Loaded Server, Repeat Interval Set to 1 Second**

```
C:\CFUSIONMX\BIN>cfstat 1
```

Pg/Sec		DB/Sec		CP/Sec		Reqs	Reqs	Reqs	AvgQ	AvgReq	AvgDB	Bytes	Bytes
Now	Hi	Now	Hi	Now	Hi	Q'ed	Run'g	TO'ed	Time	Time	Time	In/Sec	Out/Sec
0	0	0	0	0	0	0	0	0	0	41	4	0	0
8	8	7	7	0	0	0	0	0	0	43	7	11978	48736
7	8	2	7	0	0	0	0	0	0	12	9	10247	41645
8	8	4	7	0	0	0	0	0	0	19	5	11808	49235
4	8	4	7	0	0	0	0	0	0	19	0	5896	28645
5	8	5	7	0	0	0	0	0	0	13	5	7610	33202
5	8	5	7	0	0	0	0	0	0	13	10	7770	31453
4	8	4	7	0	0	0	0	0	0	11	8	6216	25073
7	8	7	7	0	0	0	0	0	0	15	0	10878	43931
5	8	5	7	0	0	0	0	0	5	19	7	7770	31235

ColdFusion Administrator Settings

No discussion of performance tuning would be complete without a discussion of the settings available within the ColdFusion Administrator, which you will find at `http://yourserver/cfide/administrator/`.

Server Settings

There are a number of server settings that can have a dramatic effect on the performance of your application. These must be tuned to the specific hardware environment and application that you are running. We'll go through them individually, taking the time to discuss the ramifications and recommended settings for each.

Limit simultaneous requests to: [*n*]

This setting controls the number of requests that ColdFusion will attempt to process at the same time. Think of the number of simultaneous requests as the number of open checkout lanes at the supermarket, with the number of CPUs in the server comparable to the number of checkers. Most ColdFusion applications will process requests faster than they arrive, so if we apply this to our supermarket scenario, the checkers will be able to handle their own checkout lanes adequately so that no lines will develop. If the number of customers picks up, and there are more open checkout lines than checkers, the checkers will need to service more than one line each, and wind up running around to service additional lanes. The same is true for process requests until the server is under significant load. When the server is very busy, the CPUs can't keep up with the requests and have to switch back and forth between them often, to try to keep everything moving. In the supermarket scenario, this would equate to the checkers running around like crazy to the different open lanes trying to check out customers in all the backed up lines while trying to keep everyone happy.

In general, the more requests each server processor is processing at the same time, the slower each request will be. For pure speed, there is not a distinct advantage to a large number of simultaneous requests. However, most ColdFusion applications involve an additional factor that is most important here—delays. In addition to the time spent actually processing requests, your ColdFusion application probably spends a lot of time waiting for external processes to complete before it can move on to the next step. Of these external processes that your application has to wait for, the most significant are probably database queries.

Most ColdFusion applications can be said to be either *CPU intensive*, or *database intensive*. The more time your application spends running the ColdFusion MX process, the more CPU intensive it is. The more time it spends waiting for database operations to complete, the more database intensive it is.

ColdFusion MX doesn't process database queries; it hands them off to another process, frequently on another server, and waits for the response. If the server is processing simultaneous requests, it can perform other work while it waits for the response from the database. So, if your application is highly database dependent, you will generally want to allow a larger number of simultaneous requests than if your application is more CPU intensive. However, this also depends your database's ability to efficiently process additional simultaneous requests. As you increase the number of simultaneous requests, you will generally also increase the number of simultaneous database queries in a database intensive application. This, in turn, should improve overall performance up to the point at which it begins to decline. This point can only be determined by experimentation because every application, database, and architecture is different, and even one poorly written SQL query or poorly indexed table can change the application's performance considerably.

There are other external requests to consider in addition to database queries. Consider a cfhttp or any other external operation that results in the ColdFusion server waiting for something; this will bring that particular CPU to a stop. This would be just like a price check in the supermarket that will bring a particular checkout lane to a stop. For instance, one request that waits 30 seconds for a bad cfldap query to timeout, would be similar to what would happen if one of our checkout lanes came to a dead stop for 30 seconds. To explain further, if we have our simultaneous requests set at 2, and 2 users attempt the same bad cfldap call at the same time, our server will not process any requests at all until those requests timeout. As a result, our server will appear to lock up for 30 seconds every time this happens. This is bad. This is also why these external calls usually provide some method for setting the amount of time the server will wait for a response and why it is important to set these timeout values carefully.

Therefore, the ideal setting for your server will be determined by the number of external calls made by your application that cause the server to wait. If your application does a lot of waiting, more threads will improve performance because the server won't waste time waiting for external processes to finish. On the other hand, if your application is CPU-bound, more threads will just tie up the processor in switching to the "lanes without a checker."

An additional factor to consider is time consuming processes. Many ColdFusion applications entail maintenance tasks, or other operations that simply take a long time to process. Whether you are re-indexing a huge Verity collection, or sending a mass e-mail to the western world, some requests take a long time. We obviously want to avoid performing long, resource intensive operations during busy periods, but we do have to run them occasionally, so we must allow for this in our settings. If we allow a larger number of simultaneous requests, the server will devote a smaller percentage of its resources to each of the tasks. With a small number of simultaneous requests, the time-consuming process will proceed faster at the expense of other requests. The reverse is true for a larger setting—the time consuming process will take longer, but the server will be more responsive to other requests.

Macromedia recommends that a good starting number for the number of simultaneous threads to use is (2 × *the number of CPUs*) + 1. For instance, a machine with 2 processors would have 5 threads—(2 × 2) + 1. Other ColdFusion experts have recommended 3 to 5 threads per CPU, or 6 to 10 for the same machine that is running 2 processors. Trial and error will determine what works in your situation.

For many high traffic applications, the adjustment of the simultaneous request limit will be among the most significant tasks affecting the performance of the server.

> **TIP**   If you are using the Scheduled Tasks feature in the ColdFusion Administrator, keep in mind that the task that is running the scheduled task and the task running on the server are separate processes. It can help matters to schedule tasks to run on a machine with lower utilization, running URLs that run on more heavily loaded machines, rather than having the heavily loaded machine that will actually run the task call itself via the Task Scheduler.

Timeout requests after: [*n*] seconds

This feature causes requests that take longer than *n* seconds to process to be aborted. Most of the ColdFusion Administrator's default settings are good starting points for most applications, except for this one—if it is left blank, it won't time out any requests at all!

For your application, determine the largest amount of time that a request might take to process normally, and set this value slightly larger. The key here is to avoid any application error that will bring down the server by using up a server thread permanently. Whether you've made an error that results in an infinite loop—by creating a `cfinclude` loop that includes a file that includes the file that called it—or whether you've got a misguided SQL query that might eventually return a bazillion more records than you intended, stuff happens. If the erroneous request doesn't time out, the server will wait for it forever, eventually stopping the server from processing requests altogether. In our supermarket scenario, this would be like effectively closing one of our checkout lanes permanently every time a request fails to stop.

Be sure to check your error logs (see Chapter 2, "Troubleshooting and Debugging ColdFusion MX Code") for templates that time out consistently; generally these templates can be tuned to work within the timeout interval you need.

Additionally, other Administrator Server Settings are dependent on the value of the timeout interval, so it's important that it be set. No live production server should have its timeout value disabled.

> **TIP**   If you are running some sort of maintenance operation that might take a really long time to process, use the `RequestTimeout` URL parameter or the `cfsetting` option. This will allow you to override the value set in the ColdFusion Administrator for individual requests that need a longer timeout interval.

Use UUID for cftoken

This setting configures the `cftoken` cookie to use a unique identifier (known as a UUID) as a token identifier, rather than a random number. If you have a very large number of users, or if you have an application with sessions spanning multiple servers, this will guarantee that sessions won't have the same identifier. However, these take longer to create and process than standard `cftokens`, and they also create longer URLs.

Enable HTTP status codes

This setting allows the system to set error codes in the HTTP header to indicate failed pages (`http 500`). See Chapter 2 for a more detailed explanation of this setting.

Enable Whitespace Management

This option first appeared in ColdFusion 4.5, along with the following tag:

```
<cfsetting enableCFoutputOnly = "Yes" or "No">
```

In ColdFusion 5.0, the following tag was added:

```
<cfprocessingdirective suppressWhiteSpace = "Yes" or "No">
```

Without the ability to suppress whitespace, ColdFusion templates have a tendency to output a significant number of needless blank lines due to the way the ColdFusion server processes requests. You can see this with the View Source option in your browser. Basically, what happens is that any space that's not part of a ColdFusion tag, including all the white space you used when you were indenting your source code for readability, is passed on to the output page.

When whitespace is suppressed, all those extra spaces, tabs, and carriage returns—which are ignored anyway in HTML files—are removed. Spaces that are part of your text are left intact.

For compatibility with older applications, you may need to disable this setting. If you leave it enabled, it is best if you manually turn off whitespace suppression for portions of the application that make use of the space created by the ColdFusion statements.

If whitespace isn't suppressed, it is possible for extraneous whitespace to represent a significant amount of additional useless data that must be sent to the client, impacting bandwidth and performance. It also makes your application look less polished to the curious observer who may happen to choose the View Source option.

NOTE The Missing Template Handler and Site-Wide Error Handler settings are discussed in Chapter 2.

Caching

ColdFusion application performance is dramatically improved through the judicious use of caching within your application's templates and database queries. These settings control the overall caching configuration of the server.

Template cache size (number of templates) *[n]*

When a page is requested, ColdFusion compiles any CFML script that will execute in Java byte codes for execution. These templates are saved in the Template Cache in memory so that the template will not have to be parsed and compiled again unless one of the files used to process the template changes or the server is restarted. Although the compiler is very fast, this is a complicated process, so you'll find that pages (especially large pages) will execute a lot faster the second time they are called because the server has skipped the entire process of reading the file from disk, compiling it, and saving it in the cache.

Normally ColdFusion MX will use whatever memory it needs to compile and cache any and all templates that run with your application. This option allows you to limit the memory that is reserved for this purpose. If you are in a memory limited application, make sure that this value is large enough to hold all your application's commonly used ColdFusion pages, and small enough to avoid lots of virtual memory paging. Macromedia recommends a starting point of one page per MB of JVM size available on your server.

If you do not allocate enough memory to hold all of your templates, the ColdFusion server will be forced to eject, or pop, the least recently accessed template from the cache. When this popped template is called again, it will have to be read from the disk and compiled again before it can be executed. As inefficient as this sounds, it is also inefficient to allocate a huge amount of memory for templates that are rarely executed. There is also a certain amount of overhead involved in keeping track of which templates are in the cache and which are the least frequently accessed. This overhead, though not large, does grow with the size of the cache.

In short, even though most ColdFusion applications will fit very neatly into the server's memory, there are times when just counting up the size of all the templates is not the best way to determine the size of the cache.

Trusted cache

With the Trusted Cache enabled, ColdFusion MX assumes that CFML templates have not changed on disk since the last time they were requested. If templates do not change very often, this setting can provide a slight performance boost. However, the overhead in determining whether a file has changed or not is rather small—the server merely checks the file's timestamp, which is usually available in the file server's disk cache for frequently accessed files. Also, though you can change the Trusted Cache setting without restarting the server, this doesn't free you from having to restart the server when content changes. You might think that flipping the Trusted Cache setting off and back on would be sufficient, but this does not clear the cache, and the server has no way of knowing that the previously trusted cache is no longer trustworthy.

WARNING   If you do use the Trusted Cache setting, you must be diligent in restarting the ColdFusion server service whenever the content changes. Otherwise, your application will exhibit strange behavior for which the cause will not be apparent.

Limit the maximum number of cached queries on the server to *[n]* queries

This setting will undoubtedly change in an upcoming release of ColdFusion because the current setting is not particularly useful. As we'll discuss in greater detail in the "Tuning the Database" section, the proper use of cached queries can improve an application's performance considerably, and improper use can bring the server to its knees. It is not the number of cached queries that is significant, but the size, and therefore the amount, of server memory consumed. The default value is 100.

Client Variables

The Client Variables section of the ColdFusion Administrator allows you to set the default storage mechanism for applications, which do not specify a client variable storage mechanism in their `cfapplication` tag, as well as create and administer client variable stores used by applications.

Client variables can be stored in the system Registry, client cookies, or in other ODBC, OLE DB, or Native Driver data sources. Each of these methods has its advantages and detractions.

Registry

This is the default value, as well as the wrong one to use. The biggest disadvantage of using the Registry as a client variable store is the impact it can have on the target system. Windows systems tend to perform better with smaller registries, and storing ColdFusion data in the Registry can impact the performance of the entire machine as the size of the Registry grows. Depending on the version of Windows you are using, the Registry may have a maximum size, and Windows will complain rather vehemently if you attempt to exceed it. Also, once your Registry has become bloated, it's not terribly easy to reclaim the space. For these reasons, Macromedia does not recommend that you store client variables in the Registry.

Cookies

Like every other method, storing client variables in client cookies has some advantages and disadvantages. The main advantage of using cookies is that this setting requires no server resources for storage whatsoever. Each client brings its own data with it.

There are some limitations with this approach, which can be significant. First, the performance degrades quickly as the size of the cookie grows because the client browser sends the entire cookie with each request to the web server. This performance degradation is not readily apparent from the server because requests have merely slowed, but performance will suffer from the client's perspective, and here's why.

Remember that each frame, image, and so on, also represents a request to the web server, if not the ColdFusion server. For example, if you are storing 2K of client variables in a cookie and the user requests a page containing 10 images, the client's browser will send the same 2K of data to your web server 11 times just for that page. If the poor client happens to be on a modem, you will have wasted about 10 seconds of the client's time and bandwidth having the browser send you 20K of completely useless redundant data. However, if the cookie is very small, the impact on performance can be negligible because the client must send a packet of data for each request anyway, and there's virtually no difference in performance when the size of each request packet increases by a small amount.

ColdFusion MX limits cookie size to 4K, and Netscape limits the number of cookies to 20, 3 of which are used by ColdFusion, so only 17 are available for us to store client variables. Not all browsers can store cookies, and some users have cookies disabled in their browsers.

In short, cookies can be a viable option for client variables only if the cookies remain very small and if you can assure that your clients' browsers will accept the cookies.

ODBC, OLE DB, or Native Drivers Data Source

This is probably the best option for most applications because it represents the fewest liabilities when compared to the other methods. The performance and efficiency is dictated by the underlying data source, and you are less limited in the type and amount of data that can be stored per client. On the local machine, an MS Access database makes a perfectly suitable client variable store. Many developers choose to store client variables in their application's primary database.

Please also see the section on Client variable storage in Chapter 17, "Clustering: Load Balancing and Failover."

NOTE   ColdFusion will happily store client variables in several data sources for which it will be unable to create the tables. For instance, ColdFusion will fail to create the tables for a client variable store in an MS SQL server database via an OLE DB connection, but it will happily create the tables if you connect to the same database with ODBC. Simply create the tables manually or through an alternate connection method, and then add the data source as a client variable store.

ColdFusion MX Data Source Settings

Unlike previous versions of ColdFusion, ColdFusion MX now communicates with databases entirely via Java JDBC connections.

ColdFusion MX Professional supports JDBC connections to ODBC data sources via a socket connection, as well as Type IV (all Java) drivers for Access in Windows, and SQL Server and mySQL drivers in both Linux and Windows. The Enterprise Edition adds Type IV JDBC support for Oracle, Informix, Sybase, and DB2 as well. The Type IV JDBC drivers are the most efficient currently available connection to these types of databases; the ODBC/JDBC connection has a significant performance penalty associated with it due to the data translation, but it will perform acceptably for smaller applications. (See "About Database Drivers" in the ColdFusion MX documentation for more information.)

There are many settings and options for ColdFusion data sources. Many are either database or driver specific, self-explanatory, or have little effect on the performance of your application. We'll concentrate on the settings that can most affect database performance.

Login Timeout (sec)

This is how long the ColdFusion server will wait for an adequate response from the server when the connection is established. This setting controls how long the user will have to wait before an error page is generated when your database is down. For most databases, this value should be shortened considerably. It is very rare for a connection to take longer than a few seconds, unless the server or database is down.

In some automatic failover applications, a longer value may be used to enable the database to switch over before responding. If you have an unreliable network connection to your database, set this option to a small timeout value and use error handling to retry your connections.

Limit Connections/Restrict Connections to [n]

By default, every thread that your application runs can create its own connection to the database server. If your database is getting bogged down with many requests from multiple application servers, you can limit the number of connections total from each application server by checking the Limit Connections checkbox and setting a maximum number of connections.

Maintain Connections

There is a certain amount of overhead involved in completing a database connection. You must establish the network connection, authenticate the username and password, and set the default database and any database options, all before you even begin the query. When the database connection is maintained, all of this extra work need only be done prior to the first query to the database, and subsequent queries are initiated much more quickly.

Once the connection is made, it will remain open and connected until it has remained idle for the number of minutes specified in the connection timeout (discussed momentarily). Most database connections can be maintained without negative affects, but there are sometimes hurdles to overcome, and the performance improvement is usually worth the effort.

For example, some automated backup programs will refuse to backup database files, which remain opened by the operating system when a database connection is maintained. On many database platforms the files also remain open whether a connection is maintained or not. In either case, the database platform usually provides for a scheduled backup procedure, which can be used either instead of, or in concert with the automated file backup procedure. Most backup programs are also capable of attempting to back up open files. This is a viable option with some database formats, and in others, it will yield unusable backups.

If you are unable to allow a connection to be maintained, you must do everything possible in your application to move as much logic and processing into the database and therefore limit the number of database queries (see the section on "Tuning the Database" for more information.) You may also be able to speed up the process of establishing some connections by placing all of your connection parameters (username, password, default database, and so on) into the connection string, rather than using the DSN defaults.

If the Maintain Connections option is set, the Connection Timeout can modify its behavior.

Connection Timeout (min)

This setting sets the maximum amount of time for which a connection will be maintained. Some database connections can become stale or unstable after a period of time, and some drivers do not correctly reestablish a connection if it has been interrupted. This setting allows you to force a database connection to be reestablished on a regular interval.

The Connection Timeout option forces database connections that have the Maintain Connections option set to reconnect after an interval of time. This can allow some connections to be maintained that would be unstable otherwise. In an extreme example, you could force a new connection to be created every minute and still avoid the vast majority of the overhead involved with recreating the connection for every query.

Connection Interval (min)

The Connection Interval option is used in conjunction with the Connection Timeout option to specify the length of time that the driver will wait for the database connection to actually close before it reopens it. When the Connection Timeout option has expired, all database operations in progress must complete before the system will close the connection, reopen it, and then allow more database operations to take place. This combination will allow your system time to recover from hung database threads, deadlocks, and other database conditions that might occur and degrade your database performance after a period of time.

CLOB/BLOB

This option can impact performance. If your database supports larger buffers, adjust the Long Text Buffer Size instead, or create an alternate connection to the database exclusively for retrieving the long text. Enable this option for the alternate connection only. You will gain the ability to retrieve the long text or binary large objects, without impacting the performance of your other queries.

NOTE In previous versions of ColdFusion, the option to allow retrieval of long text fields was enabled by default; in ColdFusion MX the default is to not allow long text retrieval. MX also adds the option that enables binary large object retrieval, which was formerly unavailable.

Connection String

As mentioned earlier, specifying database connection parameters in the connection string can expedite some ODBC database connections. You may also use connection strings with the "dynamic" database type in your queries.

The Connection String is specified as a set of name=value pairs, separated by semicolons, for example "`APP=MyApp;WSID=User001;UID=DBReader`".

Tuning the Database

Of all the factors that will affect the performance of your applications, database access is usually the most important. When the performance of a ColdFusion application is bad, it's almost always due to problems in the basic design of the database, the indexes, the SQL queries, or some combination thereof.

Database Design

If your database is poorly designed, it will be extremely difficult, if not impossible, for you to write SQL queries that the database can process quickly and efficiently. If you are having difficulty writing queries that produce the proper results, or if you find yourself having to use ColdFusion to manipulate the results of your queries, then you may need to revisit your basic table layout.

There is an excellent primer on database design in *Mastering ColdFusion MX*, by Arman Danesh, et al. (Sybex, 2002), as well as several books devoted to the subject, most notably *Database Design for Mere Mortals*, by Michael J. Hernandez (Addison-Wesley, 1996). You might also reference Chapter 1, "Designing and Planning a ColdFusion Application," for more information on this subject.

Indexes

As you know, every table in a database needs a *primary key*, which is a special type of index. Many tables need additional indexes as well. In order for you to better understand how to index your databases, it might be helpful to understand a little more about how indexes work.

Database indexes are ordered lists. They work very similarly to indexes in a book, except that books usually have only one index, and database tables have several.

Consider a residential telephone book. The book is equivalent to a table with a primary key on last name + first name. This is very convenient for looking up a person by name, but what if you want to see who lives at a given address? To do so, you would have to read the entire book from cover to cover. The same is true for every query except last name + first name. The book is not useful at all for telling you who your neighbors are, or how many people live in your zip code.

However, if you were to go through the book from cover to cover and write down the page number, line number, and zip code of every entry in the book on little index cards, and then you were to sort those cards by zip code, you could easily determine how many people live in a given zip code without ever even opening the book again—you just have to jump to the right place in your index and see if any are there. You could do the same thing for first names and street addresses. Then, you could find whatever you wanted very quickly and easily.

This is exactly the way database indexes work. If you specify a column in the `where` clause of a query that has no index, the database is forced to read the entire table looking for what you asked for. This is called a *table scan*, and table scans are to be avoided at all costs.

Consider the following query:

```
select lastname, firstname, streetnumber, streetname
from phonebook
where firstname='Fred' and zipcode='63108'
```

If our `phonebook` table has indexes on `firstname` and `zipcode`, this is a called a *fully-covering index*, or a *fully-covered query*. The database can locate and reorder the records for our result set without scanning any of the table records themselves. The database can perform these functions incredibly quickly, even for very large tables. If the `phonebook` table has an index for `firstname`, but not `zipcode`, this is a *partially-covering index*. The database will have to inspect all of the `Fred` records and look for the right zip code.

Indexing errors are sometimes difficult to spot during initial development because the database is usually very small, and the database can perform table scans very quickly. As the size of the database grows, queries will get significantly slower. With even a moderately large table, the difference in execution times can be huge. In one particular instance, a ColdFusion query that executed in 15 seconds was reduced to 50 milliseconds with a simple change in the table indexes. Usually, you will want an index for every column that you use in `where`, `order by`, or `group by` clauses.

There is some overhead in maintaining the indexes when records are added or updated, so it is possible to have too many indexes, especially with tables that have frequent additions or updates. For tables that are largely read and infrequently written (such as product catalogs), having too many indexes is a lot better than not having enough, and since most web applications have a lot more `selects` than `inserts` or `updates`, index away—you will see dramatic improvement in your query times.

On the other hand, for queries that log user actions, which are pretty much all `insert` queries, use as few indexes as possible (if any at all), since they will dramatically slow down the insert process. It can help to copy these log tables to a separate database server periodically, and create the indexes on these offline copies for querying and reporting without affecting the online application.

Common Query Pitfalls

It's quite possible to have a well-tuned database and server, and still have a poorly performing application. In this case, we have to take a close look at the structure and purpose of the application's queries. Whether your application is performing too many queries, queries that are too complex or not optimized, or is transferring too much data between the database and ColdFusion, there is usually a better way to accomplish the task.

NOTE   For more help in this area, see Chapter 11, "Advanced SQL."

Avoid Repetitive Queries

Many developers underutilize the various scopes available for storage of memory variables and queries, as well as the other methods of caching queries. As a result, the same queries are executed over and over.

Here are some tips for improving the performance of some repetitive queries:

- If your application displays a product catalog, that catalog is the same for every visitor to your site. Cache the query, or even cache the output of the main catalog pages with `cfcache` (for more information, see Chapter 18, "Caching Techniques").

- If you retrieve a customer's name for a welcome page, consider saving the value in a session or client variable. Perhaps you should retrieve the entire record and save it in a structure. As the user moves through the site, you won't have to retrieve the same information over and over, and you'll reduce the load on your database.

- If you hit the database on every request in order to load some application-specific defaults that only change daily (for example, today's news), you can save off the query result in an `application` or `server` variable and simply reload that variable when needed—for example, when the data changes in an administrative interface or when it's a new day.

- Whenever you are tempted to cut and paste a query from one part of your application to another, consider whether or not you really want to execute the query again, or whether the query or value should be stored.

Let the Database Do the Work for You

Another common mistake among ColdFusion developers is using ColdFusion to perform functions that should have been done for them by the database. Listing 16.3 demonstrates what happens when too many queries are used to perform a simple job. This listing is taken from an application that lists local area clubs and their upcoming events. This is an example of how to overwork your database by not letting it do its job.

Listing 16.3   Inefficient Use of Database Queries (/c16/clubs1.cfm)

```
<!---
   Name:         /c16/clubs1.cfm
   Description:  Inefficient select clubs from database
--->

<cfquery name="clubs" datasource="clubsSQL">
   select name, venueID, category, location, address, phone, atmosphere, notes
   from clubData
   order by name
</cfquery>
<table border="1" cellPadding="0" cellSpacing="0">
<tr>
   <th>Name</th>
<th>Location</th>
<th>Atmosphere</th>
<th>Notes/Events</th>
</tr>
<cfoutput query="clubs">
   <cfquery name="events" datasource="clubsSQL">
      select startDate, name, edesc
      from events
      where VenueID = #clubs.venueID# and endDate >= #now()#
      order by startDate
   </cfquery>
   <cfset eventNum = #events.recordCount#>
   <tr valign="top">
      <td>#clubs.Name#<BR>#clubs.category#</td>
      <td>#clubs.location#<br>#clubs.address#<br>#clubs.phone#</td>
      <td>#clubs.atmosphere#  </td>
      <td>#clubs.notes#  
         <cfif variables.eventNum is not 0>
            <br>#variables.eventNum# Event(s)<br>
            <cfloop query="events">
               #events.startDate# / #events.name# / #events.edesc#<br>
            </cfloop>
```

```
        </cfif>
      </td>
    </tr>
  </cfoutput>
```

After a query retrieves a list of clubs, it loops through the clubs with `cfoutput`, and executes an additional query for each club, retrieving any upcoming events for that club. In this case, this is fairly inefficient because it executes a large number of queries, or roundtrips to the database. This is roughly analogous to making a separate trip to the grocery store for each egg in a dozen. In this case, we make one trip, which gets all the clubs, and then we make an additional trip back for each club. The most efficient database queries get everything they need from the store/database in a single trip.

NOTE   Queries inside loops are usually avoidable. Consider modifying the original query and using the `cfoutput group` attribute or query of queries (which doesn't hit the database at all) to optimize these.

We can improve this code with a simple join:

```
select c.name, c.category, c.location, c.address, c.phone,
    c.atmosphere, c.notes,
    e.startDate, e.name as ename, edesc
from clubdata as c
left join events as e on c.venueID=e.venueID
```

This single query returns all of the data in both the original queries. This approach is not without its drawbacks, however. Though this query can return a great deal of data, that data could be redundant. For instance, all of the `clubData` fields are repeated for each event for a particular club. If many clubs have a large number of upcoming events, this could become a problem. We can alleviate this problem by reducing the number of fields displayed for each club and providing a link to the club information as a separate page, for instance. However, if we have a fast link between our web server and our database server and we limit the number of displayed records per page, this shouldn't be a serious problem.

A way around this issue is to execute the same single query for the club information, but bring back all the events at once. You could then use the query of queries to show information for a single club. Listing 16.4 shows an improved way of achieving the same result.

Listing 16.4   Use of Query of Queries to Optimize (clubs2.cfm)

```
<!---
    Name:          /c16/clubs2.cfm
    Description:   Using a query of queries to make the club selection
                   use many fewer queries.
```

```
--->
<cfquery name="clubs" datasource="clubsSQL">
    select
        name, venueID, category,
        location, address, phone, atmosphere, notes
    from
        clubData
    order by name
</cfquery>
<cfif clubs.recordCount eq 0>
    <!--- if there weren't any clubs, abort, since the clubEvents query
          will contain an empty valuelist(clubs.venueID) causing a
          syntax error --->
    No Current Events.
    <cfabort>
</cfif>
<cfquery name="clubEvents" datasource="clubsSQL">
    select
        startDate, name, edesc, venueID
    from
        events
    where
        venueID in (#valueList(clubs.venueID)#)
        and endDate >= #now()#
    order by startDate
</cfquery>
<table border="1" cellPadding="0" cellSpacing="0">
<tr>
    <th>Name</th>
    <th>Location</th>
    <th>Atmosphere</th>
    <th>Notes/Events</th>
</tr>
<cfoutput query="clubs">
    <cfquery name="events" dbtype="query">
        select
            startDate, name, edesc
        from
            clubEvents
        where
            venueID = #clubs.venueID#
    </cfquery>
    <cfset eventNum = #events.recordCount#>
    <tr valign="top">
        <td>#clubs.name#<br>#clubs.category#</td>
        <td>#clubs.location#<br>#clubs.address#<br>#clubs.phone#</td>
        <td>#clubs.atmosphere#  </td>
        <td>#clubs.notes#  
            <cfif variables.eventNum is not 0>
                <br>#variables.eventNum# event(s)<br>
                <cfloop query="events">
```

```
            #events.startDate# / #events.name# / #events.edesc#<br>
         </cfloop>
      </cfif>
   </td>
  </tr>
</cfoutput>
```

Remember, there is more than one way to get the job done, and that the first or most obvious solution is usually not the best.

Use the features your database provides. Stored procedures execute faster than standard text queries because the code has already been read, optimized, and compiled by the database, thus saving time. As discussed in Chapters 12, "Stored Procedures," stored procedures also greatly reduce the overhead involved in database transactions.

The proper use of constraints and triggers can reduce the number of queries and the complexity of your application considerably. For instance, when you delete a parent record from a table with multiple related tables, deleting all of the child records can be a complex task requiring many queries. If, you properly define the referential integrity in the database instead, the database server will delete all the child records for you automatically. However, the more platform-specific database features you use, the more difficult it will be to migrate your database from one platform to another.

cfquery and cfstoredproc Attributes

The cfquery and cfstoredproc tags contain a few attributes that may allow you to tune individual queries for better performance (see Table 16.1).

TABLE 16.1: cfquery and cfstoredproc Attributes

Attribute	Description
blockfactor	By default, Oracle connections return one row at a time. Specifying the blockfactor attribute in your queries can improve the query retrieval performance significantly.
maxRows	Specifying the maxRows attribute on a cfquery can allow you to limit the number of rows, and maximum amount of data, that ColdFusion will bring back from a query. If you only care about the first row of a large query, specify this to avoid transferring unnecessary data between the database and the application server.
timeout	The timeout attribute allows you to override the default timeout for a query as set in the JDBC driver. You can use this to allow your application to have a short default timeout time, and set it to a higher value for individual, long-running queries.
cachedAfter/ cachedWithin	These attributes allow you to specify parameters for caching individual queries. They are discussed in more detail in Chapter 11 of *Mastering ColdFusion MX*, by Arman Danesh, et al. (Sybex, 2002).

Query Tools

As you evaluate different solutions to the problem at hand, it can be quite useful to use a query tool rather than testing solutions directly in your ColdFusion templates. Even though the query information in the ColdFusion debug output is extremely valuable in helping you spot slow queries, it sometimes isn't much help when something isn't working quite right or throws an error. In the case of a query error, frequently the error isn't in the logic or syntax of the query, but it is in a parameter the template is passing (or not passing) to the query. In this case, it's helpful to execute the query with sample hard-coded data to diagnose the problem.

All major database platforms provide some sort of query analyzer or SQL interpreter for the database. Oracle provides SQL*Plus, and Microsoft's SQL Query Analyzer is an excellent tool for testing queries against an MS SQL database server. ColdFusion Studio's built-in query builder is helpful, but it doesn't offer the more advanced features of the dedicated tools, such as showing you execution plans and detailed client statistics for queries.

As you experiment with queries, remember to structure the queries so that the database can take advantage of your indexes. Also, feel free to restructure your indexes to match the queries of your application that are most important to the applications performance.

Database Tuning References

The database manufacturers have provided some excellent additional information on tuning specific databases. Check out the following links.

- For information on performance tuning for Microsoft SQL Server, see `http://www.microsoft.com/SQL/techinfo/administration/2000/perftuning.asp`.

- To take a look at a performance tuning guide for Microsoft SQL Server 7, check out `http://www.microsoft.com/SQL/techinfo/administration/70/perftuning.asp`.

- Look at the "Performance and Tuning Guide" on `http://manuals.sybase.com/onlinebooks/group-as/asg1200e/aseperf/@Generic__BookView` to learn more about Sybase ASE.

- And check out the "Introduction to Oracle Performance Tuning" at `http://technet.oracle.com/doc/server.804/a58246/intro.htm` to become more familiar with the Oracle database. To access this URL, you will need to be signed up and logged on to Oracle.com. Another excellent Oracle resource, but not from the manufacturer, can be seen at `http://www.oracletuning.com/`.

Profiling ColdFusion MX Templates

When you are monitoring performance on your web server or reading your log files, you will notice that certain templates take much longer to run than others. Sometimes the reason is obvious, such as a long-running call to an external web service, but frequently it is necessary to look deeper to figure out what's really going on within the execution of a template.

Most complex pages include calls to CFCs, functions, included pages, and custom tags, all of which may be causing the issues that cause your page to take a long time to run. Use of the `cftrace` tag or the `getTickCount` function and the debugging Report Execution Times option to see what's really taking up the time.

Profiling Template Execution

As you saw in Chapter 2, if you set the ColdFusion Administrator's Report Execution Times option, you get a detailed breakdown of the amount of time spent executing each template. The breakdown includes each page that was called during template execution, including CFCs called directly, `cfinclude`s, and custom tags that run during execution. When this option is set and after you separate your queries into included templates and put function libraries into their own templates, you will get a detailed breakdown in the debugging output that can give you a good idea of where your page is spending its time. Once you've isolated the offending page, you can use the `getTickCount` function to profile inside that page; this will help you retrieve the additional information you need to figure out exactly what's killing your application's performance.

NOTE   For more information on the `cftrace` tag and the `getTickCount` function, see Chapters 2 and 11, respectively.

Using cftrace and getTickCount to Profile within a Page

As just mentioned, the `cftrace` tag and the `getTickCount` function allow you to see how the time spent executing a template is used.

`cftrace` returns the elapsed time from the start of the template execution until the `cftrace` tag was called, along with the line number and any text you wish to display (you won't need to display a variable for this purpose). Listing 16.5 is an example of code that might be running slowly, with embedded `cftrace` tags. This code runs a CFMAIL tag, a CFHTTP, and a database query. We might like to see if the mail server used by CFMAIL, the remote server called by the CFHTTP tag, or the database is causing us performance issues.

Listing 16.5   **cftrace Profiling Example Code (trace.cfm)**

```
<!---
    Name: /c16/trace.cfm
    Description: Trace Example.  This code retrieves weather information
                 for the national parks in the exampleapps database, and
                 mails it out.
--->
<cftrace category="profile" text="Begin Code - calling query">
<cfquery name="qNatParks" datasource="exampleApps" debug>
    select
        ParkName,
        City,
        State
    from
        tblParks
    where
        ParkType = 'National Park'
</cfquery>
<cftrace category="profile" text="After qNatParks query">
<!--- only run the first 2 --->
<cfloop query="qNatParks" startRow="1" endRow="2">
    <!--- First cfhttp returns the URL we need to call to get the
          data --->
    <cftrace category="profile" text="In Loop, row=#qNatParks.currentRow#">
    <cfhttp url="http://www.srh.noaa.gov/zipcity.php" method="post">
    <cfhttpparam type="formField" name="go2" value="go">
    < cfhttpparam type="formField" name="inputString" value="#qNatParks.City#,
    #qNatParks.State#">
    </cfhttp>
    <cftrace category="profile" text="After first cfhttp">
    <!--- that first url redirects us to the URL where we can pick up
       the weather report.  The URL information is in the Location
       member of cfhttp.responseHeader, so we run a new request there.
    --->
    <cfhttp url="#cfhttp.responseHeader.location#" method="get" resolveURL="yes">
    <cftrace category="profile" text="After second cfhttp">
    <!--- we're done, now mail it out --->
    <cfmail to="kenf@macrotrain.com" from="server@macrotrain.com"
subject="Weather Report for #qNatParks.ParkName#"
type="html">#cfhttp.fileContent#</cfmail>
    <cftrace category="profile" text="After cfmail">
    <hr>
</cfloop>
```

In Figure 16.4, we can see the debug output.

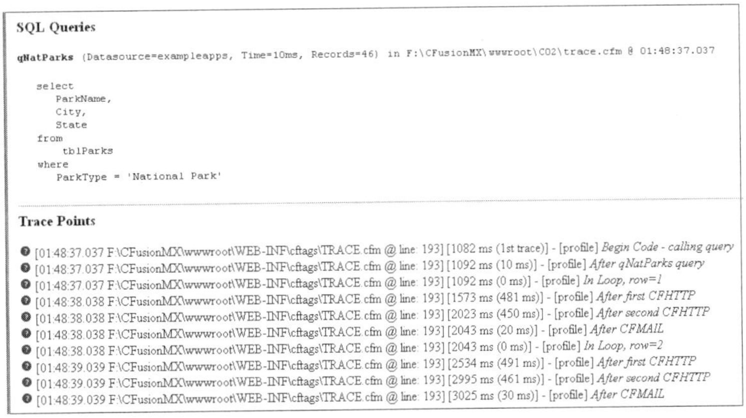

FIGURE 16.4:

Debug Output from
the cftrace example

```
SQL Queries

qNatParks (Datasource=exampleapps, Time=10ms, Records=46)  in F:\CFusionMX\wwwroot\C02\trace.cfm @ 01:48:37.037

    select
        ParkName,
        City,
        State
    from
        tblParks
    where
        ParkType = 'National Park'
```

Trace Points

```
[01:48:37.037 F:\CFusionMX\wwwroot\WEB-INF\cftags\TRACE.cfm @ line: 193] [1082 ms (1st trace)] - [profile] Begin Code - calling query
[01:48:37.037 F:\CFusionMX\wwwroot\WEB-INF\cftags\TRACE.cfm @ line: 193] [1092 ms (10 ms)] - [profile] After qNatParks query
[01:48:37.037 F:\CFusionMX\wwwroot\WEB-INF\cftags\TRACE.cfm @ line: 193] [1092 ms (0 ms)] - [profile] In Loop, row=1
[01:48:38.038 F:\CFusionMX\wwwroot\WEB-INF\cftags\TRACE.cfm @ line: 193] [1573 ms (481 ms)] - [profile] After first CFHTTP
[01:48:38.038 F:\CFusionMX\wwwroot\WEB-INF\cftags\TRACE.cfm @ line: 193] [2023 ms (450 ms)] - [profile] After second CFHTTP
[01:48:38.038 F:\CFusionMX\wwwroot\WEB-INF\cftags\TRACE.cfm @ line: 193] [2043 ms (20 ms)] - [profile] After CFMAIL
[01:48:38.038 F:\CFusionMX\wwwroot\WEB-INF\cftags\TRACE.cfm @ line: 193] [2043 ms (0 ms)] - [profile] In Loop, row=2
[01:48:39.039 F:\CFusionMX\wwwroot\WEB-INF\cftags\TRACE.cfm @ line: 193] [2534 ms (491 ms)] - [profile] After first CFHTTP
[01:48:39.039 F:\CFusionMX\wwwroot\WEB-INF\cftags\TRACE.cfm @ line: 193] [2995 ms (461 ms)] - [profile] After second CFHTTP
[01:48:39.039 F:\CFusionMX\wwwroot\WEB-INF\cftags\TRACE.cfm @ line: 193] [3025 ms (30 ms)] - [profile] After CFMAIL
```

As you can see in the example output, our cftrace call lets us know exactly how much time was spent in each interesting tag, how much time was spent in the query, and how the execution progressed. We see from the example that the CFHTTP tag has a high cost, but the CFMAIL, which we might have otherwise suspected of being a problem, was in reality quite fast.

With judicious use of the cftrace tag, you can figure out exactly which line of code is eating that valuable execution time, and optimize your application accordingly.

TIP   An important thing to watch out for in ColdFusion MX is calls to COM objects. COM calls are now wrapped in a Java-COM container with a significant performance penalty. See Tech-Note 22921 in the Macromedia Servers TechNotes Knowledge Base for more information. See http://www.macromedia.com/v1/Handlers/index.cfm?ID=22921&Method=Full.

Tuning the Operating System

Several settings can be adjusted at the operating system level for both web servers and database servers. Although these adjustments are a good idea, none will save you from a poorly performing application. Tuning your operating system can boost the capacity of a server slightly, but none of these settings will save you from a poorly written query or missing database index.

Windows NT/2000

Maximize the throughput for network applications rather than file sharing, as follows:

Windows NT   From the Network Properties page, select Services and then open the Properties page for the Server service. Select "Maximize data throughput for network applications."

Windows 2000 Server   Open the Local Area Connection Properties page, and then the access the Microsoft File and Printer Sharing Properties. Select "Maximize data throughput for network applications."

Disable any performance boost for foreground applications, as follows:

Windows NT   From the System Properties page, select the Performance tab, and slide the control for boosting foreground application performance all the way to the left—None.

Windows 2000   From the System Properties page, select the Advanced tab, and click Performance Options. For Optimize Performance For: select Background Services.

You also need to control the pagefile size. For optimum performance, the active pagefile should be located on a different physical drive from the operating system's boot partition. If you create multiple pagefiles, Windows will use the pagefile on what it considers to be the least active partition. For reliability and the ability to recover from certain types of system crashes, there should also be a pagefile on the operating system's boot partition. Microsoft recommends a pagefile of 1.5 to 2 times the amount of installed memory, but this may actually be more than you want for best performance and least paging. Only testing can tell you how much pagefile you need.

However, if your server is configured properly and you have enough memory installed, your server should use very little of the pagefile, and it will spend very little time swapping memory to disk. You should allocate enough space to the pagefile to assure that virtual memory is never exhausted under normal operation.

Internet Information Server Configuration

In Internet Information Server (IIS), the Performance Tuning slider actually tells IIS how much memory to allocate to your web server. Setting the slider to a slightly higher value than recommended causes new connections to occur faster, but it also uses more system memory. If you've got the RAM to spare, you can configure IIS for best performance by setting up IIS to conserve as few resources as possible in the name of performance. You can configure IIS from the Internet Information Services Manager as follows:

1. Highlight the server name in the left pane and select Properties. Click on the Edit button next to WWW Service Master Properties.

2. From the ISAPI Filters tab, remove any unneeded ISAPI filters.

3. Select the Performance tab, and slide the control for the number of hits per day to More Than 100,000.

4. On the Home Directory tab complete the following:

   • Disable these options: Script Source Access, Write, Directory Browsing, and Index This Resource.

- Set the Execute Permissions to Scripts Only.
- Click Configuration and remove all unused script mappings.

From the Web Site tab, configure your logging options.

For more suggestions, see the Macromedia Servers TechNotes Knowledge Base, article number 11772 (`http://www.macromedia.com/v1/Handlers/index.cfm?ID=11772&Method=Full`), which gives information on Windows platform-specific performance settings. This document will tell you how to disable unnecessary services, disable foreground application performance boost, and optimize your TCP/IP settings for server throughput.

Solaris and Linux Systems

Macromedia has published a fairly detailed Knowledge Base article (ID 23004) on the specific subject of platform tuning for Solaris, Linux, and Unix If you use one of these systems you should take the time to read this in detail. You'll find it at `http://www.macromedia.com/v1/Handlers/index.cfm?ID=23004&Method=Full`. Following are some highlights of this article's topics.

Disabling Unused Services

Any services or daemons that aren't absolutely necessary for ColdFusion or your web server's performance should be disabled (hopefully, you're not running the database on the same machine, but if you are, don't disable the database's daemons). Don't run X, CDE, or any GUI unless you are configuring your server and using the GUI tools. Specifically, you don't need `sendmail` (Solaris/Linux), `uucp`, `ntpd`, `lp`, `nfs.client`, `audit`, `autofs`, `ncsd` (Solaris), `xfs`, `postgresql`, `pulse`, `smb`, `ypbind`, `apmd`, `innd`, `snmpd`, and `gpm` (Linux).

NOTE   The foregoing list of services to disable is an "extreme" list. You may need your `nfs.client` and/or your `sendmail` server if you're going to be mounting drives or sending mail from your CF server.

In your `inetd.conf`, you should pick and choose which entries you need, and comment out the rest. Leave at least `telnet` (or SSH), `fs`, and `100235/1 tli`.

TIP   There's a handy script in the Macromedia article referenced earlier that you may want to use to comment out these nonessentials.

Remember to restart your machine after you've made these changes.

Macromedia recommends that the web server's root directory and all swap space are located on a separate physical disk than the main OS and other system files.

J2EE Tuning

On any platform, remember that ColdFusion MX is a Java application, and it only runs as well as your Java platform. The ideas discussed in this section will help you tune Windows or Unix/Linux/Solaris for good performance with the built-in JRun engine, but if you're running ColdFusion MX on top of a J2EE platform, optimizing the J2EE server can have dramatic results at runtime.

For more information on performance tuning for the various J2EE platforms, see the support sites from your J2EE application vendor.

In Sum

In all high-performance environments, it is vital that you take a sensible and ongoing approach to the performance tuning of a default installation of the machine, operating system, and application servers. This chapter covered several factors that are important to and have bearing upon your ColdFusion MX application's performance.

To achieve peak performance from your application and server, you need to do the following:

1. Observe and measure your server under load with load testing software.

2. Monitor the specific resources that are in short supply, and test to see where the problems are found.

3. Make adjustments to the system to optimize it for best performance—tune the ColdFusion MX Server, the operating system and network, and especially the database to eliminate bottlenecks and fix problems. Also watch out for your web server (Apache, IIS, Netscape Enterprise Server) and Java environment if appropriate.

4. Examine the web server logs and template performance to determine if there are application issues. As you've seen, the best way to improve template performance is to figure out which long running templates are the most important by profiling them via the load testing software, and then optimize your templates by profiling your database access, queries, and code to find and fix inefficiencies.

5. Go back to step 1 and do it all again, until the system performs as desired.

With the resources from this chapter at your disposal, you should be able to get the most out of both your hardware platform and your ColdFusion MX application.

Clustering: Load Balancing and Failover

By William Baum and Selene Bainum

- Introduction to high-availability websites

- Types of software clustering

- Hardware load-balancing options

- Planning and creating a ClusterCATS cluster

- Administering and testing a ClusterCATS cluster

- Deploying content among clustered servers

- Clustering databases

M any good books have been written solely on the topics of systems redundancy, clustering, and high-availability. Although we cannot cover all the possible options or best practices associated with these topics that are available to the ColdFusion practitioner in a single chapter, we will provide a primer on some of the options from which ColdFusion implementations can benefit. The goal is to give you some basic information and tools so that you can understand the importance of and the considerations involved in clustering and high-availability concepts.

In order to successfully design, implement, and sustain a good high-availability system, you must be able to plan a proper infrastructure. If most of your computing background has focused solely on software development and language, you'll want to solicit assistance from others with more systems administration and network engineering experience when it comes to clustering and high-availability.

This chapter focuses on techniques you can use to safeguard against systems failure by using clustering, traffic redirection, and other techniques. It also explores some fairly meaty issues, such as systems administration, network engineering, DNS, Round Robin DNS, ClusterCATS software clustering/load-balancing techniques, and hardware clustering. You will also learn to plan, install, configure, administrate, and test a ClusterCATS cluster.

NOTE   To get the most benefit from this chapter, you should have at least a basic understanding of computer networking with TCP/IP, web server configuration, and Domain Name Systems (DNS).

High-Availability Systems

High availability is a term that is used too often by marketing executives who are trying to sell customers reliable web solutions. However, the term should not simply be dismissed as a buzzword. Every person or company that has a website has a general sense of when their site should be accessible by its target audience. For a young couple who wants to make their new baby's pictures available on their personal website, their site needs to be accessible only when the grandparents want to view pictures of their baby's first days. For a large multinational company, high-availability may mean as close to 24 hours a day and 7 days a week as possible. In other words, high availability means different things to different websites.

Clustering

A *cluster* is made up of at least two web servers that can access one another over a network. Clustered servers act as a single entity to handle traffic more reliably than by any single computer. This configuration also provides system redundancy, which is lacking in a single-server environment. Here we are concerned primarily with the load balancing and failover components of clustering.

Load Balancing   *Load balancing* is the process by which traffic bound for a network service (typically a website, but it could also be used for other services such as databases) is intelligently routed to the most appropriate server according to a set algorithm that measures performance and availability. In a load-balanced environment, network traffic would be routed between two servers—or among several servers—based on existing load.

Failover   *Failover* is achieved when one device takes over for another device that is disabled in some way. Typically, network traffic will be routed to an additional server or device when one server or device fails.

NOTE   Before clustering your website, make sure it is properly tuned and configured on its existing server. Refer to Chapter 16, "Performance Tuning" for more information.

Scalability and Reliability

Moving from a single server to a clustered environment is a big step. The initial change from one server to two clustered servers is much more complicated than it is to add additional clustered servers to an already clustered environment; this is because most of the work is entailed in getting the first two clustered servers to work together.

Cluster Size

Clusters, by definition, require at least two discrete devices. Determining the number of servers—beyond the mandatory first two—you need in your cluster can be fairly simple or rather complicated, depending on your application and architecture. The process generally starts when you load test one server to determine its maximum load at acceptable performance levels. You then estimate the maximum foreseeable load you expect and divide that number by the maximum acceptable performance of each server. The result will tell you roughly how many web servers you need.

You must also take into account other factors that will limit the performance of the web servers, the most significant of which will generally be your database servers' performance. If your database and queries are well tuned, they will probably support more than one web server. Only testing will tell you how many web servers can be supported before performance significantly degrades—which you never want to happen live.

If you need more performance than you can get from a single database server, you'll have to add additional database servers into the formula and determine the level of synchronization required between the database servers. If the databases needs live synchronization, the replication will represent additional load and will have to be accounted for in your testing. If the database doesn't need live replication, then it should scale fairly linearly.

NOTE   Database replication is described later in this chapter.

NOTE   ColdFusion licensing requirements may play a role in determining the size of your cluster. In most cases, you will need a valid ColdFusion license for each server in your cluster. Check with your IT purchasing contact or Macromedia sales contact for licensing details.

Appropriate Redundancy

One of the main reasons for employing clusters is to help minimize single points of system failure. Many sites that could be served by single servers are clustered for reliability or maintainability. Although you may or may not have hardware or software failures in this arrangement, you will certainly have downtime due to maintenance. Servers have to be maintained on a regular basis—installing upgrades, patches, service packs, and so on. Make sure that you consider this when you are determining the size of your cluster or whether to cluster at all. Although everyone strives for as little downtime as possible, some applications are more mission critical than others. Frequently a certain amount of downtime, for maintenance, is perfectly acceptable.

Eliminating all of a system's single points of failure is often not feasible for any but the largest websites with astronomical budgets. It requires multiple redundant backbone connections in multiple data centers around the country, or even the world. Since you probably don't have this kind of budget, you need to draw the line somewhere and be reasonable about it. Determine what the acceptable level of risk is, and assume you will probably have some occasional downtime.

Although it is important to minimize downtime and single points of failure, there's a great deal to be said for keeping your architecture as simple as is appropriate for your needs.

Software Load Balancing

In the beginning, nobody envisioned a website big enough or busy enough that it couldn't be handled by a single computer. After all, in the really early days of the Internet, the fastest backbone was slower than the DSL or cable modems people have in their homes today. Now, of course, lots of websites are a lot bigger than can be served by any computer, so they have to be served by multiple computers, and we need a way to distribute traffic among them.

This section discusses DNS and ways to perform load balancing and failover utilizing software solutions.

WARNING When you create your first cluster for test purposes, it is a good idea to create the cluster in a test environment that will not affect any existing production servers This is so that it does not interfere with your existing configuration or slow down your network.

It is important to consider the edition of ColdFusion you are using when you go to choose a software load-balancing option. The Enterprise edition of ColdFusion includes the robust and easy-to-configure ClusterCATS technology. If you are using the Professional edition of Cold-Fusion, however, you will need to consider one of the other options discussed in this section.

DNS

DNS is a means of associating an Internet device's host and domain names with numerical TCP/IP addresses, thus eliminating the need to memorize unfriendly IP addresses for every resource that you wish to visit. When a domain name is registered, at least two authoritative DNS servers must also be registered for the domain. These are the DNS servers that other DNS servers will query for host addresses within the domain.

When you type a URL into a browser, the browser makes a DNS resolution request to the operating system. The operating system then passes the request to the first available DNS server that is configured in the computer's network properties. Assuming the address is not in the local DNS server's cache, the DNS server will query one of the root DNS servers to find out which DNS servers are authoritative for the requested domain. It will then submit the original request to one of the authoritative servers. When it receives a response, the DNS server will return it to the user's computer. This computer will then pass it to the browser, and the browser will make its HTTP request to the IP address it received. The browser and the local DNS server will cache the response so that future requests can be serviced from the cache, rather than by repeating the entire process.

Round Robin DNS

Round Robin DNS is one of the simplest and most effective methods of distributing load to more than one sever. Round Robin works simply by assigning more than one target address for a given hostname. With normal DNS, each hostname within a domain is assigned one address, and when the DNS server is queried, it returns that address. When you supply additional addresses, the DNS server returns all of the addresses, but it rotates the order in which they are returned in a round robin fashion—rotating the order of processing—hence the name.

Typically, each browser makes requests to the same IP repeatedly so it doesn't have to make multiple DNS requests. As a result, each client DNS server receives multiple IPs and picks up the round robin scheme; it changes the order of the addresses in its response to subsequent requests it serves from its cache. For instance, your ISP's DNS server is supposed to rotate the addresses for www.yahoo.com for each client that requests that site.

Round Robin DNS can play a role in your load balancing strategy but should not be relied upon alone, due to some rather severe limitations. With all of this caching going on in so many places, there is no way to reliably predict the distribution of hits. One server will invariably receive more traffic than another, and in some cases, significantly more. Proxy servers are notorious for ignoring your round robin scheme—for instance, they might send everyone to the same IP and then sometimes, they might seemingly randomly throw them all to another server, which could destroy your session integrity. This can be a problem with AOL and other "mega-proxies" as well as in situations where a large number of your application's clients will be coming from behind the same firewall or proxy server. This can happen frequently in a number of intranet or extranet applications.

Round Robin DNS also makes no provision for a server that has failed or is down for maintenance. The failed or downed server will receive the same number of requests as any other. Fortunately, most browsers will resubmit the request to another server after the first server times out, so though the initial response will be quite slow, the request will generally not actually fail and display an error in the browser.

Round Robin DNS alone is, despite its severe limitations, the simplest method of distributing load across multiple servers. Combined with other methods of balancing load and providing for high availability, it can be part of a clustering solution, but it cannot provide these capabilities alone.

ClusterCATS

ClusterCATS (Cluster Content, Application and Transaction Smart) was written by Bright Tiger Technologies, which was subsequently acquired by Allaire and then Macromedia. Originally, Bright Tiger offered ClusterCATS in various forms for different platforms and offered services for globally distributed applications, content distribution, and so on. Now, ClusterCATS exists only in the version provided by Macromedia with the Enterprise versions of ColdFusion and JRun. It is designed to provide load balancing and failover for ColdFusion- and JRun-enabled web traffic only.

NOTE For complete ClusterCATS documentation, refer to the "Using ClusterCATS" book included with the documentation for ColdFusion MX. It is also available in PDF format from the Macromedia website at http://www.macromedia.com/support/coldfusion/documentation.html.

ClusterCATS Modes

The two primary issues for consideration in planning your ClusterCATS cluster are whether to use Round Robin DNS, and whether to use ClusterCATS in static or dynamic IP mode.

Static IP Mode

If you have only one IP address assigned for each server in the cluster, ClusterCATS works in *static* mode. In this case, the ClusterCATS IP address is bound statically to the adapter. If one of the servers fails, another server will grab its IP address. When the failed server comes back up, it will generate a network IP address conflict and reboot itself. The server that grabbed the failed server's IP will detect the conflict and release the IP to be available for the rebooting server when it comes back up.

> **WARNING**   Use of static IP mode is not recommended. The static IP addresses are passed around among servers and intentionally cause IP address conflicts. Even when static failover works properly, the IP may be unavailable during the period of time in which a server is restarting. If there is any problem, your servers could end up preempting each other in a continuous loop. For these reasons, Dynamic IP mode is highly preferred for ClusterCATS operations.

Dynamic IP Mode

The preferred dynamic IP mode requires at least two IP addresses for each server in the cluster: one for the cluster, and a second *maintenance*, or dedicated address, with which the machines can communicate with each other. In this configuration, the cluster IP addresses are all allocated by ClusterCATS dynamically, and can therefore be passed around. This configuration differs from some other load balancing methods, which might use only one public IP address for an entire cluster.

ClusterCATS and Round Robin DNS

ClusterCATS works in one of two basic DNS configurations, either with or without Round Robin DNS. ClusterCATS was originally designed to overcome the limitations of Round Robin DNS, so it complements Round Robin well. In this configuration, ClusterCATS allows Round Robin to do most of the traffic distribution and only steps in to redirect traffic when a server gets busy or fails. Without Round Robin DNS, all of the traffic is sent to a single server, which then starts redirecting traffic to other servers when it gets busy.

Using ClusterCATS with Hardware Load Balancing Devices

ClusterCATS normally operates in active mode, providing active load balancing and optionally, failover for your cluster. If you are using a hardware load-balancing device, you will want that device to perform those functions for you. In this type of situation, you can use ClusterCATS in passive mode, passing only its load calculation and server health checks to your load balancing device.

NOTE   If you are using ColdFusion 5, Macromedia has an excellent knowledgebase article on the subject. See Article 21570: "ColdFusion 5 Server Monitoring & Hardware Load Balancing Devices" at `http://www.macromedia.com/v1/handlers/index.cfm?ID=21570&Method=Full`.

NOTE   Support is currently included only for the Cisco LocalDirector, and limited support for F-5's Big-IP. Hardware load balancing is discussed in more detail later in the chapter.

Windows Network Load Balancing

What was originally Convoy Cluster Software was bought by Microsoft and renamed the Windows NT Load Balancing Service (WLBS) for NT4. It is now referred to simply as Network Load Balancing on Windows 2000. Only minor differences exist between the various versions and names of this technology.

WLBS operates in either unicast or multicast mode and can be used with a single network adapter, but it is better to use it with multiple network adapters in each server. There are advantages to both multicast mode and multiple network adapters, but it's quite possible to get WLBS working properly with a single network adapter.

For NT4, WLBS is free and available for download from Microsoft, although it is intended and licensed for use only with the Enterprise version of NT. For Windows 2000, WLBS is included with Windows 2000 Advanced Server and Datacenter Server.

Drawbacks of WLBS

Although WLBS is free and can be used with the Professional version of ColdFusion, it is a very basic protocol that is not optimized for either ColdFusion or web traffic. If you are using the Enterprise edition of ColdFusion, you're much better off using ClusterCATS instead of WLBS.

Session *stickiness*—keeping a user on the same server during their entire visit to your site—is implemented in a rather blunt way in WLBS. Rather than attempting more sophisticated methods of determining sessions, WLBS will merely make sure that all incoming traffic of a given type from a single source IP or an entire Class C of IPs will be directed to the same host computer. The Class C option is intended to overcome the problem of a client that connects from behind load-balanced proxy servers, a situation that can cause a client's IP to abruptly change in the middle of a session. Since most load-balanced proxy servers will exist in the same Class C of Internet addresses, this approach is reasonable.

However, for intranet, extranet, or other applications that could have a large number of clients connecting from behind proxy servers, all clients could all wind up pounding the same server—effectively negating your load balancing. In this situation, you will need to eliminate the need for session stickiness in your application or use a different load balancing method.

Other Software Load Balancers

A number of other software-based load balancing solutions are still available, although the market for load balancing seems to be shifting more and more toward hardware load balancers, which are constantly getting better, faster, and cheaper.

The following are some other software-based load balancing technologies of note:

- Resonate Central Dispatch at
  `http://www.resonate.com/solutions/literature/data_sheet_cd.php`
- PolyServe Application Manager at `http://www.polyserve.com/`
- Linux Virtual Server Project at `http://www.linuxvirtualserver.org/`
- mod_backhand for Apache at `http://www.backhand.org/mod_backhand/`

Hardware Load Balancing

Load balancing can be performed by a hardware-based solution as opposed to software-based methods. Hardware load balancers tend to take one of two basic forms: they are either server-based load balancers like the Cisco's LocalDirector or F5's Big-IP, or they are switch-based load balancers like The Cisco Content Services Switches (CSS), Nortel's Alteon line of switches, or the ServerIron series of switches from Foundry Networks. One thing they all have in common is the ability for failover redundancy. They are all designed to work fairly seamlessly in pairs, usually in active/standby configuration, but sometimes in active/active as well.

The server-based load balancing devices are similar to some early-generation routers in that they are basically special-purpose PCs. They have motherboards, hard drives, NIC cards, and so on. Also like PCs, they boot up with an operating system and the load balancing functions they perform are controlled by software.

With a hardware load balancer, you generally assign a Virtual IP (VIP) to a logical cluster of servers. The VIP is bound to the load-balancing device, which then distributes the traffic to the actual servers through one of a few basic methods.

There are many types of hardware load balances available:

Cisco LocalDirector   The Cisco LocalDirector was among the first popular hardware load balancers, and though it is showing its age, the technology is still in use today. Information about Cisco's LocalDirector is available at `http://www.cisco.com/warp/public/cc/pd/cxsr/400/index.shtml`.

Cisco CSS Cisco recently acquired Arrowpoint Communications. Arrowpoint's line of switches has been renamed and repackaged as the CSS 11000 line of Content Services Switches. More information can be obtained about CSS at `http://www.cisco.com/univercd/cc/td/doc/pcat/11000.htm`.

NOTE Macromedia Knowledgebase Article 20404 details a problem with ColdFusion and older versions of the WebNS software. This problem has been resolved in WebNS 4.10 and later. To learn more, go to `http://www.macromedia.com/v1/handlers/index.cfm?ID=20404`.

Nortel Networks—Alteon WebSystems Alteon WebSystems, which was purchased by Nortel Networks, has been a leader in high-performance load-balancing switches for some time. Alteon offers two lines of web switches with varying capabilities and prices. They are all highly capable, high-performance ASIC based switch-based load balancers. You can find more information at `http://www.nortelnetworks.com/products/01/alt180/index.html`.

Foundry Networks ServerIron Family The Foundry Networks ServerIron family of switch-based load balancers is among the most powerful and capable of all. You can find more information about ServerIron at `http://www.foundrynet.com/products/webswitches/serveriron/index.html`.

The following hardware load balancers also warrant mention:

- Coyote Point Systems Inc. at `http://www.coyotepoint.com`
- F5 Networks, Inc. at `http://www.f5.com`
- HydraWEB Technologies Inc. at `http://www.hydraWeb.com`
- Radware, a RAD Group company at `http://www.radware.com`

NOTE Macromedia has an excellent Knowledge Base article to help you chose the hardware load balancing option that is right for you. Check it out at `http://www.macromedia.com/v1/handlers/index.cfm?ID=21780&method=full`.

Creating a ClusterCATS Cluster

Now that you've learned about some of the different types of clustering available, we'll focus on how to actually create a ClusterCATS cluster in dynamic IP mode on Windows 2000. The steps involved in this process include planning the cluster, configuring the DNS and IP address settings, and installing and configuring ClusterCATS.

NOTE   To create a cluster in Unix or Linux environments, you will need to consult the ClusterCATS documentation to modify the Windows-specific examples in this section.

Cluster Requirements

Before you plan, install, and configure a Windows 2000 cluster, you must know or have access to the elements listed in Table 17.1.

TABLE 17.1: Cluster Requirements

Requirement	Description
Web servers	At least two computers running Windows 2000 with web server software, such as IIS, and ColdFusion MX Enterprise installed.
Network	The members of the cluster must be connected to a network and be able to access one another.
IP addresses	You will need two dedicated IP addresses for each server.
DNS	An Internet name resolution service, such as DNS. If you do not have access to administer the DNS system yourself, a network administrator will need to make the DNS entries for you.
SMTP mail server	If you wish to have ClusterCATS send alert messages, you will need to know the name or IP address of your SMTP mail server as well as the e-mail addresses of the parties that should receive the alerts.

NOTE   If possible, the test cluster should be installed and configured in a test lab or non-production environment.

Planning the Cluster

Before you create a cluster, you must determine how many *members*, or servers, the cluster will contain. Each cluster member must have at least two IP addresses assigned to it: an IP address bound to the web server/website, and an IP address that will be used as the *maintenance address* for ClusterCATS. Using the maintenance address of a cluster member, ClusterCATS can still communicate with the server in case the web server service fails. This IP address also allows administrators a way to access the cluster member remotely.

Each member must also be assigned two Fully Qualified Host Names (FQHNs): the external hostname that is assigned to the web server/website, and the internal hostname assigned to the maintenance IP address.

Figure 17.1 displays a diagram of the cluster that we will study in this section.

Cluster diagram

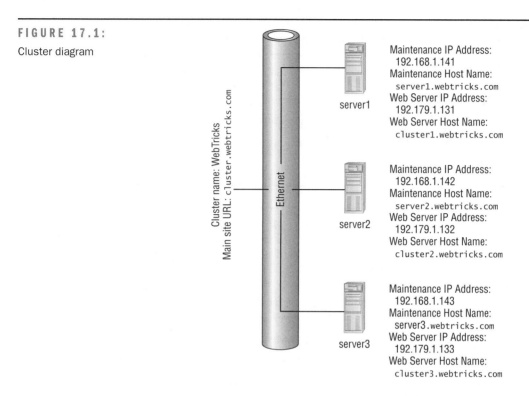

Figure 17.1 displays the members of the cluster (server1/cluster1, server2/cluster2, and server3/cluster3), including the four key components that must be known about each server. Each of these servers will be available to the `cluster.webtricks.com` domain name.

WARNING   Of course, when you plan your own cluster, you must replace the IP addresses and FQHNs that are displayed in Figure 17.1 and used throughout this section with the IP addresses and FQHNs for your domain that are compatible with your DNS configuration.

You must also decide whether or not you are going to use a Round Robin DNS configuration in conjunction with ClusterCATS.

- If you do not use Round Robin DNS, users accessing your website will all be directed to the same web server unless that server has reached its peak load or has a failure. In essence, you will have a primary and one or more backup web servers.

- If you use Round Robin DNS, users will be directed randomly to one of the web servers in your cluster, distributing the load among the servers. If one of those servers experiences a failure or reaches peak load, ClusterCATS will take over and will redirect the user to another cluster member.

Configuring DNS and IP Address Settings

Before you can create a cluster, you must ensure that the IP Address settings on your servers and the associated DNS records are properly set up.

DNS Settings

In order for the cluster members to communicate with one another and the web servers to be accessible to the Internet, an Internet name resolution system must be properly configured, containing records for each web server in the cluster. The recommended method uses a DNS server.

If you do not have access to your network's DNS server, ask a network administrator to make the necessary entries.

Because each cluster member has two IP addresses and two FQHNs, each server must also have two forward resolution DNS records created on your DNS server, one for each IP address/hostname pair. Table 17.2 displays the forward resolution DNS entries required for the cluster that will be created in this section. DNS reverse resolution records must also be created for each IP address/hostname pair in order for the cluster to operate properly.

TABLE 17.2: Cluster Forward Resolution DNS Entries

Role	IP Address	FQHN
Web server	192.168.1.131	cluster1.webtricks.com
Maintenance	192.168.1.141	server1.webtricks.com
Web server	192.168.1.132	cluster2.webtricks.com
Maintenance	192.168.1.142	server2.webtricks.com
Web server	192.168.1.133	cluster3.webtricks.com
Maintenance	192.168.1.143	server3.webtricks.com

TIP If you do not wish to use Round Robin DNS and you want users to be able to access your cluster using your main website URL (http://cluster.webtricks.com in this example), you must also create a forward resolution record with your main URL as the FQHN and the web server IP address of the cluster member that you want to be your primary web server.

Round Robin DNS Settings

If you wish to configure your DNS server to use Round Robin DNS, you must also add a forward resolution record for each web server IP address with the main URL to your site as the FQHN. Table 17.3 lists the DNS records that are needed to enable Round Robin DNS for the cluster that will be created in this section.

TABLE 17.3: Round Robin DNS Entries

IP Address	FQHN
192.168.1.131	cluster.webtricks.com
192.168.1.132	cluster.webtricks.com
192.168.1.133	cluster.webtricks.com

WARNING   Do *not* create DNS reverse resolution records for the Round Robin entries.

IP Address Settings

This section will explain how to properly bind each server's IP addresses so that they will be properly configured for ClusterCATS.

Internal IP Address

The IP address that the cluster will use as the maintenance address must be bound to the server in the TCP/IP Properties panel of the server's local area connection. Figure 17.2 displays the TCP/IP properties for the first machine in the cluster, `server1.webtricks.com`, using 192.168.1.141 as the maintenance IP address.

FIGURE 17.2:

Internet Protocol
(TCP/IP) Properties
panel

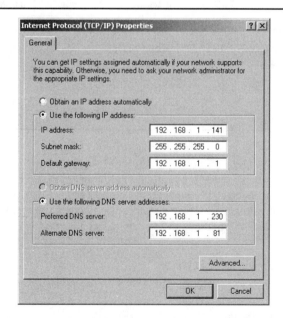

WARNING When you bind your maintenance IP addresses, you'll need to replace the IP Address, Subnet Mask, Default Gateway, and Preferred and Alternate DNS Servers in this example with the ones assigned for your network.

Web Server IP Address

In addition to the maintenance IP address, you need to have an IP address for each website that will be run on the web server. In this example, the IP address of the website is 192.168.1.131. The IP address needs to be bound to the website in your web server's software.

To change the IP address settings for Microsoft's Internet Information Server (IIS), open the IIS management console and drill down to the website that will be used for the cluster. Right-click the site and bring up the Properties window; the Web Site tab will be displayed by default. Within the Web Site Identification section, (All Unassigned) will be displayed as the IP Address. Replace that value with the web server IP address and click OK.

Figure 17.3 displays the IP address bound to the site within Microsoft's Internet Information Server (IIS).

FIGURE 17.3:
IIS website properties

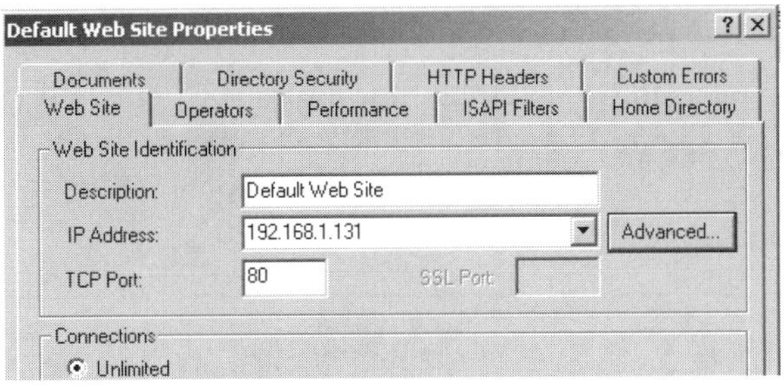

Installing ClusterCATS

Although ClusterCATS is available for use with the Enterprise version of ColdFusion, the application itself is not included on the ColdFusion MX installation CD. Instead, ClusterCATS can be downloaded from Macromedia at `http://www.macromedia.com/go/cfmx_clustercats` or by clicking the ClusterCATS option in the ColdFusion MX Enterprise edition's installation flash screen.

After downloading the appropriate file and extracting the executable file, run `setup.exe` to launch the ClusterCATS installer. ClusterCATS installs similarly to many other Windows applications, asking you to confirm installation directory, settings, and so on. When you reach the Select Components To Install window (displayed in Figure 17.4) you can select which component(s) you wish to install.

FIGURE 17.4:

Select Components To
Install window

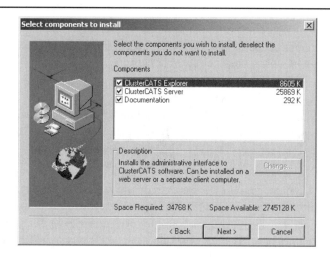

Each cluster member must have the ClusterCATS Server software installed and at least one member of your server must have the ClusterCATS Explorer installed, though you can install the ClusterCATS Explorer on each member without any problems. Installation of the ClusterCATS Documentation is optional.

After clicking the Next button, you will be presented with the Load Management Selection window (Figure 17.5). This window allows you to select a method for load management. For best results, check the option for ColdFusion MX (CFM) Performance, and click Next to continue.

FIGURE 17.5:

Load Management
Selection window

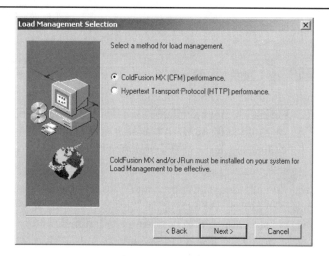

The installation continues and the ClusterCATS files are installed to the appropriate directories. After the files have been copied, you will be asked whether or not you want to configure the cluster member for Server Fail-Over. Check Yes to allow the other cluster members to pick up the IP address of this machine if it fails. If you check No, the cluster will only be enabled for load balancing.

Click Next to finish the installation. After ClusterCATS is installed, you will be asked whether or not you want to launch the ClusterCATS explorer. Check this box if you wish to configure your cluster now.

Configuring ClusterCATS

You can begin configuring your cluster as soon as you have ClusterCATS installed on at least one server. Configuration steps include creating the cluster, adding cluster members, and configuring cluster and member options.

Creating the Cluster and Adding Members

The easiest way to create a cluster is to use the Cluster Setup wizard. If you chose to launch the ClusterCATS Explorer when the installation process finished, the wizard is started automatically. To start the wizard manually, open ClusterCATS Explorer and select Configure ➤ Cluster Setup Wizard from the menu.

The first screen in the wizard asks for the cluster name, which cannot contain spaces. In this example, the cluster is named WebTricks. After clicking the Next button, you see the List Of Web Servers In The Cluster page, with a message stating that are no items to show in this view (Figure 17.6). Click the Add button to add the first cluster member.

NOTE   The name you assign to your cluster should be descriptive to you, but has no bearing on the operation of the cluster itself.

The two FQHNs for the server will be entered into the Add New Server window (Figure 17.7). The web server hostname (`cluster2.webtricks.com`) will be entered as the Web Server Name. To join the cluster using dynamic IP addressing, check the ClusterCATS maintenance support box and enter the maintenance hostname (`server2.webtricks.com`) as the Maintenance address.

WARNING   Remember, when adding servers to your own cluster, replace the web server and maintenance hostnames in this example with the appropriate hostnames assigned for your network.

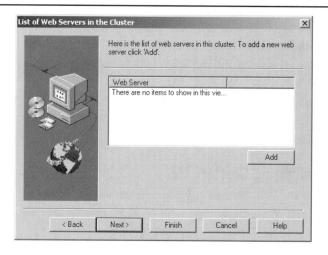

After you click the OK button, you will see a Cluster Administrator confirmation window, which displays a list of configuration conditions that must be met in order for the maintenance support to work. After ensuring that you have completed all the items in the list, click the OK button.

After the member is added, you are returned to the List Of Web Servers In The Cluster window; the name of the member you just added is now displayed. If you have already installed ClusterCATS on the other members of your cluster, you can add them to your cluster now by clicking the Add button again and repeating the process for those servers, or you can click the Next button, begin the configuration process, and add the other members later.

Configuring the Cluster

Once the cluster is created, there are several different configuration settings that can be modified.

Load Management

After adding at least one member to the cluster, the wizard proceeds to the configuration windows, starting with the Load Management window (Figure 17.8). This window lists each member in the cluster as well as each machine's load threshold values: Peak Load Threshold and Gradual Reduction Threshold.

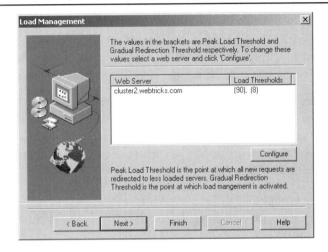

Peak Load Threshold   The peak threshold is the maximum load that the server will handle. If traffic reaches this level, all traffic will be redirected to another server, unless there are no servers available at less than their peak thresholds. If none of the servers in the cluster are available, the incoming request is aborted and the following default error message is displayed in the user's browser:

```
Requested File is not currently available in cluster
'testcluster'. Please try again later.
```

If you would like to supply your own error message, which can contain a more informative message, links to alternate mirror sites, redirections, and so on, you may do so by editing the registry values for the servers in the cluster.

To do so, just add a string value named `ErrorUrl`, which contains the name of the file you'd like the web server to present, in place of the default error message in the key for your server in:

```
HKEY_LOCAL_MACHINE\SYSTEM\CurrentControlSet\Services\BrightTiger\Servers\yo
ur-server
```

The file should be small and contain only simple HTML elements so it doesn't place additional load on the server.

Gradual Reduction Threshold   The gradual reduction threshold is the level at which ClusterCATS begins to redistribute a server's load. As long as the load factor on the server remains below this level, all traffic destined for the server will go through unabated. As the level of traffic rises above the gradual reduction threshold, ClusterCATS will begin redirecting traffic to other servers in the cluster. The redirections will become more and more aggressive as the load approaches the peak threshold. ClusterCATS will do its best to prevent load from ever reaching the peak threshold whenever possible.

Click the Next button to accept the default threshold values or select a server and click the Configure button to bring up the Load Thresholds window. After entering in the desired values, click the OK button to return to the Load Management window.

Alert Notification

The next screen in the wizard is the Alert Notification window. To setup e-mail alerts for system problems, enter in your SMTP mail server and the e-mail address(es) of those who shall receive the alerts. If you do not wish to configure alert notification at this time, you may leave both fields blank.

NOTE   For information on sending different alert messages to different people, please refer to the ClusterCATS documentation.

Session State Management

The next window asks whether or not you want to enable session state management for the cluster. If you use Session variables on any of your sites, you want to make sure Yes is checked before you proceed. If you don't, a single user who initiates a session on one server may be passed around to the various servers in the cluster, creating a session on each one. If you check Yes, the user will remain on the same server, unless that server fails during their session.

Load Balancing Device

The final window in the wizard lets you specify the name of the website that is supported by a hardware-based load-balancing device, such as Cisco LocalDirector. If none is being used, click Next and then Finish to finish the cluster configuration.

Administering a ClusterCATS Cluster

Once your cluster is created, you will need to access and administrate it. This section describes how to use the ClusterCATS Explorer and ClusterCATS Server Administrator interfaces to maintain your cluster.

NOTE   For information on the administrative tools for ClusterCATS on Linux or Unix environments, please refer to the ClusterCATS documentation.

ClusterCATS Explorer

The ClusterCATS Explorer is used to manage clusters from a central location. It is a Windows-based tool, but it can manage Unix or Linux cluster members as well. It can be run from any Windows cluster member or even from a remote computer, and it can access multiple clusters. Figure 17.9 displays the cluster configured in the last section.

FIGURE 17.9:

ClusterCATS Explorer

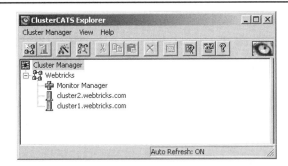

Within the ClusterCATS Explorer, existing clusters and their members are displayed. If the members are active and working, they will appear as they do in Figure 17.9. The icons displayed for a cluster member will be different if the status changes—a red "x" will appear if the server is unavailable and a yellow icon will appear if a server has reached its load threshold.

Connecting to an Existing Cluster

If you have ClusterCATS Explorer installed on a computer and wish to connect to an existing cluster, click View ➤ Show Cluster. Enter the name of a web server within the cluster (Figure 17.10) and click OK.

FIGURE 17.10:

Connecting to/showing an existing cluster

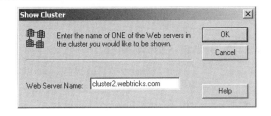

Administrating Clusters

Any of the steps that were performed in the previous section to create and configure a cluster could be performed from within the ClusterCATS Explorer as opposed to using the Cluster Setup wizard. That means you can create new clusters, add members to existing clusters, and modify clusters and cluster member configuration settings manually at any time.

The menu options in the ClusterCATS Explorer window change depending on what Explorer item is selected. The two options on the far right, View and Help, are always displayed.

When you click the name of a cluster, the Cluster, Configure, and Monitor menu items appear. You can also access these menus by right-clicking the name of a cluster.

For each cluster member, you can modify the state of the server and update the load thresholds. For clusters, you can change the administration parameters, modify the load balancing options, set alarm notifications, update the support messaging options, and add new members.

Viewing Server Loads

Using the Explorer, you can view the current load of either a single cluster member or of all the members of the server at once. To view the load of a single cluster member, select the desired server and select Monitor ➤ Load from the menu. To view the load of the entire cluster, you would basically do the same thing but you would click the cluster name instead of the server. Figure 17.11 displays the server loads for the cluster. Notice that the status of `cluster2.webtricks.com` is Busy because the load is 100 percent.

FIGURE 17.11:

Cluster load

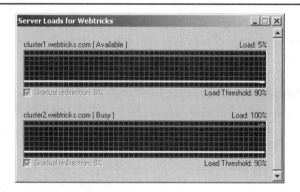

ClusterCATS Server Administrator

The ClusterCATS Server Administrator is a graphical interface that you use to modify specific settings on a server, such as those that set the configuration, those used to install/remove the ClusterCATS filter, those that stop and start the ClusterCATS service, and those that reset the server's configuration.

NOTE   Unlike the ClusterCATS Explorer, which can be run from any Windows machine with access to a cluster, the ClusterCATS Server Administrator must be run from the server that is being administered. Figure 17.12 display the Server Administrator for one of the servers in the cluster.

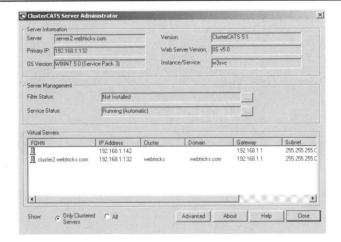

Testing a ClusterCATS Cluster

After you install and configure your ClusterCATS cluster, you are ready to begin testing and
using the cluster.

Creating a Test Home Page

The first thing you will need to do is create a test home page for each web server that will be
placed in the web server's root directory and named index.cfm. Listing 17.1 contains a page
that lists several different CGI variables that display information about the web server.

Listing 17.1   Cluster Test Home Page (c1701.cfm)

```
<!---
    Name:          /c17/c1701.cfm
    Description:   Home page for clustered servers to display
                   CGI variables.
--->
<!DOCTYPE HTML PUBLIC "-//W3C//DTD HTML 4.01 Transitional//EN">

<html>
<head>
    <title><cfoutput>#cgi.server_name#</cfoutput></title>
</head>

<body bgcolor="#ffffff">
```

```
<!--- Display the CGI variables. --->
<cfoutput>
    <table border="0">
        <tr>
            <td><b>cgi.server_name:</b></td>
            <td><b>#cgi.server_name#</b></td>
        </tr>
        <tr>
            <td>cgi.path_info:</td>
            <td>#cgi.path_info#</td>
        </tr>
        <tr>
            <td>cgi.path_translated:</td>
            <td>#cgi.path_translated#</td>
        </tr>
        <tr>
            <td>cgi.query_string:</td>
            <td>#.query_string#</td>
        </tr>
        <tr>
            <td>cgi.request_method:</td>
            <td>#cgi.request_method#</td>
        </tr>
        <tr>
            <td>cgi.script_name:</td>
            <td>#cgi.script_name#</td>
        </tr>
        <tr>
            <td>cgi.gateway_interface:</td>
            <td># cgi.gateway_interface#</td>
        </tr>
        <tr>
            <td>cgi.server_port:</td>
            <td>#cgi.server_port#</td>
        </tr>
        <tr>
            <td>cgi.server_protocol:</td>
            <td>#cgi.server_protocol#</td>
        </tr>
        <tr>
            <td>cgi.server_software:</td>
            <td>#cgi.server_software#</td>
        </tr>
    </table>
</cfoutput>

</body>
</html>
```

When a web server in the cluster is accessed, the CGI variables will display the information pertaining to that web server. Figures 17.13 and 17.14 display the browser results for cluster1.webtricks.com and cluster2.webtricks.com respectively.

FIGURE 17.13:

cluster1
.webtricks.com
home page results

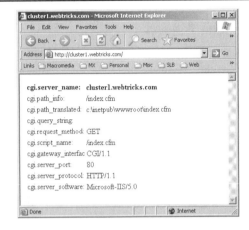

FIGURE 17.14:

cluster2
.webtricks.com
home page results

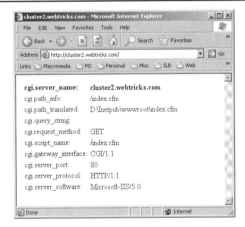

Because the two servers are configured almost identically, several of the CGI variables have the same values for each machine. However, you will notice that the *cgi.server_name* and *cgi.path_translated* variable values are different between the two servers.

Testing Load Balancing

To test the load balancing functionality of the cluster, enter your main site URL (cluster.webtricks.com in this example) into various browser types on several computers. You will notice that you may be directed to a particular server from a particular machine and browser. If you are always directed to the same server for multiple machine-browser combinations, you may want to check your ClusterCATS Explorer, as well as your DNS Round Robin or hardware load balancing devices, to ensure that all cluster members are accessible.

Testing Server Failover

One of the nice features of the dynamic IP mode configuration of ClusterCATS is that you can smoothly make a cluster member unavailable to the cluster by putting it into maintenance mode. By doing so, you can test the cluster with the remaining cluster members to ensure that they are picking up the load of the unavailable server.

NOTE   One of the steps required to place a server in maintenance mode involves ClusterCATS Server Administrator, so you must have access to the server itself. You can't just plan to access it remotely using ClusterCATS Explorer.

The first thing you need to do is set the peak threshold of the server to 0. In ClusterCATS Explorer, click the name of the cluster member you wish to put into maintenance mode and select Configure ➤ Load from the menu options. Change the peak threshold to 0 and click OK. ClusterCATS Explorer will now display the cluster member as being at being busy (see Figure 17.15).

FIGURE 17.15:

ClusterCATS Explorer displaying a busy server

Now Load the ClusterCATS Server Administrator to display the current settings. The Server Status will say Running if the server is currently up and running. Click the button with the ellipses (…) next to the status to bring up the Manage ClusterCATS Services window (Figure 17.16).

To stop the service, click the Stopped radio button within the Start Or Stop The Cluster-CATS Services section and enter the number of minutes ClusterCATS will wait before it stops the service. This setting allows users to be gracefully moved to other members in the cluster before this server is stopped. To stop the server immediately, enter 0.

Manage ClusterCATS
Services window

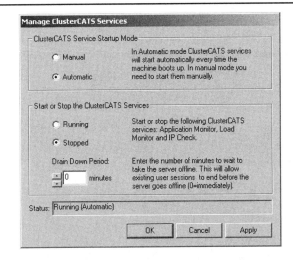

After you click the OK button, a confirm box will display; it will ask you to verify that you wish to stop the service. Click OK to stop the service. Figure 17.17 displays the ClusterCATS Explorer with the server unavailable.

ClusterCATS Explorer
displaying an
unavailable server

With the server unavailable, all hits to your main site URL will be directed to the other members in the cluster. If you try to access the inaccessible server directly through the browser (cluster1.webtricks.com in this example), the browser will be redirected to another functioning cluster member (cluster2.webtricks.com in this case).

To return this server to its proper state, start the ClusterCATS service on the server and then set the peak threshold back to its original value.

Content Deployment and Management

Once your cluster is up and running, you'll want efficient ways to deploy and manage your site's content. Deploying content is done via in one of two rather different processes, depending on whether you are installing the site for the first time or applying updates to an existing site. The initial installation is much easier because there is no existing site or content. It usually doesn't matter whether that process takes a few minutes, a few hours, or even longer.

When the site is up, however, the process of deploying new content across the servers needs to be as fast and efficient as possible to avoid downtime and errors for your website. Many of the processes and methods discussed in this section are appropriate to both the initial installation and the deployment of updates, but it will focus primarily on the latter.

Deployment Strategy

Among the most frequently overlooked aspects of a clustered website is the deployment of updated content. As the number of files and web servers increases, so does the complexity of delivering the content and assuring that all of the web servers are in synch with each other. Few things are more frustrating than attempting to diagnose an apparent code error only to discover that the cause of the problem is mismatched versions of templates across different servers.

The solution to this problem, and a whole host of others, is proper version control and a well-thought-out strategy for content delivery and deployment.

Your deployment strategy will generally involve moving either all of the content, or merely new or changed files, from the development or staging environment to one of the web servers, and then replicating or synchronizing the changes from that web server to the others. This generally involves three steps:

1. Archiving or packaging the content.
2. Delivering the content to the production environment.
3. Deploying the content across the production web servers.

This whole process can be greatly simplified with good application file layout.

Whenever possible, have the application's entire collection of template files, image files, and any other files that should be synchronized with the staging environment in one common directory tree. For instance, if you move any custom tags your application uses into a subdirectory of the application's root directory, keeping those custom tags synchronized will be considerably easier. If the application's custom tags are in ColdFusion's default location, synchronizing the custom tags between the staging and production environments will require at least one additional step in the process.

Any dynamic files, or others that should not be synchronized with the staging server (such as files uploaded via a publishing tool), should be placed in a different directory tree so that you avoid the possibility of overwriting the production site's files with files from the staging environment.

Packaging the Content

If your production servers are on the same LAN as your development or staging server, delivering the content from one environment to the other is a simple matter; but if your production servers are in a hosted or collocated environment, your access to it is limited by the speed of your Internet connection, firewalls, and so on. Delivering the content from one environment to the other can be a challenge.

Moving the content from the development or staging environment to the production environment can be done on a file-by-file basis with a number of methods, the simplest of which is the standard FTP synchronization that is offered by any number of FTP clients. Although this method can be successful for smaller sites, it tends to be fairly slow and inefficient for larger applications, especially if only a small percentage of the files have changed.

One possible solution to this problem is to *package* the new or changed files into a compressed archive file, usually a ZIP file on Windows systems, or a gzip'ed TAR file on Linux/Unix systems.

With `tar` and `gzip`, limiting the contents of the archive by date is merely a matter of adding the `--newer` attribute, but doing so with the popular WinZip application is more complicated. There is a command-line interface to WinZip available at: `http://www .winzip.com/wzcline.htm`. This command-line interface endows WinZip with considerable additional power and flexibility. Among the additional features is the ability to include or exclude multiple source directories, to exclude certain file types, and to select a file by date—all of which are arduous at best to accomplish with the standard GUI interface to WinZip.

For instance, the following command will create `myappnew.zip` with all files in the `myapp` subdirectory dated 1/2/2003 or later, but it will not include any `application.cfm` or `.mdb` files:

```
wzzip -arpt01022003 myappnew.zip  myapp\*.* -xapplication.cfm -x*.mdb
```

This approach does have a few limitations. It creates an archive file containing only newer files modified on or after a given date. It does not take into account files that should be deleted, or any files that may have been modified on the production servers. To solve these problems, one of two basic approaches can be used: you can either extend whatever method you choose to synchronize the content within the production servers to include synchronization with the staging server, or you can create and transfer a complete archive to a directory in the production environment, and then synchronize from there.

Delivering the Content

If you are transferring archive files to the production environment, you need a way to deliver the *package* to the production environment. This is usually done with a standard FTP file transfer.

Synchronizing the Web Servers

Once content has been delivered from the development or staging environment into the production environment, it needs to be moved into the actual web directories on the web servers. To do this, some sort of file synchronization utility or service needs to be used. Many such utilities are available on the market.

On Unix, there are several utilities that can do the job, including `rsync`, `rdist`, and `mirrordir`.

On Windows systems, the process is a bit more complex, and there are more alternatives. The following references cover but a few of the options available.

Microsoft Site Server   Site Server Content Deployment (SSCD) service is part of Microsoft Site Server. It allows source and target directories to be defined and can automatically replicate content. If you have use for any of Site Server's other features, the SSCD may work for you. Otherwise, there are better, less expensive utilities well suited to the task.

You can find more information about Site Server at `http://www.microsoft.com/siteserver`.

Robocopy   The Robust File Copy Utility's `robocopy.exe` (Robocopy) is a very powerful and flexible command-line utility. Microsoft provides it in the Windows NT and Windows 2000 resource kits. Robocopy is quite fast, and the output produced is suitable for redirecting to a file for logging purposes. Since Robocopy is a command-line console utility, it can be run very efficiently from a telnet or rlogin session to one of your web servers.

PeerSync from Peer Software   PeerSync is a very flexible and powerful file synchronization tool. The PeerSync Profiler is used to create a *profile*, which contains the list of source and target folders, as well as all of the file and directory inclusion and exclusion rules, and options for including NTFS permissions, reporting settings, and so on. Once the profile has been created, there are execution options, including executing by command-line or desktop shortcut, by Explorer shell extension, as a scheduled process, or by installing the program as an NT Service and performing automatic replication in real-time. In addition, some versions of PeerSync are able to connect to remote directories with FTP.

Further information about PeerSync can be obtained at `http://www.peersoftware.com/peersync.html`.

SureSync from Software Pursuits   SureSync also offers extensive file and folder selection options and true file synchronization. In addition, SureSync offers native support for *replication trees* in which a master server replicates content to two or three target web servers, which in turn replicate content to two or three more, and so on. If the cluster has a large number of web servers, file synchronization can be dramatically improved with this sort of distributed replication.

More information about SureSync can be found at `http://www.softwarepursuits.com/suresync/suresync.htm`.

Database Clustering Considerations

The secret to a website that doesn't fail is redundancy that minimizes single points of failure. However, all too often, people fail to provide for database failure in the design of their website architecture. Database servers can be configured for load balancing and failover very similarly to those employed for web servers, although more-sophisticated methods are frequently used.

Many people seem to feel that providing load balancing and failover for databases is inherently significantly more complicated than for web servers. This is not necessarily the case. Every situation is different; creating an effective distributed database environment is sometimes extremely complicated, but just as often, data can be scaled pretty easily.

If you can connect to your database with TCP/IP, then you can probably establish load balancing and failover between your web servers and database in the very same manner implemented for just your web servers. When you work with clustered databases, however, an important factor to consider is *replication*, ensuring the same data exists in all databases.

Database Replication

Virtually all major database platforms include support for one or more methods of replicating data from one server to another. These replication strategies tend to fall into one of two major categories: either bidirectional or one-directional. Oracle refers to these as *Multimaster* replication and *Snapshot* replication, while Microsoft SQL Server (MSSQL) uses the terms *Merge* replication and *Transactional* replication. Your database vendor undoubtedly uses different words, but similar concepts.

One-Directional Replication   In a one-directional or asynchronous replication scenario, the data must be updated at the master database. The target database is essentially read-only—any updates to the data will not be sent back to the master database. Much of the data accessed in most websites doesn't change very often. In a typical e-commerce website, for instance, the product catalog usually doesn't change throughout the day. Sometimes the catalog is unchanged for weeks or months. This data can be easily replicated across many database servers to provide for highly available access to the data.

Bidirectional Replication   With bidirectional replication, data can be added or updated at any of the replicated sites. The replication process merges data back together so that data that has been added anywhere becomes replicated everywhere.

Bidirectional replication can place more load on your database server, so its performance may well suffer when you establish it. In most database platforms, there are limits to the types of data that can be replicated in this manner. There are also issues with conflict resolution, which can become complicated. If the same data is modified in two places, how do you decide which change wins and which is thrown out? For data that's highly dynamic, it may be a good idea to use more of a failover strategy that assures that data is only actually updated to one server at a time. This can provide for a simpler conflict resolution strategy.

In Sum

In this chapter, you've been given a wealth of information about high-availability websites and clustering options. You should now have a better understanding of the concepts of clustering, high availability, load balancing, and which of those options are available to use in a ColdFusion environment. You have also learned the importance of DNS and how though Round Robin DNS alone is not a practical load balancing option, it is a good foundation for software and hardware clustering and load balancing systems such as ClusterCATS.

You have also learned some more in-depth information about ClusterCATS, such as how to install, configure, administer, and test a ClusterCATS cluster.

Although this chapter could not list every option available to you and how to configure each one, you are now familiar with the different types of clustering and should understand how to determine the particular method that may work for you.

CHAPTER 18

Caching Techniques

By Raymond Camden

- Identifying caching opportunities

- Using cfcache

- Query caching

- Caching in RAM

Caching, in essence, means storing data (content, query information, and so on) in such a way that it can be retrieved quickly. A simple example is a complex web page that must perform various queries and complex logic before it displays itself. This page could take close to one second to generate, which isn't horrible—until you begin to get significant traffic on the website. Caching can take the result from the first time the page is generated and store it so that the next request for the page can be taken from the cache instead of by being re-created. The actual cache can be built using files or by storing data in RAM. The point is, of course, that relevant data that takes time to construct is saved for some period of time.

This chapter helps you to identify places in your web application where caching can be employed. We discuss various ways of applying caching, including the benefits and disadvantages of each. As you become more accustomed to using caching, you will be able to employ various methods to speed up your web application. Figure 18.1 shows how the data source should be set up.

FIGURE 18.1:

Setting up the data
source

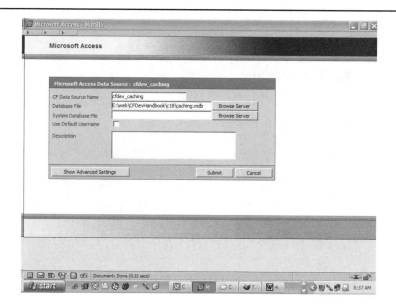

Identifying Caching Opportunities

Dynamic pages, by their very nature, will always be slower to load than static pages. Even a page that simply displays the current time has to do more work than a static page. Nevertheless, the benefits of dynamic web pages, in general, far outweigh the disadvantages. This is why we put up with the difference in speed. However, just because we take for granted that dynamic web pages are slower than static pages does not mean we should not do our best to make them as fast as possible.

Dynamic web pages consist of various parts, or tasks, that are performed to generate the resulting HTML seen in a web browser. Consider the home page for a news portal. It may do all of the following when requested:

- Check for a cookie identifying the user.
- If the cookie doesn't exist, redirect the browser to a static page that describes the benefits of becoming a user of this portal.
- If the cookie does exist, perform a database query to retrieve the users settings, including the layout scheme and the types of news that the user is interested in.
- Based on the user's preferred scheme, load a particular display template.
- Based on the types of news the user wants to read, check the database for current articles.
- If the articles are old or do not exist, perform a syndication task to retrieve the articles from various news wires.
- Display articles.

Obviously each of these tasks will take some time. There are some things in this page flow, however, that could perhaps be remembered so that we don't have to perform them again. Consider the database query to get preferences (in this case, a design layout and a list of the types of news articles the user prefers). We could store those preferences in a temporary cookie. If the user returns to the portal soon after their first hit, we won't need to perform the database query to get these values.

Required Setup for Examples in This Chapter

Before you begin this chapter, there are a few items you will need to set up in order to work with the code examples used here. First, if you haven't already done so, copy the `CFDevHandbook` folder that you downloaded from this book's page on the Sybex website (`http://www.sybex.com`) to the root of your web directory. In this chapter, we will work with the subfolder, `c18`. To create the necessary data source, go to the ColdFusion Administrator (which should be found at `http://localhost/cfide/administrator`) and select ODBC Data Sources. Name the new data source `cfdev_caching` and point it to the Access MDB file named `caching.mdb` in the c18 folder. Figure 18.1 shows a completed example of how the data source should be set up.

What about the news articles? Well, the process of gathering and displaying them was pretty complex. So what if we simply took all the text that was generated and stored it in RAM using ColdFusion session variables? If the user visits the portal before their session expires, we can just grab the value from RAM and display it.

Handling Stale Content

It's here that we hit our first snag. When it comes to things like the user's preferred layout or types of news they are interested in, we know when the user changes those values. In other words, we will be informed when the user decides they want to read news articles about the biotech industry. However, if the news stories come from an outside source, how do we know how long we can cache this information? We can make an estimate that biotech news doesn't change very often, but what about political news? The issue is timeliness. As we cache various parts of the page, they become stale. For some things, like the layout of the page, this isn't a concern, but for others, like news, we must be sure not to cache the information for too long.

What we have here, then, are two core concepts. The first is that you have to identify blocks, or sets, of information that would be helpful if cached. Second, you have to determine if the information *can* be cached, and if so, for how long. Various business rules can be applied to these decisions. You could let the user decide, or you could control what information is cached. A site providing stock market information might be set up to simply store every piece of stock information once the markets close, since there would be no reason not to. But during the trading day, information would only be cached for a few minutes, maybe even less. Taking the stock example further, you could even have caching rules based on the type of user. A user who is visiting your site for free could see stock information that is 20 minutes old, while you save the 100 percent fresh data for a premium customer.

Another obvious caching consideration is your programming environment. In our case, the ColdFusion application server provides various ways to employ caching. In another environment, your approaches to identify caching opportunities would certainly change.

> **NOTE**   Before moving into our discussion of caching techniques, remember that caching is only one way to handle slow web pages. You should *always* examine your code to make sure it is doing things efficiently. A dynamic page doesn't *have* to be slow. Are you using 40 lines of code for something that could be accomplished in two or three? If you're performing a database query and then using ColdFusion to manipulate the results, have you checked to see if SQL itself can do the manipulating? Always remember that caching is *one* of the solutions, not the only solution.

Using cfcache

After you've identified opportunities in which to cache information, you'll be faced with decisions about how to actually create the cache. In this section, we'll take a look at one of the easier forms of caching in ColdFusion, using the cfcache tag. cfcache is so easy to implement, in fact, that you can use it by simply adding cfcache, and *just* cfcache, to a page! The attributes to cfcache are described in Table 18.1.

TABLE 18.1: cfcache Attributes

Attribute	Description
action	Actions are Cache (the default, which caches on both the server and client side), Flush (remove from cache), ClientCache (tell the browser to use its cache), ServerCache (server-side only caching), or Optimal (the same as Cache).
timeSpan	The interval during which the cache should be used. The value passed to timeSpan should either be a decimal that represents the number of days (for example, .5 for half a day, 2 for 2 days) or a time span returned from the createTimeSpan() function. If not passed, the cached content will be used until the cfcache tag is passed with action="flush".
directory	The directory where the cached files should be saved. Defaults to the cache folder under the ColdFusion root. It is not recommended that you use the default directory since the flush command, even if issued by another page, can remove the current page's cache.
username	The cfcache tag performs an HTTP operation to generate the cached data. If the file requires basic authentication, you would pass a valid username here.
password	See information for username attribute.
protocol	Again, since cfcache performs an HTTP operation, you need to specify if you are using HTTPS instead of HTTP. The default is HTTP.
port	Specifies the port. The default is 80.
expireURL	Allows for dynamic flushing of flushed content based on a wildcard URL comparison.

As described in Table 18.1, cfcache essentially does this: When you request a page with the cfcache tag in it, the tag will check to see if it has already generated content for this page. If it has, it will return that result instead of regenerating the page you requested (or, in the case of client-side caching, it will return headers that let the browser know that the page has not been modified).

Adding the cfcache Tag

Let's take a look at how cfcache can be used to quickly add caching to a slow page. Listing 18.1 contains an example of non-cache-enabled code.

Listing 18.1   A slow template (cfcache_test1.cfm)

```
<!---
    Name:          /c18/cfcache_test1.cfm
    Description:    cfcache test one
--->

<!--- Do something slowly... --->
<cfsilent>
```

```
<cfloop index="x" from=10 to=150000>
    <cfset a = x * (x+1) / (x-1)>
    <cfset b = a * a>
    <cfset c = a + b>
</cfloop>
</cfsilent>

<cfoutput>
The final result was #c#.
</cfoutput>
```

As you can see, this template is pretty simple. The main block of the code is a loop from 10 to 150000. There is no real reason for these numbers except to give the ColdFusion server a lot of work to do. The mathematical statements inside the loop are there just for show. Once we are done with the loop, we output the final value of the variable c. If you run this template in your browser, it may take a good 10 to 15 seconds before you see anything—obviously not a good thing for people visiting your site. But by using the cfcache tag, we can quickly add caching to the page.

Listing 18.2 shows the modified version of our template.

Listing 18.2   **Testing cfcache (cfcache_test2.cfm)**

```
<!---
    Name:           /c18/cfcache_test2.cfm
    Description:    cfcache test two
--->

<!--- Cache the page for 20 mins --->
<cfcache timeSpan="#createTimeSpan(0,0,20,0)#">

<!--- do something slowly... --->
<cfsilent>
<cfloop index="x" from=10 to=150000>
    <cfset a = x * (x+1) / (x-1)>
    <cfset b = a * a>
    <cfset c = a + b>
</cfloop>
</cfsilent>

<cfoutput>
The final result was #c#. It was generated at #timeFormat(now())#.
</cfoutput>
```

There are only two differences in this template as compared to the original version in Listing 18.1. We added the cfcache tag on top, and then we added text at the end to let us know when the data was generated. Run this template in your browser and you'll notice that the first hit takes just as long as it did before. Every other hit, though, will be nearly instantaneous. And all we really did was to add one tag!

How cfcache Works

So, what exactly happened? As stated earlier, cfcache stores the result of the original request. By result we mean the generated text. Remember that a ColdFusion template may contain a lot of code, but it only directly outputs text. It is this text, what the browser sees, that is cached. The cached information is stored as a text file. This file is specially marked so that it not only notices updates to the original file, it also notices query strings that are different. (This enables different cache results depending on URL variables.) Our cfcache tag uses a time span of 20 minutes. We pass the createTimeSpan() function to the timeSpan attribute of cfcache to specify the amount of time the cache should be used.

Listing 18.3 shows what the cached file looks like. (Its name will vary according to your server and the time you run the example.) The times and paths will be different for your copy. You can find this file in the cache folder under your ColdFusion MX installation folder. This particular file was named cfcache_80A94FCDFF59E5955179F20CE492CF0D.tmp.

Listing 18.3   The cfcache File

```
<!---http://coruscant/CFDevHandbook/c18/cfcache_test2.cfm--->

The final result was 22500750010. It was generated at 12:17 AM.
```

This file simply contains a special header comment that specifies the filename and the HTML that was generated, which in this case, was one line of text:

```
The final result was 22500750010. It was generated at 12:17 AM.
```

A normal page would have more text and HTML, but in our case the output was simple. If you want to test the caching, you can advance your computer's system clock by 20 minutes and see what happens.

Handling Dynamic Pages with cfcache

You may wonder how cfcache handles pages that change based on certain conditions, such as form or URL parameters. Unfortunately, cfcache will not be able to detect that different form variables were passed to the template; however, it will be able to cache based on URL parameters. For a quick sample of this, see Listing 18.4.

Listing 18.4   Cache test with URL parameters (cfcache_test3.cfm)

```
<!---
    Name:            /c18/cfcache_test3.cfm
    Description:     cfcache test three
--->

<!--- Cache the page for 20 mins --->
<cfcache timeSpan="#createTimeSpan(0,0,20,0)#">

<!--- do something slowly... --->
<cfsilent>
<cfloop index="x" from=10 to=150000>
    <cfset a = x * (x+1) / (x-1)>
    <cfset b = a * a>
    <cfset c = a + b>
</cfloop>
</cfsilent>

<cfoutput>
The final result was #c#. it was generated at #timeFormat(now())#.
<p>
<cfif isDefined("url.id")>
    ID #url.id# was passed.<br>
</cfif>
<a href="cfcache_test3.cfm?id=1">Pass id=1</a><br>
<a href="cfcache_test3.cfm?id=2">Pass id=2</a><br>
<a href="cfcache_test3.cfm?id=3">Pass id=3</a><br>
</cfoutput>
```

The only change to this iteration of the template is the addition of three links. These links point back to our document and pass three different values for id. Above these links we display the value of url.id if it is passed. If you browse this page, you will notice that the first hit is slow (and each time you follow a new link the page will be slow as well) but this only applies to the first time. Once you have followed all three links, if you click on any of them again, they will load instantly. This is because the cfcache tag created a cached copy of each version of the file.

Now let's explore the situations in which the use of cfcache is *not* appropriate. First, keep in mind that it caches the entire page. As you'll see in the "Caching in Ram" section, there may be cases where we want to cache only a portion of a page. Secondly, cfcache only caches based on the filename and any URL parameters passed to it. It ignores form variables as well as other values that may affect the output of the page. Imagine a page that displays session variables:

```
<cfoutput>Good morning, #session.name#</cfoutput>
```

If cfcache were used on the first page, it would create a cached version for the first person who hit the site. If that person's session.name variable were Jacob, everyone else who visited the site would see Jacob rather than their own name. The cfcache tag does have an option to only cache on the client (action="clientCache"), but then you must trust the browser to support the caching method.

In summary, the cfcache tag is very easy to use, but it has some drawbacks of which you should be aware. As we move ahead in this chapter, we'll look at some alternatives that can handle these issues.

Query Caching

Another easy way to add caching to an application is via query caching. Unlike the cfcache tag, query caching applies only to, as you can probably guess, queries. But it's just as easy to employ in your application as cfcache is.

Before getting into the details, let's first look at a template that employs queries so that we have something to work with. Listing 18.5 displays a simple home page for a fake company.

Listing 18.5   **A template without query caching (query_caching1.cfm)**

```
<!---
    Name:           /c18/query_caching1.cfm
    Description:     Query Caching test one
--->

<!--- Get articles --->
<cfquery name="topArticles" datasource="cfdev_caching">
    select      top 10 title, left(body,100) as abstract, created,
                categoryName
    from        tblArticles, tblCategories
    where       tblArticles.CategoryIDFK = tblCategories.ID
    order by    views, created desc
</cfquery>

<!--- Get top products --->
<cfquery name="topProducts" datasource="cfdev_caching">
    select      top 10 product, cost, categoryName
    from        tblProducts, tblCategories
    where       tblProducts.CategoryIDFK = tblCategories.ID
    order by    sales desc
</cfquery>

<html>

<head>
<title>Widgets and More!</title>
</head>
```

```
<body>

<table width="100%" cellPadding=5 cellSpacing=5>
    <tr valign="top">
        <td>
        <h1>Welcome to Widgets and More!</h1>

        <h2>Latest and Most Popular Articles</h2>
        <cfoutput query="topArticles">
        <b><a href="query_caching1.cfm">#title#</a></b><br>
        <i>#dateFormat(created)#</i><br>
        #categoryName#<br>
        Abstract: #abstract#...
        <p>
        </cfoutput>
        </td>
        <td bgcolor="ghostWhite">
        <b>Top Sellers!</b><br>
        <cfoutput query="topProducts">
        <nobr>
        <a href="query_caching1.cfm">#categoryName# : #product#</a></nobr>
        <p>
        </cfoutput>
        </td>
    </tr>
</table>
```

The purpose of this web page is pretty simple. We begin with a query that grabs article information. We want to only grab the top 10 records, so we use the top keyword in our SQL:

```
select      top 10 title, left(body,100) as abstract, created,
            categoryName
```

We select a portion of the body of the article to use as an abstract, as well as the date it was written and its category of coverage. The next important part of query is the order by value. We want to order by the most popular article, so we order first by the number of times an article has been viewed, and then by its creation date.

The topProducts query works in the same way as the topArticles query. We grab the top 10 products according to the Sales column.

TIP If you are not using Access as your database, you may want to check to see if your database supports the top keyword. It's a very nice way to grab only a certain set of records. Another aspect is that it will get the top X records no matter what. So, if 3 records tie for 10th place, you may actually get 12 records back.

The rest of the template simply displays our queries.

Using Query Caching

So how does query caching help us in this situation? As with any page, we first must decide if the content can be cached. Since the two queries are based on sales and the number of views for an article, it's unlikely that the top 10 will change significantly. There is no real need for this information to be 100 percent up-to-date.

But will caching the data really help? There is an easy way to find out. Open up your browser and go to the ColdFusion Administrator. Once there, select Debugging Settings. Toward the bottom is an option for Database Activity (see Figure 18.2). Select this option and then hit the Submit Changes button. Once you have done that, information about each and every query run on a template will be displayed in the debugging text.

FIGURE 18.2:

ColdFusion debugging options

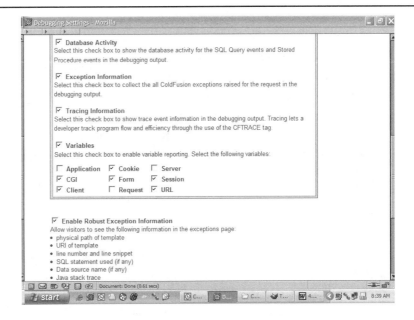

Figure 18.3 shows the bottom of our web page with the query debugging information displayed. As you can see, we not only see the name of the query, but also the amount of records return, the SQL sent, and—what's relevant for us in this discussion—the time it took to execute the query. In our case, the queries ran pretty fast. One took 60 milliseconds and the other took 10. Under normal circumstances you probably would not need to worry about queries that ran this fast. However, we have already decided that the information does *not* need to be retrieved from the database every time someone hits the site. It certainly won't hurt to cache these queries, so let's take a look at how we can do it.

FIGURE 18.3:

Query Debug
Information

Query Caching Options

We will employ query caching via attributes passed to the `cfquery` tag. Two attributes to `cfquery` affect caching:

cachedWithin   The `cachedWithin` attribute is a time span in which a query should be cached. For example, you may specify that a query should be cached for 20 minutes. The first time the query is run, the data is cached. Whenever the query is requested again within the next 20 minutes, the cached data will be returned.

cachedAfter   This value is a date. If the query is generated after the date specified, the cache will be used. You could pass a date in the past to essentially tell the tag to cache the query and use the cached version forever.

Typically the `cachedWithin` attribute is used more often than the `cachedAfter` attribute. You will normally make some decision about how long data should be cached, and then pass a time span, using `createTimeSpan()`, to the `cachedWithin` attribute.

The cached data is kept in the server's memory, so if the server is restarted, the cache will be flushed.

It's very important to keep in mind that the query is cached based on the SQL passed to it. This is a good thing. If your query uses dynamic SQL, like so,

```
select * from foo
where id = #val(url.id)#
```

you will not have to worry about one particular version of the query being cached. ColdFusion will automatically cache every different form of the query that is executed. Therefore, it would not be a good idea to cache a query that is highly dynamic, like a search engine query.

NOTE   Query caching is based on more than just the SQL passed in. It is also unique per data source name, username, password, and query name. Normally these values aren't changed while the application is running.

Let's take a look at how easy query caching is to use. Listing 18.6 is a modified version of our previous template that shows the addition of query caching.

Listing 18.6   Using query caching (query_caching2.cfm)

```
<!---
    Name:              /c18/query_caching2.cfm
    Description:       Query Caching test two
--->

<cfset timeSpan = createTimeSpan(0,0,20,0)>

<!--- Get articles --->
<cfquery name="topArticles" datasource="cfdev_caching"
        cachedWithin="#timeSpan#">
    select       top 10 title, left(body,100) as abstract, created,
                 categoryName
    from         tblArticles, tblCategories
    where        tblArticles.CategoryIDFK = tblCategories.ID
    order by     views, created desc
</cfquery>

<!--- Get top products --->
<cfquery name="topProducts" datasource="cfdev_caching"
        cachedWithin="#timeSpan#">
    select       top 10 product, cost, categoryName
    from         tblProducts, tblCategories
    where        tblProducts.CategoryIDFK = tblCategories.ID
    order by     sales desc
</cfquery>

<html>

<head>
<title>Widgets and More!</title>
</head>

<body>

<table width="100%" cellPadding=5 cellSpacing=5>
    <tr valign="top">
        <td>
        <h1>Welcome to Widgets and More!</h1>

        <h2>Latest and Most Popular Articles</h2>
        <cfoutput query="topArticles">
        <b><a href="query_caching1.cfm">#title#</a></b><br>
        <i>#dateFormat(created)#</i><br>
        #categoryName#<br>
```

```
                Abstract: #abstract#...
                <p>
                </cfoutput>
                </td>
                <td bgcolor="ghostWhite">
                <b>Top Sellers!</b><br>
                <cfoutput query="topProducts">
                <nobr>
                <a href="query_caching1.cfm">#categoryName# : #product#</a></nobr>
                <p>
                </cfoutput>
                </td>
           </tr>
        </table>
```

Most of this template is the same as it was in Listing 18.5, so we will focus on the changes. The first change is the code that creates our time span.

```
<cfset timeSpan = createTimeSpan(0,0,20,0)>
```

The `createTimeSpan` function creates a span of time, in this case, 20 minutes. I simply selected a time span that seemed to make sense. If you wanted your caches to expire earlier or later, you could simply change the values here.

To cache our two queries, we simply passed `cachedWithin="#timeSpan#"` to both queries. That's all it took! Load the page in your browser and note the execution times of the queries. Then hit the Reload button. You will notice that the times went away and the queries are marked as cached. Figure 18.4 displays this output.

FIGURE 18.4:

The cached queries

Expiring Cached Queries

The next question you are probably asking is "how do we clear the cache?" To tell ColdFusion *not* to use the cached content, you simply pass a time span of zero length. This can be done using a time span like so:

```
<cfset timeSpan = createTimeSpan(0,0,0,0)>
```

In this case the time span simply has zeros for all its values. Once the script is run, the cached queries will be removed and the data will be 100 percent fresh.

It's important to remember, however, that the SQL passed in must be *exactly* the same as the original query. This can be a problem in two ways. First, let's say you have a web-based administrator for your articles. Your page code may look something like the following pseudocode block:

```
<cfif form.saveNewArticle>
    Save a new article.
    Refresh the getArticles query used on the home page
    <cfset timeSpan = createTimeSpan(0,0,0,0)>

    <cfquery ... cachedWithin="#timeSpan#">
        SQL statements
    </cfquery>
</cfif>
```

This code has a serious problem. Notice how we placed the code within a `cfif` statement. Also notice that we nicely formatted the code using indents. These indents are enough to make ColdFusion not remove the cached query! When we say that the SQL must be *exactly* alike, we mean *exactly* alike.

How would you solve this? One way would be to simply not use any indents in your queries. This is risky, however, because it would be very easy to forget or accidentally add a space somewhere. An easier solution would be to use a custom tag. A custom tag can handle the query retrieval and optional flushing of the cache. Listing 18.7 shows a simple custom tag that handles both retrieving the cached query and updating it.

Listing 18.7   **getContent custom tag (getcontent.cfm)**

```
<!---
    Name:          /c18/getcontent.cfm
    Description:   Retrieves content
--->

<!--- default timeout --->
<cfparam name="attributes.timeSpanMinutes" default="20">

<!--- default name of article query --->
<cfparam name="attributes.r_topArticles" default="topArticles"
    type="variableName">

<!--- default name of product query --->
<cfparam name="attributes.r_topProducts" default="topProducts"
    type="variableName">

<cfset timeSpan = createTimeSpan(0,0,attributes.timeSpanMinutes,0)>
```

```
<!--- get articles --->
<cfquery name="topArticles" datasource="cfdev_caching"
    cachedWithin="#timeSpan#">
    select      top 10 title, left(body,100) as abstract, created, categoryName
    from        tblArticles, tblCategories
    where       tblArticles.categoryIDFK = tblCategories.ID
    order by    views, created desc
</cfquery>

<!--- get top products --->
<cfquery name="topProducts" datasource="cfdev_caching"
    cachedWithin="#timeSpan#">
    select      top 10 product, cost, categoryName
    from        tblProducts, tblCategories
    where       tblProducts.categoryIDFK = tblCategories.ID
    order by    sales desc
</cfquery>

<!--- copy topArticles to caller --->
<cfset setVariable("caller.#attributes.r_topArticles#",topArticles)>

<!--- copy topProducts to caller --->
<cfset setVariable("caller.#attributes.r_topProducts#",topProducts)>
```

This custom tag is pretty simple. We begin by defining a set of default attributes.

- The first attribute defines the time span value in minutes. The `createTimeSpan` function lets you specify timeout values in days, hours, minutes, and seconds, but our tool will only let you specify the minutes. This should be fine for our needs. We take this value later on and create a real time span with it:

    ```
    <cfset timeSpan = createTimeSpan(0,0,attributes.timeSpanMinutes,0)>
    ```

- The next two `cfparam` tags define the name of the queries that will be returned to the calling template. Since we will use these values as variable names, we pass the optional `type="variableName"` attribute to `cfparam`. This ensures that any value we pass to these two attributes will be valid variable names.

All of the attributes used by this tag have default values. This will make our tag easy to use.

The two queries in the custom tag are the exact same queries we defined in Listing 18.6. This hasn't changed at all.

The end of the custom tag simply copies the queries back into the calling template. We use two `setVariable()` calls to create dynamic variables that store the query information.

Using this custom tag is simple. We can remove the two queries from Listing 18.7 and simply add `cf_getContent`. This will automatically call our custom tag with all the default values. It will automatically use the cached versions of the queries as well as the default names. Now if we want to clear the cache, all we need to do is call the tag with a 0 value for the timeSpanMinutes value:

```
<cf_getContent timeSpanMinutes=0>
```

You may have heard of the cfobjectcache tag. This tag takes one attribute, action, and one value, clear. This tag will remove *all* queries from the cache. This was a hidden tag in ColdFusion 5 that has been documented in ColdFusion MX. You can use it in your own code, but be aware that it affects the entire server, not just your page.

NOTE   Since cached queries are stored in RAM, it's possible to overuse query caching to the point where server performance begins to suffer. On the ColdFusion Administrator Caching page, you can set the maximum number of queries that can be stored in cache. The default is 100. As new queries are cached, the oldest will be removed from the cache.

Caching in RAM

Caching in RAM, the last caching technique we will discuss in this chapter, is a concept that is actually a lot simpler than it sounds. In ColdFusion, three types of variables are automatically stored in RAM: server, application, and session variables. Each type has its own unique way of working and access. server variables are, of course, available from any template on the server, application variables are unique per application, and lastly, session variables are unique per user and per application.

Because these variables are stored in RAM, we can use that to our advantage. Here is a simple example in pseudocode:

```
<cfif not isDefined("Application.Result")>
    <cfset application.result = Some Piece of Logic>
</cfif>
<cfoutput>#application.result#</cfoutput>
```

This code simply checks to see if a certain application variable, Result, is defined. If it isn't, we perform some piece of logic (this could be running a database query, reading the contents of a file, or some other operation). The result of this operation is then stored in the application variable. Lastly we display the result on the page.

The interesting part of this little example is that after you run this code once, the application variable will be stored in RAM and will be available in the next request. (As long as the application variable hasn't timed out, of course.) This is a very simple way of caching data.

Let's take a look at an example. Listing 18.8 includes a simple version of the pseudocode just explained.

Listing 18.8   **Testing ram caching (ram_cache1.cfm)**

```
<!---
    Name:           /c18/ram_cache1.cfm
    Description:    Demonstrates caching in RAM
--->

<cfapplication name="c18">

<cfif not isDefined("application.topArticles")>
    <cfquery name="application.topArticles"
            datasource="cfdev_caching">
            select      top 10 title, left(body,100) as abstract,
            created, categoryName
            from        tblArticles, tblCategories
            where       tblArticles.categoryIDFK = tblcategories.ID
            order by    views, created desc
    </cfquery>
    <cfoutput>Initializing application.topArticles<p></cfoutput>
</cfif>

<cfoutput>
Query has #application.topArticles.recordCount# rows.
</cfoutput>
```

We begin this template by turning on the application framework with the `cfapplication` tag. (Normally this would be done in the `Application.cfm` file.) We then use the `isDefined()` function to check to see if our query exists in the `application` scope. If it does not, we create the query and store it in the `application` scope. The output, `Initializing application .topArticles`, is simply a debugging statement. As you can see, it outputs a message stating that we have initialized the `application` variable. The first time you run this script, the message will show up. After that, it will not. The last thing we do is simply output the `recordCount` property of the query stored in the `application` scope.

NOTE   Hey! Where are the `cflock` tags, you're asking? One of the most brilliant changes to ColdFusion MX is in the area of locking. You no longer need locks to prevent server crashes. You only use the `cflock` tag when you need to control access to a resource for logical reasons (for example, `<cfset application.hits = application.hits + 1>`).

To test this script, simply load it in your browser and pay special attention to how it looks the first time it is run. Figure 18.5 shows the output the first time the script is generated.

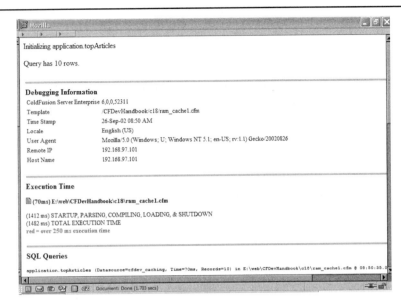

Notice how the initialization text is printed as well as the debug information from the query? The next time the script is run, we will see neither the initialization text nor the query information. Instead, the main output (the record count) will be the only thing displayed.

As you can see, this is a very simple technique, but it is also very powerful. We have much greater control over how the data is cached, how long it is cached, and how it is removed from the cache. If the query were unique per session (for example, a query that returns records based on the session preferences), the only change would be the name of the variables. The same goes for using the server scope.

> **TIP** In our example, we took a variable (a query) and copied it to a persisted scope. What if you wanted to cache something a bit more complex, like a large amount of text? The cfsavecontent tag will take any output between its beginning and end tag and store it into a variable. You could then store this value into a persisted scope.

In Sum

In this chapter we discussed caching techniques. We began by talking about how you can identify content that can be cached. We also discussed how you must determine how long that information can be cached. In one site, you may have various pieces of content, each with their own rules concerning whether or not they can be cached, and for how long.

We discussed the cfcache tag and how it can be used to cache entire pages. This solution is effective for quickly adding caching to a page, but since it applies to an entire page, it may not be something you can use that often. Again, you will need to look at the content and make a case-by-case decision about how safe it is to use cfcache.

Next, we discussed query caching, one more simple and effective caching technique for ColdFusion. Since most web applications involve queries, this type of caching can add a quick speed boost to almost every page on your site. Since the cache only affects one particular query, it's easier to have different types of lifespans for this type of cache than what you get using the cfcache tag.

Lastly, we discussed caching data in RAM. This is nothing more than using the existing ColdFusion variable scopes that store their information in RAM: server, application, and session. This technique involves the most work, but it is still simple to use. It also allows the most detailed control over how and when the cache is created and deleted.

PART V

Custom Server-Side Coding

Chapter 19: Working with Java Objects

Chapter 20: Building Java Extensions

Chapter 21: Building C++ Extensions

Chapter 22: Using cfexecute

CHAPTER 19

Working with Java Objects

By Guy Rish

- Creating Java objects with CFML

- Instantiation

- Displaying method results

- Static members

- Handling exceptions

- Class caching

- Overloading

- Datatype conversion

- Nested objects

Since version 4.5, CFML has been a relatively Java-friendly language. Now with the introduction of ColdFusion MX, the relationship between CFML and Java has gotten even friendlier because the application services have been entirely rewritten in Java! Although the CFML language elements related to Java interoperability have not really changed in any perceptible way since they were introduced, their level of collaboration has dramatically increased. Important advancements such as the ability to catch specific Java Exception subclasses with `cfcatch`, the ability to work with nested class instances, and the often automatic conversion between CFML datatypes and Java classes are just some of the highlights that will be explored in this chapter.

Introduction to Java Objects

Choosing to use Java objects to augment a ColdFusion template's functionality gives access to a broad range of APIs that are platform neutral. These APIs provide access to many technologies that have not yet been implemented in CFML or that have richer implementations in Java.

Even if you are using only the APIs available in the latest version of the Java Development Kit (JDK), there are numerous reasons for using Java objects from within a template, including the following:

- The availability of data structures, such as linked lists and binary trees, that have most robust functionality and memory management capabilities than CFML's own complex datatypes

- More robust network APIs to better handle existing protocols and for new protocols, currently unsupported by ColdFusion

- Compression APIs, the least of which are the class in the JDK for handling Zip files, which CFML has not built-in capabilities to do

- Numerous cryptographic APIs that greatly exceed the possibilities available through ColdFusion's `encrypt` function

- Numerous image file format APIs for accomplishing tasks that are extremely difficult in CFML, such as getting the pixel dimensions of a JPEG

- Robust printer-control APIs that allow for the construction of web-based tools for managing report generation

The possibilities of what could be done with ColdFusion and Java objects are even more apparent when third-party libraries from large corporations like IBM and HP, as well as numerous open-source efforts, are leveraged. The libraries available for constructing PDF files, handling iCal interfacing, manipulating various multimedia formats, telephony, and such, makes Java APIs a ready source to fill in the gaps in some ColdFusion applications.

When weighed against other external tools available to ColdFusion, such as COM or CORBA objects, some of the compelling factors in choosing Java can frequently be a simple matter of the Java library providing a platform-independent implementation, often with comparable speed and ease of implementation. Conversely, these other two component architectures have their share of detractions. COM implementations are tied specifically to a single platform, Windows, and carry a great deal of baggage from the early growth of their specification in the early-to-mid 1990s. CORBA requires a specialized server, and it is widely accepted that developing CORBA components is a laborious task with difficult APIs.

What You Should Already Know about Java

This chapter does not teach the reader the basics of the Java language; that is beyond the scope of this book. However, beginning Java students with a cursory grasp of syntax and a grounded knowledge about how Java implements many object-oriented language features should understand the content presented in this chapter.

NOTE   If you find that you need more information about Java, take a look at the following: *Mastering Java 2, J2SE 1.4,* by John Zukowski (Sybex, 2002), and *SOAP Programming with Java,* by Bill Brogden (Sybex, 2002).

Terminology

Although this chapter does make certain assumptions of the reader's knowledge of Java (as stated earlier), because object-oriented programming contains so many overused and elastic words, it is useful to clarify some of the jargon used.

An *instance* is an executing copy of the class in memory. An instance is frequently referred to as an *object*; however, because the term "object" is general abused and used generically, it is used here sparingly. If a class is analogous to a ColdFusion template, then an instance is the specific execution of a request for that template. This analogy should be taken loosely.

Instantiation is the process by which an instance of a class is created. This chapter explores the various kinds of instantiation and how ColdFusion handles them.

A *method* is an invokeable function within a class. Methods can be called like any other function in CFML using dot notation from an instance of the class in question. For example:

```
obj.method1();
```

where `obj` is an instance of some fictitious class and `method1` is a method that is defined and belongs to the class of which `obj` is an instance.

A *property* is an accessible variable belonging to a class. The value of a property may be retrieved or set using dot notation, similar to the way the members of CFML structures are handled.

One of the powerful features common in most/all object-oriented programming languages is *overloading*. In overloading, multiple methods (and in some languages properties, all of the methods) have the same name and the same general purpose but are specifically designed to handle different incoming arguments. The difference between one method of the same name and another method of the same name may be in the datatypes of the incoming arguments and in the number of incoming arguments.

A *constructor* is a special method called to create an instance of a class. The constructor takes care of various initialization tasks that prepare the instance for use. Every class has at least one constructor, sometimes called the *default constructor*, so that even if it is not specifically defined within the class's source, the runtime can still create an instance. Frequently a constructor may be overloaded so that a class can be instantiated with different starting parameters. These constructor overloads are sometimes called *alternate constructors*—alternate ways of constructing an instance.

Required Setup Examples in This Chapter

There are a number of classes in this chapter whose source would be prohibitive to list within this chapter's text. For a greater understanding of this chapter, go to the Sybex website (www.sybex.com) to obtain the source code examples for this book and, specifically, this chapter.

The Java classes discussed herein must be available to the templates discussed in the chapter. It is important to synchronize the ColdFusion Server's Class Path setting with that development environment's classpath variable; the Class Path setting is available from the ColdFusion Administrator's "Java and JVM Settings" page (see Appendix A, "Configuring ColdFusion for Java," for further details). The ColdFusion Server does not inherit any classpath environmental variables that might be set. Because of the difference between these two values, it is a frequent source of the "class not found" errors that you see when you are learning to use Java with ColdFusion.

Creating Java Objects in CFML

There are two primary ways of creating Java class instances in CFML: using the cfobject tag or the createObject function.

The Greeting Class

To better exemplify the various aspects of the CFML and Java interaction, you will primarily be working with the Greeting class. Following are descriptions of the class's various constructors and methods (Table 19.1).

TABLE 19.1: Greeting Class

method	Description
`Greeting` (constructor)	The overloaded class constructor. The default constructor sets the default salutation to "Hello," or, using an alternate constructor, the salutation is set from the incoming `java.lang.String` argument.
`error`	Throws a Java I/O exception displaying the passed `java.lang.String`.
`greet`	An overloaded method that returns a `java.lang.String` containing a concatenated greeting using the current salutation (the default is "Hello" but this could have been changed during class construction).
`hey`	A static method that returns a `java.lang.String` whose value is `"Hey, you"`.
`init`	Returns a `java.lang.String` whose value is `"not a constructor"`.

Using the cfobject Tag

As mentioned, the multifunctional `cfobject` tag is one of the two primary ways of creating instances of Java classes. Just as with creating instances of other types, creating Java instances requires the four attributes that are shown in Table 19.2.

TABLE 19.2: cfobject Attributes

Attribute	Description
`type`	The object type to be created. This attribute will be `"Java"`.
`action`	The only applicable value for creating Java instances for this attribute is `"create"`.
`class`	The fully qualified (complete with package) class name.
`name`	The CFML variable name used to identify the instance.

An example of `cfobject` can be seen on lines 12 and 13 of Listing 19.1.

Listing 19.1   Using cfobject (CreateExample1.cfm)

```
01: <!---
02:     Name:         /c19/CreateExample1.cfm
03:     Description:   A simple example of creating
04:         a Java class instance using cfobject.
05: --->
06: <html>
07:     <head>
08:         <title>Create Example 1</title>
09:     </head>
```

```
10:
11:     <body>
12:         <cfobject type="java" action="create"
13:             class="Greeting" name="obj">
14:         <cfoutput>
15:             #obj.greet()#
16:         </cfoutput>
17:     </body>
```

Using the createObject Function

This function came into being in CFML with version 4.5 with the `cfscript` tag. Instantiating a Java class with the `createObject` function requires fewer arguments than instantiating a COM or CORBA object; this is because it needs only two arguments: `type` and `class` (see Table 19.3).

TABLE 19.3: createObject Arguments

Argument	Description
type	The object type to be created. This argument will be "Java".
class	The fully qualified (complete with package) class name.

An example of this function can be seen on lines 13 and 14 of Listing 19.2.

Listing 19.2   **Using createObject (CreateExample2.cfm)**

```
01: <!---
02:     Name:           /c19/CreateExample2.cfm
03:     Description:    A simple example of creating
04:         a Java class instance using createObject.
05: --->
06: <html>
07:     <head>
08:         <title>Create Example 2</title>
09:     </head>
10:
11:     <body>
12:         <cfscript>
13:             obj = createObject("java",
14:                 "Greeting");
15:             writeOutput(obj.greet());
16:         </cfscript>
17:     </body>
18: </html>
```

Working with Java Objects in CFML

Now that the simple details of creating instances for use within ColdFusion templates have been covered, it is time to discuss the nuances. Making use of a fully object-oriented and broadly featured language such as Java through another, in this case CFML, presents a number of challenges.

Instantiation

Using either `cfobject` or `createObject` will not cause the class to be instantiated immediately. Before this can occur, ColdFusion MX Server must first load the bytecode of the class from which an instance will be created into memory. If the class has been instantiated before, then nothing is done because the bytecode is already cached into the server's memory. This early step allows for different things to happen during the instantiation, such as the process of calling alternate constructors.

Class instantiation in CFML can then be done one of two ways, either implicitly or explicitly.

> **NOTE**   Java bytecode is a compiled class, stored in the class file (`.class`). It is a binary format specific to the JVM.

Implicit Instantiation

A class is instantiated upon first use; the line of code where this instantiation occurs is not the same line of code that creates the object. The only exception to this is when you're accessing static class members (discussed later in this chapter, "Static Members"). As soon as a nonstatic property is accessed or a nonstatic method is called, the class is instantiated. When this happens the class's default constructor is called.

Implicit instantiation is the more common method of instantiation in CFML, and it requires no additional effort on the part of the developer.

Explicit Instantiation

The rationale for explicit instantiation is to call alternate constructors; this increases the flexibility of the Java/CFML integration. The CFML variable that is created to hold the instance, as a result of either a `cfobject` tag or being returned from `createObject`, has a special `init` method. The Java class being instantiated does not have to have any such method; this method is a CFML construct, an alias for the class constructor. Using the `init` method without arguments will call the default class constructor, such as the one that can be seen on line 13 of Listing 19.3.

Listing 19.3   **Instantiating a Class (InitExample1.cfm)**

```
01: <!---
02:     Name:               /c19/InitExample1.cfm
03:     Description:    Explicit instance construction.
04: --->
05: <html>
06:     <head>
07:         <title>Init Example 1</title>
08:     </head>
09:
10:     <body>
11:         <cfscript>
12:             obj1 = createObject("java", "Greeting");
13:             obj1.init();
14:             writeOutput(obj1.greet());
15:         </cfscript>
16:     </body>
17: </html>
```

Using the init method will have the same effect as an implicit instantiation. More importantly, the init method can be used to call the alternate class constructors. This is demonstrated in line 14 of Listing 19.4. Here an alternate constructor of the Greeting class is invoked.

Listing 19.4   **Using an Alternate Constructor (InitExample2.cfm)**

```
01: <!---
02:     Name:               /c19/InitExample1.cfm
03:     Description:    Explicit instance construction
04:         with alternate constructor.
05: --->
06: <html>
07:     <head>
08:         <title>Init Example 2</title>
09:     </head>
10:
11:     <body>
12:         <cfscript>
13:             obj = createObject("java", "Greeting");
14:             obj.init("Welcome, ");
15:             writeOutput(obj.greet());
16:         </cfscript>
17:     </body>
18: </html>
```

NOTE Since CFML is a typeless language, differing constructors can only be identified by the number of arguments they have as opposed to the datatypes of those arguments. Obviously, this poses challenges when you are calling the overloaded alternate constructors that are found in many of the classes in the Java API. The solution to this problem is to use the CFML javaCast function discussed later in this chapter.

Multiple calls to the constructor alias resulted in an exception being raised in ColdFusion version 4.5, but this is not the case in version 5 and later. Successive calls to the init method do not raise errors; the additional lines of code merely take up space in the source file.

The init CFML construct does, however, pose a problem when the class contains an init method of its own. This issue is exemplified in line 16 of Listing 19.5 where a call to the Greeting object's init method (with the expectation of a returned java.lang.String), not the CFML init alias, is made.

Listing 19.5   Attempting to Invoke the init Method (InitExample3.cfm)

```
01: <!---
02:     Name:           /c19/InitExample1.cfm
03:     Description:    Explicit instance construction and
04:         a call to the class's init method.
05: --->
06: <html>
07:     <head>
08:         <title>Init Example 3</title>
09:     </head>
10:
11:     <body>
12:         <cfscript>
13:             obj = createObject("java", "Greeting");
14:             obj.init();
15:             writeOutput(obj.greet());
16:             str = obj.init();
17:             writeOutput("<br>" & str & "<br>");
18:             writeOutput(obj.greet());
19:         </cfscript>
20:     </body>
21: </html>
```

When you inspect the source of the Greeting class, you will see that there is a method name init that takes no arguments and returns a java.lang.String. Obviously, as can be seen in the following message, the method is not reached by the CFML interpreter. Instead, the java.lang.String is displayed, which should contain the string "not a constructor," as indicated in the method's description in Table 19.1, is set to some identifier that the ColdFusion Server uses internally for tracking the Greeting instance.

```
Hello, World
Greeting @2b9f14
Hello, World
```

Displaying Method Results

Incorporating the output of a class's method into a page can only be done by using values returned from these method calls. Content written to the ColdFusion Server's JVM output or error streams, System.out and System.err respectively, will not be incorporated into the results sent back to the web server for eventual display in the browser. The ColdFusion MX Server does not consider content written to either of these streams as relevant to the creation of a page result.

Values must be returned to the calling logic where they can be captured to CFML variables that can in turn be incorporated into cfoutput blocks.

Static Members

Static properties and methods of classes are powerful features of the Java language. You don't have to create an instance to access these class members; they are available to you without this process, kind of like global values and "always available" functionality specific to a class. There are numerous reasons for constructing classes with static members; one of the more common reasons is that a class can be used as a logical container for similar utility functions such as the java.lang.Math class. Such a class is composed of static methods that perform certain mathematical operations but have no need to instance specific information; its existence is wholly utilitarian in purpose.

The flexibility of Java static class members is preserved when called from within CFML. Given the flexibility of the way that the ColdFusion Server loads Java classes, accessing static class members can be done without causing the implicit instantiation of a class. This is exemplified in Listing 19.6.

Listing 19.6   Calling Static Methods (StaticExample1.cfm)

```
01: <!---
02:     Name:          /c19/StaticExample1.cfm
03:     Description:    An example of using static class
04:          methods.
05: --->
06: <html>
07:     <head>
08:         <title>Static Example 1</title>
09:     </head>
```

```
10:
11:        <body>
12:            <cfscript>
13:                obj = createObject("java", "Greeting");
14:                writeOutput(obj.hey());
15:                obj.init("Welcome, ");
16:                writeOutput("<br>" & obj.greet());
17:            </cfscript>
18:        </body>
19: </html>
```

As discussed in previous listings, the code at line 13 will find a condition where the class is loaded but not actually instantiated. At this point, the ColdFusion Server has loaded, if necessary, the bytecode for the Greeting class and is ready and waiting to actually create an instance. This condition allows for static members to be accessed without actually requiring the instantiation of the Greeting class itself. Had the class been constructed, the call to the init constructor alias on line 14 would have been ignored and the greet method would return "Hello, World" instead of "Welcome, World."

Handling Exceptions

Another major enhancement in ColdFusion MX occurred in its exception handling. Not only has a try/catch capability been added to CFScript, but templates can now catch very specific Java exceptions. Additional to the 11 types that are commonly considered catch-able, the type attribute of cfcatch and the type argument of CFScript's catch can specify a Java java.lang .Exception subclass by name! Methods can throw different kinds of exceptions based upon the kind of error they encounter or wish to express. These exceptions are actually just instances or subclasses of the java.lang.Exception class. Because a method can throw different exceptions more than it throws the same kind, it is possible to write code that reacts to specific kinds of errors rather than generically as it did previous versions of ColdFusion.

The template in Listing 19.7 uses the error method of the Greeting class to exemplify this.

Listing 19.7   Catching a Java Exception (CatchExample1.cfm)

```
<!---
    Name:              /c19/InitExample1.cfm
    Description:       Explicit instance construction and
        a call to the class's init method.
--->
<html>
    <head>
        <title>Catch Example 1</title>
    </head>

    <body>
```

```
        <cfscript>
            obj = createObject("java", "Greeting");
            try
            {
                obj.error("This is a test");
            }
            catch(java.io.IOException e)
            {
                writeOutput("Caught an exception!");
                writeOutput("<br>");
                writeOutput(e.Message);
            }
        </cfscript>
    </body>
</html>
```

The `error` method specifically throws a `java.io.IOException`. The method does not really encounter an error condition; it merely throws an exception to allow for the exemplification of this point. You can see the message that is returned that tells of the thrown exception here:

```
Caught an exception!
This is a test
```

WARNING Although `cfcatch` and `catch` can be set to catch `java.lang.Exception` subclasses, they cannot be set for subclasses of `java.lang.Throwable`. To catch these `Throwable` subclasses, you must specify a `type` of "Any" for the `cfcatch` type attribute or the `type` argument of `catch`.

Class Caching

Once `cfobject` or `createObject` is used to instantiate a class, that class's bytecode is cached into the memory of the ColdFusion Server. With the singular exception of the Server's Dynamic Class Load directories, ColdFusion MX does not have any administrative or programmatic means of flushing its class cache. Thus, any time a class is recompiled, the Server must be restarted before the changes are picked up.

These problems can be demonstrated with a little work using a simple Java class called `Hi`, shown below in Listing 19.8.

Listing 19.8   **A Simple Java Class (Hi.java)**

```
/*
Name:          /c19/Hi.java
Description:    A simple with one method that
    returns a String.
*/
```

```
public class Hi
{
    public String message()
    {
        return new String("Hi");
    }
}
```

When called from the template ClassCacheExample1.cfm, shown in Listing 19.9, the output is exactly as expected: a display that says "Hi."

Listing 19.9   **Invoking the Hi Class (ClassCacheExample1.cfm)**

```
<!---
    Name:            /c19/ClassCacheExample1.cfm
    Description:     Used to help demonstrate the
        caching of Java class bytecode.
--->
<html>
    <head>
        <title>Class Cache Example 1</title>
    </head>

    <body>
        <cfscript>
            obj = createObject("java", "Hi");

            writeOutput("<h2>Message</h2>");
            writeOutput(obj.message());
        </cfscript>
    </body>
</html>
```

The following simple step-by-step process, which uses the Hi class and the template in Listing 19.9, exemplifies this point:

1. Load the ClassCaching.cfm template in your browser and observe the displayed message. It should display "Hi."

2. Open Hi.java in your editor and change the value returned from the message method from "Hi" to "Greetings."

3. Recompile the Java source. If you have changed only the enquoted value, it should recompile without errors.

4. Return to your browser and refresh the page. The display will still show "Hi."

5. Restart the ColdFusion Server.

6. Now return to your browser and refresh the page. The display will now show "Greetings."

Dynamic Class Load Directory

Even in versions as early as 4.5 there was a workaround to the class-caching problem. Any compiled class kept in the Dynamic Class Load directory would be reloaded if the bytecode was updated. Similarly, ColdFusion MX has two such "hot load" directories:

- JAR files from the `<webroot>/WEB-INF/lib`

- Class files from the `<webroot>/WEB-INF/classes`

`<webroot>` is the base web directory of the ColdFusion MX Server installation. For the standalone installation, the base directory is the `wwwroot` subdirectory of the Server's install location.

Unnecessary use of a "hot load" directory on a production server presents two crucial problems: a security risk and a performance drag.

Security Risk

The security risk associated with using a "hot load" directory may not be immediately apparent. Specifically the automatic reloading of libraries and classes has no logging, audit trail, or other checking. The class loader used by the ColdFusion Server's JVM merely checks for an updated bytecode and loads it when a change is found. Because there is no way of telling what specific bytecode is loaded (since there is no versioning feature built in for comparison), there are a number of dangerous possibilities introduced including un-auditable source control updates and malicious attacks.

For example, problems could be introduced through push mechanisms in source control systems. New code could be introduced into the staging or production environments, and depending upon the nature of the push mechanism or the source control system, insufficient logging information may be generated by the push mechanism, so exactly what version got pushed may not be known. The lack of logging on the part of an automatic mechanism makes the danger of this scenario entirely possible.

In addition, it is conceivable that a malicious version of the Java class's bytecode could be introduced. Thus, if the class was used to interact with sensitive data (either getting or setting), a subversive version could be forced to send that data to a location for easy collection.

Although this last example seems unlikely given the fact that the person injecting the malicious code would need filesystem access (which would grant far more opportunities), it does present a number of "benefits" in its attack mode. For instance, if no one spent the time thinking about how to make file permissions secure, it would be easy (especially on the Windows platform) for an attacker to replace the class file. Without some sort of filesystem-level audit or detection system, there is no trace of this replacement. In fact, no additional passwords are needed (like those that might be used to access data from the database). Well-behaved replacements could go unnoticed indefinitely; this might be more desirable than causing noticeable damage. Given the easy availability of bytecode decompilers, an attacker would not even need the original source to begin making the modifications. So even if the source files were to be kept in a safe location (for example in a CVS repository on another machine, likely behind the firewall), the attack would not need any additional access.

Performance Drag

The performance drag induced by using a "hot load" directory is slight but enough to be measurable. Each time a call to `cfobject` or `createObject` is made, a comparison must be made between the bytecode in the "hot load" directory and the content loaded into the Server's memory. The slowdown that results can become more of a problem if the ColdFusion application makes heavy use of Java.

WARNING   Because tag libraries are loaded from the `<webroot>/WEB-INF/lib` directory, the Server automatically reloads these libraries, if necessary, when the library is imported.

Overloading

In the object-oriented world, overloading is a common practice for encapsulating a piece of functionality that can be driven with a variety of differing arguments and argument datatypes under the same common method name. The transparencies provided from CFML to Java allow for this practice. This process is exemplified in Listing 19.10.

Listing 19.10   **Demonstrating Method Overloading (OverloadExample1.cfm)**

```
01: <!---
02:     Name:          /c19/OverloadExample1.cfm
03:     Description:    A simple example of using an
04:          overloaded method.
05: --->
06: <html>
07:     <head>
08:         <title>Overload Example 1</title>
09:     </head>
10:
11:     <body>
12:         <cfscript>
13:             obj = createObject("java", "Greeting");
14:
15:             writeOutput("<h2>Object No Arg</h2>");
16:             writeOutput(obj.greet());
17:             writeOutput("<h2>Object with Arg</h2>");
18:             writeOutput(obj.greet("Mr. Rish"));
19:         </cfscript>
20:     </body>
21: </html>
```

The construction of the instance occurs on line 13; then on line 16, a call to the `greet` method occurs (this causes the implicit construction of the instance, as discussed previously). The same method name is invoked on line 18 but passed an argument. Inspection of the `Greeting` source shows that the `greet` method has three overloads. There are two used in this example: the argument less one will address the world at large, and the other one takes a `java.lang.String` argument and will address a specific person by name.

Calling an overloaded method in CFML can present a few challenges. First of all, because CFML is considered a loosely typed language when simple datatypes are involved, it does little to distinguish between different kinds of numerical values or the difference between a single character and a whole string of characters the way Java does. This can often create a situation where it is difficult for the CFML interpreter to know which overload is being specified. This problem is further compounded by CFML's inability to perform type comparisons of instances. Because CFML is unable to easily differentiate instance datatypes, the strategy is to differentiate method overloads by argument count instead of argument datatypes. This applies to constructors as well, which are handled through CFML's `init` alias.

To better exemplify the challenges with overloaded methods, consider the third `greet` overload in the `Greeting` source, which takes a single `int` argument. The problem associated with the CFML interpreter's inability to seamlessly handle overloads with the same number of arguments of differing datatypes can be observed in Listing 19.11.

Listing 19.11   Overloaded Methods with Differing Datatype Arguments (OverloadExample2.cfm)

```
01: <!---
02:     Name:           /c19/OverloadExample2.cfm
03:     Description:    An example of using an overloaded
04:         method with the same number of arguments but
05:         with differing datatypes.
06: --->
07: <html>
08:     <head>
09:         <title>Overload Example 2</title>
10:     </head>
11:
12:     <body>
13:         <cfscript>
14:             obj = createObject("java", "Greeting");
15:
16:             writeOutput("<h2>Method No Arg</h2>");
17:             writeOutput(obj.greet());
18:             writeOutput("<h2>Method String Arg</h2>");
19:             writeOutput(obj.greet("Mr. Rish"));
20:             writeOutput("<h2>Method int Arg</h2>");
21:             writeOutput(obj.greet(5));
```

```
22:        </cfscript>
23:    </body>
24: </html>
```

The initial call to the `greet` method on line 17 is without arguments, and the result shown in the browser is much like what might be expected. The call to the `java.lang.String` overload, line 19, also displays what would be expected. However, on line 21, when a numerical value is passed, it is obvious that the call is not getting routed correctly. The `int` overload should display a "Hello, World" message and repeat this display the number of times indicated by the received numerical argument. Instead, interestingly enough, it calls the `java.lang.String` overload and "Hello, 5" is displayed in the browser as shown below, which is not at all the correct functionality:

Method No Arg

Hello, World

Method String Arg

Hello, Mr. Rish

Method int Arg

Hello, 5

Fortunately, CFML provides a function that helps offset this problem. The `javaCast` function provides some limited type coercion that better enables the invocation of overloaded methods. The `javaCast` function takes two arguments, shown in Table 19.4.

TABLE 19.4: javaCast Arguments

Argument	Description
type	The datatype to which to coerce. The conversion types are `boolean`, `int`, `long`, `double`, and `string` only.
variable	The CFML variable or value upon which to perform the coercion.

Usage of this function is exemplified in Listing 19.12. This template is almost identical to `OverloadTemplate2.cfm`, shown in Listing 19.11, except that the value that is being passed to the `greet` overload on lines 21 and 22 is passed via the `javaCast` function instead of passed directly.

Listing 19.12   **Using javaCast (OverloadTemplate3.cfm)**

```
01: <!---
02:     Name:              /c19/OverloadExample3.cfm
03:     Description:    An example of using an overloaded
04:         method with the same number of arguments but
05:         with differing datatypes using javaCast.
06: --->
07: <html>
08:     <head>
09:         <title>Overload Example 3</title>
10:     </head>
11:
12:     <body>
13:         <cfscript>
14:             obj = createObject("java", "Greeting");
15:
16:             writeOutput("<h2>Method No Arg</h2>");
17:             writeOutput(obj.greet());
18:             writeOutput("<h2>Method String Arg</h2>");
19:             writeOutput(obj.greet("Mr. Rish"));
20:             writeOUtput("<h2>Method int Arg</h2>");
21:             writeOutput(obj.greet(
22:                 javaCast("int", 5)));
23:         </cfscript>
24:     </body>
25: </html>
```

As can be seen here, the results are a bit different than with OverloadExample2.cfm:

Method No Arg

Hello, World

Method String Arg

Hello, Mr. Rish

Method int Arg

Hello, World
Hello, World
Hello, World
Hello, World
Hello, World

Datatype Conversion

The CFML interpreter automatically converts between Java datatypes and CFML datatypes whenever possible. This is no simple trick given the datatype-flexible nature that CFML is apt to exhibit and Java's strict and rich datatyped nature.

CFML to Java

So you may be wondering what happens under the hood when a template passes a CFML variable as an argument to a method or as an assignment to a property. The CFML interpreter converts the variable's CFML datatype into one that Java's interpreter can understand. This is easy to do with simpler datatypes, but it becomes more challenging when complex datatypes are used. Table 19.5 shows the conversion mappings between CFML and Java—this information was taken from the product documentation that ships with Macromedia's ColdFusion MX Server.

TABLE 19.5: CFML to Java Datatype Conversion

CFML Datatype	Java Type
`integer`	`short`, `int`, `long` (`shorts` and `ints` might exhibit precision loss)
`real number`	`float` or `double` (`floats` might exhibit precision loss)
`boolean`	`boolean`
`date-time`	`java.util.Date`
`string` (including Lists)	`java.lang.String`
`array`	`java.util.Vector`
`structure`	`java.lang.Map`
`query object`	`java.lang.Map`
`XML document object`	Not supported
`ColdFusion Component`	Not supported

Testing this information is not a particularly difficult task. In Listing 19.13, a simple Java class, `Passing`, is called from a template, `DatatypesExample1.cfm` (only the portion of the template where this call occurs is shown).

Listing 19.13   Passing CFML Datatypes to Java (from DatatypesExample1.cfm)

```
01: <!---
02:     Name:          /c19/DatatypesExample1.cfm
03:     Description:    An example of the automatic
04:         type conversion that takes place when
05:         CFML datatypes are passed to Java methods.
06: --->
07: <cfscript>
```

```
08:     obj = createobject("java", "Passing");
09:
10:     writeOutput("<h2>Integer (Primitive)</h2>");
11:     try
12:     {
13:         writeOutput(
14:             obj.displayPrimitiveInteger(3));
15:     }
16:     catch(Any e)
17:     {
18:         writeOutput("<strong>Error!</strong> "
19:             & e.Message);
20:     }
21:
22:     writeOutput("<h2>Integer</h2>");
23:     try
24:     {
25:         writeOutput(obj.displayInteger(3));
26:     }
27:     catch(Any e)
28:     {
29:         writeOutput("<strong>Error!</strong> "
30:             & e.Message);
31:     }
```

In Listing 19.13, the source for Passing has been elided because its source is too long for this text; a breakdown of its methods is shown in Table 19.6.

TABLE 19.6: Passing Methods

Method	Description
displayPrimitiveInteger	Receive and display an int.
displayInteger	Receive and display a java.lang.Integer.
displayPrimitiveReal	Receive and display a double.
displayReal	Receive and display a java.lang.Double.
displayPrimitiveBoolean	Receive and display a boolean.
displayBoolean	Receive and display a java.lang.Boolean.
displayDate	Receive and display a java.util.Date.
displayStructure	Receive and display a java.util.Map.
displayQuery	Receive and display a java.util.Map.
displayList	Receive and display a java.lang.String.
displayArray	Receive and display a java.util.Vector.
displayArrayOfStructures	Receive and display a java.util.Vector populated with java.util.Map instances.
identifyObject	Display the class name of the instance.

You may notice that this class does not make use of certain object-oriented features. This was a choice made because of two factors: casting problems (javaCast does not handle many of these types) and the need for simplicity of code.

If you momentarily exempt one problem (which will be discussed later), things work well with this template's execution. Even if you pass arrays of structures into Passing, the CFML to Java marshalling happens as indicated in Table 19.5. Also, if you specifically observe the array-of-structures case (within DatatypeExample1.cfm but not shown in Listing 19.13), you will see that three levels of conversion are taking place: the conversion of the CFML array itself into a Java array, the conversion of its contained structures into java.util.Map instances, and the conversion of the structure's member strings into java.lang.String instances. Figuring out exactly how deep the conversion goes without breaking, if it goes anywhere at all, would require more intensive work and is beyond the scope of this text.

When you look at the resulting display from this template, you will see that it shows a discrepancy in the Macromedia documentation. It seems that query objects are not converted to java.util.Map instances. Immediately after the call to displayQuery and its CFML try/catch block is a call to identifyObject to determine what the problem might be. The passed CFML query object is identified as coldfusion.sql.QueryTable instance, as seen here:

Structure

```
structure:
LASTNAME is Bainum
FIRSTNAME is Selene
```

Query

```
Error! Method selection Exception.
```

CFML Query object identified

```
Object class:
coldfusion.sql.queryTable
```

Obviously this poses a serious problem. Macromedia has provided no documentation on the Server's internal workings, of which coldfusion.sql.QueryTable is clearly a constituent. An enterprising developer might consider extracting that specific class file from the appropriate JAR and use the JDK's profiler to study this class at greater depth. Naturally, however, this kind of exercise runs the risk of being frowned upon in open or published forums and is thus not encouraged.

Java to CFML

Just as transferring data from a template into an instance poses certain problems, so does doing the reverse. In fact, transferring from an instance to a template has even more pitfalls given the broad variety of Java classes that are available. Table 19.7 shows the conversion mappings between Java datatypes and CFML datatypes. This was also taken from Macromedia's own product documentation.

TABLE 19.7:   Java Class to CFML Datatype Conversion

Java Class	CFML Datatype
boolean/java.lang.Boolean	boolean
byte/java.lang.Byte	string
char/java.lang.Char	string
short/java.lang.Short	integer
int/java.lang.Integer	integer
long/java.lang.Long	integer
float/java.lang.Float	real number
double/java.lang.Double	real number
java.lang.String	string
java.util.Date	date-time
java.util.List	list (comma-delimited)
byte[]	array
char[]	array
boolean[]	array
java.lang.String[]	array
java.util.Vector	array
java.util.Map	structure

Testing these conversions, despite the larger volume, is no more difficult than testing the CFML datatype to Java class conversions. For instance, if you use a simple Java class, Returning, you can devise a large number of methods for the singular purpose of returning values from Java to the calling template. As with passing, the Returning class has been elided from print for the same reasons. A breakdown of its methods is shown in Table 19.8.

TABLE 19.8: Returning Methods

Method	Description
returnPrimitiveBoolean	Return a primitive `boolean`.
returnBoolean	Return a `java.lang.Boolean`.
returnPrimitiveByte	Return a primitive `byte`.
returnByte	Return a `java.lang.Byte`.
returnPrimitiveChar	Return a primitive `char`.
returnChar	Return a `java.lang.Character`.
returnPrimitiveShort	Return a primitive `short`.
returnShort	Return a `java.lang.Short`.
returnPrimitiveInteger	Return a primitive `int`.
returnInteger	Return a `java.lang.Integer`.
returnPrimitiveLong	Return a primitive `long`.
returnLong	Return a `java.lang.Long`.
returnPrimitiveFloat	Return a primitive `float`.
returnFloat	Return a `java.lang.Float`.
returnPrimitiveDouble	Return a primitive `double`.
returnDouble	Return a `java.lang.Double`.
returnString	Return a `java.lang.String`.
returnDate	Return a `java.lang.Date` for conversion to a CFML `date-time` value.
returnList	Return a `java.lang.List` for conversion to a comma-delimited CFML `list`.
returnPrimitiveByteArray	Return a primitive `byte` array for conversion into a CFML `array`.
returnPrimitiveCharArray	Return a primitive `char` array for conversion into a CFML `array`.
returnPrimitiveBooleanArray	Return a primitive `boolean` array for conversion into a CFML `array`.
returnStringArray	Return a `java.lang.String` array for conversion into a CFML `array`.
returnVector	Return a `java.util.Vector` for conversion into a CFML `array`.
returnMap	Return a `java.util.Map` for conversion into a CFML `structure`.

You will find that if you use `Returning` from `DatatypesExample2.cfm`, excerpts of which are shown in Listing 19.14, it will work much as the `Passing` example from Listing 19.13 did.

Listing 19.14   **Converting Java Datatypes to CFML (from DatatypesExample2.cfm)**

```
01: <!---
02:    Name:         /c19/DatatypesExample2.cfm
```

```
03:     Description:    An example of the automatic
04:             type conversion that takes place when
05:             Java datatypes are returned from Java methods.
06: --->
07: <cffunction name="dump">
08:     <cfargument name="var" type="any">
09:     <cfdump var="#var#">
10: </cffunction>
11:
12: <cfscript>
13:     obj = createObject("java", "Returning");
14:
15:     writeOutput("<h2>Returned Primitive Boolean</h2>");
16:     try
17:     {
18:         b = obj.returnPrimitiveBoolean();
19:         dump(b);
20:     }
21:     catch(Any e)
22:     {
23:         writeOutput("<strong>Error!</strong> "
24:             & e.Message);
25:     }
```

Lines 7 through 10 set up a simple function called dump to wrap cfdump for use within cfscript. The bulk of the template exists within the cfscript block that begins on line 12. Lines 15 through 25 exemplify a block of code that is repeated for each of Returning's methods; in this case, within a try/catch block, the results of returnPrimitiveBoolean are captured and feed to dump. If there is an exception, it is trapped and the error message is displayed.

This template's display is considerably more interesting than that of the previous conversion exercise. Everything goes as might be expected until the class returns a primitive Java char datatype. It seems that ColdFusion MX has some problems differentiating between a primitive char and java.lang.Character instance, and in both cases, the CFML interpreter sees a java.lang.Character. Figure 19.1 shows how this would turn out in the browser.

To verify this, another template, DatatypesExample3.cfm is needed. An excerpt of this template is shown in Listing 19.15.

Listing 19.15   **Are Java Primitives CFML Objects? (from DatatypesExample3.cfm)**

```
01: <!---
02:     Name:           /c19/DatatypesExample3.cfm
03:     Description:    Verifies the object status
04:         of datatypes returned from Java method calls.
05: --->
```

```
06: <cfscript>
07:     obj = createObject("java", "Returning");
08:
09:     writeOutput("<h2>Primitive Boolean</h2>");
10:     try
11:     {
12:         writeOutput("IsObject: " &
13:             isObject(obj.returnPrimitiveBoolean()));
14:     }
15:     catch(Any e)
16:     {
17:         writeOutput("<strong>Error!</strong> "
18:             & e.Message);
19:     }
```

Lines 10 through 19 show a try/catch block where, as part of the writeOutput argument, the results of the Returning instance's returnPrimitiveBoolean method is passed to CFML's isObject. If, for some reason, there is an error with the class instance or the method call, the exception is trapped and displayed; this allows the template to continue to the next call.

If you test only the methods that return primitive values or arrays of primitive values, you will find that each one, except for `returnPrimitiveChar`, reports back as a negative answer from the `isObject`. This is likely a bug since the returning `java.lang.Character`'s `toString` method must be used to access the value, whereas the other primitive datatype conversions are automatic. Obviously, the only workaround for this is to just hardcode the template for the bug.

Nested Objects

It is a common practice in many object-oriented languages to create classes that contain subordinate classes, and even cases where those subordinate classes contain subordinate classes. This is called *nesting*. Previous versions of ColdFusion have been unable to work with nested classes directly.

Nesting is performed by stringing together a series of objects, each one subordinately contained in the previous one in the dot-notated chain. For example, if you were given a hypothetical hierarchy of a `Library` instance, `library`, that contained a `Shelf` instance, `shelf`, that contained multiple `Book` instances, it would look like this:

```
library.shelf.getBook("Age of Innocence").getAuthor();
```

This would return a `java.lang.String` with the value `"Edith Wharton"`. Basically, you would access `library`, then call the `getBook` method of the subordinately contained `shelf` so that you could call the `getAuthor` method of the returned `Book` instance.

Previous versions of ColdFusion would have required an elaborate multistep retrieval of each instance in order to drill down to the specific `Book` instance, as shown here:

```
<cfset shelf = lib.shelf>
<cfset book = shelf.book>
<cfoutput>#book.getAuthor()#</cfoutput>
```

Where larger arrangements of classes are concerned, as is often the case with an enterprise-caliber application, this style of accessing nested classes is prohibitively clumsy. But ColdFusion MX has corrected this, and the same usage of dot notation to access nested classes in Java can now be expressed in CFML, as shown here:

```
<cfoutput>
#library.shelf.getBook("Age of Innocence").getAuthor()#
</cfoutput>
```

This bit of code returns exactly what you would expect.

In Sum

The potential power that you can wield using Java class APIs within ColdFusion templates is immense. Things that seemed completely impossible within ColdFusion suddenly become possible. But as we found out in this chapter, any time two dissimilar programming languages are integrated to this degree, there are bound to be challenges. However, many of these challenges can be solved with a little forewarning about syntactical issues and mappings, which we covered.

In this chapter, the specifics of the different ways classes are instantiated and their methods can be invoked has been explained. You should now have a solid understanding of how overloaded methods are handled and datatypes are mapped. These fundamentals will form the basis for all future work along this vein, and you will find yourself employing them repeatedly when working with Java class APIs.

Chapter 20

Building Java Extensions

By Guy Rish

- Introducing Java extensions

- Installing Java CFX tags

- Java CFXAPI

- Basic Java CFX

- Debugging

- Working with Complex data: Help from WDDX

- Extending the CFXAPI

- CFML wrapped CFX tags

There are times when building a custom tag in CFML is not the best option, either because of overall system performance or functional capability. CFML custom tags are not widely known for their high performance capabilities and are wholly restricted in what they can do by the limits inherent in the CFML language itself. It is at these times when you should consider constructing or using a custom tag written in another language. A custom tag written in a language other than CFML is known as a ColdFusion Extension (CFX). Macromedia provides tools for developing CFXs in two languages, C++ and Java. CFX tags constructed in C++ become operating system–specific binaries and generally have better performance, while those constructed in Java will run on any operating system that supports Java. Although they generally run faster than CFML tags, they seldom perform as well as C++ CFXs. There are times when it is better to sacrifice the performance of a custom tag written in C++ than to deal with the difficulties associated with maintaining platform specific modifications to the code base. This is when extensions built in Java are the better choice for CFX implementation.

Introducing Java Extensions

This chapter focuses on the construction of Java CFX tags. The chapter begins with a close review of the Java CFX class library, commonly referred to as the CFXAPI. By examining the basic characteristics of the library, you will get a clear and immediate understanding of what it can and cannot do. Then we'll explore a number of workarounds for the library's limitations. We'll also discuss a few discrepancies in the Macromedia documentation and, when possible, correct them. This chapter also introduces a small set of reusable classes that can be used later in the chapter.

NOTE   The material here will relate to Chapter 7, "Advanced WDDX," and Chapter 19, "Working with Java Objects." Although these chapters are not required reading in order to understand this one, some of the concepts and work introduced in them dovetail into this one.

Rationale for Using Java CFX Tags

The broad range of available APIs and the platform neutrality associated with Java CFX tags make building them in Java an excellent middle ground between using CFML tags and C++ tags. In fact, because Java's popularity is growing fast, you may even find that a needed API is exclusive to Java. Also, since the ColdFusion MX Server is a Java server, once the CFX tag is accessed for the first time it is cached, and all subsequent executions involving this tag will be faster; this will make this tag's performance comparable to tags written in C++.

What You Should Already Know about Java

This chapter assumes that you are familiar with Java basics. None of the examples require advanced Java knowledge; in fact, they are all rather simple and are designed to demonstrate specific features of CFX construction. When you begin working with this sample code, you will need the Java Developer's Kit (JDK) to be installed, but any Java 2 JDK will suffice. In addition, you will find no special IDE requirements.

Although there is some discussion of software design patterns, you don't need to understand this topic to use the software or techniques presented herein. However, if you are a more advanced developer, these references should provide more depth to this discussion. For more information, refer to the sidebar entitled "An Overview of Design Patterns" and to the notes throughout the chapter that indicate when a pattern is in use.

An Overview of Design Patterns

A software design pattern provides a solution to some common and recurring problem. It is made up of an abstract description of how to implement some software mechanism, typically one fashioned with object-oriented constructs (classes, interfaces, aggregate relationships, and so on), to resolve some design need.

The concept of software design patterns is derived from Christopher Alexander's works on building patterns. While it seems unlikely that the world of physical architecture and building construction could have little in common with the construction of software, Alexander's work encapsulated certain conceptual abstractions that have proven broadly applicable in numerous fields of endeavor, the least of which is the software industry. The quintessential work on software design patterns, the application of Alexander's conceptual abstractions to the world of software design, is *Design Patterns: Elements of Reusable Object-Oriented Software*, by Erich Gamma, et al. (Addison-Wesley, 1995). It is impossible to properly cover the topic of design patterns in this chapter, even if work were restricted to the ones referred to herein. I strongly urge you to investigate further, either with the *Design Patterns* book, which is an excellent jumping-off point, or through research on the Web.

The standard Java libraries routinely use various basic patterns such as Factory, Adapter, and Decorator to name a few. The new classes that are presented in this chapter, some of which are meant to extend the existing CFXAPI, also make use of some patterns, including the following:

Adapter This design uses a class that acts as an intermediary between two other classes, thus changing the appearance of one so that its interface "looks" like the other. This allows a class that was previously not compatible with another class or set of classes to be integrated. There are numerous adapter-based classes in java.awt class hierarchy.

Continued on next page

> **Decorator**   This design dynamically wraps a class with another to add or remove functionality from the wrapped class without having to create subclasses. Various Reader classes in the `java.io` package provide this functionality.
>
> **Factory**   This design provides a single interface for creating instances of related or dependent classes. Many of the JDBC interfaces in the `java.sql` package act as factories for the concrete implementations of other interfaces (for specific drivers).

Chapter Setup

There is some preliminary setup and requirements work that you need to do to ensure that this chapter's examples will work correctly. You will need to install the following: a Java 2 JDK, the WDDX SDK, Apache's XML libraries, the chapter's sample code. In addition, you will need to register a sample database that is included with the chapter code.

JDK

You can download a Java 2–compliant JDK from Sun's Java website (`http://java.sun.com`). At the time of this writing, version 1.4 has been tested with and works correctly with this chapter's content. Use this JDK to compile the CFX sources presented in this chapter.

WDDX SDK

For the later examples in this chapter, you will need to install the WDDX SDK. You can download this from the OpenWDDX website (`http://www.openwddx.org`). Once you have installed the SDK, make certain that the `wddx.jar` is added to your Java IDE's `classpath` environment variable. You will need to do this before you can compile the samples for this chapter.

You will need to add the `wddx.jar` to the ColdFusion MX Server's `classpath` setting in order for some of the samples in this chapter to work. For details on how to update the Server's `classpath` setting through the ColdFusion Administrator, review Appendix A.

Apache's XML Libraries

Numerous samples later in this chapter require XML parsing and XSL transformations. Apache's XML projects provide the Java libraries you will need for these exercises. Download them from the Apache XML website (`http://xml.apache.org`). In particular, you will need to download the Xerces package, and once it is installed, you will need to add the JAR to the `classpath` environment variable to your Java IDE. You will need to do this before you can compile the samples for this chapter.

You will need to add the `xerces.jar` to the ColdFusion MX Server's `classpath` setting in order for some of the samples in this chapter to work. For details on how to update the Server's `classpath` setting through the ColdFusion Administrator, review Appendix A.

Chapter Sample Code

You can download the sample code for this chapter from the Sybex website (`http://www.sybex.com`) via a link on this book's home page. Make sure to unpack the files into a web-published directory. This chapter's directory should also appear in the ColdFusion MX Server's Java `classpath`.

NOTE   For specific details about modifying the Server's Java `classpath` see Appendix A, "Configuring ColdFusion for Java."

As you will see, a database has been included with the sample code for this chapter. It must be registered with the ColdFusion MX Server. To do this, in the ColdFusion Administrator, register the data source as `Names` and direct it to the database file, `names.mdb`, within the directory where the chapter's sample code was placed.

In addition, some of the later samples in this chapter use some specialized Java classes. These should also be included with the chapter's sample code. They are contained within a JAR called `rish_coldfusionhandbook.jar`. You will also need to include this in the ColdFusion Server's Java `classpath`. For details on how to update the Server's `classpath` setting through the Cold-Fusion Administrator, review Appendix A.

Installing Java CFX Tags

As mentioned earlier, a number of simple CFX tags will be constructed throughout this chapter, and they will need to be registered with the ColdFusion Administrator before they can be incorporated into templates. Installing a Java-based CFX tag is not very difficult and can be done in three simple steps.

1. Just launch the ColdFusion Administrator in the browser and in the Navigation area on the left, select the CFX Tags menu item from under the Extensions heading. This loads the page shown in Figure 20.1.

   As you can see in Figure 20.1, the CFX Tags page has two buttons and a table of the registered CFX tags (both C++ and Java). The two buttons, Register C++ CFX and Register Java CFX, load the different pages for the two different kinds of tags. As might be surmised, only Java CFX tag registration will be discussed in this chapter.

   The table contains four columns: Name, Description, Language, and Controls.

   Name   The Name column indicates the CFML name by which you will identify the CFX tag; this is not necessarily the same as the Java class name.

Description   The Description column contains the descriptive text that you can optionally enter when you register the tag.

Language   The Language column indicates whether the CFX tag is a C++ or Java tag.

Controls   The Controls column contains two hyperlinked images that allow you to edit or delete the CFX tag entry.

FIGURE 20.1:
The CFX Tags page

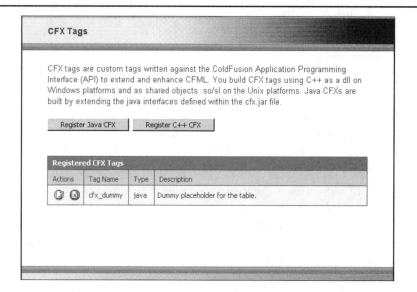

2. When you click the Register Java CFX button, it will load the Add/Edit Java CFX Tag page (as shown in Figure 20.2).

This page contains three edit fields: Tag Name, Class Name, and Description.

Tag Name   The Tag Name field specifies the CFML name for the CFX tag; this corresponds to the Name column on the CFX Tags page.

Class Name   The Class Name field contains the fully qualified class name of the CFX tag not including the `.class` file extension.

Description   The optional Description field contains any descriptive text about the tag (commercially produced tags often have copyright information here); this corresponds to the Description column on the CFX Tags page.

FIGURE 20.2:

The Add/Edit Java CFX
Tag page

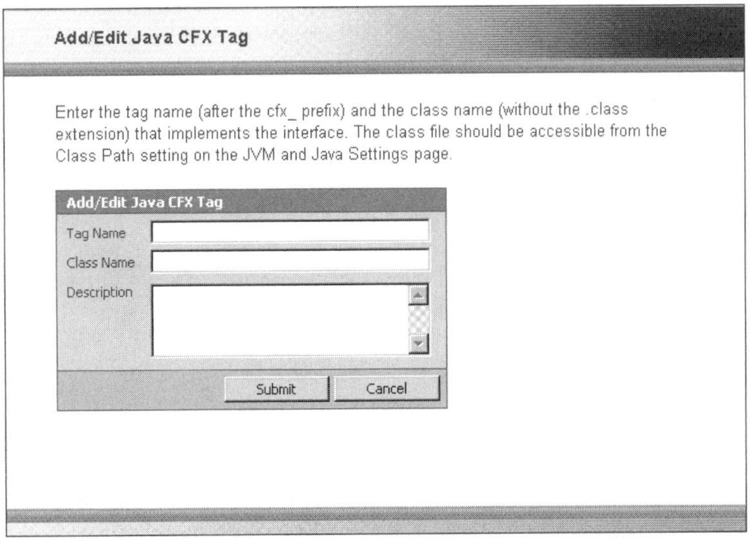

Figure 20.3 shows the registration information for a tag that will be constructed later in
this chapter. Go ahead and complete the form with this information.

FIGURE 20.3:

"Hello, World" CFX

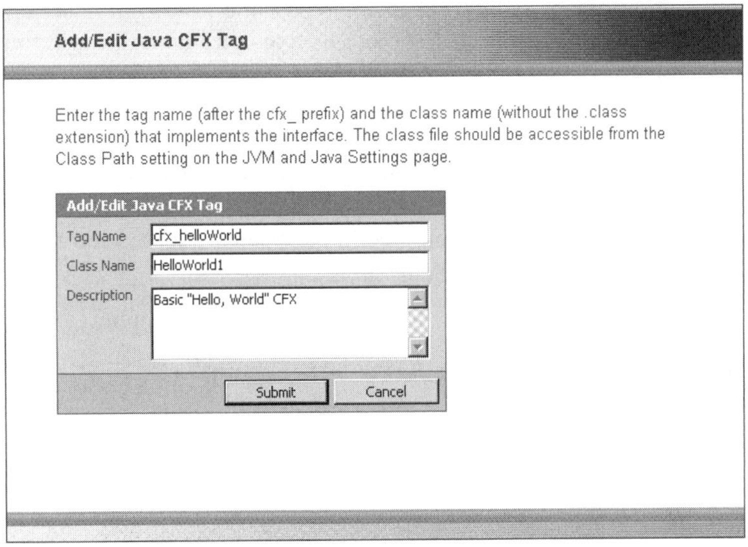

Since the ColdFusion Server does not perform any preloading or other verification of the Class Name field, you will not harm anything if you commit this information prior to the construction of the actual CFX tag.

3. Click the Submit button on the Add/Edit Java CFX Tag page. You can see the new entry in the table, and you are now done.

WARNING   Once a Java CFX tag has been registered, you must make certain that the Server's `classpath` setting includes the location or JAR containing the CFX's class file. If it does not contain this information, then when the CFX tag is called, the CFML interpreter will throw an error stating that it cannot find the tag's class files.

Java CFXAPI

When you start to study Java-based CFX tags, the CFXAPI library is a good place to start.

The Java CFXAPI is the basic kit for developing Java custom tags. The JAR that is the CFXAPI library, `cfx.jar`, contains 14 classes, many of which serve only as the scaffolding for a smaller subset. The JAR can be found in the `lib` subdirectory of the ColdFusion MX Server's installation directory.

WARNING   It is important that you include the `cfx.jar` in the `classpath` of your Java development environment (whether it is command line or IDE). Remember that the `classpath` of your development environment belongs to a different JVM than the `classpath` of the ColdFusion MX Server.

Macromedia's own product documentation, included with the software distribution, includes some standard documentation for most of these classes and information about building Java CFXs. The references below are excellent for beginners, but they have gaps in their presentation. In fact, the important bits they contain are spread across all three chapters, making the learning process a little challenging.

- *Developing ColdFusion Applications with CFML*, Chapter 12, "Building Custom CFXAPI Tags"
- *Developing ColdFusion Applications with CFML*, Chapter 32, "Integrating J2EE and Java Elements into CFML Applications"
- *CFML Reference*, Chapter 7, "ColdFusion Java CFX Reference"

Developers will use four basic classes in the construction of nearly every Java-based CFX: `CustomTag`, `Request`, `Response`, and `Query`. Because these four classes are Java interfaces, they are really just front ends for real objects and processes within the ColdFusion Server. The CFXAPI actually contains a number of classes, all of which can be seen by looking into the `cfx.jar` file.

The UML class diagram in Figure 20.4 shows how all these classes are connected.

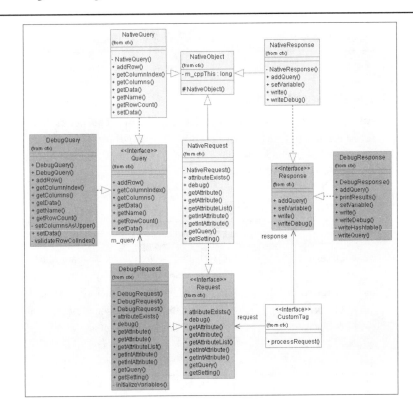

NOTE   If you need more information to understand UML diagrams like the one in Figure 20.4, see Appendix B, "Understanding UML Class Diagrams."

The model gives you a good visual overview of the relationship between the important classes in the CFXAPI. It quickly becomes apparent that mostly everything centers on these four major interfaces, which we will explore for the remainder of this section.

The CustomTag Interface

This simple interface class defines the entry point into every Java-based CFX. Any class can become a CFX tag by implementing this interface and filling out some logic in the interface's one method, processRequest, shown below in Table 20.1. The processRequest method receives, from the ColdFusion Server, a Request instance and a Response instance.

TABLE 20.1: CustomTag Interface

Method	Description
processRequest	The custom tag entry point.

The Request Interface

An instance of this interface is passed into the processRequest method of each CFX's CustomTag interface and provides all of the incoming attributes from the tag invocation. Using the various methods of the interface, shown in Table 20.2, the custom tag can find out some limited things about the calling logic.

TABLE 20.2: Request Interface

Method	Description
attributeExists	Checks for the existence of an attribute.
debug	Checks whether the debug attribute exists.
getAttribute	Retrieves the String value of an attribute.
getAttributeList	Retrieves the list of passed attributes as a String array.
getIntAttribute	Retrieves the int value of an attribute.
getQuery	Retrieves the passed Query.
getSetting	Retrieves the String value of a global setting from the registry.

The Request interface handles things like whether the tag was called with the special-purpose debug attribute set, getting a list of all of the attributes with which the tag was called, and retrieving the one Query that can be passed to a CFX.

WARNING The Request interface still maintains a getSetting method, but it is only applicable on the Windows platform. Starting with ColdFusion MX, the emulation of a Windows style registry has been discontinued on Unix. This makes it counterproductive to construct Java CFX tags with platform specific functionality.

The Response Interface

An instance of this interface is also passed into the processRequest method of each CFX's CustomTag interface and provides all of the methods, shown in Table 20.3, for passing data back to the tag's calling logic.

TABLE 20.3: Response Interface

Method	Description
addQuery	Creates a new Query instance to return to the calling logic.
setVariable	Set the String or int value of a variable in the calling logic
write	Outputs a String directly to output stream
writeDebug	Outputs a String to the debugging output stream

If you use the write method, it is possible to enter content directly into the ColdFusion Server's output stream. You can either return a simple (String or int) value to the calling logic, in the form of a wholly new variable, or you can set the value of an existing one with the setVariable method.

NOTE   Macromedia's documentation about the writeDebug method says that it will append the String argument to the debug output buffer, which will only be displayed if the tag's debug attribute is set. This information, found in Macromedia's online documentation (in its *CFML Reference*, Chapter 7, "ColdFusion Java CFX Reference," the Response Interface page), is misleading, as will be discussed later in this chapter.

The Query Interface

The Query interface provides a simple way to manipulate a CFML query object passed to the CFX custom tag. Many of the important functions for handling a Query in CFML can be found as methods of this interface (see Table 20.4).

TABLE 20.4: Query Interface

Method	Description
addRows	Adds more rows to the Query
getColumnByIndex	Gets the column by specifying its index
getColumns	Gets the column names in the form of a String array.
getData	Gets the String value of a specific row and column
getName	Retrieves the name of the Query.
getRowCount	Gets the number of rows in the Query.
setData	Sets a String value to a specific row and column.

Not only is it possible for you to retrieve data and information about the Query, it is possible to set data into the Query. Additionally, you can create a new Query, which you pass back to the calling logic through the addQuery method of the custom tag's Response instance.

Instances of the `Query` interface represent the only built-in way to pass complex data into and out of a custom tag.

Basic Java CFX

A few variations of a `"Hello, World"` custom tag, while very simplistic in nature, go a long way toward revealing the fundamentals of authoring Java CFX tags. This section will cover the four basic classes of the CFXAPI library (presented in the preceding section), which are needed for basic tag construction.

Basic Tag I/O

The first iteration of the `cfx_helloWorld` tag, implemented with `HelloWorld1.java` (Listing 20.1) shows a simple Java class that implements the `CustomTag` interface.

Listing 20.1   Simple CFX (HelloWorld1.java)

```
01: /*
02:     File            /20/HelloWorld1.java
03:     Description    A very simple Java CFX to
04:         display a "Hello, World" message.
05: */
06: import com.allaire.cfx.*;
07:
08: public class HelloWorld1 implements CustomTag
09: {
10:     public void processRequest(Request request,
11:         Response response)
12:     {
13:         String name = null;
14:
15:         name = request.getAttribute("name", "World");
16:
17:         response.write("Hello, " + name);
18:     }
19: }
```

The two important points from this example are the `getAttribute` and `write` method calls.

The CFX tag assumes that that there will be an incoming attribute: `name`. The `Request` interface's `getAttribute` method is overloaded, each returning the value of the specified attribute: one overload returns the value of the specified attribute or a `null` if the attribute is not found.

```
getAttribute(String name)
```

And one allows a default String value to be specified for the request attribute.

```
getAttribute(String name, String default)
```

In most cases, you should use the overload that allows a default value to be specified. By doing this, you will guarantee that the tag has some kind of default functionality and does not crash from null pointer exceptions.

Specifically in the case of this tag, cfx_helloWorld, if the name attribute is not provided, the value "World" is defaulted (see line 15).

A String is constructed as the argument for the call of the Response interface's write method on line 17. This causes a greeting message to be entered directly into the CFML interpreter's output buffer, which is then streamed back through the web server.

Since this CFX has already been registered (during the "Installing Java CFX Tags" section earlier in this chapter), it can be tested without further discussion. A ColdFusion template, HelloWorldExample1.cfm (Listing 20.2), does this.

Listing 20.2   Simple CFX Demonstration (HelloWorldExample1.cfm)

```
01: <!---
02:     File            /c20/HelloWorldExample1.cfm
03:     Description     Demonstrates two calls to the
04:          "Hello, World" CFX.
05: --->
06: <html>
07:     <head>
08:         <title>Hello World Example 1</title>
09:     </head>
10:
11:     <body>
12:         <cfx_helloWorld>
13:         <br>
14:         <cfx_helloWorld name="Guy Rish">
15:     </body>
16: </html>
```

Here two calls are made to the CFX: one where no name attribute is specified, and one where I specify my own name. The output, while not very exciting, is exactly as might be expected. It is composed of two lines: one says, "Hello, World" and is followed by a br, and the other says, "Hello, Guy Rish." Although this output isn't very impressive, it does demonstrate how data is passed into a CFX and how content is written back out.

However, you will find that you need a CFX tag to return content as a variable as often as you need it to enter content to the template's output buffer. You will see this addressed in the next iteration of the cfx_helloWorld tag, HelloWorld2.java (Listing 20.3).

> **Listing 20.3**   **CFX Returning a Variable (HelloWorld2.java)**

```
01: /*
02:     File              /c20/HelloWorld2.java
03:     Description      A very simple Java CFX to
04:        return a "Hello, World" message.
05: */
06: import com.allaire.cfx.*;
07:
08: public class HelloWorld2 implements CustomTag
09: {
10:     public void processRequest(Request request,
11:        Response response)
12:     {
13:        String results = null;
14:
15:        results = "Hello, " +
16:            request.getAttribute("name", "World");
17:
18:        response.setVariable("results", results);
19:     }
20: }
```

Here the code is nearly identical to HelloWorld1.java, except where that iteration called the write method, this one calls the setVariable method (see line 18). You can also see that the setVariable method takes two arguments: the first is the name of the variable to be created or set (since the variable might also already exist in the calling logic), and the second is the String value to set.

To make this CFX tag run, you need to make a quick adjustment in the ColdFusion Administrator. Call up the CFX Tags page again so that you can edit the cfx_helloWorld tag; replace the "HelloWorld1" value in the Class Name field with "HelloWorld2".

NOTE   The ColdFusion Server does not need to be restarted for this change to take place. This restart is necessary only if the class file has been modified from its first loading (the first execution of the CFX tag). Because we have specified a new Java class file to be loaded for this custom tag instead of modifying an old one, there will not be a problem.

Once the Class Name field has been updated, we can test it by launching HelloWorldExample2 .cfm (Listing 20.4). Although the results in the browser are identical to the previous iteration, the CFML is a little different—after each tag invocation cfoutput is called to display the results variable.

Listing 20.4   **Display Variables Returned from CFX (HelloWorldExample2.cfm)**

```
01: <!---
02:     File                /c20/HelloWorldExample2.cfm
03:     Description    Demonstrates two calls to a
04:        "Hello, World" CFX that returns data.
05: --->
06: <html>
07:     <head>
08:         <title>Hello World Example 2</title>
09:     </head>
10:
11:     <body>
12:         <cfx_helloWorld>
13:         <cfoutput>#results#</cfoutput>
14:         <br>
15:         <cfx_helloWorld name="Guy Rish">
16:         <cfoutput>#results#</cfoutput>
17:     </body>
18: </html>
```

Special CFX Attributes

Three attributes are optionally available to all CFX tags and are part of the CFX framework: reload, debug, and query. The reload and debug attributes dictate behavioral aspects of the CFX tag and the query attribute identifies the one CFML query that can be passed into the tag. The remainder of this section will look at each of these special attributes in more detail.

The reload Attribute

The reload attribute indicates the rule for loading or reloading the CFX's Java class to the ColdFusion Server. The Server recognizes one of three legal values for the reload attribute (see Table 20.5).

TABLE 20.5: Legal Reload Attribute Values

Value	Description
auto	Checks for changes between the loaded class files and the ones on the filesystem and reloads if discrepancies are found. This is the default action.
always	Always reloads the class files regardless of whether or not there are changes in the class files.
never	Loads the class files only once regardless of whether or not there are changes.

The debug Attribute

This Boolean attribute indicates what the CFX tag will do in a debugging mode. This attribute does not take a value; just its existence sets a special flag internal to the ColdFusion MX Server.

As it turns out, this attribute does two things for a CFX tag. First it serves as a flag to the CFX, causing the `Request` instance's debug method to return a value of `"true"`; this value informs the code that it can execute branches that are specific for debugging needs. Second, it amends the output buffer that is returned to the browser so that it includes the CFX tag execution time in milliseconds.

The simple template, `HelloWorldExample3.cfm` (Listing 20.5), demonstrates this.

Listing 20.5   Using the Special debug Attribute (HelloWorldExample3.cfm)

```
01: <!---
02:      File            /c20/HelloWorldExample3.cfm
03:      Description     Demonstrates to calls to a
04:          "Hello, World" CFX passing the special
05:          debug attribute.
06: --->
07: <html>
08:     <head>
09:         <title>Hello World Example 3</title>
10:     </head>
11:
12:     <body>
13:         <cfx_helloWorld debug>
14:         <cfoutput>#results#</cfoutput>
15:         <br>
16:         <cfx_helloWorld name="Guy Rish" debug>
17:         <cfoutput>#results#</cfoutput>
18:     </body>
19: </html>
```

As you might have noticed, this is just a slightly altered version of Listing 20.4—it now includes the debug attribute. The display that results after execution time information has been added is as might be expected (see Figure 20.5) is added.

The query Attribute

This attribute indicates the name of the CFML query to be passed into the CFX tag. The ColdFusion Server then marshals a reference into the tag, which can be retrieved through the `Request` interface's `getQuery` method. This attribute is really just the gateway to whole set of possibilities as we will explore in the next section.

FIGURE 20.5:

"Hello, World" tag
with debug attribute

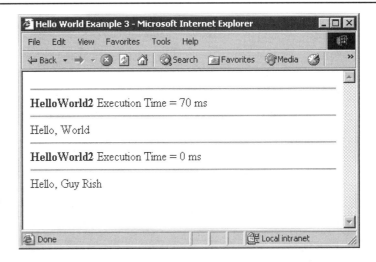

FIGURE 20.5:

"Hello, World" tag
with debug attribute

Working with Queries

Using the query attribute is the only way that complex data can be passed into and out of a
CFX tag. Since any tag can only have one attribute of any given name it is impossible to pass
more than one CFML query object into a CFX tag.

Passing a Query

The trick to passing a CFML query object into a CFX tag is that it must be done using the
special query tag attribute mentioned earlier. This is demonstrated in the template Hello-
QueryExample1.cfm (Listing 20.6), shown below.

Listing 20.6   Passing a Query to a CFX (HelloQueryExample1.cfm)

```
01: <!---
02:     File            /c20/HelloQueryExample1.cfm
03:     Description     Demonstrates a call to a
04:         "Hello, World" CFX that drives off
05:         of a query.
06: --->
07: <html>
08:     <head>
09:         <title>Query Example 1</title>
10:     </head>
11:
12:     <body>
13:         <cfquery name="names" datasource="names">
14:             select * from Name
```

```
15:            </cfquery>
16:
17:            <cfx_helloQuery query="names">
18:        </body>
19: </html>
```

As you can see, this code performs a simple cfquery to create a single columned CFML query. This query, which is populated with a few rows of names, is handed off to the CFX tag cfx_helloQuery. As stated previously, the query is passed by its name as the value of the query attribute.

The cfx_helloQuery tag is registered with the class HelloQuery1, whose source HelloQuery1 .java is shown in Listing 20.7. This simple class retrieves the Query through the Request class's getQuery. The Query is then looped over to build one "Hello" message for each name in the set; this message is then output through the Response class's write method.

Listing 20.7   Query-Enabled CFX (HelloQuery1.java)

```
01: /*
02:     File              /c20/HelloQuery1.java
03:     Description       A very simple Java CFX to
04:         display a "Hello, World" message
05:         driven from a query.
06: */
07: import com.allaire.cfx.*;
08:
09: public class HelloQuery1 implements CustomTag
10: {
11:     public void processRequest(Request request,
12:         Response response)
13:     throws Exception
14:     {
15:         int idx, length;
16:         Query attribQuery = null;
17:         String attribResults = null;
18:         String results = new String();
19:
20:         if(request.attributeExists("query"))
21:         {
22:             attribQuery = request.getQuery();
23:             length = attribQuery.getRowCount();
24:             for(idx = 1; idx <= length; idx++)
25:             {
26:                 results += ("Hello, " +
27:                     attribQuery.getData(idx, 1) +
28:                     "<br>");
29:             }
30:             response.write(results);
```

```
31:        }
32:        else
33:        {
34:            throw new Exception("Error! No Query.");
35:        }
36:    }
37: }
```

Most of the CFX's basic class construction should be familiar to you at this point, so we will not discuss each line of the listing in detail. The existence of the query attribute is checked for on line 20 as the condition of an if statement. Then within the if block, the query is retrieved on line 22 with getQuery. The row count of the retrieved Query instance is obtained on line 23; the analogous action in CFML is to get the query object's recordCount value. Using a for loop, each row of the Query instance can be obtained by using the loop variable, idx, as the row argument of the getData call on line 27. The getData method returns the value of a specific column in the query for a specific row. Columns are not accessible by name as they are in CFML; instead they are accessed by numerical index. In this case we are getting the first column.

Passthrough

It is interesting to note that when a CFML query is passed to a CFX tag, it receives the actual internal handle that the ColdFusion Server is maintaining for that query and not just some sort of copy. This means that if the data in the Query instance, returned from the Request class's getQuery method, gets modified, those modifications will be visible within the template when the CFX tag returns control. In addition, field data can be modified and rows can be added and then later used.

A new iteration of the cfx_helloQuery, HelloQuery2.java (shown in Listing 20.8) exemplifies this. Instead of just looping through the Query instance and concatenating Strings to be written out, this iteration changes the cell data of each row, using the Query interface's setData method on line 27, to include the greeting; this is done within the for loop on lines 23–28.

Listing 20.8   Altering Query Cell Data (HelloQuery2.java)

```
01: /*
02:     File            /c20/HelloQuery2.java
03:     Description     A very simple Java CFX to
04:         display a "Hello, World" message
05:         updated into an incoming query.
06: */
07: import com.allaire.cfx.*;
08:
09: public class HelloQuery2 implements CustomTag
```

```
10: {
11:     public void processRequest(Request request,
12:         Response response)
13:     throws Exception
14:     {
15:         int idx, length;
16:         Query attribQuery = null;
17:         String results = null;
18:
19:         if(request.attributeExists("query"))
20:         {
21:             attribQuery = request.getQuery();
22:             length = attribQuery.getRowCount();
23:             for(idx = 1; idx <= length; idx++)
24:             {
25:                 results = "Hello, " +
26:                     attribQuery.getData(idx, 1);
27:                 attribQuery.setData(idx, 1, results);
28:             }
29:         }
30:         else
31:         {
32:             throw new Exception("Error! No Query.");
33:         }
34:     }
35: }
```

NOTE   Updating the cfx_helloQuery Class Name setting in the ColdFusion Administrator's CFX Tags page to point at the HelloQuery2 class will make this tag example function correctly.

Then, when the CFX tag finishes and control returns to the calling template, HelloQuery-Example2.cfm (see Listing 20.9), the query is looped over to see the amended results. The output is the same as that of Listing 20.6 from the previous section. The difference under the hood is where the data came from—the query object itself.

Listing 20.9   **Altering Query Data with a CFX (HelloQueryExample2.cfm)**

```
01: <!---
02:     File            /c20/HelloQueryExample2.cfm
03:     Description     Demonstrates a call to a
04:         "Hello, World" CFX that drives off
05:         of a query that gets modified by
06:         the CFX.
07: --->
08: <html>
09:     <head>
10:         <title>Query Example 2</title>
```

```
11:      </head>
12:
13:      <body>
14:          <cfquery name="names" datasource="names">
15:              select * from Name
16:          </cfquery>
17:
18:          <cfx_helloQuery query="names">
19:          <cfoutput query="names">
20:              #names.entry#<br>
21:          </cfoutput>
22:      </body>
23: </html>
```

Return a Query

Returning a new Query from a CFX tag is not really very difficult. If you call the Response instance's addQuery method, it will return a handle to a newly created Query instance. The addQuery method takes two arguments: the name of the Query instance to be created, which can be used to reference the instance from the CFML calling logic, and a String array of the column names.

The new iteration of the cfx_helloQuery, HelloQuery3.java (shown in Listing 20.10) receives a Query containing a set of names (just as the previous CFX tag examples did).

Listing 20.10   Returning a Query from a CFX (HelloQuery3.java)

```
01: /*
02:      File            /c20/HelloQuery3.java
03:      Description     A very simple Java CFX that
04:          uses data from a passed in query to
05:          construct a simple query for return
06:          to the calling logic.
07: */
08: import com.allaire.cfx.*;
09:
10: public class HelloQuery3 implements CustomTag
11: {
12:      public void processRequest(Request request,
13:          Response response)
14:      throws Exception
15:      {
16:          int idx, length;
17:          Query attribQuery = null;
18:          String attribResults = null;
19:          String results = null;
20:
21:          String columns[] = new String[1];
```

```
22:            Query returnQuery = null;
23:
24:            columns[0] = "message";
25:
26:            attribResults =
27:                request.getAttribute("results", "results");
28:
29:            returnQuery =
30:                response.addQuery(attribResults, columns);
31:
32:            if(request.attributeExists("query"))
33:            {
34:                attribQuery = request.getQuery();
35:                length = attribQuery.getRowCount();
36:                for(idx = 1; idx <= length; idx++)
37:                {
38:                    results = "Hello, " +
39:                        attribQuery.getData(idx, 1);
40:                    returnQuery.addRow();
41:                    returnQuery.setData(idx, 1, results);
42:                }
43:            }
44:            else
45:            {
46:                throw new Exception("Error! No Query.");
47:            }
48:        }
49: }
```

Constructing a new Query is done with the Response interface's addQuery method, shown on lines 29–30. The addQuery method takes two arguments. The first argument is the name for the resulting Query instance; the name can be specified with a tag attribute, result. The result attribute is given a default value of "result" on lines 26–27. The second argument for addQuery is a String array that represents the names of the columns. This is done with the columns variable, which is an array with a single element, defined on line 24. While you are looping through the incoming Query, saved to the variable attribQuery on line 34, a greeting String is constructed from the value of the first column of the incoming Query on lines 38–39 and set to the variable result. A new row is added to returnQuery using the Query interface's addRow method (line 40). The greeting, assigned to results, is then set into the first column of the new row added to returnQuery on line 41 using the setData method.

NOTE Updating the cfx_helloQuery Class Name setting in the ColdFusion Administrator's CFX Tags page to point at the HelloQuery3 class will make this tag example function correctly.

The query object returned from the new iteration of cfx_helloQuery is displayed in Hello-QueryExample.cfm (Listing 20.11).

Listing 20.11   **Display a Query Returned from a CFX (HelloQueryExample3.cfm)**

```
01: <!---
02:     File              /c20/HelloQueryExample3.cfm
03:     Description       Demonstrates a call to a
04:         "Hello, World" CFX that drives off
05:         of a query that gets modified by
06:         the CFX.
07: --->
08: <html>
09:     <head>
10:         <title>Query Example 3</title>
11:     </head>
12:
13:     <body>
14:         <cfquery name="names" datasource="names">
15:             select * from Name
16:         </cfquery>
17:
18:         <cfx_helloQuery query="names" result="results">
19:         <cfoutput query="results">
20:             #results.message#<br>
21:         </cfoutput>
22:     </body>
23: </html>
```

This template calls the `cfx_helloQuery` tag and passes the `result` attribute value of `"results"`. Immediately after the CFX call, the template performs a `cfoutput` to dump out the rows of the new query object.

Returning Multiple Queries

With repeated calls to `addQuery`, it is possible to create multiple `Query` instances to return to the CFML calling logic. Although the query examples thus far have been very simplistic, the limits of this operation are bound solely by the imagination and business needs of the developer.

Debugging

Debugging CFX tags can sometimes be a complicated endeavor. Because the purpose of building a CFX tag is to use facilities outside the scope of the CFML language, this often means interacting with brand new or complicated mechanisms, or both. This leaves room for half-baked APIs with bugs of their own that might throw wrenches in what appears to be a well-formed CFX. Macromedia does not provide services for directly tracing through the ColdFusion Server during the execution of a template, let alone into aftermarket extensions that Macromedia has not themselves produced. Fortunately, Macromedia did provide a solution built directly into the CFXAPI.

One of the powerful benefits of building CFX tags in Java, which is not available to the C++ variety, is the debugging facility provided in the Java CFXAPI library. The Java CFXAPI has classes made specifically for debugging: DebugRequest, DebugResponse, and DebugQuery. By using these classes, you can simulate the invocation of the tag from the tag class's main. Once you have written a main in your tag's class, you can then call it directly from the command line with the Java runtime interpreter. The debugging classes can be used to set up the environment, the tag's processRequest method can be called, and the logic will be none the wiser. The CFX class will act exactly as it would if it were called by the ColdFusion Server.

So let us examine the three debugging classes of the Java CFXAPI.

The DebugRequest Class

This simple class implements the Request interface but does not provide any additional specialized methods. You can use one of its three constructors to set up the environment that you want to simulate. The first constructor takes a Hashtable that simulates the attribute names and values that will appear to be passed to the tag. The second constructor takes a Hashtable for the attributes and a Query (available through the DebugQuery class discussed later) that will masquerade as the CFML query. The third constructor takes a Hashtable for the attributes, a Query, and a Hashtable that will simulate the settings of the Strings that will be available through the getSettings method.

The DebugResponse Class

The DebugResponse class acts as a buffering device and catches all of the output String, returned variables, and constructed Query instances.

The DebugResponse class has only one constructor, the default "empty" constructor.

This class does provide one new method, printResults, beyond the basic Response interface. This method can be called when the class being debugged returns from the processResults call to dump out the buffered data. It nicely formats the Strings written, the variables, and Query instances. (See Table 20.6.)

TABLE 20.6: Additional Public DebugResponse Methods

Method	Description
printResults	Writes to System.out the buffered write messages, variables, and Query instances

The DebugQuery Class

This class simulates the one complex datatype that a CFX tag can handle, the Query. In the actual runtime of the tag, handles to the ColdFusion Server's internal Query implementation are passed around; obviously with the Server out of the picture, there is no internal Server implementation, and thus, this is a little difficult to provide. The DebugQuery implementation is quite convincing (as it should be)—it even capitalizes the column names just as a query object coming from a CFML template would do at the time of its creation.

The DebugQuery class has two constructors. The first constructor takes a String for the name of the Query and an array of Strings for the column names. The second constructor takes a string for the name, an array of Strings for the column names, and finally, an array of String arrays for the row data.

Simple Debugging

Making a debug version of a CFX tag is not difficult. Up to this point, all of the CFX classes have only required one method in them—the processRequest required by the CustomTag interface. In order to start using the debugging classes described earlier in this section you will need to implement the tried and true Java method of unit testing a class—include a main so the CFX tag's class file can be run directly from the command line by the Java interpreter

A new iteration of the most simple "Hello, World" tag constructed earlier in this chapter will serve here (see Listing 20.12).

Listing 20.12   A Simple Debug CFX (HelloWorldDebug1.java)

```
01: /*
02:    File           /c20/HelloWorldDebug1.java
03:    Description     A simple example of
04:       using the CFX debugging classes.
05: */
06:
07: import java.util.Hashtable;
08:
09: import com.allaire.cfx.*;
10:
11: public class HelloWorldDebug1 implements CustomTag
12: {
13:    public static void main(String[] args)
14:    {
15:        HelloWorldDebug1 tag = new HelloWorldDebug1();
16:
17:        DebugResponse response = new DebugResponse();
18:
19:        Hashtable attributes = new Hashtable();
20:
```

```
21:              // build attribute list
22:              attributes.put("name", "Guy Rish");
23:
24:              DebugRequest request =
25:              new DebugRequest(attributes);
26:
27:              try
28:              {
29:                  tag.processRequest(request, response);
30:
31:                  // output the response
32:                  response.printResults();
33:              }
34:              catch(Exception e)
35:              {
36:                  System.out.println(e.getMessage());
37:              }
38:        }
39:
40:        public void processRequest(Request request,
41:        Response response)
42:        {
43:            String name = null;
44:
45:            name = request.getAttribute("name", "World");
46:
47:            response.write("Hello, " + name);
48:        }
49: }
```

Here, the same processRequest implementation that can be found in HelloWorld1.java (first seen in Listing 20.1) is called from the class's main; it passes a DebugRequest and a DebugResponse. Line 22 shows the population of a Hashtable with key named "name" and a value of "Guy Rish"; as might be inferred; this serves as the tag's name attribute. Then, within a try/catch block (lines 27–37), the instantiated tag's processRequest is called (line 29). The CustomTag interface is none the wiser and processes normally. Then, when the processRequest method completes, it will return to the calling logic in main, all of the interaction that the tag performed is displayed to the console with a simple call to the DebugResponse's printResults method (line 32).

The writeDebug Method

The Response interface specifies a method called writeDebug. According to the documentation, the String argument will be written to the debug output stream. Technically, there is no apparent difference in practical operation between write and writeDebug. Any String passed to the writeDebug method will also be displayed in the normal output to the browser. All of the samples I've ever seen, including Macromedia's own published works, demonstrate checking for the existence of the debug attribute (using the `Request` instance's debug method), as shown here.

```
if(request.debug())
{
    response.writeDebug("debug message!");
}
```

Unfortunately I cannot make a claim to any better understanding of the difference between `write` and `writeDebug` than that. Interestingly enough, the same ends can be achieved with the same `if` check and a "normal" `write` call

---

NOTE   The DebugRequest class always returns a `true` value from the debug method. This is the case regardless of whether or not the debug attribute exists.

Query Debugging

You will now discover that making a debug version of a CFX tag that interacts with query object is only slightly more involved than just working with the simple attributes for debugging. First you simulate an incoming CFML query object with the `DebugQuery` class. Once the `DebugQuery` is constructed and populated, you can pass it to the `DebugRequest` constructor.

A new iteration of the query-driven `"Hello, World"` tag, `HelloQueryDebug1.java` (an excerpt is shown in Listing 20.13), does the exact same thing as `HelloQuery1.java` (see Listing 20.7) does. What is different is that this class also has a `main` that instantiates it and calls the `processRequest` method.

Listing 20.13   A Debug CFX Using a Query (from HelloQueryDebug1.java)

```
01: /*
02:     File              /c20/HelloQueryDebug1.java
03:     Description    A simple example of
04:         using the CFX debugging classes
05:         to create a query.
06: */
07: public static void main(String[] args)
08: throws Exception
09: {
10:     HelloQueryDebug1 tag = new HelloQueryDebug1();
11:
12:     DebugQuery query = null;
13:     DebugRequest request = null;
14:     DebugResponse response = new DebugResponse();
15:
16:     Hashtable attributes = new Hashtable();
17:     StringTokenizer tokenizer = null;
18:     BufferedReader reader = null;
```

```
19:        String names = null;
20:        String[] columns = new String[1];
21:        int idx = 1;
22:
23:        columns[0] = "entry";
24:        attributes.put("query", "names");
25:
26:        try
27:        {
28:            query = new DebugQuery("names", columns);
29:
30:            // read in names
31:            reader = new BufferedReader(
32:                new FileReader("names.txt"));
33:            names = reader.readLine();
34:            tokenizer = new StringTokenizer(names, ",");
35:
36:            // add names to query
37:            for(idx = 1; tokenizer.hasMoreTokens(); idx++)
38:            {
39:                query.addRow();
40:                query.setData(idx, 1,
41:                    tokenizer.nextToken());
42:            }
43:
44:            // build request
45:            request = new DebugRequest(attributes, query);
46:
47:            // call tag
48:            tag.processRequest(request, response);
49:
50:            response.printResults();
51:        }
52:        catch(Exception e)
53:        {
54:            System.out.println(e.getMessage());
55:        }
56: }
```

In this listing, an instance of DebugQuery is created on line 28 using the two-argument constructor that takes the query name and column name array. Once the query is constructed, a file containing a comma-delimited list of names is read on line 33, and this list is tokenized on line 34. On line 39 a new row is added through each pass of the loop, and then on lines 40–41 the name to the query is added.

See line 24 for a point of interest; here a key is added into the Hashtable and it is used to simulate the incoming attributes. The addition of the query attribute is important because the code inside the processRequest uses this attribute to check for an incoming query. Since the DebugRequest class does not create this attribute when it is constructed with a Query, you must do this manually. This actually works out very nicely, because in order to construct the `DebugRequest` instance, you must initialize a `Hashtable` of attributes as it will not accept a `null` value for the first argument.

NOTE   It could be argued that including a `query` attribute, as is done on line 24 of `HelloQuery-Debug1.java` (Listing 20.13), is superfluous since any tag that might use a `Query` could just assume the `query` attribute's existence and check for the return of the `Request` instance's `getQuery` method. Although this is true, the resulting process does not create an accurate simulation without this attribute. However, a number of "best practice" sources state that the existence of each attribute should be checked, and default values should always be provided. Since it is usually impractical to default a query, an error should be thrown. You will notice that all of the `HelloQueryX` classes do this.

Advanced Construction

Now that we have covered the basics of Java CFX tag construction, let's move forward to address more advanced topics. Some of the things that you will likely need understanding tools for when you sit down to begin writing serious CFX tags are:

- Techniques for passing complex data between CFML templates and CFX tags

- Extending the CFXAPI model

- A simple technique called CFML-wrapped CFX tags, which "gives" the CFX tag a start and end tag.

The remaining sections of the chapter will address these three topics and cover some advanced techniques and concepts. Many of the details of these topics have so much material that they could embody chapters and launch weeks of research unto themselves. Despite this, some care was taken to package the code in ways that would still make it immediately usable by you.

Working with Complex Data: Help from WDDX

The ColdFusion Server does not allow complex data structures to be passed into or out of CFX tags, with the exception of a single incoming query object and any number of outgoing `Query` instances, created by the `Response` instance's `addQuery` method. If you attempt to pass a CFML array or structure, the CFML interpreter will throw an exception. Sadly, this is an unrealistic restriction imposed on CFX tag developers. The point of building a CFX is to work with new and often more complex mechanisms outside the scope of the CFML language. This often means providing large amounts of data to be passed from the calling logic (the template) and, just as often, large amounts of data back. This is sometimes impossible to do without some sort of complex datatype.

Fortunately, there are techniques that can be used to circumvent this design choice. One effective approach is to serialize complex datatypes and pass them as a regular string variable that can later be deserialized back into the complex data structure, or some reasonable likeness. Although this approach can be accomplished using a variety of techniques, CFML provides a built-in tool for this—WDDX. As discussed in Chapter 7, the WDDX vocabulary is specifically designed for this kind of cross-environment data marshalling.

While CFML has a built-in tag for serializing and deserializing data into WDDX packets, Java does not. There are a few Java libraries that need to be added to the ColdFusion Server's JVM Class Path (for more details on the ColdFusion Administrator's Java Settings page, see Appendix A) before Java CFX tags can be written with this capability. First, the WDDX Java libraries (`wddx.jar`) need to be added (for details on where to get the WDDX libraries, see Chapter 7). Then you need to supply a SAX parser; I use Apache's Xerces2 library, `xerces.jar`, which you can find at `http://xml.apache.org/xerces2-j/index.html`.

Once you have completed your configuration, some simple demonstrations of this technique can be discussed: passing serialized data into a CFX and passing serialized data out of a CFX. But before we get into these, we first need to know what CFML serialized data looks like.

Serializing CFML Datatypes

You should know what CFML datatypes will look like once they are transformed into a WDDX packet. This is important when you are using any data marshalling tool but it is especially so when you are transferring values from a weakly typed language like CFML into a richly typed one like Java.

The ColdFusion template, `ComplexDataExample1.cfm` (Listing 20.14), shows the construction of a CFML structure (line 22) populated with various different values including a Boolean, a string, a list, an array, a query, numbers, and date and time formatted strings.

Listing 20.14   Serializing CFML Datatypes (ComplexDataExample1.cfm)

```
01: <!---
02:     File            /c20/ComplexDataExample1.cfm
03:     Description     Create an structure with
04:         various datatypes and serialize it
05:         to a WDDX packet.
06: --->
07: <html>
08:     <head>
09:         <title>Complex Data Example 1</title>
10:     </head>
11:
12:     <body>
13:         <cfquery name="names" datasource="names">
```

```
14:                    select * from Name
15:            </cfquery>
16:
17:            <cffile action="read"
18:                file="#expandPath("./names.txt")#"
19:                variable="nameList">
20:
21:            <cfscript>
22:                st = structNew();
23:                st.bool = true;
24:                st.number = 10;
25:                st.precision = 3.14;
26:                st.string = "Hello, World";
27:                st.list = trim(nameList);
28:                st.array = listToArray(trim(nameList));
29:                st.date = dateFormat(now(), "mm/dd/yyyy");
30:                st.time = timeFormat(now(), "hh:mm:ss");
31:                st.query = names;
32:            </cfscript>
33:
34:            <cfwddx action="cfml2wddx"
35:                input="#st#" output="packet">
36:
37:            <cfdump var="#st#">
38:
39:            <cfoutput>
40:                <br>
41:                packet contents
42:                <br>
43:                #htmlEditFormat(packet)#
44:            </cfoutput>
45:        </body>
46: </html>
```

Once a query has been created (lines 13–15) and a file of content read into a variable (lines 17–19), a structure can be made. This structure will contain various CFML datatypes. This structure is then converted into a WDDX packet on lines 34–35. The structure is dumped on line 37, and then the packet itself is displayed on line 43. It is very interesting to note that although WDDX provides for all of these types (and more), the majority of them show up in the packet as string values—even the numbers!

Passing In Serialized Data

CFML custom tags can pass attributes as a CFML structure; this is one of their more powerful features. This structure is then passed as the value to the attribute, attributesCollection. If you try to pass a structure with a CFX tag, you will find that it is impossible; the CFML interpreter will throw an error and the template will abort processing. However, you will find that if the structure is somehow serialized into a string and then passed, it can be reconstituted within the CFX tag.

This serialization of data is demonstrated with the template `ComplexDataExample2.cfm` (Listing 20.15). This template reads in a file that contains a comma-delimited list of names, which it then converts to an array. That array is added to a structure, which is serialized into a WDDX packet and passed to a CFX tag, called `cfx_complexData`, in the attribute. Notice that in addition to `attributesCollection` passing the WDDX packet, another attribute, `count`, is passing the length of the `names` array.

The use of the `attributesCollection` attribute, either for CFML custom tags or with the serialization technique demonstrated here, usually, though not always, indicates that there is some abstract process stringing values together in some dynamic process. CFML custom tags allow you to combine the use of the `attributesCollection` attribute with any number of other attributes necessary for the tag. The example here has no such dynamic process generating attribute values and grouping them in this manner, but it would be logical to want that same kind of functionality emulated with the CFX tags using this serialization technique. This way practices used with CFML tags can be, as closely as possible, replicated. This is the rationale behind passing a `count` attribute with the serialized `attributesCollection` attribute to this iteration of the `cfx_complexData` CFX tag.

Listing 20.15   Using attributesCollection with a CFX (ComplexDataExample2.cfm)

```
<!---
    File            /c20/ComplexDataExample2.cfm
    Description     Create an structure with
        various datatypes, serialize it to a
        WDDX packet and pass the packet as
        and attributesCollection attribute.
--->
<html>
    <head>
        <title>Complex Data Example 2</title>
    </head>

    <body>
        <cffile action="read"
            file="#expandPath("./names.txt")#"
            variable="nameList">

        <cfscript>
            st = structNew();
            st.names = listToArray(trim(nameList));
        </cfscript>

        <cfwddx action="cfml2wddx"
```

```
            input="#st#" output="packet">

        <cfx_complexData attributesCollection="#packet#"
            count="#arrayLen(st.names)#">
    </body>
</html>
```

As you might imagine, the cfx_complexData tag is a slight bit more complicated than the run-of-the-mill "Hello, World" example. Because of its sheer size, the next few listings will actually be excerpts from the same source, ComplexData1.java.

NOTE   Be certain to register the cfx_complexData tag in the ColdFusion Administrator. Set the tag's Class Name field to the ComplexData1 class.

The processRequest entry point into this tag is shown in Listing 20.16.

Listing 20.16   **The CFX Tag's processRequest (from ComplexData1.java)**

```
01: /*
02:     File            /c20/ComplexData1.java
03:     Description     A Java CFX that receives
04:         complex datatypes via WDDX packets.
05: */
06:
07: public void processRequest(Request request,
08:     Response response)
09: throws Exception
10: {
11:     int idx, count;
12:     Vector names = null;
13:     String name = null;
14:     Hashtable attributesCollection = null;
15:
16:     attributesCollection =
17:         buildAttributesCollection(request);
18:     names =
19:         (Vector)attributesCollection.get("NAMES");
20:     count =
21:         Integer.parseInt(
22:             (String)attributesCollection.get("COUNT"));
23:     for(idx = 0; idx < count; idx++)
24:     {
25:         name = (String)names.get(idx);
26:         response.write("Hello, " + name + "<br>");
27:     }
28: }
```

In lines 16–17, the private method, `buildAttributesCollection`, is called to build a `Hashtable` of all the attributes. Once this is done, the attributes' values are drawn from that `Hashtable` and the tag processes the names into "Hello" messages in the `for` loop on lines 23–27.

The consolidation of the incoming attributes into a single collection is a vital step and should be done prior to any other processing in the CFX tag. The `buildAttributesCollection` method takes one argument, the `Request` instance passed to the `processRequest` method of the CFX tag. This method is shown in Listing 20.17.

Listing 20.17   Building an attributesCollection (from ComplexData1.java)

```
01: /*
02:     File            /c20/ComplexData1.java
03:     Description      A Java CFX that receives
04:         complex datatypes via WDDX packets.
05: */
06: private Hashtable buildAttributesCollection(
07:     Request request)
08: throws Exception
09: {
10:     int idx, count;
11:     String attribName = null;
12:     String attribValue = null;
13:     String[] attribs = null;
14:     Hashtable attributes = new Hashtable();
15:     Hashtable collection = null;
16:
17:     attribs = request.getAttributeList();
18:     count = attribs.length;
19:     for(idx = 0; idx < count; idx++)
20:     {
21:         attribName = attribs[idx];
22:         attribValue =
23:             request.getAttribute(attribName, "");
24:
25:         attributes.put(attribName.toUpperCase(),
26:             attribValue);
27:     }
28:
29:     if(request.attributeExists("attributescollection"))
30:     {
31:         collection =
32:             (Hashtable)deserialize(
33:                 request.getAttribute(
34:                     "attributescollection", ""));
35:
36:         attributes.putAll((Map)collection);
37:     }
```

```
38:
39:     return attributes;
40: }
```

It is within this method that the `attributesCollection` is deserialized. Fortunately, CFML structures are well preserved in the WDDX format, serialized as a WDDX struct; this struct then gets deserialized into a Java `Hashtable`. First, all of the attributes passed to the tag are added to a `Hashtable`, called `attributes`, on lines19–27. Then, the `attributesCollection` packet is "reconstituted" into its own `Hashtable`, called `collection`, on lines 31–34. These two `Hashtables` are then merged with the values in the `collection Hashtable` overwriting the values in the `attributes Hashtable`, line 36.

The real meat of this process is not just the collection of the attributes into a `Hashtable`, but also the deserialization of the WDDX packet. In Listing 20.18, you can see that this functionality is packaged neatly for easy use into another private method called `deserialize`.

Listing 20.18   **Deserializing a WDDX Packet (from ComplexData1.java)**

```
01: /*
02:     File            /c20/ComplexData1.java
03:     Description      A Java CFX that receives
04:         complex datatypes via WDDX packets.
05: */
06: public Object deserialize(String packet)
07: throws Exception
08: {
09:     String parser = null;
10:     Object result = null;
11:     InputSource source = null;
12:     WddxDeserializer deserializer = null;
13:
14:     // check incoming argument
15:     if(packet == null || packet.length() == 0)
16:     {
17:         // throw error
18:         throw new Exception("Bad packet.");
19:     }
20:
21:     // TODO:
22:     // setup configuration code for retrieving
23:     // other possible SAX parsers
24:
25:     // set parser value to internal
26:     if(parser == null)
27:     {
28:         // use default parser
29:         parser = this.DEFAULT_SAXPARSER;
30:     }
```

```
31:
32:        // attempt to load the parser for verification
33:            // it is in CLASSPATH
34:        try
35:        {
36:            Class.forName(parser).newInstance();
37:        }
38:        catch(Exception e)
39:        {
40:            throw new Exception("Cannot load class: " +
41:                parser +
42:                ".\nCheck the <em>classpath</em>.\n");
43:        }
44:
45:        // create input source for the XML parser
46:        source = new InputSource(
47:                new StringReader(packet));
48:
49:        try
50:        {
51:            // create a WDDX deserializer
52:            deserializer = new WddxDeserializer(parser);
53:
54:            // deserialize the WDDX packet
55:            result = deserializer.deserialize(source);
56:        }
57:        catch(IOException ioe)
58:        {
59:            throw new Exception("Error reading packet.\n" +
60:                ioe.getMessage());
61:        }
62:        catch(WddxDeserializationException wde)
63:        {
64:            throw new Exception("WDDX error.\n" +
65:                wde.getMessage());
66:        }
67:
68:        return result;
69: }
```

There really isn't that much to this method; in fact, the first half is just made up of argument checking and setup. Lines 15–19 check the incoming argument. Then lines 21–43 determine the SAX parser class to use (which, in this case, is simply using the default static class member DEFAULT_SAXPARSER) and then making sure that the JVM can load its class file. After that, the XML InputSource is created from a StringReader on the incoming packet on line 46–47. And finally, on line 52, within a try/catch block, the WddxDeserializer is created with the SAX parser that was loaded earlier. Then the deserializer is fed the packet on line 55. The resulting instance is returned to buildAttributesCollection.

Now, to get the list of names with which the tag constructs its greetings, the code pulls from the deserialized `Hashtable` instead of the `Request` instance. What used to be a CFML array is now a Java `Vector`. Using the `count` attribute, each entry is processed and the tag is finished.

NOTE   Using the `count` attribute to loop through the elements of the `Vector` is superfluous and is not the best approach as it does not use the obvious methods of the `Vector` class like `size`. It probably would have been just as smart to use an Iterator, but that would have needlessly forced me to think up some other reason to pass an additional attribute outside of the `attributesCollection` structure.

Passing Out Serialized Data

Serializing data to be returned to CFML from Java is fairly simplistic. We will start by building upon the previous example. This next iteration of the `cfx_complexData` tag, `ComplexData2.java`, will receive an `attributesCollection` and a `count`, as in Listing 20.18. But in this iteration, the `processRequest` has undergone some alterations so that it can serialize and pass data back to the calling logic; in addition, this iteration introduces a new method to serializing this data.

Listing 20.19 shows the new tag's `processRequest` methods, an excerpt from `ComplexData2.java`.

Listing 20.19   A CFX Tag's processRequest (from ComplexData2.java)

```
01: /*
02:     File            /c20/ComplexData2.java
03:     Description     A Java CFX that returns
04:         complex datatypes via WDDX packets.
05: */
06: public void processRequest(Request request,
07:     Response response)
08: throws Exception
09: {
10:     int idx, count;
11:     Vector names = null;
12:     String name = null;
13:     String result = null;
14:     String[] messages = null;
15:     Hashtable attributesCollection = null;
16:
17:     attributesCollection =
18:         buildAttributesCollection(request);
19:
20:     names =
21:         (Vector)attributesCollection.get("NAMES");
22:     count =
23:         Integer.parseInt(
```

```
24:            (String)attributesCollection.get("COUNT"));
25:
26:        messages = new String[count];
27:
28:        for(idx = 0; idx < count; idx++)
29:        {
30:            name = (String)names.get(idx);
31:            messages[idx] = "Hello, " + name;
32:        }
33:
34:        result = serialize(messages);
35:        response.setVariable("result", result);
36: }
```

In this listing, an array of Strings is created using the count attribute (line 26). In addition, the elements of the array are populated with the individualized greeting message from within a for loop on lines 28–32. Once this array is populated, it is serialized by calling the tag's serialize method (line 34), and then it is passed back to the calling logic.

Another excerpt from ComplexData2.java, the serialize method, shown in Listing 20.20, is fairly simple and revolves around an instance of the WddxSerializer class.

Listing 20.20   Serializing Complex Data (from ComplexData2.java)

```
01: /*
02:    File             /c20/ComplexData2.java
03:    Description      A Java CFX that returns
04:        complex datatypes via WDDX packets.
05: */
06: public String serialize(Object obj)
07: throws Exception
08: {
09:    String parser = null;
10:    WddxSerializer serializer =
11:            new WddxSerializer();
12:    StringWriter buffer = new StringWriter();
13:
14:    // check incoming argument
15:    if(obj == null)
16:    {
17:        // throw error
18:        throw new Exception("Object is null.");
19:    }
20:
21:    // serialize object
22:    serializer.serialize(obj, buffer);
23:
24:    return buffer.toString();
25: }
```

The `WddxSerializer` instance is created on lines 10–11 Then, using a `StringWriter` to collect the output, the object passed to the `serialize` tag's `serialize` method is passed to the `WddxSerializer`'s `serialize` method on line 22. On line 24, the resulting packet is returned from the `StringWriter`'s `toString` method.

The setup for this new iteration of the `cfx_complexData` custom tag is fairly simple and can be observed within the template, `ComplexDataExample3.cfm`, shown in Listing 20.21.

Listing 20.21   Sending and Retrieving Complex Data (ComplexDataExample3.cfm)

```
<!---
    File            /c20/ComplexDataExample3.cfm
    Description     Create an structure with
        various datatypes, serialize it to a
        WDDX packet and pass the packet as
        and attributesCollection attribute.
        A WDDX serialized array will be
        returned and processed.
--->
<html>
    <head>
        <title>Complex Data Example 3</title>
    </head>

    <body>
        <cffile action="read"
            file="#expandPath("./names.txt")#"
            variable="nameList">

        <cfscript>
            st = structNew();
            st.names = listToArray(trim(nameList));
        </cfscript>

        <cfwddx action="cfml2wddx"
            input="#st#" output="packet">

        <cfx_complexData attributesCollection="#packet#"
            count="#arrayLen(st.names)#">

        <cfwddx action="wddx2cfml"
            input="#result#" output="a">

        <cfscript>
            length = arrayLen(a);
            for(idx = 1; idx lte length; idx = idx + 1)
            {
                writeOutput(a[idx]);
                writeOutput("<br>");
            }
```

```
            </cfscript>
          </body>
        </html>
```

Updating the `cfx_complexData` Class Name setting in the ColdFusion Administrator's
CFX Tags page to point at the `ComplexData2` class will make this tag example function
correctly.

Once the packet is returned to the calling logic, it must be reconstituted with a call to
cfwddx. The resulting CFML array is then looped over and each element is printed.

Serializing Query and ResultSet Objects

The WDDX serializers works through a series of registerable handlers that understand a
specific datatype and can correctly express it in the WDDX markup. Many of the important
basic Java datatype interfaces, such as `java.util.Map`, already have handlers constructed as
part of the stock WDDX class API. Why WDDX serialization handlers don't exist for the
CFX `Query` interface or the JDBC `ResultSet` is mystifying. These two important classes
(one of which belongs to the CFXAPI's own library set!) require handlers before WDDX can
seriously be used with the CFX model. Without these handlers, an instance of either a `Query`
or a `ResultSet` gets stored as a flattened Java beans and the column and row data is lost!

The WDDX Java library contains a very important interface class, `RecordSet`, that embodies
the WDDX recordset markup structure. You can use this interface and the Adapter pattern to
make things simple.

NOTE   For more details about the Adapter pattern see the earlier sidebar, "An Overview of
Design Patterns."

The remainder of this section will explore the use of the Adapters, conveniently constructed
for you already just for this purpose.

Serializing CFXAPI Queries

Applying an Adapter pattern to the `Query` class in the CFXAPI library is easy since the `Query`
interface and the `RecordSet` interface are so similar.

NOTE   It is beyond the scope of this chapter to detail this Adapter but the source, as well as the
needed binary, is included with the examples for this chapter.

With the template `SerializeQuery1.java` (Listing 20.22), we will test a class with a simple CFX tag, `cfx_serializeQuery`. This class, `net.rish.xml.wddx.CFXQueryRecordSetAdapter`, provides everything that is needed to serialize a CFXAPI `Query` instance through the Record-Set interface.

Listing 20.22   A Query Serializing CFX (SerializeQuery1.java)

```
01: /*
02:     File              /c20/SerializeQuery1.java
03:     Description     An example of a query
04:         serialization using the custom
05:         CFXQueryRecordSetAdapter class.
06: */
07: import java.io.StringWriter;
08:
09: import com.allaire.cfx.*;
10: import com.allaire.wddx.*;
11:
12: import net.rish.xml.wddx.CFXQueryRecordSetAdapter;
13:
14: public class SerializeQuery1 implements CustomTag
15: {
16:     public void processRequest(Request request,
17:         Response response)
18:     throws Exception
19:     {
20:         Query attribQuery = null;
21:         String attribResult = null;
22:
23:         StringWriter writ = new StringWriter();
24:         WddxSerializer serializer =
25:             new WddxSerializer();
26:
27:         CFXQueryRecordSetAdapter adapter = null;
28:
29:         attribQuery = request.getQuery();
30:         attribResult =
31:             request.getAttribute("result", "results");
32:
33:         adapter =
34:             new CFXQueryRecordSetAdapter(attribQuery);
35:
36:         serializer.serialize(adapter, writ);
37:
38:         response.setVariable(attribResult,
39:             writ.toString());
40:     }
41: }
```

This CFX tag really is like others, especially those presented previously that use the WDDX to pass complex data. The real action that this tag performs is the instantiation of the Adapter using the incoming Query. Once the Query instance has been wrapped (in lines 33 and 34), it will be treated just like a RecordSet by the WddxSerializer that was instantiated on line 24–25. The packet-ized Query can then be returned to the calling logic.

The template, SerializedQueryExample1.cfm (Listing 20.23), does very little other than create a CFML query (in the same way as you have seen in earlier cfx_helloQuery examples), pass the query to the CFX, and transform it with the cfwddx tag. It then outputs both packets for visual analysis.

Listing 20.23   Serializing a Query into WDDX (SerializedQueryExample1.cfm)

```
<!---
    File            /c20/SerializedQueryExample1.cfm
    Description     Demonstrated the hand-off of
        a query object into a CFX that retuns
        a WDDX serialized query.
--->
<html>
    <head>
        <title>Serialized Query Example 1</title>
    </head>

    <body>
        <cfquery name="names" datasource="names">
            select * from Name
        </cfquery>

        <cfx_serializeQuery query="names">
        <cfwddx action="cfml2wddx"
            input="#names#" output="packet">

        <cfoutput>
            #htmlEditFormat(results)#
            <br>
            <br>
            #htmlEditFormat(packet)#
        </cfoutput>
    </body>
</html>
```

NOTE   It is important to register the cfx_serializeQuery tag with the ColdFusion Administrator to make this example work. Set the Class Name field to the SerializeQuery1 class.

Serializing JDBC ResultSets

The Adapter for the JDBC `ResultSet` interface, `net.rish.xml.wddx.ResultSetRecordSet-Adapter`, was a little more difficult to construct than the one for the CFXAPI `Query` interface. The flexibility that the `ResultSet` interface provides for differing concrete implementations, depending upon the underlying JDBC driver, created a number of significant problems, especially since the `RecordSet` interface has no specific concept of scrollability. Further, since certain `ResultSet` instances are only capable of scrolling forward, the Adapter needed to do some investigation during construction.

NOTE   It is beyond the scope of this chapter to detail this Adapter but the source, as well as the needed binary, is included with the examples for this chapter.

Listing 20.24 shows a new iteration of the `cfx_serializeQuery` tag, `SerializeQuery2.java`.

Listing 20.24   A ResultSet Serializing CFX (SerializeQuery2.java)

```
01: /*
02:     File             /c20/SerializeQuery2.java
03:     Description       An example of a query
04:         serialization using the custom
05:         ResultSetRecordSetAdapter class.
06: */
07:
08: import java.io.StringWriter;
09: import java.sql.DriverManager;
10: import java.sql.Connection;
11: import java.sql.Statement;
12: import java.sql.ResultSet;
13: import java.sql.SQLException;
14:
15: import com.allaire.cfx.*;
16: import com.allaire.wddx.*;
17:
18: import net.rish.xml.wddx.ResultSetRecordSetAdapter;
19:
20: public class SerializeQuery2 implements CustomTag
21: {
22:     public void processRequest(Request request,
23:         Response response)
24:     throws Exception
25:     {
26:         String driver = "sun.jdbc.odbc.JdbcOdbcDriver";
27:         Statement stmt = null;
28:         Connection con = null;
29:         ResultSet rs = null;
30:
31:         try
```

```
32:            {
33:                Class.forName(driver).newInstance();
34:            }
35:        catch(Exception e)
36:            {
37:                throw new Exception("cannot load driver");
38:            }
39:
40:        try
41:            {
42:                con = DriverManager.getConnection(
43:                    "jdbc:odbc:names", null, null);
44:                stmt = con.createStatement();
45:                rs = stmt.executeQuery(
46:                    "select * from Name");
47:            }
48:        catch(SQLException sqle)
49:            {
50:                throw new Exception("failed select.");
51:            }
52:
53:        String attribResult = null;
54:
55:        StringWriter writ = new StringWriter();
56:        WddxSerializer serializer =
57:            new WddxSerializer();
58:
59:        ResultSetRecordSetAdapter adapter = null;
60:
61:        attribResult = request.getAttribute("result",
62:            "results");
63:
64:        adapter = new ResultSetRecordSetAdapter(rs);
65:
66:        serializer.serialize(adapter, writ);
67:
68:        response.setVariable(attribResult,
69:            writ.toString());
70:    }
71: }
```

NOTE   Updating the cfx_serializeQuery Class Name setting in the ColdFusion Administrator's CFX Tags page to point at the SerializeQuery2 class will make this tag example function correctly.

This listing is a little more complicated than the simple transformation of a CFX Query instance passed into a CFX tag, as was done in the previous iteration of the cfx_serializeQuery tag in Listing 20.22. Here, after loading the JDBC-ODBC bridge drivers (lines 31–38), the tag creates a connection and executes a `select` against the `Name` table (40–51). Once the `ResultSet` from that query has been produced, it can be wrapped (line 64) and serialized (line 66).

The template `SerializedQueryExample2.cfm` (Listing 20.25), which is used to call this tag, is only ever so slightly different from the one covered in Listing 20.23. This difference is in the CFX tag invocation. In this example, it is not passed a `query` attribute; this attribute is unnecessary here because the object of the serialization is derived internal to the tag itself.

Listing 20.25   **Comparing Two Serialized Queries (SerializedQueryExample2.cfm)**

```
<!---
    File            /c20/SerializedQueryExample2.cfm
    Description     Compares a WDDX serialized
        query returned from a CFX to one built
        from the same database in CFML.
--->
<html>
    <head>
        <title>Serialized Query Example 2</title>
    </head>

    <body>
        <cfquery name="names" datasource="names">
            select * from Name
        </cfquery>

        <cfx_serializeQuery>

        <cfwddx action="cfml2wddx"
            input="#names#" output="packet">

        <cfoutput>
            #htmlEditFormat(results)#
            <br>
            <br>
            #htmlEditFormat(packet)#
        </cfoutput>
    </body>
</html>
```

Extending the CFXAPI

Using the `Request` and `Response` interfaces, the data serialization techniques previously presented in this chapter can be packaged more effectively. The first step is to isolate the data serialization functionality; this is done through the `Transubstantiator` interface, discussed later in this section. Once this is done, new `Request` and `Response` implementations can be constructed using the Decorator pattern.

NOTE   For more details about the Decorator pattern, see the earlier sidebar, "An Overview of Design Patterns."

The Transubstantiator Interface

The `net.rish.pattern.Transubstantiator` interface provides generic methods (shown in Table 20.7) for converting one kind of object to another. Specifically in the case of this interface, it is a specialized Factory pattern that is used to create serialize objects.

TABLE 20.7: Transubstantiator Interface

Method	Description
demote	Transforms an object of "greater form" into an object of "lesser form"
isDemotedForm	Checks to see if the passed object is of a "lesser form"
promote	Transforms an object of "lesser form" into an object of "greater form"

Because this class is an interface, the details of how and where and what specific classes are used are given to the specific implementation. The `Transubstantiator` interface serves as a high-level abstraction, a shield (following the Shield metapattern concept), to the specifics not only of the format of the serialization but of other underlying tools for serialization like Java's own `ObjectStream` class hierarchy versus other third-party class libraries.

A specific implementation of the `Transubstantiator` interface, `net.rish.xml.wddx.Wddx-Transubstantiator`, makes use of the WDDX serialization and deserialization code that was presented in the previous section. If you use this implementation, it is possible to create new classes that implement the `Request` and `Response` interfaces. These new classes use a Decorator pattern to wrap the `Request` and `Response` instances passed into a CFX, and they add methods that can be used to pass complex data in the form of WDDX packets in and out of a CFX tag.

The ComplexRequest Class

A data marshalling equipped `Request` implementation, the `net.rish.coldfusion.Complex-Request` class, provides a simple way to deserialize incoming complex data. This class uses the Decorator pattern to draw its data from the existing `Request` instance (to be provided at construction). Of all its methods (shown in Table 20.8 below), the `getSerializedAttribute` and `getSerializedSettings` methods are the most important to the `ComplexRequest` class.

These methods provide a simple way to retrieve serialized complex data that has been passed from the calling CFML logic.

TABLE 20.8: ComplexRequest Methods

Method	Description
getAttributesCollection	Retrieves the specialized Hashtable that serves as the collection of all attributes
getRequest	Gets the wrapped Request instance
getSerializedAttribute	Retrieves and deserializes a complex attribute
getTransubstantiator	Gets the active Transubstantiator instance
setRequest	Sets the base Request instance
setTransubstantiator	Sets the Transubstantiator instance

The ComplexResponse Class

A data marshalling–equipped Response implementation, the net.rish.coldfusion.Complex-Response class, provides a simple way to serialize outgoing complex data. Like the Complex-Request class, it also uses the Decorator pattern and requires an existing Response instance (also to be provided at construction). Also like the ComplexRequest class, the ComplexResponse class contains an overridingly important method, setSerializedVariable (see Table 20.9) for handling serialized data. This method provides a simple way to serialize Java objects into string values that can be passed back to the CFML calling logic.

TABLE 20.9: ComplexResponse Methods

Method	Description
getResponse	Gets the wrapped Response instance
getTransubstantiator	Gets the active Transubstantiator instance
setResponse	Sets the base Response instance
setSerializedVariable	Serializes and sets a complex variable
setTransubstantiator	Sets the Transubstantiator instance

A Complex Look

Using the Decorator classes, ComplexRequest and ComplexResponse, the code applied in the CFX class ComplexData2.java can be greatly simplified. A new iteration, ComplexData3.java, shown in Listing 20.26, uses these classes, and as a result, the source file is lightened by nearly 100 lines. True, the code is actually just relocated, but it is this relocation that allows the developer to concentrate more effectively on what the CFX is supposed to be doing instead of how to shuffle data in and out.

Listing 20.26   Better Complex Datatype Handling (ComplexData3.java)

```
01: /*
02:     File            /c20/ComplexData3.java
03:     Description      Handling complex datatypes
04:         with the Decorator classes
05: */
06: import java.util.Vector;
07:
08: import com.allaire.cfx.*;
09:
10: import net.rish.coldfusion.ComplexRequest;
11: import net.rish.coldfusion.ComplexResponse;
12: import net.rish.xml.wddx.WddxTransubstantiator;
13:
14: public class ComplexData3 implements CustomTag
15: {
16:     public void processRequest(Request request,
17:         Response response)
18:     throws Exception
19:     {
20:         int idx, count;
21:         Vector names = null;
22:         String name = null;
23:         String result = null;
24:         String[] messages = null;
25:
26:         WddxTransubstantiator trans =
27:             new WddxTransubstantiator();
28:
29:         ComplexRequest cRequest =
30:             new ComplexRequest(request, trans);
31:         ComplexResponse cResponse =
32:             new ComplexResponse(response, trans);
33:
34:         names = (Vector)
35:             cRequest.getSerializedAttribute("names");
36:         count = cRequest.getIntAttribute("count");
37:
38:         messages = new String[count];
39:         for(idx = 0; idx < count; idx++)
40:         {
41:             name = (String)names.get(idx);
42:             messages[idx] = "Greetings, " + name;
43:         }
```

```
44:
45:            cResponse.setSerializedVariable("result",
46:                messages);
47:     }
48: }
```

The `WddxTransubstantiator` class is instanced on lines 26–27; this is the engine that makes the rest of the process possible. The `processRequest` method's incoming `Request` and `Response` instances are wrapped on lines 29–32. After this is done, the Decorator instances are used to handle all of the interaction normally done with their unDecorated selves.

Notice that there is no explicit handling of the `attributesCollection` attribute; this is all taken care of behind the scenes when the `Request` instance is wrapped. It is a small matter to retrieve the array of names passed into the CFX as part of the `attributesCollection` structure—this is done on lines 34 and 35 with the `ComplexRequest`'s `getSerializedAttribute`. After this, line 36 shows the easy retrieval of the `count` attribute again using the `getInt-Attribute` method from the `ComplexRequest`.

The greeting messages are then constructed just as they were in the previous iteration of this CFX, with the slight adjustment to the salutation text. Finally, lines 45 and 46 pass the array back with the `ComplexResponse` instance's `setSerializedVariable` method.

Now update the Class Name field of the `cfx_complexData` tag registration to point to the new `ComplexData3` class and reload the `ComplexDataExample3.cfm` template. You will see the altered greeting message constructed in `ComplexData3` confirming the execution of the new CFX tag.

CFML Wrapped CFX Tags

There is one major shortcoming of the CFX model—a CFX tag can't have a body or subordinate tags. This makes CFX tags little more than aggrandized inline command statements. This shortcoming, however, is where CFX custom tags get an opportunity to mesh with their "lesser" siblings, the CFML custom tags. While arguably less broad in terms of possible functionality, a CFML custom tag does have the ability to have a body and track subordinate tags.

The simple trick here is to create a CFML tag that handles these organizational matters, gathers all of the needed data, and then calls the CFX for the heavy lifting. The CFML tag needs to take a number of concerns into account:

- Handling situations where the tag body is optional and the CFML tag needs to determine whether to call the CFX tag when `thisTag.executionMode` equals "start" or "end."

- Determining if the `thisTag.generatedContent` value should be blanked out.
- Propagating variables returned from the CFX tag to the calling logic of the CFML tag.

A perfect way to examine most coding challenges is simply to build it and see what happens.

A Simple XSLT Tag

It is not difficult to use the Java XSL transformation APIs; in fact, if you use the `TrAX` interfaces, this process becomes even simpler.

Building a Java CFX to use these APIs seems like a simple idea. The tag could take an attribute that specifies the input XML file, the input style sheet, and the output file or it could just dump the output to the result stream. But what if the goal was to build a document dynamically and then transform it based upon the browser client—say, to make a presentation between regular HTML and WML. Then your template could focus on the dynamic construction of data for presentation logic rather than the minutia of various tags.

The `Transformation` tag set, `cf_transformation` and `cfx_transformation`, allows for this. The front-ending `cf_transformation` tag accepts a number of attributes as detailed in Table 20.10.

TABLE 20.10: cf_transformation Attributes

Attribute	Description
`factory`	An optional attribute for specifying alternate XSLT `TransformationFactory` classes. This allows different XSLT engines to be plugged into the tag and used.
`result`	An optional attribute to which the resulting XML content can be saved.
`source`	An optional attribute that contains a string of XML content to be transformed.
`stylesheet`	A required attribute that indicates the name of the XSLT style sheet file.

ColdFusion MX has built-in XSLT capabilities that are available through the CFML `xslTransform` function, but it does not provide the same kind of functionality that is described here. The `xslTransform` function requires content being passed to already be an XML document object, and it requires the style sheet content to have already been read into a variable. Instead, the `Transformation` tag set creates a body within which XML content can be dynamically created and filenames can be specified but cannot already be buffered. Additionally, the tag set, using the pluggable settings in the `TrAX` interface, allows for different XSLT engines to be easily used, whereas ColdFusion MX's own XML functionality does not. This lets the tag keep pace with changes to the XSLT standards, such as embedding ECMA scripts into style sheets, independent of the version of the ColdFusion Server.

The CFML wrapper tag, `Transformation.cfm` (Listing 20.27), provides the start and end tag capabilities that don't exist in the CFX model.

Listing 20.27   CFML Wrapper Tag (Transformation.cfm)

```
001: <!---
002:     File            /c20/Transformation.cfm
003:     Description     A CFML custom tag for
004:         wrapping an XSLT CFX tag with pluggable
005:         XSLT engines.
006: --->
007: <cfsetting enableCFOutputOnly="yes">
008:
009: <cfparam name="requiredAttributes"
010:     default="STYLESHEET">
011:
012: <cfparam name="attributes.factory"
013:     default="">
014:
015: <cfswitch expression="#thisTag.executionMode#">
016:     <cfcase value="start">
017:         <!--- check for required attributes --->
018:         <cfloop index="idx"
019:             list="#requiredAttributes#">
020:             <cfif not isDefined("attributes.#idx#")>
021:                 <cfset msg =
022:                     "Missing Attribute: " & "#idx#">
023:                 <cfthrow message="#msg#">
024:             </cfif>
025:             <cfif len(attributes[#idx#]) eq 0>
026:                 <cfset msg =
027:                     "Empty Attribute: " & "#idx#">
028:                 <cfthrow message="#msg#">
029:             </cfif>
030:         </cfloop>
031:
032:         <cfif isDefined("attributes.source")
033:             and len(attributes.source) gt 0>
034:             <cfif thisTag.hasEndTag eq false>
035:                 <cfx_transformation
036:                     factory="#attributes.factory#"
037:                     stylesheet=
038:                         "#attributes.stylesheet#"
039:                     source="#attributes.source#"
040:                     result="results">
041:
042:                 <cfif isDefined("attributes.result")>
043:                     <cfset
044:                         caller[#attributes.result#]
045:                         = results>
```

```
046:                         <cfelse>
047:                             <cfoutput>
048:                                 #results#
049:                             </cfoutput>
050:                         </cfif>
051:                     </cfif>
052:             <cfelse>
053:                 <cfif thisTag.hasEndTag eq false>
054:                     <cfset msg =
055:                         "Missing body and no SOURCE.">
056:                     <cfthrow message="#msg#">
057:                 </cfif>
058:             </cfif>
059:         </cfcase>
060:
061:         <cfcase value="end">
062:             <cfif isDefined("thisTag.generatedContent")
063:                 and len(thisTag.generatedContent) gt 0>
064:
065:                 <cfset content = thisTag.generatedContent>
066:                 <cfset thisTag.generatedContent = "">
067:
068:                 <cfx_transformation
069:                     factory="#attributes.factory#"
070:                     stylesheet="#attributes.stylesheet#"
071:                     content="#content#" result="results">
072:
073:                 <cfif isDefined("attributes.result")>
074:                     <cfset caller[#attributes.result#]
075:                         = results>
076:                 <cfelse>
077:                     <cfoutput>
078:                         #results#
079:                     </cfoutput>
080:                 </cfif>
081:             <cfelse>
082:                 <cfif isDefined("attributes.source")
083:                     and len(attributes.source) gt 0>
084:
085:                     <cfx_transformation
086:                         factory="#attributes.factory#"
087:                         stylesheet=
088:                             "#attributes.stylesheet#"
089:                         source="#attributes.source#"
090:                         result="results">
091:                     <cfif isDefined("attributes.result")>
092:                         <cfset
093:                             caller[#attributes.result#] =
094:                             results>
095:                     <cfelse>
096:                         <cfoutput>
```

```
097:                         #results#
098:                     </cfoutput>
099:                 </cfif>
100:             <cfelse>
101:                 <cfset msg =
102:                     "Missing body and no SOURCE.">
103:                 <cfthrow message="#msg#">
104:             </cfif>
105:         </cfif>
106:     </cfcase>
107: </cfswitch>
108:
109: <cfsetting enableCFOutputOnly="no">
```

The tag switches on the `thisTag.executionMode` variable to determine its entry state: either "start" or "end". When the state is "start", the tag checks all the required incoming attributes (lines 18–30). Then the logic checks for combinations of the `source` attribute and an end tag (lines 32–58). If a `source` attribute is specified, the tag does not need to have an end tag and then the CFX can be called if the other required attributes, like `stylesheet`, are present. If no `source` attribute and no end tag are specified, then an exception is called; otherwise it is assumed that content in the body is to be processed.

When the tag's state is "end" the logic checks the `thisTag.generatedContent` variable; if there is a value, it is saved to an internal variable and then `thisTag.generatedContent` is set to an empty string (lines 65 and 66). This is done because the CFX tag will be generating content meant to replace what is in the body currently. If `thisTag.generatedContent` is empty, then the logic checks for a `source` attribute. If the `source` attribute exists and has a value, then the end tag is assumed to be superfluous and the CFX tag is called (lines 85–90), otherwise an exception is generated (line 103).

A major point of interest in this listing is where variables that are returned from the CFX tag are transferred to the CFML tag's calling logic. This happens in three places: lines 42–50, lines 73–80, and lines 91–99. In these places, the `result` attribute of the CFX tag is always set so that the CFML tag can control what happens with the CFX tag results. If the `result` attribute of the CFML tag is set, then the CFX tag results are passed back into a variable of that name in the CFML tag's calling logic; otherwise the output of the CFX tag is outputted directly.

The tag presented in `Transformation.java` is, in terms of actual CFX construction, unremarkable. The bulk of the complexity of creating CFML-wrapped CFX tags, such as gathering up the content of the body between start and end tags, is handled in the CFML custom tag itself; there is seldom any different handling needed in the actual construction of the CFX tag itself. Listing 20.28 shows the tag's `processRequest` method.

Listing 20.28   **XSLT CFX Tag (Transformation.java)**

```
001: /*
002:     File              /c20/Transformation.java
003:     Description       A XSLT CFX tag intended
004:         for use with a CFML custom tag wrapper.
005: */
006:
007: // standard Java stuff
008: import java.io.*;
009: import java.util.*;
010: // Allaire's CFX interfaces
011: import com.allaire.cfx.*;
012: // Imported TraX classes
013: import javax.xml.transform.*;
014: import javax.xml.transform.stream.*;
015:
016: public class Transformation implements CustomTag
017: {
018:     // custom tag entry point
019:     public void processRequest(Request request,
020:         Response response)
021:     throws Exception, TransformerException,
022:         TransformerConfigurationException,
023:         FileNotFoundException, IOException
024:     {
025:         // attributes
026:         String attribContent = null;
027:         String attribStylesheet = null;
028:         String attribResult = null;
029:         String attribSource = null;
030:           String attribFactory = null;
031:
032:         File sourceFile = null;
033:         StringReader str = null;
034:         StringWriter writ = null;
035:         StreamSource stylesheet = null;
036:         StreamSource xmlsource = null;
037:         StreamResult xmlresult = null;
038:
039:         // retrieve/default the incoming argument
040:         attribContent =
041:             request.getAttribute("content", null);
042:         attribStylesheet =
043:             request.getAttribute("stylesheet", null);
044:         attribResult =
045:             request.getAttribute("result", "result");
046:         attribSource =
047:             request.getAttribute("source", null);
048:           attribFactory =
```

```
049:            request.getAttribute("factory", null);
050:
051:        if(attribContent == null
052:            && attribSource == null)
053:        {
054:          throw new
055:            Exception("No CONTENT or SOURCE");
056:        }
057:
058:        if(attribContent != null
059:            && attribSource != null)
060:        {
061:          throw new
062:            Exception("Combine CONTENT and SOURCE");
063:        }
064:
065:        if(attribStylesheet == null)
066:        {
067:          throw new Exception("No STYLESHEET");
068:        }
069:
070:        if(attribContent != null)
071:        {
072:          str = new StringReader(attribContent);
073:          xmlsource = new StreamSource(str);
074:        }
075:
076:        if(attribSource != null)
077:        {
078:          sourceFile = new File(attribSource);
079:          xmlsource = new StreamSource(sourceFile);
080:        }
081:
082:          // install a specific transformation library
083:          if(attribFactory != null &&
084:            attribFactory.length() != 0)
085:          {
086:            System.setProperty(
087:            "javax.xml.transform.TransformerFactory",
088:              attribFactory);
089:          }
090:
091:        writ = new StringWriter();
092:        xmlresult = new StreamResult(writ);
093:        stylesheet = new StreamSource(
094:            new File(attribStylesheet));
095:
096:        TransformerFactory factory =
097:            TransformerFactory.newInstance();
098:
099:        Transformer transformer =
```

```
100:              factory.newTransformer(stylesheet);
101:
102:         transformer.transform(xmlsource, xmlresult);
103:
104:         response.setVariable(attribResult,
105:              writ.toString());
106:    }
107: }
```

Lines 39–49 show the retrieval of the needed attributes, all of which have default values of `null`, with the exception of the `result` attribute. Then on lines 51–63, attribute combinations are checked; any checks that the wrapping CFML tag has performed are disregarded. (This is important because the CFX tag is still useful without the wrapping CFML tag.) Lines 91–94 instantiate the needed streams for the transformation, and lines 96–102 perform the actual work by invoking the transformation engine passing the XML and the stylesheet. The transformed content is then returned to the calling logic, the wrapping CFML tag, into the variable specified in the `result` attribute.

NOTE   Be sure to register the `cfx_transformation` tag in the ColdFusion Administrator. Set the Class Name to the Transformation class.

One practical way of stitching this set together could be for presentation purposes. For instance, you might want to use style sheets to target different markups, like HTML versus WML. The template `TransformationExample1.cfm` (Listing 20.29) demonstrates this.

Listing 20.29   CFML Wrapped CFX Example (TransformationExample1.cfm)

```
01: <!---
02:    File              /c20/TransformationExample1.cfm
03:    Description       Uses the XSLT CFML wrapped CFX
04:       to create a dynamic display either for
05:       HTML or WML.
06: --->
07: <cfparam name="url.sheetType" default="html">
08: <cfset stylesheet =
09:    expandPath("./booklist.#url.sheetType#.xsl")>
10: <cfset bookList = expandPath("./booklist.txt")>
11: <cffile action="read"
12:    file="#bookList#" variable="books">
13:
14: <cf_transformation stylesheet="#stylesheet#">
15: <cfoutput>
16: <booklist>
17:    <cfloop index="idx" list="#books#"
18:        delimiters="#chr(13)##chr(10)#">
19:       <book>
```

```
20:          <name>#listGetAt(idx, 1, "|")#</name>
21:          <link>#listGetAt(idx, 2, "|")#</link>
22:        </book>
23:      </cfloop>
24: </booklist>
25: </cfoutput>
26: </cf_transformation>
```

This template opens by cfparaming a URL variable, sheettype, to "html" for default viewing. It uses this variable to dynamically construct the style sheet name (the two style sheets, booklist.html.xsl and booklist.wml.xsl, are not shown here for the sake of brevity) on lines 8–9. A data file, whose path is dynamically figured on line 4, is read in; on line 10, the contents of this file will dynamically drive the display. It then enters the cf_transformation tag block passing the style sheet, on line 14. Within the tag body, the XML is constructed by looping over the contents of the data file, which is a list of book titles and their Amazon.com links.

NOTE   I use Apache Software Consulting, Inc.'s (http://www.apachesoftware.com) Klondike WAP browser to view my WML pages. This free non-commercial version serves most of my simple needs very well. It even does WMLScript!

In Sum

The numerous topics covered in this chapter are only the core concepts involved in constructing CFX tags in Java. This chapter also explored the CFXAPI library, from its basic interfaces, its debugging tools, and its specialized attributes, and some of the shortcomings of the Java CFX model. In addition to these basics, we dealt with a number of the techniques and tools that are used to extend the CFXAPI beyond the core library and to circumvent the imposed limitations of the CFX model.

Unfortunately, it is beyond the scope of this book to cover the specifics of all of the radical directions CFX development could take you. Many of the examples in this chapter were simple in nature, but they served to give you a fundamental understanding of the APIs. This chapter's work with wrapping CFX tags with CFML and wrapping classes in the CFXAPI with custom Decorator classes demonstrates that many of the shortcomings of the CFX model can be overcome with any special tricks that could make your code unstable. These kinds of techniques can serve as templates for future endeavors.

CHAPTER 21

Building C++ Extensions

By Guy Rish

- Setting up your system and selecting a C++ compiler

- Exploring the C++ CFXAPI library

- Creating CFX tags and learning CFX construction basics

- Passing and returning queries

This chapter introduces the C++ library for writing *ColdFusion Extensions (CFXs)*. A CFX is a custom tag that was written in a language other than CFML. Because ColdFusion MX can bind with externally created modules, like CFXs, ColdFusion applications can effectively use vast external libraries, which provide whole tangents of functionality that don't exist within CFML. While ColdFusion MX has become a very evolved application server, there are still things it cannot accomplish or keep pace with as industry standards rapidly evolve. Wisely, Allaire, and now Macromedia, perceived this and supplied tools like CFXs to provide for the extension of CFML.

Since C++ is such a broadly used language, it is an excellent choice for building CFXs. Many of the emerging standards in XML and network protocols, as well as operating system services, are typically written in either C++ or Java, or both. CFXs written in C++ have an edge over custom tags written in CFML or CFXs written in Java; as a compiled binary they typically run faster. However, this speed improvement comes at a serious cost: as a binary the CFX is specific to the operating system for which it is compiled. This detraction is frequently compounded by the usage of platform-specific extensions used in the source code of the CFX as well.

To respond to the challenge, this chapter will not only cover the basics of the C++ CFXAPI but will introduce some techniques for making the source code more portable. These techniques will be introduced right away so that all of the code presented herein is immediately viable whether you are initially targeting Microsoft's Windows platform or any of the Unix-based platforms supported by ColdFusion MX.

NOTE   The chapter assumes you have a basic familiarity with C++ and the C++ Standard Library. None of the examples require advanced knowledge. They are all rather simple and are designed to demonstrate specific features of CFX construction.

Chapter Setup

For the examples in this chapter to work correctly, you'll need to do some setup and have a few things in place: a C++ compiler, the chapter sample code, and the registration of the sample database.

Choosing a C++ Compiler

Because this chapter addresses two different basic platforms, Windows and Unix-based, providing specific details about compiler use does present some difficulties. It would be impossible to address all of the different IDEs and compiler options across all the ColdFusion MX supported platforms, so this chapter will focus on two, Microsoft Visual C++ and GNU's C++ compiler.

Microsoft Visual C++   Numerous quality C++ compilers are available for the Windows platform, but the clear standard, not surprisingly, is Microsoft's own Visual C++ product (often bundled as part of Visual Studio). Although you can use other compilers such as the ones that are available from Intel, Borland, or even the relatively new OpenWatcom compiler, this chapter assumes that you are using Microsoft's product, version 6.0 or later.

NOTE Technically, any C++ compiler suite that is capable of producing a Win32 DLL is a viable solution.

GNU C++ Compiler   Again, many good C++ compilers are available for the non-Windows platforms that are supported by ColdFusion MX, but again, there is one whose popularity and platform diversity make it the clear choice: the GNU C Compiler. It is available for Linux, Solaris, and HP/UX, thus covering the "other" ColdFusion platforms. If you are working on any of the non-Windows platforms, this chapter assumes that you are using the GNU C Compiler, 2.95 or later.

NOTE As is the case for the Windows platform, any compiler that is capable of producing a shared object/shared library for the OS in question is a viable solution.

While this chapter will use Microsoft Visual C++ throughout, care was taken to create code that would be viable with other compilers. Whether the target platform is Windows or Unix-based, operating system or compiler, the resulting code from the examples should work.

Chapter Sample Code

You can access this chapter's sample code from this book's web page on the Sybex website (http://www.sybex.com). Once you have downloaded the code, unpack the files into a web-published directory.

Part of the sample code that you'll download is a Microsoft Access database. This needs to be registered in the ColdFusion Administrator with the names data source name.

Installing C++ CFX Tags

A number of simple CFX tags will be constructed throughout this chapter, and they must be registered with the ColdFusion Administrator before you can incorporate them in your templates.

You will find that installing a Java-based CFX tag is not very difficult; just follow these steps:

1. Launch the ColdFusion Administrator your browser.

2. From the navigation on the left-hand side of the screen, select the CFX Tags menu item from under the Extensions heading to load the page shown in Figure 21.1.

FIGURE 21.1:

The CFX Tags page

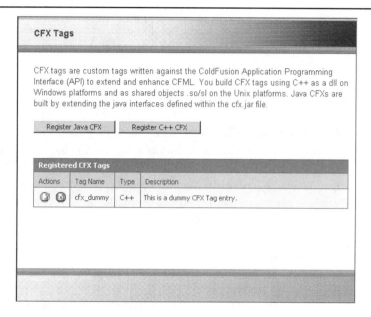

The CFX Tags page has two buttons and a table of the registered CFX tags (both C++ and Java). The two buttons, Register C++ CFX and Register Java CFX, load the pages for the two different kinds of tags. As you might have surmised, only C++ CFX tag registration will be discussed in this chapter.

The table contains four columns:

Actions   This column contains two hyperlinked images that allow the CFX tag entry to be edited or deleted.

Tag Name   This column indicates the CFML name by which the CFX tag will be identified; this is not necessarily the same as the Java class name.

Description   This column contains the descriptive text that can be optionally entered at the same time the tag is registered.

Type   This column indicates whether the CFX tag is a C++ or Java tag.

To load the Add/Edit C++ CFX Tag page in Figure 21.2, just click the Register C++ CFX button.

FIGURE 21.2:

The Add/Edit C++ CFX
Tag page

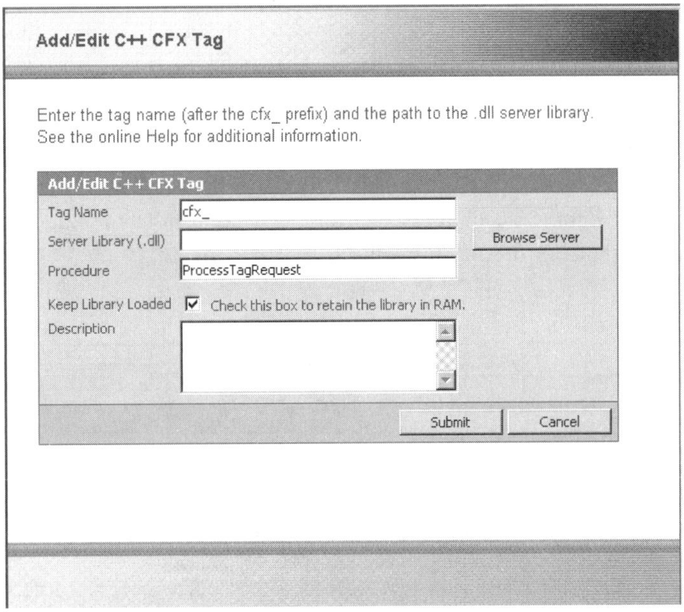

Add/Edit C++ CFX Tag

Enter the tag name (after the cfx_ prefix) and the path to the .dll server library.
See the online Help for additional information.

Add/Edit C++ CFX Tag	
Tag Name	cfx_
Server Library (.dll)	
Procedure	ProcessTagRequest
Keep Library Loaded	☑ Check this box to retain the library in RAM.
Description	

This page contains the following features:

Tag Name field   This field specifies the CFML name for the CFX tag. This should correspond to the Tag Name column on the CFX Tags page (Figure 21.1).

Server Library (.dll) field   This field is where you indicate the DLL or shared object that contains the CFX tag. As an interesting side note, the text label of this field reads "Server Library (.dll)" even on the Unix-based platforms.

Procedure field   This field identifies the function to call in the DLL or shared object; by default, this is `ProcessTagRequest`.

WARNING   While previous versions of ColdFusion allowed for the specification of different procedure names, the function name to be called as the entry point into the DLL or shared library, ColdFusion MX does not. It will only execute the `ProcessTagRequest` procedure, regardless of what is specified in this field. This prohibits multiple CFXs from existing in the same DLL or shared library.

Keep Library Loaded check box   This lets you indicate whether or not the ColdFusion MX Server should maintain the DLL or the shared object loaded in memory for better performance.

Description field   This optional field contains any descriptive text about the tag (commercially produced tags often have copyright information here); this corresponds to the Description column on the CFX Tags page.

Now that we have covered these screens, we will be jumping ahead a bit to show the registration information for a tag that will be constructed later in this chapter (see Figure 21.3).

NOTE   Since the ColdFusion Server does not perform any preloading or other verification of the Server Library field, it will not harm anything to commit this information before you construct the actual CFX tag.

FIGURE 21.3:

The Hello, World CFX

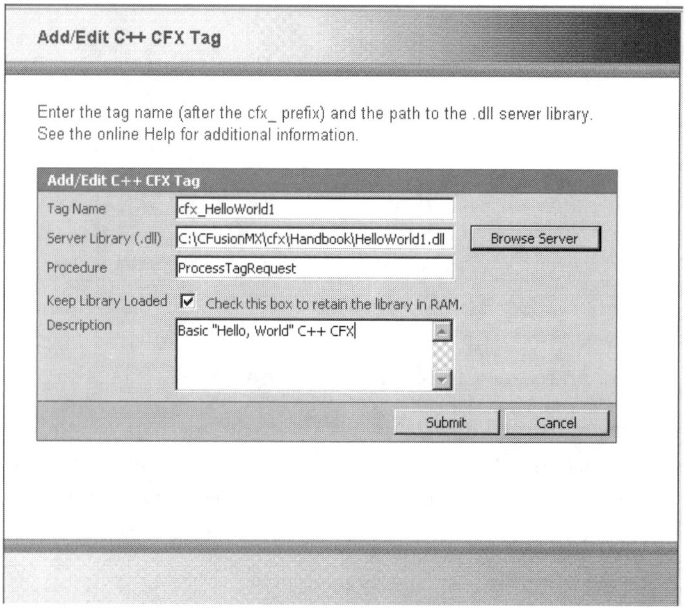

Introducing the C++ CFXAPI

When you begin to study C++-based CFX tags, the best place to start is with the CFXAPI library itself. The C++ CFXAPI is the basic kit that you can use to developing C++-based custom tags. There are four classes identified within the cfx.h include file that you will use when you are constructing a CFX: CCFXRequest, CCFXQuery, CCFXStringSet, and CCFXException. Figure 21.4 shows a UML class diagram of these classes.

FIGURE 21.4:

The CFXAPI UML model

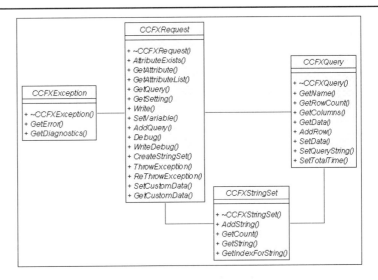

NOTE   UML diagrams are explained in Appendix B, "Understanding UML Class Diagrams."

The classes are all abstract, meaning that they act as interfaces with deferred implementations internal to the ColdFusion MX Server. In other words, you will not need to supply an external library to link them, only the header.

The CCFXRequest Class

An instance of this abstract class is passed into every custom tag; this instance provides the mechanism for the tag to receive data and to pass it back. Table 21.1 shows the methods of this class.

TABLE 21.1: The Methods of the CCFXRequest Class

Method	Description
AttributeExists	Checks for the existence of the specified attribute
GetAttribute	Retrieves the value of the specified attribute
GetAttributeList	Retrieves a list of all of the attributes passed from the calling logic
GetQuery	Retrieves the one query passed from the calling logic
Write	Writes text to the output stream and back to the calling logic
SetVariable	Sets a variable in the calling logic
AddQuery	Creates a query to be returned to the calling logic

Continued on next page

TABLE 21.1 CONTINUED: The Methods of the CCFXRequest Class

Method	Description
Debug	Checks for the existence of the debug attribute
WriteDebug	Writes text to the debug stream of the calling logic
CreateStringSet	Creates a CCFXStringSet instance
ThrowException	Throws an exception to the calling logic, interrupting the processing of the tag
ReThrowException	Rethrows a previously caught exception to the calling logic, interrupting the processing of the tag

NOTE   Additional methods not listed in this table are used for interfacing with the system registry. Since Macromedia has officially declared cross-platform registry functions deprecated in ColdFusion MX, these methods will not be covered in this chapter.

The CCFXQuery Class

The CCFXQuery class provides the interface in which you can manipulate the data it receives from a CFML query object or data that is destined to become a CFML query object when it is returned to the CFX's calling logic (see Table 21.2).

TABLE 21.2: The Methods of the CCFXQuery Class

Method	Description
GetName	Retrieves the name of the query
GetRowCount	Returns the number of rows in the query
GetColumns	Returns a CCFXStringSet containing the names of the columns in the query
GetData	Returns the value of the column from a specific row of the query
AddRow	Adds a new empty row to the query
SetData	Sets the value of a column on a specific row of the query

NOTE   The CCFXQuery class contains two other methods that are not listed in Table 21.2; SetQueryString and SetTotalTime. These methods are not discussed here because they have been officially deprecated from the API.

The CCFXStringSet Class

This class represents a rather simplistic data structure, a string array. A class to do only this might seem foolish given the various data structure libraries today, but the class was constructed at a time before the C++ Standard Library was much of a cross platform standard. This class provides a platform- and compiler-independent implementation that lets you manage strings in an internal buffer. However, it does not provide any basic string functionality of its own. Table 21.3 lists the class's methods.

TABLE 21.3: The Methods of the CCFXStringSet Class

Method	Description
AddString	Adds a string to the end of the set
GetCount	Returns the number of strings in the set
GetString	Returns the string located at the indicated index within the list
GetIndexForString	Finds the index for the indicated string

This class is used in a few places, most notably as the return value of the CCFXRequest's AttributesList and AddQuery methods.

The CCFXException Class

The CCFXException class wraps string data that can be caught in a normal C++ catch statement or thrown with one of two CCFXRequest methods: ThrowException and ReThrowException. By itself, this class is passive. Table 21.4 lists the class's methods.

TABLE 21.4: The Methods of the CCFXException Class

Method	Description
GetError	Returns the error string of the exception
GetDiagnostics	Returns the error's diagnostic information for the exception

C++ CFX Basics

Building a C++ CFX tag is fairly simple for the intermediate to experienced C++ developer. However, with the various tools that are available and a little help, even a novice C++ developer can begin the work necessary to create a CFX tag. Among other things, this section introduces

- The CFX Tag Wizard
- Basic CFX construction
- Portable CFX construction

To introduce the basic concepts of CFX construction, this section initially relies on Visual Studio's tools for creating CFX tags that are specific to the Windows platform. Once the basics are established, this section introduces some techniques for making the code more portable; at this point, we will no longer rely as much upon Visual Studio and Windows specific constructs.

The CFX Tag Wizard

Microsoft's Visual Studio is an extremely powerful IDE. One of its more useful extensibility features is Project Wizards. As part of the pre-MX product packaging, the ColdFusion Server installed a Project Wizard when a Visual Studio installation was detected. The CFX Tag Wizard was a simple but helpful tool for quickly generating the skeleton of a Windows-based C++ CFX. Since its value has not diminished, in spite of the fact that Macromedia no longer includes the Wizard as part of its installation package, this chapter will show you how to use the Wizard to build basic CFX tags.

NOTE   This Wizard may be downloaded from the Macromedia website (`http://www.macromedia.com/v1/handlers/index.cfm?ID=5825&Method=Full&PageCall=/support/index.cfm`). This Wizard was originally targeted at Visual Studio 5.*x* and 6.*x*. It was never intended for use with Microsoft's newer Visual Studio .NET product.

Basic CFX Construction

The quickest way for you to get a grasp on how CFXs work is just to dive in and build one. In this section you will construct a simple "Hello, World" CFX using the CFX Tag Wizard in Visual Studio.

When you launch Visual Studio, you can create a new workspace in a directory called `Handbook`, which you can create subordinate to the `cfx` subdirectory of your ColdFusion MX installation. You will use this workspace to house all of the Windows-based work you do throughout this chapter.

To begin creating this CFX, follow these steps:

1. Create a new project to the Workspace (File ➢ New).

2. Select the Cold Fusion Tag Wizard from the Projects tab of the New dialog box.

3. Enter **HelloWorld1** into the Project Name field to create a project as part of the current workspace (see Figure 21.5).

FIGURE 21.5:

HelloWorld1 project creation

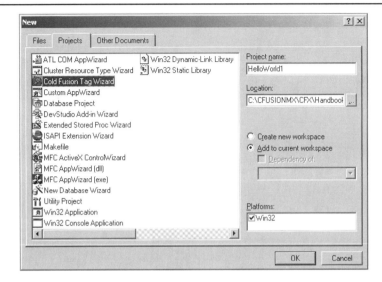

4. Click OK to launch the CFX Tag Wizard as shown in Figure 21.6.

FIGURE 21.6:

CFX Tag Wizard for HelloWorld1

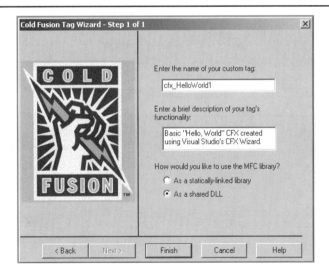

5. In the "Enter the name of your custom tag" field, type **cfx_HelloWorld1**.

6. You can leave the Description field blank if you want, but be certain to select the As a shared DLL radio button below the Description field; this makes the resulting DLL file smaller.

7. Select the Finish button to close this one-step wizard. A summary of the generation actions displays in the New Project Information screen (see Figure 21.7).

If you open the IDE's Workspace browser, shown in Figure 21.8, you can see that the resulting project contains a copious number of generated files. In this view, you can see three C++ source files (the files with the `.cpp` extension), but the one of overriding interest is the `Request.cpp` file, shown in Listing 21.1.

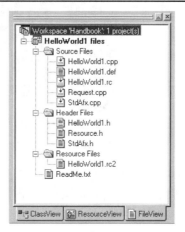

Listing 21.1   HelloWorld1 CFX (Request.cpp)

```cpp
01: //////////////////////////////////////////
02: //
03: // CFX_HELLOWORLD1 - Cold Fusion custom tag
04: //
05: // Copyright 2002. All Rights Reserved.
06: //
07: #include "stdafx.h"      // Standard MFC libraries
08: #include "cfx.h"         // CFX Custom Tag API
09:
10: void ProcessTagRequest( CCFXRequest* pRequest )
11: {
12:     try
13:     {
14:         // Retrieve attributes passed to the tag
15:         // For example:
16:         // LPCSTR lpszColor =
17:         //      pRequest->GetAttribute("COLOR") ;
18:
19:         // Write output back to the user here...
20:         pRequest->Write(
21:             "Hello from CFX_HELLOWORLD1!" ) ;
22:
23:
24:         // Output optional debug info
25:         if ( pRequest->Debug() )
26:         {
27:             pRequest->WriteDebug( "Debug info..." ) ;
28:         }
29:     }
30:     // Catch Cold Fusion exceptions & re-raise them
31:     catch( CCFXException* e )
32:     {
33:         pRequest->ReThrowException( e ) ;
34:     }
35:
36:     // Catch ALL other exceptions and throw them as
37:     // Cold Fusion exceptions (DO NOT REMOVE! --
38:     // this prevents the server from crashing in
39:     // case of an unexpected exception)
40:     catch( ... )
41:     {
42:     pRequest->ThrowException(
43:     "Error occurred in tag CFX_HELLOWORLD1",
44:     "Unexpected error occurred while processing tag.");
45:     }
46: }
```

The source file created by the wizard is verbose and even includes snippets within comments that show you how to accomplish some basic tasks.

Let's now examine what is going on in this listing line by line. Lines 7 and 8 handle the CFX tag's two includes: `stdafx.h` is a wrapper that includes numerous MFC headers, and `cfx.h` is the CFX API header. After that, the DLL's entry point is set up. It is represented by the function `ProcessTagRequest`, which receives a pointer to a `CCFXRequest` instance, pRequest.

The body of the `ProcessTagRequest` function contains a try/catch block that spans lines 12–45. The `try` block calls the `Write` method of the `CCFXRequest` instance to display `"Hello from CFX_HELLOWORLD1!"` on lines 20–21. Lines 25–28 check the `CCFXRequest` instance for its "debug" mode indicated by the presence of the debug attribute. If it is present, the instance will call `WriteDebug` to output some diagnostic information.

Moving on, you can see that there are two `catch` blocks: the first for catching CFX exceptions and the second for catching all other exceptions. The first `catch` merely calls the `CCFXRequest`'s `ReThrowException` method. The second `catch` catches all other unforeseeable errors and throws a wholly new exception with a call to `CCFXRequest`'s `ThrowException` method.

Now that we have reviewed what is going on in Listing 21.1, it is time to build the CFX's DLL (Build ➤ Rebuild All) and copy the resulting DLL to the Handbook subdirectory (the base directory of the Visual Studio Workspace). Since we already reviewed how to fill out this configuration information for this CFX (see "Installing C++ CFX Tags"), this tag is all ready to go. We'll put it to work in Listing 21.2.

Listing 21.2   **Calling HelloWorld1 CFX (HelloWorld1.cfm)**

```
<!---
    Name:          /c21/HelloWorld1.cfm
    Description:   Calling a simple C++ CFX.
--->
<html>
<head>
    <title>"Hello, World" C++ CFX Example 1</title>
</head>

<body>
    <h2>Basic C++ CFX</h2>
    <cfx_HelloWorld1>
</body>
</html>
```

To see the output in the browser, which is exactly what you might expect, see Figure 21.9.

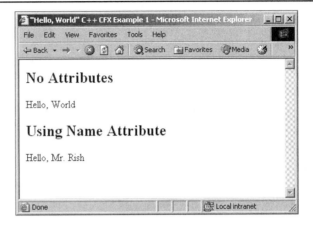

Handling Attribute Values

Sadly, getting a chunk of software to spit out a hardcoded Hello, World is not terribly impressive. People might be more impressed if you got it to actually address the user by name.

This can be accomplished with just a few more lines of code. In the following code, you see an updated `try` block from the `Request.cpp`. Within this block, you give the CFX a `name` attribute to spruce up the display. This listing also demonstrates how to get information passed from the CFXs calling logic.

```
01: CString attributeName("World");
02: try
03: {
04:     if(pRequest->AttributeExists("NAME"))
05:     {
06:         attributeName = pRequest->GetAttribute("NAME");
07:     }
08:
09:     attributeName = "Hello, " + attributeName;
10:
11:     // Write output back to the user here...
12:     pRequest->Write(attributeName) ;
13: }
```

By using the code in the snippet to replace the entire `try` block in `Request.cpp` (which can be done with a simple cut and paste), you can see that making the CFX tag a little smarter isn't difficult. You just need a way to retrieve the value of the `name` attribute and create something within which to store that value. Line 1 of this excerpt shows the declaration of an MFC `CString`, `attributeName`, that has a defaulted value of `"World"`.

Where it is obvious that this `try` block is pretty different from the previous iteration of this code is in lines 2–13. In this section, the first thing you do is check for the existence of the `name` attribute, using the `AttributeExists` method of the `CCFXRequest` class as the driver of a conditional statement (line 4). If `name` does exist, its value is assigned to `attributeName` on line 6 with `GetAttribute`. On line 9, you concatenate the salutation with the value of `attributeName`, which will be either `"World"` or the value passed in the tag's `name` attribute. Then on line 12 (similar to the previous iteration), you make a call to `Write` to output the newly fashioned string.

Naturally these change make it possible for you to conduct another invocation from within a ColdFusion template. This is shown in Listing 21.3 with an updated version of `NewHelloWorld1.cfm`.

Listing 21.3   **Invoking the Revised CFX (NewHelloWorld1.cfm)**

```
<!---
    Name:           /c21/NewHelloWorld1.cfm
    Description:    Calling a simple C++ CFX.
--->
<html>
<head>
    <title>New "Hello, World" C++ CFX Example 1</title>
</head>

<body>
    <h2>Basic C++ CFX</h2>
    <cfx_HelloWorld1>
    <br>
    <h2>Using the Name Attribute</h2>
    <cfx_HelloWorld1 name="Mr. Rish">
</body>
</html>
```

Portable CFX Construction

While using the CFX Tag Wizard makes creating a CFX tag easier by adding all the plumbing you need to use the Microsoft Foundation Classes (MFC), it makes the code dependent upon the Windows platform. This is true of even the most basic output of the Wizard that uses Windows specific data structure libraries.

Making a CFX tag's source code more portable is entirely possible, but you will have to wean yourself from the CFX Tag Wizard to make a few subtle adjustments to mask platform-specific extensions.

Making Subtle Changes to Your CFX Code

Although the C++ CFX API was not intended to be platform-specific, it does rely on a number of datatype definitions that are common to the Windows platform and are not commonly defined on the Unix-based platforms. Because of this Macromedia maintains two different cfx.h header files to support this dependency. The appropriate, platform-specific one comes installed with the ColdFusion MX. The Unix version defines these datatypes but the Windows version does not because the Windows version of cfx.h assumes that various Windows header files are being included before it.

You need to make subtle, not drastic, changes in the way you write the CFX tag because it assumes the inclusion of header files that will define the needed datatypes. Because of this, you can no longer use the standard cfx.h include directly. You will use the new header, shown in Listing 21.4, which really isn't a replacement, but more of a wrapper around the original cfx.h.

Listing 21.4   New CFX Header (cfx_lean.h)

```
/*
    Name:           cfx_lean.h
    Description:    CFX include wrapper.
*/
/* [BEGIN] check for need types flag */
#ifdef WIN32
/* [BEGIN] check for Windows includes */
#ifndef _WINDOWS_

#ifndef _SYS_TYPES_H
#include <sys/types.h>
#endif

/* Porting help */
typedef unsigned short BOOL;
typedef unsigned char BYTE;
typedef unsigned short WORD;
typedef unsigned int DWORD;
typedef char *LPSTR;
typedef const char *LPCSTR;
typedef unsigned int UINT;
typedef BYTE    BOOLEAN;
typedef BYTE *LPBYTE;
typedef DWORD *LPDWORD;
typedef void *LPVOID;
#endif
/* [END] check for Windows includes */
#endif
/* [END] check for need types flag */

/* pull in the standard CFX header */
#ifndef __CFX_H__
#include "cfx.h"
#endif
```

```
/* Solaris thread handling */
#if defined(sun)
#define _POSIX_PTHREAD_SEMANTICS
#endif
```

The first thing this include file does is check for the existence of the precompiler tags for a Win32 binary, the Windows include, and the types include. Then, if appropriate, it defines the necessary datatypes. This is important, especially since the datatypes that were originally defined in the header files (included for MFC compatibility by the CFX Tag Wizard) will no longer be used!

TIP   Remember that these definitions are already defined in the Unix platform's cfx.h.

After the include defines the datatypes, it adds in the original cfx.h header. And finally, it adds a Solaris directive for better thread handling. This last was extracted from Macromedia's own C++ CFX sample files included with the standard production installation; there is no specific Tech Note to relate any additional information on the matter.

Using the C++ Standard Library

When you remove the MFC dependency from the CFX's source you get rid of much of the overtly Windows-platform-specific code, you create a serious problem—the loss of classes for complex data structures. But there is a simple way for you to solve this.

C++'s own Standard Library is one of the most powerful tools for making a CFX's source more portable. This package supplies a standardized set of features that were sorely missing from C++, not the least of which are complex data structures like strings and vectors.

Before a stable and robust implementation of the Standard Library was available, the CFX developer had to work with a plethora of incompatible third-party libraries. Most likely, the Windows developer would have used the MFC to fill the gap and the Unix developer would have used OS-specific extensions, expensive (but high-end) libraries, or open source libraries (which commonly port to the Windows platform last, making portable code even more difficult). So, even if CFXs were performing basic functions that could be done relatively easily on Windows and Unix-based systems, the fact that they used incompatible class libraries made porting a daunting task.

Following the steps in this next section you will be able to produce a basic C++ CFX whose source code is platform independent.

Creating a Portable CFX Tag

To create a portable CFX tag, follow these steps:

1. Return to Visual Studio and create a new project (File ➤ New) within the Handbook Workspace.

2. This time, select Win32 Dynamic-Link Library, and type **HelloWorld2** in the Project Name field, as shown in Figure 21.10. This will launch the wizard, shown in Figure 21.11.

3. In the first screen of this wizard, select the "An empty DLL project radio." radio button and click Finish. You will now see a summary of the generated actions, like that shown in Figure 21.12.

FIGURE 21.10:

HelloWorld2 project creation

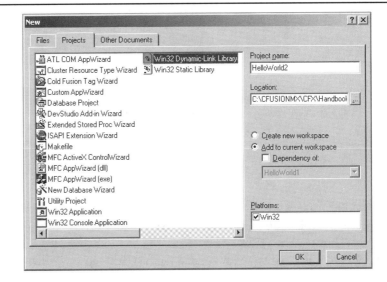

FIGURE 21.11:

Win32 Dynamic-Link Library Wizard for HelloWorld2

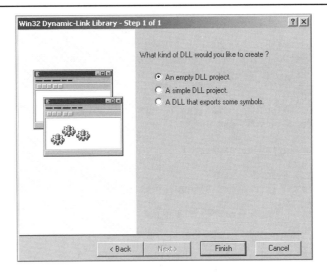

Summary for
HelloWorld2

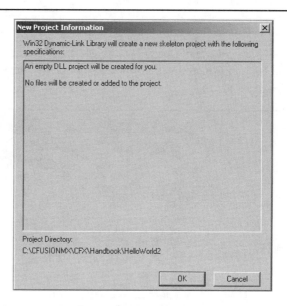

The project that you just created will not contain any generated files; you will have to produce these. To do so, you have to add a new C++ source file to HelloWorld2 project, (HelloWorld2.cxx). The new source, shown in Listing 21.5, does not look dramatically different from what was generated by the CFX Tag Wizard, but it is a little cleaner.

Listing 21.5   HelloWorld2 CFX (HelloWorld2.cxx)

```
01: /*
02: Name: /cfx/handbook/HelloWorld2/HelloWorld2.cxx
03: Description: A simple platform inspecific
04:     CFX tag.
05: */
06:
07: #include "cfx_lean.h"
08: #include <string>
09:
10: using namespace std;
11:
12: extern "C"
13: void ProcessTagRequest(CCFXRequest* request)
14: {
15:     string attributeName("World");
16:
17:     try
18:     {
19:         if(request->AttributeExists("NAME"))
20:         {
```

```
21:                attributeName =
22:                    request->GetAttribute("NAME");
23:            }
24:
25:            attributeName = "Hello, " + attributeName;
26:            request->Write(attributeName.c_str());
27:        }
28:        /* ColdFusion exception */
29:        catch(CCFXException* e)
30:        {
31:            request->ReThrowException(e);
32:        }
33:        /* IMPORTANT catch all */
34:        catch(...)
35:        {
36:            request->ThrowException("Unknown Error!",
37:                "A processing error occurred.");
38:        }
39: }
```

As you can see, the previously discussed custom CFX header wrapper (Listing 21.4) is included on line 7, and the String library from C++'s Standard Library is on line 8. Line 10 helps to minimize the verbosity of the code by declaring that C++'s Standard Library `std` namespace will be used throughout the source.

The real work begins on lines 12 and 13 where the CFX's handler function, `ProcessTag-Request`, is declared. This is the function that will be externally accessible from this project's resulting DLL or shared object. On line 15, the Standard Library's `string` class is used instead of the MFC `CString` class that was necessary in `cfx_HelloWorld1`. The `attributeName` instance, which also appears on line 15 is constructed with a default value of `"World"`. This instance will hold the value of the CFX tag's `name` attribute.

The differences between the `cfx_HelloWorld1` tag and this one begin to become less noticeable after line 15. The `try` block, which spans lines 17–27, does pretty much what its predecessor did. First it checks for the existence of the `name` attribute (see line 19), and if it is present, it retrieves its value using `GetAttribute` (line 21 and 22). It then concatenates the salutation and the `name` together on line 25. This is all very familiar, right? But there is a point of interest on line 26. Although you probably expected the call to the `Write` method, that the `string`'s `c_str` method is used is a reminder that the C++ CFXAPI was not constructed with the Standard Library in mind. The `Write` method is expecting an `LPCSTR`, so passing the `string`, `attribute-Name`, directly will not work. The `c_str` method returns a `LPCSTR` to the contents of the `string` instance, matching the excepted argument datatype of the `Write` method.

Now that we have added the code to the HelloWorld2 project, we only need to create export declarations for DLL construction, `HelloWorld2.def`; this is shown in Listing 21.6.

Listing 21.6   HelloWorld2 Module Definition (HelloWorld2.def)

```
; Name:         /cfx/handbook/HelloWorld2/HelloWorld2.def
; Description: cfx_HelloWorld2 CFX exports
LIBRARY        "HelloWorld2"
DESCRIPTION    'HelloWorld 2 CFX'
EXPORTS
   ProcessTagRequest  @1
```

Once you have added the module definition file to the HelloWorld2 project, you can compile this project, copy the resulting DLL to the cfx/Handbook subdirectory, and register a new C++ CFX in the ColdFusion Administrator called cfx_HelloWorld2 and specify this new DLL in the Server Library field. You execute a quick call to this new CFX from the template HelloWorld2.cfm that is shown in Listing 21.7. The results are identical to that of the previous CFX and template, as they should be.

Listing 21.7   Calling the HelloWorld2 CFX (HelloWorld2.cfm)

```
<!---
    Name:          /c21/HelloWorld2.cfm
    Description:    Calling a simple C++ CFX.
--->
<html>
<head>
    <title>"Hello, World" C++ CFX Example 2</title>
</head>

<body>
    <h2>No Attributes</h2>
    <cfx_HelloWorld2>
    <br>
    <h2>Using the Name Attribute</h2>
    <cfx_HelloWorld2 name="Mr. Rish">
</body>
</html>
```

Portability Payoff

At this point, you might be wondering what, if anything, is really all that different between these two CFXs other than a few syntactical point of interest. These differences are more apparent when you copy the following three files to a Unix machine: the new include (cfx_lean.h), the CFX source (HelloWorld2.cxx.), and the template (HelloWorld2.cfm).

First, place the `cfx_lean.h` in the compiler's include path. There are three typical options for placement:

- The CFX `include` subdirectory with `cfx.h`
- The `/usr/include` directory
- The `/usr/local/include` directory

Which of these you choose depends on where the machine's support staff, with whom you should consult, would prefer such things to be located.

After you place the header, you are ready to place the CFX source, `HelloWorld2.cxx`. Put it in the `cfx` subdirectory of the ColdFusion MX installation directory. Then, you can use the GNU C++ compiler to build the CFX tag with a simple invocation. The command line on Linux will look like this:

```
g++ -shared HelloWorld2.cxx -o HelloWorld2.so
```

You can use the Administrator to register the resulting shared object with the machine's ColdFusion MX Server, as shown previously in the "Installing C++ CFX Tags" section. Just be certain to register it as `cfx_HelloWorld2` so that the template will work without alteration.

Now place the template in a published web directory, perhaps one that is specific to this book's and this chapter's code. The template should be immediately browseable and should yield the same results as were demonstrated previously.

NOTE   Naturally, the foregoing process is a wholly impossible course of action with the source for the `cfx_HelloWorld1`, due to its heavy reliance upon Windows specific libraries.

Returning Variables

As has been demonstrated, it is relatively easy to receive data from tag attributes and then create strings to be added to the templates output buffer. The next progressive step is to be able to return data specifically into variables in the calling logic.

This is actually rather simple to do using the `SetVariable` method of the `CCFXRequest` class. When you are constructing the `cfx_HelloWorld3` tag, as is shown in Listing 21.8, you can use a technique that allows the calling logic to specify the name of the variable.

To ensure the best portability, you will need to use the Win32 Dynamic-Link Library Wizard again to create a new project in Visual Studio called `HelloWorld3`. You will then need to add an empty C++ source file called `HelloWorld3.cxx` to the project. The code for this file is shown in Listing 21.8.

Listing 21.8   HelloWorld3 CFX Source (HelloWorld3.cxx)

```
01: /*
02: Name: /cfx/handbook/HelloWorld3/HelloWorld3.cxx
03: Description: A simple platform-inspecific
04:     CFX tag that returns a value to the
05:     calling logic.
06: */
07:
08: #include "cfx_lean.h"
09: #include <string>
10:
11: using namespace std;
12:
13: extern "C"
14: void ProcessTagRequest(CCFXRequest* request)
15: {
16:     string attributeName("World");
17:     string attributeResult("RESULT");
18:
19:     try
20:     {
21:         if(request->AttributeExists("NAME"))
22:         {
23:             attributeName =
24:                 request->GetAttribute("NAME");
25:         }
26:
27:         if(request->AttributeExists("RESULT"))
28:         {
29:             attributeResult =
30:                 request->GetAttribute("RESULT");
31:         }
32:
33:         attributeName = "Hello, " + attributeName;
34:         request->SetVariable(attributeResult.c_str(),
35:             attributeName.c_str());
36:     }
37:     /* ColdFusion exception */
38:     catch(CCFXException* e)
39:     {
40:         request->ReThrowException(e);
41:     }
42:     /* IMPORTANT catch all */
43:     catch(...)
44:     {
45:         request->ThrowException("Unknown Error!",
46:             "A processing error occurred.");
47:     }
48: }
```

The source for this CFX tag is not unlike that shown in `cfx_HelloWorld2` (Listing 21.5). The difference is that, within the `try` block, an additional attribute, `result`, is retrieved on lines 27–31. Then on lines 34 and 35, instead of using the `Write` method to pass content back, you invoke the `SetVariable` method. The first argument of `SetVariable` is the name of the variable to be created in the calling logic; this is defined by the value of the `result` attribute. This argument allows the tag's user to indicate the name of the variable. The second argument is the value that is to give the variable; in this case it is the concatenated greeting that was passed back into the output buffer in the previous version of this tag.

Now you add a module definition file to the project, called `HelloWorld3.def`, similar to the one shown in Listing 21.9.

Listing 21.9   HelloWorld3 CFX Module Definition (HelloWorld3.def)

```
; Name:          /cfx/handbook/HelloWorld3/HelloWorld3.def
; Description: cfx_HelloWorld3 CFX exports
LIBRARY       "HelloWorld3"
DESCRIPTION  'HelloWorld 3 CFX'
EXPORTS
    ProcessTagRequest  @1
```

You should now build the project and copy the resulting DLL to the `cfx/Handbook` subdirectory. After you have done this, register the DLL as `cfx_HelloWorld3`. Once this is done, you can demonstrate its functionality by using a template like `HelloWorld3.cfm`, shown in Listing 21.10.

Listing 21.10   Returning a Variable (HelloWorld3.cfm)

```
<!---
    Name:          /c21/HelloWorld3.cfm
    Description:    Calling a C++ CFX that returns
        a value to the calling logic.
--->
<html>
<head>
    <title>"Hello, World" C++ CFX Example 3</title>
</head>

<body>
    <cfx_HelloWorld3 name="Mr. Rish" result="greeting">
    <cfoutput>#greeting#</cfoutput>
</body>
</html>
```

Working with Queries

The CCFXQuery class provides an interface that allows you to work with CFML query objects. Although only one query can be passed into a CFX, numerous queries can be returned.

Passing a Query

There is a trick to passing a CFML query object into a CFX—it must be done using the special tag attribute: query. This is demonstrated in the template HelloQuery1.cfm shown in Listing 21.11.

Listing 21.11   Passing a Query (HelloQuery1.cfm)

```
<!---
    Name:            /c21/HelloQuery1.cfm
    Description:     Calling a C++ CFX that produces
        greeting messages from names passed in a query.
--->
<html>
<head>
    <title>"Hello, World" Query C++ CFX Example 1</title>
</head>

<body>
    <cfquery name="names" datasource="names">
        select * from Name
    </cfquery>

    <cfx_HelloQuery1 query="names">
</body>
</html>
```

This template calls a new CFX that needs to be constructed. To do so, create a new project in Visual Studio called HelloQuery1 using the Win32 Dynamic-Link Library Wizard. Add a C++ source file called HelloQuery1.cxx to the project. The code for this file is shown in Listing 21.12 below.

Listing 21.12   HelloQuery1 CFX Source (HelloQuery1.cxx)

```
01: /*
02: Name: /cfx/handbook/HelloQuery1/HelloQuery1.cxx
03: Description: A simple platform inspecific
04:     CFX tag using queries.
05: */
06:
07: #include "cfx_lean.h"
08: #include <string>
```

```
09:
10: using namespace std;
11:
12: extern "C"
13: void ProcessTagRequest(CCFXRequest* request)
14: {
15:     string msg;
16:     string name;
17:     CCFXQuery* query;
18:     int rows;
19:     int index;
20:
21:     try
22:     {
23:         if(request->AttributeExists("QUERY"))
24:         {
25:             query = request->GetQuery();
26:         }
27:         else
28:         {
29:             request->ThrowException(
30:                 "Missing Attribute",
31:                 "The QUERY Attribute is missing.");
32:         }
33:
34:         rows = query->GetRowCount();
35:         for(index = 1; index <= rows; index++)
36:         {
37:             name = query->GetData(index, 1);
38:             msg = "Hello, " + name + "<br>";
39:             request->Write(msg.c_str());
40:         }
41:     }
42:     /* ColdFusion exception */
43:     catch(CCFXException* e)
44:     {
45:         request->ReThrowException(e);
46:     }
47:     /* IMPORTANT catch all */
48:     catch(...)
49:     {
50:         request->ThrowException("Unknown Error!",
51:             "A processing error occurred.");
52:     }
53: }
```

The source for this CFX starts out almost entirely as expected prior to the try/catch block.
Notice line 17, where a pointer to a CCFXQuery instance is declared. Once you move inside the
try block, you will see that the query attribute's existence is verified on line 23, and when it is
found, a reference is returned with GetQuery on line 25.

The query object's record count is retrieved on line 34; it is this value that is used as the conditional break in the for loop that spans lines 35–40. Also in this span, you can see that the greeting that will be written back to the calling logic. This greeting is constructed from the person's name obtained from each record of the query object, which is retrieved using the GetData method of CCFXQuery on line 37. The retrieved name is concatenated with the salutation on line 38 and written on line 39.

Even after all the work above, the project still needs a module definition file: this is shown in Listing 21.13. Once you have added this to the project, you can compile the CFX.

Listing 21.13   **HelloQuery1 CFX Module Definition (HelloQuery1.def)**

```
; Name:        /cfx/handbook/HelloQuery1/HelloQuery1.def
; Description: cfx_HelloQuery1 CFX exports
LIBRARY        "HelloQuery1"
DESCRIPTION    'HelloQuery 1 CFX'
EXPORTS
   ProcessTagRequest  @1
```

Once you have successfully compiled the CFX, copy the DLL to the cfx/Handbook subdirectory and register it as cfx_HelloQuery1 in the ColdFusion MX Administrator.

If you browse HelloQuery1.cfm, you will see results similar to those shown in Figure 21.13.

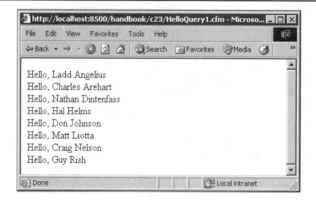

Reference Altering a Passed Query

When a CFX gets access to the passed CFML query object by using the GetQuery method of the CCFXRequest reference passed to the CFX library's entry point, it receives a pointer to the query object, not a copy of the data. The significance of this is that the calling template can see alterations made directly to the data of the query object after the CFX has returned.

We'll demonstrate this with a new CFX. First create a new project in the Handbook workspace in Visual Studio, called HelloQuery2, using the Win32 Dynamic-Link Library Wizard. Then add a C++ source file to the project called HelloQuery2.cxx; its code is shown in Listing 21.14.

Listing 21.14   HelloQuery2 CFX Source (HelloQuery2.cxx)

```
01: /*
02: Name: /cfx/handbook/HelloQuery2/HelloQuery2.cxx
03: Description: A simple platform-inspecific
04:     CFX tag that modifies query fields.
05: */
06:
07: #include "cfx_lean.h"
08: #include <string>
09:
10: using namespace std;
11:
12: extern "C"
13: void ProcessTagRequest(CCFXRequest* request)
14: {
15:     string msg;
16:     string name;
17:     CCFXQuery* query;
18:     int rows;
19:     int index;
20:
21:     try
22:     {
23:         if(request->AttributeExists("QUERY"))
24:         {
25:             query = request->GetQuery();
26:         }
27:         else
28:         {
29:             request->ThrowException(
30:                 "Missing Attribute",
31:                 "The QUERY Attribute is missing.");
32:         }
33:
34:         rows = query->GetRowCount();
35:         for(index = 1; index <= rows; index++)
36:         {
37:             name = query->GetData(index, 1);
38:             msg = "Hello, " + name;
39:             query->SetData(index, 1, msg.c_str());
40:         }
41:     }
42:     /* ColdFusion exception */
43:     catch(CCFXException* e)
```

```
44:     {
45:         request->ReThrowException(e);
46:     }
47:     /* IMPORTANT catch all */
48:     catch(...)
49:     {
50:         request->ThrowException("Unknown Error!",
51:             "A processing error occurred.");
52:     }
53: }
```

The HelloQuery2.cxx source is nearly identical to its predecessor, cfx_HelloQuery1. The point where these two source files differentiate is within the for loop, which again spans lines 35–40. In particular, line 37 retrieves the person's name from the query object as it did in the earlier example, and the person's name is likewise concatenated with a salutation on line 38. But there are some differences. For instance, notice the missing br from the constructed string. Since the new greeting will not be directly incorporated into the output stream with a Write there is no longer any need to format the output with a br. This newly constructed string is then placed into the query, overwriting the previous value, on line 39 using the CCFXQuery class's SetData method. This replaces the person's name with the greeting, incorporating the person's name.

As before, this project will require a module definition, as shown in Listing 21.15.

Listing 21.15   HelloQuery2 CFX Module Definition (HelloQuery2.def)

```
; Name:        /cfx/handbook/HelloQuery2/HelloQuery2.def
; Description: cfx_HelloQuery2 CFX exports
LIBRARY      "HelloQuery2"
DESCRIPTION  'HelloQuery 2 CFX'
EXPORTS
    ProcessTagRequest  @1
```

Once the project is built and the DLL moved, you will register it as cfx_HelloQuery2. The new CFX tag can be called from the template HelloQuery2.cfm, shown in Listing 21.16.

Listing 21.16   Query Alteration by Reference (HelloQuery2.cfm)

```
<!---
    Name:          /c21/HelloQuery2.cfm
    Description:    Calling a C++ CFX that alters
        the contents for fields in a query.
--->
<html>
<head>
    <title>"Hello, World" Query C++ CFX Example 2</title>
</head>
```

```
<body>
    <cfquery name="names" datasource="names">
        select * from Name
    </cfquery>

    <h2>Query Before Alteration</h2>
    <cfdump var="#names#">

    <cfx_HelloQuery2 query="names">

    <h2>Query After Alteration</h2>
    <cfdump var="#names#">
</body>
</html>
```

When you browse this template, you get results like those shown in Figure 21.14.

FIGURE 21.14:

Query Alteration by
Reference

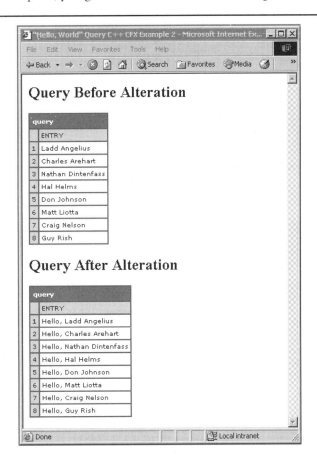

Returning a Query

You can create entirely new query objects using the CCFXRequest's AddQuery method. This method also introduces you to the CCFXStringSet class, which is an interesting construct that compensates for the lack of complex data structures in C++ that stems back to a time when the Standard Library wasn't so standard.

To demonstrate how to create and return a CCFXQuery instance, we will create a new CFX. Create a new project in the Handbook Workspace in Visual Studio, called HelloQuery3, using the Win32 Dynamic-Link Library Wizard. Then add a C++ source file to the project called HelloQuery3.cxx; its code is shown in Listing 21.17.

Listing 21.17   HelloQuery3 CFX Source (HelloQuery3.cxx)

```
01: /*
02: Name: /cfx/handbook/HelloQuery3/HelloQuery3.cxx
03: Description: A simple platform-inspecific
04:     CFX tag that returns a query sourced
05:     from a file.
06: */
07:
08: #include "cfx_lean.h"
09: #include <fstream>
10: #include <string>
11:
12: using namespace std;
13:
14: extern "C"
15: void ProcessTagRequest(CCFXRequest* request)
16: {
17:     string name;
18:     string filename;
19:     CCFXQuery* query;
20:     CCFXStringSet* set;
21:     int row;
22:
23:     try
24:     {
25:         if(request->AttributeExists("FILENAME"))
26:         {
27:             filename =
28:                 request->GetAttribute("FILENAME");
29:             if(filename.size() == 0)
30:             {
31:                 request->ThrowException("Error",
32:                     "Empty FILENAME attribute.");
33:             }
34:         }
35:         else
36:         {
```

```
37:                    request->ThrowException("Error",
38:                        "Missing FILENAME attribute.");
39:                }
40:
41:                // open input file
42:                ifstream inputFile(filename.c_str());
43:                if(!inputFile)
44:                {
45:                    request->ThrowException("Input Problem",
46:                        "Unable to open the filename.");
47:                }
48:
49:                // create query
50:                set = request->CreateStringSet();
51:                set->AddString("NAME");
52:                set->AddString("MESSAGE");
53:                query = request->AddQuery("names", set);
54:
55:                // process file to add content to query
56:                while(getline(inputFile, name))
57:                {
58:                    row = query->AddRow();
59:                    query->SetData(row, 1, name.c_str());
60:                    query->SetData(row, 2,
61:                        ("Hello, " + name).c_str());
62:                }
63:            }
64:            /* ColdFusion exception */
65:            catch(CCFXException* e)
66:            {
67:                request->ReThrowException(e);
68:            }
69:            /* IMPORTANT catch all */
70:            catch(...)
71:            {
72:                request->ThrowException("Unknown Error!",
73:                    "A processing error occurred.");
74:            }
75: }
```

This CFX tag is considerably more complex than the others in this chapter. In this example, the try block spans lines 23–63. In this block, the tag will get the data to load into the query object from names it will obtain from a file on the filesystem. The name of this file is indicated by filename attribute, which is the first thing to be checked in the try block (on line 25). If the filename attribute is missing, an exception is thrown (lines 35–39); otherwise the attribute's value is retrieved and assigned to the filename string (lines 27 and 28). Then on line 42, the tag attempts to open the file with an input file stream; if it fails, it throws an exception.

Before a query object can be created you will need to create a CCFXStringSet. This class creates and manages a collection of strings. Using the CCFXRequest class's CreateStringSet method, a CCFXStringSet can be instantiated; this is done on line 50. The collection of strings that set will manage are the column names of the query object you are going to create. Using the CCFXStringSet method AddString, two values, "NAME" and "MESSAGE," are added to set; this is done on lines 51 and 52. A CCFXQuery instance is gotten by calling the CCFXRequest instance's AddQuery method on line 53. AddQuery takes two arguments, the name of the query object, in this case "names," and a CCFXStringSet instance, in this case set.

The names to be entered into the query are stored in the filename specified by the filename attribute; the names are stored one name per line. The file will be processed one line at a time using the Standard Library's getline function as the driver of a while loop that spans lines 56–62. First a new row is added with the query object's AddRow method on line 58. Then the two columns are populated with SetData: first with the name from the file on line 59, and then with a greeting concatenated from the name on lines 60 and 61.

As before, this project will require a module definition file to be created, as shown in Listing 21.18.

Listing 21.18   HelloQuery3 CFX Module Definition (HelloQuery3.def)

```
; Name:        /cfx/handbook/HelloQuery3/HelloQuery3.def
; Description: cfx_HelloQuery3 CFX exports
LIBRARY      "HelloQuery3"
DESCRIPTION  'HelloQuery 3 CFX'
EXPORTS
   ProcessTagRequest  @1
```

Once the project is built and the DLL moved, you will register it as cfx_HelloQuery3. The new CFX tag can be called from the template HelloQuery3.cfm, shown in Listing 21.19.

Listing 21.19   Returning a Query (HelloQuery3.cfm)

```
<!---
    Name:        /c21/HelloQuery3.cfm
    Description:   Calling a C++ CFX that creates
       a query object from the contents of a file
       whose name is passed into the CFX.
--->
<html>
<head>
    <title>"Hello, World" Query C++ CFX Example 3</title>
</head>

<body>
```

```
        <cfx_HelloQuery3
            filename="#expandPath("./names.txt")#">
        <cfdump var="#names#">
    </body>
    </html>
```

When you browse this template, you see results similar to those shown in Figure 21.15.

FIGURE 21.15:

Returning a new query

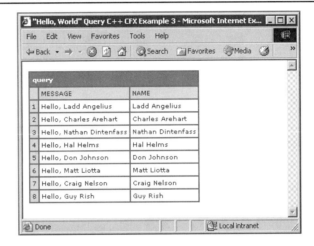

Returning Multiple Queries

With repeated calls to AddQuery you can create multiple query objects that will be available to the calling logic. Although the examples in this chapter have been very simplistic, the limits of this operation are bound solely by the needs of the developer.

In Sum

Becoming familiar with the basic framework for building CFX tags in C++ is a fairly straightforward task. The four constituent classes of the API are well coordinated and their interaction is obvious. In addition, when combined with the adjustments you need to make to incorporate the C++ Standard Library, you can expand this API to work cooperatively with any modern C++ library.

Although the examples in this chapter relied heavily upon Microsoft's Visual Studio, the specific steps taken to make the code more portable will allow you to use them on any of the ColdFusion MX supported platforms. Further, because the alterations are necessary to make your code more portable, using them as part of your common practice should not inhibit the rest of your personal development processes.

CHAPTER 22

Using cfexecute

By Arman Danesh

- Why use cfexecute?

- Specifying the application to run

- Passing multiple parameters in argument

- Using timeouts to avoid endless loops

- Effective use of output

- Security issues with cfexecute

C fexecute allows you to run a process on the server just as if you were issuing a command at the command prompt. Many ColdFusion developers, including those with extensive experience, rarely, if ever, use the cfexecute tag in their applications. Indeed, there are compelling security concerns about the cfexecute tag that can expose serious security holes on a server when the tag is misused. Nevertheless, it offers a powerful mechanism for extending the capabilities of your ColdFusion applications.

This chapter starts by examining the reasons to use cfexecute. Then, we'll briefly review the attributes and syntax of the cfexecute tag. Then we'll discuss the motivations for using the tag and some effective ways to implement it. Finally, we'll take a careful look at the security issues surrounding this tag so that you can make an informed decision about using the tag in your work.

Why Use cfexecute?

The cfexecute tag allows you to execute any process on the server just as if you were issuing a command at the command prompt. This holds true in the Unix, Linux, and Windows versions of ColdFusion: any command you can execute at the command prompt should, in theory, be possible to execute through cfexecute. Any output generated by the command is returned as part of the HTML stream sent to the browser. It is also possible to send arguments and input to the command being invoked with cfexecute.

NOTE   The commands executed by cfexecute are run in the same user space as the ColdFusion server process. This means that the commands you can execute are restricted to those that the ColdFusion server process can execute. Your environment, including the default path and any environment variables, will be the environment of the ColdFusion server process. As discussed later in the section "cfexecute Security Issues," this helps minimize the risk of allowing ColdFusion to execute arbitrary applications on the server, but it still allows fairly free access to run useful commands on the server as part of your ColdFusion applications.

Reasons for Using cfexecute

The immediate question many developers ask when they are considering the cfexecute tag and its security risks is: why would I need to use this tag? After all, ColdFusion is a flexible and powerful programming environment for building web applications. You can use it to access Internet protocols, communicate with a database, process text files, generate e-mail, use server-side Java objects, and much more. However, as with all web application environments, there are limitations on what can be done. Some of the instances where `cfexecute` might be useful in extending ColdFusion's capabilities include the following:

- Accessing Internet protocols other than those directly supported by ColdFusion
- Running system utilities such as monitoring system load
- Using third party applications or databases not support directly by ColdFusion
- Using the capabilities of an outside scripting language such as Perl
- Submitting batch processes to legacy applications

Of course, it is always possible that you could consider building COM objects or Java objects and using these through the `cfobject` tag to achieve similar extensibility. However, this solution requires building custom objects in C++ or Java, which may be beyond the skill or time resources available to a ColdFusion developer (see, for example, Chapter 20, "Building Java Extensions"). It is often quicker and easier to add these sorts of extensions to a ColdFusion application using the `cfexecute` tag by using an existing application, a third-party tool, or even simple scripts that you write yourself in Perl or other scripting languages.

Specifying the Application to Be Run

The main attribute of the `cfexecute` tag is the `name` attribute, which indicates the full path and command name of the outside application to execute:

```
<cfexecute name="program to execute">
```

For instance, consider the case where you want to monitor statistics about the ethernet interfaces on your web server as part of an administrative application for remotely monitoring the health of your server. On a Windows system, the `netstat.exe` command provides this output.

With the -e argument, `netstat.exe` displays information about the current active connections on the server as in the following example from the Windows command prompt:

```
C:\>netstat.exe -e
Interface Statistics

                        Received            Sent

Bytes                 18107392        10456945
Unicast packets         101493           97766
Non-unicast packets       2608            1135
Discards                     0               0
Errors                       0               3
Unknown protocols            0
```

This output can be displayed in a ColdFusion application with the following tag:

```
<cfexecute
  name="c:\windows\system32\netstat.exe"
  arguments="-e"
  timeout="1">
```

In Windows NT 4, the usual path to `netstat.exe` was `c:\winnt\system32\netstat`
`.exe`. It was in Windows 2000, and later in Windows XP, that the Windows directory was
moved to `c:\windows` and the path to `netstat.exe` typically became `c:\windows\`
`system32\netstat.exe`.

A partial ColdFusion template would look like this:

```
<body>
  <cfexecute
    name="c:\windows\system32\netstat.exe"
    arguments="-e"
    timeout="1">
  </cfexecute>
</body>
```

The result looks like those in Figure 22.1.

FIGURE 22.1:

Displaying output of
the `netstat.exe`
command in a web
browser

There are a few important points to note in this sample template:

- We have closed the `cfexecute` block with a closing tag. You have to do this even though you typically will not include any code between the opening and closing tags of the block.

- We have passed arguments to the command with the `arguments` attribute. Arguments cannot be passed as part of the command in the `name` attribute. For instance, the following tag is not a correct use of `cfexecute`:

```
<cfexecute
 name="c:\winnt\system32\netstat.exe -e"
 timeout="1">
```

The passing of arguments is discussed more in the section "Passing Multiple Arguments to Commands."

- We have specified the complete path and filename of the command. This is necessary with `cfexecute`. In Windows environments, it is especially important to remember that the file-name extensions (such as `.exe`) must be included in the command in the `name` attribute in order for the tag to work. This differs from the Windows command line where the file-name extensions of common executable file formats can be excluded when a command is being executed.

- It is generally necessary to specify a timeout in seconds when using the `cfexecute` command, as we've done here with the `timeout` attribute. Timeouts are discussed in more detail later in the section "Using Timeouts to Avoid Endless Loops." Without a timeout, it is not possible for ColdFusion to display the output from a command.

The resulting output from this template appears formatted as one continuous line of text. This is because the output of the `netstat.exe` command ends up as part of the HTML stream and spaces and new line characters do not affect the formatting of HTML when it is rendered. To resolve this, you could wrap the `cfexecute` block with opening and closing `pre` tags to generate results as shown in Figure 22.2.

```
<body>
  <pre>
    <cfexecute
     name="c:\windows\system32\netstat.exe"
     arguments="-e"
     timeout="1">
    </cfexecute>
  </pre>
</body>
```

FIGURE 22.2:

Formatting output of the `netstat.exe` command in a web browser

Passing Multiple Arguments to Commands

You can send more than one argument to a command using a single `argument` attribute. This can be done in two ways:

1. As a string of arguments as they would appear on the command line after the command

2. As an array containing one element for each argument

For instance, with the `netstat.exe` command you can combine arguments to generate more detailed output. Including the `-s` argument in the command adds the output of protocol-specific statistics to the report:

```
C:\>netstat.exe -e -s
Interface Statistics
```

	Received	Sent
Bytes	18107392	10456945
Unicast packets	101493	97766
Non-unicast packets	2608	1135
Discards	0	0
Errors	0	3
Unknown protocols	0	

```
IPv4 Statistics

  Packets Received                      = 123771
  Received Header Errors                = 0
  Received Address Errors               = 6
  Datagrams Forwarded                   = 0
  Unknown Protocols Received            = 0
  Received Packets Discarded            = 219
  Received Packets Delivered            = 123552
  Output Requests                       = 116730
  Routing Discards                      = 0
  Discarded Output Packets              = 2
  Output Packet No Route                = 0
  Reassembly Required                   = 0
  Reassembly Successful                 = 0
  Reassembly Failures                   = 0
  Datagrams Successfully Fragmented     = 0
  Datagrams Failing Fragmentation       = 0
  Fragments Created                     = 0

ICMPv4 Statistics

                              Received      Sent
  Messages                    14            16
  Errors                      0             0
  Destination Unreachable     1             2
  Time Exceeded               0             0
  Parameter Problems          0             0
  Source Quenches             0             0
  Redirects                   0             0
  Echos                       0             14
  Echo Replies                13            0
  Timestamps                  0             0
  Timestamp Replies           0             0
  Address Masks               0             0
  Address Mask Replies        0             0

TCP Statistics for IPv4

  Active Opens                          = 5560
  Passive Opens                         = 476
  Failed Connection Attempts            = 3704
  Reset Connections                     = 510
  Current Connections                   = 5
  Segments Received                     = 113808
  Segments Sent                         = 100699
  Segments Retransmitted                = 7470
```

```
UDP Statistics for IPv4

   Datagrams Received    = 9154
   No Ports              = 589
   Receive Errors        = 0
   Datagrams Sent        = 8420
```

You can generate the same output in a ColdFusion template by just passing both arguments in the arguments attribute of the cfexecute tag:

```
<cfexecute
  name="c:\windows\system32\netstat.exe"
  arguments="-e -s"
  timeout="1">
```

Alternately, however, you can pass an array to the cfexecute tag. In Listing 22.1, an array named commandArguments is created, populated with two entries reflecting the two arguments and that array is passed to the arguments attribute.

Listing 22.1   **Passing Arguments to cfexecute Using an Array (2201.cfm)**

```
<!---
    Name:          /c22/2201.cfm
    Description:   Passing arguments through an array
--->

<body>
  <cfset commandArguments = arrayNew(1)>
  <cfset commandArguments[1] = "-e">
  <cfset commandArguments[2] = "-s">
  <pre>
     <cfexecute
       name="c:\windows\system32\netstat.exe"
       arguments="#commandArguments#"
       timeout="1">
     </cfexecute>
  </pre>
</body>
```

Notice that this code sample creates a one-dimensional array, populates it with two arguments, and then passes the value of the array to the arguments attribute using the hash marks (#commandArguments#) to evaluate the array before passing it to the tag. Without the hash marks, the text "commandArguments" would be sent as an argument to the netstat.exe command instead of the contents of the array.

In both cases, whether you're passing arguments as a string or as an array, the end result will be output similar to that illustrated in Figure 22.3.

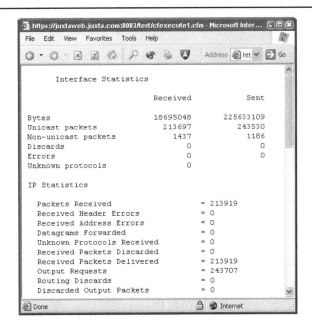

The result of passing multiple arguments with `cfexecute`

NOTE   If you are using ColdFusion 4.5.1 for Windows, you need to apply Service Pack 1 or higher from the Macromedia website to pass arguments as arrays. If you don't, ColdFusion will return an "Unknown exception condition" error when the template is processed. You can find Service Pack 2 for ColdFusion 4.5.1 for Windows at http://www.macromedia.com/ software/coldfusion/downloads/update/. ColdFusion 5 and ColdFusion MX do not require service packs or other updates to use `cfexecute` in this way.

Keep in mind that arguments do not simply have to be flags such as -e; they can be arbitrary text. In the command `dir c:\windows`, for example, `c:\windows` is an argument.

Similarly, arguments can also be flags followed by arbitrary text. For instance, in the command `netstat.exe -p tcp`, the `-p tcp` indicates that the command should display statistics for only TCP. When you are passing arguments through an array, if you have compound arguments such as `-p tcp` both pieces of the argument should be assigned to a single array element instead of split into two elements.

Using Timeouts to Avoid Endless Loops

We haven't had much to say about the `timeout` attribute, although it appears in all the examples we have seen so far. Technically an optional tag, it is nevertheless widely used with the `cfexecute` tag, depending on the programmer's goal. Up to this point, we have seen examples of the cfexecute tag being used to send output of a command to the HTML stream that is being sent to the browser. However, there are other uses of the cfexecute tag:

- Executing a command and sending its output to a file (which is also discussed in the section "Effective Use of Output")

- Executing a command that generates no output

Depending on which of these you want to do and the results you want to see, you will use the timeout attribute in different ways.

The timeout attribute specifies how many seconds ColdFusion should wait for a command to complete execution before proceeding with the rest of the template. This is an important attribute. If you launch a program or script with cfexecute, which has bugs, it may run endlessly without completing. Similarly, extenuating circumstances such as a high CPU load or a congested network can make a program or script take a long time to complete. In these cases, your template processing will halt until the outside program or script completes, and the user will not be able to receive the web page until the program finally finishes. Using the timeout attribute, you tell ColdFusion when to stop waiting and continue processing the rest of your template.

In the worst case scenario, a command will never complete, and any template that invokes it with cfexecute will run endlessly until ColdFusion's default page processing timeout is met. The danger of this is that if that template is requested frequently, you could have numerous instances of the faulty command running taking CPU and other system resources from your other ColdFusion templates.

Controlling Timeout's Effect on the Output

The result of the timeout value depends on where the output of a cfexecute tag is directed.

First, let's consider the case where the output of a command is directed to the HTML stream and sent to the browser. In this case, you need to set the timeout value so that it is greater than 0. This indicates how long ColdFusion should wait in seconds for the command to complete. If the command completes within this time, then the output is included in the output of the template to the browser, but if the command has not completed after the specified number of seconds, an error is returned, as illustrated in Figure 22.4.

In the next case, if you want to send the output to a file instead of the browser, you can leave out the timeout value since ColdFusion will not wait for the output to complete template processing. Instead, ColdFusion will launch the command, direct the output to the specified file for later use, and then immediately continue processing the rest of the template even if the command hasn't finished executing. (The section "Effective Use of the Output" discusses the direction of output to a file.)

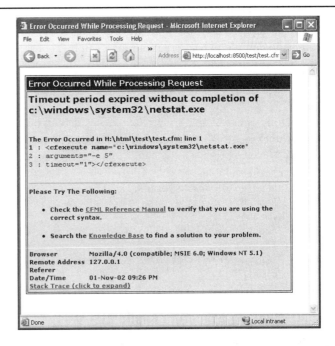

FIGURE 22.4:

If a command takes
too long to execute,
an error is generated.

Finally, there is the case in which a command should be launched and the output should simply be ignored: you want the command to execute, but don't need to use the output in your template or store it in a file. In this case, you should set the timeout to 0 and not specify an output file. Then, ColdFusion will simply launch the command and immediately proceed with processing the rest of the template.

These various output options are summarized in Table 22.1.

TABLE 22.1: Use of the timeout Attribute of the cfexecute Tag

timeout Value	Output File	Result
0	No	Command is executed and processing immediately continues. The output of the command is not saved or used.
Greater than 0	No	Command is executed and ColdFusion waits for the command to finish or the specified time to elapse before continuing to process the template or generating an error if the time has elapsed without completion.
0	Yes	Command is executed and processing immediately continues. The output of the command is saved to the specified file.
Greater than 0	Yes	Command is executed and ColdFusion waits for the command to finish or the specified time to elapse before continuing to process processing the template or generating an error if the time has elapsed without completion. The output of the command is saved to the specified file.

Capturing Timeout Errors

As has been previously mentioned, if a timeout is specified and the time elapses without the command completing, an error message will be generated by ColdFusion, processing will stop, and the user will see the error message. In most cases, you will want to catch this error and handle it in your own way with custom ColdFusion code. This can be done using the cftry and cfcatch tags.

The following example shows how these tags can be used to catch the error that occurs when the timeout value is exceeded and displayed custom output at that time:

```
<cftry>
    <cfexecute
      name="c:\windows\system32\netstat.exe"
      argument="-e -s"
      timeout="1">
    </cfexecute>
    <cfcatch>
        Custom Error CFML/HTML Code Here
    </cfcatch>
</cftry>
```

Limitations on Executing Applications

When using cfexecute, you need to consider the actual applications you choose to execute. Certain types of applications are inappropriate and others will not be accessible from within ColdFusion using cfexecute. In general, keep in mind the following limitations and guidelines:

- Any command you execute should work non-interactively. That is, the user shouldn't need to provide input or interact with the application in order for it to complete.

- You can't run graphical user interface-based applications; instead, you are restricted to command-line tools that don't invoke a graphical front-end for the user.

- The commands you run will run inside the user space of the ColdFusion server. In the case of Unix and Linux systems, this will typically be the nobody user who is highly restricted in their access to the system and commands. On Windows systems this is typically the system user who has moderate access to the system.

- You can only run applications that the user space of the ColdFusion server has permissions to execute. Other commands will not work.

In addition to these guidelines, you should also be closely familiar with the behavior of the script or program you intend to run. In addition, you should know what the result of the command should be in cases where bad input or a bug in your template causes the command to execute in a manner that you had not intended when you were building your ColdFusion application. This ensures that you won't be surprised by the behavior of the cfexecute tag when you use it.

System Environment and the Use of Outside Applications

When you are running a command through `cfexecute`, remember that the command will inherit the environment of the ColdFusion server process, including the default path and all environment variables. This is especially significant when you write custom scripts or programs that you want to use with `cfexecute`. Don't assume that your commands will behave identically to those that you issue at the command line, especially if the scripts or programs make use of environment information in their execution. Instead, test this carefully and if you are developing your own applications or scripts, make them as independent of the environment as possible (for instance, by fully-specifying all paths within the code).

Effective Use of Output

There are several options available for utilizing the output of a `cfexecute`-run command in ColdFusion. So far in this chapter we have seen examples of displaying output to the browser by including it in the HTML stream generated by processing the template. However, this is not the only option available. In particular, there are two useful ways to handle output other than by displaying it as part of a template:

- Storing it in a file for later use
- Capturing it in a variable for immediate use

Storing Output in a File

The `cfexecute` tag provides the optional `outputFile` attribute, which allows you to specify the full path and filename of a file where the output of the command can be stored. For instance, if you wanted to stored the output of the `netstat.exe` command shown earlier in the file `c:\output.txt`, you would alter the tag to look like this:

```
<cfexecute
  name="c:\windows\system32\netstat.exe"
  arguments="-e"
  outputFile="c:\output.txt">
```

This causes the template to continue processing without interruption while `netstat.exe` processes in the background, and when it is done, the output is saved to a file.

When a file is specified, the output cannot be directed to the HTML stream sent to the browser, so there is no way to both display the output and capture the output to a file. In this circumstance, you would want to combine output to a file with an appropriate timeout. The logic works like this:

1. Use the `outputFile` attribute to direct output of the command to a file that is within the web server document tree.

2. Specify a `timeout` value greater than 0 to cause the template to stop processing while the command executes. This `timout` value should be large enough to ensure that the command is guaranteed to complete in normal circumstances.

3. After the `cfexecute` tag finishes, `cfinclude` can be used to incorporate the resulting output file back into the ColdFusion template.

The resulting code would look something like the following; in this code, `c:\html` is the web server's root document directory:

```
<cfexecute
 name="c:\windows\system32\netstat.exe"
 arguments="-e"
 outputFile="c:\html\output.txt"
 timeout="50">
</cfexecute>
<pre>
   <cfinclude template="/output.txt">
</pre>
```

If you take this approach, you will probably want to catch any timeout errors that occur and display an intelligent message to the user instead of simply allowing ColdFusion's error display to appear in the user's browser. Listing 22.2 does this.

Listing 22.2   Catching Timeout Errors (2202.cfm)

```
<!---
   Name:          /c22/2202.cfm
   Description:    Catching timeout errors
--->

<cfset successful = 1>
<cftry>
   <cfexecute
    name="c:\windows\system32\netstat.exe"
    arguments="-e"
    outputFile="c:\html\output.txt"
    timeout="50">
   </cfexecute>
   <cfcatch>
      <cfset successful = 0>
   </cfcatch>
</cftry>
<cfif successful is 1>
   <pre>
      <cfinclude template="/output.txt">
   </pre>
<cfelse>
```

```
        Sorry. Maximum processing time elapsed without the command completing. No
    results are available at this time.
    </cfif>
```

In order to run the template in Listing 22.2, you should change the path of the output file in your `cfexecute` tag and the path of the resulting `cfinclude` tag to the appropriate directories on your system.

In this example, the `successful` variable is used to track the successful completion of the command and the `cfcatch` block is used to set the variable to a value that indicates that the command failed to complete. Then, this variable can be used to decide whether the output file should be included in the HTML stream sent to the browser or whether an appropriate error message should be displayed to the user.

Capturing the Output in a Variable

There are times when it is useful to capture the output of a command for processing prior to sending the output to the browser. For instance, you may want to search the output for specific values and display only those values to the user, or you may want to use regular expressions to change the resulting output in some systematic way before providing the results to the user.

In this case, you could send the output to a file, load the contents of the file into a variable, and then perform the necessary processing. However, this is an inefficient process in that it requires the use of two filesystem interactions (creating the output file and then reading from the output file). Instead, you can use the `cfsavecontent` tag to directly save the output from the command to a variable.

With the `cfsavecontent` tag, all the output generated by ColdFusion code within the `cfsavecontent` block is saved to the specified variable instead of sent in the HTML stream to the browser. For instance, in the following example, the result of the `netstat.exe` command is stored in the variable `netStatOutput`:

```
<cfsavecontent variable="netStatOutput">
  <cfexecute
   name="c:\windows\system32\netstat.exe"
   arguments="-e"
   timeout="1">
  </cfexecute>
</cfsavecontent>
```

NOTE   In the preceding example, notice that the `cfexecute` command looks exactly the same as it would look if it were sending the output directly to the browser. This is the way it should be. The role of the `cfsavecontent` tags is to define the block of code you want saved in a specified variable instead of being sent as regular output to the browser.

Once the content is saved in the variable, processing can be performed. For instance, imagine that you want to replace any value of 0 with the text "zero". This can be done with the `replace` function:

```
<cfset Rresults = replace(netStatOutput,"   0","zero","all")>
```

The resulting template might look like Listing 22.3.

Listing 22.3   **Saving Output to a Variable (2203.cfm)**

```
<!---
    Name:          /c22/2203.cfm
    Description:    Saving output to a variable with cfsavecontent
--->

<body>
    <cfsavecontent variable="netStatOutput">
        <cfexecute
        name="c:\winnt\system32\netstat.exe"
        arguments="-e"
        timeout="1">
        </cfexecute>
    </cfsavecontent>
    <cfset results = replace(netStatOutput,"   0","zero","all")>
    <cfoutput>
        <pre>#results#</pre>
    </cfoutput>
</body>
```

cfexecute Security Issues

Security is a critical issues with the `cfexecute` tag. Because it exposes many system commands and tools so that they can be accessed, the tag can be abused and misused. Examples of this include the following:

- A poorly designed template that takes form input and sends it as an argument to a command. This could be abused to send arguments to a command that trigger unwanted, possibly destructive, results.

- If the server is compromised so that an attacker can upload web content, the attacker can then upload templates that use `cfexecute` to execute arbitrary commands on the server.

- The server itself may be poorly configured allowing excessive permissions to the Cold-Fusion server user space to run commands and access system resources that would allow a ColdFusion template the potential to perform unwanted actions.

- The use of a buggy program as a command from `cfexecute` can affect the stability of the entire server and all ColdFusion applications running on the server.

For these and other reasons, careful consideration needs to be given to the security of your ColdFusion environment and your decision to use the `cfexecute` tag (or not).

Risks of cfexecute on a Server with FTP/RDS Access

When you use `cfexecute`, security is of particular concern if your server allows any type of remote content development and management (for instance using FTP or ColdFusion's own remote development services). This problem is made even worse if this type of remote content management is allowed across public networks such as the Internet.

If a developer's username and password for managing content are compromised, then a malicious attacker could upload their own templates that use the `cfexecute` tag to execute unwanted, malicious actions. Even worse, they can upload their own executable files to the server and, potentially, use the `cfexecute` tag to execute these programs. This allows an attacker great flexibility to attack a system once remote content management has been compromised.

Limiting the Risks of Using cfexecute

Given the security risks of using the `cfexecute` tag, you need to analyze your requirements, and if you determine `cfexecute` is not necessary, you can take steps to eliminate the tag as the source of a possible attack against your server.

ColdFusion provides a mechanism for disabling a handful of tags that are considered potential security risks. In addition to `cfexecute`, these tags include `cfcontent`, `cfdirectory`, `cffile`, `cfobject`, `cfregistry`, `cfadminsecurity`,`cfftp`, `cflog`, and `cfmail`. Controlling access to all of these tags, including `cfexecute`, is done through the ColdFusion Administrator's Security section, in the CF Tags section of Resource Security page, which is illustrated in Figure 22.5. You simply move selected tags between an enabled list and a disabled list.

NOTE   In the Enterprise Edition of ColdFusion MX, tag restriction is specified within individual sandboxes in the sandbox security system.

FIGURE 22.5:

Controlling tag restrictions in the ColdFusion Administrator

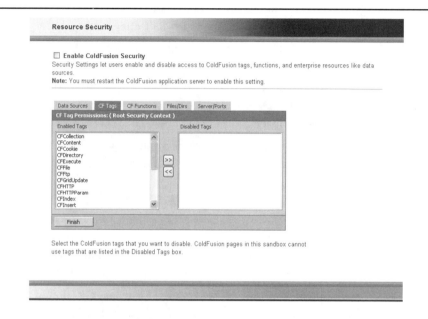

In Sum

In this chapter you have learned the details of using the `cfexecute` tag to run external commands and then work with the output of those commands. With `cfexecute`, the output can be sent to a browser or saved to a file or variable for later processing and, if desired, it can be displayed in the browser. This allows you to leverage capabilities not available in ColdFusion but available in the form of external programs or scripts. Of course, with this power come security issues. As a result, you need to weigh carefully your use of `cfexecute` and only use it if it provides needed functionality and doesn't expose you to unnecessary security risk. If used improperly, `cfexecute` can allow developers to execute commands on your system that are potentially destructive or produce unwanted results in terms of system performance or reliability.

PART VI

Integrating with External Services

Chapter 23: Integrating with Flash MX

Chapter 24: Web Services

CHAPTER 23

Integrating with Flash MX

By Jen and Peter deHaan

- Using the Flash MX authoring environment

- Understanding ActionScript

- Integrating ColdFusion using LoadVars

- Flash Remoting MX

- Working with Recordsets in Flash

- Understanding and using DataGlue

- Working with server-side ActionScript

- Integrating Flash Remoting and web services

- Using ColdFusion, Remoting, and web services

Flash MX can be integrated with a back-end technology in many different ways. In the past couple Flash generations, you could use technologies such as PHP, ASP, and ColdFusion to help transfer data. Such integration was useful but rudimentary when compared to what we can now accomplish using Flash as a front end. With the introduction of Flash Remoting MX and the LoadVars object, you are now capable of creating fully dynamic and easily updatable websites using ColdFusion and Flash.

This chapter begins by explaining how to use Flash MX. Although we limit our discussion to what you need in order to understand and complete the examples within this chapter, there are more than enough books on Flash MX and ActionScript available for your further study on the subject. We understand that you are probably only interested in the basics, so we'll help you create a basic GUI that works hand-in-hand with Flash designers. We'll also give you enough information about Flash to allow you to expand upon the examples we provide on your own.

You also explore how to use LoadVars to transfer information to and from the server using ColdFusion. You can easily apply this to other languages such as ASP or PHP. A new way of accomplishing data transfer between a server and Flash MX is by using Flash Remoting. Most of the chapter is devoted to Flash Remoting, perhaps the most exciting integration of technologies available when it comes to Flash. We wrap up with a discussion of integrating web services with ColdFusion and Flash Remoting. By the end of this chapter, you'll be able to go and create your own dynamic Flash interfaces.

Using Flash MX

Flash "movies" have traditionally been used to bring animation to an online audience. However, in recent years, these movies have been used more often as a front end for dynamic server-side applications. The Flash authoring tool now offers much more to developers, particularly with the introduction of Flash Remoting.

This section covers how to set up a basic interface of text fields, buttons, and scroll bars, and the terminology you most commonly use in Flash. We also explain the fundamentals of writing ActionScript. In addition, you learn how to set up interface elements on the Stage, and how to write code to make the application work. Both of these skills take you a long way toward mastering the skills you need to work with a designer.

NOTE   If you are already familiar with the terminology and tool sets within Flash and Action-Script, move on to the section "Integration Using LoadVars," where you begin to integrate Flash MX with ColdFusion.

Building Applications Using Flash

This section gives you a "crash course" in how to create simple Flash movies. We are not going to get into any design or animation elements. Instead, we simply cover what you need to know to make a basic movie that can display information after interacting with ColdFusion. This information enables you to work with Flash designers by creating a prototype application from which they can create an interesting front end.

Setup for the Examples in This Chapter

For the examples in this chapter, you use ColdFusion MX, and you'll also need to install the following:

The Flash MX authoring tool   Download Flash MX or a trial from `http://www.macromedia.com/downloads/`.

The Flash Remoting MX component set for ColdFusion   Install these components after you have installed the Flash MX authoring tool. Download the component set free from `http://www.macromedia.com/software/flashremoting/downloads/components/`.

The latest version of the Flash Player   Make sure you have version 6,0,40,0 or later. The Flash Player is a free download from `http://www.macromedia.com/shockwave/download/download.cgi?P1_Prod_Version=ShockwaveFlash&P5_Language=English`.

The Flash Authoring Environment

Using Flash may be new to many of you, so we will start at the very beginning. When you initially open Flash MX, you have the option of choosing a designer or developer panel layout. Because we assume that you plan to focus your efforts on adding functionality and ActionScript to a Flash movie, it is likely that you will feel most comfortable using the developer layout. This is the layout that we use in this chapter.

Each layout defines a default set of panels that open in the program each time you start it up. *Panels* are where you enter code, select tools, grab components, set properties, and more. (You will take a further look at these panels later in this chapter.)

Refer to Figure 23.1 for an overview of the Flash MX authoring environment.

Animations, applications, and websites can be built using the Flash authoring environment. They are saved as editable `.fla` documents. These files are usually published into a SWF (`.swf`) file or executable for a CD-ROM.

FIGURE 23.1:

The Flash MX developer authoring environment

Actions panel

Tools

Panels

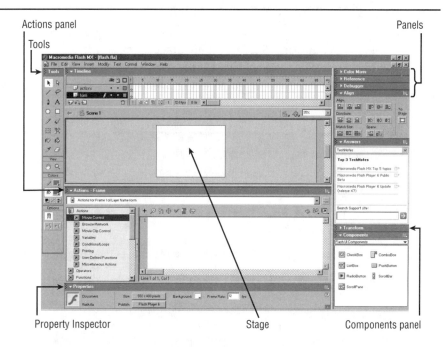

Property Inspector   Stage   Components panel

The Timeline and the Stage

Flash movies are based around a Timeline that contains a sequence of numbered frames. The Timeline helps organize content such as code, graphics, and labels. If you have more than one frame in a movie, a playhead moves along the Timeline until it reaches the last frame containing content (see Figure 23.2).

FIGURE 23.2:

The Timeline

Lock Layers

Layers

Layer name

Actions on frame 1

Playhead

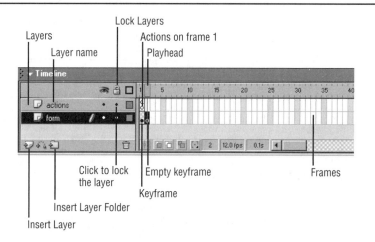

Click to lock the layer

Empty keyframe

Frames

Keyframe

Insert Layer Folder

Insert Layer

Along the Timeline you can have keyframes. A frame with a solid black dot is a keyframe, and an empty circle represents an empty keyframe. *Keyframes* are frames with new or changed content. If you have tweened (animated) content, successive frames between two keyframes are spanned with an arrow that represents the calculations Flash makes to animate the content.

To create a keyframe, select a frame and press F6. You can add content to or remove it from this frame. If you want several frames to span the Timeline with the same content, select a frame later on the same Timeline and layer (these elements are explained in the following paragraph), then press F5. If you want to add content to an empty frame, select the frame and then choose Insert ➤ Blank Keyframe—this adds an empty keyframe to which you can add new content.

The Timeline can contain one or more layers, which are stacked on top of one another. Though it is not necessary to do so, it is common to have all of your ActionScript in a frame called Actions, on the topmost layer. The reason why most Flash developers make a habit of adding code on a layer separate from other content (such as components and movie clips) is because it helps them avoid bugs, conflicts, and unexpected results.

You can name a layer by double-clicking the default name and typing a new one. You might want to organize by putting all components, movie clips, and graphics on their own layers. To add new layers, go to Insert ➤ Layer or press the Insert Layer button below the Layer column. Layers can be grouped together intuitively using Layer folders; just use the Insert Layer Folder button, also under the Layer column, to create these.

NOTE   *Load order,* which determines the order in which your layers are published, is set when you are publishing your movie. If you have code in more than one layer in the same frame, loading it in a different order can affect how this code loads and executes. Publishing is discussed later in the section called "Putting Flash Documents Online."

The Stage represents the front end of your Flash movie. This is where you lay out your interface of text, graphics, and animation. You can use the Toolbox (Ctrl+F2) to add text and graphics, and to access the Select and Zoom tools (see Figure 23.3).

The Library, Panels, and Property Inspector

Flash MX is a multimedia tool, and many different kinds of media can be imported into your movies. Sound (such as MP3 or WAV files), video (MOV, AVI, DV), images (JPG, GIF), or even specialized file formats such as Adobe Illustrator and Macromedia FreeHand and Fireworks can be imported into Flash using File ➤ Import. These are all stored in the Library (F11) as symbols. If these elements are placed on the Stage (by dragging them from the Library), they are then referred to as *instances*.

FIGURE 23.3:
The Toolbox

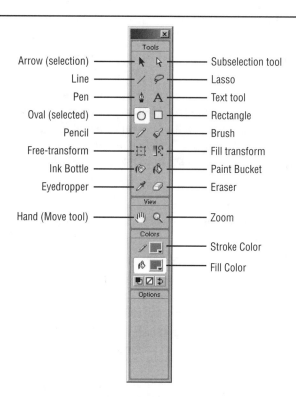

Arrow (selection) —————— Subselection tool
Line —————— Lasso
Pen —————— Text tool
Oval (selected) —————— Rectangle
Pencil —————— Brush
Free-transform —————— Fill transform
Ink Bottle —————— Paint Bucket
Eyedropper —————— Eraser
Hand (Move tool) —————— Zoom
—————— Stroke Color
—————— Fill Color

NOTE You can change the properties of an instance on the Stage. This does not change the properties of other instances, nor does it change the symbol in the Library. If you edit the symbol in the Library, all instances on the Stage will be changed as well.

You can access a special menu in the Library by clicking the button on the upper-right corner of the Library panel. This opens the Options menu where you can create new symbols (see Figure 23.4).

There are many other panels in the Flash interface. The ones you use the most in this chapter are the Components panel, the Library, and the Property Inspector. You can access any panel from the Window menu, and then you can maximize or minimize it using the small arrow button in its upper-left corner. The Property Inspector is context sensitive, meaning what it contains will change depending on what is currently selected in the Flash authoring environment.

FIGURE 23.4:

The Library and its
Options menu

You change the properties of text instances, movie clips, buttons, the Stage, components, and so on, by using the Property Inspector (Ctrl+F3). The Property Inspector is an extremely valuable tool (see Figure 23.5). When you select an instance on the Stage you can use the Property Inspector to give it a name, or you can use it to change properties such as size, coordinates, font, or color. If you select the Stage with your mouse, you can change the dimensions and background color of the Stage, and even the movie's overall frame rate using the Property Inspector.

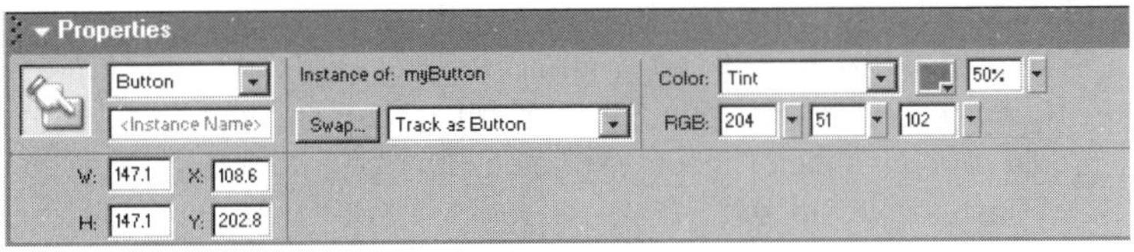

FIGURE 23.5:

The Property Inspector

WARNING Instance names are used to target the object instance using ActionScript. One way to give an instance an instance name is in the `<Instance Name>` field within the Property Inspector. When doing so, do not save your movie with the cursor still in this text field—if you do, a bug in the program reverts your instance name back to whatever was in the field previously (if anything at all). So make sure you click the Stage or the blank area around it before you press Ctrl+S to save your file.

Working with Symbols, Instances, and Components

So far, you have learned that imported elements are stored in the Library as symbols, and when they are on the Stage, they are instances of these symbols. Movie clips, buttons, and graphics created in Flash are also symbols in the Library. Text fields are not stored in the Library, but they are instances of the predetermined `TextField` object in ActionScript.

TIP There is a library of premade buttons and movie clips available right inside Flash. Go to Window ➤ Common Libraries to open it. Premade components (such as buttons, tool-tips and user interface elements) are available online, which you can download and then install into Flash. To access them, go to the Flash exchange at `http://www.macromedia` `.com/exchange/flash`.

Buttons, movie clips, components, and dynamic or input text fields can be controlled using ActionScript if they are given a unique instance name. In the following sections, you will learn about these different kinds of instances and how you use them in your documents.

Text Fields

You certainly use a lot of text fields in the following exercises. There are three kinds of text fields: *static*, *input*, and *dynamic*. As you might have guessed, static text fields don't change. Input text fields are fields in which the end user types in text. Dynamic text fields are used to display text or variables that are internally set, externally loaded, or dynamically changed during runtime.

You can select a font and a font size for your dynamic and input text in the Property Inspector, but the end user must have this font installed on their system. If the end user does not have the font, a default font is used.

TIP You can create new font symbols in your movie by selecting the Library's Options menu and choosing New Font. Font symbols are useful when you want to use a specialized font in your dynamic or input text fields. Just be aware that using font symbols increases the Flash movie file size.

Static text is unchanging text, and the outlines of it are embedded in your movie. Therefore, the end user does not need to have the font type installed on their computer.

Movie Clips

Sometimes called MCs, movie clips are usually an integral part of your Flash movie. Movie clips are like mini-movies because they each have a Timeline that runs independently from the main Timeline. You can have many instances of a movie clip on the Stage, and you can give each one a separate instance name so that you can control each one independently.

To create a movie clip, select an object or graphic on the Stage, and press F8. From the Convert To Symbol dialog box, select the Movie Clip radio button. The selected item, now a movie clip, can be given an instance name and manipulated using ActionScript. In this chapter, you use components for many exercises; be aware that many such tasks could use movie clips as well. When you are working with Flash designers, you run across movie clips frequently.

Buttons

Either movie clips or button instances can be used for buttons in Flash. Movie clips offer you more functionality, but for basic applications or prototypes (as in this chapter), simple buttons will certainly suffice. Buttons typically have four states: up, over (hover), down (press) and hit (the area where the button is clickable).

You do not create buttons in this chapter; instead you use prebuilt instances from the Common Libraries and Components panels (described in the next section). The Flash UI Component set that ship with Flash includes what is called a PushButton component, which has four states already built for you. You'll see how to use the PushButton component later in this chapter.

TIP   Graphics are imported and drawn in a raw state. Before you publish a movie, you want to make each raw graphic a symbol. To do so, select it, press F8, and select the Graphic radio button.

Components

Components are self-contained movie clips that you can drag and drop onto the Stage. You will find components especially useful when you are reusing applications or code blocks that are needed for multiple applications. Components are easily transferred to other movies or to other developers. They can also expedite the interface building process; this is especially evident when you use the Flash UI Component set. This set ships with Flash and is already installed within the Flash authoring environment. To access this set, open up the Components panel (Ctrl+F7), and use the drop-down menu at the top of the panel to select Flash UI Components (see Figure 23.6).

FIGURE 23.6:

The Flash
UI Component
set in the
Components panel

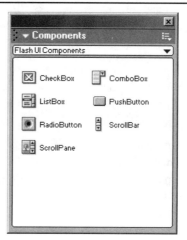

This component set includes some of the most commonly used interface elements: buttons, scroll bars, panes, and list and selection boxes. They are made to function like traditional GUIs, as is seen in Table 23.1.

TABLE 23.1: Flash UI Component Functionality and HTML Equivalents

Component	Functionality	HTML Equivalent
CheckBox	Typical check box	Input type = `checkbox`
ComboBox	HTML select box	Select and Option
ListBox	Multiple select box	
PushButton	Button	Input type = `button` or Input type = `submit`
RadioButton	Typical radio button	Input type = `radio`
ScrollBar	Typical scroll bar	n/a
ScrollPane	n/a	n/a

Now that you have an idea of how the components function, let's try them out. The Property inspector is where you can enter values that can be used in conjunction with ActionScript to control components, or change what they look like. Drag and drop a component onto the Stage, select it, and open the Property Inspector. The Property Inspector includes two tabs:

The Parameters tab   This tab allows you to enter labels, data, and variables. You can also use the options on this tab to designate a Click or Change Handler for the component or give the component an instance name.

The Properties tab   This tab allows you to change the component visually.

NOTE   The Flash UI Component Set uses Change Handlers and Click Handlers to call named functions on the Timeline on which the component is placed. Simply add the function name for this value and the function is called.

Putting Flash Documents Online

You need to publish a Flash document in order to create a SWF file. The SWF file can be put online, and the Flash plug-in (player) is used to play the SWF movie in a browser.

NOTE   You can also create Flash movies as executables (or Projectors), which are commonly put on CD-ROMs. *Projectors* are self-contained movies that contain your SWF movie as well as the Flash player all within an `.exe`.

You must publish your movie as a Flash 6 document (Flash MX corresponds to the Flash Player 6) for the examples in this chapter. This is because you will be writing ActionScript (and using Remoting) that is specific to Flash MX. You must also use the ColdFusion MX server for the same reason.

To publish a movie, begin by selecting File ➤ Publish. This creates a SWF and an HTML file, which are set to the default (or current) settings, that you can upload to your server. These files are created in the same directory the current FLA file is in.

If you want to change the settings, select File ➤ Publish Settings, which opens the Publish Settings dialog box shown in Figure 23.7.

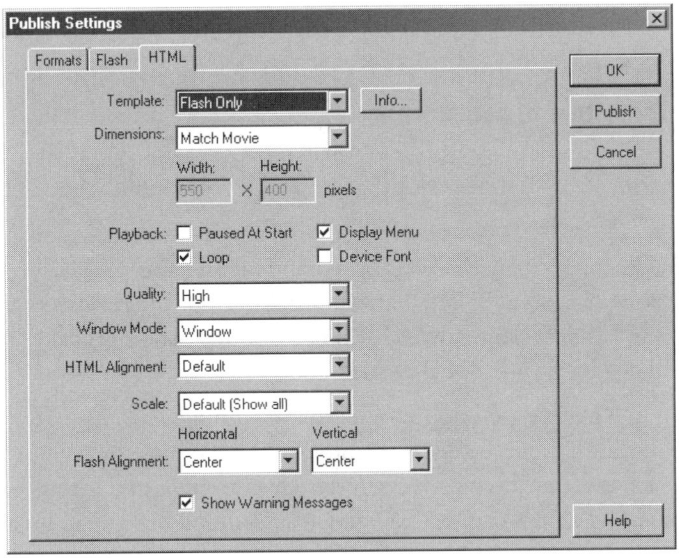

FIGURE 23.7:

The HTML tab of the Publish Settings dialog box

In the Publish Settings dialog box, the Flash tab is used to select a player version. You can leave the default settings as they are for the duration of this chapter. However, you might want to select Omit Trace Actions to slightly decrease the file size and run times, and Protect From Import so others cannot import the SWF file into a new Flash document. Remember to select the Omit Trace Actions after you have finished editing your ActionScript because trace actions are disabled in the testing environment as well.

Movies are usually embedded within HTML pages. The HTML tab includes settings that allow you to change the HTML code in your document. You probably want to leave these settings at their defaults. You can either customize the code in the HTML file that is written to your directory or add the `<object>` and `<embed>` content from the published file to an existing web page.

> **TIP**   By no means is this a comprehensive section on using the Flash interface. However, what you have explored so far is ample to enable you to build the files that you create in this chapter. If you are interested in learning more about using Flash MX, check out *Flash MX Savvy*, by Ethan Watrall and Norbert Herber (Sybex, 2002).

An Overview of ActionScript

Since you are using Flash MX to develop prototype applications, you are mainly using the Flash scripting language, ActionScript, to create interactive movies. Over the past few generations of Flash, ActionScript has developed into a robust and transferable scripting language.

> **NOTE**   Flash can be so developer-centric that you can create entire working applications using it, without placing a single graphic element on the Stage or in the Library.

The Nature of ActionScript

ActionScript is a scripting language that uses dot syntax. It is extremely similar to JavaScript, so if you are familiar with that language you certainly have a head start when you go to write ActionScript.

ActionScript is ECMA-262-compliant and generally follows ECMA's restrictions and standards. You should note that ActionScript follows the *scope chain* concept, as defined by ECMA standards. Meaning, you are able to define local or global variables, global objects (all predefined objects are global), and so forth.

You delve right into ActionScript beginning with the section "Integration Using `LoadVars`," but throughout the entire chapter we explain how the script is used as you progress through each exercise. If you are interested in the details and intricacies of ActionScript, check out *Flash MX ActionScript: The Developer's Edge*, by Scott Hamlin and Jennifer Hall (Sybex, 2002).

Flash and Objects

Predetermined objects in Flash are objects that are already built into Flash. You make a new instance of these objects using a new constructor, such as:

```
var myVars = new LoadVars();
```

which in this case makes a new instance of the LoadVars object. Then you are able to work with the methods, events, and properties of the object.

LoadVars is an example of a predetermined object that you use later on in the section called "Integration Using LoadVars." Others include TextField, String, Array, MovieClip, and XML. These built-in objects have methods, properties, and sometimes events.

NOTE   In Flash, you are also able to define your own class and instantiate "homemade" objects of your own. The particulars are beyond the scope of this chapter, but you might want to check out a book or website that contains advanced topics in ActionScript for details.

Case Sensitivity

Some words in the ActionScript language are case-sensitive (for example, function, instanceof, and for), but in most cases, they are not. This is one difference between strict compliance to ECMA-262 and ActionScript; in strict ECMA-compliant languages, strict case-sensitivity is necessary. Just make sure that your ActionScript actions are color-coded in the Actions panel or match its entry in the ActionScript Reference (Shift+F1). However, it is good practice to double-check the case of your code when you are troubleshooting because incorrectly capitalized case-sensitive ActionScript does not work when the movie is tested or published.

Common Naming Conventions

It is common practice to adopt naming conventions when you are writing code in ActionScript. If you poke around tutorials or sources files, you find that mixed capitalization (myVar) and underscores (my_var) are both used.

If you want to use code hinting, however, you must use specific suffixes. This concept is discussed in the upcoming section "Code Hints." Typically, mixed capitalization is used, followed by an underscore suffix such as myClip_mc.

WARNING   ActionScript has many keywords, including predetermined object names. These keywords—in fact, any ActionScript object, method, property, or action—should *never be used* as instance or variable names in your code. If you do this, your movie might not work or it may run in an unexpected manner.

It's unwise to begin your variable names with numbers or underscores. Similarly, you shouldn't use special characters in your variable names. Macromedia makes specific recommendations in a white paper on coding best practices for ActionScript; these can be found at the following URL:

```
http://www.macromedia.com/desdev/mx/flash/whitepapers/actionscript_standards.p
df
```

Using Dynamic Content

You are probably familiar with the annoying tendency of movies to have long loading processes. Using new advancements in Flash, developers are striving to keep this loading to a minimum.

A good way to do this is to dynamically load JPG images, MP3 sounds, variables, and textual content, when the end user requests them. You can accomplish this using ActionScript such as `loadMovie`, `loadSound`, `XML.load`, and the `LoadVars` object. You can also use Flash Remoting to load dynamic content to minimize load times. By using some or all of these methods, the end user's wait time can be kept to a minimum.

Where to Put Your Code

Before you can write code, you need to know where to put it. There are two places you can put ActionScript: on a frame (called *frame code*), or on an instance (called *object code*).

NOTE   For ease of use, editing and transferability, it is best to *put all of your code in frame scripts and avoid object code altogether*. All of the instances on the Stage can be targeted from ActionScript on a Timeline. One of the most annoying aspects of version 5 and earlier editions of Flash is that the code wound up in many different locations, which made it very difficult to dissect and edit the FLA files. This is not the case in Flash MX, which is developer-friendly, so it's a good idea to try to put all of your code in one place.

Let's take a look at the Actions panel. Open up Flash MX, and then press F9 to open the Actions panel, which is shown in Figure 23.8. ActionScript is entered in the Script pane within this panel. In this chapter, you need to use Expert mode, which allows you to type ActionScript freely into the Script pane. Select the Options menu on the upper-right corner of the Actions panel to switch to Expert mode.

FIGURE 23.8:

The Actions panel

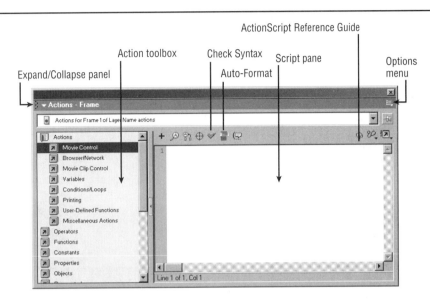

Inside the Actions panel there is an Actions toolbox that contains actions, methods, properties, and object constructors. Even when you are using Expert mode, you can still double-click the elements in the ActionScript toolbox to add them automatically to your code.

Two useful features on this panel are the Check Syntax and Auto Format buttons, both of which are found above the Script pane. Respectively, these features help you find errors in your code, and make it much easier to read. Also in the Actions panel is the Reference button, which opens the ActionScript Reference Guide. This Reference explains and gives examples for all of the objects and actions in ActionScript. These features can be extremely useful when you are new to the language.

Code Hints

A discussion on the Actions panel is not complete unless code hints are mentioned. When you are creating instance or object names, you might consider writing a suffix that enables *code hinting* in the Actions panel.

To do so, open the Actions panel and type the following line:

```
myXML_xml.
```

When you do, a code hint pop-up menu appears in the Actions panel. This menu allows you to select methods and properties for predetermined objects (such as XML). The suffixes that are available are shown in Table 23.2.

TABLE 23.2: ActionScript Suffixes

Object	Suffix Required
Array	_array
Button	_btn
Color	_color
Date	_date
MovieClip	_mc
NetConnection	_conn
Sound	_sound
String	_str
TextField	_txt
TextFormat	_fmt
XML	_xml
XMLSocket	_xmlsocket

NOTE   There are more suffixes, most of which are only used with the Flash Communication Server and components. Refer to Flash Help (F1) where you can search for a complete list.

Integration Using LoadVars

Now that you have a grasp on Flash's authoring environment, and the code structure and features of ActionScript, you should be ready to start integrating your knowledge of ColdFusion MX with Flash. Essentially, there are two different ways you can integrate ColdFusion with Flash MX, and each has its own pros and cons. You can use LoadVars to send name/value pairs, or for a more robust technology (and if you are planning on taking advantage of web services), you can use Flash Remoting, which is discussed in the last section of this chapter.

Of course, Flash Remoting might be too complicated for your application. If you simply want to pass variables or simple text content, you may want to use LoadVars to load a .txt document. If this is too complicated, perhaps simply using getURL to load a variable into Flash will be sufficient.

NOTE   Both LoadVars and Flash Remoting require the end user to have the Flash Player 6 installed.

Flash and the LoadVars Object

Integrating Flash and ColdFusion is quite simple when you are using the LoadVars object. LoadVars allows you to transfer variables to and from a server in name/value pairs. It is a useful technology to know, because it is also what you use to integrate other languages such as PHP or ASP.

Before you can use the LoadVars object to transfer data, you must use a constructor to create a new instance of the object, as shown here:

```
myVars = new LoadVars();
```

Some of the most common uses for LoadVars involve downloading data, posting variables, or posting and then sending a response back to the movie. Table 23.3 lists the methods used in this section.

TABLE 23.3: Methods Used in This Section

Commonly Used Method	What It Does
load	Downloads variables from a specified server to a Flash movie.
send	Posts variables from the Flash movie in name/value pairs to a specified server.
sendAndLoad	Posts variables from the Flash movie in name/value pairs to a server and then loads the response from the server into an object.

You also employ the onLoad event handler in this section. This handler is used to call a function when data from either the load or sendAndLoad processes has finished loading to Flash.

You can also use the properties of the LoadVars object to check that the data has been loaded, and to check the data MIME type. You can also create a callback function to indicate when the data has been loaded. For more information on callback functions, refer to the section "Your First Flash Remoting Document" later in this chapter.

TIP   You may hear mention of the loadVariables action. This now-deprecated action was an earlier and more simplistic way of working with server-side integration. The LoadVars object is more robust, and we strongly recommend that you work with this new object instead.

LoadVars can be used with many different server-side languages to transfer name/value pairs to and from a Flash movie. It is quite useful, allowing you to send data and then receive the server's reply back to the movie.

TIP   The XML object in Flash works similarly to the LoadVars object. It is useful when you need to transfer XML formatted structures, even out of ColdFusion!

Building a Mail Application Using LoadVars

In this example, you create a simple mail application that connects a Flash movie to the ColdFusion application server using the `LoadVars` object in ActionScript. Let's start by setting up the Stage.

1. Create a new document in Flash by selecting File ➢ New. You'll see a blank Stage, and the Actions panel (F9) Script pane is empty.

2. Save your file in `<webroot>\CFMXHandbook\mail\` as `sendMail.fla`.

3. Rename your default layer, currently called Layer 1, to **actions** by simply double-clicking the existing name, and typing in a new one.

4. Then click the dot beside the layer name and under the Lock icon. This locks the actions layer so that you can't place or move any objects on this layer by accident. (You should work with the actions layer locked throughout this chapter.)

5. Create a new layer by going to Insert ➢ Layer and rename the layer to **form**. Move this layer to the bottom of the Layers column by clicking it and dragging it below the actions layer. The following graphic shows how your Timeline should now look.

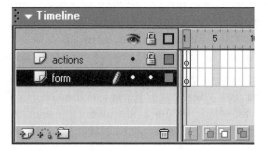

Next you need to create several text fields on the Stage to start building the mail form.

1. Begin by selecting the Text tool by clicking it (or by pressing T on the keyboard), and then open the Property Inspector (Ctrl+F3).

2. You have to set the Text properties before you create the fields. Set the Text type to Static Text in the Property Inspector and then set the Font and Font Size so they are legible on the Stage. You can also change the text color and justification as you see fit.

3. With the Text tool still selected, click anywhere on the Stage to create the first of four text fields.

4. For the first field, type **From:**. Since static text cannot be manipulated using ActionScript, you cannot assign it an instance name.

5. Create three more text fields and type in **To:**, **Subject:**, and **Message:** and position them on the Stage.

TIP You can use the Align panel (Ctrl+K) to align instances or objects on the Stage. This is particularly useful for forms. This panel can be used to center, space, or align instances to each other or to the Stage. If you want to align them to the Stage, make sure that you have the To Stage button activated. You can also position instances by selecting the instance and setting precise coordinates using the X and Y text fields in the Property Inspector.

6. Reselect the Text Tool and change the Text Type from Static Text to Input Text. Make sure that the Render Text As HTML button is *not* selected and that Show Border Around Text is turned on. If you are using HTML tags, you have to enable the Render Text As HTML button for the text field, and set the `.htmlText` property instead of the `.text` property. Your settings should match those in the Figure 23.9.

NOTE The following HTML tags and attributes are supported: `<a>`, `<b>`, `<font color>`, `<font face>`, `<font size>`, `<i>`, `<p>`, `<u>`, LEFTMARGIN, RIGHTMARGIN, ALIGN, INDENT, and LEADING.

7. Click the Stage and drag a rectangle that represents the size you want your input text field to be.

8. Make sure the text field is selected, and give it an instance name of **from_txt** in the `<Instance Name>` field of the Property Inspector. Position it beside the From: label you created earlier.

9. Repeat this process for two more input text fields. Assign them instance names of **to_txt** and **subject_txt** and align them accordingly. The Property Inspector should now look like Figure 23.9.

FIGURE 23.9:

The Property Inspector for an Input Text field

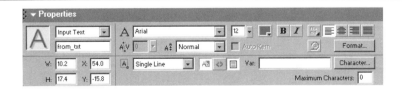

Next you'll create a text field for the body of the e-mail.

1. Create a larger text field for the e-mail message, and give it an instance name of **message_txt** in the Property Inspector.

2. Change its Line type from Single Line to Multiline.

NOTE   Multiline is similar to using `<textarea>` in HTML.

3. Open the Components panel (Ctrl+F7) and drag an instance of the ScrollBar component over the new `message_txt` text field, and it attaches (snaps) to the field. Make sure that in the Parameters tab of the Property Inspector the Target text field value has changed to `message_txt`.

   This component attaches a scroll bar resized to the height of the text field. If the end user types a long message, then they can easily scroll the text up and down if they need to edit it.

WARNING   Make sure that you have Snap enabled (View ➤ Snap To Objects) or the Component will not attach to the text field. If you are having problems with it snapping, try dragging the component from left to right, releasing it when it is directly over the field.

4. Now drag an instance of the PushButton component onto the Stage. Position it at the bottom of the form and give it an instance name of **send_btn**.

5. Select the PushButton instance on the Stage and then open the Property Inspector. Make sure that you have the Parameters tab selected, as shown in Figure 23.10.

FIGURE 23.10:

The Property Inspector for with Parameters tab selected

6. Then select the Label field in the Parameters tab to and type in **Send**. Select the Click Handler field and type **sendMessage**. Figure 23.11 shows the Stage layout that you just produced.

TIP   The Label parameter is the text labeling that appears on the PushButton, similar to `<input type="button" name="send_btn" value="Send">` in HTML. The Click Handler is the name of the function that is executed when a user clicks the `button` instance. It is similar to adding `onClick='sendMessage();'` to the HTML input button analogy that we discussed earlier.

FIGURE 23.11:

The Stage layout

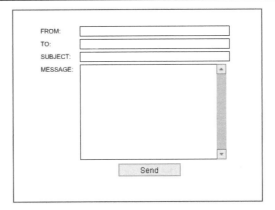

Now that you have everything created and ready to use, the only thing left to do for the Flash application is to open the Actions panel and write some ActionScript. Select frame 1 of the actions layer in the Timeline, and type the code in Listing 23.1 into the Script pane of the Actions panel:

Listing 23.1   Send Mail (sendMail_final.fla)

```
/*
   Name:          /c23/ sendMail_final.fla
   Description:   Send mail using LoadVars
*/

function sendMessage() {
  var params = new LoadVars();
  params.from = from_txt.text;
  params.to = to_txt.text;
  params.subject = subject_txt.text;
  params.message = message_txt.text;
  params.sendAndLoad("sendMail.cfm", params, "POST");
  params.onLoad = function(success) {
    if (success) {
      from_txt.text = "";
      to_txt.text = "";
      subject_txt.text = "";
      message_txt.text = "";
    }
  };
}
```

Let's go over this code line by line. The first line is simply the name of the function. You'll notice that the name of the function, sendMessage(), is the same name that you typed into the Click Handler for the send_btn PushButton instance earlier. When a user clicks on the Send button, this function is invoked.

Next a local variable called params is created, and it in turn creates a constructor for the LoadVars object. In the next four lines, four parameters are added to the params object. The values of these parameters are taken from what the user enters into the text input fields in the Flash application. Also, as you can see in the code block, you must reference each text field by adding a .text suffix to each instance name.

The LoadVars sendAndLoad method is then called. It is used to post the variables in the params object to the sendMail.cfm template. The three parameters in the sendAndLoad method are the URL to submit to, the object used to receive any variables that are passed back to Flash from the CF template, and the method you are using when submitting the variables. The two options for the method are POST and GET, which behave the same as they do when you are submit an HTML form. These options affect how variables are referenced in the CF template (either FORM or URL scoped variables).

Now consider the next section of code:

```
params.onLoad = function(success) {
  if (success) {
    from_txt.text = "";
    to_txt.text = "";
    subject_txt.text = "";
    message_txt.text = "";
  }
};
```

onLoad is what's known as an event handler and is invoked when the sendAndLoad() or load() function has received data. For this example you are using an inline function (also referred to as an anonymous function) that is executed when the event handler is triggered. You have one parameter, success, which is a Boolean value holding whether or not the operation is successful. If no errors occur in the ColdFusion template, then success is true and you clear the Flash form.

You could create one more text field instance as static text and use the status flag to show the user a message about whether the operation completed successfully. However, note that this cannot be used to detect whether or not the e-mail address was valid or a real person, it can only detect if ColdFusion threw an exception while parsing the sendMessage.cfm template.

The final code you need to write for the mail application is for the .cfm template. To do so, create a new file called sendMail.cfm in the same directory as your .FLA file and enter the code in Listing 23.2.

Listing 23.2   **Send Mail (sendMail.cfm)**

```
<!---
   Name:          /c23/ sendMail.cfm
   Description:   send mail
--->

<cfsetting enableCFOutputOnly="Yes" />

<cftry>
  <cfparam name="Form.From" type="string" />
  <cfparam name="Form.To" type="string" />
  <cfparam name="Form.Subject" type="string" />
  <cfparam name="Form.Message" type="string" />

  <cfmail to="#Form.To#" from="#Form.From#"
          subject="#Form.Subject#"> #Form.Message#
  </cfmail>
  <cfset result = 1 />

  <cfcatch type="Any">
    <cfset result = 0 />
  </cfcatch>
</cftry>

<cfoutput>&result=#result#</cfoutput>

<cfsetting enableCFOutputOnly="No" />
```

By using `enablecfoutputonly="Yes"`, this code begins by making sure that any extra white-space that might be generated by ColdFusion is suppressed. Then the `cfparam` tag is used to make sure all the required fields have been passed to the template.

Following this, the `cfmail` tag is used to send an e-mail message using the supplied parameters. If no exceptions have been caught in the `cftry` block then a variable called `result` is set. This variable is given a value of 1. If you do encounter an error, then `result` is set to 0. Finally the value of the `result` variable is output, the results of which are sent back to Flash. This output can be used to provide some additional error checking.

With all the code in place, you can now test and publish the e-mail application. Save all of the files in the same directory, and test your movie in a browser window by pressing Ctrl+F12. Another way to go is to publish the movie by selecting File ➤ Publish, and then test the documents by uploading them to your server.

Now that you have experienced transferring data using the `LoadVars` object between Flash and an application server, it is time to try accomplishing this in a different manner. The following section incorporates the principles of Flash Remoting, using a service to transfer data between a SWF file and an application server such as ColdFusion.

Flash Remoting MX

Flash Remoting MX is used to connect an application server to Flash MX so that data can be transferred between the two. Flash Remoting uses a binary transmission method called *Action Message Format (AMF)* to transfer data. AMF is also the method of transmission used by the Flash Communication Server (FlashCom).

Flash Remoting can connect to .NET, Java, and SOAP applications as well as ColdFusion and JRun 4. However, if you use any of these technologies other than CFMX or JRun 4, you need to download a trial version or purchase Remoting software from Macromedia. The trial reverts to a developer edition after 30 days.

Using Remoting for Communication

Flash Remoting is a service facilitating communication between a Flash movie and an application server. Remoting is essentially two things put together:

- First of all, the ColdFusion Application Server includes a built-in server Gateway that is specifically for Remoting. This allows Flash to connect directly to the application server.

NOTE *A* Gateway simply refers to what is enabling Flash to directly communicate with an application server such as ColdFusion when it is running in a Flash player. All data transfer between the player and the application logic running on the server is handled by the Gateway.

- Flash Remoting is also a set of components installed on your computer. This includes APIs for the Flash authoring environment, and the ActionScript (.as) files that are compiled into your movie when it's published.

As you can see in Figure 23.12, Remoting works by making calls to the application server for certain procedures. A call is made for the service, and then the application waits until the data is returned to process it. Callback functions are used to handle these events.

FIGURE 23.12:

How Flash Remoting transfers data

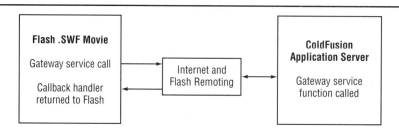

Flash .SWF Movie

Gateway service call

Callback handler returned to Flash

Internet and Flash Remoting

ColdFusion Application Server

Gateway service function called

Every Remoting application fundamentally works in the following way:

- The Flash movie must include the ActionScript files (.as files) that are functions specific to Flash Remoting.

- A connection to the Flash Remoting service Gateway must be made.

- Service functions are called from Flash and parameters are passed to the application server.

- The data is returned to the SWF file and then it is processed using callback functions (event handlers).

Installing the Remoting Components

In order to get started with Flash Remoting and ColdFusion, you need to download the Remoting component set. See the "Setup for the Examples in This Chapter" sidebar earlier in the chapter.

The components you install are not visual—that is, they are APIs and ActionScript include files that are installed on the client side (in Flash) and are unlike the components you drag from the Components panel to the Stage. When you download the component set, it installs APIs that are required in the Flash MX authoring environment for Remoting to work. The component set also includes the classes that you need to compile into your movies for Remoting to work using `include` statements.

Flash Remoting has several classes that are used to connect to a server, manipulate content, and help process it in Flash. These classes are defined when you use the `#include` action to compile them in a Flash Remoting movie. These classes are `NetConnection`, `NetServices`, `DataGlue`, `NetDebug`, and `RecordSet`, and each is explained in relation to the exercises later in this chapter.

NOTE   The Flash Remoting service does not have an administrator like the one in ColdFusion Application Server.

The following section runs through a basic Flash Remoting document, covering the fundamental steps for setting up a service. You learn how to use the Remoting service to call a ColdFusion component, and then use the NetConnection Debugger to debug your Flash movie. Start up Flash MX, and let's get going!

Your First Flash Remoting Document

In this section, you begin by creating a new Flash Remoting project from a template. The HelloWorld example is a simple Flash Remoting application that shows you how Flash communicates with ColdFusion Components (CFCs) and templates. It also demonstrates the roles of each application.

Here, you use Flash as the visual interface and have it call remote functions in the CFCs and then receive data back from the ColdFusion Application Server.

NOTE   In this section you return simple strings from the server. In later examples we'll work with queries and their ActionScript equivalent, RecordSets.

This example walks you through the basic layout of a Remoting file and the general syntax used to call remote templates and functions. We also explore an excellent tool for debugging Flash/ColdFusion communication using the NetConnection Debugger.

Setting Up Flash and Adding ActionScript

To set up Flash, follow these steps:

1. In Flash MX, select File ➢ New From Template....

2. When the New Document dialog box opens, select Web from the Category list and then Basic from the Category Items list.

3. Then click the Create button. A new document opens, and if you open the Actions panel (F9), you see the code shown in Listing 23.3. (This listing has been slightly reformatted for readability and spacing.)

Listing 23.3   Template

```
/*
    Name:           /c23/template.fla
    Description:    default template
*/
#include "NetServices.as"
// uncomment this line when you want to use
//the NetConnect debugger
//#include "NetDebug.as"
// ----------------------------------------
// Handlers for user interaction events
// ----------------------------------------
// This gets called when the "aaaa" button is
//clicked
function aaaa_Clicked() {
// ... put code here
// For example, you could call the "bbbb"
//function of "my.service" by doing:
// myService.bbbb(123, "abc");
}
// ----------------------------------------
// Handlers for data coming in from server
// ----------------------------------------
```

```
// This gets called with the results of calls
//to the server function "bbbb".
function bbbb_Result(result) {
// ... put code here
// For example, if the result is a
//RecordSet, you could display it in a
//ListBox by doing:
// myListBox.setDataProvider(result);
}
// ----------------------------------------
// Application initialization
// ----------------------------------------
if (inited == null) {
  // do this code only once
  inited = true;
  // set the default Gateway URL (this is used
  //only in authoring)

  NetServices.setDefaultGatewayUrl(
    "http://localhost:8100/flashservices/gateway");
  // connect to the Gateway
  gateway_conn = NetServices.createGatewayConnection();
  // get a reference to a service
  myService = gateway_conn.getService("my.service", this);
}
stop();
```

Let's step through Listing 23.3 line by line.

First you have the include files. The ActionScript #include action is the equivalent to ColdFusion's cfinclude tag. The external template is compiled into the movie when you select Control ➤ Test Movie, File ➤ Publish, or File ➤ Export Movie.... Take note that the include action, unlike other ActionScript actions, isn't terminated by a semicolon (;).

For this example you only need to include the NetServices.as file. This file is responsible for setting out the default Gateway URL, which is used to specify where Flash locates the Flash Remoting Gateway. This file also handles another function called createGatewayConnection, which creates a NetConnection object used to make connections to the application server using the Flash Remoting service.

NOTE   The actual connections aren't established until you call a remote function (such as when you invoke a CF component function).

The second include is NetDebug.as, which is used when you want to use the NetConnection Debugger (which can be accessed in Flash MX by selecting Window ➤ NetConnection Debugger). The Debugger allows you to view information being passed between the Flash client and the Flash Remoting server, which is described later in this section. You will find the debugger to be very helpful when you are debugging your application and seeing which data has been returned to your Flash application from the application server. We'll cover the NetConnection Debugger in more detail in the section called "Using the NetConnection Debugger."

NOTE By default the `NetDebug.as` isn't included in your application and the line is commented out. This line should only be restored when you are developing or debugging your application. `NetDebug.as` should never be included in the final production code because it adds unnecessary overhead.

Next you see the following code:

```
function aaaa_Clicked() {
// For example, you could call the "bbbb"
// function of "my.service" by doing:
// myService.bbbb(123, "abc");
}
```

This code is only executed when a user clicks a button in your movie with the instance name aaaa. You won't be using this code for the sample application, so you can delete these lines.

The next code block you encounter is as follows:

```
function bbbb_Result(result) {
// For example, if the result is a RecordSet,
//you could display it in a ListBox by doing:
// myListBox.setDataProvider(result);
}
```

Function bbbb_Result is what is known as a *callback function*. The function is executed when Flash receives a successful result from the ColdFusion Application Server via Remoting. Being able to have methods trigger when the data arrives is the true power of Flash Remoting.

NOTE The important thing is that this function is only executed if you had a ColdFusion component function named bbbb or a ColdFusion template called bbbb.cfm. This is discussed in the section "Creating the Hello World CFC."

The following code is where you initialize the Flash application:

```
if (inited == null) {
  inited = true;
  // set the default Gateway URL (this is used
  // only in authoring)
  NetServices.setDefaultGatewayUrl(
    "http://localhost:8100/flashservices/gateway");
  gateway_conn = NetServices.createGatewayConnection();
  myService = gateway_conn.getService("my.service", this);
}
```

First, this code checks to see if the application has already been initialized and, if it has, the code block is ignored.

This block is where the Flash Remoting Gateway and connections get defined. You begin by setting the default Gateway URL to the local server.

NOTE   There is a slight error in the default template that Flash creates. The template sets the Gateway URL to port 8100 on the local server. If you are using the internal ColdFusion web server, then you will need to change this to port 8500 unless you have remapped the default port number. If you are using IIS or another web server, then you will likely have to modify the port to which you are trying to connect.

Next you define your Gateway connection by calling `NetServices.createGateway-Connection()`. It is important to understand that the actual connection is not established at this point. The connection is made when you call your remote CFC functions or CFML templates.

Next, you name your handle to a CFC or CFML template:

```
myService = gateway_conn.getService("my.service", this);
```

`my.service` is a string allowing you to identify the name of the Flash Remoting service. If you are connecting to a CFC, then it becomes a file named `<webroot>/my/service.cfc`, or if you are connecting to a CFML template, then Flash tries to find a directory named `<webroot>/my/service/`.

The final `this` defines how Flash will handle responses from the Flash Remoting service. You will see how this all ties together in a minute, but first let's create the Hello World application.

Creating the Hello World CFC

Begin by creating a file named `HelloWorldCFC.cfc` in the `<webroot>\CFMXHandbook\HelloWorld\` directory. To do so, open the CFC and type in the following code:

```
<cfcomponent>
  <cffunction name="sayHelloWorld"
access="remote" returntype="string" output="No">
    <cfreturn "Hello World (cfc)" />
  </cffunction>
</cfcomponent>
```

This is a very simple component that doesn't really require any explanation other then the fact that you've set the `access` parameter to `remote` so that Flash can access this function.

Adding the ActionScript

Now return to Flash so that you can revise the file; at this point you are going to call the remote function. Do this by first opening the Actions panel (F9) and enter the code from Listing 23.4.

Listing 23.4   **Hello World (helloWorld_final.fla)**

```
/*
   Name:          /c23/ HelloWorld_final.fla
   Description:   HelloWorld example
*/
#include "NetServices.as"
// uncomment this line when you want to use
//the NetConnect Debugger
// #include "NetDebug.as"
// -------------------------------------------
// Handlers for data coming in from server
// -------------------------------------------
function sayHelloWorld_Result(r) {
  trace("result: "+ r);
}
function sayHelloWorld_Status(s) {
  trace("error: "+ s.description);
}
// -------------------------------------------
// Application initialization
// -------------------------------------------
if (inited == null) {
  inited = true;
  NetServices.setDefaultGatewayUrl(
    "http://localhost:8500/flashservices/gateway");
  gateway_conn = NetServices.createGatewayConnection();
  myService = gateway_conn.getService(
    "CFMXHandbook.HelloWorld.HelloWorldCFC", this);
  myService.sayHelloWorld();
}
stop();
```

You can see that most of this code is similar to the default template discussed earlier. However, a couple of functions have been added to the Handlers section, and some minor changes and additions have been made to the initialization section. In addition, some comments have been removed for readability. Let's continue by stepping through the initialization section.

You may have noticed that some small changes have been made to this section. First, the port number on the default Gateway URL has been changed to port 8500.

TIP   You can easily create a custom Remoting template in Flash. Make the changes you want to the FLA file, and then select File ➢ Save As Template. A dialog box opens where you can name the template, and give it a location and description. Press Save, and the next time you open a new template the file will be available.

Modifications have been made to the `getService` function so it works with the file structure. This is very similar to referencing a component using `cfinvoke`. This method will look for the CF component named `HelloWorldCFC.cfc` in the `<webroot>\CFMXHandbook\HelloWorld\` directory.

```
myService = gateway_conn.getService(
  "CFMXHandbook.HelloWorld.HelloWorldCFC", this);
```

Then the `sayHelloWorld()` function is called in the CFC. Let's take a closer look at what is going on behind the scenes. You have a CFC with a function named `sayHelloWorld`, and you can also see that there are two functions defined in the Handlers section near the beginning of the ActionScript listing. There are two functions: `sayHelloWorld_Result()` and `sayHelloWorld_Status()`.

The first one, `sayHelloWorld_Result()`, is automatically called when you receive a response from the `myService.sayHelloWorld()` function call. The `sayHelloWorld_Result()` function should only be invoked when the Flash movie successfully receives data back from the `sayHelloWorld()` function. If there is an error, then the second function, `sayHelloWorld_Status()`, is invoked and the application shows you the error message in the Output window.

NOTE   The `trace` action only outputs information when you are testing the movie. Nothing is displayed when you publish the movie and test it live on a web server.

Testing the Application

What we have just done in this exercise is all that you need in order to test the Flash Remoting application. You can test the code by selecting Control ≻ Test Movie or by pressing Ctrl+Enter on the keyboard. If everything works, then the Output window in Flash appears and you see "`result: Hello World (cfc)` " in this window. If there is an error, then you will see something similar to "`error: Service threw an exception during method invocation: ...` " followed by an error message that may (or may not) help you diagnose and correct the problem.

To test this in action, return to the CFC and break some code. Let's see what happens when we return an invalid data type to the Flash application. Find the following line in your CFC:

```
<cfreturn "Hello World (cfc)" />
```

and change it to

```
<cfreturn QueryNew( "This,Will,Not,Work") />
```

This will throw an error because you are trying to return a Query and you have set the *return type* to `string` in the `cffunction`.

Now return to Flash and retest the code by pressing Ctrl+Enter. You now see the error-catching in action! Now when you test the movie, you will get the following error message in the Output window:

```
error: Service threw an exception during method invocation:
 The value returned from function sayHelloWorld() is not of
 type string.
```

Using the NetConnection Debugger

A very useful tool for debugging Flash Remoting applications is the NetConnection Debugger (sometimes also referred to as the NetConnect Debugger in the Macromedia documentation). To use the NetConnection Debugger first make sure you include the `NetDebug.as` file in your ActionScript code. Then open the Actions panel for frame 1 of the Actions layer, and uncomment the following line of ActionScript:

```
//#include "NetDebug.as"
```

Once you have done this, open up the NetConnection Debugger window in Flash by selecting Window ➤ NetConnection Debugger (see Figure 23.13). Press Ctrl+Enter to test the movie. Again you see the error in the Output window, but you can also see the communication between the Flash application and the ColdFusion component.

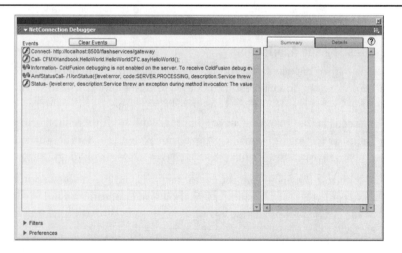

There are five items in the Debugger's Events pane shown in Figure 23.13, including a Connect to the Gateway and a Call to the CF function in the component. The last item is a status message that tells you that the service threw an exception while it was trying to invoke the `sayHelloWorld` function. The other two entries are just information telling you that ColdFusion debugging is not enabled on the server, and that an error occurred while trying to invoke the function.

WARNING The following warning message, "ColdFusion debugging is not enabled on the server," will appear in your NetConnection Debugger when your pages encounter a syntax error. You will get this error even if you have debugging enabled in the CF Administrator. This known bug is detailed at `http://www.macromedia.com/support/flash/flashremoting/releasenotes/releasenotes.html#cf` and there are no workarounds.

Now that you have enabled and used the Debugger, your next step is to return and fix the CFC and try to use the NetConnection Debugger again. First change the `cfreturn` statement back to

```
<cfreturn "Hello World (cfc)" />
```

and then save the template. In Flash, test the movie again; the results in the NetConnection Debugger will be as shown in Figure 23.14.

FIGURE 23.14:

NetConnection Debugger window with new results

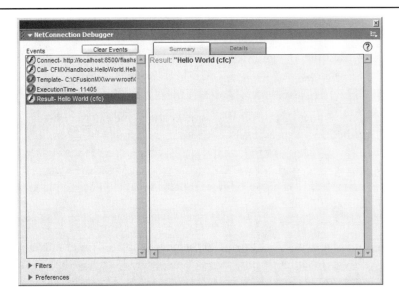

This time there are five entries in the Debugger's Events pane. The first two are the same, but if you select the third one, you can see that ColdFusion parsed an `Application.cfm` template if it found one. The fourth entry reports the execution time, and the final entry shows you the result that is returned from the CFC function.

Using a CFM Template Instead

You can also modify the HelloWorld application to use CFM files instead of CFCs. With very few revisions to the template, you can duplicate the functionality of the component.

1. First you will need to create a ColdFusion template named sayHelloWorld.cfm and save it in your <webroot>\CFMXHandbook\HelloWorld\ directory.

2. Then enter the following code in the document:

   ```
   <cfset FLASH.Result = "Hello World (cfm)." />
   ```

3. Next, modify your template to work with the new file in the Flash Actions panel. Because of the simple nature of this example, you only have to change one line of code to use the new template. Change the following line:

   ```
   myService = gateway_conn.getService(
   "CFMXHandbook.HelloWorld.HelloWorldCFC", this);
   ```

   to this:

   ```
   myService = gateway_conn.getService("CFMXHandbook.HelloWorld", this);
   ```

4. Test the Flash movie again and you will see the following result appear in the Output window:

   ```
   result: Hello World (cfm)
   ```

How does this work? Well, you changed the call to getService to be just the directory rather then a specific CFC. By doing this, your Flash Remoting application attempts to find a sayHelloWorld.cfm in that specific directory and then run that template. This was the only change necessary because you named the CFM file the same as the function in the earlier CFC example. If you chose a different name for the CFM template, then you would have had to change this line:

```
myService.sayHelloWorld();
```

in order to match the name of the new template. For example, if you chose to name the new file HelloWorldCFM.cfm, then not only would you have had to change the previous line of code to

```
myService.HelloWorldCFM();
```

but you also would have had to change your function names in the Handler section of the ActionScript from:

```
function sayHelloWorld_Result(r) {
  trace("result: "+ r);
}
function sayHelloWorld_Status(s) {
  trace("error: "+ s.description);
}
```

to:

```
function HelloWorldCFM_Result(r) {
  trace("result: "+ r);
}
function HelloWorldCFM_Status(s) {
  trace("error: "+ s.description);
}
```

If you want, you can launch the NetConnection Debugger again and see how things change when you use the CFC instead of the CFM (see Figure 23.15).

FIGURE 23.15:

NetConnection Debugger window with new results

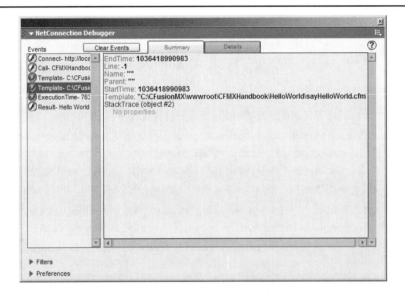

Notice that there are now six entries in the Events pane. The one new entry is another template that is processed by the ColdFusion Application Server, sayHelloWorld.cfm. The last entry in the Events pane shows the result that was passed back from the Flash application.

Using the FLASH Scope

Finally, let's take a look at the sayHelloWorld.cfm template. This simple template has a few points that are worth mentioning—this is probably the first time that you have seen the new FLASH scope.

When you are using Flash Remoting with CFM templates there are a few special variables that you can use to send and receive variables between Flash and ColdFusion:

FLASH.Result   Sends variables from ColdFusion to the Flash application. You can only return one variable to Flash, but you can always return a structure that contains a number of variables or queries.

FLASH.Params   This useful variable is an array of the parameters that are passed to Cold-Fusion templates. Parameters can either be passed using an ActionScript object, or as a comma separated list.

Let's modify the basic HelloWorld application to accept a name so that you can personalize your greeting using the FLASH scope.

1. First change your ActionScript to the following and pass a parameter to the sayHelloWorld .cfm template:

    ```
    myService.sayHelloWorld("Jeremy");
    ```

2. Next make the following slight change to the CFM file and then save the template:

    ```
    <cfset FLASH.Result = "Hello, #FLASH.Params[1]#." />
    ```

3. Now, switch back to Flash MX and test your movie using Ctrl+Enter. You will see "result: Hello, Jeremy. " in the Output window.

Passing Variables to ColdFusion Using the FLASH Scope

Passing variables to ColdFusion using Flash Remoting is very similar to doing it in JavaScript and most other programming languages, but you might notice that the syntax for dereferencing the variables in ColdFusion isn't always easy to read. However, there is another method for passing variables that is very similar to how the ArgumentCollection attribute works in cfinvoke.

1. First create a new object in Flash and pass that object as a parameter to the ColdFusion template. In the Actions panel, change the following code:

    ```
    myService.sayHelloWorld("Jeremy");
    ```

    to this:

    ```
    params = new Object();
    params.name = "Jeremy";
    myService.sayHelloWorld(params);
    ```

    Now you can refer to the parameter in the CFM template as #FLASH.name# instead of #FLASH.Params[1]#, which makes it much easier to debug later on.

3. Finally, update your CFC to mirror the changes made to the sayHelloWorld.cfm template. This process is fairly straightforward and self-explanatory. The revised CFC looks like this:

    ```
    <cfcomponent>
    <cffunction name=
      "sayHelloWorld" access="remote" returntype="string" output="No">
    <cfargument name="Name" type="string" required="yes" />
    <cfreturn "Hello, #Arguments.Name#." />
    </cffunction>
    </cfcomponent>
    ```

Calling this function works exactly the same as when you called the CFM template. You can use either method of passing variables to this function (either by using an object, or directly embedding the parameter in the function call).

4. Before you test this new CFC, make sure that you modify the `getService()` function call so that it looks to the CFC instead of the directory containing the CFM.

```
myService = gateway_conn.getService(
"CFMXHandbook.HelloWorld.HelloWorldCFC", this);
```

5. Also, if you named your CFM template something other than the name of the function in the CFC, then rename the functions in the Handler section to the same name as your CFC's function name.

6. Press Ctrl+Enter to test the movie and make sure that it still works using the modified component. If it is successful, "`result: Hello, Jeremy.`" will appear in the Output window.

This section has covered everything you need to know to get started on full-fledged Flash Remoting applications. We now move on to working with `RecordSets` in Flash, and the `DataGlue` class. After these topics have been covered, you will create a Flash Remoting image gallery.

RecordSets and Flash Remoting

The `RecordSet` is the Flash equivalent to ColdFusion's `query`, and it allows you to control query results returned from ColdFusion or create your own client-side `RecordSet` objects. Before you can use `RecordSets` in Flash, you need to include `NetServices.as` and have Flash Remoting installed. Each individual record in the `RecordSet` is simply an ActionScript object that can be accessed using dot notation to get at the columns.

There are 17 methods in the `RecordSet` object and two properties. This section briefly explains these methods, but we encourage you to consult the Flash Remoting documentation at the following URL to learn more about each of them.

```
http://livedocs.macromedia.com/frdocs/Using_Flash_Remoting_MX/asDict25.jsp
```

addItem()and addItemAt()   These methods add records to a client-side `RecordSet`. The difference between these two methods is that `addItemAt()` inserts a record into a specific index in the `RecordSet`, and all other records will be shifted as necessary. `addItem()` adds a record at the end of a `RecordSet`.

filter()   This method filters records in a `RecordSet`. By passing the name of a user defined function and a filter criteria, you are able to filter out records from a `RecordSet` that do not match a certain condition. It is worth noting that the original `RecordSet` is unchanged, and a new `RecordSet` object is returned instead.

getColumnNames()   This method retrieves a list of column names from a RecordSet object. This is the same as using the #QueryName.ColumnList# variable in ColdFusion.

getItemAt()   This method retrieves specific records from a RecordSet. This method takes one parameter, which is the index of the record to retrieve.

getLength()   This method returns the number of records contained in a RecordSet. This is the same as ColdFusion's #QueryName.RecordCount# variable.

NOTE   The getLength() method will return the total number of records in a RecordSet, even if the records haven't been downloaded from the server yet.

getNumberAvailable(), isFullyPopulated(), and setDeliveryMode()   These are used to incrementally return large RecordSets from ColdFusion to Flash using a variable in Cold-Fusion named FLASH.Pagesize. This allows you to return records to the Flash application without having to wait for the entire RecordSet to completely load. Let's look at of them each in detail:

getNumberAvailable()   This method simply tells you how many records have been completely downloaded from the server.

isFullyPopulated()   This is a read-only Boolean property that signals if all records have been fully downloaded to our Flash application.

setDeliveryMode()   This method controls how the records are paged. There are three options to choose from: ondemand, fetchall, and page. Explaining these three methods is beyond the scope of this chapter, but they are covered in detail in the Flash Remoting documentation.

isLocal()   This property is read-only and checks whether a RecordSet came from a remote server or was created client-side.

removeAll() and removeItemAt()   These methods remove records from a RecordSet. When you remove a record at a specific index using removeItemAt(), any items after the deleted record will be shifted accordingly.

replaceItemAt()   This method is used to replace an existing record in the RecordSet with an entirely new record.

setField()   This method is used when you only need to change one field in an existing record.

sort() and sortItemsBy()   These methods sort existing RecordSets. sortItemsBy() takes two parameters that represent the column to sort on, and the direction to sort them by. This is similar to using the ORDER BY statement in SQL, although SQL only allows you to sort by a single column. The sort() method takes a single parameter, a user-defined function that is used to compare two records, to create a custom sorting method. This is used when you need to create a sorting method that sorts records based on multiple columns.

addView()   This method allows you to watch a RecordSet and then trigger an event when a record is changed. Again, this is beyond the scope of this book and you can find details on it in the Flash Remoting documentation.

Using the DataGlue Class

The DataGlue class allows you to bind a Flash RecordSet to Flash UI Components, such as the ComboBox or ListBox. This class provides two methods to help bind and format the data. The first method is DataGlue.bindFormatStrings(), which has the following syntax:

```
DataGlue.bingFormatStrings(dataConsumer, dataProvider, labelString, dataString)
```

This method is similar in concept to using the cfselect tag in ColdFusion as seen in the code below:

```
<cfselect name="dataConsumer" query="dataProvider"
display="labelString" value="dataString" />
```

The first argument, dataConsumer, is the component instance on the Stage to which you want to bind the RecordSet. This is slightly different from the cfselect tag because cfselect is creating the HTML select tag for you. However, in Flash the instance must already exist on the Stage.

The next argument, dataProvider, is the actual RecordSet that you want to bind. This is the same as the Query attribute in the cfselect tag. The labelString argument defines the output (or label) that is shown in the ComboBox or ListBox component. In the case of the cfselect tag, this is the text generated after the option tag that the reader sees on the screen.

In ActionScript, you wrap pound signs (#) around the column names you want to display. But in the ColdFusion tag, you just type the column name without pound signs. You will see an example of this in exercises later in this chapter. The labelString in ActionScript can also display several columns and any other text you want to be displayed. For example, if you want to show the name of a category and the number of products in that category, you use a labelString similar to this: #CategoryName# (#numCategoryProducts# products)—assuming the RecordSet has columns named CategoryName and numCategoryProducts.

The final argument, dataString, is the value (or data) for each item in the ComboBox or ListBox component. Similar to the labelString already described, dataString can be formatted using any combination of columns from the RecordSet, but each column must be enclosed in pound signs (#). This is similar to the value attribute in an HTML <option value="#data String#"> tag.

The second function in this object, `DataGlue.bindFormatFunction`, has the following syntax:

```
DataGlue.bindFormatFunction(dataConsumer, dataProvider, formatFunction)
```

The first two arguments are the same as for the `DataGlue.bindFormatStrings()` method. However, the third argument is the name of a user-defined function that takes a single record as a parameter. The user-defined function must return an ActionScript object consisting of two items: `label` and `data`. This is useful when you need to further format records from a `RecordSet` before binding them to a component. Let's look at an example:

```
#include "NetServices.as"
#include "DataGlue.as"
myQuery_rs = new RecordSet(["ID", "Name", "CalendarDate"]);
myQuery_rs.addItem({ID:1, Name:'Christmas',
  CalendarDate:'Thu Dec 25 00:00:00 GMT-8:00 2003'});
myQuery_rs.addItem({ID:2, Name:'New Years Day',
  CalendarDate:'Wed Jan 1 00:00:00 GMT-8:00 2003'});
myQuery_rs.addItem({ID:3, Name:'Canada Day',
  CalendarDate:'Fri Jul 1 00:00:00 GMT-8:00 2003'});
myQuery_rs.addItem({ID:4, Name:'Independance Day',
  CalendarDate:'Fri Jul 4 00:00:00 GMT-8:00 2003'});
function myUDF(record) {
  var date_array =
    record.CalendarDate.toString().split(" ");
  var myLabel = record.Name+" ("+date_array[0]+
    " "+date_array[1]+" "+date_array[2]+
    ", "+date_array[5]+")";
  var myData = record.ID;
  return {label:myLabel, data:myData};
}
DataGlue.bindFormatFunction(myComboBox_cb, myQuery_rs, myUDF);
function traceData() {
  trace(myComboBox_cb.getValue());
}
myComboBox_cb.setChangeHandler("traceData");
```

Notice there are two `#include` statements as usual. `NetServices.as` is required to create the `RecordSet` object, and you need `DataGlue` to be able to use the `bindFormatFunction` method.

Following this, you create a local `RecordSet` using the new `RecordSet` method. You also need to pass an array of strings as an argument. Then you add four records to the `RecordSet`, which are holidays and their dates. Next you create the user-defined function, which controls how each record is formatted as it is displayed. The function returns an object consisting of the label that displays in your Flash component and the data value that belongs to each record.

Finally the `DataGlue.bindFormatFunction()` method is called and you pass the `dataConsumer` (the `myComboBox_cb` instance), the `dataProvider` (the `myQuery_rs` RecordSet), and finally the name of the user-defined function that was just created (`myUDF`). `DataGlue` then binds each record of the `RecordSet` to the Flash component with the formatting specified in the user-defined function.

Building a Dynamic Image Gallery

Now that you understand the fundamentals of Flash Remoting, and are more familiar with the Flash MX authoring environment, it's time to build something a little bit more interesting than a Hello World example! In this section, you are going to build an image gallery that dynamically pulls JPG files from a database into a Flash front end, using Remoting.

Building the Database

This example uses Flash Remoting to call a CFC that grabs gallery information from a database. First you set up the database and then build the Flash document. SQL Server is used for this example, but you can use Access, or MySQL, or any other data product with a couple of minor changes.

1. First create the necessary tables in the database. You need to create a new table, called `Galleries`, and add the following columns:

   - `GalleryID - int - PrimaryKey - Identity`
   - `GalleryName - nvarchar(64)`
   - `GalleryDate - smalldatetime`
   - `GalleryActive - bit` (default: 1)

2. Then create another table, called `GalleryImages`, with the following columns:

   - `GalleryImageID - int - PrimaryKey - Identity`
   - `GalleryImageSrc - nvarchar(64)`
   - `GalleryImageAlt - nvarchar(512)`
   - `GalleryID - int`
   - `OrderID - int`

   These tables are fairly straightforward. The last two columns in the `Galleries` table are included so that you can sort galleries by date instead of alphabetically, and the `GalleryActive` column is included so you could easily hide a gallery without having to delete it from the database.

   The `GalleryImages` table has a `GalleryImageSrc` column that holds the filename of the image that is going to be displayed. The `GalleryImageAlt` column is used to house descriptions of each image in the gallery, and `GalleryID` is the foreign key that allows you to tie images to their respective galleries. `OrderID` is simply there to allow a developer to order images.

NOTE   Flash only dynamically loads non-progressive JPG files.

Creating the Flash Interface

Now that you have set up the database you are ready to create a new file in Flash as you have done in previous examples.

1. Select File ➢ New From Template..., and then choose Web and select Basic. Click the Create button. This opens the document and gives you a basic framework.

2. Next you need to set up your layers. You should already have one layer called Actions from the template. Lock the Actions layer by clicking the dot under the lock icon in the Timeline.

3. Create a new layer by selecting Insert ➢ Layer; name it Form. With the Form layer active, drag an instance of the ComboBox component onto the Stage and give the component an instance name of GalleryID_cb. Set the component's width to 300 pixels in the Property Inspector as shown here.

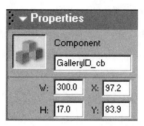

4. Below the ComboBox instance on the Form layer, create a dynamic text field and name it GalleryInfo_txt. Near the bottom of the Stage create a large Multiline dynamic text field and give it an instance name of GalleryImageAlt_txt.

5. With the Form layer still active, you need to add four buttons to the Stage for navigation. To do so, select Window ➢ Common Libraries ➢ Buttons and expand the Circle Buttons folder. Drag the following button instances onto the Stage and name them as shown here:

Button Type/Action	Instance Name
Circle button/to beginning	firstImage_btn
Circle button/previous	previousImage_btn
Circle button/next	nextImage_btn
Circle button/to end	lastImage_btn

6. Drag a ScrollPane instance from the Components panel onto the Stage and give it an instance name of GalleryImageSrc_sp. Set the width and height to the size of your images using the Property Inspector. Since you are going to disable the horizontal and vertical scroll bars on the ScrollPane, if there is an image with dimensions larger than the Scroll-Pane, you won't be able to scroll to see all of it.

7. Select the ScrollPane instance on the Stage. In the Parameters tab of the Property Inspector set both the Horizontal Scroll and Vertical Scroll values to false. The Stage setup should now look like Figure 23.16.

FIGURE 23.16:

The completed Stage setup

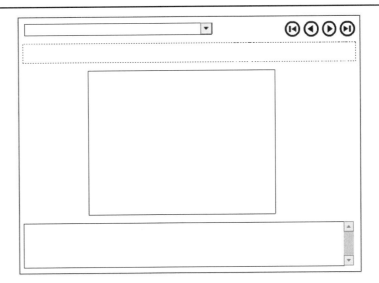

Writing ActionScript for the Image Gallery

Now let's go over the ActionScript code you need for the application. Select frame 1 of the Actions layer, and add the code from Listing 23.5 into the Actions panel.

Listing 23.5   Gallery_final.fla

```
/*
   Name:          /c23/Gallery_final.fla
   Description:   Flash Remoting image gallery
*/

#include "NetServices.as"
#include "DataGlue.as"
// uncomment this line when you want to use the NetConnect
//debugger
//#include "NetDebug.as"
```

```
// --------------------------------------------------
// Handlers for user interaction events
// --------------------------------------------------
function updateGallery() {
  var thisGalleryID_int = GalleryID_cb.getValue();
  galleryService.getGalleryByGalleryID(thisGalleryID_int);
  galleryService.getGalleryImages(thisGalleryID_int);
}
previousImage_btn.onRelease = function() {
  previousImage();
};
nextImage_btn.onRelease = function() {
  nextImage();
};
firstImage_btn.onRelease = function() {
  firstImage();
};
lastImage_btn.onRelease = function() {
  lastImage();
};
// --------------------------------------------------
// Handlers for data coming in from server
// --------------------------------------------------
function getActiveGalleries_Result(result) {
  _global.Gallery_rs = result;
  DataGlue.bindFormatStrings(GalleryID_cb,
    _global.Gallery_rs,
    "#GalleryName# (#GalleryDateString# -
    #numGalleryImages# images)", "#GalleryID#");
}
function getGalleryImages_Result(result) {
  _global.GalleryImages_rs = result;
  _global.GalleryImageID_int = 0;
  loadGalleryImage();
}
function getGalleryByGalleryID_Result(result) {
  var thisRecord_obj = result.getItemAt(0);
  var output_str = "<font size='14'><b>"+
    thisRecord_obj.GalleryName+"</b></font>";
    output_str += " ("+thisRecord_obj.GalleryDateString+
    " - "+thisRecord_obj.numGalleryImages+" images)";
  GalleryInfo_txt.htmlText = output_str;
}
// --------------------------------------------------
// Application initialization
// --------------------------------------------------
if (inited == null) {
  // do this code only once
  inited = true;
  // set the default Gateway URL (this is used only in
  //authoring)
```

```
    NetServices.setDefaultGatewayUrl(
      "http://localhost:8500/flashservices/gateway");
    // connect to the Gateway
    gateway_conn = NetServices.createGatewayConnection();
    // get a reference to a service
    galleryService = gateway_conn.getService(
      "CFMXHandbook.Gallery.GalleryCFC", this);
    galleryService.getActiveGalleries();
}
GalleryInfo_txt.html = true;
GalleryID_cb.setChangeHandler("updateGallery");
function loadGalleryImage() {
  var thisImage =
    _global.GalleryImages_rs.getItemAt(
    _global.GalleryImageID_int);
  GalleryImageSrc_sp.loadScrollContent(thisImage.Gallery ImageSrc);
  GalleryImageAlt_txt.htmlText = thisImage.GalleryImageAlt;
  if (isFirstImage()) {
    firstImage_btn._alpha = 50;
    previousImage_btn._alpha = 50;
    firstImage_btn.enabled = false;
    previousImage_btn.enabled = false;
  } else {
    firstImage_btn._alpha = 100;
    previousImage_btn._alpha = 100;
    firstImage_btn.enabled = true;
    previousImage_btn.enabled = true;
  }
  if (isLastImage()) {
    nextImage_btn._alpha = 50;
    lastImage_btn._alpha = 50;
    nextImage_btn.enabled = false;
    lastImage_btn.enabled = false;
  } else {
    nextImage_btn._alpha = 100;
    lastImage_btn._alpha = 100;
    nextImage_btn.enabled = true;
    lastImage_btn.enabled = true;
  }
}
function isFirstImage() {
  return (_global.GalleryImageID_int<=0);
}
function isLastImage() {
  return (_global.GalleryImageID_int >= _global.GalleryImages_rs.getLength()-1);
}
function nextImage() {
  if (_global.GalleryImageID_int < _global.GalleryImages_rs.getLength()-1) {
    _global.GalleryImageID_int++;
  } else {
    _global.GalleryImageID_int = 0;
  }
```

```
    loadGalleryImage();
}
function previousImage() {
  if (isFirstImage()) {
    _global.GalleryImageID_int
    _global.GalleryImages_rs.getLength()-1;
  } else {
    _global.GalleryImageID_int--;
  }
  loadGalleryImage();
}
function firstImage() {
  _global.GalleryImageID_int = 0;
  loadGalleryImage();
}
function lastImage() {
  _global.GalleryImageID_int
  _global.GalleryImages_rs.getLength()-1;
  loadGalleryImage();
}
stop();
```

In the first section of the ActionScript you have one new `include` that hasn't been used before.

```
#include "NetServices.as"
#include "DataGlue.as"
```

`DataGlue.as` handles the binding of data from a `RecordSet` or array to a ListBox or ComboBox component. This is a huge improvement from having to loop over each item in a collection and manually add rows to the ComboBox or ListBox `DataGlue.as`.

Following these includes, you see the Handler section that contains a handful of functions associated with the gallery navigation and a function called `updateGallery()`, which is the Change Handler for the ComboBox.

The next section handles data that is returned from the remote functions. The first function, `getActiveGalleries_Result()`, returns a `RecordSet` object of active image galleries that contain at least one image. In this section, you set a global variable called `Gallery_rs` that contains the `RecordSet` returned from the CFC, and then you use a method from the `DataGlue` class to bind the `RecordSet` to the ComboBox component, as seen here:

```
function getActiveGalleries_Result(result) {
  _global.Gallery_rs = result;
  DataGlue.bindFormatStrings(GalleryID_cb,
  _global.Gallery_rs, "#GalleryName#
  (#GalleryDateString# - #numGalleryImages# images)",
  "#GalleryID#");
}
```

The `bindFormatStrings()` function takes four parameters:

- The `dataConsumer` to which you are binding the `RecordSet`. In this case it is the ComboBox instance, `GalleryID_cb`.

- The `dataProvider`, which is the `RecordSet` itself. In this case it is the `RecordSet` `_global.Gallery_rs`.

- A `labelString` that is displayed in the ComboBox/ListBox. This is similar to the following HTML: `<option>{label}</option>`. Column names are enclosed in pound signs. `GalleryName`, `GalleryDate`, and `numGalleryImages` are being displayed in that gallery.

- A `dataString` that determines the value of the items in the ComboBox/ListBox. This is similar to the following in HTML: `<option value="{value}">...</option>`.

The second function, `getGalleryImages_Result()`, receives a `RecordSet` of images for the gallery selected in the ComboBox instance, `GalleryID_cb`. It sets two global variables: the `RecordSet` that was returned from the server, and a counter used to track the current image being displayed.

```
function getGalleryImages_Result(result) {
  _global.GalleryImages_rs = result;
  _global.GalleryImageID_int = 0;
  loadGalleryImage();
}
```

The final function in this section, `getGalleryByGalleryID_Result()`, receives a `RecordSet` and displays the information to the `GalleryInfo_txt` text field.

There is one new method that you probably haven't seen yet, called `getItemAt()`. It is responsible for retrieving a single record from a `RecordSet` in ActionScript. In the code, the method grabs the first record from the returned `RecordSet`.

WARNING   ActionScript uses 0-based indexes, unlike ColdFusion, which is 1-based.

Keeping this in mind, you need to put the first record into a variable and then reference columns in the record using dot syntax.

```
function getGalleryByGalleryID_Result(result) {
  var thisRecord_obj = result.getItemAt(0);
  var output_str = "<font size='14'><b>"+
    thisRecord_obj.GalleryName+"</b></font>";
  output_str += " ("+thisRecord_obj.GalleryDateString+
    "- "+thisRecord_obj.numGalleryImages+" images)";
  GalleryInfo_txt.htmlText = output_str;
}
```

Next, you have the initialization section, which is responsible for setting up the application with default settings and a few functions that you will need later on. One new thing you see in the initialization section is that you can turn on HTML formatting programmatically instead of enabling it in the Property Inspector.

```
GalleryInfo_txt.html = true;
```

Then you programmatically set the Change Handler for the ComboBox named GalleryID_cb.

```
GalleryID_cb.setChangeHandler("updateGallery");
```

In the loadGalleryImage() function, you use the getItemAt() method to grab the current image from the global GalleryImages_rs RecordSet. Then you use a new function, load-ScrollContent(), to load the current image into the ScrollPane.

Next, you set the image description text to the GalleryImageAlt_txt text field. At this point, the function isFirstImage() is called and it returns a Boolean value that reports whether or not the current image is the first image in the RecordSet. If it is the first image, it fades out the first image button and the previous image button and disables them both. If it isn't the first image, then the alpha is set to 100 percent (fully visible) and both of the buttons are enabled. In addition another if statement checks whether or not the current image is the last image in the RecordSet; this statement is similar to the previous if statement.

The next two functions are used to test whether or not the current image is the first or last image in the RecordSet. The last four functions: nextImage(), previousImage(), firstImage(), and lastImage() are responsible for changing the current image counter and reloading the image.

In the next section, you are going to create the CFC file for the application. Following this, you will integrate the two files and test the application.

Writing the CFC for the Image Gallery

Now let's look at the code for the CFC. First create a new document and save it as GalleryCFC .cfc in the same directory as your FLA file. Then enter the code from Listing 23.6 into the document.

Listing 23.6   **GalleryCFC.cfc**

```
<!---
    Name:          /c23/GalleryCFC.cfc
    Description:    image gallery component
--->
<cfcomponent>
  <cffunction name="getActiveGalleries" access="remote"
    returntype="query" output="No">
    <cfset Var returnQuery = "" />
```

```
  <cfquery name="returnQuery"
  datasource="#Request.Site.Dsn#">
    select
      G.GalleryID,
      G.GalleryName,
      G.GalleryDate,
      convert(char(12), GalleryDate, 107) as GalleryDateString,
      (select count(GI.GalleryID) from GalleryImages
        GI where G.GalleryID = GI.GalleryID) as
        numGalleryImages
    from
      Galleries G
    where
      G.GalleryActive = 1
    group by
      G.GalleryID,
      G.GalleryName,
      G.GalleryDate
    having
      (select count(GI.GalleryID) from GalleryImages
        GI where G.GalleryID = GI.GalleryID) > 0
    order by
      G.GalleryName ASC
  </cfquery>

  <cfreturn returnQuery />
</cffunction>

<cffunction name="getGalleryByGalleryID" access="remote"
  returntype="query" output="No">
  <cfargument name="GalleryID" type="numeric" required="No" />
  <cfset Var returnQuery = "" />

  <cfquery name="returnQuery"
    datasource="#Request.Site.Dsn#" timeout="15">
    select top 1
      G.GalleryID,
      G.GalleryName,
      G.GalleryDate,
      convert(char(12), GalleryDate, 107) as GalleryDateString,
      (select count(GI.GalleryID) from GalleryImages GI
        where G.GalleryID = GI.GalleryID) as
        numGalleryImages
    from
      Galleries G
    where
      G.GalleryActive = 1 and
      G.GalleryID = <cfqueryparam
        value="#Arguments.GalleryID#"
        cfsqltype="cf_sql_integer" />
    order by
      G.GalleryName asc
```

```
      </cfquery>
      <cfreturn returnQuery />
   </cffunction>

   <cffunction name="getGalleryImages" access="remote"
     returntype="query" output="No">
     <cfargument name="GalleryID" type="numeric" required="Yes" />
     <cfset var returnQuery = "" />

     <cfquery name="returnQuery" datasource="#Request.Site.Dsn#">
       select
         GI.GalleryImageID,
         GI.GalleryImageSrc,
         GI.GalleryImageAlt
       from
         Galleries G inner join GalleryImages GI on G.GalleryID = GI.GalleryID
       where
         G.GalleryID = <cfqueryparam
         value="#Arguments.GalleryID#"
         cfsqltype="cf_sql_integer" />
     </cfquery>
     <cfreturn returnQuery />
   </cffunction>

</cfcomponent>
```

These three functions are relatively basic and each one returns a query to Flash. The first function, getActiveGalleries, selects all galleries from the database that are active, and have at least one image. SQL Server's convert function is being used to format the dates in SQL Server. By moving the formatting to the database, you can easily use bindFormatStrings() function in ActionScript when you need to use the DataGlue class. Conversely, we could use bindFormatFunction to format the records in Flash.

The last two functions both accept a single parameter, GalleryID, and return queries to Flash. getGalleryByGalleryID simply gets a specific gallery from the Galleries table based on its PrimaryKey, and getGalleryImages is responsible for getting all records from the GalleryImages table that match the supplied GalleryID argument.

Creating an Application.cfm File

You also have to create an Application.cfm file and define the #Request.Site.Dsn# variable. Create an Application.cfm file in your <webroot>\CFMXHandbook\ directory and type in the following code:

```
   <cfapplication name="CFMXHandbook"
                  applicationtimeout="#CreateTimeSpan(0,0,15,0)#" />

   <cfscript>
     Request.Site = structNew( );
```

```
    Request.Site.Dsn = "CFMXHandbook";
</cfscript>

<cfsetting showDebugOutput="No">
```

Now go to your database and enter a few records. Type in the filename of the images in the `GalleryImageSrc` column and make sure that you have at least two active galleries with at least one image in each gallery. Save your images in the same folder as your `*.fla` and `*.swf` files.

Return to the Flash authoring environment, and press Ctrl+Enter to test the application. Now you should be able to navigate through the image galleries that are dynamically loading the JPG files into the Flash interface. Refer to Figure 23.17 to see the finished Gallery.

FIGURE 23.17:

The finished Image Gallery movie

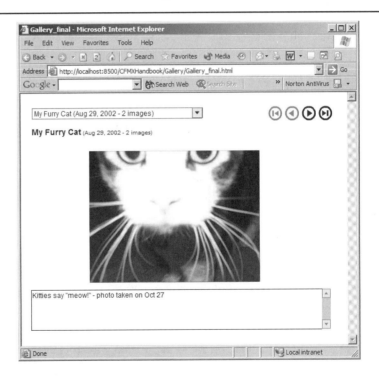

Working with Server-Side ActionScript

Another way to use Flash Remoting with Flash MX and ColdFusion MX is by using a new server-side language called server-side ActionScript, or SSAS for short. Aimed at the Flash developer, SSAS allows you to integrate server-side functionality by using syntax similar to Flash ActionScript. You are able to write SSAS functions that use the same basic functionality as two of ColdFusion's most powerful operations, `cfquery` and `cfhttp`. SSAS files are saved with an `.asr` extension.

With only two functions, SSAS isn't nearly as robust or as powerful as using CFCs. Therefore, it is a technology mostly aimed at Flash developers who are already familiar with ActionScript syntax.

NOTE
For the next example, you only use SSAS's CF.http function, but you can go to http://livedocs.macromedia.com/frdocs/Using_Flash_Remoting_MX/usingFRCF4. jsp to read more on this subject in the section called "Using Flash Remoting MX with server-side ActionScript."

You use CF.http to grab a remote URL and return the result to a Flash application. However, CF.http is capable of using both GET and POST methods, resolving URLs, and saving the file content to a local file on the web server.

First, you'll create an SSAS file. Save a file called getPageASR.asr into the <webroot>\CFMXHandbook\SSAS\ folder. Here are the contents of this short file:

```
function getPage(url) {
return CF.http(url);
}
```

The file only has a single function, but you could have as many functions as you need in the file; this is similar to how a CFC works.

WARNING
If you have a CFC with the same name as an ASR in a directory, Flash Remoting seems to invoke the CFC before attempting to find ASR files. Therefore, do not use the same name for an .asr file as a .cfc file in the same directory.

Now you need to create a Flash application. Begin by setting up the Stage in Flash.

1. Create a new file from a template by going to File ➤ New From Template....

2. In the New Document dialog box, choose Web from the Category list and Basic from the Category Items list.

3. Click the Create button.

4. Save this file as httpinfo.fla in the same directory as the ASR file.

5. Next, lock the Actions layer so that you don't accidentally place any instances on that layer.

6. Then create a new layer called Form and position it below the Actions layer. Make sure this layer is selected in the Timeline.

7. Select the Text tool and change the settings in the Property Inspector to Static Text. Click near the top of the Stage and type **http://**.

8. Click the Stage again and create another text field, but this time type in **headers:** and position it below the previous instance.

9. Create another text field on the Stage large enough for a user to type in a URL.

10. Select this instance and change its Text type to Input Text in the Property Inspector. Then give it an instance name of **targetUrl_txt** and enable the Show Border Around Text button. Position this instance to the right of the http:// label that you created in step 7.

11. Create one more large Multiline text field that takes up a large part of the Stage.

12. Position the instance at the bottom of the Stage, but leave enough room to the right of this instance to fit a ScrollBar component.

13. In the Property Inspector, give the text field an instance name of **output_txt**, set the Line type to Multiline, and select Show Border Around Text.

14. Then set the Text type to Dynamic Text, as shown just in Figure 23.18. Then attach a ScrollBar component onto this text field.

FIGURE 23.18:

The Property Inspector

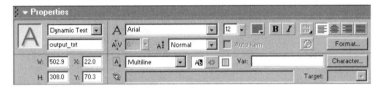

15. Now drag a PushButton instance from the Components panel onto the Stage and give it an instance name **submit_pb**. Position it to the right of your targetUrl_txt text field.

16. Next drag a ComboBox instance onto the Stage, give it an instance name of **headers_cb**, and align it to the right of the headers: label. The results are shown in Figure 23.19.

FIGURE 23.19:

The stage setup

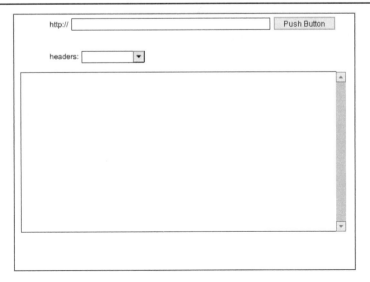

Now that the Stage is set up, take a look at the client-side ActionScript, shown in Listing 23.7. In this example, you'll be using a few new techniques so we'll go over this carefully following the listing.

To get started, select frame 1 of the Actions layer and type the code from Listing 23.7 into the Actions panel:

Listing 23.7   **Server-side ActionScript (httpinfo_final.fla)**

```
/*
    Name:            /c23/httpinfo_final.fla
    Description:     server side actionscript
*/
#include "NetServices.as"
#include "DataGlue.as"
// uncomment this line when you want to use the NetConnect
//debugger
//#include "NetDebug.as"
// --------------------------------------------------
// Handlers for user interaction events
// --------------------------------------------------
function showData() {
  var tempStr_str = headers_cb.getSelectedItem().data;
  output_txt.text = (tempStr_str.length == 0) ? "null" : tempStr_str;
}
function getUrl() {
  myService.getPage(targetUrl_txt.text);
}
// --------------------------------------------------
// Handlers for data coming in from server
// --------------------------------------------------
function ServiceHandler() {};
ServiceHandler.prototype.getPage_Result = function(result){
  var tempRecordSet_rs = new RecordSet(["HeaderName", "HeaderValue"]);
  for (var i in result) {
    tempRecordSet_rs.addItem({HeaderName:i, HeaderValue:result[i]});
  }
  tempRecordSet_rs.sortItemsBy("HeaderName");
  DataGlue.bindFormatStrings(headers_cb,
    tempRecordSet_rs, "#HeaderName#","#HeaderValue#");
};
// --------------------------------------------------
// Application initialization
// --------------------------------------------------
if (inited == null) {
  inited = true;
  NetServices.setDefaultGatewayUrl(
    "http://localhost:8500/flashservices/gateway");
  gateway_conn = NetServices.createGatewayConnection();
  myService = gateway_conn.getService(
```

```
      "CFMXHandbook.SSAS.getPageASR", new ServiceHandler());
}
submit_pb.setLabel("submit");
submit_pb.setClickHandler("getUrl");
headers_cb.setSize(150);
headers_cb.setChangeHandler("showData");
stop();
```

The first four lines of this listing (not including the header information) are simply the #include statements. If you wish to use the NetConnection Debugger, then you'll have to uncomment the #includes at the beginning of the listing.

The next two functions are simply the Change Handlers for the PushButton and ComboBox components. The showData() function checks the length of the value in the combo box, and if it has a length of zero, then it inserts a null into the large text box at the bottom of the Stage. Otherwise, there is a value for a currently selected item in the ComboBox, so we show that text. The second function, getUrl(), simply calls our getPage() function in the ASR file.

The next section is where event handling occurs a little differently than it did in the image gallery example. Rather then each instance having _Result and _Status handlers, you create a class and have that class handle the events instead. The syntax is similar, but the advantage of this method is that it tends to handle the user's memory more efficiently. This is achieved by assigning memory to functions and parameters instead of allocating it for every instance. You create a class as follows:

```
function ServiceHandler() {};
```

Then you define functions in the class by assigning them to the prototype property of that class, as shown here:

```
ServiceHandler.prototype.getPage_Result = function(result){
  var tempRecordSet_rs = new RecordSet(["HeaderName", "HeaderValue"]);
  for (var i in result) {
    tempRecordSet_rs.addItem({HeaderName:i, HeaderValue:result[i]});
  }
  tempRecordSet_rs.sortItemsBy("HeaderName");
  DataGlue.bindFormatStrings(headers_cb, tempRecordSet_rs, "#HeaderName#",
#HeaderValue#");
};
```

You can see that you still have getPage_Result but now you can assign this function to your ServiceHandler class. This is an advanced concept, and Object-Oriented ActionScript is beyond the scope of this book, but learning this key concept will pay off in the long run. For more information on this topic, please refer to the excellent book by Branden Hall and Samuel Wan called *Object-Oriented Programming with ActionScript* (New Riders, 2002).

Next you create a local variable from the results of the ASR function that you use to hold a `RecordSet`. (Creating this `RecordSet` is similar to manually creating a query in ColdFusion.) The new `RecordSet` method takes one parameter, which is an array of strings that are used as column names. In your case, these columns are named `HeaderName` and `HeaderValue`.

After this, the object returned by the ASR function is looped over using a `for..in` loop. This allows you to iterate through the key/value pairs. This situation is similar to how you loop over a collection in ColdFusion using `<cfloop collection="#result#" item="i">...</cfloop>`.

For each key in the object, you are adding a record to the `RecordSet` and passing an object as a parameter. You set the `HeaderName` to the current key—or, in ColdFusion terms, the "item"—when you are looping over a collection You then set the `HeaderValue` to the value of that key (or `#result[i]#`). After you finish looping over each item in the object, the `RecordSet` is sorted by the `HeaderName` and the records are bound to the `headers_cb` ComboBox using the `bindFormatStrings()` method.

The remaining code is all fairly straightforward, with one notable exception.

```
myService = gateway_conn.getService("CFMXHandbook.SSAS.getPageASR",
    new ServiceHandler());
```

The previous examples all had functions that caught their own results, but now you are using a class to handle them. Here, one change was made to the `gateway_conn.getService()` method. Now it is using `new ServiceHandler()` to catch events instead of using `this` as was used in all previous examples.

NOTE Since we are constructing an instance of this class, we must use "new" before our `ServiceHandler()` method.

Finally you set up labels for the PushButton, set the width of the ComboBox, and set up the handler functions for each of the components:

```
submit_pb.setLabel("submit");
submit_pb.setClickHandler("getUrl");
headers_cb.setSize(150);
headers_cb.setChangeHandler("showData");
```

Notice that several new techniques are incorporated into this example as seen in Listing 23.7. Nevertheless, there are no real differences between invoking a CFC and using an ASR file as you have done here. The most significant change is that you use an object-oriented approach to handle events in the application. Indeed, this technique can be used both with CFCs and SSAS.

Web Services and Flash Remoting MX

One of the great benefits of using Flash Remoting MX is how it enables you to use web services in your Flash front ends. With the release of Flash Remoting, you can even directly consume remote web services in Flash. Or, you can use ColdFusion to process the information before it is brought into your Flash front end. As you will discover in this final section, it is very easy to transfer this data to the Flash movie.

In the following examples, two different ways of integrating Flash with web services will be explored. In the first example, Flash and web services will be integrated using Flash Remoting without using ColdFusion. The exercise demonstrated in this part will be an example of Flash and web services being used without a ColdFusion intermediary. In the second example, ColdFusion is used as a proxy in the data transmission process.

Determining the Weather Using Flash Remoting and Web Services

In this exercise, you are going to build a simple Flash application that will directly call a weather service and get the current weather report for any valid U.S. Postal Service zip code. If you enter any valid five-digit zip code, the weather service will return the city/state, the current temperature, the visibility, the barometric pressure, the dewpoint, and wind speed/direction, as well as several other values.

You will be using a service from `http://www.ejse.com`, which you can demo at the following URL:

```
http://www.ejse.com/WeatherService/Service.asmx?op=GetWeatherInfo
```

Web services will be covered in much greater detail in Chapter 24, "Web Services," but here we want to demonstrate how you can directly consume a remote web service in Flash instead of creating a CFC to call each of the methods in the web service.

NOTE   Several other options can be found on `http://www.xmethods.net` although some require you to register or get demo licenses before you can begin developing.

Preparing the Flash Interface

Let's begin by setting up the Flash movie.

1. Create a new movie by selecting File ➢ New From Template.... and then choose Category ➢ Web and Category Items ➢ Basic. Save your file as `weatherRemoting.fla`.

2. Lock the Actions layer by clicking below the lock icon next to the Actions layer name in the Timeline. This prevents you from accidentally placing instances on that layer.

3. Create a new layer by selecting Insert ➢ Layer, and rename it **Form**. This is where you place all your text fields and other components.

4. Select the Text Tool and create a text field on the Stage. Type **Zip Code:** into the field.

5. Then open the Property Inspector and set the text type to Static Text.

6. Create another Text field on the Stage that is large enough to hold a five-digit zip code.

7. In the Property Inspector, change the text type to Input Text and then name the instance **ZipCode_txt**. We will add some ActionScript in Listing 23.8 that will set the maximum number of characters that can be entered into this text field. Also, we will add some code so users are only able to enter numbers and not any other characters.

8. Add a dynamic text field to the Stage below the Zip Code field. Make this field large enough to hold a short message that will be displayed when the user is waiting for data or when there is a transmission error from the web service. Name this instance **status_txt**, and deselect the Show Border Around Text button.

9. The last text field on the Stage will be a large dynamic text field used to display the result from the web service. To set this text field up, open the Property Inspector, and name the instance **output_txt**, then enable the Show Border Around Text button and set the line type to Multiline.

Now that we have finished adding the text fields to the Stage, we need to add a couple components to complete the interface.

1. Open the Components panel (Ctrl+F7).

2. Drag an instance of the ScrollBar component and snap it to the output_txt text field.

3. Open the Property Inspector and give the ScrollBar an instance name of scrollbar_sb. We're naming the scroll bar so we can target the instance using ActionScript. Then we can dynamically control whether or not the ScrollBar instance and the associated text field are visible while the movie is waiting for a result from the web service.

4. Drag an instance of the PushButton component onto the Stage. Position it beside the ZipCode_txt instance and give it an instance name of **submit_pb**. We'll use ActionScript in Listing 23.8 to change the label on **submit_pb** as well as set the Click Handler for it.

5. Select frame 1 of the Actions layer, and then open the Actions panel. Type the code Listing 23.8 into the Script pane.

Listing 23.8   Weather Service (weatherRemoting.fla)

```
/*
   Name:          /c23/weatherRemoting.fla
   Description:   Return a weather report
*/
#include "NetServices.as"
// uncomment this line when you want to use the NetConnect
// debugger
//#include "NetDebug.as"
// -------------------------------------------------
// Handlers for user interaction events
// -------------------------------------------------
```

```
function sendZipCode() {
  myService.GetWeatherInfo(ZipCode_txt.text);
  status_txt.htmlText = "fetching data from server.";
  output_txt._visible = false;
  scrollbar_sb._visible = false;
}
// -------------------------------------------------
// Handlers for data coming in from server
// -------------------------------------------------
// This gets called with the results of calls to the server
// function "GetWeatherInfo".
function GetWeatherInfo_Result(result) {
  status_txt.htmlText = "";
  var output_str = "";
  for (i in result) {
    output_str += "<b>"+i+":</b> "+result[i]+"<br>";
  }
  output_txt.htmlText = output_str;
  output_txt._visible = true;
  scrollbar_sb._visible = true;
}
function GetWeatherInfo_Status(error) {
  status_txt.htmlText = "an error has occurred";
  trace(error.description);
}
// -------------------------------------------------
// Application initialization
// -------------------------------------------------
if (inited == null) {
  inited = true;
  NetServices.setDefaultGatewayUrl(
    "http://localhost:8500/flashservices/gateway");
  gateway_conn = NetServices.createGatewayConnection();
  myService =  gateway_conn.getService(
    "http://www.ejse.com/WeatherService/Service.asmx?WSDL",
    this);
  submit_pb.setClickHandler("sendZipCode");
  submit_pb.setLabel("submit");
  ZipCode_txt.restrict = "0-9";
  ZipCode_txt.maxChars = 5;
  output_txt.html = true;
  output_txt._visible = false;
  scrollbar_sb._visible = false;
}
stop();
```

The first function in this code, sendZipCode(), is invoked when a user clicks on the Push-Button component. The code is used to set the Click Handler for the PushButton component, which you will find covered later in this example. Then a brief message is displayed in the `status_txt` text field; it states that the search has been sent to the server. In this initial function, you also set the `_visible` property for both the `output_txt` instance and the associated Scroll-Bar instance to false. This essentially hides both the text field and the scroll bar when the user clicks the Submit button.

The next function is `GetWeatherInfo_Result()`. It is triggered when the web service successfully returns data to the Flash application. At this point, `GetWeatherInfo_Result()` clears the `status_txt` message and creates a new variable called `output_str`. This will hold a string that will eventually be displayed in the `output_txt` text field. This text instance will be populated from the data returned from the web service.

In this listing, the next piece of code you will recognize as a typical `for..in` loop. The `for..in` loop allows you to loop over an object, and for each iteration you will append the key/value pair to the `output_str` variable. ActionScript's `for..in` loop is very similar to looping over a structure in ColdFusion using `<cfloop collection="#result#" item="i">` syntax. The last part of the `GetWeatherInfo_Result()` function copies the contents of the `output_str` variable into the `output_txt` field on the Stage, and finally you make both the text field and the ScrollBar component instance visible.

The final function is `GetWeatherInfo_Status()`, which simply displays a brief error message to the `status_txt` field saying that the service was unsuccessful.

NOTE   If an error occurred during our call to the remote web service, we don't unhide the large text field and ScrollBar.

The remaining code is all the initialization section, where you set up the Gateway, service, and a few items on the Stage.

```
myService = gateway_conn.getService(
  "http://www.ejse.com/WeatherService/Service.asmx?WSDL",
  this);
```

Notice that you are directly consuming a web service from Flash using Flash Remoting, so instead of the `gateway_conn.getService()` function trying to connect to a local CFC or CFM template, you pass a complete URL to the web service. If you had to write CFC functions to invoke each of the web service methods, then you'd essentially be doubling the amount of resources you need to access a remote service.

The following two lines in the initialization section cover the Submit PushButton. The first line sets the click handler for the button, and the second line sets the text that appears on the button:

```
submit_pb.setClickHandler("sendZipCode");
submit_pb.setLabel("submit");
```

The following two lines are very useful when you are building forms in Flash.

```
ZipCode_txt.restrict = "0-9";
ZipCode_txt.maxChars = 5;
```

The `restrict` property filters out which characters are allowed in the text field instance. For this simple application, you are only allowing U.S. zip codes and you only need digits 0–9. If you were dealing with currency, you would want to allow numbers, decimals, commas, and possibly the dollar sign.

The next property, `maxChars`, sets the maximum number of characters that can be entered into this text field. This is similar to the `maxlength` attribute in HTML text input fields.

Finally you enable HTML content in the `output_txt` text field, and then hide the `output_txt` and `scrollbar_sb` instances by default:

```
output_txt.html = true;
output_txt._visible = false;
scrollbar_sb._visible = false;
```

These two instances will be visible only if the Flash application successfully receives a response from the web service.

This was a fairly simplistic example. You will definitely want to filter out the information that is shown to the end user, and clean up the interface a lot more. By using Flash instead of HTML to display things like the weather, you can request new data from a web service without refreshing the entire page. You can simply use Flash's `setInterval()` function to call the `myService.GetWeatherInfo()` function every five minutes and Flash can take care of refreshing the information as necessary. You can also add a users' postal code to the database so they won't have to reenter the value every time they visit your site or go to a new page.

There are a few other important issues we should to cover that deal with Flash Remoting and ColdFusion. First and foremost, when you return a Boolean value from a CFC or CFM page to Flash, the value gets improperly cast as a string. If you have a CFC or CFM page that needs to return a Boolean, then you can do one of two things: you can return a numeric 0 or 1, which Flash will then convert to Boolean values; or you must explicitly set the `returntype` in your CF Component to `Boolean`. Similarly, if you are returning numeric data from ColdFusion to Flash, you must explicitly set the `returntype` to `numeric`, otherwise it will be cast as a string instead of a numeric value.

More information can be found at the following URLs:

```
http://livedocs.macromedia.com/frdocs/Using_Flash_Remoting_MX/UseASData4.jsp#1
171141
http://www.macromedia.com/support/flash/flashremoting/releasenotes/releasenote
s.html#cf
```

Passing Variables to a Web Service

Something that you have not seen yet in this chapter is how a variable can be passed to a remote web service. Flash has a shortcut for creating objects, similar to the shortcut for writing conditional `if` statements. Instead of having to write

```
var params = new Object();
params.age = _global.Age;
cfTips.Browse(params);
```

you can just type

```
{Age:_global.Age}
```

The curly brackets `{ }` tell ActionScript that an object is being created. The `Age:` tells Action-Script that `Age` is the key, and `_global.Age` will be evaluated and passed to the remote function.

If you needed to pass multiple parameters to a function using this method, you just separate each key/value with a comma:

```
myService.myFunction({ID:132,size:32,var3:'on sale'});
```

There is also a shortcut for creating arrays in ActionScript. Instead of using curly brackets `{ }` as in the `myService` example above, you use square brackets `[]` and pass a comma-separated list of values, as seen here:

```
var names_array = ['Danesh', 'Camden', 'Bainum', 'Rish'];
```

This is shorthand for

```
var names_array = new Array();
names_array[0] = 'Danesh';
names_array[1] = 'Camden';
names_array[2] = 'Bainum';
names_array[3] = 'Rish';
```

Calculating Distance with Flash, ColdFusion, and Flash Remoting

In the following exercise, you integrate Flash Remoting, ColdFusion, and web services together in one application. This application calculates the distance in miles between two locations. The locations are input using phone numbers.

NOTE   Because of the nature of the web service being used, this application only works with phone numbers from the United States.

Creating the Flash Interface

The Flash interface is going to be a simple combination of text fields and components. To build it, follow these steps:

1. Create a new file in Flash by choosing File ➢ New From Template.... Then choose Web and finally Basic from the Category Items list.

2. Then lock the Actions layer.

3. Then create a new layer by selecting Insert ➢ Layer and name it **Form**.

4. In the Property Inspector, select the Text tool and set it to Static Text.

5. Click on the Stage to create a field, and type **Phone 1:**. Create a second static text field below this, and type **Phone 2:**. Refer to Figure 23.17 for guidance.

6. In the Property Inspector, change the Text tool to Input Text and turn borders on by selecting Show Border Around Text.

7. Create two text fields on the Stage that are each large enough to hold a phone number. Name these instances **ph1_txt** and **ph2_txt** and position them beside the two static text instances that were created in step 5.

8. With the ph1_txt text instance selected, go to the Property Inspector and press the Character button near the bottom right. The Character Options dialog box will open (see Figure 23.20).

9. Select the radio button beside Only and click the checkbox beside Numerals (0–9). In the text input box below these characters, enter a dash (-). This will allow users only to enter numbers and dashes for phone numbers. When you are finished, press Done to close the dialog box.

FIGURE 23.20:

The Character Options dialog box

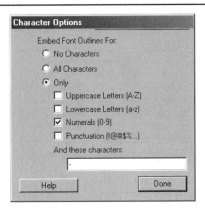

10. Repeat steps 8 and 9 for the ph2_txt text field instance.

11. Draw a large text field on the Stage large enough to accommodate approximately 12 lines of text. Name this instance `results_txt` and set the Line type to Multiline (see Figure 23.21).

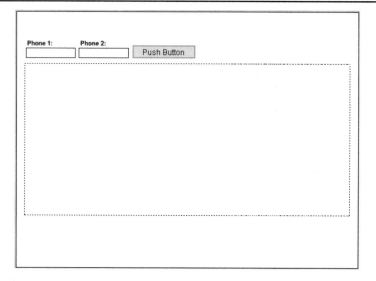

Now that you have set up the interface for your application, you need to add the code that will make it work.

Adding the ActionScript

Now select frame 1 of the Actions layer, and type the content of Listing 23.9 into the Actions panel.

Listing 23.9   Phone distances (phone_final.fla)

```
/*
   Name:          /c23/phone_final.fla
   Description:   calculate the distance between two          phone numbers
*/

#include "NetServices.as"
// uncomment this line when you want to use
//the NetConnect Debugger
//#include "NetDebug.as"
// -----------------------------------------------
// Handlers for user interaction events
// -----------------------------------------------
function printResult() {
  if (ph1_txt.length == 0) {
```

```
      return;
  }
  var ph1_array = ph1_txt.text.split("-", 3);
  if (ph2_txt.length == 0) {
    ph2_txt.text = ph1_txt.text;
  }
  var ph2_array = ph2_txt.text.split("-", 3);
  var params = new Object();
  params.orgAreaCode = ph1_array[0];
  params.orgSwitch = ph1_array[1];
  params.destAreaCode = ph2_array[0];
  params.destSwitch = ph2_array[1];
  phoneLookup.getAddressFromPhone(params);
  results_txt._visible = false;
}
// -------------------------------------------------
// Handlers for data coming in from server
// -------------------------------------------------
function getAddressFromPhone_Result(result) {
  var output_txt = "";
  output_txt += headerPrefix_str+ph1_txt.text+headerSuffix_str+"<br>";
  output_txt += "<b>City: </b>"+result.City1+"<br>";
  output_txt += "<b>State: </b>"+result.State1+"<br>";
  output_txt += "<b>Zip: </b>"+result.Zip1+"<br>";
  if (ph1_txt.text != ph2_txt.text) {
    output_txt += "<br>";
    output_txt += headerPrefix_str+ph2_txt.text+headerSuffix_str+"<br>";
    output_txt += "<b>City: </b>"+result.City2+"<br>";
    output_txt += "<b>State: </b>"+result.State2+"<br>";
    output_txt += "<b>Zip: </b>"+result.Zip2+"<br>";
    output_txt += "<br>";
    output_txt += headerPrefix_str+"Mileage:"+result.Mileage+headerSuffix_str;
  }
  results_txt.htmlText = output_txt;
  results_txt._visible = true;
}
function getAddressFromPhone_Status(status) {
  trace("failure!");
}
// -------------------------------------------------
// Application initialization
// -------------------------------------------------
if (inited == null) {
  inited = true;
  NetServices.setDefaultGatewayUrl(
    "http://localhost:8500/flashservices/gateway");
  gateway_conn = NetServices.createGatewayConnection();
  phoneLookup = gateway_conn.getService(
    "CFMXHandbook.Phone.PhoneCFC", this);
}
ph1_txt.maxChars = 12;
```

```
ph2_txt.maxChars = 12;
submit_pb.setLabel("submit");
submit_pb.setClickHandler("printResult");
results_txt.html = true;
headerPrefix_str = "<font color='#0099FF' size='12'><b>";
headerSuffix_str = "</b></font>";
stop();
```

In the event handlers section we have a single function named `printResult()` that looks like the following:

```
function printResult() {
  if (ph1_txt.length == 0) {
    return;
  }
  var ph1_array = ph1_txt.text.split("-", 3);
  if (ph2_txt.length == 0) {
    ph2_txt.text = ph1_txt.text;
  }
  var ph2_array = ph2_txt.text.split("-", 3);
  var params = new Object();
  params.orgAreaCode = ph1_array[0];
  params.orgSwitch = ph1_array[1];
  params.destAreaCode = ph2_array[0];
  params.destSwitch = ph2_array[1];
  phoneLookup.getAddressFromPhone(params);
  results_txt._visible = false;
}
```

The first thing that happens in this code is that it checks to see if the user has entered some data into the text field. This code does not perform any kind of data validation for the sake of simplicity in this example. If the length of the string is zero then function is exited.

Next the phone number is converted from a string into an array using the dashes as a delimiter.

The second parameter in the ActionScript `split` method is optional, but it tells Action-Script the number of items to put into the array. Here it is set to three because you're only interested in the first three tokens in the phone number.

TIP   ActionScript's `split` method is similar to using `<cfset ph1_array = ListToArray(` `ph1_txt, "-" ) />` in ColdFusion.

The next part of the code checks to see if the user has entered anything for the second phone number in the Flash form. If there is no phone number specified in the ph2_txt text field, then the value is copied from ph1_txt into the ph2_txt field. The second phone number is similarly split into an array. Then an object is created that will hold the variables being sent to the CFC.

You will notice that only the first two elements in the array are passed to the remote function. This is because a third party remote web service (these will be covered in greater detail in the next chapter) is being used, and this particular one only requires the first two elements of each phone number to determine the mileage between the two Zip codes. Finally the remote function is called, the necessary parameters are passed, and the results_txt text field is hidden.

The callback function section has two functions, both of which respond to events from the getAddressFromPhone() function. Let's take another look at the function here:

```
function getAddressFromPhone_Result(result) {
  var output_txt = "";
  output_txt += headerPrefix_str+ph1_txt.text+headerSuffix_str+"<br>";
  output_txt += "<b>City: </b>"+result.City1+"<br>";
  output_txt += "<b>State: </b>"+result.State1+"<br>";
  output_txt += "<b>Zip: </b>"+result.Zip1+"<br>";
  if (ph1_txt.text != ph2_txt.text) {
    output_txt += "<br>";
    output_txt += headerPrefix_str+ph2_txt.text+headerSuffix_str+ "<br>";
    output_txt += "<b>City: </b>"+result.City2+"<br>";
    output_txt += "<b>State: </b>"+result.State2+"<br>";
    output_txt += "<b>Zip: </b>"+result.Zip2+"<br>";
    output_txt += "<br>";
    output_txt += headerPrefix_str+"Mileage:"+ result.Mileage+headerSuffix_str;
  }
  results_txt.htmlText = output_txt;
  results_txt._visible = true;
}
```

When data from the application server is received by the Flash movie, the _Result handler is triggered. This creates a local variable in the function that will contain the output that will be displayed in the results_txt text field. In this snippet, first the phone numbers are displayed as headers. The formatting is in the headerPrefix_str variable, which is defined at the end of the ActionScript for the initialization section. The formatting is put into a variable because it is usually easier to change the font color and size in one location instead of multiple places in your code.

Then the City, State, and Zip are saved for the first phone number into the output variable. The code then checks to see if the user has entered two different phone numbers. If they did, the City, State, and Zip are saved into the output variable for the second phone number along with the mileage between the two phone numbers. Finally, the contents of the output variable are copied into the results_txt instance and the visibility of the text area is set to true.

The last section of ActionScript code in this example is the initialization section that sets up the Gateway connection. This is the same as it was in previous examples. However, some code that hasn't been discussed or seen yet is shown below:

```
ph1_txt.maxChars = 12;
ph2_txt.maxChars = 12;
submit_pb.setLabel("submit");
submit_pb.setClickHandler("printResult");
results_txt.html = true;
headerPrefix_str = "<font color='#0099FF' size='12'><b>";
headerSuffix_str = "</b></font>";
```

The first two lines of this segment simply set the maximum number of characters a user can type into a text field. This is similar to the `maxlength` attribute in the following HTML code:

```
<input type="text" name="ph1_txt" maxlength="12">
```

Then a label is set for the `submit_pb` button and the Click Handler is set to the `printResult()` function that is defined near the beginning of the ActionScript listing. The `html` property is set to true for the `results_txt` instance so that HTML formatting can be used in the application. The last two lines of code simply describe the HTML formatting that is being used for the headers in the results window.

Writing the CFC

In this section you will step through the code for the ColdFusion component. Create a file called `PhoneCFC.cfc` in your `<webroot>\CFMXHandbook\Phone\` directory and type in Listing 23.10's code.

Listing 23.10   **Phone distances (PhoneCFC.cfc)**

```
<!---
   Name:          /c23/PhoneCFC.cfc
   Description:    Calculating distance
--->
<cfcomponent>

  <cffunction name="getAddressFromPhone" access="remote"
             returntype="struct" output="No">
    <cfargument name="orgAreaCode" type="numeric" required="Yes" />
    <cfargument name="orgSwitch" type="numeric" required="Yes" />
    <cfargument name="destAreaCode" type="numeric" required="Yes" />
    <cfargument name="destSwitch" type="numeric" required="Yes" />

    <cfset var returnObj = structNew( ) />
    <cfset var phoneInfo = "" />
```

```
<cfinvoke method="RateBasicInformation" returnVariable="PhoneInfo"
          webService="http://www.xeeinc.com/RateInformation/
                      RateInfo.asmx?WSDL">
  <cfinvokeargument name="orgAreaCode" value="#Arguments.orgAreaCode#" />
  <cfinvokeargument name="orgSwitch" value="#Arguments.orgSwitch#" />
  <cfinvokeargument name="destAreaCode" value="#Arguments.destAreaCode#" />
  <cfinvokeargument name="destSwitch" value="#Arguments.destSwitch#" />
</cfinvoke>

<cfscript>
  returnObj.Mileage = phoneInfo.getMileage( );

  returnObj.City1 = phoneInfo.getOrigCity( );
  returnObj.State1 = phoneInfo.getOrigState( );
  returnObj.Zip1 = phoneInfo.getOrigZip( );

  returnObj.City2 = phoneInfo.getDestCity( );
  returnObj.State2 = phoneInfo.getDestState( );
  returnObj.Zip2 = phoneInfo.getDestZip( );
</cfscript>

<cfreturn returnObj />
  </cffunction>
</cfcomponent>
```

Web services will be covered in detail in the next chapter, so we don't need to explain them in detail here. In Listing 23.10, you are simply passing the four arguments that were sent to the CFC to the web service. PhoneCFC.cfc expects four required, numeric arguments to be passed to it. The service is returning a structure that contains a series of functions that allow you to retrieve the City, State, and Zip for both of the phone numbers as well as the mileage between the two Zip codes. You'll save each one of these values into the local variable and return the struct to Flash.

After this happens, two local variables are created one will hold the return value of the component, and the other will contain the results of the call to the external web service

Once you have saved the phoneCFC.cfc, return to the Flash authoring environment to test the application. First, press Ctrl+Enter to open the movie and make sure that everything is running smoothly. You will then be able to enter two American phone numbers, and submit them so information about the numbers and a distance between the two points can be gathered. The results are shown in Figure 23.22.

FIGURE 23.22:

The final movie

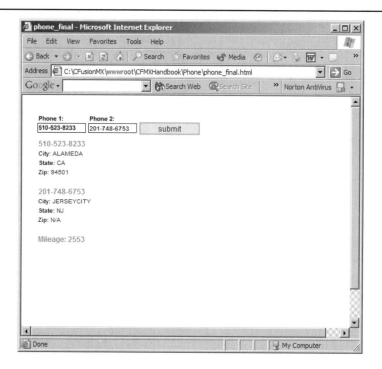

Resources for Flash Remoting

Check out the following resources and communities for more information or help on the topic of Flash Remoting:

- Macromedia LiveDocs for Flash Remoting at `http://livedocs.macromedia.com/ frdocs/Using_Flash_Remoting_MX/contents.htm`.

- Documentation on CF Server side actions at `http://download.macromedia.com/ pub/coldfusion/documentation/cfmx_server_side_actions.pdf`.

- The FlashComm mailing list at `http://chattyfig.figleaf.com`.

- The Macromedia newsgroup for Flash Remoting (`http://www.macromedia.com/ support/forums`) at `macromedia.flash.flash_remoting`.

- A new community for those using Flash and ColdFusion `http://www.devmx.com`.

In Sum

You have covered a lot of ground in this chapter. Not only have you learned some of the fundamentals of a programming language—ActionScript—you've also studied an entire new technology—Flash Remoting MX. By this time, you should be able to create working prototypes that are ready to take to a front-end designer. You can now use `LoadVars` to pass name/value pairs between Flash and a server, or use the Remoting Gateway to transfer data between a movie and your server.

If you are familiar with Java, .NET, or SOAP technologies, you can also use the Flash Remoting technology. You will need to download software from Macromedia to take advantage of Remoting with these technologies.

There are alternative ways of loading data into Flash. For example, XML structures can be loaded into Flash and parsed instead of using ColdFusion. In addition, the new Flash Communication Server (FlashCom) can be used to create real-time communications using video, audio, and text. FlashCom can also be integrated with Flash Remoting, databases, and an application server to create truly dynamic and real-time environments.

Further information and tutorials on the topics in this chapter can be found at `www.flash-mx.com`.

CHAPTER 24

Web Services

By Matt Liotta

- What do web services provide?

- Consuming web services automatically

- Understanding the hidden details of web services

- Consuming web services manually

- Producing web services

Web services are a disruptive technology in much the same way that the Internet is. A *disruptive technology* is one that significantly changes how people and systems operate. Such technologies allow different applications and organizations to communicate, using established standards, no matter what platform or language the application uses. Those of you who are familiar with technologies such as Remote Procedure Call (RPC), Electronic Data Interchange (EDI), and Electronic Application Integration (EAI) will recognize that web services follow a similar arrangement. However, unlike these other technologies, web services are built on top of open standards.

In this chapter, I will be covering what web services are, how to consume them, and how to produce them. You will see how these open standards cover all facets of using RPC for distributed applications, how ColdFusion applies these standards allowing for Rapid Application Development (RAD) of web services, and finally, how to get around any limits ColdFusion's RAD capabilities have.

Web Services Defined

Web services are very similar to other disruptive technologies. Specifically, web services are a form of RPC that can be consumed using standardized, application-independent technologies that let you consume and publish remote application functionality over the Internet. The implementation of a web service is very much like working with a class in an object-oriented system in that they both have properties and methods. The main difference between a web service and a class is that a web service's methods are invoked (consumed) remotely. In fact, in many cases, a web service is actually nothing more than a proxy to an existing object-oriented implementation.

Web services use a client/server model for communication, so you as a developer are either consuming a web service or producing one.

Web services can also be managed using an additional set of standardized technologies, UDDI. Exhaustive discussion of these management technologies is beyond the scope of this chapter.

WSDL

The Web Service Description Language (WSDL) is an XML document that describes a web service's purpose and how to access it. It includes information about what operations (methods) can be preformed on the web service and the datatype signatures associated with those operations as needed. A web service cannot be consumed unless the WSDL is available. I will cover WSDL on an as-needed basis throughout this chapter, but I won't cover it in-depth because WSDL will generally be hidden from you.

SOAP

The Simple Object Access Protocol (SOAP) is an XML document that encapsulates the sending and receiving of web service requests and responses. It is often best to think of these requests and responses as messages enclosed in an envelope. This envelope describes what is in the message and what to do with it and contains rules for datatype mapping as well as a convention for handling RPC.

UDDI

Universal Description, Discovery, and Integration (UDDI) is a standard that allows you to programmatically locate web services with specific capabilities. Various companies have created public UDDI registries with which any web services producer can register. Thus, a web services consumer can use these UDDI registries like a "yellow pages" and find web services to meet their specific needs. UDDI gives developers the ability to discover web services, describe their business purpose, and integrate them into their applications. As you can imagine, UDDI is a large subject that is out of scope for this chapter. However, if you are going to be developing web services, it is worth looking into, but it is certainly not needed.

More about the Technologies Discussed in This Chapter

To learn more about these technologies, visit the following websites:

- For WSDL visit `http://www.w3.org/TR/wsdl`.
- For SOAP visit `http://www.w3.org/TR/SOAP`.
- For UDDI visit `http://www.uddi.org`.

Interoperability Stack

Web services combine many different standardized technologies. Each one of these technologies is layered on top of each other to form the *interoperability stack* (see Figure 24.1). The technologies that make up this stack can be divided into two types: transport and data marshalling.

Transport   The bottom-most layers of the stack are made up of transport technologies. Generally speaking, the two bottom-most layers will always be Internet Protocol (IP) and Transmission Control Protocol (TCP). Hyper Text Transport Protocol (HTTP) is the most common technology to layer on top of TCP, although some web services make use of the Simple Mail Transfer Protocol (SMTP). I am going to focus on HTTP for simplicity.

Data Marshalling   On top of the transport layers are the data marshalling layers. The bottom-most data marshalling layer will generally be Extensible Markup Language (XML). SOAP is most commonly the layer on top of XML; however, some web services use XML-RPC or Web Distributed Data eXchange (WDDX). I am going to focus on SOAP since that is by far the most common.

FIGURE 24.1:

The interoperability stack

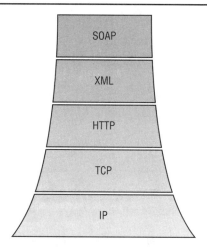

Consuming Web Services

In this section, I will describe how to consume web services—automatically, using `cfinvoke` and `createObject()`, and manually, using CFML and Java.

The first method makes use of a new tag for ColdFusion MX (CFMX), `cfinvoke`. This tag can be used for many different purposes, but I will only show how to use it with web services. I will also show how to make use of `createObject()`, which is similar in function to `cfinvoke`, but stylistically different.

After consuming some web services with `cfinvoke`, I'll move on and show you how to consume web services manually using CFML.

Consuming Web Services Automatically with cfinvoke

Before you can consume any web service, you need to know three things: the URL to the web service's WSDL file, what method you want to call, and what parameters the method expects. The WSDL file describes all of the available methods and their respective parameters.

The XMethods website (`http://www.xmethods.net`) has a large number of publicly available web services that are great for learning about consuming web services without immediately understanding all the ins and outs. To get started with this chapter's discussion of consuming a web service, I chose to use the TemperatureService example from XMethods, which has a single method, `getTemp`. This method expects a zip code as a string and returns a temperature for that zip code as a float. I figured all this out by reading the TemperatureService's WSDL file, which is available at `http://www.xmethods.net/sd/2001/TemperatureService.wsdl`.

Getting to Know the WSDL File

The XMethods website also provides a more-readable form of the WSDL file at `http://www.xmethods.net/ve2/WSDLAnalyzer.po?serviceid=8`. However, not every web service producer will provide this helpful tool for you. So it is worth learning how to read this file on your own.

When looking at a WSDL file, you should try and find the appropriate method's request and response definitions. These are easy to find because they follow a standard naming convention. The following is a portion of the TemperatureService's WSDL file that shows the request and response definitions:

```
<message name="getTempRequest">
  <part name="zipcode" type="xsd:string" />
</message>
<message name="getTempResponse">
  <part name="return" type="xsd:float" />
</message>
```

By reading this, you should be able to tell what parameter `getTemp()` expects and what its type is as well as what type it returns.

At this point, you may be asking yourself how CF deals with web services types since it is a typeless language. I will cover this topic later in the WSDL-to-ColdFusion datatype mapping section when I show you how CF handles web services under the hood. For now, just assume that the type issues will be taken care of for you automatically.

Consuming the TemperatureService

Thanks to XMethods, I now have the three requirements for consuming their sample TemperatureService: the URL to the TemperatureService's WSDL file, the method name, and what parameters the method expects. These are used for the attributes of the `cfinvoke` tag, which allows me to consume this web service. The syntax for the `cfinvoke` tag is as follows and its attributes are further described in Table 24.1.

```
<cfinvoke
    webservice = "URLtoWSDL"
```

```
    method = "operationName"
    [username] = "username"
    [password] = "password"
    inputParam1 = "val1"
    inputParam2 = "val2"
    ...
    returnVariable = "varName"
>
```

TABLE 24.1: The cfinvoke Tag's Attributes

Attribute	Required	Description
webService	Yes	The URL of the web service's WSDL file
method	Yes	The name of the method you wish to call
username	No	The username to use for remote authentication
password	No	The password to use for remote authentication
returnVariable	Yes	The name of the variable to which to assign the result

You can also specify parameters for the web service in two other ways. First, you can nest the cfinvokeargument tag inside of the cfinvoke tag for each parameter. Or, second, you can create a struct of key/value pairs for each of the parameters and pass it to the cfinvoke tag using the argumentCollection attribute. All three methods are demonstrated in the code below.

```
<cfinvoke
  webService =
    "http://www.xmethods.net/sd/2001/TemperatureService.wsdl"
  method = "getTemp"
  zipcode = "94105"
  returnVariable = "result"
>
<cfoutput>#result#</cfoutput>

<cfinvoke
  webService =
    "http://www.xmethods.net/sd/2001/TemperatureService.wsdl"
  method = "getTemp"
  returnVariable = "result"
>
  <cfinvokeargument name="zipcode" value="94105">
</cfinvoke>
<cfoutput>#result#</cfoutput>

<cfscript>
  params = structNew();
```

```
    params.zipcode = "94105";
</cfscript>
<cfinvoke
  webService =
     "http://www.xmethods.net/sd/2001/TemperatureService.wsdl"
  method = "getTemp"
  argumentCollection="#params#"
  returnVariable = "result"
>
</cfinvoke>
<cfoutput>#result#</cfoutput>
```

Consuming Web Services Automatically with createObject()

Besides the `cfinvoke` tag, CF also has one other built-in way to consume web services—`createObject()`. Below is an example of calling the TemperatureService using the `create-Object()` function.

```
<cfscript>
  ts = createObject("webService",
    "http://www.xmethods.net/sd/2001/TemperatureService.wsdl");
  result = ts.getTemp("94105");
  writeOutput(result);
</cfscript>
```

For the most part, using `createObject()` has the same effect as using the `cfinvoke` tag, albeit with a different style syntax. However, it is not possible to pass authentication information with `createObject()`. If you need to be able to pass authentication information, you will need to use the `cfinvoke` tag.

Consuming Web Services Manually

In this section, I'll show you how to consume web services manually using CFML. This method will use `cfhttp` and `cfxml` to make raw SOAP requests. This will allow me to cover some of the underlying mechanics of web services that have been hidden from you by `cfinvoke`. Finally, I will make use of Apache Axis (an open source web services package) to manually consume web services using Java. After I cover these three methods, you should feel comfortable with how web services work and appreciate all the work `cfinvoke` does for you.

WSDL-to-ColdFusion Datatype Mapping

As you may have seen earlier, web services support strong datatyping. Because CF is a typeless language, this can lead to some confusion. According to the CF documentation, datatypes are mapped as shown in Table 24.2.

TABLE 24.2: WSDL-to-CF Datatype Mappings

CF Datatype	WSDL Datatype
numeric	SOAP-ENC:double
boolean	SOAP-ENC:boolean
string	SOAP-ENC:string
array	SOAP-ENC:Array
binary	xsd:base64Binary
date	xsd:dateTime
struct	complex type

Because CFML is a typeless language, it may have seemed surprising to see these CF datatypes listed in Table 24.2. Nevertheless, at runtime, CF can determine whether a given variable can be evaluated as one of these types. However, there is really only one datatype mapping with which you should concern yourself. Any WSDL datatype that is not listed in Table 24.2 will be considered a complex type, and according to the table, mapped into a struct. At least according to the documentation that is the case.

In practice, the resulting variable will seem like a struct in that you can use dot notation to reference its nested elements, but none of the structure functions will work. This has two implications. First, if you want the resulting variable to be a struct, you will need to manually map each nested element to an actual struct. Second and more importantly, you will have no way to programmatically determine what nested elements even exist. You can try this yourself: simply call the isStruct() function on the variable; it will return false.

The mapping of datatypes will also be a problem when you go to produce a web service with CF. However, I will be covering those issues in a later section, ColdFusion-to-WSDL datatype mapping.

NOTE   A WSDL datatype of queryBean will map to a CF query.

Web Services Parameters

I explained earlier that web services methods specify which parameters and types they expect as input as well as what type of data they return. This is not altogether different from how a function works. Some languages support functions for passing parameters by value or reference. Although ColdFusion doesn't let you do this, it does it implicitly for you. Specifically, if you pass a simple value to a CF function, it will be passed by value. If you pass a complex value to a CF function, then it will be passed by reference.

As you can imagine, it would be impossible for web services methods to support parameters being passed by reference. On the other hand, returning more than one result is an important feature and must be supported. So, WSDL allows you to define *inout parameters*.

Recall that in the "Consuming the TemperatureService" section above I passed the `zipcode` parameter to the `getTemp()` method of the TemperatureService; this was passed as a value, `"94105"`. I could have declared a variable named zip earlier and assigned `"94105"` to it, but I would still have needed CF to evaluate the variable before passing it to the method. However, if a web service method defines a parameter as inout, then I would need to pass the parameter a variable name, not a value. CF would still evaluate the variable and pass it to the method, but the method would be able to overwrite the variable's value as a result.

The Process Flow for Consuming Web Services

Although the `cfinvoke` tag allows you to consume a web service in a single step, the process is actually quite a bit more complicated. In Figure 24.2, I have shown the process flow for a typical web service call. As you can see, calling a web service is a multiple step process.

FIGURE 24.2:

The process flow of consuming a web service

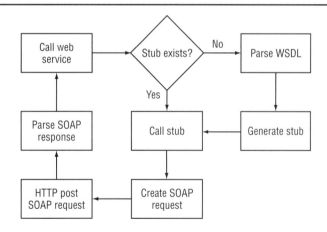

CF, like many other languages, uses stubs to lower the overhead associated with doing RPC. The idea of a stub is simple—figure out ahead of time what the remote procedure's interface is and build a local module with which to call it. Languages like Java do this at compile time, but since CF is a dynamic language, it does its web service stub generation the first time it calls a web service. This allows the subsequent requests to that web service to be faster. Thus, the first step in the process flow is to determine if a stub exists for the remote web service. If it doesn't, CF will need to parse the WSDL file, generate a stub, and register the web service with the CF Administrator.

NOTE   Using the CF Administrator you can preregister web services. This allows you to remove the overhead of creating a stub.

Once the stub has been created, the remote web service is ready to be called; the ColdFusion Server will accomplish this in three steps.

1. First, the Server will create a SOAP request. The format of the message contained in the SOAP request is specified by the remote web service's WSDL file.

2. Next, the Server will post the SOAP request to the appropriate URL. Again, the URL is specified by the remote web service's WSDL file.

3. Finally, the SOAP response will be parsed in order to obtain the result.

Although you can procedurally do these same three steps manually, the stub takes care of all of this for you. In addition, the process of generating the stub and making use of it is hidden when you use `cfinvoke`.

In the next section, I will explain how to consume a web service without using ColdFusion's built-in capabilities for calling web services.

Consuming Web Services Manually with cfhttp and cfxml

As explained earlier, the `cfinvoke` tag does much of the work needed to consume web services. Although the `cfinvoke` tag does make it easy, you sacrifice a certain amount of control. For example, as of this writing, some web services are not compatible with ColdFusion's web services implementation. For those web services, you can only use them by consuming them manually. In this section, I will explain how to consume web services using two CF tags, `cfhttp` and `cfxml`. I will encapsulate the use of these tags into a ColdFusion Component (CFC) that will act like a stub for the TemperatureService.

To get started, I create a new CFC named `temp.cfc`, which will be my stub for all interactions with the remote TemperatureService. (Recall that the TemperatureService has a single method named `getTemp` that accepts a `zipcode` parameter as a string and returns the temperature for that zip code as a float.) Thus, my new CFC, `temp.cfc`, will have a single public method with the same signature. Listing 24.1 is the code for my CFC.

Listing 24.1   TempartureService stub (temp.cfc)

```
<!---
    Name:         /c24/temp.cfc
    Description:  TempartureService stub
--->

<cfcomponent>
```

```
<cffunction name="getTemp" returnType="numeric" access="public">
  <cfargument name="zipcode" type="string" required="true">
  <cfreturn parseResponse(postRequest(generateSOAP(arguments.zipcode)))>
</cffunction>

<cffunction name="generateSOAP" returnType="string" access="private">
  <cfargument name="zipcode" type="string" required="true">
  <cfxml variable="soap">
    <SOAP-ENV:Envelope
      xmlns:SOAP-ENV="http://schemas.xmlsoap.org/soap/envelope/"
      xmlns:xsi="http://www.w3.org/1999/XMLSchema-instance"
      xmlns:xsd="http://www.w3.org/1999/XMLSchema">
      <SOAP-ENV:Body>
        <ns1:getTemp
          xmlns:ns1="urn:xmethods-Temperature"
          SOAP-ENV:encodingStyle="http://schemas.xmlsoap.org/soap/encoding/">
          <zipcode xsi:type="xsd:string">
            <cfoutput>#arguments.zipcode#</cfoutput>
          </zipcode>
        </ns1:getTemp>
      </SOAP-ENV:Body>
    </SOAP-ENV:Envelope>
  </cfxml>
  <cfreturn toString(soap)>
</cffunction>

<cffunction name="postRequest" returnType="string" access="private">
  <cfargument name="soapRequest" type="string" required="true">
  <cfhttp
    url="http://services.xmethods.com:80/soap/servlet/rpcrouter"
    method="POST">
    <cfhttpparam
      name="xml"
      value="#arguments.soapRequest#"
      type="XML">
  </cfhttp>
  <cfreturn cfhttp.fileContent>
</cffunction>

<cffunction
  name="parseResponse"
  returnType="numeric"
  access="private">
  <cfargument name="soapResponse" type="string" required="true">
  <cfset xml = XmlParse(arguments.soapResponse)>
  <cfreturn xml.Envelope.Body.getTempResponse.return.XmlText>
</cffunction>

</cfcomponent>
```

As stated earlier, the first task the stub needs to do is generate a SOAP request, so I created a method named `generateSOAP`. Although the method is several lines long, it doesn't really do anything exciting. Using the `cfxml` tag, I created my SOAP request and assigned it to a variable named `soap`. In the body of my SOAP request, I specified what method the message is intended for by creating a tag named `getTemp`, which corresponds to the method name I am calling. The fact that the name of the tag is preceded by the string "`ns1:`" indicates a namespace that I wish to use. In this case, the namespace, `ns1`, simply means `namespace1`, but it could have been anything or nothing at all.

For each parameter I want to pass to the method, I need to nest a parameter tag inside the method tag (`getTemp`) that specifies the parameter's value. In this case, the `getTemp` method expects a single parameter (`zipcode`), so I create a tag named `zipcode`. The `zipcode` tag has a single attribute representing its type, which is a string, if you recall. I need to specify the value of the parameter by nesting it inside the parameter tag, `zipcode`. Since the actual zip code is passed as an argument to this method, I use `cfoutput` to evaluate the value of `arguments.zipcode`. Once I have created the SOAP request as an XML document, I return its string value.

Now I can call the `generateSOAP` method with a `zipcode` anytime I want to create a SOAP request for the TemperatureService. The next step is to post the SOAP request to the remote web service. To do this, I create a method named `postRequest`, which takes a single argument—the SOAP request—and posts it to the remote web service using the `cfhttp` tag.

As you can see, this method is very straightforward. I specify two attributes for the `cfhttp` tag, `url` and `method`. I obtained the `url` attribute by reading the WSDL file associated with the TemperatureService. Specifically, the `url` is located in the following snippet.

```
<service name="TemperatureService">
  <documentation>
    Returns current temperature in a given U.S.zip code
  </documentation>
  <port name="TemperaturePort" binding="tns:TemperatureBinding">
    <soap:address
      location="http://services.xmethods.net:80/soap/servlet/rpcrouter"
    />
  </port>
</service>
```

For the `method` attribute, I chose to use `post` because that is what the SOAP standard specifies. SOAP supports all types of HTTP posts, but some SOAP-based web services only support certain types of posts. Unfortunately, the WSDL file does not specify what types of posts the TemperatureService accepts, so you have to use trial and error to determine it. Almost all SOAP-based web services will support "raw" posts as does the TemperatureService, so that is what I used. To do a raw post, I specify a `cfhttpparam` tag with a type of XML. The value of the `cfhttpparam` tag is, of course, the SOAP request itself.

After cfhttp makes a successful request, it creates a variable named cfhttp, which is a struct that contains the response. The body of that response is available by referencing the key fileContent in the cfhttp struct. My method simply returns the value of the fileContent key. I have included an example response here:

```
<SOAP-ENV:Envelope
  xmlns:SOAP-ENV="http://schemas.xmlsoap.org/soap/envelope/"
  xmlns:xsi="http://www.w3.org/1999/XMLSchema-instance"
  xmlns:xsd="http://www.w3.org/1999/XMLSchema">
  <SOAP-ENV:Body>
    <ns1:getTempResponse
      xmlns:ns1="urn:xmethods-Temperature"
      SOAP-ENV:encodingStyle="http://schemas.xmlsoap.org/soap/encoding/">
      <return xsi:type="xsd:float">68.0</return>
    </ns1:getTempResponse>
  </SOAP-ENV:Body>
</SOAP-ENV:Envelope>
```

As you can see, the response is a SOAP response that I need to parse in order to get the actual result. Again, I create a method to do this, which I name parseResponse.

Thanks to CFML's new XML capabilities, parsing out the result from the SOAP response is quite easy. First, I create a new XML document by calling the xmlParse function and assigning its result to variable named xml. Then, I simply return the value of the return tag nested in the SOAP response using dot notation.

Now that I have the three steps required to consume the TemperatureService encapsulated into methods, I am ready to finish the getTemp method. Because all the work has been done by the other methods, I simply chain them together to complete the entire process. With the getTemp method complete, so is my TemperatureService stub. Much like using the cfinvoke tag or the CreateObject function, I can now make use of the TemperatureService very easily.

```
<cfobject type="component" name="temp" component="temp">
<cfoutput>#temp.getTemp(94105)#</cfoutput>
```

With these two lines of code, I create an instance of the temp CFC and then output the results of calling the getTemp method.

At this point, it's probably very clear how much work the cfinvoke tag saves you as a developer. Also, you might be wondering if CF uses a similar approach for generating the stubs it uses for cfinvoke. It does indeed, but the stubs are not created using CFML. In fact, the stubs are Java based and are created using an open source project from the Apache Foundation named Axis. The next section covers how to use Apache Axis to consume web services.

Consuming Web Services Manually with Apache Axis

ColdFusion has always offered a simplified interface for web developers, one that includes the cfquery tag and the cfsearch tag; when this was first offered, it seemed like cutting edge technology. CFMX has followed this precedent with the introduction of the cfinvoke and cfxml tags discussed in this chapter. All of these tags share one thing in common; they are interfaces to third party technology. In the case of cfinvoke and consuming web services, CF makes use of Apache Axis.

Apache Axis is a Java-based framework for web services. It simplifies the consumption and production of web services using Java and is compliant with the Java API for XML Remote Procedure Calls (JAX-RPC). There are two important things to realize about Apache Axis and CFMX. First, CFMX ships with an embedded version of Apache Axis, which is not the same as the publicly distributed one available directly from Apache. Second, and more importantly, not only does the ColdFusion Server use Apache as its underlying technology for handling web services, but you can use Apache Axis without using ColdFusion's built-in interfaces.

In this section, I am again going to consume a web service in two lines, except this time, I will create my TemperatureService stub using Apache Axis and Java. As you can imagine, creating a web service stub in Java would take considerably more work than with CFML. However, I won't need to worry about this because Apache Axis can generate all the necessary Java code for me.

Apache Axis provides a command-line tool named wsdl2java. This tool takes the URI to a WSDL file as a command-line parameter. The tool downloads and parses the WSDL file and then generates the Java code needed to make use of that web service. You can find this tool in a directory named bin nested under a directory named runtime, which is in the base ColdFusion installation directory.

Using the following command-line, I was able to generate four Java classes, Temperature-BindingStub.java, TemperaturePortType.java, TemperatureService.java, and Temperature-ServiceLocator.java.

```
w2dsl2java http://www.xmethods.net/sd/2001/TemperatureService.wsdl
```

Now that I have these four Java classes created for you, all you need to do is compile them. In order to compile them, you will need two things. First, you will need JDK 1.4.*x*. Second, you will need JAX-RPC. Once you have the JDK and JAX-RPC installed, you can compile the Java classes using the Java compiler (javac). You will need to include jaxrpc.jar and web-services.jar in your classpath. You can find the webservices.jar file in your ColdFusion installation base directory in the directory lib, which is nested under runtime. The jaxrpc .jar file's location will vary depending on the installation of the JDK and JAX-RPC.

Once all four Java class files have been compiled, make sure they are available to CF by placing them in the ColdFusion Server's classpath. Once they are available to the Server, you can consume the TemperatureService using the following code:

```
<cfobject
  type="java"
  name="temp"
```

```
        class="net.xmethods.www.TemperatureServiceLocator"
        action="create">
 <cfoutput>#temp.getTemperaturePort().getTemp(94105)#</cfoutput>
```

The first line creates a new instance of the `TemperatureServiceLocator`. With the `TemperatureServiceLocator` you can call the `getTemperaturePort` method to get an instance of `TemperatureBindingStub`. Once you have an instance of `TemperatureBindingStub`, you can call its `getTemp` method by passing a zip code as a parameter; this will return the temperature for that zip code as a float.

Producing Web Services

Producing web services simply means making functionality available to remote clients using web services standards. As stated earlier, web services can use a variety of transport and marshalling protocols. For simplicity, I am going to focus on producing web services using HTTP and SOAP because they are the most common.

This section works through a simple web service example much like the TemperatureService studied in the section on consuming web services. The IdentityService example used here will produce *identities*; an identity is simply an object that is unique in a given context. For example, a primary key in a database is considered an identity in the context of a table.

The IdentityService has two methods, `getGUID` and `getSessionID`. The `getGUID` method returns a Globally Unique Identifier (GUID), which is a 36-character string that is theoretically guaranteed to be unique in any context. The `getSessionID` method returns an integer representing the session that belongs to the remote client.

Using CFCs

To get started, I am going to produce the IdentityService using a CFC. As you know, a CFC is a CFML way of encapsulating functionality. Additionally, CFCs can be used to produce web services by making that functionality available to remote clients. This is done by changing the `access` attribute of the appropriate CFC methods to `remote`. According to the documentation, for a CFC to be published as a web service, the following list of requirements must be met.

- The value of the `access` attribute of the `cffunction` tag must be `remote`.

- The `cffunction` tag must include the `returnType` attribute to specify a return type.

- The `output` attribute of the `cffunction` tag must be set to `false`.

- The attribute setting `required="false"` for the `cfargument` tag is ignored because CF considers all parameters as required.

Only the first and last requirement of the above list seems to be true. First, not specifying a `returnType` attribute seems to have no effect; nor does specifying an `output` attribute. However, if you actually try and output anything, the code will produce undefined results. Simply consider the elements of the above list to be good practices. Listing 24.2 is the CFC I created to represent the IdentityService.

Listing 24.2   **The IdentityService (identity.cfc)**

```
<!---
    Name:          /c24/identity.cfc
    Description:   IdentityService
--->
<cfcomponent output="false">
  <cffunction
    name="getGUID"
    returnType="guid"
    access="remote"
    output="false">
    <cfreturn insert("-", createUUID(), 23)>
  </cffunction>

  <cffunction
    name="getSessionID"
    returnType="numeric"
    access="remote"
    output="false">
    <cfreturn session.sessionID>
  </cffunction>
</cfcomponent>
```

As you can see, my CFC has two remote methods, `getGUID` and `getSessionID`. There is absolutely nothing special about these methods except that their `access` attribute is set to `remote`. If I put the CFC in my web root and request it via a URL with "?wsdl" appended to the end of it, I will be able to get the WSDL file generated by the ColdFusion Server for this CFC. I have included the relevant parts of the WSDL file here:

```
<wsdl:message name="getSessionIDRequest" />
<wsdl:message name="getSessionIDResponse">
  <wsdl:part name="return" type="SOAP-ENC:double" />
</wsdl:message>
...
<wsdl:message name="getGUIDRequest" />
<wsdl:message name="getGUIDResponse">
  <wsdl:part name="return" type="SOAP-ENC:string" />
</wsdl:message>
...
```

```
<wsdl:service name="identityService">
  <wsdl:port
    name="identity.cfc" binding="intf:identity.cfcSoapBinding">
    <wsdlsoap:address location="http://localhost/identity.cfc" />
  </wsdl:port>
</wsdl:service>
```

My IdentityService is now ready to go. Any web services client should be able to parse the above WSDL and be able to make use of it. CFMX has certainly made producing web services quite easy.

ColdFusion-to-WSDL Datatype Mapping

As explained earlier, web services are strongly typed, while CFML is not. This requires the CFML interpreter to map remote web services' datatypes to CFML variables when you consume a web service.

When you produce a web service with a CFC, the CFML interpreter also needs to map datatypes, but the table of mappings is expanded as compared to the table of mappings from WSDL to ColdFusion (see Table 24.3).

TABLE 24.3: CF-to-WSDL Datatype Mappings

CF Datatype	WSDL Datatype
numeric	SOAP-ENC:double
boolean	SOAP-ENC:boolean
string	SOAP-ENC:string
array	SOAP-ENC:Array
binary	xsd:base64Binary
date	xsd:dateTime
uuid	SOAP-ENC:string
guid	SOAP-ENC:string
query	QueryBean
struct	Map
cfc	Complex type

CFML is able to expand this table of mappings because it is contextually aware of the web services it produces from CFCs. This has a few implications of which you should be aware. First, the mapped datatypes could lose contextual information that the client might need. For example, supposed you return a GUID to a client, and it gets mapped to a string. There is no way for the client to know or expect that the string will contain a GUID. Another implication is that *round tripping* might not work. Round tripping is essentially consuming a web service you produce. This is because once you map some datatypes, you can't map them back.

Things get even trickier with complex datatypes like structs and queries. As you know, a CFML structure can contain an arbitrary number of keys with values of any valid type. This leads to CFML structures being treated as complex types, but the nested types aren't explicit. Here is the WSDL for such a CFML structure:

```
<complexType name="Map">
  <sequence>
    <element name="item" minOccurs="0" maxOccurs="unbounded">
      <complexType>
        <all>
          <element name="key" type="xsd:anyType" />
          <element name="value" type="xsd:anyType" />
        </all>
      </complexType>
    </element>
  </sequence>
</complexType>
```

What this implies is that any strongly typed language attempting to consume a CFC-based web service that returns structures will be unable to know what type of variables the struct contains.

The Process Flow for Producing Web Services

Although producing a web service is quite easy with a CFC, the ColdFusion Server does quite a bit of work behind the scenes. Figure 24.3 illustrates the typical processing of a web service request.

As you can see from the process flow, there are two types of requests a web service needs to handle, WSDL and SOAP. If the request is for the WSDL of the web service, then a WSDL file needs to be generated and returned to the client. The generated WSDL file can, of course, be cached if performance is an issue.

If the request is a SOAP request, then several steps need to happen. First, the SOAP request needs to be parsed to determine what method to invoke and its parameters. Next, the method requested is invoked with the supplied parameters and a result is created. A SOAP response then needs to be generated that contains this result. Finally, the result is returned to the client.

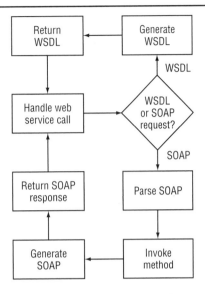

In Sum

Covering the topic of web services could easily fill a book all by itself, but using ColdFusion allows for less time to be spent covering this technology while still allowing you to quickly understand how to practically use web services. Even though web services is a complex subject, it can be broken down into the following major pieces of technology:

- Web Services Description Language (WSDL), which describes the service and how to make use of it

- Simple Object Access Protocol (SOAP), which gives you a programming language–independent way of marshalling data between endpoints no matter what technology those endpoints were developed in

Consuming web services with ColdFusion turned out to be really easy. However, you learned that with that ease you pay a price in control. You then learned how to overcome this lack of control by manually consuming web services using two different techniques.

- Using `cfhttp` and `cfxml`

- Using Apache Axis

Producing web services with ColdFusion was also quite easy. You learned how to take a CFC and make it into a web service, and you also learned the various implications of what happens when ColdFusion-based web services interoperate with other languages.

Appendix A

Configuring ColdFusion for Java

O ne of ColdFusion's many compelling features is its ability to incorporate and interoperate with other technologies. Beginning with version 4.5, ColdFusion began to incorporate a Java 2 Java Virtual Machine (JVM) that was embedded directly into the ColdFusion Server. When the JVM was embedded directly into the server, ColdFusion templates could manipulate a Java class. It even became possible to write a ColdFusion Extension (CFX) in Java.

This marriage granted access to platform-neutral APIs that paved the way for custom CFX tags that could be written once and run without modification from within any ColdFusion server, regardless of what platform it was running on. This platform neutral capability meant the end of the requirement that said a CFX's C++ code had to be recompiled, or—worse—that two different code bases had to be maintained to compensate for platform discrepancies.

Making Java work with previous versions of ColdFusion was once a challenging task. Now that ColdFusion MX *is* a Java server under the hood, things are bit different, and numerous configuration concerns have been alleviated.

JVM Requirements

Every ColdFusion MX Server has a Java Runtime Engine (JRE) configured during installation even if it is the JRE that comes as part of the default package. Upgrading that JRE can be done after the installation, but it must be done with a Sun Microsystems Java 2–compliant JRE. Given the variety of platforms on which ColdFusion runs, this can sometimes be a bit challenging.

Since Microsoft officially dropped support for Java (though their support truly stopped long before the Java 2 platform was released) there are only three major sources of Java 2–compatible JREs for the ColdFusion supported platforms: Sun Microsystems, IBM, and HP.

Sun Microsystems

For Windows and Solaris, getting a JRE is as simple as visiting Sun's Java website (http://java .sun.com/products/) and selecting one of the many versions available there.

IBM

IBM's developerWorks (http://www.ibm.com/developerworks/java/) and alphaWorks (http:// www.alphaworks.ibm.com/) provide a broad selection of Java tools for Windows and Linux for the Java 2 platform specification.

HP

As is true for many things in the HP fold, you have to go directly to HP (http://devresource .hp.com/JTK/) to get a JRE for HP-UX.

The Administrator's Java Settings

In all cases, when you make adjustments to the Java and JVM Settings panel in the ColdFusion Administrator (see Figure A.1), you have to restart ColdFusion MX Server before the settings will take effect.

FIGURE A.1:

ColdFusion Administrator's Java and JVM Settings Page

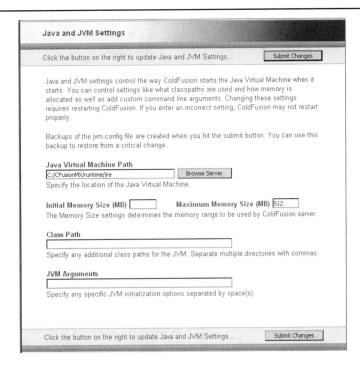

All of the settings managed through this panel can be manually edited through the server's jvm.config file. This is not regularly advised, but it can sometimes be the most direct route when there are problems with the server. Each configurable value in the Java Settings panel, shown in Table A.1, has a related entry in the Java configuration file.

TABLE A.1:   Relationship of Java Settings to Configuration File Entry

Setting	Configuration File Entry
Java Virtual Machine Path	java.home
Initial Memory Size	java.args
Max Memory Size	java.args
Class Path	java.class.path
JVM Arguments	java.args

Java Virtual Machine Path

One of the most fundamental settings in the entire configuration is the location of the JVM itself. Without this setting, everything else is pointless because the ColdFusion MX Server will fail to work correctly.

NOTE   As is the convention with other Java settings, paths use forward slashes, *even Windows paths*, which normally uses backslashes. Naturally, this is not a problem on the Unix platforms.

The default path for the stand-alone ColdFusion MX Server is the JRE that comes with the server.

```
C:/CfusionMX/runtime/jre
```

Installing a new version of Java for use with the ColdFusion MX Server is as easy as installing the new JRE and changing the JVM Path setting. It is unlikely, with the possible exception of some JVM arguments, that additional changes would be required.

Memory Sizes

By adjusting the Initial Memory and Maximum Memory Size settings, it is possible to tune the JVM operation. The server's defaults are an unspecified (empty) value for the Initial Memory Size, and the maximum physical system memory amount for the Maximum Memory Size. ColdFusion applications that make use of a heavy number of objects (such as DOM-oriented XML parsers), static objects, or threaded services (such as with network communications) should serve as indicators to tune the Memory Size settings on the server.

Using the Initial Memory and Maximum Memory Size settings is analogous to using the JVM runtime switches -Xms (initial) and -Xmx (maximum). In fact, these are the same JVM switches that are set as part of the java.args entry in the jvm.config file to reflect the values entered in the ColdFusion Administrator. When you combine these switches with the -verbose:gc switch, you help determine the proper memory sizes to use. The -verbose: gc switch will log the garbage collector's actions to the standard output. It is important to actually examine the utilization and garbage collection, since making the memory allocation arbitrarily large can actually decrease performance when the JVM's memory manager tries to defragment and compact the memory space.

Class Path

The JVM's Class Path is managed with the Class Path setting. The server does not inherit environmental variables set at the system level. This is often a hard thing to remember if Java components are being built and tested from the command line and then later invoked from within ColdFusion templates.

If the object or CFX tag being invoked leverages anything outside of the standard API, then that path or JAR needs to be included in the Class Path setting.

JVM Arguments

The JVM arguments provide a way to configure the JVM's runtime environment directly, such as by allowing all of the name/value pairs to be supported through the -D command-line switch of the Java interpreter. The variety of options that can be expressed this way allows for a high degree of configuration. Multiple name/value pairs can be included with this setting, separated by semicolons.

One of the more common Java system configurations to be adjusted, and not just through ColdFusion, is the JVM's Security Manager. You can override the built-in Security Manager of the JVM by setting the `java.lang.Security` to point to an alternate implementation. An example of this would be the installation of Java's `RMISecurityManager` class as the default Security Manager:

```
java.security.manager=java.rmi.RMISecurityManager
```

Additionally, the JVM implementation-specific switches, often called *x-switches*, can be set using this form field in the ColdFusion Administrator. In the case of the ColdFusion MX Server's default JRE, there are files called `Xusage.txt` installed in the JVM subdirectories of the `runtime/jre` directory that list all of the *x-switches*.

APPENDIX B

Understanding UML Class Diagrams

This appendix provides a cursory explanation of UML class diagrams and how they are used within this book.

UML

The Unified Modeling Language (UML) is a graphical and textual language for expressing (primarily) object-oriented systems. It can be used for analysis and design of new systems as well as for documentation of existing systems. UML has its roots in the efforts of numerous contributors whose work began over a decade ago. UML is now a committee-run standard driven by the Object Management Group (OMG), which is made up of various academic and commercial contributors.

NOTE   The complete UML documentation is available at the OMG's UML website, `http://www.uml.org`. UML is currently a version 1.4 specification, but the committee is currently working on a major 2.0 upgrade.

The major components of UML are the various specifications for document formats and diagrams that are used to describe systems. The UML class diagrams discussed in this appendix are used to describe one or more classes, their properties and methods, and their relationships with other classes in the diagram. Hierarchies of classes can be visually displayed as well as their linkage, through inheritance, aggregation, or association.

Specific symbols and text conventions, called *notation*, are used to describe nearly every object-oriented feature of class structure.

Elements of a Class Diagram

As might be expected with any tool used to describe a system, the nomenclature within a class diagram is very specific and intended to remove ambiguity. The elements of a class diagram that will be discussed herein are classes, relationships, packages, and notes.

Classes

In UML, a class is rendered graphically as a rectangle with multiple internal sections (usually three), as shown here.

```
        SimpleClass
  + publicProperty
  - privateProperty
  # protectedProperty

  + publicMethod()
  - privateMethod()
  # protectedMethod()
```

This figure describes a class called, `SimpleClass`, that has three properties and three methods. The rectangle representing this class is divided into three very specific compartments that contain the name, the properties, and the methods of the class. Each property and method is named according to its visibility scope; the privately scoped method is called `privateMethod` and the privately scope property is called `privateProperty`. The notation symbol that prefixes the name of each property and method depicts its visibility scope. Privately scoped items are noted with a minus sign (–), protected scope items are noted with a pound sign (#), and publicly scoped items are noted with a plus sign (+); this is all part of the UML specification.

The compartment containing the class' name can also contain an additional notation element called a *stereotype*. This further qualifies the kind of class being represented. A class called `SimpleInterface`, which has been stereotyped as an interface class, is shown here.

Notice that the stereotype appears above the name enclosed within double angle brackets, specifically called guillemets. A stereotype means much the same in UML as it does in real life, implying a certain set of qualities to something, in this case a class, that are descriptive of its general intent or usage.

Types of Relationships

Depicting individual classes within a diagram does not correctly express a system unless the relationship between these classes can also be expressed. UML is capable of directly expressing almost any kind of relationship between classes.

NOTE   There are specific rules within UML for extending the notation to handle new logical and language specific constructs. You can read about these rules in the UML specification.

This section will look at four kinds of relationship in class diagrams: generalization, realization, dependency, and association.

Generalization

The UML term for the more common term inheritance is *generalization*. A generalization is a relationship between a more general kind of class, also known as the *superclass* or *parent*, and a specific kind of that general class known as the *subclass* or *child*.

This relationship is depicted on a diagram as a solid line with an open arrowhead, as shown here. The arrowhead points at the superclass.

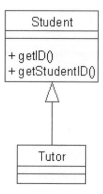

Realization

A *realization relationship* is a special mechanism often used to express a class' implementation of an interface.

This relationship is depicted on a diagram as a dashed line with an open arrowhead, as shown here. The arrowhead points at the class that is being implemented or realized.

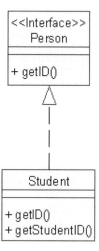

Dependency

A dependency relationship expresses the reliance of one class on another. Changes in the specification of one class may have an impact on the other class, but this is not necessarily a bidirectional relationship. A dependency relationship is often used to show that one class makes use of the instances of another class.

This relationship is depicted on a diagram as a dashed line being directed at the class upon which the dependency exists, as shown in here.

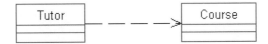

Association

An *association* is a very common structural relationship and implies a simple connection between classes.

This relationship is depicted on a diagram as a solid line between two classes, as shown here.

There are four notational adornments that can be applied to an association relationship to better define the nature of the relationship: name, role, multiplicity, and aggregation.

Name

An association can be named to provide a degree of information about the relationship. For even greater clarification, a direction can be indicated using a direction triangle in the name.

Role

The class at either end of an association relationship can be said to play a specific role—the purpose of the class. This notation allows that role or purpose to be displayed as shown here.

Multiplicity

Frequently an association may include multiple instances of a specific class on either or both ends of the relationship. One-to-Many relationships, among others, are expressed with this notation.

Aggregation

An *aggregation* is a specialized form of association used with structural relationships that expresses a "whole/part" kind of relationship, where a class in the model is contained within another class in the model.

Aggregation is depicted on a diagram as a solid line with an open diamond on the end of the "whole" or containing class.

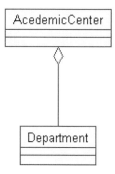

Packages

Related classes can be logically grouped into packages. Although packages can be reflected in programming language structures such as Java packages, this is merely serendipitous. UML packages and Java packages should not be assumed to be isomorphic constructs where one strictly and interchangeably means the other. Java packages are appropriately represented as UML packages, and tools like Rational Rose, which generate code from UML models, will use the Java package keyword to express UML packages. However, it is entirely possible to create a UML package just for groups that should not be expressed in Java.

Packages are depicted on a diagram as tabbed folders, as shown here.

Notes

Frequently there is a need to include textual content on a class diagram. Not as jotted notes but as real pieces of documentation about various elements that are to accompany the diagram. This type of information is what becomes a UML Note.

Notes are depicted as rectangles with a folded upper-right corner, like a dog-eared note card, with a dashed line that connects it to the diagram element to which it pertains. The textual content is written within the rectangle as shown here.

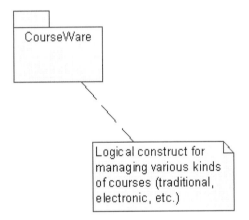

Using the Code from This Book

Each chapter of *ColdFusion MX Developer's Handbook* has its own instructions on how to set up the code it presents for your study. However, you may want to download the entire code archive for the whole book before you begin reading. Here's how you can download the book's code:

1. Go to `http://www.sybex.com`.

2. Browse the online catalog (there's a link on the left side of the page) or use the Search function to find the page for the *ColdFusion MX Developer's Handbook*. You can enter the title or the ISBN (0-7821-4029-7).

3. Look for the Download link button on the right side of the screen, and click.

4. You will now be able to download the code for each chapter.

You should also consider using a good-quality code editor. Dreamweaver MX, the newest release of Macromedia's flagship editor, can be downloaded from

```
http://www.macromedia.com/software/dreamweaver/download/
```

You can also use ColdFusion Studio 5 or any other editor you are comfortable with.

And of course, you'll want to have ColdFusion MX installed. You can download a free trial of the server here:

```
http://www.macromedia.com/software/coldfusion/downloads/
```

Even after the trial period expires, you can continue to use the server in an IP-limited Developer edition.

Index

Note to the reader: Throughout this index **boldfaced** page numbers indicate primary discussions of a topic. *Italicized* page numbers indicate illustrations.

SYMBOLS & NUMBERS

& (ampersand), WML errors from, 511–512, *512*

! (bang) symbol, 473

&, for passing URL attributes, **511–512**, *512*

(pound sign)
  in ActionScript, 803
  errors from, 35, 36
  for temporary stored procedure, 391

#include action, in ActionScript, 791

$ (dollar sign), to access variables in WML, **512–513**

% (percent sign), as SQL wildcard, 363

.asr file extension, 815
  vs. .cfc file extension, 816

@ symbol, for stored procedure variables, 392

_Result handler, creating class for, 819

_Status handler, creating class for, 819

{ } (curly brackets), in ActionScript, 826

5-tiered application, 12, *12*

A

<a> tag, for WML links, **507–508**

abort attribute, of <cftrace> tag, 61

abstracting component types, **193–194**

acceptance tests, 141

Access. *See* Microsoft Access

access keys, for WML links, 509–510

accessor methods, 182–183

act_ fuse, 144
  for sample application, 174–175

action attribute
  of <cfcache> tag, 605
  of <cfcollection> tag, 211
  of <cfindex> tag, 212
  of <cfobject> tag, 627
  of <cfwddx> tag, 250
  of event handlers, 457

Action Message Format (AMF), 788

action requests. *See* fuseactions

Actions panel, code for send mail application, 785–786

ActionScript
  # (pound sign) in, 803
  #include action in, 791
  adding to ColdFusion component, 793–795
  adding to Flash, **790–793**
  case sensitivity, 777
  code location, **778–780**
  curly brackets ({ }) in, 826
  for dynamic image gallery with Flash, 807–812
  for..in loop, 824
  LoadVars object, 777, **780–787**

nature of, 776–778
  naming conventions, 777–778
server-side, **815–820**
suffixes for objects, 780
variables for formatting in, 831
white paper on coding best practices, 778
Adapter pattern, 653, 690
Add/Edit C++ CFX Tag page (ColdFusion
    Administrator), *713*
Add/Edit Java CFX Tag page, 656, *657*
addColumn method, of WddxRecordset
    class, 260
addItem() method, of RecordSet object, 801
addItemAt() method, of RecordSet object, 801
AddQuery method, of CCFXRequest class, 740
addQuery method, of Response interface, 661
addRows method
  of Query interface, 661
  of WddxRecordset class, 260
addView() method, of RecordSet object, 803
administrator, home page for, 299–300
aggregate functions in SQL, **364–366**
aggregation for UML association, 868
alert notification, ClusterCATS configuration
    for, 588
Alexander, Christopher, 653
aliases
  for circuits, **125–126**
  for database columns and tables, **363–364**
Align panel (Flash), 783
all-in-one templates, **525–526**
AllowZeroLength properties, as upsizing
    trouble spot, 426
alter procedure statement, 392
  including parameters in, 393
alter statement (SQL), **355**
alternate constructors, 626
AMF (Action Message Format), 788
ampersand (&), WML errors from,
    511–512, *512*

<anchor> tag (WML), **508–509**
and operator in Verity queries, 207
anonymous function, 786
Apache Axis, **849–851**
Apache XML libraries, 654–655
application attribute, of <cflog> tag, 65
application planning and design
  architecture design, **6–18**
    physical architecture, 6–7, *7*
  coding standards, **26–30**
    cohesion and coupling, 26–28
    exception handling, 30
    methodology, 29–30
    security issues, 29
  comments and documentation, 23–26
    template headers, 24–25
    using Program Design Language (PDL),
        25–26
  database and data model design, **8–9**
    database selection, **10**
  development tips, **75**
  front-end prototype, **18–20**
  gathering technical requirements, **4–6**
  importance of, 4
  logical architecture, **16–17**
  naming conventions, **20–23**
    database tables/columns, 22–23
    for files/directories, 21–22
    for variables/queries/structures/arrays, 21
  third-party products, **17–18**
  tiered applications, **10–16**
    business logic tier, 14–16
    client tier, 13
    data integration tier, 16
    data tier, 16
    n-tiered, 10–13, *11*
    presentation tier, 14
    single and 2-tiered, 10
application syndication, 277

application variables, 617
Application.cfm file, 101, 290–291
    authentication logic in, 293, 297–298,
        304–305
    for dynamic image gallery with Flash,
        814–815
    variables to handle styles, 490–491
application.log file, 64
applications. *See also* mail application; sample
        application
    Hello Universe application, **119–121**
    Hello World for Flash Remoting, 793
        adding ActionScript, 793–795
        testing, 795–796
    specifying for <cfexecute> tag, **747–757**
Archive Wizard, **321–328**
    accessing, 321
    Archive Information page, *321*, 322
    Archive Summary page, *327*, 327–328
    Build CAR File Archive page, *328*, 328–329
    CF Mappings page, *325*, 325
    CFX Tags page, 326
    Data Sources page, 326, *326*
    Include/Exclude Associated Files and
        Directories page, *322*, 322
    Java Applets page, 326
    Scheduled Tasks page, 326, *327*
    Server Settings page, 323–325, *324*
    Verity Collections page, 326
archives
    building, *328–329*
    defining and generating definition, **319–329**
    deployment, **330–332**, *332*
    as part of deployment, **318–319**
    preparation and generation, **319**
    sample application for, 320
    specifying location, 328–329
argumentCollection attribute, of <cfinvoke>
        tag, 842

arguments
    for methods, 456
    passing multiple <cfexecute> commands,
        750–753
arguments attribute, of <cfexecute> tag, 749
<array> element, for <fusedoc> <in>/<out>
        element, 150
Array object (ActionScript), 777
arrays
    exceptions from attempt to pass, 679
    naming conventions for, 21
    to pass arguments to cfexecute tag, 752
Arrowpoint Communications, 578
as operator (SQL), 363
<assertions> element, for <fusedoc>, 147
association in UML, 867–868
Astra LoadTest and LoadRunner (Mercury
        Interactive), 535
asynchronous replication, 599–600
attributeExists method
    of CCFXRequest class, 724
    of Request interface, 660
attributes
    for URLs, passing with &,
        511–512, *512*
    values for CFX tags, **723–724**
attributesCollection attribute, 681–682, 699
authentication, **289–296**
    for Access Upsizing Tools, 430
    for data source, 93–94, *94*
    for Microsoft SQL Server, 430
    of users, 287
authorization, 287, **296–297**
Auto Format in Flash Action panel, 779
average database time, monitoring, 544
average queue time, monitoring, 543
average request time, monitoring, 543
avg function (SQL), 365

B

Backslash XML vocabulary, 281
  fields, 283
backup
  and open database files, 554
  planning, **31**
bang (!) symbol, 473
Beck, Kent, 134
begin keyword, for if code block, 408
benchmarks, for server load, 84
bidirectional replication, 600
bindFormatFunction function, of DataGlue
    class, 804
bindFormatStrings() method, of DataGlue
    class, 803, 811, 814
BlackBox, 30, 112
blockfactor attribute, of cfquery and
    cfstoredproc, 561
body attribute, of <cfindex> tag, 212
<boolean> element, for <fusedoc> <in>/<out>
    element, 149–150
Boolean queries
  user assistance in building, **233–238**
  in Verity, 206–207
Boolean values, returning to Flash, 825
break keyword, 409
Brooks, Fred, *The Mythical Man-Month: Essays
    on Software Engineering*, 114
browsers. *See* web browsers
buildAttributesCollection method, 684–685
business logic tier, 14–16
business objects, 189
business rules, for login process, 15, *15*
buttons, in Flash authoring environment, 773
bytecode in Java, 629
  caching, **634–637**
bytes incoming per second/bytes outgoing per
    second, monitoring, 544

C

C++
  choosing compiler, **710–711**
  for ColdFusion Extensions, 652
  installing CFX tags, **711–714**, *712*
  Standard library for CFX portability, 726
C++ CFXAPI, **714–717**
  CCFXException class, **717**
  CCFXQuery class, **716**
  CCFXRequest class, **715–716**
  CCFXStringSet class, **716–717**
  UML model, *715*
cached queries, limiting maximum number, 551
cachedAfter attribute
  of <cfquery> tag, 561, 612
  of <cfstoredproc> tag, 561
cachedWithin attribute
  of <cfquery> tag, 561, 612, 614
  of <cfstoredproc> tag, 561
caching
  with <cfcache> tag, **604–609**
    adding, **605–607**
    for dynamic pages, **607–609**
    how it works, **607**
  ColdFusion MX Administrator performance
      settings, **549–551**
  handling stale content, **604**
  identifying opportunities, **602–604**
  Java classes, **634–637**
  queries, **609–617**
    expiring, **614–617**
  in RAM, **617–619**
  with WDDX
    for database, **254–256**
    for database queries, **250–253**
callback function, 792
  for LoadVars object, 781
<card> tag (WML), 504

cards in WML, 503
   navigation, **506–510**
      links with a tag, **507–508**
      links with access keys, 509–510
      links with anchor tag, **508–509**
car.log file, 64
cascading style sheets, **488–492**
case sensitivity
   in ActionScript, 777
   of files and directories, Windows vs.
      Unix, 257
   of JavaScript object names, 453
   of WML tags, 506
Category attribute, of <cftrace> tag, 61
CCFXStringSet class, 742
CDATA database table
   in client variable database, 83
   code to create, 96–97
   structure of, *99*
<cfabort> tag, in WML, **529–530**
<cfadminsecurity> tag, disabling, 761
<cfapplication> tag, 618
   enabling domain cookies, 88
   session management attributes, 86, 87–88
.cfc file extension, vs. .asr file extension, 816
<cfcache> tag, **604–609**
   adding, **605–607**
   for dynamic pages, **607–609**
   how it works, **607**
<cfcatch> tag, 756
<cfcollection> tag, 209, **211**
   to optimize collection, 244
<cfcontent> tag
   for content type setting, **514**
   disabling, 761
CFCs. *See* ColdFusion Components (CFCs)
<cfdirectory> tag, disabling, 761
<cfdump> tag, **59–60**, *60*
<cferror> tag, 524

<cfexecute> tag
   disabling, 761
   effective use of output, **757–760**
      file storage, **757–759**
      output capture in variable, **759–760**
   limitations on executing applications,
      756–757
   passing multiple arguments to commands,
      750–753
   reasons for using, **746–747**
   security issues, **760–761**
   specifying application to run, **747–757**
   timeouts to avoid endless loops, **753–756**
<cffile> tag, disabling, 761
<cfform> tag, integrating custom JavaScript
      with, **474–478**
<cfftp> tag, disabling, 761
CF.HTTP function (SSAS), 816
<cfhttp> tag, **846–849**
   and ColdFusion server delays, 547
<cfhttpparam> tag, 848
CFID variable, 81
   allocating in cluster, 82–83
   storage in database, 99
<cfif> tag, 357
   Transact-SQL replacement for, **407–409**
<cfinclude> tag, 73
   for <cfexecute> output, 758
<cfindex> tag, 209, **211–213**
   in indexing template, 242–243
<cfinsert> tag, and form fields, 468
<cfinvoke> tag, **840–843**
   syntax, 841–842
<cfinvokeargument> tag, 842
<cflocation> tag, 71
<cflock> tag, 292, 618
   to lock session variables, 87
   for user and password changes, 295
   and Verity, **208–209**

<cflog> tag, 65, 75
  disabling, 761
<cflogin> tag, 304, 306
<cfloginuser> tag, 304
<cflogout> tag, 304
<cfloop> tag
  Transact-SQL alternative, **410–412**
  while statement to replace, **409–410**
.cfm template, for e-mail application, 786–787
<cfmail> tag, disabling, 761
CFML
  conversion to JavaScript, **257–259**
  object-oriented concepts, **180–189**
    application example, **190–197**
    applying, **189–190**
    encapsulation, **182–183**
    inheritance, **183–187**
    instance construction, **180–182**
    polymorphism, **187–189**
  serializing data to be returned to, **687–690**
  tools for WDDX, **249–250**
CFML Code Analyzer, **65–66**, *66*
CFML datatypes
  conversion from Java objects, **644–648**
  conversion to JavaScript, 641
  serializing, **680–690**
CFML Reference, 658
CFML wrapped CFX tags, **699–707**
  XSLT tag, **700–707**
cfml2js action, 250
cfml2wddx action, 250
<cfobject> tag, 29–30, 112, **627–628**
  disabling, 761
<cfobjectcache> tag, 617
<cfoutput> tag
  group attribute of, 461
  for grouping, 379
  nesting, 383
  to return or display parameter value, 394
  Transact-SQL alternative, **410–412**

<cfparam> tag, 185–186
  and form fields, 468
<cfpop> tag, 214
<cfprocparam> tag, **399**
  to pass parameters to stored procedure,
  400–402
<cfprocresult> tag, **400**, 403
<cfquery> tag
  attributes, and query performance, 561
  attributes for caching, 612
  to call stored procedure, **397–398**
  in data integration tier, 16
  dbtype attribute of, 384
  debug attribute, 58
  passing results to CFX tag, 668
<cfregistry> tag, disabling, 761
<cfsavecontent> tag, 128, 759–760
  nesting tags, 128–130
<cfsearch> tag, 200, 204–208
  attributes, 205
  and paging through results, **229–233**
<cfselect> tag, vs. bindFormatStrings()
    method, 803
<cfset> tag, 406
<cfsetting> tag, showDebugOutput attribute, 59
CFSQL (ColdFusion SQL), **384–386**
cfSQLType attribute, of <cfprocparam>
  tag, **399**
CFSTAT utility, **545**
<cfstoredproc> tag, 59
  attributes, and query performance, 561
  in data integration tier, 16
  to execute stored procedure, **398–399**,
  400–405
  ExecutionTime variable, 398
  StatusCode variable, 398–399
cftoken, UUID for, 549
CFTOKEN variable, 81
  allocating in cluster, 82–83

storage in database, 99
value assignment, 83
<cftrace> tag, **61–64**, 75, **563–565**
cftrace.log file, 64
<cftransaction> tag, 358, 361
<cf_transformation> tag, 700
<cftry>/<cfcatch> block, nesting error, *37–39*
<cftry> tag, 756
<cfupdate> tag, and form fields, 468
<cfwddx> tag, **249–250**
CFX Tag Wizard (Visual Studio), **718**, *719*
CFX tags, installing C++, **711–714**, *712*
CFX Tags page, *712*
CFXAPI. *See* Java CFX class library (CFXAPI)
cfx.h file
   as CFX Tag include, 722
   and portability, 725
cfx.jar, 658
<cfxml> tag, 846–849
<cfx_transformation> tag, 700
CGI variable, for browser type, 484
cgi.http_accept variable, for browser type, **515**
cgi.http_referer variable, 75
CGLOBAL database table
   in client variable database, 83
   code to create, 96–97
   structure of, *100*
change requests, DevNotes to manage, *140*, 140–141
Character Options dialog box, *827*, 827
charIndex() function (SQL Server), 439
Check Syntax in Flash Action panel, 779
CheckBox component (Flash), 774
checkBoxValidate() function, 479, 480
checkForm() function, 475
child class in UML, 865
child table, 351
circuits
   creating, 123
   defining aliases, **125–126**

fuse integration into, 158
fuseaction identification with, 142
in Fusebox framework planning, 114
identification, 142
integration into application, 159
nesting, **123–125**
testing, 158
Cisco Content Services Switches, 577, 578
Cisco LocalDirector, 85, 577
clarity, of Fusebox, 113
class attribute
   of <cfobject> tag, 627
   for HTML object with custom rule, 490
class caching, for Java objects, **634–637**
"class not found" error message for Java, 626
classes in UML, 864–865
Classic.cfm template, 56
classpath variable, 626
client affinity, 84
Client Network Utility, 90, *91*
client/server performance, Access vs. SQL Server, 422–423
client-side processing, vs. server-side, **450–451**
client tier, 13
client variables
   ColdFusion MX Administrator performance settings, **551–552**
   database setup, **89–106**
      CF servers configuration to use database, **96–98**
      creating, 89, *90*
      netwok client connections setup, 90–91
      ODBC data source configuration, **91–95**, *92*
   database use, **99**
   datatypes for, 88
   precautions for using, 100
   for state maintenance, 80, 81–82
   storing complex datatypes, **100–106**

CLOB/BLOB, setting for database
    connection, 555
closed model, 112
closing tags, in WML, 506
Cluster Setup wizard, 585–586
cluster variables, and inter-session state, 88
ClusterCATS, 85
    cluster administration, **588–590**
        ClusterCATS Explorer, 589–590,
            594, 595
        ClusterCATS Server Administrator,
            590, *591*
    configuration, **585–588**
        alert notification, 588
        gradual reduction threshold, 587–588
        load management, 586–587, *587*
        peak load threshold, 587
        session state management, 588
    content deployment and management,
        596–599
        packaging content, **597**
        strategy, 596–597
    creating cluster, **578–588**
    installing, **583–585**, *584*
    stopping service, 594–595
    testing cluster, **591–595**
        home page for testing, 591–593
        load balancing, 593–594
clustering, 78, **570–571**
    allocating CFID and CFTOKEN in, 82–83
    cluster database setup, **89–106**
        CF servers configuration to use database,
            96–98
        creating, 89, *90*
        netwok client connections setup, 90–91
        ODBC data source configuration,
            91–95, *92*
        storing complex datatypes, **100–106**
        use of database, **99**
    databases, **599–600**

fundamentals, **83–85**
    configurations, **84–85**
    and sideways scalability, **84**
    guidelines in ColdFusion environment,
        85–88
    CFID and CFTOKEN management,
        85–86
    inter- and intra-session state, **87–88**
    session variables, **86–87**
    planning, **579–580**, *580*
    scalabililty and reliability, **571–572**
    size, 571
code hints in Flash Action panel, 779–780
code sweeper, 24
coding. *See also* program code; source code
        management
    vs. planning and design, 115
cohesion in code, **26–28**
ColdFusion
    as server, **451**
    variables for state management, **80–83**
        allocating CFID and CFTOKEN in
            cluster, 82–83
        state variable storage, 80–82
ColdFusion 4.5.1 for Windows,
        Service Pack 1, 753
ColdFusion Components (CFCs), 14, 180
    abstracting types, **193–194**
    vs. CFM template, **798–799**
    creating, **189–190**
    identification in application example,
        191–193
    to produce web service, **851–854**
"ColdFusion debugging is not enabled on the
        server" message, 797
ColdFusion Extensions (CFX), 652. *See also* Java
        extensions
ColdFusion Extensions (CFX) with C++, 710
    attribute values, **723–724**
    basic construction, **718–724**

CFX Tag Wizard, **718**, *719*
portable CFX construction, **724–731**
   porting to Unix, 730–731
   steps for creating, **726–730**
queries, **734–743**
   passing to CFX, **734–736**
   reference altering passed, **736–739**
   returning, **740–743**
returning variables, **731–733**
ColdFusion MX
   downloading, 872
   error types, 34
ColdFusion MX Administrator
   Archives and Deployment page, *320*
   archiving settings of, 324–325
   CFML Code Analyzer, **65–66**, *66*
   to check and verify data source settings,
      97, *97*
   debug settings, **43–55**, *44*
      classic style information, *46*
      Database activity, *51*, 51–52
      debugging IP addresses, 53–55, *54*
      docked information, *48*
      Enable cfstat, 53
      Enable Debugging, 45
      Enable Performance Monitoring, 53
      Enable Robust Exception Handling,
         38, 53
      Exception Information, 52
      floating information, *47*
      output format, 45, 48
      Report Execution Times, 48–51, *50*
      Tracking Information, 52
      variables, *52*, 52–53
   Debugging Settings, Database Activity,
      611, 611
   Java settings, *859*, **859–861**
   performance tuning settings, **546–555**
      caching, **549–551**
      client variables, **551–552**

      data source settings, **553–555**
      server settings, **546–549**
   registering C++ CFX tags with,
      711–714, *712*
   Verity Collections page, 201, *201*
ColdFusion server
   configuration to use client variables database,
      96–98
   troubleshooting hung, 75
collection attribute
   of <cfcollection> tag, 211
   of <cfindex> tag, 212
   of <cfsearch> tag, 205
collections
   <cfcollection> tag for, 209, **211**
   in Verity, 200
      creating, **200–202**
      locking, 209
columns
   in database table
      aliases for, **363–364**
      alter statement, **355**
      including in select statement, 362
   naming conventions, 22–23
COM objects, ColdFusion MX calls to, 565
ComboBox component (Flash), 774
   DataGlue for binding RecordSet to, 810
command prompt, <cfexecute> tag vs., 746
comments, **23–26**
commit and rollback, Access vs.
      SQL Server, 422
communication, planning and, 108–109
complex data structures, **679–695**
   sending and retrieving, 689–690
ComplexRequest class, **696–697**
ComplexResponse class, **697**
components. *See* ColdFusion
      Components (CFCs)
concurrency, 341

Concurrent Versions System (CVS), 31, 336, 344–345

conditional processing, of form fields, 472–473

Configure RDS Server dialog box (Dreamweaver), 340, *340*

connection string, for database server connection, 555

connections

between cluster servers and remote client database server, 90

to database server

maintaining, 553–554

settings to limit, 553

timeout, 554

to existing cluster, 589

constructor, 180, 626

Construx coding standard, 26

consuming web services, **840–851**

automatically with cfinvoke, **840–843**

automatically with createObject(), 843

manually, **843–845**

manually with Apache Axis, **849–851**

manually with cfhttp and cfxml, **846–849**

process flow for, *845*, **845–846**

continue keyword, 409

Control Panel, Data Sources (ODBC) applet, 91, *92*

convert() function (SQL Server), 439, 814

Convoy Cluster Software, 576

<cookie> element, for <fusedoc> <in>/<out> element, 151

cookies

for persisting authentication, 304

for simulating multiple sessions, 537

to store client variables, 81, 551–552

Corfield, Sean A., 20

count function (SQL), 365–366

coupling in code, **26–28**

Coyote Point Systems, 578

.cpp file extension, 720

CPU utilization, monitoring, **540**

create procedure statement, 391–392

including parameters in, 393

create table statement (SQL), 353–354

createObject() function, **628**

to consume web services, **843**

createTimeSpan() function, 607

createUUID function, 101

criteria attribute, of <cfsearch> tag, 205

cross-site scripting, **312–314**

.css file extension, 489

curly brackets ({ }), in ActionScript, 826

cursor, associating with select statement, 410

custom tags. *See also* ColdFusion Extensions (CFX); Java extensions

in CFML, 652

for query retrieval and cache flush, 615–616

customers

feedback from, 134

initial meeting in FLiP, 136

and software development, **110–111**

CustomTag interface (CFXAPI), **659–660**

Customtag.log file, 64

CVS (Concurrent Versions System), 31, 336, 344–345

D

data integration tier, 16

sample code, 12–13

data marshalling, 680

for web services, 840

data models, design, **8–9**

data source, setup for security, 286, *287*

Data Sources (ODBC) applet (Control Panel), 91, *92*

data structures, complex, **679–695**

data syndication, 277

data tier, 16

Data Transformation Services (DTS), **434–438**
   running Import/Export wizard, *435*,
      435–436, *437*
   verifying import, 437–438
database
   caching with WDDX, **254–256**
   choosing the right one, 10
   for dynamic image gallery with Flash, 805
   recaching records to include status
      information, 267–268
   for user authentication data, 293
database hits per second, monitoring, 544
database interaction, fuse for, 143–144
database servers
   CPU utilization, 540
   disk activity monitoring, 542
database tables
   aliases for, **363–364**
   naming conventions, 22–23
   SQL to manipulate, **353–356**
      alter statement, **355**
      create table statement, 353–354
      drop statement, 356
databases
   clustering considerations, **599–600**
   ColdFusion applications waiting for,
      546–547
   design, **8–9**
   maintenance, 420
   performance monitoring, **555–562**
      database design, 555
      indexes, **556–557**
      queries, **557–562**
      references, 562
   relational data, **350–351**
   tuning references, 562
DataGlue class, 789, **803–805**
datasource attribute
   of cfstoredproc tag, 398

datatypes
   in CFML
      conversion from Java objects, **644–648**
      conversion to JavaScript, 257–259, 641
      serializing, **680–690**
   for client variables, 88
   ColdFusion to WSDL mapping, **853–854**
   handling complex, 697–699
   storing complex, **100–106**
   as upsizing trouble spot, 426–427
   for WDDX, 247
   WSDL-to-Coldfusion mapping, **843–844**
<datetime> element, for <fusedoc> <in>/<out>
      element, 150
dbtype attribute, of <cfquery> tag, 384
dbVarName attribute, of <cfprocparam>
      tag, **399**
de function, 357
deadlocks, 99
deallocate statement, 410
debug attribute, for CFX tags, 666
debug method, of Request interface, 660
debugging
   in code development, 35
   ColdFusion MX Administrator settings for,
      43–55, *44*
      classic style information, *46*
      Database activity, *51*, 51–52
      debugging IP addresses, 53–55, *54*
      docked information, *48*
      Enable cfstat, 53
      Enable Debugging, 45
      Enable Performance Monitoring, 53
      Enable Robust Exception Handling,
         38, 53
      Exception Information, 52
      floating information, *47*
      output format, 45, 48
      Report Execution Times, 48–51, *50*

Tracking Information, 52
variables, *52*, 52–53
in Dreamweaver MX, **55–56**
Java CFX tags, **673–679**
DebugQuery class, **675**
DebugRequest class, **674**
DebugResponse class, **674**
making debug version of tag, **675–677**
queries, **677–679**
on live server, 67–74
Missing Template Handler, **71**
by team, **72–74**
using error handlers, **67–70**
server-side, **386–387**
tag-based, **58–65**
template for, **56–57**
DebugQuery class, **675**
DebugRequest class, **674**
DebugResponse class, **674**
decks in WML, 503
basic structure, 504–505
declaration in style rule, 488
declare cursor statement, 410
declare statement (Transact-SQL), 406
Decorator design, 654
default constructor, 626
default template, for debugging information, 56
default values
for stored procedure parameters, 393
upsizing wizard control of, 431
DefaultLayout.cfm file, 131
DefaultValue property, of fields, as upsizing
trouble spot, 425
delete statement (SQL), **361**
deleting
indexes, 211
stored procedures, 392
users, 303
demote method, of Transsubstantiator
interface, 696

dependency relationship in UML, 866–867
deployment, 318
archiving as part, **318–319**
deserialization, 248
of WDDX packet, 251
deserialize method, of WddxDeserializer
class, 263
deserializeURL method, of WddxDeserializer
class, 263
design. *See* application planning and design
design patterns, 117
overview, **653–654**
*Design Patterns: Elements of Reusable
Object-Oriented Software* (Gamma), 653
DevEdge Online (Netscape), 492
developer layout, for Flash authoring
environment, 767
*Developing ColdFusion Applications with
CFML*, 658
development environment, moving content to
production from, 597
DevNotes to iterate through prototype, *140*,
140–141
DHTML (Dynamic HTML), **482–496**
browser compatibility, 482
testing with ColdFusion, 484–485
testing with JavaScript, 483–484
for debugging output format, 45
hiding and showing elements, **492–496**
image rollovers, **485–488**, *486*
styles, **488–492**
applying, 488–489
controlling with ColdFusion, 490–492
custom rules, 490
precedence, 490
when to use and not use, 485
directories
for archiving, 322
case sensitivity, Windows vs. Unix, 257

for HTML and WML
  separate, **528–529**
  shared, **526–528**
  naming conventions for, 21–22
directory attribute, of <cfcache> tag, 605
disk activity, monitoring, **542**
displayArray method, of Passing class, 642
displayArrayOfStructures method, of Passing class, 642
displayBoolean method, of Passing class, 642
displayDate method, of Passing class, 642
displaying method results, for Java objects, 632
displayInteger method, of Passing class, 642
displayList method, of Passing class, 642
displayPrimitiveBoolean method, of Passing class, 642
displayPrimitiveInteger method, of Passing class, 642
displayPrimitiveReal method, of Passing class, 642
displayQuery method, of Passing class, 642
displayReal method, of Passing class, 642
displayStructure method, of Passing class, 642
disruptive technology, 838
distances, integrating with Flash Remoting and web services to calculate, **826–833**
distinct keyword (SQL), 364, 366
DLL construction, export declarations for, 729–730
DNS, **573**
  cluster configuration, **581–583**
  cluster requirements, 579
dockable format for debugging output, 45
dockable.cfm template, 56
document structure, in WML, **503–505**
Document Type Definition (DTD), for Fusedoc, 114
documentation, **23–26**
  Fusedocs, **145–151**
    listing, 146–147

subelements, 147–149
  syntax, 148
with template headers, **24–25**
dollar sign ($), to access variables in WML, **512–513**
DOM (Document Object Model), *452*, *452–457*
  object components, **455–457**
    event handlers, **456–457**
    methods, **456**
    properties, **455–456**
  object references, **453–455**
dot notation, to access nested Java classes, 648
downloading program code for book, **872**
downtime, acceptable levels, 572
Dreamweaver MX
  debugging in, **55–56**
  for prototyping, 18
  with RDS, **338–343**
  support for WML, 530
  warning when opening file already checked out, 342
dreamweaver.cfm template, 56
drop constraint clause, in alter statement, 355
drop procedure statement, 392
drop statement (SQL), 356
dropDownRequired() function, 480
dsp_ fuse, 143
  for sample application, 165, 169–172, 175–177
DTD (Document Type Definition), for Fusedoc, 114, 145
DTS (Data Transformation Services), **434–438**
  running Import/Export wizard, *435*, 435–436, *437*
  verifying import, 437–438
dynamic backups, Access vs. SQL Server, 422
Dynamic Class Load directory, **636–637**
dynamic content in Flash, 778

dynamic image gallery with Flash, **805–815**
   ActionScript, 807–812
   Application.cfm file, 814–815
   ColdFusion Component, 812–814
   database, 805
   Flash interface, 806–807, *807*
dynamic IP mode for ClusterCATS, 575
dynamic pages
   <cfcache> tag for, **607–609**
   and performance, 602–603
dynamic query results
   indexing, **213–215**
   searching, **215–219**
dynamic text fields, in Flash, 772

E

e-mail address, UDF to validate, 14–15
e-TEST suite (Empirix), 536
Edit Sites dialog box (Dreamweaver), 338, *339*
else statement, 409
embedded style sheets, 489
Empirix, e-TEST suite, 536
empty keyframe, 769
emulators for WML browsers, **501–503**
encapsulation in CFML, **182–183**
end keyword, for if code block, 408
endless loops, timeout to avoid in cfexecute tag, **753–756**
environment variables, FBX_Settings.cfm file for, 122
ER/Studio, 9
Ericsson, WapIDE SDK Browser, 502
error handling
   for debugging on live server, **67–70**
   for WML and HTML, 527
error logs, checking for timedout templates, 548

error messages, **34–43**
   "class not found", 626
   "ColdFusion debugging is not enabled on the server", 797
   cryptic, **42–43**
   from Flash, 795–796
   invalid line numbers in, 43
   and Java dump, 42–43
   missing in Internet Explorer, **40**
   MX, **36–43**, *37*
      default, **36–39**
   ODBC Timeout error, preventing during upsizing, 432
   "Overflow" error, from Upsizing Wizard, 430
   search engine cataloging of, 40
   for server at peak load threshold, 587
   syntax vs. logic errors, **34–35**
   "Unknown exception condition", 753
error streams, and browser display, 632
errors
   ColdFusion errors and WAP/WML, **523–524**
   timeout to capture in cfexecute tag, 756
   WML response to, **510–511**
escape() method (JavaScript), 463
eval() method (JavaScript), 479
event handlers, of DOM objects, **456–457**
exception handling, 30
   for Java objects, **633–634**
exceptions.log file, 64
excluding files from archive, 322, *323*
exclusive locks
   in source code management, 335–336
   in Verity, 209
exec statement, **395–396**
   in cfquery tag, 397
executables, Flash movies as, 775
exists keyword, **375–376**

exit fuseactions (XFAs), 116, **126–127**
  assignment to exit points, 142
exit points, identification in FLiP, 141–142
Expert mode for ActionScript, 778
expireURL attribute, of <cfcache> tag, 605
expiring cached queries, **614–617**
explicit instantiation, of Java class, 629
explicit queries in Verity, 208
export declarations for DLL construction,
    729–730
exporting database, vs. upsizing, 420
extensions attribute, of <cfindex> tag, 212
external attribute, of <cfindex> tag, 212
external style sheets, 489
Extreme Programming (XP), 134–135

F

F5 BigIP, 85, 577
F5 Networks, 578
factory attribute, of <cf_transformation>
    tag, 700
Factory design, 654
failover, 571
  for databases, 599
  testing, **594–595**
failure rates on corporate software projects, 109
  FLiP and, 133–134
FBX structure, 131
FBX_Circuits.cfm file, 123, 125–126
  for sample application, 161–162
FBX_Fusebox30_CFnn.cfm file, 121–122
FBX_Layouts.cfm file, 123, 130–131
  for sample application, 162, 163–164
FBX_Settings.cfm file, 122
  for sample application, 161
FBX_Switch.cfm file, 123
  for sample application, 164–165, 167–168
fetch into statement, 410

fetch next statement, 411
fields, examining for upsizing, 425–426
file attribute, of <cflog> tag, 65
<file> element, for <fusedoc> <in>/<out>
    element, 151
file extensions, Verity limitations, 239
file formats
  Verity indexing for, 203
  Verity indexing for multiple, **240–242**
file sizes, upsizing Access to SQL Server, 436
files
  for archiving, 322
  case sensitivity, Windows vs. Unix, 257
  from CFX Tag Wizard, 720, *721*
  locking, 335–336
  naming conventions for, 21–22
  sending cfexecute output to, 754, **757–759**
filter() method, of RecordSet object, 801
.fla file extension, 767
Flash MX, **766–780**. *See also* ActionScript
  authoring environment, **767–775**, *768*
    Actions panel, 778–779, *779*
    buttons, 773
    code hints in Action panel, 779–780
    Library, 769–772, *771*
    movie clips, 773
    Panels, 769–772
    Property Inspector, 769–772, *771*
    Stage, *768*, 768–769
    symbols, instances and components,
      772–775
    text fields, 772–773
    Timeline, *768*, 768–769
    Toolbox, *770*
  Boolean values returned to, 825
  creating application for server-side Action-
    Script, 816
  custom Remoting template, 794
  dynamic content, 778
  initializing application, 792–793

for presentation tier, 14
putting documents online, **775–776**
scripting language. *See* ActionScript
setup, **790–793**
Flash Remoting Gateway, defining, 793
Flash Remoting MX, 780, *788*, **788–820**
   for communication, *788*, **788–789**
   component set, 767
   DataGlue class, **803–805**
   dynamic image gallery, **805–815**
      ActionScript, 807–812
      Application.cfm file, 814–815
      ColdFusion Component, 812–814
      database, 805
      Flash interface, 806–807, *807*
   first document, **789–801**
   installing remoting components, **789**
   integrating with web services to calculate
      distance, **826–833**
   RecordSets and, **801–802**
   resources for, 834
   and web services, **820–834**
      for weather determination, 821–825
FLASH scope, 799
   to pass variables to ColdFusion, **800–801**
Flash UI Component set, 773–774, *774*
FlashComm mailing list, 834
flash.log file, 64
FLASH.PARAMS variable, 800
FLASH.Result variable, 799
flexibility, in database design, 9
FLiP. *See* Fusebox Lifecycle Process (FLiP)
flowcharting, 134
flushing cached queries, **614–617**
focus() method, of form field, 457
for..in loop in ActionScript, 824
foreground applications in Windows, disabling
      performance boost for, 566
foreign key in database table, 351
forking, 335, **337**

form field validation, **465–482**
   client-side, *469*, **469–482**
   server-side, **465–467**
   server-side by ColdFusion, **467–469**, *468*
form variables, cfcache and, 608
formatting HTML, in <cfexecute> tag, 749
forms
   dynamic updates using WddxRecordset,
      260–262
   in WML, **516–523**, *517*
      selection lists in, **521–523**, *522*
      submitting data to another WML docu-
      ment, 518–519
Foundry Networks ServerIron switches,
      577, 578
FQHNs (Fully Qualified Host Names), for
      clusters, 579
frames
   for ActionScript code, 778
   ColdFusion and, 451
framework, 111
freezing prototype, 139, 141
front-end prototype, **18–20**, *19*
FTP, cfexecute risks on server with, 761
fully-covered query, 556
fully-covering index, 556
Fully Qualified Host Names (FQHNs), for
      clusters, 579
fuseactions, 119
   identification with circuit, 142
Fusebox, 29
   attributes scope, 131–132
   building application, **119–121**
   code reuse with, **115–116**
   overview, **116–133**
      circuit aliases, **125–126**
      complexity syndrome solution, **117–121**
      exit fuseactions (XFAs), **126–127**
      nested circuits, **123–125**

nested layouts, **126–131**
query sims, **132–133**
sample application, **159–177**, *172*
    act_ fuse, 174–175
    circuits and fuseactions, 160
    directory structure, *160*
    dsp_ fuse, 165, 169–172, 175–177
    FBX_Circuits.cfm file, 161–162
    FBX_Layouts.cfm file, 162, 163–164
    FBX_Settings.cfm file, 161
    FBX_Switch.cfm file, 164–165, 167–168
    index.cfm file, 161
    limitations, 160
    qry_ fuse, 168–169
    url_ fuse, 173
skeleton, **121–123**
what it is, **113–116**
    benefits, 113–115
Fusebox Lifecycle Process (FLiP), 113,
    133–159
benefits, 135
steps, 135–159
    1-initial customer meeting, 136
    2-wireframe creation, 136, *137*
    3-prototype creation, 137–139, *139*
    4-DevNotes to iterate through prototype,
        140, 140–141
    5-freezing prototype, 141
    6-acceptance testing design, 141
    7-sign-off prototype and acceptance
        tests, 141
    8-exit points identification, 141–142
    9-exit fuseactions assignment to exit
        points, 142
    10-circuit identification, 142
    11-fuseaction identification with
        circuit, 142
    12-fuse identification for fuseaction,
        143–145
    13-fuse consolidation, 145
    14-Fusedocs, 145–151
    15-fuse coding, 152
    16-test harnesses, 152–154
    17-fuse testing, 155–158
    18-fuse integration into circuits, 158
    19-circuit testing, 158
    20-circuit integration into
        application, 159
    21-testing, 159
Fusedocs, 114, 145–151
FuseMinder, 152
fuses, 119
    coding, 152
    consolidation, 145
    in Fusebox framework planning, 114
    identification for fuseaction, 143–145
    integration into circuits, 158
    tasks for, 120
    testing, 155–158

G

Gamma, Erich, *Design Patterns: Elements of
    Reusable Object-Oriented Software*, 653
gateway
    for Flash communication with application
        server, 788
        default port, 794
        defining, 793
    between WAP and HTTP networks,
        499, *500*
generalization in UML, 865–866
get methods, 182–183
getAttribute method, of Request interface, 660,
    662–663
getAttributeList method, of Request
    interface, 660
getAttributesCollection method, of Com-
    plexRequest class, 697

getAuthUser() function, 304

getColumnByIndex method, of Query interface, 661

getColumnNames() method, of RecordSet object, 802

getColumns method, of Query interface, 661

getData method, of Query interface, 661

getDate() function (SQL Server), 439

getField method, of WddxRecordset class, 260

getGalleryImages_Result() function, 811

getIntAttribute method, of Request interface, 660

getItemAt() method, of RecordSet object, 802, 811

getLength() method, of RecordSet object, 802

getName method, of Query interface, 661

getNumberAvailable() method, of RecordSet object, 802

getQuery method, of Request interface, 660

getRequest method, of ComplexRequest class, 697

getResponse method, of ComplexResponse class, 697

getRowCount method
    of Query interface, 661
    of WddxRecordset class, 260

getSerializedAttribute method, of ComplexRequest class, 697

getService() function, 801

getSetting method, of Request interface, 660

getTickCount function, **387–388**, 563

getTransubstantiator method
    of ComplexRequest class, 697
    of ComplexResponse class, 697

global search and replace, to change functions, 439

GNU C++ Compiler, 711

<go> tag (WML), 508–509

gradual reduction threshold, ClusterCATS configuration for, 587–588

Greeting class
    creating, 626–627
    error method, 633

group attribute, of <cfoutput> tag, 461

group by clause, 379, 380–381

grouping, **379–383**, *381*
    in output, **381–383**
    in query, **379–381**

groups
    in authorization process, 296–297
    displaying for user, 301
    matching users to, 297

guest book, cross-site scripting and, **312–314**

gzipped TAR file, to package content for clusters, 597

H

hackers, Robust Exception Handling data and, 53

Hall, Branden, *Object-Oriented Programming with ActionScript*, 819

handheld devices. *See* WAP (Wireless Application Protocol); WML (Wireless Markup Language)

hardware
    constraints in technical requirements, 5
    cost estimates, 7
    for load balancing, **577–578**
        ClusterCATS with, 575

having clause, 379, 381

header, for WML, 505

Hello Universe application, **119–121**

hiding and showing elements, in DHTML, **492–496**

high-availability systems, **570–572**

historical log reports, of source code changes, 337

<history> element, for <fusedoc> <properties>
        element, 147, 148
HKEY_LOCAL_MACHINE\SOFTWARE\
    Allaire\ColdFusion\CurrentVersion\
        Clients\LastID, 82–83
    Allaire\ColdFusion\CurrentVersion\
        Clients\UuidToken, 83
    Microsoft\Jet\4.0\Engines\ODBC\
        QueryTimeout, 432
HKEY_LOCAL_MACHINE\SYSTEM\,
    CurrentControlSet\Services\
        BrightTiger\Servers\, 587
HomeSite+
    automatic backup, 31
    code sweeper, 24
    default template with header, 25
"hot load" directories, 636
HP, Java Runtime Engine (JRE) from, 858
HTML (HyperText Markup Language)
    basic form, 454
        object model, *454*
    DOM as API for, 452
    Flash movies embedded in, 776
    Flash support for tags, 783
    for presentation tier, 14
    turning on formatting programmatically, 812
htmlEditFormat() function, 314
HTTP (HyperText Transport Protocol), 839
    to retrieve WDDX packet, 252
    state management over, **78–80**
http_host CGI variable, 71
HydraWeb Technologies, 578
HyperText Transport Protocol (HTTP), 839

I

IBM, Java Runtime Engine (JRE) from, 858
icons for representing relevance score from
        search engines, 222–223, *224*

ID, automatically generated, in SQL, **358–360**
identifyObject method, of Passing class, 642
identity fields
    manually generating sequential, 442–443
    query for in Microsoft SQL Server, 359
    upsizing and, **440–443**
IdentityService (web service), 851–854
if/else logic, in Transact-SQL, **407–409**
iIf function, 357
IIS. *See* Microsoft Internet Information Server
image files, server for, 542
image rollovers, **485–488**, *486*
implicit instantiation, of Java class, 629
importing database, vs. upsizing, 420
<in> element, for <fusedoc> <io> element, 149
in keyword, **374–375**
#include action, in ActionScript, 791
index number for JavaScript, 455
index.cfm file, 123
    for sample application, 161
    and WML/HTML shared directories
        architecture, 526, 527
Indexed properties, as upsizing trouble
        spot, 426
indexes
    <cfindex> tag for, 209, **211–213**
    dynamic query results, **213–215**
    performance tuning settings, **556–557**
    upsizing wizard control of, 431
    in Verity, 200, **202–204**
        automating, **242–243**
index_html.cfm file, and WML/HTML shared
        directories architecture, 526, 527
index_wml.cfm file, and WML/HTML shared
        directories architecture, 526
information display, fuse for, 143
inheritance, in CFML, **183–187**
init method, 629, 630–631
Initial Memory setting, for Java Virtual
        Machine, 860

initializing Flash application, 792–793
inline attribute, of <cftrace> tag, 62
inline function, 786
inline styles, 489
inner joins, **376–377**
inout parameters for WSDL, 845
input attribute, of <cfwddx> tag, 250
input parameters
    for stored procedures, **392–394**
        <cfprocparam> tag to pass, 400–402
input points for web application, security for,
    307–312
<input> tag, type attribute of, 516
input text fields in Flash, 772, 783
    Property Inspector for, *783*
insert statement (SQL), **356–360**
installing
    ClusterCATS, **583–585**, *584*
    Java CFX tags, **655–658**, *656*
instances
    for ActionScript code, 778
    construction in CFML, **180–182**
    in Flash, 769
    in Java, 625
instantiation for Java objects, 625, **629–632**
instr() function (Access SQL), 439
int() function (Access SQL), 439
integrated authentication, 93
integration, planning, **31–32**
inter-session state, **87–88**
interface components, 188
    in application example, 191–193
Internet Explorer
    missing error messages in, **40**
    testing for, 484
Internet Information Server, configuration,
    566–567
Internet Options dialog box, Advanced tab, *41*
Internet Protocol (IP), 839

Internet Protocol (TCP/IP) Properties dialog
    box, *582*
intra-session state, **87–88**
"Invalid CFML construct found on line *xx*"
    error message, 35
<io> element, for <fusedoc>, 148–151
IP addresses
    cluster requirements, 579
    configuration for cluster, **581–583**
    for web servers, 583
IP (Internet Protocol), 839
isDebugMode() function, 59, 61
isDefined() function, 618
isDemotedForm method, of Transsubstantiator
    interface, 696
isFullyPopulated() method, of RecordSet
    object, 802
isLocal() method, of RecordSet object, 802
isStruct() function, 844
isUserInRole() function, 304, 306
isWddx function, 250

J

J2EE, performance tuning, 568
Java
    ColdFusion MX Administrator settings, *859*,
        859–861
    dot notation to access nested classes, 648
    error causing dump, *42*, 42–43
    for web service stub, 850
Java applets, archiving, 325
Java CFX class library (CFXAPI), 652, **658–661**
    CFML wrapped CFX tags, **699–707**
        XSLT tag, **700–707**
    CustomTag interface, **659–660**
    debugging facility, **674–675**
        DebugQuery class, **675**

DebugRequest class, **674**
DebugResponse class, **674**
extending, **695–699**
ComplexRequest class, **696–697**
ComplexResponse class, **697**
Transsubstantiator interface, 695–696
model, *659*
Query interface, **661**
rationale for using, 652
Request interface, **660**
Response interface, **660–661**
returning variable, 664
rule for loading or reloading class, 665
Java CFX tags
basics, **662–673**
queries, **667–673**
special attributes, **665–666**
tag I/O, **662–665**
debugging, **673–679**
DebugQuery class, **675**
DebugRequest class, **674**
DebugResponse class, **674**
making debug version of tag, **675–677**
queries, **677–679**
installing, **655–658**, *656*
Java Developer's Kit (JDK), 653, 654
Java extensions, **652–658**
software needed, **654–655**
Java objects
CFML to work with, **629–648**
class caching, **634–637**
datatype conversion, **641–648**
displaying method results, 632
exception handling, **633–634**
instantiation, 625, **629–632**
nesting, **648**
overloading, **637–640**
static members, **632–633**
creating in CFML, **626–628**
with cfobject tag, **627–628**

with createObject function, **628**
Greeting class, 626–627
datatype conversion from CFML, 641
datatype conversion to CFML, **644–648**
reasons for using, 624
terminology, **625–626**
Java Runtime Engine (JRE), 858
Java Virtual Machine (JVM)
arguments, **861**
class path, **860–861**
memory sizes, **860**
path, **860**
requirements, **858**
javaCast function (CFML), 631, 639
JavaScript
building with ColdFusion, 451
as client, **451**
ColdFusion communication with, **457–462**
form field validation, **465–482**
client-side validation, *469*, **469–482**
server-side validation, **465–467**
server-side validation by ColdFusion,
467–469, *468*
integrating with <cfform> tag, **474–478**
passing variables to ColdFusion, **462–464**
tutorials, 496
JavaScript libraries, **478–479**
sample, 479–482
for WDDX, **256–276**
accessing, **256–257**
CFML conversion to JavaScript, **257–259**
WddxDeserializer class, **262–266**
WddxRecordset class, **260–262**, **273–276**
WddxSerializer class, **266–273**
JDBC connections, 553
JDBC ResultSets, serializing, **693–695**
joins, **376–377**
jvm.config file, 859

K

k2server.ini file, 209
key attribute, of <cfindex> tag, 212
keyframes in Flash, 769
keys in relational databases, 351
keywords in ActionScript, 777
Klondike WAP Browser for Windows, 501, *502*

L

language
    for indexing collections, 202, 204, **239–240**
    settings for data source, *95*
language attribute
    of <cfcollection> tag, 211
    of <cfindex> tag, 212
language settings, for data source, 95
layers in Flash timeline, 769
    locking, 782
layouts
    FBX_Layouts.cfm file for, 123
    nested, **126–131**
lcase() function (Access SQL), 439
left function, 367
left outer join, 377
len() function, 473
Library, in Flash authoring environment,
    769–772, *771*
licensing, and cluster size, 572
like keyword, in SQL queries, 209
line numbers
    invalid in error messages, 43
    jumping to specific, 39
Linux, performance tuning, **567–568**
Linux Virtual Server Project, 576
<list> element, for <fusedoc> <in>/<out>
    element, 151

ListBox component (Flash), 774
    DataGlue for binding RecordSet to, 810
live server, debugging on, **67–74**
    Missing Template Handler, **71**
    by team, **72–74**
    using error handlers, **67–70**
load balancing, 571
    for databases, 599
    device comparison, 85
    hardware, **577–578**
        ClusterCATS with, 575
    session-aware, 81
    software for, **572–577**
        ClusterCATS, **574–576**
        DNS, **573**
        Round Robin DNS, **573–574**
    testing, 593–594
load capacity, 78
load management, ClusterCATS configuration
    for, 586–587, *587*
load method, of LoadVars object, 781
load order in Flash, 769
load spikes, 543
load testing software, **535–536**
loadVariables action, 781
LoadVars object (ActionScript), 777, **780–787**
    for mail application, **782–787**, *785*
locks
    RDS to manage, **341–342**
    for session variables, 87
log files, errors recorded in, **64–65**
logging in and out, **292–294**
logic errors
    <cftrace> tag to locate, 64
    vs. syntax errors, **34–35**
logical architecture, **16–17**
login timeout, 553
Lookup fields, as upsizing trouble spot, 426
loops, endless, timeout to avoid in cfexecute tag,
    753–756

lower() function (SQL Server), 439
ltrim() function (SQL Server), 439

M

Macromedia
  Developer Exchange, 18
  Knowledgebase article on WebNS software, 578
  LiveDocs for Flash Remoting, 834
  product documentation on building Java CFXs, 658
  web site to download CFX Tag Wizard, 718
mail application
  Actions panel code, 785–786
  .cfm file, 787
  LoadVars object (ActionScript) for, **782–787**, *785*
mail.log file, 64
maintenance address, for ClusterCATS, 579, 582
Manage ClusterCats Services window, 595
mappings, archiving, 325
max function (SQL), 366
maxChars property, for Flash forms, 825
Maximum Memory Size setting, for Java Virtual Machine, 860
maxLength attribute, of <cfprocparam> tag, **399**
maxRow attribute, of <cfstoredproc> tag, 405
maxRows attribute
  of <cfprocresult> tag, 400
  of cfquery and cfstoredproc, 561
  of <cfsearch> tag, 205, 229
MDAC (Microsoft Data Access Components), 92
Medinets, David, 30

memory
  caching in, and server performance, 617
  for Java Virtual Machine, **860**
  monitoring allocation, **540–541**
  for template cache, 550
Merant SQL Server driver, 427
Mercury Interactive, Astra LoadTest and LoadRunner, 535
merge replication (MSSQL), 599
method attribute
  for <cfhttp> tag, 848
  of <cfinvoke> tag, 842
methodologies, 111
methods
  of DOM objects, **456**
  for Java objects, 625
  overriding, 184–187
Microsoft
  Application Center Test, 535
  Web Application Stress Tool, 535, *536*, **536–539**
  recorded requests, *537*
Microsoft Access, 9, 420
  Access Upsizing tools, **424–438**
    database check for trouble spots, **424–429**, *425*
    known problems, **434**
    report review, 433, *433*
    running wizard, **429–434**
  automatically generated ID, 358–359
  create table statement, 354
  inserting new record, 357
  limitations, 89
  vs. Microsoft SQL Server, 10
  SQL functions that map to TSQL functions, 428
  SQL, vs. SQL Server, 438–439
  VB functions that transfer to SQL Server, 426

Microsoft Cluster Server, 78
Microsoft Data Access Components
    (MDAC), 92
Microsoft Data Engine (MSDE), 421
Microsoft Internet Information Server
    configuration, **566–567**
    IP address settings, 583
Microsoft MSDN Library, 450
Microsoft Site Server, 598
Microsoft SQL Server, 432. *See also* stored
        procedures
    authentication, 430
    automatically generated ID, 359–360
    create table statement, 354
    database design tools, 9
    DTS (Data Transformation Services),
        434–438
        running Import/Export wizard, *435,*
            435–436, *437*
        verifying import, 437–438
    inserting new record, 357–358
    performance tuning information, 562
    SQL, vs. Access, 438–439
    transaction log, upsizing and, 433
    upsizing to, 420
Microsoft Visio, 9
Microsoft Visual C++, 710–711
Microsoft Windows NT/2000 Load Balancing
        Server, 85
MIME type, <cfcontent> tag to set, **514**
min function (SQL), 366
mirrordir utility, 598
Missing Template Handler, **71**
mixed-mode authentication, 94
MKS Source Integrity, 31
mod_backhand for Apache, 576
modularity, of Fusebox, 113
Moreover.com using WDDX, **278–281**
    news category selection, 278–279

news frameset, 278
news headline display, 280
movie clips, in Flash authoring
        environment, 773
MovieClip object (ActionScript), 777
MSDE (Microsoft Data Engine), 421
multilingual indexing, **239–240**
multimaster replication (Oracle), 599
multimedia, importing to Flash, 769
multiple tasks
    ColdFusion for multiple, 413–414
    stored procedure for, 415–416
multiplicity for UML association, 868
multiSelectValidate() function, 480–481
MVC (Model-View-Controller) pattern, 189
MX error messages, **36–43**, *37*
mySQL, 9

N

n-tiered applications, 10–13, *11*
name attribute
    of <cfexecute> tag, 747
    of <cfobject> tag, 627
    of <cfprocresult> tag, 400
    of <cfsearch> tag, 205
    of object's tag, 453
name for UML association, 867
name/value pairs
    LoadVars to transfer, 781
    to pass parameters to stored procedure, 395
named lock, 295
naming conventions, **20–23**
    in ActionScript, 777–778
    database tables/columns, 22–23
    for files/directories, 21–22
    for stored procedures, **390–391**
    for variables/queries/structures/arrays, 21

native drivers, for client variables, 552
near operator in explicit query, 208
nesting
    <cfoutput> tag, 383
    cfsavecontent tags, 128–130
    circuits, **123–125**
    error in<cftry>/<cfcatch> block, *37–39*
    Java objects, **648**
    layouts, **126–131**
    WML tags, 505
NetConnection class, 789
NetConnection Debugger, 791–792, *796,*
    796–797
NetDebug class, 789
NetDebug.as file, 791
Netscape
    DHTML for, 492
    testing for, 484
NetServices class, 789
NetServices.as file, 791
    for RecordSets in Flash, 801
netstat.exe, cfexecute to run, 747–748
network traffic, monitoring, **541–542**
networks, cluster requirements, 579
New dialog box (Visual Studio), *719*
New Project Information Screen, for
    CFX tag, *720*
Nokia, Mobile Internet Toolkit, 502
Nortel Alteon switches, 577, 578
not exists keyword, **375–376**
not in keyword, **374–375**
not operator, 473
    in Verity queries, 207
notation in UML, 864
<note> element, for <fusedoc> <properties>
    element, 147, 148
notes in UML, **869**
now() function (Access SQL), 439
null attribute, of <cfprocparam> tag, **399**

null values, Access vs. SQL Server, 444,
    445, 446
nullIf function (SQL Server), 357–358
<number> element, for <fusedoc> <in>/<out>
    element, 149

O

Object Management Group (OMG), 864
object-oriented concepts in CFML, **180–189**
    application example, **190–197**
        abstracting component types, **193–194**
        basic requirements, 191
        component identification, 191–193
        record search, **194–197**
    applying, **189–190**
    encapsulation, **182–183**
    inheritance, **183–187**
        overriding methods and variables,
        184–187
    instance construction, **180–182**
    polymorphism, **187–189**
Object-Oriented Programming with ActionScript
    (Hall and Wan), 819
objects in DOM, **455–457**
    event handlers, **456–457**
    methods, **456**
    properties, **455–456**
    references, **453–455**
objects in Java. *See* Java objects
obscurity, security through, **312**
ODBC data source
    for client variables, 552
    for cluster database
        configuration, **91–95**
        verifying, *97*
ODBC Timeout error, preventing during
    upsizing, 432

ODBC, to import Access file to
    SQL Server, 436
off-line work with source code, synchronization
    and, **337**
OLE DB data source, for client variables, 552
OMG (Object Management Group), 864
one-directional replication, 599–600
onLoad() event handler, 457, 786
onMouseOut() event, 486, 487
onMouseOver() event, 486, 487
onSubmit() event handler, 470
open source projects, SourceForge hosting of,
    345–346
open-standard methodologies, benefits, 112
Open WDDX, 654
OpenSTA, HTTP/S Load, 536
OpenWave, SDK, 502
Opera browser, WML and HTML
    support, 515
operating systems
    performance monitoring, **565–568**
        Internet Information Server configura-
            tion, **566–571**
        Solaris and Linux, **567–568**
        Windows NT/2000, **565–566**
    portability of CFX tag, 724–731
optimizing Verity, **244**
<option> tag, 521
or operator in Verity queries, 207
Oracle
    database design tools, 9
    replication, 599
order by clause, in unions, 379
orders of precedence, for Boolean queries, 207
<out> element, for <fusedoc> <io> element, 149
outer joins, **377**
output attribute, of <cfwddx> tag, 250
output parameters for stored procedures,
    392, **394**
    <cfprocparam> tag to pass, 400–402
    returning, **396–397**

outputFile attribute, of <cfexecute> tag, 757
"Overflow" error, from Upsizing Wizard, 430
overloading, 626
    for Java objects, **637–640**

P

<p> tag, 504
packages in UML, **868–869**
packaging content for cluster deployment, **597**
packets in WDDX, **247–248**
    HTTP to retrieve, 252
    PacketBuilder for, **253–254**
    PacketReader, 254, *254*
    transformation to JavaScript object,
        WddxDeserializer class for, **262–266**
page hits per second, monitoring, 544
page size, DHTML and, 485
pagefile, controlling size, 566
paging through recordset results, hiding and
    showing elements for, 492–496
paging through search results, 229–233
Panels, in Flash authoring environment, 767,
    769–772
paragraph operator in explicit query, 208
parallel projects, in source code
    management, **337**
parameterized constructor, 182
parameters
    for methods, 456
    for stored procedures, <cfprocparam> tag to
        pass, **399**, 400–402
    of technical requirements, 4–5
parent class in UML, 865
parent table, 351
partially-covering index, 556
Passing class (Java), 641–643
password attribute
    of <cfcache> tag, 605
    of <cfinvoke> tag, 842

password for authentication, 289
    changing, 294–295
path attribute, of <cfcollection> tag, 211
pcAnywhere, 545
peak load threshold
    ClusterCATS configuration for, 587
    setting for testing, 594
PeerSync, 598
PengoWorks.com, 482
performance
    Access vs. SQL Server, 422
    code and, 604
    database selection and, 10
    "hot load" directories and, 637
    metrics for technical requirements, 5
Performance Monitor. *See* System Monitor for
        Windows
performance monitoring
    database tuning, **555–562**
        database design, 555
        indexes, **556–557**
        queries, **557–562**
        references, 562
    operating system, **565–568**
        Internet Information Server
                configuration, **566–571**
        Solaris and Linux, **567–568**
        Windows NT/2000, **565–566**
    templates, **563–565**
    tools and methods, **544–545**. *See also*
            ColdFusion MX Administrator
        CFSTAT utility, 545
        System Monitor for Windows, 544–545
performance testing, **386–388**, **534–544**
    ColdFusion MX performance counters,
        543–544
    GetTickCount function, **387–388**
    load testing software, **535–536**
        Web Application Stress Tool, *536*,
            536–539

metrics, **540–542**
    CPU utilization, 540
    disk activity, 542
    memory allocation, **540–541**
    network traffic, 541–542
    server-side debugging, **386–387**
    testing environment, **535**
persistence, and memory requirements, 79
persistent sessions, 84
Peters, Jeff, 158
physical architecture, setup, **6–7**, *7*
planning. *See also* application planning and
        design
    backup, **31**
    communication and, 108–109
    integration, **31–32**
    projects, **30**
    version control, **31**
point-to-point system, 117
polymorphism, in CFML, **187–189**
PolyServe Application Manager, 576
POP3 mail server, query of user inbox on, 214
    links to details, 218–219
    template changes, 217, *218*
Popkov, Albert, 485
port attribute, of <cfcache> tag, 605
port, for default Gateway URL, 794
pound sign (#)
    in ActionScript, 803
    errors from, 35, 36
<pre> tag, 749
precedence
    order for Boolean queries, 207
    of styles, 490
predetermined objects in Flash, 777
premade components, for Flash, 772
presentation tier, 14
    sample code, 12, 13
press releases, 287–288, *288*
    editor, 289–290, *290*

<prev /> tag (WML), 508–509
primary key of table, 351, 556
   naming conventions for, 22
   referencing, and delete process, 361
printResults method, of DebugResponse
     class, 674
procedure attribute, of cfstoredproc tag, 398
processing, server-side vs. client-side, **450–451**
processRequest method, of CustomTag
     interface, 659–660
ProcessTagRequest function (CFX), 729
producing web services, **851–854**
   with CFCs, 85
   process flow for, **854**, *855*
production environment, moving
     content to, 597
profile, from PeerSync, 598
program code. *See also* source code management
   in application development, 134, *134*
   application specificity and reuse, 116
   creating stubs for, 152
   development testing, 158
   jumping to line in, 39
   maintenance costs, 116
   standards, **26–30**
   third-party products, **17–18**
   using from book, **872**
Program Design Language (PDL), **25–26**
programmer tunnel vision, 35
project planning, **30**
projectors from Flash, 775
promote method, of Transsubstantiator
     interface, 696
properties, 625
   of DOM objects, **455–456**
   of fields, examining for upsizing, 425–426
   of instance in Flash, 770
   of queries, ignored in upsizing, 428
<properties> element, for <fusedoc>, 147–148

<property> element, for <fusedoc> <properties>
     element, 147, 148
Property Inspector in Flash, 771, *771*
   tabs, 774
proprietary model, 112
protocol attribute, of <cfcache> tag, 605
prototype in FLiP, 138
   creating, 137–139, *139*
   DevNotes to iterate through, *140*, 140–141
   freezing, 139, 141
   sign-off for, 141
prototype of front-end, **18–20**, *19*, 135
proxy servers, and round robin scheme, 574
Publish Settings dialog box, HTML tab, *775*,
     775–776
publishing Flash document, 775–776
purging indexes, 211
push mechanisms in source control systems,
     security risk from, 636
PushButton component (Flash), 774, 784

Q

qry_ fuse, 143–144
   for sample application, 168–169
queries. *See also* SQL (Structured Query
     Language)
   with C++ ColdFusion Extensions, **734–743**
     passing to CFX, **734–736**
     reference altering passed, **736–739**
     returning, **740–743**
   caching, **609–617**
     expiring, **614–617**
   with Java CFX tags, **667–673**
     alterations in query, 670–671
     debugging, **677–679**
     passing query, **667–669**
     passthrough, **669–670**
     returning new query from, 671–673

limiting maximum number cached, 551
maintaining, 16
naming conventions for, 21
performance monitoring, **557–562**
    ColdFusion vs. database functions, 558–561
    queries within loops, 559
    repetition, 557–558
  vs. stored procedures, 391
  as upsizing trouble spot, 427–428
  WDDX for caching, **250–253**
query attribute
  of <cfindex> tag, 212
  for CFX tags, 666, 679
Query interface (CFXAPI), **661**
query objects
  problem converting to java.util.Map instances, 643
  serializing, **690–692**
query sims, **132–133**, 169
  results, *133*
QuerySim.cfm, 132
queued requests, monitoring, 543

R

RadioButton component (Flash), 774
RadView Software, WebLOAD, 536
Radware, 578
RAM. *See* memory
RDBMS (relational database management systems), 351
rdist utility, 598
RDS (Remote Development Services), 336, **338–343**
  cfexecute risks on server with, 761
  configuration, **338–341**
  to manage locks, **341–342**
  security management, **343**

rds.log file, 64
readOnly locks, during Verity searches, 209
realization relationship in UML, 866
record count, for query object, 736
record search, **194–197**
RecordSet class, 690, 789
  binding Flash to Flash UI Components, 803
RecordSet, DataGlue for binding to ListBox or ComboBox, 810
<recordset> element, for <fusedoc> <in>/<out> element, 150
RecordSet method, 804
RecordSets, Flash Remoting MX and, **801–802**
recoverability, Access vs. SQL Server, 422
recoverable errors, 34
recurse attribute, of <cfindex> tag, 212
redundancy, 78
  with clusters, 572
Reference in Flash Action panel, 779
referential integrity, 351, 561
<refresh /> tag (WML), 508–509
refreshing indexes, 211
regional settings, for data source, *95*, 95
registerWddxRecordsetExtension function, 273
Registry, as client variable store, 81, 82, 551
related selects, 457–462, *458*
relational data, **350–351**
relational database management systems (RDBMS), 351
relationships in UML, **865–868**
relevance score from search engines, *220*, 220–223, *221*
  as percentages, 222
reload attribute, for CFX tags, 665
Remote Development Services (RDS). *See* RDS (Remote Development Services)
Remote Procedure Call (RPC), 838
removeAll() method, of RecordSet object, 802
removeItemAt() method, of RecordSet object, 802

replication of databases, **599–600**

repositories, for source code, 334

request definition, for web service, 841

Request interface (CFXAPI), **660**

Resonate Central Dispatch, 576

response definition, for web service, 841

Response interface (CFXAPI), **660–661**

    writeDebug method of, **676–677**

<responsibilities> element, for <fusedoc>, 147

restrict property, for Flash forms, 825

result attribute, of <cf_transformation> tag, 700

_Result handler, creating class for, 819

result sets

    <cfprocresult> tag for, 400

    multiple from stored procedure,
        402–405, *405*

resultSet attribute, of <cfprocresult> tag, 400

returnCode attribute, of cfstoredproc tag, 398

Returning class (Java), 644–648

    methods, 645

returnVariable attribute, of <cfinvoke> tag, 842

right outer join, 377

Robocopy, 598

Robust File Copy utility, 598

role for UML association, 867

roles-based security, **303–307**

Round Robin DNS, **573–574**

    ClusterCATS and, 575, 580

        settings, 581–582

round-trip design, 9

round tripping, 854

rows in database table, returning unique, 364

RPC (Remote Procedure Call), 838

rsync utility, 598

rtrim() function (SQL Server), 439

running requests, monitoring, 543

S

sample application, **159–177**, *172*

    for archiving, 320

    database for, **351–353**, *352*

    with Fusebox

        act_ fuse, 174–175

        circuits and fuseactions, 160

        directory structure, *160*

        dsp_ fuse, 165, 169–172, 175–177

        FBX_Circuits.cfm file, 161–162

        FBX_Layouts.cfm file, 162, 163–164

        FBX_Settings.cfm file, 161

        FBX_Switch.cfm file, 164–165, 167–168

        index.cfm file, 161

        limitations, 160

        "Numbers by Vinny" application,
            159–177

        qry_ fuse, 168–169

        url_ fuse, 173

    with object-oriented concepts, **190–197**

        abstracting component types, **193–194**

        basic requirements, 191

        component identification, 191–193

        record search, **194–197**

SaveContent.cfm file, 122

SAX parser, 680

scalability

    Access vs. SQL Server, 422

    and state management, 79

scalar functions in SQL, **366–370**

scope chain concept, 776

scope creep, 19, 109

scope variables, shared, 87

<script> tag, 256–257

scripting, cross-site, **312–314**

ScrollBar component (Flash), 774, 784

ScrollPane component (Flash), 774

search and replace, global, to change
        functions, 439

search engines, 75. *See also* Verity
searching
    dynamic query results, **215–219**
    indexes, **204–209**
security
    Access vs. SQL Server, 422
    basics, **286–307**
        authentication, **289–296**
        authorization, **296–297**
        <cfexecute> tag and, **760–761**
        cross-site scripting, **312–314**
        "hot load" directories and, 636
        logging in and out, **292–294**
        and program coding, 29
        roles-based, **303–307**
        session management, 291–292
        settings as upsizing trouble spot, 429
        through obscurity, **312**
        for Web applications, **307–315**
            input point protection, **307–312**
Segue Software, SilkPerformer, 535
select statement (SQL), 350, **362–363**
    top keyword for, 610
<select> tag, 521
selection lists, in WML forms, **521–523**, *522*
selector in style rule, 488
self variable, 120
send method, of LoadVars object, 781
sendAndLoad method, of LoadVars object,
    781, 786
sentence operator in explicit query, 208
serial correlation in software development, 114
serialization, 248
    of CFML datatypes, **680–690**
    of JDBC ResultSets, **693–695**
    of query objects, 251, **690–692**
serialize method, of WddxSerializer class, 267
serializeValue method, of WddxSerializer
    class, 267

serializeVariable method, of WddxSerializer
    class, 267
server-based load balancers, 575
server-side ActionScript, **815–820**
    creating Flash application for, 816
server-side debugging, **386–387**
server-side processing, vs. client-side, **450–451**
server variables, 617
server.log file, 64
servers
    cached queries in memory, and
        performance, 617
    in cluster, viewing loads, 590, *591*
    ColdFusion MX Administrator performance
        settings, **546–549**
    failover, testing, **594–595**
    scalability of, 79
services, disabling unused, **567**
session-aware load balancing, 81
session ID (SID), 101–102
session-instance variable, nesting, 87
session management, 291–292
session state management, ClusterCATS
    configuration for, 588
session stickiness, in Windows NT Load
    Balancing Service, 576
session variables, 617
    locking, 87
    proper use, **86–87**
    for state maintenance, 80
        storage, 80–81
set methods, 182–183
set noCount on/off (SQL Server), 359
set statement (Transact-SQL), 406–407
setData method, of Query interface, 661
setDeliveryMode() method, of RecordSet
    object, 802
setField method
    of RecordSet object, 802
    of WddxRecordset class, 260

setInterval() method, 825

setRequest method, of ComplexRequest
    class, 697

setResponse method, of ComplexResponse
    class, 697

setSerializedVariable method, of
    ComplexResponse class, 697

setTransubstantiator method
    of ComplexRequest class, 697
    of ComplexResponse class, 697

<setvar> tag, **512–513**

SetVariable method, of CCFXRequest class,
    731, 733

setVariable method, of Response interface,
    661, 664

severability, of Fusebox, 113

shared directories, for HTML and WML,
    526–528

shared scope variables, 87

showImage() function (JavaScript), 487

SID (session ID), 101–102

sideways scaling, 79

sign-off, for prototype and acceptance tests, 141

SilkPerformer (Segue Software), 535

Simeonov, Simeon, 246

Simple Mail Transfer Protocol (SMTP), 840

Simple Object Access Protocol (SOAP),
    839, 848

simple queries in Verity, 208

simulation. *See* query sims

simultaneous requests, setting to limit, **546–548**

simultaneous users, 84

Site Definition dialog box (Dreamweaver),
    339, 339

Site Server Deployment Deployment
    service, 598

Site-wide Error Handler, 68
    path, 67

Slashdot Effect, 281

Slashdot.org, **281–283**

SMTP (Simple Mail Transfer Protocol), 840
    mail server, cluster requirements, 579

snapshot replication (Oracle), 599

SOAP (Simple Object Access Protocol),
    839, 848

software
    development
        current practices, **109–113**
        and customers, **110–111**
        methodologies, **111–113**
        testing in, 158
    for load balancing, **572–577**
        ClusterCATS, **574–576**
        DNS, **573**
        Round Robin DNS, **573–574**

Software Pursuits, SureSync, 599

Solaris, performance tuning, **567–568**

sort() method, of RecordSet object, 802

sortItemsBy() method, of RecordSet object,
    802–803

soundex operator in explicit query, 208

source attribute, of <cf_transformation>
    tag, 700

source code management
    benefits, **334–337**
        locking and concurrency, **335–336**
        parallel projects and forking, **337**
        synchronization, **337**
        versioning and history, **336–337**
    tools, **337–346**
        CVS, 31, 336, 344–345
        RDS (Remote Development Services),
            338–343
        SourceForge, 345–346
        SourceSafe, **343–344**
        WebDAV, **344**
    what it is, 334

SourceForge, 345–346

SourceSafe, **343–344**

spaghetti code, 119

SQL (Structured Query Language)
    Access vs. SQL Server, 438–439
    basics, **350–353**
    in cached queries, 615
    CFSQL, **384–386**
    for data manipulation, **356–361**
        automatically generated ID, **358–360**
        delete statement, **361**
        insert statement, **356–360**
        null value, 356–358
        update statement, **360**
    database, for client variables, 82, 89
    functions, **364–370**
        aggregate, **364–366**
        scalar, **366–370**
    grouping, **379–383**
        in output, **381–383**
        in query, **379–381**
    joins, **376–377**
    modifying for database upsizing, **438–440**
    performance testing, **386–388**
        GetTickCount function, **387–388**
        server-side debugging, **386–387**
    queries
        aliases for columns and tables, **363–364**
        exists/not exists keywords, **375–376**
        in/not in keywords, **374–375**
        with select statement (SQL), **362–363**
        subqueries, **370–376**
        unique rows, 364
        where clause subqueries, **373–374**
    for table manipulation, **353–356**
        alter statement, **355**
        create table statement, **353–354**
        drop statement, 356
    unions, **378–379**
SQL Server. *See* Microsoft SQL Server
SSAS. *See* server-side ActionScript
Stage, in Flash authoring environment, *768,*
    768–769

staging environment, moving content to
    production from, 597
stale content in cache, handling, **604**
standards for team projects, 20
Standish Group, 109
Starbase StarTeam, 31
startRow attribute, of <cfsearch> tag, 205, 229
state management, **78–83**
    with ColdFusion variables, **80–83**
        allocating CFID and CFTOKEN in
            cluster, 82–83
        state variable storage, 80–82
    over HTTP, **78–80**
    and scalability, 79
stateless protocol, HTTP as, 78
static files, indexing, 202–204
static IP mode for ClusterCATS, 575
static members, for Java objects, **632–633**
static text fields in Flash, 772
    creating, 782, *782*
_Status handler, creating class for, 819
stdafx.h file, 722
stem operator in explicit query, 208
stereotype in UML, 865
sticky sessions, 84
stored procedures
    calling from ColdFusion, **397–405**, 416–417
        with cfquery tag, **397–398**
        with cfstoredproc tag, **398–399**, **400–405**
    creating, **391–392**
    executing, **394–396**
        with exec statement, 395–396
    multiple result sets from, **402–405**, *405*
    for multiple tasks, 415–416
    naming conventions, **390–391**
    parameters, **392–394**
        returning output, **396–397**
    and performance, 561
    vs. queries, 391

string concatenation operator, Access vs.
    SQL Server, 440
<string> element, for <fusedoc> <in>/<out>
    element, 149
String object (ActionScript), 777
strings, class to create and manage
    collection, 742
<structure> element, for <fusedoc> <in>/<out>
    element, 150
structures
    exceptions from attempt to pass, 679
    naming conventions for, 21
    for session variables, 88
    WSDL datatypes as, 844
stubs
    for program code, 152
    for remote web service, 845–846
        with Java, 850
    TemperatureService, 846–847
style sheets, to target different markups,
    706–707
<style> tag (HTML), 489
stylesheet attribute, of <cf_transformation>
    tag, 700
subclass, 184
    in UML, 865
subqueries, **370–376**
suffixes
    for ActionScript objects, 780
    for ColdFusion validation fields, 468
sum function (SQL), 366
summary display in search results, 224–228, *225*
    enabling or disabling, *226–227, 228*
Sun Microsystems, Java Runtime Engine (JRE)
    from, 858
superclass, 184
    in UML, 865
SureSync (Software Pursuits), 599
SWF file, creating, 775–776
switch-based load balancers, 577

switch statement, 119
Switch_box, 30, 112
symbols, in Flash, 772
symbols in Flash, **772–775**
synchronization
    between database servers, 571
    in source code management, **337**
    web servers, **598–599**
syntax errors, vs. logic errors, **34–35**
system environment, and cfexecute tag, 757
System Monitor for Windows, 543, 544–545
System.err error stream, 632
System.out error stream, 632

T

table relationships, upsizing wizard control
    of, 431
table scan, 556
TCP/IP, for connection between cluster server
    and client database server, 90
TCP (Transmission Control Protocol), 839
team debugging, **72–74**
team development, file locking for, 335–336
technical requirements of application, in plan-
    ning, **4–6**
TemperatureService, 841
    consuming, 841–843
    stub, 846–847
templates
    all-in-one, for HTML and WML, **525–526**
    cache size, 550
    vs. CFCs, **798–799**
    checking error logs for timedout, 548
    for debugging, **56–57**
    headers, **24–25**
    for indexing, **242–243**
    performance monitoring, **563–565**

profiling, **563**
terminating processing at point in, **529–530**
test harnesses, 152–154
tool to automate writing, 158
testing, 159
acceptance testing design, 141
circuits, 158
fuses, 155–158
text attribute, of <cftrace> tag, 62
text fields in Flash, 772–773
restrict property, 825
Text tool (Flash), 782–783
text truncation, Access vs. SQL Server, 443–444
textAreaValidate() function, 481, 482
textBoxRequired() function, 480
TextField object (ActionScript), 777
thesauras operator in explicit query, 208
this keyword (JavaScript), 274
this scope, 184
thisTag.executionMode variable, 701
thisTag.generatedContent variable, 701
tiered applications, **10–16**
business logic tier, 14–16
client tier, 13
data integration tier, 16
data tier, 16
n-tiered, 10–13, *11*
presentation tier, 14
time estimates for development, 7
time span
for expiring cached queries, 614–615
for query caching, 614
timed out requests, monitoring, 543
Timeline
in Flash authoring environment, *768*, 768–769
timeout
in cfexecute tag
to avoid endless loops, **753–756**
capturing errors, 756, 758–759

ColdFusion MX Administrator settings, **548**
for database server connection, 554
for login process, 553
server values, 547
for session management, 292
timeout attribute
of <cfexecute> tag, 749
of cfquery and cfstoredproc, 561
timeSpan attribute, of <cfcache> tag, 605, 607
timestamps, upsizing wizard control of, 431
title attribute, of <cfindex> tag, 212
title of document, Verity identification of, 240, *241*
Toolbox in Flash, *770*
Tools menu (Internet Explorer), ④ Internet Options, Advanced tab, 40, *41*
top keyword, for select statement, 610
topLevelVariable attribute, of <cfwddx> tag, 250
Transact-SQL, **406–412**. *See also* SQL (Structured Query Language); stored procedures
function conversion when upsizing, 425
if/else logic, **407–409**
looping over query result set, **410–412**
variables in, cfset alternatives, 406–407
while statement to replace cfloop, **409–410**
transactional replication (MSSQL), 599
transactions, Access vs. SQL Server, 422
Transmission Control Protocol (TCP), 839
transport technologies, for web services, 839–840
Transsubstantiator interface, 695–696
TrAX interfaces, 700
trim() function, 439, 473
truncated text, Access vs. SQL Server, 443–444
trusted cache, 550–551
tunnel vision of programmer, 35
type attribute
of <cfindex> tag, 212
of <cflog> tag, 65

of <cfobject> tag, 627
of <cfprocparam> tag, **399**
of <cfsearch> tag, 205, 207–208
of <cftrace> tag, 62
of <input> tag, 516
typo operator in explicit query, 208

U

ucase() function (Access SQL), 439
UDDI (Universal Description, Discovery, and
     Integration), 839
UDFs (User Defined Functions), 14
Unicode fields, as upsizing trouble spot, 427
Unified Modeling Language (UML), 17, 134,
     864–869
   C++ CFXAPI model, *715*
   elements of class diagram, **865–869**
      classes, 864–865
      relationships, **865–868**
      notes, **869**
      packages, **868–869**
unions, **378–379**
Universal Description, Discovery, and
     Integration (UDDI), 839
Unix
   porting CFX to, 730–731
   web server synchronization, 598
"Unknown exception condition" error
     message, 753
unreserved locks, in source code
     management, 336
update statement (SQL), **360**
updating indexes, 211
upper() function (SQL Server), 439
upsizing
   with Access Upsizing tools, 423, **424–438**
      database check for trouble spots,
         424–429, *425*

known problems, **434**
running wizard, **429–434**
decision process, **421–424**
   need for, 421–423
   user management of SQL Server
      data, 423
   modifying ColdFusion applications for,
      438–446
      Access vs. SQL Server, **443–446**
      identity columns, **440–443**
      SQL syntax changes, **438–440**
   with SQL Server DTS (Data Transformation
      Services), 423–424, **434–438**
      running Import/Export wizard, *435*,
         435–436, *437*
      verifying import, 437–438
   what it is, **420–421**
url attribute, for <cfhttp> tag, 848
URL attributes, passing with &,
      511–512, *512*
url_ fuse, 144
   for sample application, 173
URL parameters, cache based on, 607
URL tokens, tracking sessions with, 541
urlEncodedFormat function, 463
urlPath attribute, of <cfindex> tag, 212
URLTOKEN, 82
user, code to create and display, 56–57
USER_AGENT variable, for browser
      information, 484
username
   for authentication, 289
      changing, 294–295
username attribute
   of <cfcache> tag, 605
   of <cfinvoke> tag, 842
users
   help in building queries, **233–238**
   management of SQL Server data, 423

useTimeZoneInfo attribute, of <cfwddx>
    tag, 250
UUID, for cftoken, 549

V

validate attribute, of <cfwddx> tag, 250
validating fields. *See* form field validation
validation fields, in ColdFusion, 468
validation functions, library of, 479–482
validation rules, upsizing wizard control of, 431
ValidationRule property of fields, as upsizing
    trouble spot, 425
ValidationText properties, as upsizing trouble
    spot, 426
value attribute, of <cfprocparam> tag, **399**
var attribute, of <cftrace> tag, 62
variable attribute, of <cfprocparam> tag, **399**
variables
    $ to access in WML, **512–513**
    capturing cfexecute output in, **759–760**
    CFX returning, 664
    FLASH scope to pass to ColdFusion,
        800–801
    for formatting in ActionScript, 831
    in JavaScript, passing to ColdFusion,
        462–464
    naming conventions for, 21
    overriding, 184–187
        direct assignment vs. cfparam, 185–186
    passing to web service, **826**
    returning from CFX, **731–733**
    saving code content to, 128
    in Transact-SQL, cfset tag alternatives,
        406–407
Vector class, 687
Verity
    automating indexing, **242–243**
    and cflock, **208–209**

creating collections, **200–202**
for dynamic query results, **213–219**
    indexing, **213–215**
    searching, **215–219**
helping users build queries, **233–238**
indexing, **202–204**
K2 server, **209–210**
multiformat indexing and searching,
    240–242
multilingual indexing and searching,
    239–240
operators, 208
optimizing, **244**
paging through results, **229–233**
search interfaces, **219–238**
    summary display, 224–228, *225*
    usefulness of results, **219–228**
searches of document indexes, **204–209**
    Boolean queries, 206–207
    query result columns, 205
    simple vs. explicit, 207–208
    wildcards in, 207
version control
    and deployment strategy, 596
    planning, **31**
    in source code management, **336–337**
View menu, ④ Code View Options, ④ Line
    Numbers, 39, *40*
Virtual IP (VIP), for hardware load
    balancer, 577
virtual memory paging, 541
Visual Basic, functions in Access that transfer to
    SQL Server, 426
Visual Mind, 142, *143*
    notes about io variables, 151, *152*
visual outliner, 142
Visual SourceSafe (Microsoft), 31
Visual Studio, 718

W

Wan, Samuel, *Object-Oriented Programming with ActionScript*, 819
WAP (Wireless Application Protocol)
    application using ColdFusion, *500*, 500–501
        HTTP servers, 501
        WAP gateways, 500–501
        WML browsers, 501
    what it is, **498–501**
WDDX SDK, 654
WDDX (Web Distributed Data eXchange), 246
    for complex data structures, **679–695**
        serializing CFML datatypes, **680–690**
        serializing JDBC ResultSets, **693–695**
        serializing query objects, **690–692**
    concepts, **247–248**
        deserialization, 248
        packets, 247–248
        </wddxPacket> serialization, 248
    deserializing packet, 685–686
    history, **246–247**
    JavaScript library, **256–276**
        accessing, **256–257**
        CFML conversion to JavaScript, **257–259**
        WddxDeserializer class, **262–266**
        WddxRecordset class, **260–262**, **273–276**
        WddxSerializer class, **266–273**
    language tools, **249–256**
        and CFML queries, **250–253**
        CFML tools for WDDX, **249–250**
        database caching, **254–256**
        packet construction and display, **253–254**
    required setup for examples, 249
    syndication, **277–283**
        Slashdot.org, **281–283**
        use with Moreover.com, **278–281**
wddx2cfml action, 250

wddx2js action, 250
WddxDeserializer class, **262–266**
WddxRecordset class, **260–262**, **273–276**
wddxSerialize method, of WddxRecordset class, 260
WddxSerializer class, **266–273**
weather service, Flash application to call, 821–825
Web Application Stress Tool, *536*, **536–539**
Web applications
    security for, **307–315**
        restricting display, 310–312
web browsers
    cgi.http_accept variable to determine type, **515**
    as client tier, 13
    ColdFusion and, 451
    compatibility, 450
    compatibility with DHTML, 482
        testing with ColdFusion, 484–485
        testing with JavaScript, 483–484
    WML (Wireless Markup Language)
        browser emulators for PC, **501–503**
        browsers, 501, 515
web cluster, 79
Web Distributed Data eXchange (WDDX).
    See WDDX (Web Distributed Data eXchange)
web farm, 79
web server software, and ColdFusion Application Server, 451
web servers
    cluster requirements, 579
    CPU utilization, 540
    IP addresses, 583
    memory allocation, 541
    network adapters, 542
    network traffic monitoring, 541
    synchronization, **598–599**

Web Service Description Language
        (WSDL), 838
web services
    consuming, **840–851**
        automatically with cfinvoke, **840–843**
        automatically with createObject(), 843
        manually, **843–845**
        manually with Apache Axis, **849–851**
        manually with cfhttp and cfxml, **846–849**
        process flow for, *845*, **845–846**
    defined, **838–839**
    and Flash Remoting MX, **820–834**
        for weather determination, 821–825
    integrating with Flash Remoting to calculate
        distance, **826–833**
    interoperability stack, **839–840**
    options, 821
    parameters, 844–845
    passing variables to, **826**
    preregistering, 846
    producing, **851–854**
        process flow for, **854**, *855*
    publicly available, 841
    requesting new data without page
        refresh, 825
    syndication, 277
WebDAV, **344**
WebLOAD (RadView Software), 536
<webroot> directory, 636
webroot/WEB-INF/debug directory, 56
webService attribute, of <cfinvoke> tag, 842
where clause
    for delete statement (SQL), 361
    in select statement (SQL), 362
    for subqueries, **373–374**
    for update statement (SQL), 360
while statement (Transact-SQL), **409–410**
whitespace management, ColdFusion MX
        Administrator settings, 549

wildcards, in Verity queries, 207
Windows
    Klondike WAP Browser for Windows,
        501, *502*
    performance counters, WAST data
        collection from, 538
    System Monitor, 544–545
    web server synchronization, 598
Windows NT/2000, performance monitoring,
        565–566
Windows NT Load Balancing Service,
        576–577
WinWap, 501
WinZip, 597
wireframe creation in FLiP, 136, *137*
Wireless Application Protocol (WAP). *See* WAP
        (Wireless Application Protocol)
Wireless Markup Language (WML). *See* WML
        (Wireless Markup Language)
WML/HTML web site, 528–529
    architecture, **525–529**
        all-in-one templates, 525–526
        separate directories, 528–529
        shared directories, 526–528
<wml> tag, 504
WML (Wireless Markup Language)
    basics, **503–513**
        $ to access variables, **512–513**
        card navigation, **506–510**
        document structure, **503–505**
        header, **505**
        intolerance for coding errors, **510–511**
        syntax rules, **505–506**
        URL attributes passing with &,
            511–512, *512*
    browser emulators for PC, **501–503**
    browsers, 501
    with ColdFusion, **513–524**
        <cfabort> tag, **529–530**

<cfcontent> tag for content type, 514

cgi.http_accept variable for browser
  type, 515

error handling, **523–524**

forms, **516–523**, *517*

document, *499*

what it is, **498–501**

word operator in explicit query, 208

World Wide Web Consortium, 452

write method

  of Response interface, 661, 662

  of WddxSerializer class, 267

writeDebug method, of Response interface,
  661, **676–677**

WSDL (Web Service Description
  Language), 838

  datatypes mapping to ColdFusion, **843–844**

  getting to know, 841

X

x-switches, 861

XFAs (exit fuseactions), 116, **126–127**

XMethods website, 841

XML. *See also* WDDX (Web Distributed Data
  eXchange)

  DOM as API for, 452

  WSDL as, 838

XML object (ActionScript), 777

XP (Extreme Programming), 134–135

XSLT scripting, 282

XSLT style sheets, to transform XML to WML
  or HTML, 529

XSLT tag, **700–707**

xslTransform function (CFML), 700

Z

ZIP file, to package content for clusters, 597

TELL US WHAT YOU THINK!

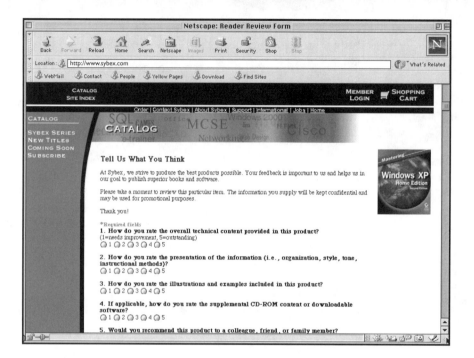

Your feedback is critical to our efforts to provide you with the best books and software on the market. Tell us what you think about the products you've purchased. It's simple:

1. Go to the Sybex website.
2. Find your book by typing the ISBN or title into the Search field.
3. Click on the book title when it appears.
4. Click **Submit a Review.**
5. Fill out the questionnaire and comments.
6. Click **Submit.**

With your feedback, we can continue to publish the highest quality computer books and software products that today's busy IT professionals deserve.

www.sybex.com

SYBEX Inc. • 1151 Marina Village Parkway, Alameda, CA 94501 • 510-523-8233